INTERPRETATIVE REPORTING

NINTH EDITION

Curtis D. MacDougall, Ph.D., Litt.D.
Late Professor of Journalism,
Northwestern University

Robert D. Reid
Professor of Journalism,
University of Illinois

D0162068

MACMILLAN PUBLISHING COMPANY
NEW YORK

COLLIER MACMILLAN PUBLISHERS
LONDON

Earlier edition entitled *Reporting for Beginners* copyright 1932 by Macmillan Publishing
Co., Inc. Earlier editions entitled *Interpretative Reporting* copyright 1938 and 1948 and ©
1957 and 1963 by Macmillan Publishing Co., Inc., copyright © 1968, 1972, and 1982 by
Curtis D. McDougall.
Copyright renewed 1960, 1966, 1976, and 1981 by Curtis D. MacDougall.

Macmillan Publishing Company
866 Third Avenue, New York, New York 10022

Collier Macmillan Canada, Inc.

Library of Congress Cataloging-in-Publication Data

MacDougall, Curtis Daniel,
    Interpretative reporting.

    Includes index.
    1. Reporters and reporting.   I. Reid, Robert D.
(Robert Delaware),   II. Title.
PN4781.M153   1987   070.4′3   86-17984
ISBN 0-02-373140-0

Printing: 1 2 3 4 5 6 7   Year: 7 8 9 0 1 2 3

ISBN 0-02-373140-0

INTERPRETATIVE REPORTING

Preface

This ninth edition of *Interpretative Reporting* is the first that is not solely the work of Dr. Curtis D. MacDougall. "Dr. Mac" died on November 10, 1985, at the age of 82, about eleven months after he had asked me to become his co-author for this latest edition of his classic work. Thus, what began as a joyous collaboration between "Dr. Mac" and a former student became a bittersweet effort to preserve the central thoughts about journalism of a great teacher who had a significant influence on modern American reporting.

As "Dr. Mac" has pointed out in prefaces to previous editions, this book is not intended as a complete journalism education but rather as a starting point for would-be journalists. It covers the basics of reporting and newswriting and is intended to serve as a supplement to the instruction of good teachers in the first two or three semesters of reporting and newswriting courses. The text also instructs future journalists in ethical and social responsibilities and elaborates on the interaction of journalists with the law and new technology.

In this edition, with the help of those listed in the Acknowledgments, I have tried to maintain the substance of "Dr. Mac's" thinking about reporting and how it is best learned. Thus, the bulk of this new edition remains the work of "Dr. Mac," updated with many new examples and much new information that I have added about reporting in the 1980s. As "Dr. Mac" and I agreed in our detailed exchanges before his death, the new edition expands and moves to greater prominence throughout the text the importance of the nature and quality of the interpretation that inevitably enters into all reporting. "Dr. Mac" became seriously ill before he could carefully review my execution of what we agreed to in this new edition, so I bear full responsibility for any shortcomings in this revision.

"Dr. Mac's" was the first modern textbook to analyze systematically and to popularize the interpretative aspects of reporting. He recognized that journalists are human and cannot help but have their perceptions and values shape their reporting and writing. Thus, he emphasized that the news needs context, clarity, nuance and explanation and that reporters need to be fair-minded and thorough in their research and writing. Over 50 years and in eight previous editions of this book, Professor MacDougall lucidly defined reporting and urged would-be journalists to acquire a humane, rounded education so that they might then be better equipped to report with intelligence, fairness and common sense. He believed strongly that in doing their work, reporters should seek out the widest possible range of sources and perspectives on the subject at hand.

I have attempted to preserve "Dr. Mac's" Jeffersonian approach to journalism. He believed that ordinary Americans could govern themselves effectively if the men and women of the press have the humility to recognize that "the truth" is something they can never be sure they have found. I uphold this notion not only because of my love and respect for "Dr. Mac" but also because of my conviction, based on 20 years as a working journalist and seven years as a journalism educator, that journalism students need exposure to it now more than ever. This remains the most accurate textbook on the demands of reporting in a democratic society. In it, "Dr. Mac" encourages his readers to raise their own journalistic standards and to think independently. His basic message is that reporting well is vitally important and extraordinarily difficult but that it is a task that can be accomplished if reporters work hard and care deeply about their work.

Along with the thousands of people around the country who learned from "Dr. Mac" and whose lives were affected by his challenging approach to journalism, I lament his passing more than words can convey. I hope that this book will allow those who study it to see why those who best knew "Dr. Mac" came to respect him so much. I also hope it helps the next generation of American journalists, now preparing themselves for one of society's most noble and rewarding callings, to see how they can meet the journalistic challenges that "Dr. Mac" delineated so effectively.

ROBERT D. REID

Acknowledgments

This book remains primarily the work of Dr. Curtis D. MacDougall. He took it through eight editions over 50 years and shaped the basic concepts of this ninth edition before his death in November 1985. Its strengths are his. More than any other teacher I ever had, he showed me what learning, thinking and citizenship are about.

I am certain "Dr. Mac" would wish to thank his many friends and former students who helped him with the eight previous editions. They truly are a constructive part of this book.

I wish to thank "Dr. Mac's" family for their courtesy, patience and assistance as the work on this edition progressed during Dr. MacDougall's decline and then after his death. They were gracious and supportive beyond measure, especially Priscilla Ruth MacDougall, who kept the project moving when it could have faltered, and A. Kent MacDougall with his tough-minded critiques of key portions of the revision.

Others among Dr. MacDougall's long-time associates who offered helpful suggestions under difficult conditions were journalism educators Daniel Thornburgh, Gene Burd, Les Brownlee, Charles-Gene McDaniel, and R. Neale Copple. William Wylie made some important comments to Dr. MacDougall that led to my substantial reshaping of the chapters on business, labor and agriculture in this edition.

I am indebted to many of my colleagues. Both Thomas Littlewood, head of the University of Illinois journalism department, and Richard Stegeman, a long-time associate first in our work in daily newspapers and now as a faculty colleague, helped me far more with the beginning stages of this edition than I expect they realize. In a less direct way, my other faculty colleagues in the University of Illinois journalism department and in the communications college were very helpful. They are a cantankerous lot but stimulating and a pleasure to work with because of their independent thinking about the nature of journalism and journalism education. Littlewood and James Carey, who is the dean of the college in which I teach, were patient and supportive during my work on this project, for which I am especially grateful.

I also owe much to all my many former colleagues with the now defunct

Lindsay-Schaub Newspapers group in Illinois. They showed me how enjoyable and stimulating journalism can be. They furthered my education as a journalist, citizen and human being in ways I never can hope to repay. The same is true for those with whom I worked as a very young journalist at the Freeport (Ill.) *Journal-Standard* in the 1950s and 1960s, especially Donald L. Breed and Ford Fuller. Those people at Lindsay-Schaub and the *Journal-Standard* showed me that major metropolitan newspapers have no monopoly on competent, thoughtful and sensitive journalists and that caring about others is not incompatible with the practice of journalism—popular images in the media notwithstanding.

I would be remiss, too, not to thank students at the University of Illinois. Their lively responses to the challenges and demands of a journalism education have been stimulating and often inspiring. These students and their counterparts in classrooms and newsrooms all across the United States are the future of American journalism. I retain the faith that they will do much to improve journalism and America in the decades ahead.

Kathryn Brown, then the secretary and glue of the journalism department at the University of Illinois, was an invaluable help during my year of working on this project and especially in the first half of 1985 when I was also acting department head.

Finally, I must express my loving appreciation to my wife, Marilyn, who was a tremendous help with this book.

Robert D. Reid

Contents

NEWS REPORTING

Journalism presents a continuous, never-ending moving picture of the world and its occurrences, of mankind and its conduct, depicting comedy, tragedy, vice, virtue, heroism, devotion, enterprise, discovery, calamity, beneficence, sorrow and joy—human life in all its kaleidoscopic and inexplicable changes. And accompanying all this editorial comment upon the news, interpreting the meaning of events, associating views with information, opinion with facts, and thereby aiding the reader to a better understanding and to an opinion of his own which becomes an element in the creation of public opinion, that "sovereign mistress of effects," which rules the modern world. Such is journalism, a profession that exists upon the events of the day, that mirrors all life and presents it to the view of every individual, thereby bringing all mankind to a closer unity and a clearer conception of its kinship.

—CASPER S. YOST, editor, St. Louis *Globe-Democrat*

A newspaper should seek what is original, distinctive, dramatic, romantic, thrilling, unique, curious, quaint, humorous, odd, apt to be talked about, without shocking good taste or lowering the general good tone and above all without impairing the confidence of the people in the truth of the stories or the character of the paper for reliability and scrupulous cleanness.

—JOSEPH PULITZER, New York *World*

WHOSE FIRST AMENDMENT?

Whose First? It belongs to every man, woman and child.

Whose right to use it? It is the right of every man, woman and child.

Whose responsibility to protect it? It is the responsibility of every man, woman and child.

The First Amendment protects freedoms, separately defined, yet indivisible. We share these rights:

- To believe.
- To speak.
- To publish.
- To support or criticize our government.

These rights belong to the people and never are to be denied nor controlled by the government.

We share, as citizens, a responsibility to understand that the First Amendment protects, with equal force, the ideas we despise as well as those we cherish. Government infringement on any one of these fundamental rights threatens them all.

Whose First? One infringement will raise another question: Who's next?

As Irving Brant, the distinguished constitutional authority and journalist, thoughtfully pointed out in his history, "The Bill of Rights," James Madison and his colleagues "knew what they were doing. . . . English history had demonstrated to them that without complete religious liberty, without freedom of conscience and separation of church and state, there could be no freedom of speech, or of the press, or the right of assembly. Both English and American experience had taught them that without all these freedoms there could be no free government. And they had learned that even in a country where the people are sovereign, no words of lesser force than 'shall not'—enforceable in independent courts of law—could restrain the servants of the people from acting as if they were the masters."

We owe ourselves and those who follow an obligation to recapture the concern and spirit which Madison referred to as the "Great Freedoms."

If freedom is a growing thing, it can mean no less today and tomorrow than it meant to those who wrote the First Amendment.

The First Amendment distinguishes us from all other societies. And it works. Every time the First Amendment works, it makes us stronger.

The preceding was passed as a resolution by the delegates to the First Amendment Congress in Williamsburg, Va., in March, 1980.

2

CHAPTER

1

The Modern Newsgatherer

The content of American newspapers is changing dramatically. So is the nature of the newspaper reporter's work and the background that reporters need to bring to that work. Newspapers are printing more stories or packages of stories that do more than just tell what happened. They also attempt to put what happened in a larger context, to examine causes, to explore consequences—and to do it all in writing that is clear and humane. Doing such stories requires an excellent and continuing education, good street sense and a skeptical but sensitive human touch on the part of reporters. No longer do many editors and reporters pretend that the news does not involve their interpretations. Instead, they are conceding that interpretation is a fundamental part of all journalism and are trying, to the extent that time and their capacities allow, to make their interpretations intelligent, compassionate and illuminating. Thus, the demands of reporting are growing, but so are the rewards for reporters, financially and otherwise.

Interpretation in Action

To get at the changing nature of reporting, let's examine two approaches to a kind of happening that, sadly, still occurs far too often in almost any community—rape. The first story involves what is called in newspaper lingo a straight, breaking story. The second approach is a set of three stories that apply the concept of interpretation to a similar incident with more intensity.

A Case Study: Reporting Rape

The first story appeared in the Chicago *Tribune* on Dec. 29, 1985, one of several brief items in a column called "Metropolitan Report." The story carried a small headline that said, "Cleaning Woman Raped in Office":

> A 45-year-old cleaning woman was raped on the 23rd floor of a Loop office building Friday evening by a man who said he was looking for a lawyer, according to police. "She said nobody was there and he continued to follow her and pulled a knife on her. He said he needed car fare" said Detective Patricia Hickey, of the Wentworth Police Area Violent Crimes Unit. The woman told him she had no money and offered him her gold cross and chain, Hickey said. He told her that wasn't what he wanted and he pulled her into a bathroom, raped her and fled the building at 100 N. LaSalle St., Hickey said. "She screamed and called for help and nobody answered."

The story is a news story in its simplest form, an account from a police report of the basic facts of a crime with no effort to examine deeper motives or consequences, no attempt to establish a larger context for what happened. Although the story sensitively protected the victim's identity, it nevertheless is almost abstract.

Such reporting once was the staple of the American press. That is no longer the case. While newspapers still run stories like this, most of them de-emphasize them, as the Tribune did, and instead attempt to put such incidents into context and explore their larger meaning.

The difference is great between the routine daily police story about a rape and reporting that takes a larger perspective, displays a sensitivity to human feelings and seeks answers to such questions as "What does it mean to be raped in our culture? Why does rape occur so often? What can be done about rapes? What should be done?"

The difference between a brief daily newspaper story about a rape and reporting that answers such larger questions is highlighted clearly in stories that appeared in the June 10, 1984, edition of the Corpus Christi (Tex.) *Caller Times*. Written by Karen Brandon, a reporter then only three years out of the University of Illinois journalism program, the stories show what an energetic, thoughtful and sensitive reporter can do in applying the interpretative reporting concept to help readers better understand the news. Her stories demonstrate the nature and utility of the interpretative concept that is the foundation of this book. Her articles, excerpts of which are reprinted here by permission of the *Caller-Times,* show that even fairly young reporters working for publications not as well known or celebrated as giant metropolitan newspapers can do reporting that goes beyond the routine if only they will ask intelligent, humane questions, seek to explore below the surface of events and apply their liberal arts and sciences studies to their journalism.

The first of Brandon's three stories that day in June 1984 appeared under a headline, "A Case of Rape: For a Victim of the Crime, Life Becomes More Brutal." In this story, Brandon portrayed the human dimensions of rape. Excerpts follow:

Ellen finds herself living a series of little rapes now. In life's daily frustrations, when another driver cuts ahead of her in traffic, or a co-worker does something underhanded, or an acquaintance makes a cruel remark, everything is disturbingly different.

Life became more brutal for Ellen, a 52-year-old Corpus Christi mother of three, as of 4:27 one spring morning when she was raped. The rape took less than half an hour and left no physical scars, so her perceptions might seem like exaggerations to someone who has never been raped, or to men who are skeptical of the reality of rape, or to women who think themselves immune from it.

Ellen (which is not her real name) knew to keep her car doors locked and to avoid notoriously dangerous areas of the city. She never thought of herself as a potential rape victim, and she never expected that being raped would have such a drastic effect. "Before, you think, 'What difference does one more act of sex make?' And then this happens, and you think, 'All the difference in the world.'"

Ellen woke up when her cat, Ming, padded onto her bed. It was still dark in the apartment she has called home since her divorce. She looked at the clock; it was 4:27 a.m. and she had 13 minutes before she had to get up for work.

"No, Ming, it's too early," she said. But looking at the clock, she thought, "Well, what's 13 minutes? I'll get up." She crossed the dark hall of her two-bedroom apartment to use the bathroom and was heading back toward the bedroom when someone grabbed her from behind, gripping her with his forearm. "It's a friend of mind playing a joke on me," she thought. "He's always fussing at me because I leave the window open."

A voice said. "I have a gun. If you make a sound I'll blow your head off. . . ."

During the ordeal she was obsessed with the question of how he had gotten in. She wondered if she had simply forgotten to lock the door. She asked, "How did you get in?" so many times that he finally told her he entered by taking the screen off the window.

Then guilt slapped her, too. She had always left her window open to enjoy the fresh air and to let her cat look out. One of her neighbors had told her, "You know, you ought not to do that. There have been burglars here." But Ellen always thought she had little to lose, only a TV set and stereo.

She forced her mind away from her body, trying to feel almost physically dead until he had finished, and she told him to withdraw. "I meant withdraw from my body, my house, my life, from what you have done to me, from what you have taught me. . . ."

After he had gone, she lay there for maybe a minute and thought, "He said he won't tell anybody, and I won't tell anybody, and no one will know."

Then she changed her mind. "No, I'm not the only woman in the world this has ever happened to, and I'm not the only woman in the world that he might go after."

It was about 5 a.m. when Ellen called the police. Though she knew she should not wash away any evidence, she was too disgusted and did wash herself a little.

She called a relative in town. She called her boss, and, without explaining what had happened, told him she would not be in to work that day. . . .

They went to Memorial Medical Center, where a nurse began asking the intimate, detailed questions of the rape, and Ellen realized, "This is a story I'm going to be telling over and over again."

The rape had been a relatively short ordeal. The hospital ordeal was not. She waited two hours for the doctor to arrive, a wait that she found the worst part of the entire episode. The rape scene became like a videotape, playing over and over in her mind. . . .

It was 10:30 a.m. when Ellen went home, flipped the mattress on the bed and tried to get through the day.

"Part of me didn't want to tell anybody, And part of me wanted to tell everybody," she said. "I thought, 'Who am I going to tell? And why am I going to tell them?. . . .'"

More than a month after the rape, Ellen no longer thinks about it constantly. It is unlikely she is pregnant or infected with venereal disease.

But there are constant reminders. The windows are braced. A 16-gauge shotgun leans on the wall by her bed, and she has learned to use it. Though she is a cat lover, she has given Ming to her mother and now owns a guard dog. She carries the pewter bookend with her to escort a guest to the parking lot. . . .

In a way, she thinks it would have been easier to deal with the devastation of war, rather than rape, because her neighbors and friends would understand that kind of devastation.

War is the only situation she feels bears comparing with rape. But it is not easy to relate such a personal war. "I guess the best description I could use is we're at war. There's a war going on in Corpus Christi and we don't even know it."

In the two accompanying stories (called sidebars in newspaper lingo), Brandon supplied a larger context and setting to her first story, showing how the experience of one rape victim connected with important public policy questions and other forces and trends at work in society.

The first of these sidebar stories was entitled, "Both Laws and Attitudes Regarding Rape Are Changing." An excerpt follows:

Rape has become more of a speakable crime than a hidden shame. Through social and legal changes, survivors of rape are treated as victims rather than as people bearing stigmas.

In the past nine months Texas law has undergone major changes designed to help rape victims. Over the past three years, the Coastal Bend Rape Crisis Center has counseled victims and helped educate the public. For nearly a decade, the Corpus Christi Police Department rape investigation team has tried to ease the trauma of reporting rape.

Despite the progress, the push forward isn't always steady. Locally, a program that was to help in the collection of physical evidence, considered crucial for a successful trial, has all but stalled out. Remnants of earlier attitudes about women, social and sexual roles, and who does and doesn't "invite" rape still exist. And public attitude about the new laws has yet to be tested in Nueces County courts.

Though the legal system still doesn't effectively deter rape, new laws are less likely to deter victims from reporting rapes. Texas law took a significant step Sept. 1, 1983, when the "rape as sexual assault" law went into effect, making five major changes of both substance and thought.

The changes . . . (The story then lists the specific changes made by the law).

What most successful cases still demand is solid evidence that can only be collected immediately after the rape.

A year ago District Attorney Grant Jones said a program designed to secure evidence should be operating within months. The plan would have had volunteer nurse practitioners examine rape victims, gather evidence and later testify, if necessary.

Today he says, "The status sort of got stalled. I still think it's a good idea. It's on hold."

Though Jones says the program hasn't met any opposition, the key problem has been the district attorney's office "not having the time. . . ."

But attitudes about rape seem to be progressing. Fifteen years ago, rape crisis centers really didn't exist in Texas, says Kay West, sexual assault coordinator with the Coastal Bend Rape Crisis Center. Now more than 36 centers in the state offer services such as education and prevention information, individual and group counseling and 24-hour hotlines. Ms. West estimates the Coastal Bend services alone came into contact with more than 10,300 people last year.

"I see more understanding on the part of the public toward the survivor," she says. "More and more people are willing to be open about it. They're being very businesslike about it, not just trying to forget it happened. . . ."

In her other sidebar story, Brandon supplied statistical information that, had it been presented in a standard straight newspaper story, unaccompanied by the main article about the human effects, would have seemed dry, abstract and even unimportant to many readers. The second sidebar was entitled, "More Than 1,000 Rapes Reported in the Last Five Years." Here is an excerpt from that sidebar:

The story of Ellen's rape is a grim one in itself, but more grim is the fact that she is far from alone.

Two other rapes were reported in Corpus Christi the weekend Ellen Hantle was raped. In the first four months of this year, 46 rapes were reported to Corpus Christi police, figures from Commander C.F. Wimbish show. Over a five-year period, more than 1,000 rapes were reported in the Coastal Bend, statistics gathered by the Rape Crisis Center show.

Ellen asked that her real name not be used but that her story be told to help those who have become victims and the many others who are potential victims.

There is very little about rape that falls into a predictable pattern, except that it continues to happen, according to area and national figures from the Coastal Bend Rape Crisis Center. . . .

Brandon's stories exemplify the interpretative reporting concept in action, employed by a young reporter, but a reporter nevertheless clearly in touch with both the human beings and the larger forces at work in her community. She was looking for the story behind the story. She had done a good deal of background research. She was willing to do legwork beyond the facts to be found on easily obtainable police reports. And she spent a good deal of time trying to write her package of stories in ways that would be clear and interesting.

Another Case Study: Reporting Government

Many other reporters—young and older—around the country are using the interpretative reporting concept to find good stories that might be missed by journalists unwilling to look for the larger meaning of what might seem boring to reporters looking for news only in older and more conventional ways. One of them is Kevin Davis, who in 1985 was in his first year as a reporter for the Fort Lauderdale *News and Sun-Sentinel* daily newspaper. Davis graduated in late 1984 from the University of Illinois.

Davis spends a good deal of time covering governmental meetings and writes his share of routine news stories. But using the interpretative concept, he is coming up with significant, readable stories that provide good insights into the life of the area of Florida he covers as his beat. What follow are excerpts from three of his stories that, like those of Brandon in Texas, show how the interpretative reporting concept can make journalism more interesting for both the journalist applying the concept to daily reporting work and to readers. The excerpts are reprinted with permission of the News and Sun-Sentinel Company.

In the first of these stories, which appeared on Sept. 22, 1985, Davis provided a readable, fresh perspective on the nature of local government as it is working today in Florida. The story was headlined, "Steady Tax Rates Make for Quiet Budget Hearings":

> Davie Mayor Bud Jenkins looked at the rows of chairs in Town Hall, where about a dozen people were seated, and asked if anyone wanted to speak against the proposed $11.8 million budget.
>
> No one said a word.
>
> Did any one care to speak in favor of the budget? he asked.
>
> No one said a word.
>
> "This is unreal," Jenkins said at the town's first public hearing on the budget last week. "I think it gets easier every year."
>
> Town Finance Director Chris Wallace had just given a short budget presentation on an overhead projector complete with the standard pie charts and bar graphs. He was ready to answer any questions the public might have.
>
> But no one asked.
>
> "There're no issues," Wallace said after the half-hour public hearing. "If there were issues, people would show up."
>
> Town Administrator Irv Rosenbaum's proposed budget does not raise taxes and it increases city services. So who wants to argue?
>
> But a few miles to the southwest in Cooper City, about 50 residents were at City Hall protesting a proposed 21 percent increase in property taxes during that city's first public hearing on a $4.7 million budget.
>
> There were some people at Cooper City interested in the budget. Or at least they were interested in their taxes.
>
> Taxes.
>
> That's what gets people's blood rushing, especially when those taxes are going up, city officials say. Otherwise, there's not much interest in the municipal budget process. . . .

Davis had found news where less alert reporters would have seen none. In an unrelated story a month later, Davis again used the interpretative reporting concept to illuminate another aspect of public life in Florida. This story appeared on Oct. 20, 1985, and was headed, "Mobile Home Owners Fight Park Policies":

Every day for nearly six months angry residents, most of them senior citizens, marched with picket signs in front of the Paradise Village mobile home park on State Road 84 protesting rent hikes and decreasing park services.

Just down the road at Rexmere Village mobile home park, residents got together one day last summer and burned their leases.

And a few miles west at Sunshine Village mobile home park in Davie, several families are now preparing to do battle with their landlord after receiving eviction notices accusing them of breaking park rules.

These are not isolated incidents. Residents of mobile home parks in Broward are increasingly challenging their park policies. They are challenging rent increases and speaking up when services decline.

Most mobile home owners are in an unusual position. They own their homes but they don't own the property where their homes sit. So they pay rent, generally from $200 to $250 per month, and are subject to park rules. And many say they are always subject to unfair and unreasonable rent increases.

But an unhappy mobile home owner just can't pack up and move. Moving is expensive, usually costing thousands of dollars. Moreover, there is no place to put the homes. There's just no room.

Residents also say that most parks will not accept a used mobile home. So if a mobile home owner can't find a place to put his home he is stuck, and there's not much of a market for used mobile homes.

James Lyon, who edits the homeowners newsletter at Paradise Village, put it this way: "This simply is not a free market situation. We're trapped. . . ."

Rep. Tom Armstrong, D-Plantation, has recognized the numbers, and he has recognized the concerns of mobile home owners. He also has become their advocate.

Armstrong is sponsoring what is expected to be a huge mobile home owner rally on Oct. 29, which will include a panel of appointed area homeowners association representatives, legislators and local officials.

"We're trying to unify the residents of mobile home parks into a voting bloc so they know what their rights are and what the issues are," Armstrong said. "We're trying to get rid of some of the homelessness that some mobile home residents feel."

In the third of his stories that we are examining here, Davis used the interpretative reporting concept to add context, perspective and feeling to the concerns of a bereaved father in a way that defined a public policy issue with life-saving potential. This story appeared on Oct. 30, 1985, and was entitled, "Father Wants Deadly Canals Made Safe":

Charles Reynolds rented a small motorboat several weeks ago and began searching the canals of far southwest Broward for his son, David, who had been missing for several days.

He had a gut feeling, one he hoped was wrong.

Reynolds felt his son wouldn't just pack up and run away from home. He knew something was wrong when David did not return home after going out with his friends on a Saturday night.

He also knew David, 20, had been driving in far southwest Broward county the night he disappeared. And Reynolds knew that cars can easily end up in the many canals that run along the roads out there.

While dragging the canals on Oct. 8, Charles Reynolds discovered his son's submerged 1981 Toyota Celica. His son's body was found in the auto.

The car was in a canal off of Griffin Road near Southwest 188th Avenue. The intersection where the accident occurred has a short S-curve near the new Interstate 75 exchange.

"The road has a very big dip and it automatically throws you to the north side of the road," Reynolds said.

Reynolds is angry because he said he believes his son's life could have been saved had there been guardrails at this intersection.

"I would do anything I have to to get it corrected," Reynolds said, adding that he thinks it's ridiculous if money is the only thing preventing the installation of guardrails.

"It doesn't make sense," Reynolds said. "You can't put a price on a human life."

Since 1983 there have been at least six drownings and dozens of injuries resulting from cars plunging into canals in southwest Broward. Those statistics are based on reports from local police agencies and the Broward Sheriff's Office.

According to the latest available records through July, at least 75 cars have run into the canals in Davie since 1983. Cooper City reported 10 canal accidents during the same period, while Pembroke Pines reported eight such accidents through 1984.

In many cases the roads that run along canals have no shoulders, few guardrails, and cars drive within only a few feet of the canals.

The problem, say traffic engineers and police, is that many of these roads were never intended for the amount of traffic traveling on them daily. At one time, most were just rural dirt roads, with few, if any, warning signs for motorists to slow down near dangerous spots. . . .

The stories by Brandon and Davis that we have examined were written with a bit of distance in time from when they appeared in print. That made providing the setting, context, perspective and human touch a bit easier than the task of a reporter who has only a few hours between learning something and getting a story into print, who is covering what is called in newspaper jargon a breaking story.

Interpretative Reporting on Deadline

But the interpretative concept also can improve breaking stories (stories done close to deadline), which is why the concept should be the cornerstone of even the beginning journalism student's thinking about how to do quality reporting.

Eugene Roberts, executive editor of the Philadelphia *Inquirer,* one of the nation's finest newspapers, had some wise things to say about reporting in the February 1985 edition of the *Washington Journalism Review.* In a symposium addressing the question "What Makes a Great Reporter," Roberts said:

There is no perfect way, no wallet size guide to great reporting. The newsroom that becomes a shrine to one type of reporting is in danger of keeling over, out of balance. The editor ought to applaud the person who wrote the well-crafted brief as readily as the one who did the definitive nine-part series. Thanks, sure, to the reporter who single-handedly detects the next trend; but hooray, too, to the one who succinctly and accurately reports the news conference. Hosanna to the film critic, but hot damn to the beat reporter. . . . Reporting, like anything else is a learning process. . . . The best reporters, whatever their backgrounds or their personalities, share that consummate drive to get to the center of a story and then put the reader on the scene.

Roberts also observed in that article that he has a prejudice in favor of reporters starting out on smaller newspapers, as Brandon and Davis did, rather than on larger ones such as the Chicago dailies. On a smaller paper, Roberts said, you are more likely to learn to cover all kinds of stories—trials, floods, politics and crime—and do breaking stories as well as non-breaking news and features. On the largest metros, he said, young reporters often do not get that diversity of experience early enough. Thus they sometimes have to learn instantly, under great pressure, too late in their careers all the things that a young reporter learns early on a smaller newspaper.

This book shares the attitudes toward reporting expressed by Roberts and therefore will emphasize the basic reporting and newswriting skills along with examining the demands and requirements of more complex, specialized reporting. Throughout, recognizing the realities of modern newsgathering, the book keeps as a central, basic concept the fundamental importance of interpretation in all reporting.

The Nature of Newspaper Work _____

The Newspaper As a Business

Of necessity a newspaper is a business enterprise that must be economically profitable to survive. It is a peculiar business enterprise because its social service is considered so important that it is protected by the First Amendment to the Constitution.

Freedom of the press pertains to gathering and printing the news only, however, and not to the commercial aspects of publishing. Like all other businesses, news media must obey laws pertaining to child labor, wages and hours, antitrust, taxation and so forth.

As commercial enterprises, newspapers have been affected by the same economic trends that are present in all other phases of the economy. Most importantly that means mergers, consolidations and purchases to eliminate small independent businesses. Despite anti-trust laws there are huge monopolies, financial conglomerates and international multinationals whose holdings are widely diversified. Newspapers, magazines and other journalistic enterprises are bought and sold as are businesses dealing in food, clothing, machinery or anything else.

In 1910, when the population of the United States was approximately 92 million, there were 2,202 daily newspapers. In 1985 there were approximately 1,800 daily newspapers to serve a population of 238 million. Whereas in grandfather's day virtually every city of 15,000 or over had rival newspapers and the largest cities—New York, Chicago and others—had from five to ten papers each, today only a few of the largest cities have second newspapers and most of those are under the same ownership.

There is, however, competition for advertising and news from independently owned radio and television stations and from a growing number of community, suburban and special interest periodicals. There are about 9,000 weeklies and about 13,500 other nondailies, mostly community gossip sheets or throwaway shopping newspapers, which are becoming more editorial in content.

The existence of these nondailies means more job opportunities for beginners. Many of them are gadflies, often embarrassing the larger dailies by scooping them on important stories, mostly exposés.

In the '80s newspapers began taking advantage of modern technological advances and marketing practices to experiment with new methods of gathering, displaying, and selling information. Their production processes are in a state of rapid and continuing change. But their need for clear, imaginative writing, and bright, well-educated reporters capable of perceptive interpretation of the events and forces of our time remains and is intensifying.

The Reporting Life

Any experience, from the high school or college campus newspaper to the most standardized of the metropolitan dailies, is valuable. Monetary reward is seldom the prime motivation of a would-be newspaper reporter, although, as will be related in Chapter 4, the starvation wages and long working hours of yesteryear are no more.

Good reporters today quickly move from beginning salaries of $12,000–$20,000 a year (in 1985 dollars) to salaries that range from $30,000–$50,000 and sometimes higher on large metropolitan papers.

Understandably applicants ask themselves:

1. How do I know I would like it?
2. How do I know I am qualified?
3. How should I prepare myself?
4. Can I preserve my integrity?

Television and movies notwithstanding, newspaper reporters do not often emulate detectives in exposing murderers, kidnappers and subversives, nor do they shout "stop the presses" and compose headlines over the telephone after profanely "telling off" unreasonable superiors. Rather, they put in a regular full day's work in and out of remarkably quiet and orderly newsrooms, where they remove their hats.

In large cities, some reporters spend their entire working days in the pressrooms at police headquarters, city hall, the county buildings, the federal building and other places where it is certain important news will originate or be reported. Some still telephone their information to rewrite persons in note form or they dictate it, composing as they go along. Many now send copy from personal computers to the main newspaper computer. On smaller newspapers, beat reporters visit their news sources once or twice daily, returning to their offices to compose their own accounts. They also may double as general assignment reporters, covering news that occurs at places other than the familiar spots. In all instances they are under the careful direction and scrutiny of the city editor, who in turn is responsible to the managing editor, who has general charge of the entire news-editorial operation.

To satisfy the cosmopolitan interests of their readers, newspapers are becoming increasingly departmentalized. The geographical beats are giving way to interest or subject beats. How departmentalized a newspaper operation is and how split up the managerial and operational functions are depend upon its size. Someone is in charge of handling news that reaches the office via the press associations (Associated Press and United Press International), so there may be a telegraph or wire desk or, on larger papers, a foreign news department desk. Some large newspapers also have a central copy desk where most stories from whatever department are checked for style, accuracy, and so forth, and given headlines. Makeup (deciding where stories and other, mostly illustrative, materials are to appear) may be handled by a separate makeup editor, by a news editor or by someone else performing multiple duties. Pagination—the computerized make-up of newspaper pages—is being introduced into more and more newsrooms.

Most newspapers, large and small, have had autonomous sports departments for decades. Society pages that enjoyed equal longevity, however, have virtually disappeared in recent years. For a time they were replaced by women's pages. Today there is considerable experimentation to determine both the format and contents of a substitute department.

Already the need is recognized for specialists on energy, environment, education, religion, civil liberties, health, housing and planning and some other fields. Beat reporters covering any of these cannot remain stationed in a single pressroom. There are a large number of offices, public and private, that the reporter must visit or maintain contact with by telephone. Service clubs, church groups, women's organizations, labor unions and other groups have become actively interested in many fields related to social welfare. The reporter must be familiar with the magazines, books, reports and other material related to a specialized field.

A warning to such colleagues is sounded as follows by Casey Bukro, Chicago *Tribune* environment reporter:

> Specialists must avoid falling into a trap, in which they begin to view themselves as "experts" and begin writing stories that have little meaning to the average reader. Specialists do this by writing over their readers' heads, giving little explanation, or by writing about rarefied issues of little consequence other than to show that the writer knows something nobody else knows. A specialist should not be an elitist. He should be an interpreter, an explainer.

Although the reporter may be haunted constantly by deadlines (the last minutes at which copy can be submitted to make editions), there is generally less monotony and consequently danger of "getting into a rut" in newspaper work than there is in almost anything else one could do today. This is the age of the Organization Man in which white-collar as well as blue-collar workers increasingly are becoming comparatively smaller and smaller cogs in huge industrial machines whose total operations (or even purposes) it is difficult for them to understand. Many recent authors have deplored the extent to which the contemporary economy puts a premium on conformity, stifles imagination and originality, causes boredom and, consequently, destroys initiative and even self-respect.

There is, of course, considerable similarity in the news from the same source day after day. Nevertheless, no two stories ever are exactly alike. The principals at least are different and so are their reactions to whatever befalls them, such as arrest, accident, or honor. And, even though the swashbuckling days of Richard Harding Davis are long since past, there is still a thrill, or at least a satisfied feeling, with every assignment successfully concluded. There is a greater pride of workmanship and sense of accomplishment than is possible for workers in most industries and offices in the late twentieth century. Even though low on the press's totem pole, young reporters carry more prestige with the public than do apprentices in most other fields. At the scene of a fire or riot they flash their credentials and are allowed to cross police lines. On the routine beat they are courted by those who want to get something in or to keep something out of the paper. From the very start of a journalistic career, by the very nature of the work, a reporter, "is somebody," and this fact cannot help but be gratifying to the human ego.

The reporter is an influential person. Several others will have a part in determining how news appears in the paper. Nevertheless, the reporter has "first crack" at it, exercising original judgment to determine whether and/or how something is to be reported. The reporter, in other words, is the backbone of the newsgathering and disseminating operation. Truly, every reporter is also an editor and, conversely, the best editors continue throughout their future careers to maintain the attitudes of reporters.

The occupational disease that journalists must guard against is cynicism. Whereas skepticism is a journalistic asset, a hard-boiled or flippant attitude toward the so-called realities of life can lead not only to a flagrant disregard of the public interest but also to personal deterioration. Many of the public figures with whom they come into contact, reporters know, do not deserve public adulation but are, to use the vernacular, stuffed shirts or phonies. Disillusionment comes also with discovery that the "rules of the game"—as the game actually is "played" in politics, business and many other aspects of life—are often crass, mercenary and hypocritical. Overcoming gullibility and learning the "facts of life" can be valuable, provided they lead to intelligent sophistication.

The reporter who has a professional attitude will be happier and more effective. Professionalism can be present or absent among carpenters, hotel clerks, nurses, doctors, lawyers, taxi drivers, newspapermen, and anybody or everybody else. As for journalism, there is no field that offers greater opportunities for the development of a professional point of view, idealism, public service and the like. There is no better calling for those who want to help make democracy work more effectively.

Another important advantage of newspaper reporting is that one is paid while learning. On every new assignment one gets valuable experience for any future occupational venture. Reporting is a continuing education.

Personality Traits of Reporters

Successful journalists are not born; they are made. Most of the personality traits usually listed as valuable for the journalist are ones that would be equally essential for success in most other professional fields: intelligence, friendliness, compassion, reliability, imagination, social conscience, ingenuity, nerve, speed, accuracy, courage, endurance, ability to organize one's activities, perseverance, mental alertness, honesty, punctuality, cheerfulness, the power of observation, shrewdness, enterprise, optimism, humor, adaptability, initiative and the like.

Altogether too many college students think training for journalism consists primarily in learning how to write. They are mostly students who did well in high school English and were inspired with literary ambitions by teachers who were surprised and grateful to find fewer than the average number of grammatical errors in their themes. Unfortunately, there is no such thing as "just writing," in journalism or any other field. William Shakespeare is immortal not because of vocabulary or style but because of greatness of thought. He had an incomparable knowledge of history, psychology, geography, philosophy, and many other fields. He and other masters of past centuries are read today because they had something extraordinarily worthwhile to say.

Because great ideas rather than beautiful words and phrases make for superior writing, everything that a journalism student studies is of potential value. The subject matter of journalism includes all that is taught in courses in political science, history, economics, sociology, chemistry, physics and other subjects too numerous to mention. Students who recognize this fact as freshmen have a big advantage. By the time they take their first journalism course in the sophomore, junior or senior year, they will have more than the average liberal-arts student's superficial interest in and knowledge of the contents of innumerable textbooks. The reporter's head and files should be full of information on which to rely when exploring on or off campus in search of news. Journalism courses should make textbook knowledge come to life. This background should enable the reporter to understand and interpret the contemporary scene. Through experience in hiring both liberal arts and journalism school graduates, editors have learned that a so-called broad background of general courses is not in itself adequate preparation for newspaper reporting. However, because the journalist deals mostly with news related to the subject matter of courses in the different social sciences, students who have little or no interest in political science, economics and sociology should take stock to determine whether to aspire to a career in journalism.

The young person who should be encouraged to go into journalism, therefore, is the one who wants very badly to spend an adulthood saying or writing worthwhile things about contemporary problems. The more cosmopolitan one's interests, the better.

Among the courses that relate to the kind of news the future journalist will cover are ones in criminology, urban sociology, business, labor problems, public finance, taxation, political parties, population problems, state and local government and others in the fields of sociology, political science and economics. Taking them is the comparatively easy way to learn what any successful journalist must know; the hard way is on the job. A student supposedly goes to college to get a head start.

Nose for News

Usually listed first among the special qualifications that a newsgatherer needs is a nose for news, which means the ability to recognize the news possibilities of an item of information and involves

1. The ability to recognize that the information can be made of interest to readers.
2. The ability to recognize clues that may be very casual but may lead to the discovery of important news.
3. The ability to recognize the relative importance of a number of facts concerning the same general subject.
4. The ability to recognize the possibility of other news related to the particular information at hand.

Common sense is indispensable for the reporter. In these days of public relations counsels and press releases, news sources often are difficult to see. Reporters must ask question after question to draw out whoever they get to interview to learn about less obvious but important phases of the subject at hand. They should, in other words, be inquisitive, perceptive and healthfully skeptical.

What Is News? _____

At any given moment billions of simultaneous events occur throughout the world. Someone is born, dies, gives a speech, attends a meeting, takes a trip, commits a crime and so on ad infinitum. All of these occurrences are potentially news. But they do not become so until some purveyor of news gives an account of them. The news, in other words, is the account of the event, not something intrinsic in the event itself.

Professional newsgatherers judge the potential interest and/or importance of an event before deciding whether to render an account of it, thus making it news. These newsgatherers are humans, not deities. They possess no absolutistic yardstick by which to judge what to report and what to ignore. There is nothing that cannot be made interesting in the skillful telling; and only a supernatural power could say with absolute certainty what is important and what is unimportant.

Nothing is news until it is reported, no matter when it occurred. After an important person dies hitherto unknown facts about him or her become known as in the iconoclastic anecdotes about J. Edgar Hoover, John F. Kennedy and others. Sometimes the events occurred many years earlier, as the revelation that William O. Douglas wrote to Harry S Truman offering his support in 1948, or that Dwight Eisenhower secretly taped conversations in the Oval Office that included a criticism of Richard Nixon for attacking the foreign policy of the Democrats.

The first-rate newsgatherer does not ask himself what the potential use or effect of his information will be or how many "gatekeepers" will handle it; rather, his sole duty is to concentrate on discovering as much of the truth about a matter as is possible in the time available.

The Interpretative Viewpoint _____

To climb the ladder of success modern journalists have to be more than thoroughly trained journeymen. They must be capable of more than routine coverage and able to intelligently interpret as well as simply report what is going on.

To interpret the news it is necessary to understand it, and understanding means more than just the ability to define the jargon used by persons in different walks of life. It involves recognizing the particular event as one of a series with both a cause and an effect. The historians of the future, with their perspective, may be better able to depict the trends and currents of the present, but if today's gatherers of information are well informed, through reading of history, the study of economics, sociology, political science and other academic subjects, and are acquainted with the attempts of other observers to interpret the modern scene in books and magazine articles, they will at least be aware of the fact that an item of news is not an isolated incident but one inevitably linked to a chain of important events. That kind of insight is vital to convey to the larger citizenry and electorate that need it to function themselves and to help make democratic institutions function better.

The first important impetus to interpretative handling of the news was provided by World War I. When it broke out most Americans were surprised and utterly unable to explain its causes. In his doctoral dissertation at the University of Wisconsin in the mid-'30s, the late Maynard Brown suggested the extent to which the newsgathering agencies were responsible for this phenomenon. Brown wrote in part:

> Where the Associated Press failed most was in preventing its reporters from sending background and informative articles based on politics and trends. It smugly adopted the attitude of permitting correspondents to report only what had definitely transpired. It wanted no interpretation of events but the mere factual reporting of the obvious. Some of its correspondents were trained in

foreign affairs, but too few were able to interpret or discern significant events and tendencies.

Not only the Associated Press but other press associations and newspapers as well learned a great lesson from the experience of being totally unprepared either to understand the final steps that plunged the world into war or adequately to report the war once it started. During the '20s and '30s they peopled the capitals and other important news centers of the world with trained experts qualified not only to report but also to explain and interpret factual occurrences. Among the best of these journalistic scholars were Walter Duranty, John Gunther, Vincent Sheean, Edgar Ansel Mowrer, Edgar Snow, Quentin Reynolds, William Shirer and W. M. Fodor. In newspaper stories, magazine articles, authoritative books and radio commentaries, they and others did such a thoroughly competent job that, by contrast with 1914, for years before World War II began in 1939, an overwhelmingly majority of Americans expected it or at least knew it was possible if not probable.

Reader demand for more than mere drab basic reporting of domestic news grew tremendously after the stock-market crash of 1929 and during the depression years of the '30s and the period of New Deal experimentation, which brought with it nationwide awareness of the increased importance in the life of every citizen of the federal government. Readership of the recently created weekly news magazines, *Time, Newsweek* and others, skyrocketed; so did the circulation of *Reader's Digest* and a multitude of other monthly digest magazines. So did the number and readership of how-to-do-it and other easily read books, allegedly compendious accounts of how to understand what was happening in a variety of fields of human interest and activity. So also did newsletters for general and specialized audiences.

Slow to modify their basic news formula, newspapers nevertheless expanded their contents to include signed columns by political analysts, most of which were syndicated at reasonable cost so as to be available for moderate-and small-sized newspapers. In the mid-'30s newspapers also experimented with weekly news reviews, some of which (notably that of the New York *Times*) have survived. They also tried out various forms of daily reviews, expanded Sunday magazine or feature sections and increased the number of supplemental articles to provide historical, geographical, biographical and other background information to help make current news more understandable and meaningful. A whole new vocabulary developed to categorize these writings. Instead of lumping them all under the general heading of "think pieces" as in the past, newsmen talked of sidebars, explainers, situationers, wrap-ups, button-ups, blockbusters and other types of explanatory, enterprise, offbeat, background, subsurface, creative, speculative or interpretative reporting and writing.

Today, the debate is virtually over, with only a few still arguing against the necessity for interpretative reporting. This means that to become more than a humdrum journeyman the future reporter must prepare himself to help meet the increasing need and demand for "subsurface" or "depth" reporting, to "take the reader behind the scenes of the day's action," "relate the news to the reader's own framework and experience," "make sense out of the facts," "put factual news in perspective," "put meaning into the news," "point up the significance of current events," and so on, to use the expressions of various authorities.

Foremost defender of interpretative reporting against its critics was Lester Markel, longtime associate editor of the New York *Times,* who, in the heat of debate over the concept, once wrote:

> Those who object to interpretation say that a story should be confined to the "facts." I ask, "What facts?" And I discover that there is in reality no such thing as an "objective" article in the sense these objectors use it—or in any sense, for that matter.
>
> Take the most "objective" of reporters. He collects fifty facts; out of these fifty he selects twelve which he considers important enough to include in his piece, leaving out thirty-eight. This is the first exercise of judgment.
>
> Then the reporter decides which of these twelve facts shall constitute the lead of the story. The particular fact he chooses gets the emphasis—which is important because often the reader does not go beyond the first paragraph. This is the second exercise of judgment.
>
> Then the editor reads the so-called objective story and makes a decision as to whether it is to be played on page 1 or on page 29. If it is played on page 1 it may have considerable impact on opinion. If it is put on page 29 it has no such emphasis. The most important editorial decision on any paper, I believe, is what goes on page 1. This is the third exercise of judgment.
>
> In brief, this "objective" news is, in its exponents' own terms, very unobjective and the kind of judgment required for interpretation is no different from the kind of judgment involved in the selection of the facts for a so-called factual story and in the display of that story.

In other words, just as the Constitution is said to mean what the Supreme Court says it means, so is news what newspapers and other media of communication decide it is to be.

How to Prepare _____

Informational Background

The rule to follow in preparing for a career in journalism is this: learn as much about as many things as possible and stay intellectually alert. Ignorant reporters are at a tremendous disadvantage. They annoy news sources, fail to obtain all of the essential facts, and may make gross errors of fact as well as emphasis.

To cover intelligently a police station, criminal court, city hall, county, state or federal office, or political headquarters, reporters must understand the setups of government, the nature and functions of various offices. They must be able to read and quickly digest the contents of legal documents. They must know the meanings of such terms as *corpus delicti, habeas corpus, injunction* and *certiorari.* A reporter cannot say *divorce* when *separate maintenance* is meant, or *parole* when it should be *probation.* The reporter must be able to read a bank balance sheet, know when a financial market is bullish and when bearish and what it means to *sell short, hedge* and *stockpile*. A reporter must understand what it means to *refinance a bond issue* or *liquidate the assets of a corporation*.

It is impossible for interpretative reporters to write that the last obstacle to beginning a slum-clearance program has been removed unless they know the procedure by which such projects are developed. One can't explain the status of a pending city ordinance without understanding what the rules provide for future consideration of it. It is impossible to interview a prosecuting attorney regarding a possible course of action in a particular case unless one knows what the alternatives are.

Although most editorial offices today are equipped with good libraries, or morgues as they often still are called, the reporter has to know which reference books and clipping files to consult to obtain historical and other explanatory information to "round out" a story. As reporters gain experience they become veritable storehouses of knowledge. Aware of the nature of different organizations, public and private, the trained newsgatherer knows which ones to consult on which occasion and what each group's slant or interest is likely to be.

Without background knowledge of a subject a reporter cannot fill out an account by declaring that the home run was the longest ever hit in the park; that this was the first time a certain ward gave a voting majority to the candidates of a particular party; that a fatal accident occurred at an intersection where the city council once refused to permit the erection of stop signs; that what seems to be a new proposal for civic reform really was resurrected from a decade-old report by an elder statesman.

At an Associated Press Managing Editors meeting, Robert Paine of the Memphis *Commercial Appeal* once cited the following story:

> Grand Junction, Tenn., Feb. 19.—(AP)—A smooth-working hound flushed seven bevies of quail in a three-hour trial yesterday for the top performance of the national championship.

Commented Paine:

> I imagine that every bird-dog owner in the country shuddered in horror at the word HOUND. That would be about the same as saying a cow won the Kentucky Derby. There are strictly different kinds of dogs and bird-dog fanciers have a habit of shooting from the hip when one of their dogs is called a hound.
>
> Secondly, the word FLUSH is the exact opposite of the word that should have been used. That would be about like saying Babe Ruth won the game by striking out. Flush means to frighten the birds into flying away. The correct word is point.

It was not that many years ago when a journalistic ignoramous asked the Nobel prize-winning physicist Dr. Robert Millikan what cosmic rays were "good for." Those were the days when science was treated more or less as a joke in editorial offices and reporters assigned to science news stories were capable of little more than asking when the scholars expected to fly to Mars, find the missing link or take the smell out of the onion. No wonder that many scientists still are reluctant to talk to reporters.

The interpretative reporter seeks in stories to answer the intelligent reader's query, "What does it mean?" To keep a particular news event "in focus," the interpretative reporter shows its comparative importance. Darrell Huff began his *How to Lie with Statistics,* a book every journalist of whatever kind would find valuable reading, with a warning that widespread reporting of a particular type of news, such as crime, easily can create a distorted impression as regards a social situation.

Mere figures showing total numbers of different types of crime committed in two or more areas only suggest the real story. Explanations of why styles in lawbreaking differ in different places at the same time, and at the same place at different times, are to be found in such variable factors as size and complexion of population, police policies and activities and many others.

To present anywhere near a true picture of the housing situation in any community, a reporter must consider the age of the community and of the dwelling units; the adequacy of zoning and building codes and their enforcement; the influx of newcomers and the effect, including that caused by prejudice against certain types of persons because of race, national origin, religion or other reasons; the extent of overpopulation; transportation and parking facilities; educational, cultural and recreational advantages; the income and cost of living indices; nearby urban and suburban growth and similar factors. With such data the reporter can provide readers with an understanding of the situation and enable them properly to evaluate proposals for change.

Mere announcement that consumer credit outstanding at any given time is such-and-such means little or nothing unless the reader knows how the figures given compare with similar ones for comparable periods in other months or years. Tables, graphs and charts help show trends. For a broader picture of the state of the economy as a whole, more than comparative figures in any one economic category is necessary. In addition to installment buying, price indices, extent and kind (savings or checking) of bank deposits and withdrawals, a breakdown of the types of depositors (by size of deposits), purchase and cancellation of government securities (with comparable breakdown) bank loans, mortgages, new businesses, business failures, growth of chains and monopolies and other similar factors must be considered.

Just as sports writers explain in considerable detail the reasoning behind the strategies and tactics of coaches, managers and contestants, so could reporters dealing with political affairs explain that rivals of a political leader often are made candidates for judgeships in order to remove them from active politics. The interpretative reporter knows that cornerstone layings, dedications of buildings, openings of parks and other public facilities and similar acts are timed so as to have the maximum beneficial effect for the officeholders in charge. After they have been around long enough, reporters know the tricks of the trade and can at least suggest probable causes for the behavior of many newsworthy persons. Failure to do so means that readers are often left in the position of just not knowing what's going on.

To write with the perspective of the cultural anthropologist or historian of a century means to be aware of schools of thought, climates of opinion and social, economic and political trends. Scholarly journalists should know when the views of an educator are consistent with those of an outstanding scholar or organization or with what has been attempted elsewhere. Education reporters should know what *progressive* versus *traditional* in pedagogical methods means. To cover social welfare they should know the difference between the missionary (settlement house or boys club) and the self-help (area or community project) approaches.

Of this the studious interpretative reporter is certain: nothing just happens. A wave of intolerance has a cause. So has a revival movement, excessive hero worship, a bullish stock market, an increase in superstition, or any fad, fashion, craze or mass movement. Sometimes what seem to be isolated phenomena in several different fields really stem from the same causal roots. At any rate, there are always explanations for how we got that way. For instance, when violence erupts and persists simultaneously in many parts of the world, it is shortsighted to treat one incident as an isolated phenomenon.

Academic Preparation

Although there probably always will be exceptions, most journalists need college educations, including a degree in journalism. The proportion of those with master's and other higher degrees also is increasing among candidates for the better paying, more satisfying, more challenging of today's reporting positions.

Modern journalism schools are not trade schools. From two-thirds to four-fifths of a student's classwork is taken in the liberal arts or other divisions. Anything and everything that a future journalist studies has potential future value and it is frustrating not to be able to take the entire curriculum in the humanities and the natural and physical sciences. Those who are ambitious to specialize ultimately in particular fields should do so, but the majority should strive for a thorough and well-rounded background in the social sciences: political science, sociology and economics in particular. The student should try to get in courses in public finance, criminology and labor problems among others. History courses provide perspective and psychology enables one to come closer to understanding both individual and crowd behavior. The reporter should have some idea about what public opinion is that journalists are supposed to influence.

In advanced journalism courses the student should expect to be taught how to utilize the background and theoretical knowledge acquired all over the rest of the campus in reporting and interpreting the contemporary scene. On assignments, the students observe theory becoming action, and by taking some philosophy they will be better able to comprehend and evaluate the immediate incident in terms of the general and eternal.

A strict journalism instructor, simulating the exactness of a hard-boiled city editor, can teach sound methods of research. The journalistic fact-finder does not begin with a hypothesis to prove, but rather tries, by background research and legwork, to devise various hypotheses and then to test them thoroughly. Good, open-minded seekers after truth explore every possible avenue of investigation; and only after exhausting every chance to obtain additional information do they attempt to draw conclusions regarding the acumulated data. In the process, the student-reporter becomes familiar with the nature of reference or source material and will learn about the day-to-day realities of such important things as how to read and understand a county board's budget or the complicated declaration filed to begin a civil law action.

Since World War II, a number of social scientists have become interested in quantitative analysis of various aspects of social behavior and in communication theory. They use the tools of the statistician and the language of the sociologist to examine the effects of various ways to influence human thought and behavior. Many of their findings are of value to the propagandist, advertiser, public relations counsel and others who have ideas or products to sell. Knowledge of what they are up to is important for the true journalist who is a protector of their potential victims. The journalist, however, should be wary of academic fads and should examine the so-called behavioral sciences and communications theory courses to determine whether they have relevance to anything journalistic and whether the teachers of them have any practical knowledge of the profession of newsgathering. *Social Science As Sorcery* by Stanislav Andreski is an edifying critique by a Reading University scholar.

Prospective employers usually want to see samples of an applicant's published work. The student who has any thought of becoming a journalist should start accumulating clippings as early as possible. Certainly there should be stories written for high school and college papers. Even better, and more important to today's editors, there should be stories written during summer internships, which are available on most newspapers today for students energetic enough to seek them out. There are many opportunities for young journalists and persistence in pursuing them will impress editors looking for good young journalists to hire.

CHAPTER

2

Getting It Right

Sometimes a reporter is present at an event such as a meeting, speech, court hearing or athletic contest. More often, however, the newsgatherer must rely on secondhand information obtained by interviewing eyewitnesses, authorities and others, or from press releases, reports and documents. Even when the reporter is at the scene, facts and details must be checked with police, firefighters, convention chairpersons and the like.

Usually these sources are approachable and cooperative. As much cannot always be said of others from whom the reporter seeks supplementary background information, comments, explanations or predictions of the consequences of an event. Maybe the news source doesn't want to become involved in some matter, for fear of being summoned to court as a witness or of arousing the displeasure of public officials, gangsters and others. Possibly a person whose opinion is solicited does not want to reveal ignorance or to risk betraying a business or other secret. The reasons a news source slams the door or telephone or clams up may be many and diverse, but the obligation of the reporter is the same: to learn any facts that it is in the public interest to make known, consistent with considerations of ethics and human decency.

"Getting it right," the title of this chapter, describes concisely what is probably the most difficult task of the reporter, just as it is the most challenging task of the scientist or historian. For journalists, the task is even more imposing because they work against much shorter deadlines than scientists or historians. Fundamentally, that is because the decisions in a representative system of government such as ours cannot be postponed for later mulling over the way scholarly inquiries can be delayed.

What journalists, scientists and historians do have in common, however, is their unique individuality as human beings, each with varied experiences, values and psyches, each with sensory perception systems somewhat different from those of anyone else. The net effect of those differences is that each human being interprets the world uniquely. Those differences are precious—the sources of our humanity and our creative, critical, analytical capacities of thought. They also are a part of the insurmountable barrier that blocks the path to the objectivity that good thinkers pursue as a goal, even though they know it is impossible to attain. Scientists follow the scientific method in an effort to eliminate personal bias and find THE TRUTH. Professional historians spend long hours in graduate school studying techniques they can use to help them try dispassionately to evaluate evidence about our past. But like the reporter, most of what such scholars think they have discovered is THE TRUTH eventually turns out to be something less than THE TRUTH. That is because sooner or later some other scholar sees something that others missed, despite their best efforts. So it is with reporters and their pursuit of facts, their efforts to get things right.

The best reporters usually are the best mainly because they recognize that THE TRUTH is perpetually elusive, that all reporting, as with all other kinds of human study, is subject to selective individual perceptions and interpretations. Good reporters strive to be fair and thorough. They treat their story ideas as hypotheses to be tested rather than as truths to be documented. They level with their readers and with themselves about the sources of their "facts" and the foundations of their interpretations. They are skeptical without being cynical about most everything, especially their own perceptions.

Reporters of that quality are loved by good editors, but such reporters can drive editors, if not nuts, at least to frustration. Really good reporters always have one more fact to check, one more phone call to make, one more sentence with which to tinker, even when the deadline is undeniably at hand. The very best reporters know in their bones that they are likely to be wrong a good deal of the time, just as the best scholars are humble rather than arrogant about their discoveries. It is a quality of thought that can paralyze some reporters, but one that energizes others, making them incredibly persistent and attentive to detail. If their mother says she loves them, they are nevertheless driven by the inclination to check it out.

Without that state of mind in some human beings through the long history of our species, we most likely would be extinct, or alternatively, at best probably still would live in dark caves, fearing both the dark inside and the light outside. It is that skeptical state of mind which gives us the courage and wisdom to acknowledge that nothing ever is quite what it seems, but also to realize that such uncertainty is a strong argument for trying to make better sense of what is true today than we were able to make of what seemed true yesterday. It is that state of mind, rather than a desire to make life blissful for prosperous groups of powerful publishers, which the framers of the First Amendment to the United States Constitution sought to encourage. It is the state of mind of the very best reporters.

Getting it right is not easy, which is why the best reporters relish the task even as they recognize the difficulty of fulfilling it. They are at once arrogant enough to try to get it right and humble enough to realize they probably will not. What follows in the rest of this chapter is some specific advice to help you in your struggles to be a good reporter, to get it as close to right as you can. But remember as you go about that important task to realize that what you think is THE TRUTH of the matter is almost certainly only your individual perception of the truth, your personal interpretation of reality. Alas, Walter Cronkite to the contrary, what you report probably never will be precisely "the way it is." But that is not an argument to give up. It is an argument for reporters to get going.

The Q Is the Mother of the A _____

Questions are the basic implements in the reporter's toolbox, whether the reporter is interviewing, observing someone or something firsthand, doing research in a library, combing through stacks of official documents or using the most modern social science methods of gathering statistics. The questions you decide to pursue, the questions you reject or the questions that never occur to you inevitably will determine the answers you discover and the answers that elude you. What is true for computers is also true for reporters: Garbage in, garbage out.

In that sense, one of the best definitions of news—best in the sense of its seering simplicity of insight—is the observation made some years ago by Thomas Griffith, a former editor of *Life* magazine.

A news story, Griffith said, originates in a collision of a fact with an interested mind. What makes one journalist "see" a story and another not see anything worth reporting has to do with the individual reporter's imagination, curiosity and temperament, he added.

In seeking to define the essence of reporting, of the attempts to get things right, Griffith put the emphasis where it belongs: not just on what the reporter beholds, but also on what a reporter decides to behold. His view recognizes that even if news did grow on trees, was simply a fruit there for the plucking, it would be up to a reporter to get to the orchard and to decide what to pick.

The controlling decision of what will be news rests with the reporter, not with the phenomenon the reporter may decide to report or to ignore, however much either editors or critics of the media would like it to be otherwise. Whether something becomes news depends on what the reporter decides to ask of whom, how, when, where and under what circumstances. Without a reporter to ask a question, and to frame that question, there will be no answer for the readers.

Those may seem like self-evident propositions. They are not. Much of the journalism of yesterday and today pretends to operate on an opposite premise. That premise holds that reporters are or should be little more than unfeeling, unthinking robots. According to this school of thought, reporters can and should be programmed to ask only totally objective questions according to predetermined formulas for deciding what's news and what is not. If a dog bites a man, this school holds in its simplest form, that is usually not news. But if a man bites a dog, that is certainly news. Such definitions represent a view of journalism that is useful in marketing news as a product. After all, few Americans want to believe that the news really is the product of a newspaper employee's subjectivities. It is a definition, too, that allows a publisher or editor to feel fair in trying to keep a news staff's reporting more or less within the control of the publisher's or editor's own concerns and viewpoints, without a lot of differing values being left free to roam indiscriminately among things and events that might become news. But it is a definition that does not describe what reporting really is or how reporting gets done, even though it is a definition that many reporters try to follow as much as they can. Reporting is something individual human beings do. It is, whether readers or bosses or even reporters feel comfortable with its inherent nature, an inevitable function of a reporter's curiosities, questions and even angers.

Because of that reality, it is extraordinarily important that reporters take great care asking themselves what to report in the first place, and then in shaping their questions, in considering how and from whom or what to seek answers and in conveying to readers what answers they think their reporting has found. Like it or not, the Q is the mother of the A. The question determines the answer to a great extent. In that sense, all reporting is interpretative reporting, including that done in the seemingly simple, but actually complex, forum of the interview.

Interviewing

Reliability of Witnesses

Even when news sources are cooperative the shrewd reporter should seek corroboration of whatever he is told. Editors often hold stories until at least two witnesses or authorities have verified their contents.

Beginning with Hugo Munsterberg's *On the Witness Stand* almost a century ago, there have been many scholarly investigations of the reliability of human testimony. An excellent article on the subject was "Eyewitness Testimony" by Robert Buckhaout in the December 1974 *Scientific American*. The author concludes, "Human perception is sloppy and uneven," and "the ideal observer does not exist, nor does the ideal physical environment to make testimony trustworthy."

It is human to distort an impression to conform to one's preconceived notions, prejudices and experiences. No instant recall is possible as it is when televising sports events. The closest approximation is the classroom exercise of staging a dramatic event and then asking students to prepare memoranda on what they observed. The differences in the reports are fantastic and constitute a strong warning to the journalistic truth-seeker.

Journalists are also suggestible human beings likely to be influenced by the prestige of informants. Their visual impressions are often distorted because of their preconceptions.

Getting the Interview

When seeking additional facts about a fast-breaking incident, a reporter does not have time to write or telephone for an appointment. A great deal of such interviewing is by telephone. For best results reporters should be straightforward, identifying themselves by name and newspaper. Pretending to be a police official or coroner's deputy is self-defeating, because the untruth is bound to be discovered, at least when the paper appears. Since the first 30 seconds of a telephone interview may be the most important, come to the point at once, politely, but making clear the nature of the information that is being sought. When seeking opinions as well as fact, avoid a negative approach as "You wouldn't want to say something on this matter, would you?" Rather say, "We want your opinion."

If someone has recommended that the reporter contact the interviewee that fact usually can be stated unless the tipster requested anonymity and the reporter guaranteed it. Unless it seems necessary to gain the confidence of the interviewee, it usually is better to postpone mention of other mutual acquaintances, as one never can be certain what the relationship between the interviewee and the third party is.

In all situations, whether face-to-face or by telephone, the interviewer must be flexible. Ordinarily it is better to postpone asking potentially embarrassing or irritating questions until after a friendly relationship has been established. However, when using the telephone, if the reporter fears the interviewee will hang up, it may be expedient to reveal whatever the reporter already knows with a request that the interviewee comment upon it.

When the time factor is not urgent, appointments can be made by mail or telephone. Some important people surround themselves with secretaries, public relations counsel, bodyguards and others to protect their privacy, which they often believe all journalists want to destroy. In such cases reporters are lucky if they have influential friends to put in a good word. It is important to make friends with people on the way up as well as those who are already in influential positions with an eye to their future value as sources. Friendly secretaries can be of great assistance.

Reportorial perseverance is usually rewarded. If a man deliberately evades the press by refusing to answer the telephone or by hiding in an office or at home, he plays a losing game. If he is a person whose information or opinion the newspaper has a right to request, his refusal to grant an interview does not make him appear in a very favorable light to readers. The reporter must be careful in stating that a man has disappeared to avoid being interviewed, but it can be said that a person could not be reached. In fact, such a statement should be included to let readers know that the effort was made. If a person answers the phone but still refuses to talk, his silence may be even more important news than any statement would have been. Once the reporter has questioned a person and has received a non-committal answer or no answer at all, he can say that Mr. So-and-So refused to make any comment. Then readers can draw their own conclusions as to why Mr. So-and-So would not talk.

> Mayor Alvin R. Potter had nothing to say today regarding the accusation that city employees, including himself, obtain free gasoline from the city yards.
> The charge was made yesterday by Ald. Leonard Ball, chairman of the streets committee. The chief executive's only reply to inquiring reporters was: "I have no statement to make at this time."

Sometimes the reporter may be able to convince a subject that it is better to make some statement. If interviewees know that the paper will run a story of their refusal to comment, they may be prodded into speaking against a previous resolution not to do so.

In *Inside Story,* Brit Hume, then assistant to columnist Jack Anderson, says it is a "common technique" to persuade a person that you have been told a truly lurid story to inspire him to reveal the truth. Hume often was sly in identifying himself with the syndicate that distributed the Anderson column rather than with his employer. And he recommends the two-questioner technique popular with police whereby one interrogator assumes a belligerent attitude while the other seems protective. *Washington Post* reporters Carl Bernstein and Bob Woodward, Pulitzer prize winners for their exposé of the Watergate scandal, reveal in their book *All the President's Men* that they inspired confidence when Bob said he was a registered Republican and Carl expressed a sincere antipathy for both parties. When an interviewee asked who gave the reporters his name, they could explain the necessity of protecting their sources, thus inspiring confidence from a jittery interviewee. They often called at interviewees' homes unannounced and always created the impression of seeking the truth regarding partial information they possessed. The confessions of these and several other top flight reporters inspired a great deal of soul searching throughout the entire journalistic world. The ethical beginner who is studying this textbook should become acquainted with the memoirs of many contemporary reporters.

The veteran foreign correspondent, Georgie Ann Geyer, who has interviewed the heads of many of the world's governments, relates how when foreign correspondents were not allowed to enter Cambodia, she obtained a tourist visa. That, she says, was the only time in 20 years that she misrepresented herself. On another occasion, however, she got herself invited to a dinner as a state guest rather than as a journalist.

The Reluctant Interviewee

Once the reporter has an audience the first task is to win the confidence of the interviewee. It is impossible to lay down rules for all occasions. Sometimes it is possible to break the ice by irrelevant conversation, perhaps inspired by a painting or other object in the room or by a comment on some hobby of the interviewee's. But unless the reporter is sincerely interested and, above all, well-informed, the effort may repulse the interviewee as being contrived.

The best way for reporters to impress the interviewee is by making clear what they are after and that they have prepared for the occasion by learning about the interviewee and the subject of the interview. Reporters should make it clear that they do not know all the facts; otherwise they would not be there.

Beginners and even some experienced reporters often yield to the temptation to argue with interviewees. If one hopes to convert the interviewee this is usually a futile effort, and one runs the risk of antagonizing the person from whom information is sought. It is possible, without being belligerent, to ask potentially embarrassing questions by requesting comments on statements or situations about which others have ideas different from those of the interviewee. Interviewers should have specific questions in mind but must be flexible enough to follow any leads to other points arising from the interviewee's responses.

If a person evades questions or changes the subject and talks about extraneous matters, the reporter must be tactful about interrupting. The source should not, however, be permitted to escape responding to the purpose of the interview. The reporter should not give up but should come back to vital unanswered questions. Continued dodging of them usually indicates that the interviewer is on the right track in the quest for knowledge. Reporters do not terminate an interview until they have asked all the questions they had in mind and have obtained some response from the subject.

Sometimes a lucky guess disarms a reluctant interviewee, as when the reporter asks whether a certain meeting is in the offing and the news source is startled into believing the reporter has more information than the interviewee had assumed to be the case.

When the interviewee is cautious or antagonistic it usually is best to take as few notes as possible. In fact, it might be disastrous to take a single note. If reporters can get their subject to relax, they will obtain much more than if the person is constantly reminded that the interviewer is taking down verbatim what is being said.

Sometimes the interviewee requests that the reporter take verbatim notes. Or the reporter at the end of an interview may remark, "By the way, would you mind spelling that name for me?" Or the reporter may ask for exact figures or addresses, for example, which the interviewee will be glad to have correct. The reporter must be careful in asking for such information, however, so as not to suggest to the interviewee that it is acceptable to start designating which remarks were for publication and which not. A good way to close an interview is for the reporter to ask an open-ended question such as: "Is there anything I haven't asked you that I should have to make my story fair and complete?"

Reporters should train their memories to recall, an hour or so afterward, the essence of the important remarks of the interviewee.

They should make immediate mental note of any startling statement which they will want to use verbatim, and should keep turning it over in their mind during the rest of the interview. They should seize the first opportunity after leaving the scene of the interview to write down such a statement and to make any other necessary notes.

In writing a story based on an interview, it often is wise, for the sake of authority, to mention that the statements were made during an interview. If so, "Mr. White stated in an interview today" is better than "Mr. White told a *News* reporter today."

Off the Record

A reporter must always be reluctant to allow the interviewee to go off the record. It usually is understood that newsgatherers expect to use whatever information they obtain. It can happen that, in the course of an interview, a principal says, "I'll answer that but only off the record." The reporter must make a fast decision whether to proceed on such terms. If the answer probably can be obtained from other sources, the reporter may advise the interviewee that an attempt will be made to get the desired information from others. What the reporter never should permit is for an interviewee to make statements and later designate that they were off the record. If other sources for the information do not exist, reporters would be killing their own story by promising not to use it.

Reporters sometimes leave news conferences when the interviewee goes off the record, fairly certain that some colleague will fill them in later. Once the reporter agrees to accept something off the record, that promise must be kept. To do otherwise is to risk ostracism by one's fellows as well as to lose the trust of the news source. Sources accustomed to dealing with reporters, such as elected officials, understand these customs. But ordinary people usually do not and the ethical reporter should take pains at the outset of an interview to explain the ground rules, except in the most extraordinary circumstances.

Friendships on Beats

Because nobody is as grammatically correct while speaking as while writing, it is common practice to fix up unprepared oral statements of persons in the news so as not to embarrass them or create a wrong impression. The sense of any quotation must, of course, be retained. On occasion, it may not be in the public interest to protect a source. If, for instance, despite overwhelming evidence to the contrary, a public official declares that he knows nothing of a scandalous situation with which he should be familiar, it is not unfair to quote him verbatim. When such necessity arises, the best reporter who has daily contact with the news source would be pleased to have a special or general assignment reporter sent over to handle that particular story. Often beat reporters find it wise to warn someone with whom they have made friendly contact that an unfavorable story is going to appear. In other words, reporters cannot be effective if they make enemies of those on whom they must depend for information. How to maintain personal relationships of friendship and at the same time fulfill one's newsgathering obligations is one of the most vexatious problems with which the beat reporter has to contend.

A serious pitfall the young reporter must avoid is naïveté. No matter how pleasing the personality of the interviewee, the reporter must realize that it is necessary to check, corroborate, diligently seek the other side and in general not be gullible. With complete sincerity a news source usually presents a one-sided version of whatever is at issue. Reporters may be tremendously impressed with the account of how a business, governmental unit or social agency operates if they rely entirely on what an interested party says. Omissions, misplaced emphases and distortions may become apparent only by interviewing other persons known to be critical. Otherwise the reporter may become only a messenger for press releases or one-sided "good" news. Probing, both by intensive interviewing of original news sources and of others, will not always end in complete reversal of original impressions, but it is a necessary precaution against error through excessive exuberance.

Publicity Seekers

By no means are all persons reticent about granting interviews. The person who attempts to cajole or bulldoze reporters or to hand out statements promoting himself or a cause is commonplace. Reporters must be constantly on guard to spot the phony.

Entertainers and authors advertising their books are eager to be interviewed, especially on television. They have secretaries or press agents who may have typewritten or mimeographed answers to stock questions. The enterprising reporter, of course, wants much more. If the primary purpose of the interview is to obtain information or opinion on some public matter, the reporter may encounter the unhappily growing tendency on the part of celebrities to expect monetary reward. Magazines occasionally offer huge sums for memoirs.

A musician, scientist, writer, politician or any other person who has become prominent scorns the reporter who betrays ignorance or lack of preparation in seeking or conducting an interview. Anyone with a speciality is bored to have to talk to another who is utterly uninformed. There are numerous biographical reference books which the reporter can consult to learn something about a person's life and achievements. The newspaper's reference department, probably computerized or about to be, should be able to supply information as to what the interviewee actually has done.

Not only national celebrities but also local persons who have won honors, taken new positions of importance, or been in the news prominently are the frequent subjects of reportorial inquiry. Reporters follow candidates for public office around during a day of campaigning to make a full report on their activities. Articles written after interviews with newly appointed school superintendents, bank presidents, chairmen of civic organizations and the like may resemble the profiles (combined biography, character sketch and description) originally made popular by *The New Yorker*. The object is to give readers the "feel" of the person, not just old facts.

When people are being written up primarily because of their information or opinions regarding a matter, personality traits and description should be kept to a minimum or ignored. If a man shouts, bangs on the table, hesitates before giving an answer or in some other way behaves so that proper understanding of his comments requires mention of such circumstances, they may be included. Unless such is the case, references to "the balding professor" or "the slight soft-spoken man" may be inconsistent and out of place.

Entirely the opposite is true when the object is to make readers thoroughly acquainted with the subject of the interview as a person. In such cases, the subject's opinions are secondary and are used to help build a total word picture. How a person appears, talks and behaves during the interview may be pertinent, especially if the reporter elects to write in the first person.

By George Esper

Rogers, Ark. (AP)—He dances the disco and partakes in transcendental meditation. At age 75.

Casual dress has replaced the dark blue suit, vest with gold chain and high collar with pin that were his trademark.

He has become a health food enthusiast.

He has taken a new wife, 40 years his junior, and moved from New York to the idyllic manmade lakes of northern Arkansas.

Life has taken some curious turns for Dr. Benjamin Spock, the grand adviser to mothers whose "Baby and Child Care" book has sold more than 28 million copies and has been translated into more than 30 languages since it was first published in 1946.

Ten years ago this month, he was convicted in Boston of conspiracy to aid, abet and counsel young men to avoid the draft for the Vietnam War. He was sentenced to two years in prison, but the conviction was overturned by a higher court.

Looking back now, he says he has no regrets except that it took so long to stop the war. . . .

These rules are applicable to all kinds of subjects, including the off-the-beaten-path characters who may be the subjects of feature articles: retiring lifeguards, octogenarians, persons with unusual hobbies or reminiscences, and the like. Pictures supplement and confirm written accounts in such cases, not the other way around. Questions should be related to the interviewee's field of interest and yet should not be too elementary. The reporter should try to find some new angle of approach. Reporters should not try to cover their subject's entire field of interest. To do so would mean failure to cover any aspect with any degree of thoroughness. The best stories following interviews with celebrities are on specific points about which the interviewer has questioned his subject thoroughly. In such interviews, strive for a relaxed, conversational tone. Be sure to ask follow up questions such as "Why?" "For example?" or "Would you tell me more about that?"

News Conferences

Persons who wish to make an announcement or be interviewed often arrange for news conferences at which representatives of all the newspapers and perhaps electronic and other media in the community are present.

From the standpoint of the reporter, such an interview is less desirable because none of the information is exclusive and because the reporter cannot control the course of the dialogue.

An advantage of the news conference, however, lies in the fact that there are several minds thinking up questions to ask.

If the news conference is televised, as are many of those in the White House, it may take days or weeks to verify or supplement misstatements or incomplete remarks that have already been heard by large audiences. In nonbroadcast interviews government officials may designate which of their remarks are to be (1) on the record and usable as coming from the source; (2) background information usable but not to be attributed to the source; (3) off-the-record, for the reporter's information only, not to be used without further permission.

Even when interviewing someone in the company of other reporters, it is possible to obtain material from which to write a superior story. The keenest listener and the sharpest wit present writes the best story. Comparison of several write-ups based on a joint interview often discloses several different methods of handling the subject. One reporter plays up one statement and another reporter picks an entirely different one for the feature. Still a third writer concentrates on the personality of the interviewee rather than upon the source's remarks.

Denials

Sometimes a person quoted in an interview as having made a certain statement issues a denial. He may even deny that he never saw the reporter who wrote the story. This can happen when a reporter plays up some extemporaneous remark that the person would not have made in a formal interview.

A denial of the facts of an interview, of course, can be avoided by presenting the copy of the write-up to the subject, but few newspapers favor such a practice. To do so means that the interviewee may delete everything the least bit unfavorable. It also means delay that a newspaper may not be able to afford, and a surrender of the newspaper's privilege to gather its information and write its stories as it sees fit.

If the reporters are not guilty of misquotation they may refuse to correct or retract. In a second story the reporter may add evidence that the original report was accurate. Then the public can choose whom to believe. Reporters frequently do not use remarks that they suspect the interviewee would deny. If reporters wish to make sure that the interview will not be denied, they can phone or call upon the interviewee again to obtain verification of whatever they wish to write. When the reporters do so, or even when obtaining the original interview, they may take a person along as a witness to the interview. This, however, seldom is feasible, as the presence of a third person may prevent informality.

A tape recording is the best defense that any interviewer can have of accuracy. Most of the problems considered so far in this chapter would be reduced or eliminated if it were possible to use electronic recording devices on all occasions. That is, of course, impossible. Unless there is surreptitious use of the devices, which would raise legal as well as moral questions, most interviewing for spot news stories will continue to be of the old-fashioned pencil and notebook kind. At present effective use of tape recorders must be limited to feature interviews with the time element not so pressing as daily press deadlines. Some people, especially those not used to being interviewed, are self-conscious when a tape recorder is used. Often their discomfort disappears. It should be the reporter's goal to put them at ease.

There is no succinct set of simple rules for a beginning interviewer to master. It is impossible to advise a novice always to do this, generally avoid doing that, and so forth. No two situations are the same, but it is essential that the reporter (1) know about the interviewee, (2) know the subject matter and (3) be sharp, which means flexible, perceptive, penetrating and ethical.

Accuracy

There has been considerable research to determine news story accuracy, usually by questioning persons involved in the news or in positions to recognize errors in the reporting. The first study, conducted in 1936 by Prof. Mitchell Charnley of the University of Minnesota, revealed that of 591 straight news stories in three Minneapolis dailies only 319, or 54 per cent, contained no errors of any kind. In 1965 Charles Brown found a 59.5 per cent accuracy score for 143 stories in 42 small weeklies. In 1966 Fred C. Berry Jr. reported 270 stories in two metropolitan and one suburban dailies were 47.3 per cent accurate and in 1967–68 Prof. William B. Blankenburg of the University of Wisconsin got a 40.1 per cent accuracy score for 332 stories in one suburban and one rural daily. A summary of these and other studies appeared in an article by Blankenburg, "News Accuracy: Some Findings on the Meaning of Error," in the *Journal of Communication* for December 1970. A more detailed review of more than 40 years of research was prepared by Prof. Michael Singletary of Shippensburg State College for the American Newspaper Publishers Association, which published it Jan. 25, 1980, as its Research Center Report No. 25.

Whereas there seems no doubt that most people mistrust newspapers, until recently little research has been attempted to determine the reasons for that distrust. Nearly everyone at times has questioned the news judgment of an editor. Historically the bearer of bad tidings has been scapegoated. A reader may carry a lifetime grudge against journalism because of an error in fact or judgment concerning an event of which the reader had firsthand knowledge.

A study of Ottawa newspapers showed society stories are 90 per cent accurate and sports stories 77 per cent accurate. According to researchers Gary C. Lawrence and David L. Grey, two major causes of subjective error are (1) reporters' insufficient background information and (2) news desk and editing practices and policies. These results may be explained by the facts that most society news is written from press releases and sports writers were experts in their field long before their counterparts were considered necessary in other fields. Other studies have shown that information obtained face-to-face is more accurate than that received by telephone.

Avoiding Error

One of the first lessons the beginning reporter must learn is how to avoid making mistakes. There are some newsrooms even in large cities where a certain amount of carelessness is condoned, but not many. A standard of accuracy way beyond anything to which the recent college graduate has been accustomed in his English composition classes is maintained by a large majority of those newspapers worthy of being called first-rate. Lucky is the reporter who starts a career under an editor who "raises the roof" whenever he detects a misspelled word or incorrect middle initial in a piece of copy.

The reporter who has had time to prepare for an interview by acquiring knowledge of the background of the subject matter and of the interviewee is less likely to accept misinformation than one who must handle the assignment without the opportunity to prepare.

Fairness and caution both require that, when two persons interviewed differ greatly as to what is the truth, the statements of both be included in the news story. To achieve this objective, newspapers go to extremes of which the general public hardly dreams. The sentence saying that Mr. Smith could not be reached for a statement may have been added to a story after hours of futile effort to attain either accuracy or fairness or both.

Newsgatherers increasingly are up against what has been called hand-outitis, which means the refusal of many news sources to provide any more information than is contained in carefully prepared publicity releases. Between the reporter and a principal in the news is the public relations or public affairs counsel, as spokespersons and press agents like to call themselves today. On the whole, these intermediaries perform a useful function, as no newspaper could possibly employ a staff large enough to cover all a community's activities. They also can be helpful to the reporter who wants additional information not included in a press release or who is seeking an original story. It must not be lost sight of, however, that public relations or public affairs persons are employed to advance the best interests of their employers, which means that often ways to circumvent them must be sought. The reporter who is content with what is included in a mimeographed press release may become little more than a transmission belt for self-service or duplicitous statements.

The veteran investigative reporter I. F. Stone warned that any newsgatherer concerned with governmental sources should assume that every officeholder is a liar and that it is the journalist's duty to discover the truth of what is being covered up.

Within our generation, presidents, vice presidents, and other high-up national leaders have appeared on television to lie publicly. In September 1971 New York Gov. Nelson Rockefeller deliberately lied to the press about the Attica prison riot. He and other state officials said prisoners were responsible for the deaths of 29 prisoners and 10 guards who were held as hostages. The coroner's report proved that all bullets came from the guns of state troopers, and a Special Commission called the assault "the bloodiest attack by Americans on Americans" since the massacre of Indians at Wounded Knee, S.D. in 1890. The reporters covering the riot were held at bay and had to rely on official bulletins, which they had no way of verifying.

Shortly before the disaster at the Three Mile Island nuclear plant near Harrisburg, Pa., in April 1979, the York (Pa.) *Record* ran a series of articles warning that there were inadequate safety devices at the plant. Walter Greitz, president of Metropolitan Edison Company, which ran the plant, lambasted the *Record*'s series as tantamount to crying fire in a crowded theater. Two days later he confessed, "We should have listened."

James Panyard, veteran Philadelphia *Bulletin* investigative reporter, said, "We've been given complete misinformation and conflicting statements from the Nuclear Regulatory Commission here and the NRC in Washington, the governor's office and the utility." He said that authorities who condescended to meet the press seemed to speak a foreign language. If a reporter asked a straight question about how much radiation was escaping the answer would be mumbo jumbo about millirems, manrems, rods and picocuries. One needed a nuclear physics degree to come up with the proper follow-up question.

To deal with such situations it is important to know what information is to be found at what place. The Investigative Reporters and Editors, organized in 1974, maintains a resource center on the campus of the University of Missouri at Columbia, Mo. It services members who want to know where to go to find material and makes available the results of reporting projects conducted by other papers. Journalism students may become associate members. The address is Steve Weinburg, IRE Executive Director, Box 838, Columbia, Mo. 65205. IRE has an annual convention and regional workshops. Its *Journal* is a 12-page periodical.

Verification

Verifying a story means more than checking the statements of different news sources against each other. It also means making use of the standard books of reference to check spellings, addresses, middle initials and many similar details. In many police and court stories more than the newspaper's reputation for accuracy may be at stake; innocence or carelessness is no defense against libel.

The newspaper takes a chance whenever it prints an unverified story. Mere rumor it generally can detect, but when a story contains something that seems improbable it is safer to delay publishing the story than use it before checking. Often persons in public life say things to reporters that they later regret. It may seem to laymen that the newspaper should quote them regarding what they have let slip and then stand by its guns and insist upon its own accuracy. It is the same laymen, however, who with few exceptions believe an important personage's denial even though it be a gross lie. For this reason many editors have held up a story until they have had a chance to check on even a reliable reporter's work.

Telephone books, city directories, electronic data banks, clippings in the newspaper's library and books of reference are available to the newspaper reporter for a purpose—so that they will be used. In interviews, it is possible to repeat information to be sure it has been heard correctly. Over the telephone, difficult words can be spelled in code: A as in Adam, B as in Boston, and so on. A humorous incident once occurred on the Dayton *Journal-Herald* that emphasizes the need for great care in taking news by telephone. A reporter, doing a late phone check of police/fire, wrote a story that 2,003 pigs had been killed in a barn fire. A check by a skeptical desk man revealed that the accurate casualty list was two sows and three pigs. How the error occurred as the result of a telephone interview can easily be imagined.

If reporters have profited by their high school and college education, they should avoid many errors that the uneducated might commit, such as giving a ship's speed as "knots per hour," the office as chief justice of the Supreme Court instead of chief justice of the United States, the Court of St. James instead of the Court of St. James's, Noble instead of Nobel prizes, half-mast instead of half-staff, John Hopkins University instead of Johns Hopkins University, and many other "teasers," mastery of which is a journalistic prerequisite.

IRE leaders stress the importance of asking the same questions of different persons, being careful not to change the wording as from "Do you think the mayor should?" to "Do you think the mayor could?"

Qualification

When certain about the main facts of a story but doubtful about others, a way to make the earliest edition before complete verification is possible is to qualify what is written, as

> A man believed to be Hillyer Swanson, 30, of Salt Lake City, was found by police today wandering in Forest Park, apparently an amnesia victim. Partial identification was made by means of a billfold and checkbook found in his possession.

It is when the reporter guesses or takes a chance that error is most likely to occur. Careless habits not only are bad practice from the newspaper's selfish standpoint, but reprehensible ethically as well. The speed with which newspapers are produced and the other obstacles to accuracy in reporting make a minimum number of errors inevitable. If the newspaper is generous in publishing corrections of the most serious errors and if it gives evidence of striving to attain the ideal of absolute accuracy, the supercilious reader is less likely to be "off" a newspaper for life because on one occasion it made a mistake in the middle initial of a friend or relative.

Systematic Checking

The practice is growing among newspapers of soliciting the comments of readers in much the same way that scientific researchers do. Increasingly, readers also are urged to take the initiative in pointing out errors and many newspapers have institutionalized their handling. Many of the nation's best newspapers now have a full-time, experienced staffer to field complaints and investigate whether reporters have made errors. Others send out forms asking people mentioned in a story how accurate the story is. Most papers run corrections, and more are doing it in a prominent, designated place in each edition.

Since 1971 newspapers in Minnesota have been under constant surveillance of the Minnesota Press Council which, in 1980, changed its name to Minnesota News Council to reflect the fact that broadcast stations also fall within its purview. The professional journalists and general public are represented on the council.

Similar local councils exist in several other places. All are in their experimental infancy and there has not yet been any "big news" or "test case" to determine their value.

The National News Council, founded in 1973 by the Twentieth Century Fund to investigate complaints against the major television and radio networks, major wire services and a few prestigious newspapers, closed down in March 1984 for lack of financial support and cooperation from the media.

Total Effect

An account can be devoid of errors in facts, spellings and the like and still be inaccurate if the impression it gives as a whole is wrong. This can happen when pertinent facts are omitted, when motivations are disregarded, when cause and effect relationships are not made clear and in many other, similar ways.

Thorough reporting is the best protection against unintentional distortion. For example, a story telling of an arrest for reckless driving could be error-free, but would it be accurate unless it were explained that the apparently careless motorist was trying to get to his injured child's side?

Here is an example of how a reporter digging for the whole story rather than just poking at the surface can help a reader to a deeper understanding of an important public issue. In this 1985 article, Chicago *Tribune* education writer Jean Latz Griffin could have settled for one of those "Gee whiz, aren't computers wonderful, let's all get on the bandwagon" stories of which readers have seen so many these days. But she went beyond that, proving context and interpretation in the following story, the first six paragraphs of which appear here:

> Marilyn Pollock's 5th grade class in Wheaton is what many believe the classroom of the future will be like: 27 children using 15 computers to learn everything from math to creative writing and American history.
>
> "I am a facilitator and model learner," said Pollock, a 28-year-old veteran of teaching who designed the all-computer class, which began in September in Madison Elementary School.
>
> "The computers have given the students what I have always tried to create in my classrooms, a sense of learning through exploration."

But for every teacher who, like Pollock, believes that computers will revolutionize education, at least one critic predicts that the current rage of bits and bytes will fade much as educational television did.

Even some who expect computers to shape the future of schooling worry that they could end up widening the gap between students in affluent areas and their counterparts in poorer locales—that children in areas such as Wheaton will be taught to use computers to their fullest potential, while disadvantaged students will receive little or no training.

Others worry that in the rush to buy expensive computers, many schools are not laying the groundwork for their effective use by training teachers in their applications and the evaluation of software. . . .

It is clear from this example that the thoughtful, skeptical reporter can get answers that come a little closer to the truth of the matters under examination by deciding to ask much more than just the obvious questions for which another reporter might have settled.

The "Other Side"

Deadpan reporting of the contents of a report, speech or the like, even when the source is reputable, may be misleading in that it does not give readers the "whole" or "essential" truth. When the news source is irresponsible, grave disservice may be done the reading public. It certainly is newsworthy when someone important in public life attacks another person. Such news often cannot be ignored. It can, however, be put in better perspective if there is simultaneous opportunity for reply by the accosted party. Readers want to know how those most affected by any news event react to it. Unless their curiosity is satisfied, the account is incomplete.

Attribution

A newspaper's reputation for credibility is the best guarantee a reader has of the reliability of the news. Nevertheless, the most authoritative publications are the most careful to attribute every important fact to some source. "Who said this?" a hard boiled city editor may bawl to a young reporter. "Why, Mr. Smith, whose name is in the lead as having given the speech," is no defense but merely provocation for a further remark such as, "You don't say he said this unquoted part down in the fifth paragraph. I know he made the statement in the lead, but the rest of your story reads like an editorial."

Direct Quotation

To avoid such reprimands, reporters "document" their stories by attributing the information to a source. How to attain accuracy and authority in different types of news stories will be considered more fully in the chapters devoted to them in Part Three. Including authority in the lead adds emphasis, satisfies the reader's curiosity and partially protects the newspaper against error in a situation where it cannot immediately verify a statement as fact.

> Police Chief Walter Johnson was fired Friday night by Mayor William Washington because he had lost the confidence of the black community, the mayor's press secretary said today.
> Neither Johnson nor Washington was available for comment.

When the news consists in the fact that an announcement or statement has been made, especially if it is one which has been expected for some time, authority should be given the greatest emphasis possible by beginning the lead with it, as

> Mayor William Washington said today that he wants the City Council to investigate fully recent Chamber of Commerce charges of shakedowns in the collection of business license fees by city employees.
> The mayor pledged full cooperation with alderman in the investigation.

When someone in public life makes an attack on another, the lead should begin with the attacker's name, as

> State Sen. Rollin A. Bishop today called Gov. Joseph B. Dilling a "crackpot" and described his plan to consolidate seven state departments as "the wild idea of a neophyte in public life."

That type of lead is much better than the following:

> Gov. Joseph B. Dilling is a "crackpot" and his plan to consolidate seven state departments is "the wild idea of a neophyte in public life," State Sen. Rollin A. Bishop said today.

It is a fact that Senator Bishop attacked the governor that is news; what he said is opinion unless he was much more definite than either lead would indicate. If he did make specific charges, then what has been said regarding efforts to obtain "the other side" applies.

In stories growing out of public reports, statements or announcements, mention of the authority may be delayed until the second paragraph but seldom should be any later than that.

> Milltown users of natural gas pay a higher rate than consumers in any other American city of comparable size, but local rates for electricity are among the lowest in the United States.
> These facts were revealed by a Federal Power Commission report released today. . . .

Care, however, must be exercised to avoid a "tag line" type of lead that, standing alone, is misleading, as

> Rep. Y. S. Owen could defeat Mayor L. L. Wood.
> That is the opinion of Judge K. K. Wendell who spoke at noon today.

Caution must be exercised so as not to declare as certain something that still is a matter of debate or further official action. For instance, a reporter erred when he wrote

> Baxterville will have a new 20-story office building by next spring.
> Plans for it will be presented tonight to the City Planning commission.

In this instance the Planning commission disapproved the project, which the reporter might have anticipated if he had interviewed more than its enthusiastic proponents. The hoary adage that applies is never to count your chickens before they hatch.

The extent to which a careful newspaper goes to give adequate authority throughout a controversial story is indicated in the following example.

By Anthony Man

Illinois Power Co. *was blamed for* $294 million to $463.6 million of needless spending on its costly and long-delayed Clinton nuclear plant *in an independent audit* released Thursday.

Auditors faulted ineffective management for causing excess spending ranging from 7.7 percent to 12.2 percent of the plant's latest $3.8 billion estimated cost.

Illinois Power was most culpable for problems that led to stop work actions, which delayed construction for 18 months, *the audit said.*

The company and contractor Baldwin Associates needed to prove effective quality assurance programs to get a license from the Nuclear Regulatory Commission. Failure to offer adequate proof—rather than construction quality problems themselves—led to those 1982 stop work actions, *the audit said.*

The document, prepared by Touche Ross & Co. and Nielsen-Wurster Group, *attributes* a year of the delay fully to the company. The problems were *"controllable and avoidable."*

The 1,300-page audit is designed to help the Illinois Commerce Commission decide what portion of cost overruns should be paid by Illinois Power customers and how much by shareholders. State law bans charging consumers for *"unreasonable"* costs.

Illinois Power had little to say. "They sprang it on us kind of late," *Harold Deakins, manager of public affairs, said.*

The company will provide evidence today showing "there were no decisions or actions on the part of Illinois Power Co. that resulted in costs which should be categorized as unreasonable," *Deakins said.*

Commerce commission members, who have not seen the five-volume document, are unable to discuss contents, *spokeswomen Beth Bosch said. She added* they could not talk about something on which the panel will rule.

The audit argues against cancellation of the nearly complete facility because it would be most economically beneficial to the utility and its customers for the unit to be completed. However, *it warned* additional increases could invalidate that finding.

"Should the costs of (Clinton) continue to escalate to a significant degree, the economic advantage of the project may well be lost."   [Southern Illinoisan]

Indirect Reference

No reporter should write a story supplied by an anonymous source, which means that practical jokers and persons with grievances who telephone and write to newspapers in the hope of giving news without disclosing their identity seldom are successful. When taking, over the telephone, information about which any question may arise, the reporter should obtain the informant's number, hang up and call him back. This practice often will expose impersonators, provided the reporter also checks the telephone numbers in the directory. Sometimes, at the request of high public officials, newspapers thinly veil sources of information by referring to "sources close to," "a source known to be reliable," "an official spokesman," "a high official" and the like.

It is irritating to any reputable reporter to have to write this way, and protests against the refusals of public officials to permit their names to be used as authorities are frequent. Such vagueness weakens the confidence of readers in any newspaper that practices it on its own volition.

High government officials, including the president, may designate into which of four classes what they say at a press conference falls: (1) quotable directly, (2) quotable as from a reliable source, (3) not quotable but valuable as background information or (4) completely off the record. Reporters begrudgingly acquiesce unless they defiantly boycott the session and then try to learn what happened secondhand from someone who did attend. Such an informant might be another journalist.

John D. May in _Columbia Journalism Review_ for September–October 1978, called it "Goosing the Public" to write "Vyacheslav Kuzrin, believed to be the KGB officer, etc.," or Bishop Abel Muzorewa, "believed to have the largest following . . ." or "decisions on money . . . are expected to dominate the 1978 General Assembly." He deplored what he called "a standardized way of treating events, in which journalists allude, often in the guise of doing 'straight' reportage, to what is believed, estimated, expected, perceived by, well—by nobody in particular, by everybody, by unidentified and yet implicitly credible witnesses, by ghosts."

When Attribution Unnecessary

One way excessive attribution can be avoided is by being careful not to cite authority for old, especially widely known, facts. You wouldn't, for instance, write: "The capital of Wyoming is Cheyenne, according to Sen. Blimp." Neither, unless there was uncertainty regarding it, would you give authority when mentioning the capital of Tibet, Afghanistan or any other place. Such facts, though probably unfamiliar to most people, are easily obtained from standard reference books.

To cite authority for old facts can be misleading. It is likely to create the impression that the information is new. For example,

> To be eligible for low-cost public housing a person must not earn more than $5,000 annually, Theodore McCoughna, economist for the Public Housing Administration, said today.

The statement would be bad if the $5,000 ceiling had been in effect for some time. It would be worse if "revealed," "announced," "admitted," or some similar verb had been used. When a statement of fact is inserted in a story as part of the background to enable readers properly to evaluate some item of news, it should not be attributed to any authority unless, in the newsman's judgment, it might not be accepted as true otherwise. Then dictionaries, encyclopedias, public laws and other authoritative reference works can be mentioned.

In short, trying to get it right means that the reporter must take great care with such nuances of writing and reporting as we have considered in this chapter. That reporters have biases and that absolute truth is never possible to attain hardly constitute an argument for carelessness or lack of attention to detail. Rather, those realities make it more important that reporters strive for accuracy and for the truth, with all their energy, intellect and sensitivity.

The Reporter and the Law

The First Amendment

As 1985 drew to a close, American editors were spending much of their time worrying about the credibility of their newspapers to readers.

Part of their concern stemmed from surveys that showed many people critical of what they saw as excesses on the part of reporters pursuing news and of what readers thought as too much negative news in relation to positive in the news media. But much of the editors' worrying was related to what Eugene Roberts, editor of the Philadelphia *Inquirer,* called an epidemic of libel suits, with damage awards much greater than previously granted by juries.

Meanwhile, the Reagan administration was clamping down on reporters' access to officials and records of the federal government, and watering down the federal Freedom of Information Law. The president was holding far fewer press conferences than his predecessors. And when he did appear in public, reporters were kept at great distances from him, meaning that they often had to shout questions at him to try to get his personal reaction to many important events of the times. In doing so, they invariably seemed rowdy, if not downright rude, to many watching Reagan's public appearances on television.

In the face of all this, many thought they saw a large segment of the American press beginning to pull its punches, fearing to undertake vigorous investigative projects and settling for less tough-minded reporting of

governments from the local to federal levels. The buzzword for that phenomenon was "the chilling effect." The press was confronted with a popular president who knew how to make himself look good and the press look
bad, with a public seemingly increasingly indifferent to the importance of
First Amendment protections and tired of hearing "bad news," with well-
financed attacks on journalistic credibility from big businesses seeking more
friends in the public arena, and with a Supreme Court inclined to weaken
earlier libel law decisions that have allowed reporters wide latitude in
writing about public policy issues. Many editors frankly admitted that the
threat of costly libel suits and the difficulty of getting increasingly expensive libel insurance was making them cautious about all their reporting
and especially reluctant to do potentially controversial investigative reporting.

That modern crisis is serious because of the reliance the Founding Fathers placed in a free press to help create an informed public capable of
making the American experiment in democratic self-government possible.
The First Amendment was not a guarantee that every journalistic attempt
would be praiseworthy. Quite the contrary, the authors of the Bill of Rights
(the first ten amendments to the Constitution), weighed the consequences
of allowing some form of government censorship other than libel laws, and
decided the risk was worth taking. A free press was, and has continued to
be for more than two centuries, the most important cornerstone of American democracy.

The Right to Report

Freedom of the press thus is a means to an end, not an end in itself. It
is the right of the people to know, not the special privilege of those who
own the media to profit therefrom. During the current debate concerning
the precarious status of press freedom, some legal and other scholars have
contended that freedom of the press protects only the right to publish and
not the right to obtain news. The response of the neo-Jeffersonians is that
if the desideratum is an informed public, those scholars' attitudes are self-
defeating. As James Russell Wiggins, a former president of the American
Society of Newspaper Editors argued:

> How futile it would have been to give constitutional and legal protection to
> circulation of the facts while denying the right to gather the facts. Information
> is the raw material of opinion. . . .
>   A people who mean to enjoy the benefits of a free press must have a govern-
> ment that protects

1. The right to get information.
2. The right to print without public restraint.
3. The right to print without threat of sanguinary reprisal for mistaken publication.
4. The right of access to the means of publication.
5. The right to distribute.

Problems of Access

Unless forewarned, one of the first big surprises that young reporters may experience is the discovery that they can invoke the freedom of the press clause in the Constitution from morn to night and still be denied access to some documents that they might believe are public records open to all.

It is regrettable that there is no place to which reporters can be directed for a clearcut statement of what their rights and privileges are in particular instances. Not only are the laws of different states different, but also the same law is likely to have been interpreted differently by two or more courts of law in what would seem to be cases involving identical issues. As regards a number of important legal problems involving newspapers, there is little or no law, either statute or common. For this, newspapers themselves are partly if not largely to blame because they often prefer to settle law suits out of court.

The principle generally observed, regardless of the clarity of state or municipal law, is that the public—which includes the press—has the right to inspect public documents except when the public interest would be harmed thereby. The frequent clashes between newspapers and public officials result from differences of opinion as to what constitutes a public record and what constitutes public interest. Some states have been careful to define public documents; others haven't. In either case, and regardless of the fact that there have been few tests in court, newspapers do not expect to be allowed to cover grand jury proceedings, executive sessions of lawmaking bodies, or to be shown records of unresolved cases in the police detective bureau, the report of an autopsy before it is presented to a coroner's jury, the report of an examiner to either a fire marshal or public banking official or a number of other similar documents.

Reporters should learn what both the law and general practice are in the states and communities where they work and what the policy is as to defiance or circumvention of public officials seeking to conceal news. Some editors encourage reporters to search for leaks whereby grand jury and executive session news may be obtained and they have defied judges' orders with resultant citations for contempt. Most state bar associations now publish media-law handbooks and update them regularly. Reporters should obtain one for the state in which they work. Many papers have written policies on legal matters. The beginning reporter should inquire of his editors about these policies by the first day on the job.

Most states have passed open-record and open-meeting laws. Nevertheless, reporters continue to be frustrated by the evasive practices of some governmental bodies, such as city councils and school boards, which go into executive session and hold informal meetings in private places. Often important matters are decided at such clandestine rendezvous so that what transpires in public legally is merely a confirmation and leaves the newsgatherer ignorant of the factors that went into the decision making.

Most serious has been a steady increase in judicial orders forbidding reporters to attend court proceedings. In July 1976 the United States Su-

preme Court declared unconstitutional a Nebraska judge's gag order restricting press coverage of a mass murder case. Three years later, however,
in *Gannet v. DePasquale,* the Burger court, 5 to 4, in effect reversed itself.
Specifically the court upheld the closing of a pretrial hearing to the press.
The language of Justice Stewart's majority opinion, however, was so broad
that 45 attempts were made in all parts of the country to close entire trials.
Of these requests 32 succeeded, and there were about 200 other attempts,
about half of them successful, to exclude press and public from preliminary
hearings. And then, July 2, 1980, exactly a year after the Gannet decision,
the Supreme Court, 7 to 1, declared that criminal trials under most circumstances must be public. The case involved a Virginia murder trial from
which Richmond reporters were excluded.

As the press learned quickly, the decision in the Richmond newspapers
case did not invalidate the earlier one regarding preliminary hearings at
which more than 90 percent of cases are settled. Judges in different parts
of the country continued to bar reporters from many pre-trial negotiations
and were still doing so as late as 1986.

In 1982 the Supreme Court did rule in *Globe Newspaper v. Superior Court,*
that the press should not be excluded from selected parts of trials. Two
years later, in *Press Enterprise v. Superior Court,* the court held that the
press should be allowed to cover the jury selection process at the outset of
trials. But at the end of 1985 the law still remained murky as to whether
the First Amendment allowed access to pre-trial proceedings. As 1986 began the press was hoping for a favorable ruling in a case taken to the
Supreme Court by the Riverside (Calif.) *Press-Enterprise.* In that case, the
California Supreme Court held that there was no First Amendment right
of access to preliminary hearings that lasted forty-one days in a highly
publicized murder case. At the request of the defense lawyer, every one of
those 41 day of hearings was closed. The judge sealed the transcript for
many months. A Supreme Court decision was expected sometime in 1986
on the *Press-Enterprise*'s appeal of the state court finding.

Invasion of Privacy _____

In 1890 two young lawyers, Samuel Warren and future Supreme Court
Justice Louis Brandeis, wrote an article for the *Harvard Law Review* in
which they attempted to establish a common-law right to privacy—the right
to be left alone. They deplored the yellow journalism of their times and
argued that persons should have legal recourse if they were victims of gossip from journalistic overstepping of the "obvious bounds of propriety and
decency" and pandering to "idle or prurient curiosity."

Although most states have laws allegedly to protect against invasions of
privacy, the concept is virtually impossible to define in any but subjective
terms and is hence susceptible to various judicial interpretations.

Despite the lack of specificity in privacy laws it generally is accepted
that those who court public attention, such as politicians or entertainers,
sacrifice much or most of their privacy. How much of a celebrity's private

life it is legitimate to publicize as distinguished from their professional life has been tested in many courts with no consistent results and is mostly a matter of journalistic ethics.

Some people lose their privacy temporarily through no fault of their own if they witness an accident or crime or other newsworthy event. It is not surprising in these computerized days, with everyone being the subject of many dossiers, that the press should be the object of complaint and legal action when people think there has been an invasion of privacy through unjustified disclosure of facts of their private lives, by physical intrusion or trespass in the course of newsgathering, by infringement of their right to advertise their own talent or by being placed in a false light.

Fiction Based on Facts _____

In the early '70s several writers and novelists gave the name New Journalism to their use of the literary devices of the fiction writer to retell news stories in works of fiction. Thus Truman Capote's *In Cold Blood* and Gerold Frank's *The Boston Strangler* were novels based on recapitulations of facts familiar to newspaper readers for a couple of years.

The style was neither new nor journalism, but no one was sued for invasion of privacy or libel until a California psychologist successfully sued Gwen Davis Mitchell and her publisher because she modeled a character in *Touching* after him. Doubleday thereafter tried to recover $138,000 damages from Mitchell.

Regarding the U.S. Supreme Court's refusal to review the Mitchell case, Townsend Hoopes, president of the Association of American Publishers, said: "I think it's one of the most destructive and wrongheaded decisions that any court has made in the area of First Amendment rights."

If such suits become popular a freedom that writers have enjoyed for centuries will be in jeopardy. Cervantes, Proust, Ernest Hemingway, Somerset Maugham and other literary greats have been guilty. Robert Penn Warren's *All the King's Men* was a fairly accurate biography of Huey Long. Theodore Dreiser's *An American Tragedy* was a by-product of his reportorial coverage of a murder trial; he changed the name of the murderer from Chester Gillette to Clyde Griffiths and similarly camouflaged others. Orson Welles "did" William Randolph Hearst in *Citizen Kane*. The testimony in *Inherit the Wind* is verbatim from the Scopes trial where the rival attorneys were William Jennings Bryan and Clarence Darrow, not Matthew Harrison Brady and Henry Drummond as in the play.

The use of literary devices worked fine so long as reporters remembered they were not free to make up facts and still call their work journalism. Some inevitably stepped over the line. In April 1981, for the first time in history, a Pulitzer prize was awarded, then taken away because a story's facts were discovered to have been fabricated. The New Journalism was blamed by some. Others, however, found the Washington *Post* more blameworthy for not verifying Janet Cooke's background and facts and for not insisting she tell editors the identity of her sources. The incident threatened to damage seriously the *Post*'s reputation. Some similar exposures have followed involving other publications, and they certainly have caused some public lack of faith in media credibility.

Libel _____

There is no aspect of newspaper law about which reporters must be more knowledgeable than that of libel—and that means keeping up with United States Supreme Court decisions.

Public Figures

The first of a succession of libel decisions that have kept publishers and lawyers wondering "what next?" was *New York Times v. Sullivan* in 1964. The case began when L. B. Sullivan, Alabama commissioner of public affairs, sued the paper because of an advertisement soliciting support for Dr. Martin Luther King's Southern Christian Leadership Council. It was captioned "Heed Their Rising Voices" and charged that a reign of terror against black students existed in Alabama. Sullivan won in lower courts but in 1964 the United States Supreme Court declared that a public official may not receive damages for defamatory statements relating to his official conduct unless he proves that the statements were made with "actual malice," with knowledge that they were false or in "reckless disregard" of truth or falsity.

Five years later the court extended the "public official" rule to include "public figure." The main case was *Curtis Publishing Co. v. Butts*. It resulted from a *Saturday Evening Post* article charging that Wally Butts, University of Georgia football coach, had conspired to throw a game to the University of Alabama. Butts won because the court held that the magazine failed to investigate adequately after Butts had told the magazine's writer the charge was untrue.

In 1971 the court came close to making state libel laws obsolete when it extended the "actual malice" rule to cover a private individual projected into the news limelight. The case was *Rosenbloom v. Metromedia*. George Rosenbloom, a nudist magazine distributor in the Philadelphia area, sued radio station WIP after he was acquitted of criminal obscenity charges. The station had branded him "smut distributor," "a girlie book publisher" and similar unflattering things. Rosenbloom lost his libel action. As a result, the law of libel seemed to be dead and many newspapers canceled their libel insurance.

And then came *Gertz v. Robert Welch, Inc.*, publisher of the John Birch Society magazine, *American Opinion*. In 1974 Elmer Gertz, a Chicago lawyer, successfully sued the magazine for falsely accusing him of having framed a policeman who was convicted of murdering a 19-year-old boy. The judge, however, set aside the $50,000 judgment on grounds that the publisher had not shown reckless disregard for the truth. The Supreme Court decided that Gertz was not a public figure and so needed only to prove that the publisher acted negligently. Abandoned was the principle that a private citizen speaking on public issues had to prove actual malice and so, as journalistic publications now declared, there were "new ground rules for the old ball game." A retrial of the case in April, 1981 resulted in a jury award to Gertz of $400,000.

Since then there have been other cases in which the decisions have upheld the Sullivan principle, but narrowed and fuzzed it up so much that there is now great uncertainty whom courts will decide is a public figure and what constitutes negligence or reckless disregard for the truth. In the confusion of those decisions, moreover, procedures have been permitted to determine journalists' states of mind in handling stories in which libel is alleged. Those procedures have created the potential for great difficulties—and considerable embarrassment—for reporters.

In *Time v. Firestone* in 1976 the court ruled that May Alice Firestone, a prominent Palm Beach society woman, was not a public figure except in her home area. The woman had sued because the magazine reported that her husband divorced her for adultery. Actually the decree, which followed a nasty trial, mentioned other grounds; adultery was omitted so that under Florida law she could receive alimony. The case commanded nationwide attention partly because of her news conferences.

On June 26, 1979, the Supreme Court handed down two significant opinions. In one it declared that members of Congress can be sued for statements made in press releases, newsletters and television interviews. At issue was a suit by Dr. Ronald Hutchinson, director of research for a Michigan mental hospital to whom Senator William Proxmire (Dem., Wis.) awarded a Golden Fleece award adversely critical of the $500,000 Dr. Hutchinson received for research of the behavior of monkeys such as clenching of jaws when they were exposed to various "aggravating stressful stimuli." The court remanded the case for trial after declaring the grant did not obtain sufficient public attention and comment to make the doctor a public figure.

The same day the court ruled that Ilya Wolston was not a public figure despite his conviction for criminal contempt when he failed in 1958 to appear before a grand jury investigating Soviet espionage. In 1974 *Reader's Digest* published a book incorrectly naming Wolston as having been indicted for espionage. The court found no evidence of malice inasmuch as the book reference was based on the FBI report.

In a footnote to the *Hutchinson v. Proxmire* decision the court questioned the routine awarding of summary judgments in public figure libel cases, declaring "the proof of actual malice calls a defendant's state of mind into question . . . and does not readily lend itself to summary disposition."

By far the most significant decision was in *Herbert v. Lando,* intended to make it possible to obtain just such proof. Former Lt. Col. Anthony Herbert demanded that Barry Lando and Mike Wallace of CBS's "Sixty Minutes" be compelled to answer questions during pretrial discovery proceedings about their thoughts, conversations and conclusions while preparing their program questioning Herbert's accusation that the Army had covered up reports of civilian killings in Vietnam. Only by such questioning would it be possible to prove actual malice in public figure cases.

In January 1981 the court let stand an appellate court ruling that consultants hired by the government are not public officials or public figures. The case concerned the accounts in the London (Va.) *Times-Mirror* of the hiring of the Iroquois Research Institute by the Fairfax County Water Authority. Specifically the institute objected to the paper's report that an archeologist was critical of its work.

The Big Chill

As the '80s progressed, the state of libel law protection for journalists deteriorated. A big chill set in.

In 1984 the Supreme Court in rulings in *Calder v. Jones* and *Keeton v. Hustler Magazine* made it possible for plaintiffs to sue national publications in almost any jurisdiction of the plaintiff's choosing, meaning that the media would have to defend against libel in states where the legal climate would be most unfavorable to them and most favorable to plaintiffs. In the same year Dow Jones & Company settled out of court a $5 million libel suit against the *Wall Street Journal* and one of its reporters. The company agreed to pay $800,000 to two former federal prosecutors who claimed the *Journal* had libeled them. It was the largest payment up to that time in a libel suit that had not gone to trial.

But 1985 was the year that really caused the libel law alarm bells to clang among journalists.

One reason was a case that set no new libel law precedents, but substantially increased the chilling effect among journalists. The Alton (Ill.) *Telegraph* in 1980 had been ordered by an Illinois jury to pay $9.2 million in damages for a libel committed against a local contractor. In the '70s, two *Telegraph* reporters had sent a confidential memo to a representative of the U.S. Justice Department as part of an investigation they were conducting into whether the Mafia was laundering money through a financial firm in Alton. A man mentioned in the memo sued for libel, claiming the memo amounted to publication, even though neither it nor its contents ever appeared in the Alton newspaper. The local jury awarded the man $9.2 million in damages, the largest judgment ever up to that time in a libel case against any American newspaper. The newspaper's financial structure buckled under the costs of legal fees in defending itself and trying to appeal. It could not post the bond required for an appeal to a higher court, ended up in bankruptcy court and eventually settled the case for more than $1.5 million, partly because of legal complications that developed in trying to appeal the case while caught up in the bankruptcy proceedings. In the early '80s the case got widespread national attention. In 1985, after the national attention had faded and while the newspaper was struggling financially to stay alive, the paper was sold by its long-time independent family ownership to a chain. Apart from the huge damage award and eventual settlement, the chilling effect of the case flowed from the facts that a paper known for its aggressive investigative reporting had been forced to become more meek and that the family owners had been driven to sell to a chain. Around the country editors of other feisty, smaller independent papers took note and realized the potential costly consequences of investigative reporting. Many became more cautious.

More than just those smaller papers were jolted in 1985. *Time* magazine and CBS both were caught up in highly publicized, extraordinarily expensive defenses of themselves in trials during which their innermost internal reporting and editing procedures were opened up to intense public scrutiny. The probing sought to determine to what extent there had been malice or negligence in coverage of the stories in dispute. The Washington *Post* had gone through a similar process in a case brought by the head of Mobil Oil, had won a victory of sorts at the trial court level, then lost at the appeals court level and, as 1985 ended, was still struggling with an appeal of its own to reduce the damages awarded. And the Boston *Globe* faced similar difficulties in defending itself against a suit brought by a failed candidate for governor of Massachusetts. The candidate claimed that *Globe* reporting about his earlier life had cost him an election victory. In the *Globe* case, both the plaintiff and the newspaper hired nationally known and expensive public relations firms to argue their cases in public while their lawyers fought the case out in the courtroom.

All these cases involved people who clearly were public figures. And while the outcomes were varied, they underlined how expensive, time consuming, energy draining and image battering defending a libel suit could be, even if the defendant eventually won the case. They also showed that the Sullivan principle was no certain refuge for the media from retribution from public officials seeking either money, vengeance or a spiffed-up public image through libel suits. For reporters, the cases provided dramatic examples of how the effort to explore journalists' states of mind while doing a story could lead to the toughest questioning of their motives and work habits in full public view. By the end of 1985 there was such chaos in libel law that even the nation's most expert media lawyers were either divided or undecided on the basic question by reporters about whether they were better off to save or destroy the notes they took while covering stories.

Nor were those cases all the bad news for the press in 1985. In June of that year, the Supreme Court in the case of *Dun & Bradstreet v. Greenmoss Builders* handed down a ruling that said, in effect, that the protections of the Sullivan and Gertz cases would not be available when a libelous statement or report deals with "matters of purely private concern." That meant that, in addition to the confusion over whether a person who claimed to have been libeled was a public or private person, there also would be confusion over whether the subject matter of an alleged libelous account dealt with clearly public matters or purely private matters. How considerable such confusion can be was suggested again in late 1985 when the Supreme Court let stand an Ohio court ruling that a well-known high school teacher and wrestling coach was neither a public official nor a public figure under the libel laws. Thus, the coach-teacher was able to press a libel suit against an Ohio paper without having to prove that the paper, if it published a story about him, acted with malice. Instead, he only would have to prove that the paper acted with the less difficult to establish standard of negligence.

Insurance companies, going through financial difficulties of their own related to matters other than libel, took note. Libel insurance rates more than doubled and, for papers involved in considerable investigative reporting, it became difficult to get any coverage at all without paying even much higher increases. The situation was not crucial, even though it was expensive, for large national newspapers or newspaper chains. But it was a big problem for smaller newspapers, and they became much more cautious in what they reported or commented upon.

Researchers at the University of Iowa and elsewhere noted that an increasing number of libel suits were being filed by public officials seeking not so much the money involved in damage requests, but rather either revenge or to preserve their public image. Noting that, some lawyers and students of the media suggested that the courts be allowed to make rulings on whether a story was true or false without there being any legal remedy of damage payments involved. Others doubted the constitutionality of that alternative to the epidemic of multi-million dollar libel suits. By the end of 1985 many newspapers were trying to clean up their newsroom procedures for dealing with complaints from those about whom stories had been written in the hope that more politeness and faster corrections, retractions and/or apologies would head off libel suits before they were filed. What no one mentioned, but probably should get more attention, is whether the lack of a national news council or of similar councils in most states was a contributing factor in aggrieved parties taking to the courts more frequently. It may be that the folding of the National News Council and the lack of such councils in most states give those with a complaint against the press no place to turn except the courts.

In short, as matters stood at the end of 1985, the law of libel remained hazy at some of its most crucial points, not just in regard to reporting about those who clearly are government and political officials, but also about those people who are prominent in other fields where the public either has much at stake or considerable interest. The law was equally unclear as to what the courts would regard as non-malicious or non-negligent journalism. It was virtually impossible for a reporter or editor to know before a story was published whether or not that story would be libelous. It was equally clear from the public climate and the action of many juries that if the reporter or editor published the story, but guessed wrong as to whether it was libelous, the costs in legal fees alone might be staggering, to say nothing of the damages a jury might award if the story were determined libelous. Perhaps just as troubling to journalists as all this was the apparent inclination of a majority of Supreme Court justices to do nothing to clarify the situation and a great deal to further muddy it up.

About the only safe course for reporters to follow is to proceed as responsibly as possible under the circumstances, which means continuing to pursue stories that are in the public interest with energy and sensitivity and without fear of libel law consequences, but to make sure that good libel lawyers are consulted before publication. To put it metaphorically, in this big chill reporters should wear mittens, but not be afraid to go out in the cold. Reporters are the life-blood of our democracy and our representative government. If they stay meekly in the office rather than risk the frigid winds of the courts, then our society will be in big trouble.

What Is Libel?

According to the *American and English Encyclopedia of Law*

> A libel is a malicious defamation expressed either by writing or printing or by signs, pictures, effigies or the like; tending to blacken the memory of one who is dead, or to impeach the honesty, integrity, virtue or reputation, or to publish the natural or alleged defects of one who is alive and thereby expose him to public hatred, contempt, ridicule or obloquy; or to cause him to be shunned or avoided, or to injure him in his office, business or occupation.

Many publications contain libels that do not result in lawsuits because the law stipulates defenses for libel under certain circumstances. Those defenses are discussed later in this chapter. Cartoons, photographs and other illustrations can be libelous. So can picture captions and headlines on stories as well as letters to the editor.

Before the advent of broadcasting, libel was considered more serious than slander because a written statement appearing in a publication with a wide circulation had greater possibilities of injury. Today radio and television reach millions and the same judicial interpretations apply to electronic journalism. This does not mean that courts will be consistent. In fact just the opposite often is the case from state to state and even within the same jurisdictions. Ordinarily, however, it is considered defamatory to

1. Charge that a person has committed or has attempted to commit a crime, or that he has been arrested for the commission of a crime, has been indicted for a crime, has confessed to committing a crime or has served a penitentiary sentence.
2. Impute that a person has committed an infamous offense, even though the words do not designate the particular offense.
3. Tend to diminish the respectability of a person and to expose him to disgrace and obloquy, even though they do not impute commission of a crime.
4. Tend to disgrace, degrade or injure the character of a person, or to bring him into contempt, hatred or ridicule.
5. Tend to reduce the character or reputation of a person in the estimation of his friends or acquaintances or the public from a higher to a lower grade, or tend to deprive him of the favor and esteem of his friends or acquaintances or the public.
6. Impute that one has a perverted sense of moral virtue, duty or obligation, or that he has been guilty of immoral conduct or has committed immoral acts.
7. Impute commission of fraud, breach of trust, want of chastity, drunkenness, gambling, cheating at play, violation of duties imposed by domestic relations, swindling, and so forth.

8. Impute weakness of understanding or insanity.
9. Impute a loathsome pestilential disease, as leprosy, plague or venereal disorders.
10. Tend to expose a person in his office, trade, profession, business or means of getting a livelihood to the hazards of losing his office, or charge him with fraud, indirect dealings or incapacity and thereby tend to injure him in his trade, business or profession.

A libel may be committed by mere insinuation. It is necessary only that the insinuation contain the elements of libel and that the readers of the paper understand it in its derogatory sense.

Likewise, allegory and irony may be libelous, as imputing to a person the qualities of a "frozen snake in the fable" or heading an article in regard to a lawyer's sharp practices "An Honest Lawyer."

The following list of "Red Flag Words" is taken from the Scripps-Howard *Synopsis of the Law of Libel and the Right to Privacy* by Bruce W. Sanford. They are words that may lead to libel suits if not handled carefully in news stories.

Adulteration of products	divorced	kept women
adultery	double-crosser	Ku Klux Klan
altered records	drug addict	
ambulance chaser	drunkard	liar
atheist		
attempted suicide	ex-convict	
		mental disease
bad moral character	false weights used	moral delinquency
bankrupt	fascist	
bigamist	fawning sycophant	Nazi
blackguard	fool	
blacklisted	fraud	
blackmail		paramour
blockhead	gambling house	peeping Tom
booze-hound	gangster	perjurer
bribery	gouged money	plagiarist
brothel	grafter	price cutter
buys votes	groveling office seeker	profiteering
		pockets public funds
cheats	humbug	
collusion	hypocrite	rascal
communist (or red)		rogue
confidence man	illegitimate	
correspondent	illicit relations	scandalmonger
corruption	incompetent	scoundrel
coward	infidelity	seducer
crook	informer	sharp dealing
	intemperate	short in accounts
deadbeat	intimate	shyster
deadhead	intolerance	skunk
defaulter		slacker
disorderly house	Jekyll-Hyde personality	smooth and tricky

sneak	suicide	unsound mind
sold his influence	swindle	unworthy of credit
sold out to a rival		
spy	unethical	vice den
stool pigeon	unmarried mother	villain
stuffed the ballot box	unprofessional	

Damages

Damages resulting from libel suits are of three major kinds: (1) general, (2) special and (3) punitive or exemplary.

General damages are awarded in cases of proof of libel when injury is recognized as the natural consequence of such publication. There must, however, be proof of actual injury to reputation.

Plaintiffs may receive special damages when they can prove particular loss. When special damages are asked, proof of specific injury must be established by the plaintiff. Special damages may, however, be awarded in addition to general damages.

Punitive damages are inflicted as punishment for malice on the part of the offending publication. Proof of malice must be established by the plaintiff. Punitive damages may be awarded upon proof of gross negligence or if a newspaper reiterates its libelous statement after being warned that it is untrue.

Defenses

The following are five major defenses or mitigating factors that apply in libel cases. Like other aspects of libel law, however, they are open to varying interpretations, and it cannot be predicted with certainty that they will be accepted by a court in a given instance.

1. *Truth.* In civil actions the truth of a publication is a complete defense, even though natural inferences of a defamatory character might be drawn which would be untrue. If malicious intent can be proved, however, truth may not be a defense. In criminal prosecutions, unless the publication was made for the public benefit or with good motives and for justifiable ends, truth is not a defense. The law in this respect differs in different states.

A publication must not only know the truth of what it has printed, but it must be able to submit legal proof. It is not a defense to claim that the libelous matter was printed upon the authority of another person. For example, publication of libelous statements made in a public address is not privileged, and the injured party can sue both the individual making the statement and all publications which reported it.

2. *Privilege.* Publication of the contents or of extracts of public records and documents for justifiable purposes and without malice, even though they contain libelous matter, is privileged by law. Publication of the contents of complaints or petitions before a public hearing has been held on them is not privileged; neither is publication of the proceedings of a private hearing, the contents of a warrant before it is served, confessions to police, news of arrests unless by warrant and many other exceptions.

3. *Fair comment*. Authors, playrights, actors, officeholders and other public characters who invite the attention of the public to their work are liable to fair comment and criticism. This privilege, however, extends only to an individual's work and not to his private life, and there must be no malice.

In the case of officeholders, comment or criticism must be confined to official acts or actual qualifications, and there must be an honest purpose to enlighten the community upon the matter under discussion.

The language of such criticism cannot be so severe as to imply malice, and the statement or comment must, in fact, be comment and not an allegation of fact. It, furthermore, must be on a matter of public interest, such as comment on public affairs, the church, the administration of justice, pictures, moving pictures, architecture, public institutions of all kinds, other publications and the like.

4. *Absence of malice*. As indicated, malice is an important element of all libel actions. It must be proved, as the previous discussion indicated, in cases involving public officials and public figures. Its presence in those or any other kinds of cases leads to larger damages than its absence. Malice is either *in fact,* which means that it springs from ill will, intent, hatred and so on, or *in law,* which is disregard for the rights of the person without legal justification.

Absence of intent to libel is no defense, but proof of unintentional libel helps to mitigate damages. In proving absence of malice the defendant in a libel suit may show

a. That the general conduct of the plaintiff gave the defendant "probable cause" for believing the charges to be true.
b. That rumors to the same effect as the libelous publication had long been prevalent and generally believed in the community and never contradicted by the accused or his friends.
c. That the libelous article was copied from another newspaper and believed to be true.
d. That the complainant's general character is bad.
e. That the publication was made in heat and passion, provoked by the acts of the plaintiff.
f. That the charge published had been made orally in the presence of the plaintiff before publication, and he had not denied it.
g. That the publication was made of a political antagonist in the heat of a political campaign.
h. That as soon as the defendant discovered that he was in error he published a retraction, correction or apology.
i. That the defamatory publication had reference not to the plaintiff, but to another person of a similar name, concerning whom the charges were true, and that readers understood this other person to be meant.

5. *Retraction*. Often a newspaper can avoid a suit by prompt publication of a retraction. If a suit does result, such retraction serves to mitigate damages, especially if it is given a position in the paper equally prominent to that given the previously published libelous statement.

Confidentiality _____

Journalistic defendants in libel actions are handicapped by the growing inclination of judges to grant plaintiff requests that they be compelled to reveal the source of their information and often to turn over all notes and other material used in the writing of their accounts.

Similar requests are made by attorneys engaged in almost any kind of newsworthy litigation. The Reporters Committee for Freedom of the Press reports that from 1960 to 1968 about a dozen subpoenas were served on news organizations. In the next two years the number jumped to about 150. From 1970 to 1976 about 500 subpoenas were served on reporters. After that the committee stopped counting because subpoenas were being issued all over the country and it was impossible to keep track of them. It estimates there are at least 150 new cases annually. Often lawyers use the tactic to delay a trial or to save themselves the trouble and expense of investigation.

Even when the information has not been obtained in confidence most newspapers refuse to comply with court orders. Hundreds of journalists, mostly reporters, have gone to jail and been fined as a consequence.

What inspired lawyers and judges to crack down on the press was a Supreme Court 5 to 4 decision upholding the conviction of Earl Caldwell, a west coast New York *Times* reporter, for contempt of a grand jury to which he refused to reveal the identity of sources from whom he obtained information concerning the Black Panthers.

Also upheld by the court was the contempt conviction of Paul M. Branzburg, who refused to tell a grand jury whom he saw converting marijuana into hashish as he reported for the Louisville *Courier-Journal*. The court also upheld the conviction of Paul Pappas, reporter-photographer for The New Bedford (Mass.) WTEV-TV station, who attended a Black Panther meeting in anticipation of a police raid that did not occur.

A New Jersey case that attracted widespread attention was the jailing for 45 days in mid-1978 of Myron Farber, New York *Times* reporter, because he refused to reveal who caused him to write a series of articles calling for a reinvestigation of five deaths ten years earlier in a hospital. Attorneys defending Dr. Mario Jascalevich on murder charges demanded to see all of the reporter's notes in the case. The *Times* backed its reporter and paid a total of $285,000 in contempt fines. Without Farber's notes, the doctor was acquitted.

More than half of the states have adopted so-called shield laws, presumably to protect journalists from being compelled to reveal confidential sources. It is the same kind of protection that is provided priests, lawyers and doctors. Supporters contend that without such laws not more but fewer crimes would go undetected because tipsters would cease to confide in reporters. Until recently many newspersons opposed such laws in the belief that the First Amendment provided adequate protection and that if lawmaking bodies started legislating about journalistic procedures, the results might be oppressive laws.

In some states, shield laws apply to reporters, but not to columnists or editorial writers.

Believers in the First Amendment have additional reasons for worry, including the ruling of the U.S. Court of Appeals in Washington in August 1978 that journalists do not need to be warned that their long-distance telephone records are being subpoenaed in criminal investigations. Especially alarming was the Supreme Court's 5 to 3 decision June 1, 1978, in *Zurcher v. Stanford Daily,* in which it held that Palo Alto police acted constitutionally in 1971 when they raided and ransacked the office of the Stanford University student newspaper allegedly in search of photographs of demonstrations by which they hoped to identify participants. No member of the paper's staff was suspected of any wrongdoing. The police found nothing of any value to them.

Noteworthy raids in the wake of the Stanford case decision occurred when the Minneapolis Vice Squad raided the offices of a tabloid, the *Metropolitan Forum* and police did the same at the Flint, Mich., *Lafeer County Press,* and KBCI-TV of Boise, Idaho.

As a result of tremendous pressure from journalistic organizations, Congress acted and on Oct. 10, 1980, President Carter signed a bill, the Privacy Protection Act, which ended the practice in federal courts. President Carter declared that the Supreme Court decision in the Stanford case had had "a chilling effect" on the ability of reporters to develop sources and pursue stories. "This bill requires federal, state and local authorities either to request voluntary compliance or to use subpoenas—with advance notice and the opportunity for a court hearing—instead of search warrants when they seek reporters' material as evidence," the president explained. He urged the states to enact similar legislation, as Washington already had done.

Clark R. Mollenhoff, a Pulitzer prize-winning former Washington correspondent for the Des Moines *Register* and *Tribune,* has offered the following "Rules for Thoughtful Dealing with Confidential Sources":

1. Know the law applicable to dealing with confidential sources in your jurisdiction. Know the limitations of that law. Do not be misled by your own notion of what the law should be. The law as it is now, and as it has been, does not provide an absolute right for reporters to keep their sources confidential. Read the applicable state and federal statutes and read the opinions of the United States Supreme Court.

2. Know the views of prosecutors and judges in your jurisdiction as well as the views of your own editors and publishers. The law permits considerable discretion for prosecutors and judges in the search for evidence. It is expensive to fight for a principle, and you would be well advised to have an informed judgment as to how far your editors and publishers will go with you even if there is a shield law that seems to afford some limited protection.

3. Try to limit your area of vulnerability in the discussions with your confidential source. In most instances the source is interested in protection only for a certain amount of time, or until after certain events take place. Do not be too quick to offer or give blanket assurances of confidentiality that could put you in jail. It is a serious business and you should give great consideration to the value of the information and to the possible consequences.

4. Do not con your source by giving the false impression that a shield law protects your confidential relationship or that the United States Constitution gives you a firm right to keep your sources confidential. The Court has stated that newsmen do not have an absolute right to refuse to disclose information

to a grand jury. The Sixth Amendment rights of a defendant to subpoena all witnesses who may be favorable to him represents such a serious limitation that Myron Farber and the prestigious and wealthy New York *Times* could not overcome it.

5. If you take information in confidence keep the source totally confidential. Use that source properly as leads to public records, documents and other witnesses who may be used in support of the story. Do not mention in the story that you have a confidential source for that is waving a red flag in the face of defense attorneys, law enforcement officials, the courts and others. You are not being true to your confidential source if you risk disclosure by mentioning the undisclosed source in your story, and particularly if you mention a source and give any leads as to the position of the source in any specific agency. In the rare case in which it is believed necessary to indicate a confidential source in the story, make sure there is a specific agreement with the source as to how he (or she) will be identified in the story.

6. Do not keep notes that might identify the confidential source. In any highly sensitive situation the original notes should be destroyed after the reporter has transcribed them into "random notes" that might be produced without identifying or pointing to the confidential informant. To destroy these notes after a subpoena is issued would risk a contempt of court charge.

7. If litigation is initiated to force you to disclose your source with threats of jail and fines, you should seek permission from your source to be relieved of the obligation of confidentiality unless it is obvious why the disclosure would seriously endanger his life, health, ability to earn a living or his family life.

8. Unless you are relieved of the responsibility of the confidential relationship you should be prepared to serve a substantial jail term, to pay a fine, and to pay legal fees. Your publisher can pay your fine and your legal fees to uphold your pledge to confidentiality, but he cannot serve your jail term for you.

9. Do not sign a contract to write a book that is related in any manner to your confidential source, until all litigation is concluded. Even if you are pure of heart in your motivation, the existence of any money contract provides defense lawyers, the court, prosecutors, and any other critics with an argument that you have a financial stake in the outcome of the litigation. It can leave the impression that you are remaining silent for a price rather than a principle.

Investigative reporting is a precarious profession, and no one with any real understanding of the business would tell you it is an easy and comfortable way to make a living. Confidential sources are important to investigative reporting, and it is vital that reporters and editors give those sources a real protection by using them properly and by avoiding any actions that may risk identification of the source even within the confines of the newsroom. Most often it is a trust the source has in an individual reporter, editor, or news organization. That personal trust is not influenced so much by the opinions of the courts or the ulterior motivations that various prosecutors and defense lawyers may have as it is by the faith in the specific news reporter, and his track record for decency and common sense.

Reports of newsmen dealing in a dishonest manner with their sources are as destructive of the confidence of sources in reporters as are the questionable tactics of any defense lawyer or prosecutor or the arbitrary overreaching of any wrong-headed or dishonest judge.

There are many situations in which confidential sources are invaluable in getting the full story, but it is a disservice to the cause to wrongly argue that Watergate (or any other big story) would have remained buried if it had not been for some "deep throat" source. Make sure that you understand the detailed development of any story situation before using it as an argument on the vital role of confidential sources. If there are good cases in your own experience, they are much better than repetition of a fallacious argument built upon a widely circulated myth.

After the Janet Cooke incident, most editors now insist on their reporters telling them, if necessary, the names of any sources with whom a deal of confidentiality is made. Many also want the source to know of that possibility. Editors increasingly discourage the use of confidential sources.

Reporters should think carefully before making a pledge of confidentiality to a source. Once given, such pledges should not be broken, but keeping the pledge can mean an expensive court fight to stay out of jail for contempt of court. Such fights, moreover, are not always successful, even in states with shield laws.

Government Secrecy

The ghastly extent to which the American people were uninformed and misinformed about many matters, especially the conduct of foreign affairs, was revealed during the congressional hearings into the Watergate scandals and by subsequent exposés of the censorship and propaganda activities of earlier administrations. Revelations of infringements of the Bill of Rights by the CIA, FBI, IRS, military branches and other agencies were shocking. Some charged the press with overplaying the news but most came to realize that American democracy was saved by the so-called Fourth Estate which accelerated its activities when the three official branches floundered.

Systematic post-World War II infringement of the people's right to know began Sept. 24, 1951, when President Harry S Truman ordered all federal departments and agencies to classify and withhold news as the State and Defense departments already were doing, the categories being "classified," "top secret," "secret," "confidential" and "restricted." Under pressure from all of the journalistic organizations, President Eisenhower eliminated the "restricted" category, which proved meaningless as "classified" became the catchall.

With the support of the ANPA, ASNE, SDX and other journalistic groups, a House committee chaired by Rep. John Moss of California embarrassed a number of bureaucrats who tried to justify their censorship actions, using a 1789 "housekeeping" statue intended to help George Washington get his administration started. Congress passed an amendment to the 1789 law to state it "does not authorize withholding information from the public or limiting the availability of records to the public." However, President Eisenhower, on signing the bill, declared it did not "alter the existing power of the head of an executive agency to keep appropriate information or papers confidential in the public interest."

In 1966 President Lyndon B. Johnson used virtually the same language when he signed the Freedom of Information Act, which established the right of the public, including the press, to inspect the *Federal Register* descriptions of the operations of federal agencies, their rules and records. Several kinds of information, mostly allegedly related to national security or privacy, were excepted and the measure was of little help to journalists. Whereas private law firms and businesses utilized the law 640 times, the press used it only 90 times. In 1975 passage of 17 amendments over President Ford's veto supposedly simplified and accelerated use of the privilege. However, bureaucratic stalling and exorbitant service charges still were obstacles.

A sizable library exists of books by frustrated journalistic scholars who tried to "set the record straight" as regards such events as the U-2 incident, the Bay of Pigs, the Cuban missiles crisis, the invasion of the Dominican Republic, the Vietnam War, America's attitude during the Indo-Pakistani War, the role of the CIA in insurrections, including assassinations in several countries such as the Congo, Guatemala, Iran, Indonesia and Chile. Fresh facts regarding these and other incidents are still emerging, in congressional investigations, from confessions of repentant principals, and, not the least, from journalistic activity. In the meantime the American public has had to wait to know the truth about important historical events.

Whereas there have been several attempts by states to impose prior restraint or to suppress periodicals (the Minnesota gag law of 1925 and the Louisiana advertising 1934 tax were the most notorious), since colonial days the federal government had made no such attempts. Then in July 1971 the United States Supreme Court ruled, 6 to 3, that the New York *Times* and Washington *Post* could publish articles based on the so-called Pentagon Papers, documents detailing much of the behind-the-scenes diplomacy which led to American military involvement in Southeast Asia. The papers were leaked to the press by a former Rand Corporation researcher, Dr. Daniel Ellsberg, whose trial for conspiracy and other offenses ended with the revelation of the attempted burglary of his psychiatrist's office by members of the White House Plumbers group, which also burglarized the National Democratic headquarters in the Watergate. Some of the Plumbers' leaders had been prominent in the fiasco of the Bay of Pigs invasion of Cuba a few years earlier.

In permitting publication of the Pentagon Papers the Supreme Court did not invalidate the classification system, which remains intact. Perhaps 20,000,000 documents remain inaccessible because of the actions of about 30,000 federal governmental bureaucrats with censorship powers.

A second case on which practicing newspapermen split was the injunction issued by U.S. District Judge Robert W. Warren in Milwaukee against publication of a magazine article by free-lance writer Howard Morland on "The H-Bomb Secret; How We Got It. Why We're Telling It" scheduled for publication in the May 1979 issue of *The Progressive*. Morland revealed that he had obtained all of his information from government publications, which fact American Civil Liberties Union investigations confirmed. The contention of most atomic scientists that there is no secret was substantiated in September when *The Press Connection,* a Madison daily operated by former strikers against the *Capital-Times,* ran a letter from a 32-year-old computer programmer, Charles Hansen, who used unclassified information to describe the bomb. After several other papers published the Hansen letter, the government dropped its suit and the original Morland article appeared in the November 1979 *Progressive.*

An excellent article on the scope of the problem of access to truthful information about the federal government appeared in the March–April 1985 *Columbia Journalism Review.* It was written by Anthony Marro, managing editor of *Newsday* and a former Washington correspondent. Its title is "When the Government Tells Lies."

Under President Reagan, the Freedom of Information Act's limited effectiveness was even more watered down. Reagan supported bills to exempt the Secret Service, the Central Intelligence Agency and most Federal Bureau of Investigation activities from the Freedom of Information Act. He made mandatory lie detector tests of any defense employee with access to classified information who is asked to take such a test. Reversing a policy of the preceding administration, Reagan authorized the FBI and CIA to infiltrate journalistic organizations if the attorney general approved it in the name of national security. He also approved FBI and CIA infiltration of many domestic institutions, including the press, if those federal agencies deem such undercover work necessary in their investigations of organized crime or terrorism. He took other steps, including rewriting the classification system to diminish available information, encouraging fewer fee reductions to journalists in FOIA requests and attempting to require all officials who had access to classified information while in office to seek government approval for the rest of their lives of any public writing or speaking they would do that involved that information.

In late 1985 a bill largely inspired by the Society of Professional Journalists, Sigma Delta Chi, was introduced in the U.S. House of Representatives. Its intent was to roll back some of those Reagan actions and to strengthen access to federal government information for the public, including reporters. The major provisions of the bill were to reduce the material exempt from FOIA disclosure, increase the number of agencies exempt from the law, increase penalties for agencies that fail to comply with requests in timely fashion, cut the fees charged for answering requests and speed up responses for requests. In addition, the bill would transfer responsibility for endorcing compliance from the Justice Department to the archivist of the United States, who the drafters believed would be more likely to sympathize with a free flow of information than the attorney general. Sponsors hoped the bill would be debated in 1986, but as this textbook was being prepared for publication, it seemed likely the debate would be long and that the prospects for passage in anything like the proposed form were poor so long as the president's party controlled at least one chamber of the Congress.

All states now have some kind of freedom of information law, but there, too, reporters often have trouble making it work in a way that comes close to living up to the name of such legislation. A good example of the difficulties at the state level was illustrated in Illinois. In 1984, after a long fight to enact such a law by journalistic and other organizations, the state became the last in the nation to pass such a comprehensive freedom of information statute. But the measure was so severely amended by the governor and legislature that most of its main sponsors concluded that the law makes it more difficult to obtain many kinds of information from the government than before the law was passed.

According to Jack Anderson in *Confessions of a Muckraker:* "Any government agency in which men connive to court the favor or dodge the obloquy of politicians is bound to be a spawning ground for one of the most valuable species in American life—the informer. The informer is our principal protection against the design of public wrongdoers who have built massive walls to hide their activities."

Copyright

Facts (news) cannot be copyrighted. The actual wording of an account of those facts, however, can be. A Conference of Press Experts called by the League of Nations in 1927 at Geneva stated the principle as follows:

> The Conference of Press Experts lays down a fundamental principle that the publication of a piece of news is legitimate, subject to the condition that the news in question has reached the person who publishes it by regular and unobjectionable means, and not by an act of unfair competition. No one may acquire the right of suppressing news of public interest.
>
> The Conference affirms the principle that newspapers, news agencies, and other news organizations are entitled after publication as well as before publication to the reward of their labor, enterprise and financial expenditure upon the production of news reports, but holds that this principle shall not be so interpreted as to result in the creation or the encouragement of any monopoly in news.

Although facts cannot be copyrighted, newspapers can seek redress for pirating of news as a violation of fair business practices. In the case of *Associated Press v. International News Service,* the United States Supreme Court declared Dec. 23, 1918:

> Except for matters improperly disclosed, or published in breach of trust or confidence, or in violation of law, none of which is involved in this branch of the case, the news of current events may be regarded as common property. . . . Regarding the news, therefore . . . it must be regarded as quasi-property, irrespective of the rights of either as against the public.

A newspaper that wishes to rewrite or quote a copyrighted article appearing in another publication either buys the copyright privilege or requests permission to quote. In either case, credit must be given to the publication that originally printed the material. If the copyright privilege is purchased, this credit line appears at the top of the article, as

By Larry Green and Rob Warden
© 1975, CHICAGO DAILY NEWS

A Chicago undercover policeman operated as a double agent, spying on antiwar groups and at the same time selling those groups information on police intelligence operations, a Daily News investigation has found.

Otherwise, if permission to quote is given, the newspaper that copyrighted the article is given credit in the story itself. Unless permission is received, the paper using material in this manner is in danger of being sued for violation of copyright laws.

Usually, the copyright device is employed by newspapers to ensure that they get credit for their enterprise when the wire services and networks circulate paraphrased versions of the story around a region, the nation or world.

Reportorial Ethics

For years groups such as the American Society of Newspaper Editors, the American Newspaper Publisher Association, Sigma Delta Chi/Society of Professional Journalists and the National Conference of Editorial Writers have had ethics codes. The codes are guidelines for responsible conduct in various aspects of journalistic work.

Still, in 1974 a survey by the Associated Press Managing Editors revealed that only 9 percent of the respondents' newspapers had written codes or guidelines. A decade later, more than half of daily newspapers had ethics codes and guidelines of varying content.

New Concerns Over Ethics

In part, the reason for the increase of such formal policy attention to ethics on the part of newspapers was their growing concern over the costs of libel suits, discussed in the previous chapter. In part, it was the result of the red faces caused by a series of incidents during the '70s and '80s in which a few reporters were discovered to have fabricated entire stories, or parts of stories.

But mostly it was the result of more newspapers getting involved in the same kind of customer and marketing surveys that many other industries, including the broadcasting media, had conducted for years. Those surveys made editors more conscious than ever before of what readers thought about newspapers, and newspaper owners and publishers were putting editors under pressure to pay attention to the results. What the surveys seemed to show was that readers did not always love what newspapers did. All of this concern came to be known among editors as "the credibility crisis," and they worried a lot about it. By 1984, the worry had become the dominant topic of many newspaper editors' national meetings. Reporters in newsrooms around the country were feeling the effects of their bosses' concerns, in the form of, among other things, renewed attention to matters reflected in the growing number of ethics codes, in the presence of ombudsmen in many newsrooms, in more checks with outside sources about the accuracy of reporters' stories and the like.

Editors As Business People

Newspapers being business enterprises, part of the worry about credibility and ethics was related to such matters as advertising and circulation revenue, the main direct sources of newspaper profits. Newspapers remained among the nation's most profitable industries. But there were signs that among younger, more affluent people—those most desirable to many of the biggest advertisers—fewer people were buying or reading newspapers than made publishers or their marketing consultants feel comfortable when they pondered the industry's future. And major metropolitan papers were not penetrating as high a portion of their potential markets as they once did.

Many editors became more concerned about marketing a product than with their old preoccupation with editing good newspapers, to the point when you attended meetings of newspaper editors, it sometimes was difficult to determine if you had walked into a gathering of journalists or one of sales managers for soap companies. Discussions of ethics reflected journalistic concerns, but also had a tone of the attention of other industries to "quality control" in the manufacture and distribution of their products.

Nationally, this was apparent, among other places, at the 1984 meeting of the Associated Press Managing Editors organization. One of the reports circulated at the meeting was that of the Media Competition Continuing Study Committee. The report was a glossy facsimile of *Time* magazine. It contained excerpts of the responses of more than 100 members of the organization to the following question: "Just who or what is our (newspapers') competition? Us? Apathy? HBO? Barbara Tuchman? Trivial Pursuit? Male Go-Go Nights for the ladies? USFL? Nursing home rocking chair marathons? VCRs? Barbara Mandrell? Lower reading skills? Time? Michael Jackson? Higher priorities? Happy Hour? Radio Shack? Barbara Walters? Higher reading skills?" Most of the editors responded with answers similar to those implied in the list of the questions, revealing both their confusion about how to respond to new kinds of competition and their concern about the diversity of that competition.

Editors As Journalists

One of the few respondents in that 1984 APME survey who saw things less as a marketer and more as a public affairs journalist was Herb Robinson, editor of the editorial page of the Seattle *Times*. Said Robinson: "Our 'competition' in the main may well be an intangible—the growing complexity of the news, which is so difficult to understand that many readers are tempted to simply throw up their hands and say 'to hell with it.' I've long had the suspicion that what often passes for hostility to the press is a combination of public bewilderment and the old 'kill the messenger' syndrome—not only do many people fail to understand contemporary developments, they have a sense of powerlessness in dealing with the perception that it's bad news. The challenge, of course, is to do a better job of explaining what's going on in a world fraught with conflict and complexity."

In a paper in another report to that APME meeting, this on the matter of ethics, the then president and editorial chairman of the Des Moines Register and Tribune Co., took a dim view of the writing of ethics codes that had been going on in so many American newsrooms. Michael Gartner noted that the First Amendment does not talk about a responsible press, only a free press. He pointed out that most ethics codes were made up of vague generalities, many of their provisions conflicting with one another, and mainly serving the purpose of allowing editors to discipline reporters for doing something wrong or stupid, when they could be disciplined for doing such things even without a code. Furthermore, he said, the codes of ethics were dangerous because they could be used in courtrooms to suggest that reporters had done something wrong as professionals, when in fact journalism is not in a legal sense a profession with enforceable standards by which its practitioners must do their work. Gartner argued that the First Amendment allows anybody to write what they want to write, subject only to the discipline of libel laws, their employers and the pressures of the marketplace. Codes of ethics might end up destroying that right, Gartner contended. He said he subscribed to the goals of the ethics codes, but asserted that nobody else had any business telling him how to edit his newspaper in terms of having the power to take disciplinary action. All newspapers, he said, deserved such freedom.

Gartner also looked askance at all the worrying about the credibility of the newspaper industry among his fellow editors. He pointed out that if you read the surveys closely, you found that most people had a more favorable attitude toward the newspaper they read regularly than they did toward newspapers generally. "Maybe," he said, "this whole question of worrying about our image, about regulation, about policing, about ethics codes, about standards and behavior is a real waste of our time. Maybe we should, instead, be talking about story ideas, about quality of writing, about how to put out even better papers, papers that are more accurate, that are more thorough. . . ."

Bias, Conscious and Unconscious _____

When a presidential candidate came to town, a reporter for Paper A wrote: "Despite the rain a wildly enthusiastic crowd of thousands gave him a warm welcome at the airport." His rival on paper B saw it this way: "Although the rain had stopped before his plane landed, only 5,000 persons—most of them loud teenagers—were present when he arrived."

Both accounts are accurate but obviously biased, one pro and the other con.

These prejudices, on the part of owner, publisher, editor or reporter, may be unconscious. To the extent that they are conscious convictions, their holders may try not to allow them to distort or suppress the truth. Reporters' academic training should have made them aware of the importance of stereotypes, taboos, superstitions and other factors influencing attitudes and opinions. The journalism student is encouraged to be as open-minded and fair as it is humanly possible to be and to be aware of any emotional obstacles to be overcome in seeking so-called truth and to understand the behavior of others who may go through life unaware of their inhibitions.

Overwhelmingly newspaper ownership is conservative. A large majority of newspapers always endorse the most conservative presidential candidate. Moreover, with few exceptions editorial pages historically have opposed measures generally considered liberal. In editorials and sometimes in their news columns, the majority of newspapers fought Woodrow Wilson's New Freedom, which meant the income tax, woman suffrage, federal reserve bank, child labor laws and similar measures. Many publishers joined the economic royalists in despising Franklin D. Roosevelt and the New Deal. Many of them disliked Harry Truman's Fair Deal, John F. Kennedy's New Frontier and Lyndon Johnson's Great Society. Likewise, ever since the press helped drum up support for the Spanish-American war, the majority of the papers have been chauvinistic, often uncritically supporting America's foreign policy. Only voluntary censorship was needed to obtain their cooperation during World Wars I and II and in support of aggressive actions in Korea and Vietnam. Until recent years, much of the press has been hawkish in support of increases in military expenditures despite their inflationary effect. Only a handful of papers vigorously opposed Sen. Joseph McCarthy, the House Committee on Un-American Activities, witch hunters and red baiters.

Professional journalists sometimes become more liberal as the result of their firsthand observations covering assignments. It is possible to maintain one's integrity even on a paper whose policies are personally repugnant. The time to say "no" when asked to do something contrary to one's principles is on the first occasion. Those who show a willingness to do dirty work will get the assignments. This strong warning should not be interpreted as meaning that such disagreeable experiences occur frequently. In fact, they occur infrequently enough to be newsworthy, as when a Texas editor was fired because he ran a comparative shoppers' list and when two Michigan editors were replaced because they refused to publish what they considered to be unfair criticisms of the president distributed by the chain's headquarters.

Conflict of Interest _____

There is no unanimity among journalists as to how much they, from the owner to the young reporter, should participate in community affairs. Many allow and encourage it, but many others discourage it, to the extent that they can draw up clear, rational policies to do so.

The role of the owner, who has ultimate authority over a newspaper's content, is often the most difficult to control, and frequently leaves employees believing that there is a double standard within newspapers in respect to conflict of interest guidelines. When a reporter for the Hackensack (N.J.) *Record,* for example, once made a routine examination of campaign donation funds he discovered that William Dean Singleton, publisher of the Paterson (N.J.) *News,* had given $1,000 to the election campaign of that city's Mayor Lawrence "Pat" Kramer. He had done so through the Westfield (Mass.) *Evening News,* which he also owned. Singleton explained that he made the contribution as an individual, not as a newspaper publisher. Malcolm "Mac" Borg, publisher of the Hackensack paper, replied, "You cannot separate the individual from the publisher." Singleton said his paper covered the campaign fairly; the paper endorsed Kramer, who won handily. Then he recalled that both the executive editor and Trenton correspondent of the *Record* had at different times taken leaves of absence to act as the governor's press agent. Borg also serves on the board of the Bergen Pines County Hospital, some units of which lost their accreditation. Singleton asked what went through the mind of the *Record* reporter who covered the story.

Although some newspaper managements permit or even encourage employees to join organizations and accept positions on the boards of philanthropic institutions, most frown on staff persons being candidates for public office. When Julianne Agnew filed papers to run for the Duluth (Minn.) City Council, she was promptly discharged as Living editor of the Duluth *Herald* and *News-Tribune* by managing editor Robert. A. Knaus, who said her decision "placed her in a position of conflict of interest with her responsibilities to these newspapers." Subsequently a county grand jury indicted Knaus and other members of the paper's management for violating the state's fair campaign practices law. The case eventually reached the Minnesota Supreme Court, which dismissed the charges.

In nearby Minneapolis, John Cowles Jr., owner of the Minneapolis *Star* and *Tribune,* became chairman of the Greater Minneapolis Chamber of Commerce Stadium Task Force, and gave $4.9 million of the company's money to the campaign to construct a domed stadium in midtown Minneapolis on land owned by the newspaper. The following paid advertisement signed by 49 *Tribune* newsroom staffers appeared in the *Tribune:*

> As journalists, our responsibility is to be dispassionate and fair in covering public issues. Our role is to report, not to participate in these issues. Because we work for the Minneapolis Tribune, we recognize some people may question our fidelity to that principle when John Cowles Jr., chairman of the board of the Star & Tribune Co., is a leading advocate in the debate over whether and where the sports stadium should be built. We bought this advertisement to assure our readers that our professional principles have not been undermined by Cowles' involvement in the stadium issue. We neither advocate nor oppose building a stadium, domed or un-domed, at any location. Furthermore, neither Cowles nor any other company executive has tried to influence the Tribune's coverage of this issue. But to prevent even an appearance of such a conflict of

interest, we believe management should avoid a leadership role in sensitive political and economic issues.

Unusual as the incident was, it was not the first time working journalists resorted to advertising to promulgate viewpoints at variance with those of management. The New York *Daily News* twice refused to accept advertisements signed by staff members. The first, signed by 58 employees of the paper, opposed the American incursion into Cambodia and the killing of Kent State University demonstrators by state troopers. The second, with 150 signers, called on President Nixon "to live up to his preelection promise of peace in Southeast Asia." Both ads were accepted by the New York *Times*.

In 1971 after the Chicago *Daily News* endorsed Richard J. Daley for reelection as Chicago's mayor, 88 staff members bought a half-page advertisement to oppose the endorsement. Then 61 staffers of the Chicago *Sun-Times* did likewise.

The paper's liberal attitude, by comparison with that of the New York *Daily News,* recalled the Republican candidacy for vice president of Frank Knox, when he owned the Chicago *Daily News*. The paper's editorial page columnist, Howard Vincent O'Brien, wrote several uncensored columns opposing the Landon-Knox ticket, even declaring he didn't think his boss would be good in the job.

After the officers of the Newspaper Guild, a labor union whose members include many reporters, endorsed Sen. George McGovern for president in 1972, the Washington *Post* ran a full-page advertisement signed and paid for by nearly 300 Washington Guild members declaring the Guild had no business interjecting its members into a partisan political role. "We in the news business have an obligation to inform the public," the ad read, "The fulfillment of this obligation depends on maintaining credibility with the public."

Reporter Power _____

The model Newspaper Guild contract includes an integrity clause as follows:

> EMPLOYEE INTEGRITY: Employees shall be protected by contract against use of their by-lines or credit lines over their protest. Employees shall also be protected by contract against having to perform under protest any practice compromising their integrity. Substantive changes in material shall be brought to the employee's attention before publication. Provision shall be made that no employee shall be required to write, process or prepare anything for publication in such a way as to distort any facts or to create an impression that the employee knows to be false. Provision shall be made that if a question arises as to the accuracy of printed material, no correction or retraction of that material shall be printed without prior consultation with the employee concerned. Any employee whose work or person is mentioned in a letter to the

editor shall be informed of such letter immediately and shall have the right to respond to such letter simultaneously and adequately on the page on which it is published. Provision shall be made that no employee shall be required to use his or her position as an employee for any purpose other than in carrying out his or her work for the employer.

The Guild demands elimination of secret surveillances of employees as well as the use of electronic supervisors, tape recordings, telephone-monitoring systems and similar procedures and devices. It seeks management's support of anyone who "refuses to give up custody or disclose any knowledge, information, notes, records, documents, files, photographs or tapes or the source thereof, that relate to news, commentary, advertising or the establishment and maintenance of his or her sources, etc."

Citing *Le Monde* of Paris and some other European publications, the Guild seeks regular, generally monthly discussions between representatives of management and the reportorial staff, also possibly delegate attendance at regular editorial board and similar high-level meetings.

When the Burlington (Iowa) *Hawk Eye* needed a managing editor, the publisher, John McCormally, invited all members of the news-editorial department and the heads of other departments to veto his first or second appointee if they wished to do so. As a result, the new man, an outsider who subjected himself to thorough interviewing by all, received unanimous approval.

The *News Policy Manual* of the Lexington (Ky.) *Leader* stipulates: "During the first week of every month a news policy committee made up of the editor, the managing editor, the city editor and two reporters or copy editors, will meet to consider suggested changes and additions."

One of the strongest deterrents to injustices is the adverse publicity that often results. That was the case when Jude Dippold was fired by the Greensburg (Pa.) *Tribune-Review* for remarking, "one down and one to go" after Spiro Agnew resigned as vice president. The publisher, Richard Mellon Scaife, had contributed $1 million to the Nixon campaign. Twelve other reporters resigned in protest.

Because she refused to shake hands with a congressional candidate, Karen Kelly was fired by the Oak Park (Ill.) *Pioneer Press*. Her reason was Edward Hanrahan's role, when Cook County state's attorney, in the police raid that resulted in the murders of Black Panther leaders Fred Hampton and Mark Clark. Even Hanrahan objected to the firing.

Special Interests

Policy decisions are made by management, with or without consultation with labor groups or any others, and are communicated to the rank and file. Nevertheless, it is to everyone's advantage for reporters to know the reasons as well as the decisions themselves. That means, among other things, understanding the special interests that seek favorable treatments by the press.

Public Relations

Many persons who quit newspapers or other journalistic media go into pubic relations work. Often this is because of the lure of a fatter paycheck, in which case the more basic reportorial experience the better. Others have been cynical failures in their attempt to find adequate means of self-expression where they were. They become jaded and bored, weary of being "a daily historian" and believe public relations provides a greater variety of experiences. Still others seek opportunities to promote causes in which they believe.

Their most recent attempt to improve their public image is to call themselves directors or vice presidents in charge of public affairs. Most of the nation's largest corporations now use the terms "public affairs" or "corporate relations" instead of "public relations." The trend is also for governmental agencies at all levels to do the same.

To Edward L. Bernays, who coined the term "public relations" in 1919, the phenomenon is partly the result of "the operatives in the White House who called themselves public relations experts and who were not." Bernays is dubious about the value of name change, saying that "a group of highbinders" could commit some "kind of professional mayhem" and then "another name would have to be sought." As he has since 1923 in *Crystallizing Public Opinion,* the first book ever written on the subject, Bernays advocates state licensing of public relations counsel to safeguard the public from quacks.

Adverse Criticism

Until recently, practicing journalists were almost unanimous in condemning public relations persons as brazen if not unscrupulous space-grabbers and fakers. Today, this harsh judgment has been considerably modified, partly because of the impossibility of covering the wide range of potential news without assistance, and partly because of the considerable elevation of standards within the public relations field. Once they were mostly press agents, whose forte was the manufacturing of stunts, and, more recently, they were mere publicity men whose success was determined largely by the amount of space their clients got in the legitimate news columns of the media. Now the best of them are skillful participants in top-level policy making who have the total image of their clients in mind. Instead of courting publicity they may, in fact, advise against seeking any journalistic mention. They concern themselves with internal problems of personnel and morale, advertising, product, salesmanship and total behavior. In their exalted positions they may be considered by some to be even more dangerous as hidden persuaders, pressure boys, masters of the invisible sell, space-grabbers, ballyhoo boys, hucksters or malicious engineers of public consent, to use some of the titles by which they are known to their detractors.

A great danger is the extent to which public relations people erect a barrier between the reporter and original news sources. If all news is obtained through carefully prepared news releases, the reporter becomes little more than a glorified messenger. Good newspapers and magazines consist of more than such handouts with proper headlines and picture captions added by the editors. No matter how cooperative and sensible, public relations counsels never can lose sight of the fact that the primary obligation is to their employer. The reporter, on the other hand, is a kind of unofficial public servant in a democracy, and can argue that point with a publisher seeking to browbeat the reporter. The publisher may still fire the reporter, but does so at the risk of appearing a hypocrite about the claims of his paper to print the news without prejudice. It is a subtle, but significant distinction. There are bound to be at least occasional clashes of interest. News releases today are usually well written and reliable but often there are omissions and obscurities that can be corrected only by personal contact between newsgatherer and news source.

Large news conferences, especially with the president and other prominent public figures, can be extremely frustrating because no reporter present has the opportunity to probe deeply into any matter. Too often a reporter is limited to a single question so that as many as possible can have a turn. Planted questions are asked by friendly reporters who have been advised by press agents. It's impossible under such circumstances to be thorough in one's fact finding. Even if better conditions prevail, a public relations counsel may hover over the shoulder of the interviewee to advise, augment and correct his statements. Reporters often are infuriated and feel that their dignity has been injured. Serving one's editor and the public is extremely difficult under such circumstances.

If the interview is broadcast live, the nonelectronic media newsgatherers may be at great disadvantage to follow up misconceptions that already have become familiar to millions of watchers. It is possible for public figures to misuse television to the detriment of all. The task of the print media to correct errors and to supplement incomplete details is becoming tremendous.

In Defense

In their own defense, the estimated 80,000 persons who perform public relations functions contend that their activities are of great social benefit. They take credit for having converted business and industry completely away from the public-be-damned attitude and say that they have humanized business, helped give it good manners and, most important, a conscience; and that they have taught it that he profits most who serves best. They define public relations or its synonym as simply doing the right thing and letting people know about it, applying the Golden Rule in everyday activities while not letting one's light shine unnoticed under a basket. To them, sound public relations means the daily application of common sense, common courtesy and common decency in accordance with a continuous program of enlightened self-interest through good works that not only earn one a good reputation but also cause him to deserve it as a good neighbor. There is a growing sense of professionalism among corporate public relations counsel and increasingly they are seeing the wisdom of training and preparing chief executives to face the media. Several major agencies run sensitivity courses for corporate executives on dealing with the media.

In further defense of public relations as it relates to news media, it is indisputable that almost every legitimate news item that appears in public print has publicity value for someone. Even unfavorable mention or scandal doesn't seem to be fatal to national heroes, especially in the entertainment world. Readers' memories are short and inaccurate and when they go to the polls the familiar name has advantage, no matter how unsavory the situation in connection with which it was publicized. Organized baseball and other professional sports are commercial enterprises that have thrived on free publicity, through good-sized sports sections, for generations. The same is true of the theater, book publishing, concert stage and other artistic enterprises, which are not generally philanthropies.

Since John D. Rockefeller II hired Ivy Lee early in the century, the policy of the public relations profession has been increasingly toward more cooperation with the newsgathering media rather than agencies to suppress unfavorable news or retard newsgatherers in their efforts to obtain it. Public relations departments of railroads, airlines and industries today are a great asset to reporters at times of fires, accidents and other disasters, whereas a generation ago exactly the opposite was the case.

The news or publicity or information division of a public relations department provides a quantity of legitimate news handouts, full texts of speeches by important people, notices of meetings and conventions, plans for changes in policies and operations of both private and public institutions, and other services that no newspaper or magazine could afford to obtain by means of its own paid employees. To some extent, the media are today at the mercy of the public relations people to keep them informed of what is going on in large segments of society. Reporters should not be cynical about public relations people, but they should be skeptical.

Freebies and Payola

Reporters covering large meetings, conventions, athletic contests and similar events expect that there will be pressrooms and tables with desks, telephones, refreshments and other necessities. Newspapers differ as to how much, in addition to the mere necessities, their employees should be permitted to accept. Some even refuse passes to games or plays and pay for the books they review.

Because it is important to make contacts with newsworthy people, the reporter finds it impossible to boycott all cocktail parties and receptions at which there often are elaborate refreshments. Reporters are guided by office rules as to what, if any, gifts they can accept at Christmas or any other time. Sometimes it is stipulated that a newsroom employee must return any gift that costs more than a certain amount, possibly the price of a fifth of whisky. Sports writers today mostly have their expenses paid by their offices rather than by the management of the teams they accompany on trips. Usually, however, they are allowed to accept season passes just as music and drama critics go free to entertainments and book editors do not have to pay for books they review.

When the Strand bookstore in New York wrote a letter of solicitation to a book editor whose managing editor was president of the Associated Press Managing Editors, an investigation was undertaken to reveal that for years book review editors in many parts of the country were making thousands of dollars annually by selling unreviewed books to the used-book company. Most newspapers consider the books the property of the paper, not the reviewer. To avoid the gigantic payola some donate the books to libraries or charitable institutions. According to the used-book stores, some of these institutions then offer them for sale.

There have been a few cases of financial writers who used their inside knowledge of the market for personal profit. The Securities and Exchange Commission has taken action against writers who purchased stock just prior to boosting it in their columns, after which they sold at considerable profit. The practice is growing for newspapers to require financial writers to reveal their holdings, to their editors at least.

The importance of journalists seeing something of the world cannot be denied. Only a few of the larger papers can adhere consistently to a pay-as-you-go policy. So many newspapers allow their staff people to accept invitations from foreign governments to visit other nations, usually in parties with representatives of other papers, and they are represented on junkets paid for by their own government to inspect military establishments or to visit battlefields. They take inspection cruises and go on inaugural flights as the guests of private aviation companies. It is a wise policy for a reporter to avoid taking any more freebies than appear absolutely essential to doing good reporting. When in doubt, do not take something for what appears to be nothing. There almost certainly will be a cost, sooner or later.

Contests

A more subtle way of influencing news judgment is the awards that are given in recognition of stellar performance in a particular field. The decision in such a case as to what constitutes good journalism is that of the donor of the prize. Some newspapers are eager to wallpaper their offices with plaques and certificates, and some keep a careful tab on announcements of such honors in the offing. *Editor & Publisher* issues a fat annual *Directory of Journalism Awards*. Too much ambition may develop into exaggerated emphasis on news of a certain character rather than unprejudiced evaluations of the happenings of the day. In other words, conscious efforts to please the donors of prizes can badly warp good editorial performance. The commendations that accompany the certificates or plaques or medals in addition to money prizes, are flattering to recipients and creators of good will for the donors.

Reporters should be wary of how the pursuit of prizes can shape their story selection and their reporting. Trying to interpret reality accurately and fairly is a far more noble goal than winning awards.

Deceptions _____

In earlier days it was common practice for reporters to pretend to be policemen, deputy coroners or some other public officials. To avoid deliberate misrepresentation without identifying themselves they might begin a telephone conversation with a news source by saying, "I'm calling from police headquarters." Or they might ask, "Has the sheriff arrived yet? If not would you tell me . . . ?"

Concealed Identities

Reporters still occasionally crash gates merely by not identifying themselves and acting as though they were within their rights. Mark Butler of the Suburban and Wayne (Pa.) *Times* attended a Kennedy family wedding reception after chauffeuring a part of the bridal party in a car rented from a garage for which he occasionally moonlighted as an extra driver. A Detroit *News* Washington correspondent witnessed the signing of an Israeli-Egyptian peace treaty in the White House by taking the bus seat intended for a congressman who, he knew, would be absent. No special credential had been issued and police were too busy to check attendance carefully.

Inasmuch as both of these incidents were successful evasions of security measures they led to official condemnations of reporters, the police and the Secret Service. In another case a $1-million suit for invasion of privacy was brought against a radio reporter who eavesdropped on a Panax corporation stockholders' meeting as well as a closed directors' meeting. He did it by putting on overalls and checking wall sockets with an electric circuit tester.

Eugene Patterson, editor of the St. Petersburg *Times,* has said: "All of us engage in plainclothes reporting. Our restaurant reviewer doesn't wear a press card on her lobster bib; she takes pains, in fact, not to be recognized in the joints she's casing for our readers' guidance. Neither does our consumer reporter reveal her noncustomer status when she sets out to nail a bait-and-switch advertiser. She's not even above driving a rigged car into a series of garages in order to report the wildly varying cost and effectiveness of auto repairs."

Stunts

Nevertheless, Patterson has soured on such stunts as planting a masquerading reporter on a nursing home's payroll to do an inside job on the nature of the care provided patients. Most newspapers, however, do believe that the best, often the only, way to investigate a situation is from the inside. Edgar May of the Buffalo *Evening News* won a Pulitzer prize for his series of articles after working for three months as a caseworker for the Erie County Department of Social Welfare. Ted Smart of the Chicago *Daily News* won several citations for his exposé of conditions in the Chicago Bridewell, to which he got himself committed as a common drunk.

Several official investigations resulted after Edward Williams, Milwaukee *Journal* reporter, spent ten days in the House of Correction posing as a vagrant. By becoming an applicant himself, Sam Washington of the Chicago *Sun-Times* exposed an examiner who was soliciting bribes from students taking a General Educational Development Test.

When the late William Jones, Chicago *Tribune* reporter, heard unconfirmed reports alleging that Chicago police were bribed to steer hospital call cases to private ambulance companies, he thought it worthwhile following up. So he trained as a first-aid man and got a job as an ambulance driver. The results: a six-part exposé of official collusion; a grand jury that handed up 16 indictments; and a Pulitzer prize for special local reporting for Jones.

Other reporters have obtained employment as guards or attendants in prisons, mental hospitals and other public institutions. The existence of illegal gambling has been exposed by investigative reporters who were supplied with money and told to find bookmakers with whom to place bets. Because of the growing complaint by teachers that students are unruly, reporters with the proper credentials have obtained teaching positions or have acted as substitutes in the classroom to observe firsthand.

The opportunities for such "undercover" journalism are boundless. Usually, some properly qualified official, as a judge or social worker, is "in" on the stunt, often to legalize it and, in any case, to soften adverse criticisms of entrapment or other unethical conduct. Certainly the responsibility is great not to yield to the temptation to merely "make a case" in the interest of a sensational story. It is easy to find that for which one earnestly is looking. The reporter and newspaper are vulnerable unless the highest principles of ethical journalism are observed. Impersonation is not illegal except of police and public officials.

The investigative stunt that perhaps caused the most debate in journalistic circles was that of the Chicago *Sun-Times,* which purchased a tavern that was then operated by reporters with cameramen taking surreptitious pictures of attempts by city inspectors and others to solicit bribes or payoffs. The revelations shook the city that was supposed to work and was considered a cinch for a Pulitzer prize. Although it won eight state and national contests sponsored by organizations including the Associated Press, United Press International and the Society of Professional Journalists, Sigma Delta Chi, the public service committee judging the Pulitzer prizes decided the *Sun-Times'* enterprise involved entrapment, so the prize went to the Philadelphia *Inquirer* for exposing systematic police violence. The best policy for a reporter is not to resort to deceptions unless it is a matter of great importance to the public interest and unless there are no other ways to get information. To lie is a serious matter for anyone, especially a reporter.

Impersonations

When the roles are reversed, journalists usually protest impersonations of reporters by policemen. The Welch (W. Va.) *Daily News,* however, hired an undercover policeman to pose as a reporter to gather evidence of the illicit drug traffic. After several journalistic organizations were critical of the imposture, the paper's publisher, Rollo Taylor, wrote to the Charleston (W. Va.) *Mail:*

> For over 100 years newspaper reporters have posed as ditch diggers, diplomats, welders, Indians, Jews, blacks, truck drivers, and criminals to obtain stories.
>
> Such a pose is a deception—a lie—but I don't recall that anybody was ever offended by that, nor do I recall that any newspaper ever lost its credibility by it.
>
> It now seems to offend some newspaper people that a policeman posing as a reporter is all wrong despite the fact that a reporter is applauded for posing as a policeman.

Much more serious were the revelations by two special congressional committees, one in the Senate with Frank Church of Idaho as chairman, the other in the House with Rep. Otto Pike of New York as chairman. Both reports revealed that almost since its origin shortly after World War II, the Central Intelligence Agency had employed journalists abroad as covert agents or informers. At the time of the reports, 1976, it was estimated that approximately 50 foreign correspondents for American newspapers and news services, freelancers and stringers were in CIA's employ. They helped plant stories in publications all over the world, falsified accounts and supplied the CIA with information that didn't get into any news dispatches.

The disclosures of the Church and Pike committees and revelations contained in several books by former CIA agents resulted in new CIA guidelines containing the following: "Effective immediately the CIA will not enter into any paid or contractual relationship with any full-time or part-time news correspondent accredited by any U.S. news service, newspaper, periodical, radio or television network or station."

The order was almost universally applauded by journalists. However, when Congress enacted new legislation governing clandestine CIA and FBI activities, there were few provisions to prevent a recurrence of the old practices.

Codes of Ethics _____

Professional public opinion polls show an increasing number of persons favoring strict control of the media. This situation is one of the facts of life that the young journalist must be aware of. To combat the bad public image that newsgatherers have to the detriment of the credibility of the media, almost every journalistic organization has prepared a code of ethics for the guidance of reporters on how to be on their good behavior. The National Labor Relations Board has ruled that the management of the Madison (Wis.) *Capital-Times* can unilaterally issue a code of ethics but it cannot establish penalties without negotiating with the Guild. The paper's managing editor had declared in a speech to the New Jersey Press Association, "Can a reporter who dates news sources be objective? We can't prevent such associations but in order to protect as much as possible the newspaper's objectivity we must know about them." This inspired many reporters to prepare memoranda telling of their social engagements, including menus, size of bills and conversations. Some who received tips or ideas for news stories requested overtime pay.

The Society of Professional Journalists, Sigma Delta Chi, has the largest membership of any journalistic organization. Its code of ethics, revised in 1973, follows:

The Society of Professional Journalists, Sigma Delta Chi, believes the duty of journalists is to serve the truth.

We believe the agencies of mass communication are carriers of public discussion and information, acting on their Constitutional mandate and freedom to learn and report the facts.

We believe in public enlightenment as the forerunner of justice, and in our Constitutional role to seek the truth as part of the public's right to know the truth.

We believe those responsibilities carry obligations that require journalists to perform with intelligence, objectivity, accuracy, and fairness.

To these ends, we declare acceptance of the standards of practice here set forth:

RESPONSIBILITY

The public's right to know of events of public importance and interest is the overriding mission of the mass media. The purpose of distributing news and enlightened opinion is to serve the general welfare. Journalists who use their professional status as a representative of the public for selfish or other unworthy motives violate a high trust.

FREEDOM OF THE PRESS

Freedom of the press is to be guarded as an inalienable right of the people in a free society. It carries with it the freedom and the responsibility to discuss, question, and challenge actions and utterances of our government and of our public and private institutions. Journalists uphold the right to speak unpopular opinions and the privilege to agree with the majority.

ETHICS

Journalists must be free of obligation to any interest other than the public's right to know the truth.

1. Gifts, favors, free travel, special treatment or privileges can compromise the integrity of journalists and their employers. Nothing of value should be accepted.

2. Secondary employment, political involvement, holding public office, and service in community organizations should be avoided if it compromises the integrity of journalists and their employers. Journalists and their employers should conduct their personal lives in a manner which protects them from conflict of interest, real or apparent. Their responsibilities to the public are paramount. That is the nature of their profession.

3. So-called news communications from private sources should not be published or broadcast without substantiation of their claims to news value.

4. Journalists will seek news that serves the public interest, despite the obstacles. They will make constant efforts to assure that the public's business is conducted in public and that public records are open to public inspection.

5. Journalists acknowledge the newsman's ethic of protecting confidential sources of information.

ACCURACY AND OBJECTIVITY

Good faith with the public is the foundation of all worthy journalism.

1. Truth is our ultimate goal.

2. Objectivity in reporting the news is another goal, which serves as the mark of an experienced professional. It is a standard of performance toward which we strive. We honor those who achieve it.

3. There is no excuse for inaccuracies or lack of thoroughness.

4. Newspaper headlines should be fully warranted by the contents of the articles they accompany. Photographs and telecasts should give an accurate picture of an event and not highlight a minor incident out of context.

5. Sound practice makes clear distinction between news reports and expressions of opinion. News reports should be free of opinion or bias and represent all sides of an issue.

6. Partisanship in editorial comment which knowingly departs from the truth violates the spirit of American journalism.

7. Journalists recognize their responsibility for offering informed analysis, comment, and editorial opinion on public events and issues. They accept the obligation to present such material by individuals whose competence, experience, and judgment qualify them for it.

8. Special articles or presentations devoted to advocacy or the writer's own conclusions and interpretations should be labeled as such.

FAIR PLAY

Journalists at all times will show respect for the dignity, privacy , rights, and well-being of people encountered in the course of gathering and presenting the news.

1. The news media should not communicate unofficial charges affecting reputation or moral character without giving the accused a chance to reply.

2. The news media must guard against invading a person's right of privacy.

3. The media should not pander to morbid curiosity about details of vice and crime.

4. It is the duty of news media to make prompt and complete correction of their errors.

5. Journalists should be accountable to the public for their reports and the public should be encouraged to voice its grievances against the media. Open dialogue with our readers, viewers, and listeners should be fostered.

PLEDGE

Journalists should actively censure and try to prevent violations of these standards, and they should encourage their observance by all newspeople. Adherence to this code of ethics is intended to preserve the bond of mutual trust and respect between American journalists and the American people.

Ethical Sensitivities _____

Michael Gartner's paper in the APME ethics report of 1984, discussed at the beginning of this chapter, illustrated that the question of ethics codes is highly debatable in the context of preserving the First Amendment protections of freedom of speech and freedom of the press. Moreover, like the Bible and the Bill of Rights, important ethical and moral principles often conflict with one another in important gray areas of many situations. Journalists are not only journalists, they also are citizens and human beings. Knowing the right thing to do in playing all those roles at once is not easy. Precisely because it is not easy is the reason that journalists young and old should constantly strive to remain sensitive to the gray areas and try to reason through them carefully, being sensitive to as many perspectives as is humanly possible in the time available in a given situation.

The best way to prepare for such introspection is to study philosophy in college and to keep studying it after college, trying to apply its precepts to the journalistic situations at hand.

More university journalism programs are offering courses in media ethics, a healthy development, and if such a course if available, the young reporter should take it.

Three of the best recent books to help journalists think through the ethical questions that face them daily are _Media Ethics_ by Cliff Christians, Kim Rotzoll and Mark Fackler, and two books, _Secrets_ and _Lying,_ by Sissela Bok. A classic work on the dilemma of the journalist trying to respect individual privacy and dignity yet report important social injustices is James Agee's _Let Us Now Praise Famous Men._

The intellectual and moral challenges of reporting are so great that it takes a certain arrogance for any human being to undertake them. The arrogance in that sense is as essential as the task is daunting. Human nature remaining less than perfect, human perceptive capacities being flawed, human language being less than completely precise, however, should make journalists temper their arrogance with large amounts of humility. Journalism, like most other kinds of human thought, is more than a little like trying to chip away at the mightiest of mountains armed only with a toothpick. Yet to live honorably and with humanity, those of us alive at any given time nevertheless should undertake the challenge as energetically, gracefully and thoughtfully as we can.

Those who consider themselves too humanly sensitive for the rigorous ethical demands of journalism should, before they shirk them, consider that if they do, the odds are that the less sensitive among journalists and would-be journalists will prevail.

PART
II

News Writing

A high standard of style is repeatedly found in the great newspapers; it is one of the qualities that make them great.

—ERNEST BERNBAUM, professor of English.

Always be aware you're running a magic show—creating an illusion—when you're writing. Be responsible about it and remember that you're not telling "The Truth." . . . Good writing is a dangerous commodity. It creates a kind of reality for readers. You can make people believe things.

—HENRY ALLEN, reporter, Washington *Post*

5

Organizing the Facts

Starting in the mid '70s, accelerating in the early '80s and then in mid-decade running into a barrage of second thoughts and reservations, there was a movement among American daily newspaper editors and reporters to rethink traditional newswriting styles. Because the content of stories is shaped by the reporting done before the writing process begins, inevitably the movement to reconsider writing styles led to a reappraisal of traditional reporting techniques, too.

'Suddenly We Care . . .'

The spirit of that movement was captured in an edition of the *ASNE Bulletin,* the magazine of the American Society of Newspaper Editors. In the introduction to that edition, which appeared as the movement was gathering momentum, James Gannon, then executive editor (now editor) of the Des Moines (Iowa) *Register and Tribune,* summarized what was occurring when he wrote:

> As editors, we're searching for ways to improve the writing in our newspapers. In the past three or four years, the "writing movement" has spread from newspaper to newspaper, spawning a new crop of writing coaches, writing

seminars, writing awards and an effort to develop new approaches to telling old stories.

We are re-inventing the wheel—-but it's about time.

What does a newspaper have to offer the reader if not good stories well-told? Perhaps we are getting back to the basics of good reporting and good writing after realizing the folly of competing on the other guy's terms.

We've realized that our pictures can't move and talk and appear instantaneously as they do on television; we can't beat the competition with pictures. We've learned that color helps, but you can't out-dazzle the magazines. We know that sex sells, but you can't beat Playboy and Penthouse at their game in a family newspaper.

That drives us back to our basics—or at least, it should. What readers want from newspapers is news. And they want it written in a way that won't confuse them, bore them or waste their time. They want writing that clarifies complex issues, writing that illuminates people, places and things with the subtle light of well-used language, writing that builds on a rock-solid foundation of fact and a structure of clear thinking with the tools and the trimmings of well-chosen words.

This is, in short, what we owe our readers, and what they will not get elsewhere.

Yes, suddenly we care about writing—because it is the heart of our enterprise, and our medium of exchange. . . .

Historical Perspective _____

The movement to which Gannon referred was not an effort to tear up the traditional conceptions of reporting and writing for the newspages of the mainstream daily commercial press in the United States. If anything, it was an effort to maintain as many of those traditions as possible in the face of a changing setting in which newspapers were operating.

The movement reflected a recognition of the presence of television, with its emphasis on visuals and narrative story-telling forms. It reflected the existence of competing, specialized alternative print media. It reflected changing American lifestyles, more loose in many ways than in the past, yet in many ways conservative still. It reflected, too, the discovery by daily American newspapers of modern marketing techniques. Those techniques were based on the utilitarian premise of giving readers what they wanted rather than something that was shaped openly by the newspaper owner's social, political or economic prejudices.

Alternative media of the sort with which daily newspapers were trying to compete long had existed in America, but not in the form they came to take in the '60s and afterwards.

In the early days of American journalism, newspapers were blatantly partisan, often organs of political parties or of political factions. Their accounts of events were full of opinions, deliberate distortions and sometimes downright lies.

In the 19th century, though, more newspapers gradually switched from such fare in their newspages to what they said was factual reporting. Stories were based on reality as best a reporter could perceive and communicate it through the written word. Attempts were made, not always successfully, to limit opinion to either editorials (opinion essays run in a separate, clearly distinctive space that represented the owner's viewpoint on public issues) or to signed columns, in which individual writers could express their personal opinions. News became a product to sell, something of value to readers not just for its entertainment value or political slant, but because it was presumed to be something approaching fact rather than just partisan opinion or exaggerated drama posing as reality.

As the 20th century unfolded, most daily American newspapers followed, or said they did, that new formula. Most did so with gradually increasing maturity and responsibility.

But existing side by side with the mainstream press throughout the period were journals of opinion that did not pretend to be fully objective. Instead, they combined fact and opinion in the same accounts, rather than trying to separate fact from opinion, objectivity from subjectivity. They were the outlet for a style of public affairs journalism that President Theodore Roosevelt eventually labelled muckraking, though in reality it was far more responsible and less sensational than that term implied. The muckrakers of the early 20th century were serious writers who, rather than indulging in the kind of sensationalized reality-based melodrama of publishers like William Randolph Hearst, dug into such subjects as the performance of large corporations and municipal or state governments. Today, we would regard them as investigative reporters, although most of the muckrakers of Teddy Roosevelt's area included more outright opinion along with their facts than do today's daily newspaper investigative reporters.

Gradually, that kind of muckraking as a magazine form faded. But public opinion journals such as *The Nation, The Progressive, The New Republic, National Review* and *Commentary* remained, magazines whose specialty was long essays of opinion on public affairs, popular culture and the fine arts. Those essays combined facts, analysis and opinion all in the same package.

Then, in the '60s, when a counterculture developed on the university campuses in reaction to American foreign policies in Indochina, there emerged the modern version of the alternative press. The alternative media took many forms, but if they had a common trait, it was a negative reaction to the rules that applied in almost all daily newspapers and serious journals of opinion. At the extreme edge of these alternative media, there was no pretense at objectivity and little concern for facts except those facts that supported the view of the writers' critiques of government policies or various aspects of American culture. Rules of grammar were disregarded. There was considerable experimentation with varied forms of writing, including a more ample dosage of profanity than anyone had dared to use in earlier journalism. Not all alternative publications were so extreme. Some took such forms as *I.F. Stone's Weekly,* which used fairly traditional techniques of fact-based reporting mixed with opinion to critique government's foreign and civil-rights policies. Stone's weekly was published in newsletter form with a highly personalized but formal writing style.

When American troops finally were withdrawn from Vietnam and when the civil-rights movement came in from the streets, the alternative press calmed down. Many publications disappeared. Others remained, most gradually becoming much more conventional in their content, which was targeted toward younger readers with considerable buying power, mostly in large and medium-sized cities.

But combined with the effects of television and the more free-wheeling commentary of such popular art media as the movies, radio, records and videocassettes, all of which experimented with less restrictive forms of presentation and various sorts of commercialized social commentary, the alternative press had a powerful effect on the expectations of media consumers. Americans had grown accustomed to media that experimented with criticism of dominant social values, that emphasized the individual, that expressed messages in language of the streets and that tried, in one way or another, to have a human touch. And what was called "the new journalism," reporting and writing that had similar traits, had become popular with many younger consumers, the people whom daily newspapers' demographic studies and marketing experts told them they must reach if they were to retain their audiences and appeal to advertisers.

It was in that context that the rethinking of the reporting and writing in American daily newspaper occurred. Editors had co-opted as much as the content of the alternative press, of television and of popular media as they could, in one way or another. But the co-option was tricky business, because many of the best customers of daily newspapers were people accustomed to the more traditional fare. They often were offended by the counterculture symbols and values. What's more, politicians knew that and tried to appeal to the disaffected by urging "the silent majority" to speak up about these fads that seemed to threaten traditional American values and customs as well as America's way of doing business with governmental policy at home and abroad. If they were to hang on to older readers and to fend off government attempts to nibble away at First Amendment protections that were vital to their papers' newsgathering, editors were limited in how far they could go in appealing to the new tastes of younger Americans without risking a backlash from those with different appetites.

Thus, while reconsidering their old ways of reporting and writing, few editors were willing to tinker too much with such concepts as keeping news separate from opinion. They were wary about moving too far from a goal of objectivity into the murky waters of subjectivity, about changing traditional story forms of American newswriting, about altering traditional rules of American newsgathering. And apart from the politics of dealing with readers and the government, most editors thought it would be a mistake, as they saw the public interest, to drift too far from those traditional values, though they realized they had to make their papers more lively and more attuned to the interests and expectations of young readers.

Newswriting: Looking Ahead _____

That theme of experimentation tinged with cautious conservatism remains in the mid-'80s. It is likely to remain for some time to come among American daily newspaper editors. Those editors know, in their bones and from the marketing surveys that increasingly guide them, that America has changed from what it was in the '50s. The country is more open in many ways to social and political experimentation, but also still quite conservative, still easily shockable in many of the older shocking ways and in some new ones as well. For that reason, while experimental forms of reporting and writing now go on in the work of news staffs in American daily newspapers, the older forms are still the rock of that work, from which young reporters must swim, towline tied to the waist, only with the greatest caution and with the realization that somebody may yank them back quickly if they make too many waves in exploring the journalistic waters.

Success in reporting for the American daily newspapers of the late 20th century thus seems likely to require a mastery of the traditional fundamentals of newsgathering and newswriting—the five W's and H, the inverted pyramid story form, and an intuitive street-wise grasp of such basic determinants of news as proximity, prominence, timeliness, conflict, significance and the like. It also will require, though, more attention than most reporters of earlier periods paid to the human touch in reporting and writing, to the skillful uses of the devices of literature and to penetrating intellectual insights. But whether the reporting and writing forms are traditional or innovative, the basics remain trying your darndest to get it right, to write clearly and interestingly, and to interpret with intelligence, feeling and an open-minded quest for setting, significance, nuance and context. Those always have been the best yardsticks of good reporting and good journalistic writing. They will remain so even in a period of cautious experimentation with reporting and writing forms other than those that held sway in the mainstream press for most of this century.

The Five W's and H _____

Even before the task of gathering the facts concerning a particular news event has been completed, the reporter starts thinking of how to organize them into a news story. The more experienced the newsgatherer, the more automatic or unconscious this habit becomes. As new information is obtained, earlier ideas regarding the theme or central idea coming out of the assignment may be modified.

Because the five *w*'s have been taught to journalistic novitiates for several generations, they often seem to be trite and academic. Nevertheless, no matter what writing or speaking style is used, regardless of whether the contents are objectively descriptive or subjectively analytical, the reader or listener's curiosity has to be satisfied as regards the *who, what, when, where* and *why,* as well as the *how* of a newsworthy occurrence. What has happened, largely as a result of the blandishments of the readibility conscious and statistically conscious communications researchers and the socially conscious rank-and-file, is a considerable loosening of the rigid rules regarding the structure of a news story. Whereas a generation ago it was virtually mandatory that as many as possible of the five *w*'s and *h* be mentioned in the first paragraph of a news story, today considerably greater freedom is permitted in presenting them. Now that radio and television have taken the edge of the spot news, stories important enough to have been broadcast may be written with some disregard of the old principles. Nevertheless, though delayed, the five *w*'s must be included somewhere in the full account.

The Inverted Pyramid Form _____

Because by far most of the stories a newspaper prints every day have not been broadcast by radio or television, the great majority, perhaps 90 per cent, of news stories still are written in accordance with the traditional rule that the first part—whether it be a conventionally written single paragraph or a half-dozen or more short paragraphs—contain a succinct resume of the story as a whole. The beginner ambitious to achieve stylistic originality does well to master the rules first in order to break them intelligently later.

The striking difference between traditional news writing in the United States and other forms of written composition, such as the essay, poetry, drama, novel and short story, continues to be this: whereas the authors of these other forms of composition usually begin with minor or incidental details and work to a climax near or at the end of their compositions, the news writer in one way or another reverses this plan of organization. That is, the climax or end of the story comes first or near the beginning of the article. Given a schedule of facts to arrange in the form of a newspaper article, the writer selects the most important fact or climax of the story and puts it at the beginning. The second most important fact comes second, the third most important fact third and so on.

The traditional form of news writing is called the *inverted pyramid form*. It is said to have originated in Civil War days when correspondents used the telegraph for the first time. From fear that their accounts would not be transmitted all at one time, the war correspondents crowded as much information as possible into their first paragraphs.

Throughout the decades since that time, press associations, which transmitted stories by telegraph, have perfected the system. Before the teletypesetter was introduced about mid-century, few leading stories ever were transmitted in one piece. Instead, a few paragraphs of several important stories were sent first and then the later paragraphs. Throughout a day's sending, there were numerous new or substitute first paragraphs (leads), inserts and additions. That continues to be the predominant form, even though stories are now delivered electronically from one computer to another and the added material now is included in a full version of the updated story, called a *write-thru*.

Locally written news followed the press association pattern. The inverted pyramid form of organization was defended in several different ways:

1. *To facilitate reading.* The reading matter of the average newspaper, if printed in book form, would fill a large volume. The American

newspaper reader hasn't time to read that much daily. Neither is anyone interested in all the articles appearing in any newspaper. If the climax of every story is at the beginning, the reader can learn the gist of the news quickly and, if interested, can continue to the details. No one should have to read any article to its conclusion to learn what it is about.

2. *To satisfy curiosity.* This is the natural way of telling an important item of news. If someone drowns while swimming, the average person would not begin telling of the incident by narrating the dead person's preparations for a visit to the beach with a group of friends. Rather, the important fact would be first—John was drowned while swimming. The supplementary details of how, when and where it happened would follow.

3. *To facilitate makeup.* In rectifying a page, the makeup editor often finds it necessary to cut the length of some articles. If the least important details are at the end of a story, this can be done without harming the story. The makeup editor should feel free to cut ordinary articles without consulting other editors.

4. *To facilitate headline writing.* The headline consists of the key words or their synonyms necessary to give an idea of what a story contains. If the story is well written, the headline writer should not have to look beyond the first paragraph or two to find these words.

The writing committee of the Associated Press Managing Editors once cited the story in the right-hand column below as one of the best examples of news writing of the year. It was written in the traditional inverted pyramid style. In the left-hand column below, the same facts, using the identical phraseology as much as possible, are rearranged in chronological order.

Chronological Style

About 1 a.m. today, Mrs. Harry Rosenberg was awakened by the sound of a car roaring out of the driveway of her home. She rushed to the living room where she discovered that her granddaughter, Judith Ann Roberts, 7, no longer was sleeping on the studio couch and that the front door was standing open.

Mrs. Rosenberg called her daughter, Mrs. Shirley Roberts, wife of a Baltimore attorney and labor leader, who was visiting her parents. Mrs. Roberts, the missing child's mother, notified police of her daughter's kidnapping at 1:10 a.m.

Police said the kidnapper sneaked into the home of the grandparents, stole the keys to the Rosenberg's car

Newspaper Style

Judith Ann Roberts, blue-eyed, 7-year-old daughter of a Baltimore attorney and labor leader, was kidnapped from the home of her grandparents here today, raped and beaten to death.

Police found the child's nude and brutally battered body in a clump of bushes off fashionable Bayshore Drive five hours after her mother, Mrs. Shirley Roberts, reported her missing.

She had been beaten on the head with a heavy instrument and a piece of gauze was knotted about her throat. Her flimsy seersucker nightgown, white with red polka dots, lay eight feet from the body.

Judith Ann's little body was caked

from the grandfather's trousers pocket and took the child away.

Four hours and ten minutes after they were called, police found the Rosenberg car abandoned in the strip of sandy land between Bayshore Drive and the shore of Biscayne Bay. Its wheels were mired in the sand and the tire marks showed the driver tried frantically to get it out.

Judith Ann's nude and brutally battered body was found a block from the car in a clump of bushes off fashionable Bayshore Drive. It was caked with blood and dirt, indicated she put up a brave fight for her life. The blue-eyed child had been raped and beaten on the head with a heavy instrument and a piece of gauze was knotted about her throat. Her flimsy seersucker nightgown, white with red polka dots, lay eight feet from her body.

with blood and dirt, indicating she put up a brave fight for her life.

Police said the killer sneaked into the home of the grandparents, Mrs. and Mrs. Harry Rosenberg, about 1 a.m., stole the keys to Rosenberg's car from his trousers pocket and took the child from the studio couch in the living room where she was sleeping.

Mrs. Rosenberg was awakened by the sound of the car roaring out of the driveway. She found the child missing and the front door standing open.

Police were called at 1:10 a.m. Four hours and ten minutes later, they found the Rosenberg car abandoned in the strip of sandy land between Bayshore Drive and the shore of Biscayne Bay. Its wheels were mired in the sand and the tire marks showed the driver tried frantically to get it out.

Judith's body was found a block from the car.

"Note, please," the APME Writing committee asked, "the many fine points . . . 'the seersucker nightgown, white and red polka dots, lay eight feet from the body.'

"How many little nightgowns like that are all over this land? And *eight feet* . . . no guess-work there; the reporter was seeing it for you. Too, the killer sneaked in about 1 a.m. and 'police were called at 1:10 a.m.' The car was found *four hours and ten minutes later* . . . not simply later in the day."

Although few would argue with an unnamed news editor with more than forty years' experience, whom the committee quoted as saying, "That Miami story is one of the finest writing jobs I've ever seen," the points cited by the committee indicate that the story's strength derived primarily from the fact that an extraordinary job of reporting, involving keen observation, had preceded its composition. In other words, *the most important step in communication is obtaining something worthwhile to communicate.* Stated still another way, the basis of all good journalism is thorough reporting. Shorter words, sentences and paragraphs, desirable as they may be for clarity, cannot add important details to a journalistic account. *There is no substitute for good reporting no matter what writing style is used.*

The Lead

The Miami story was written in traditional inverted pyramid style. That is, the first paragraph contained the gist or skeleton outline of the entire story in a minimum of words. Subsequent paragraphs elaborated upon various aspects of the lead, making them more definite; or they supplied additional details in the order of their importance as the reporter judged them.

Because, for more than a half-century, this has been the orthodox form of news writing, the _lead_ of a straight news story came to be defined as the first paragraph, which contained all of the elements (five _w_'s and _h_) necessary for the complete telling of the essential facts.

This practice often led to long and crowded first paragraphs. The lead of the Miami story, for instance, might have read something like this:

> The nude and brutally beaten body of Judith Ann Roberts, blue-eyed, 7-year-old daughter of a Baltimore attorney and labor leader, was found by police in a clump of bushes off fashionable Bayshore Drive here at 1 a.m. today after she had been kidnapped from the home of her grandparents, Mr. and Mrs. Harry Rosenberg, and raped.

In the effort to avoid such cumbersome lead paragraphs, and to increase readability, some newspapers have gone to the opposite extreme of invoking the "one-fact sentence" rule, which would lead to something like the following:

> A 7-year-old girl has been kidnapped, raped and beaten to death.
> She was blue-eyed Judith Ann Roberts of Baltimore. Her father is a lawyer and labor leader.
> Police found the child's body in a clump of bushes off fashionable Bayshore Drive.
> The body was nude and brutally battered.
> The child's mother, Mrs. Shirley Roberts, reported her daughter missing at 1:10 a.m.
> That was four hours and ten minutes before the body was found by police.

It is difficult to determine exactly how many of the one- or two-sentence paragraphs of a story written in this manner constitute the lead, or first unit of the story. Every sentence relates to some word or fact in a preceding sentence, and it takes a half-dozen or more of them to present all of the information which one would have been crowded into half the space or less. This form of writing says less in more words but is perhaps more readable. The original version of the Miami story was a compromise between the new and the old extremes.

Because the inverted pyramid form still is adhered to, even in the staccato type of paragraphing illustrated above, in that facts are arranged in the order of their supposed importance, the traditional definition of a news story lead holds: the first unit of the story performs the function of telling the entire story in epitomized form.

A good lead, no matter how much it is strung out, answers all the questions that a reader wants answered when hearing of a particular incident. These include the cause and result (the _how_ or _why_ and the _what_), the _who_ and often the _where_ and the _when_. These elements are called the _5 w_'s and the _h_. Not all of them must be present in every lead, but no important one should be omitted. The lead also plays up the feature of the story if there is one, is attractive and induces the reader to continue with the rest of the story. It, of course, observes the canons of good writing. A good lead suggests or gives the authority on which the news is printed and identifies the persons mentioned in the story (or the story itself) by relating them (or it) to previous or current news.

The Miami story fulfilled these requirements in this way:

Who—Judith Ann Roberts.
What—Killed.
When—July 7; time of day (1 a.m.) given later.
Where—Miami, Fla.
How—Kidnapped, raped and beaten to death.
Authority—Police and relatives obvious sources of information.
Identification—Seven-year-old daughter of a Baltimore lawyer and labor leader.
Feature—Kidnapped from home of grandparents.

The Body

In view of the tendency to reduce the first sentence of a news story to the fewest possible words, the function of the sentences and paragraphs that immediately follow is clearly to restate the facts of the first sentence so as to make them more definite. Loosening of the rule that the first paragraph contain all of the five *w*'s and the *h* means that succeeding paragraphs often must supply some additional pertinent facts crowded out of the lead in the interest of brevity.

It doesn't make any difference what academic labels are placed on units of a news story, and it is difficult or impossible to chart news stories so that units do not overlap. If you wish, you can consider the extreme attempt at epitomized writing ("A 7-year-old girl has been kidnapped, raped and beaten to death") as the lead and call all the rest of the story by its traditional name, *body*. Or you can insist that the lead proper include as many sentences as are necessary to make the basic elements (five *w*'s and *h*) definite.

In either case, there often remain a number of additional paragraphs which can be labeled either "body" or "second part of body." If new details are added in the same sentences or paragraphs in which there is further amplification of the lead, telling exactly where the last unit of the story begins isn't easy.

Unity

A method of obtaining rhetorical unity as one short paragraph follows another is by the use of *linkage* words. Note in the following example how their skillful use creates a flow and, at the same time, enables the writer to introduce new facts. This story could be cut at the end of almost any paragraph and there still would be a rhetorically complete account.

By Associated Press

Mighty rivers on a late winter rampage surged through south central sections of Alabama, Georgia and Mississippi Wednesday, leaving wide trails of muddy ruin amounting to millions.

Except around Jackson, Miss., the highest levels of the flooding rivers were spread largely across rural areas as they continued toward their common draining point, the Gulf of Mexico.

However, more flood menace lies ahead for downstate residents, and even in ravaged mid-state sections where the worst is over, it will be days before the rampant rivers fall within their banks.

At Selma in central Alabama, *for example,* the Alabama River reached its crest of 58.3 feet Tuesday night, but the muddy waters are not expected to creep back to the 45-foot flood level until March 9.

In hard-hit Selma and Montgomery and Demopolis, Ala., *as well as* Jackson, Miss., and West Point and Columbus, Ga., thousands in evacuation centers looked to more days of waiting for water to seep out of their homes.

To relieve the tension of Montgomery refugees, many facing their fifth night in shelters, the Red Cross put on recreation programs.

Damage to Alabama's public facilities *has already topped* $10 million in preliminary estimates. That includes only roads and bridges and county and municipal places—not homes, businesses, farmland and livestock.

In central Alabama's Montgomery and Elmore Counties alone, a livestock broker estimates that about 2,500 head of cattle worth $500,000 have drowned *during the current flood.*

As the swollen Pearl River swirled around the Jackson, Miss., area Tuesday night and Wednesday, cutting a three-mile swath in some places, about 850 residents left their low-lying homes and most flocked to refuge centers.

[Tampa *Tribune*]

Other useful linkage words or phrases include the following: in the meantime, before, after, earlier, later, sooner, previously, furthermore, also, therefore, because, moreover, nevertheless, however, but, by contrast, inconsistently, here, there, above, below.

Block Paragraphing

In longer stories, regardless of whether the lead was one or several paragraphs long, paragraphs are so written as to include a single subtopic each.

This type of paragraphing differs from the type that English composition students are taught is best. Because newspaper paragraphs of necessity (appearance) must be short, they do not follow the orthodox rule of rhetoric that every paragraph should include a complete thought or topic sentence. Rather, in newspaper paragraphing the idea-unit is broken up into subtopics. In other words, news writers paragraph their paragraphs.

This type of *block paragraphing* is distinctly advantageous for news writing. It permits the insertion or deletion of paragraphs without disarranging a story. Frequently it is necessary, in the light of new information, to recast certain paragraphs, to add additional paragraphs and to remove others. For example, note in the following story how additional information might be added without serious trouble. The paragraphs in italics quite conceivably could have been added after the story was written. Furthermore, several of them could have been inserted at other places in the story. Quite a few of the paragraphs, italicized or not, could be shifted around without destroying the effectiveness of the story. Often, different inserts are written by different reporters.

Flights were back on schedule Monday at Kent County International Airport after being disrupted this weekend with fog canceling most flights.

Air traffic during the busy holiday season came to a near standstill Saturday and Sunday because of dense clouds of fog which kept most planes grounded and prevented flights from arriving from other cities.

Passengers coming here from Chicago were being ferried in on buses, while those trying to leave Kent County either had to wait and hope for the fog to clear or take a bus to Detroit in hopes of catching a flight there.

The airport terminal was cluttered with luggage and impatient passengers most of the weekend.

"Fog closed it down yesterday from the early morning to about two in the afternoon. It was closed back down again at night," said an airport spokesman. "It was basically the same thing Saturday. Nobody could get in."

Flights were back to normal by 7:30 a.m. Monday. Some passengers were able to catch flights out of Kent County, while others were bused to Detroit for flights there.

"Everything got so far behind this weekend that they (airlines) decided not to divert planes here to take out the passengers," said a spokeswoman from Republic Airlines. "Those that could not be accommodated on a flight from here are going to Detroit.

"It's better this way than to try and play catch up."

Travelers faced the possibility of a foggy Christmas in wide sections of the country with poor visibility contributing to traffic accidents that pushed the death toll toward the 300 mark in the third day of the long holiday weekend.

[Grand Rapids (Mich.) *Press*]

Chronological

A widely used method of organizing the material after the lead is chronological, at least for a number of paragraphs, after which new facts can be added in block paragraph style. This type of organization is effective in stories in which action is described, as in the following example:

A gunman robbed the Eastwood Federal Savings and Loan Assn. of about $7,000 while scores of noonday shoppers walked past the building at 118 S. Jeffrey St.

The bandit walked in at 12:45 p.m., normally the busiest time of day, and found the office empty of customers. A teller, Miss Virginia Kole, one of four employees present, asked the man if she could help him.

"Yeah. There's a lot you can do to help me," the man answered as he leaped up on the 4-foot high counter and pulled out an old rusty revolver.

"Get back, get back," he ordered from his perch. "I'm not fooling. I'll shoot the woman first. Don't step on the alarm."

Joseph Dierks, vice-president, said he was sitting in the back of the office and did not move, waiting to see what the man would do next.

The bandit jumped down on the floor behind the counter and ordered the four to a rest room in the rear. The other two workers were Howard K. Jacobs, secretary-treasurer of the association, and Robertson Evans, a teller.

As the holdup man was directing the group to the rear room, a customer came in. He was Walter Mather, 2130 W. Otis Ave., who also was ordered to the back room.

The robber closed the door on the five and went back to the front of the office where he rifled three cash drawers and the open safe.

When Evans heard the front door close, he hurried from the back room and ran to the front door hoping to see which way the bandit fled. The man apparently became quickly lost in the crowd, and Evans could not see him.

Dierks said an early count indicated the stolen money totaled $6,829.15, but he thought the final tally would be higher, perhaps as much as $8,500.

The vice-president considered the holdup man an extremely lucky amateur. He pointed out that an experienced robber probably would have looked over the office several days in advance and would have realized that the association usually was busiest between 12:15 and 1:15 p.m. when many customers come in on their lunch hours.

Dierks said the gunman was probably a very athletic person, judging from the way he moved about the office. He appeared to be in his early twenties, about 5 feet 6 inches tall, and weighed about 140 pounds. He wore a blue cap, green shirt, and khaki trousers.

What must be avoided is making the lead sentence merely a "peg line." For example, "Alderman John F. Gates today called Mayor Henry R. Penrose a liar" is superior to "An alderman today called the mayor a liar." It is inferior to "Alderman John R. Gates today charged that Mayor Henry R. Penrose lied when he said he never owned any west-side real estate." If by some grotesque error the former lead sentence were to appear alone, there would be considerable embarrassment if not worse. There is, in other words, a limit beyond which it is unwise to be brief. Too often brevity necessitates being vague or indefinite, which requires more rather than less effort on the part of the reader who seeks the facts of a news story.

Variations _____

Increasingly, in stories in which the human interest is paramount, the rule that it should be possible to cut final paragraphs without ruining the news interest is violated. There are some stories that must be read in their entirety.

Sequence

In a story written in sequence style all facts are arranged in strictly chronological order. The climax or satisfaction of the reader's curiosity is postponed until the end. Thus a sequence story cannot be edited from the bottom up as could be the chronological story which has a news lead.

Three-year-old Byron Halpert opened a second-story window Tuesday a few minutes after his mother had left to take her daughter to school.

Byron leaned out to see what he could see. But he leaned so far that he lost his balance, fell through the opening and wound up hanging from the window sill by his finger tips, 20 feet above a concrete walk.

Just then a police car came by. Officer William Watson, sizing up the situation, ran to the spot below the window just as little Byron let go. The boy landed squarely in the policeman's arms, unhurt but tearfully scared.

Cumulative Interest

The lead of this type of story contains some sort of news peg. In addition to emphasizing the tone or situation of the story as it progresses, this kind of story incites reader interest, which cumulates as each succeeding sequence and paragraph makes for greater definiteness.

Long Beach, Calif. (AP)—The young woman said a friend had given a bottle to her with instructions to throw it at anyone who tried to mug her.

Police officials said Miss Jackie Lynn Samay, 22 years old, had telephoned to ask them what to do with the bottle in her refrigerator, "a pint of nitro-glycerine."

Bomb-squad officers rushed to her residence, ordered a four-block downtown area evacuated, packed the bottle in ice from a nearby liquor store and had Army experts transport it carefully in a thick metal box to nearby Fort MacArthur. Traffic was cleared from all streets along the route.

The next day the Army reported the liquid was glue.   [New York *Times*]

Suspended Interest

A suspended interest story is one in which the writer "strings along" the reader to the very end before giving him the news peg on which the item is based. Such stories resemble magazine short stories in that they must be read in their entirety. Frequently, the climax may be a surprise; in any case, it satisfies the reader's interest which has been suspended because of the indefiniteness of early details.

An ice-cream cone failed to have a cooling effect Saturday night on Patrolman Harry O'Brien.

O'Brien, assigned to the burglary detail, was parking his car on Auburn Street near Wilson Avenue, when a man approached the car, mumbling incoherently.

"What did you say?" O'Brien asked.

Without another word, the man suddenly jammed an ice-cream cone into the policeman's face.

O'Brien alighted, drew his gun, seized the man and was told, "You'll have to fight to take me in."

With that, the prisoner punched O'Brien in the mouth. O'Brien countered with an uppercut which knocked the man flat.

At the Kenton Avenue Station the arrested man identified himself as Willis C. Solano of 1768 W. Tree St. and said he thought policemen were "too hot" and he wanted to "cool one off."

Delayed News Peg

Because most readers of sports pages are fans who already know how their favorite teams or players fared, sports writing has undergone a great change. Today the fan who didn't attend the game or watch it on television has to hunt for the score in the fourth or fifth paragraph. Then he may or may not return to read the description or evaluative or philosophical earlier paragraphs. Here are a couple of typical examples of this type of story or organization, both from the Chicago *Sun-Times*.

By Bob Pille

Ann Arbor, Mich.—Being very mindful of tradition and honoring the 100th anniversary of local collegiate football, the folks at Michigan should have been wary of omens Saturday.

It was equally tradition-encrusted Notre Dame against the Wolverines in the nation's biggest game of this early season with 105,111 in the house on one of those sunny autumn afternoons invented for football and most of the country watching on television—when the cameras were working, that is.

So they had to know that the Irish came in with a two-game winning streak at Michigan—from victories in 1909 and 1943—and that Dan Devine, the Notre Dame coach, had been the last from outside the Big Ten to beat the Wolverines here. Devine, in his Missouri days, did it to Bo Schembechler's first team in 1969 just as he had to Bump Elliott's first Michigan team in 1959.

And the Irish and Devine did it again 12–10 in a moderate upset in a strange sort of game dominated by defenses and field goal kickers. . . .

By Taylor Bell

All Scott Parzych could remember was that he was the goat last year and Lockport's 6–7 All-Stater wasn't about to let it happen again. In the end, however, he could only watch as Jim Stack lofted a 20-foot shot with one second to play.

"In last year's game," recalled Parzych, "there was one second left and Kevin Boyle took a rebound away from me and he beat us. The ball rolled off my fingertips and he got it. I felt terrible. And tonight, when that shot went off, my heart was 'way down here in my stomach."

But Stack's shot rimmed out, and Lockport, which trailed by five points with four minutes left, rallied to pull out a 42–41 victory over St. Laurence Wednesday night in a showdown between the state's two ranking Class AA powers in the sectional tournament at Downers Grove North. . . .

Direct Address

Beginning reporters are admonished to keep out of their own stories, only an occasional reference to the fact that a reporter asked a certain question or made an unsuccessful effort to obtain an important fact being permitted. Use of either the first or second person is discouraged. Columnists, special writers who sign their articles, and writers of feature stories are exempt from this rule when effectiveness cannot be obtained otherwise. The following are examples to show how the first or second person occasionally may be used in an ordinary news or news feature story such as a beginning reporter might write.

Kids, when Mom and Dad take a look at your report card then start the sermon about how smart they were in high school, do you see red? Do you want to chew nails?

Relax, kids, you've got a friend.

He is Dr. F. H. Finch of the University of Illinois, and he takes your side today in a monograph of the American Psychological Association. . . .

If you haven't heard of it, and wouldn't believe it if you had, it probably will be on display today at the National Inventors' Congress in the Palmer House.

Window glass that can't be seen through, lamps that give invisible light and solid water pipes that have no hollow space for the water—those are some of the things you may expect to find. . . .

The Reporter's Notes

Prerequisite to a well-organized news story is a careful rearrangement of the reporter's notes. For the experienced reporter, the task of dictating a story over the telephone to a rewrite person from a handful of notes scribbled on copy paper while standing in a stuffy booth is an everyday matter. The reporter who uses a video display terminal does not write "false start" leads one after another on it. It is to the writer's interest to make as few false starts as possible, thus avoiding the push-buttoning involved in making corrections. While learning, young reporters profit by making an outline of the facts they have gathered. The reporter has, first of all, to pick the feature to go into the lead; next, to be certain essential questions are answered and there is sufficient identification and authority; then, to decide which phases of the lead need amplification in the first part of the body of the story and how it is to be provided and, finally, to arrange the other facts which should be included.

Seldom, if ever, does the reporter while reporting jot down facts in the order in which they should be used. As the reporter learns more and more about the incident one or more lead possibilities are seen. There are few if any reporters, regardless of experience, who fail to profit by a study of all notes taken and an outlining of them, if only mentally, before beginning to write or dictate. The young reporter frequently finds it profitable to number the facts included in his or her notes in the order of importance.

The necessity for rearranging and discarding notes can be seen by imagining how the reporter who covered the Judith Ann Roberts case gathered the facts. If he were stationed at police headquarters, the first information obtained was: Mrs. Shirley Roberts called to report that her child had been kidnapped from the home of her parents whose address was given. Either then or when policemen, accompanied by reporters, arrived at the residence, the mother gave a complete description of the child's appearance and habits. She and her parents told how the child's disappearance was discovered and the condition of the room, including the empty couch and open door. Mr. and Mrs. Rosenberg provided a description of their automobile: its make, model, color, license number, mileage and distinguishing features.

In the search for clues, police and reporters asked the three adults and other residents about the visit of the mother and child to Miami. They wanted to know how the family and child spent the preceding day, especially what they did during the evening. They asked about Mr. Roberts and whether either he or any of the others had any enemies who might wish them ill. They wanted to know whom Judith had met, talked with, played with, where she had gone and so on.

Before the body was found, reporters made notes on the activities of the police: how many and who were assigned to the search, where they went and whom they questioned, what alarms were sent out, what clues, if any, they considered important and the like. They inquired carefully into how discovery of the body was made—whether as part of a careful plan of investigation or by accident.

Bear in mind that the example given was written for a press association, which means it was intended for publication in cities other than Miami. In that city the story received much longer treatment with many additional details of interest to local readers.

To summarize: The first step in good news writing is good reporting. No story writes itself. The factual material must be gathered first. The person who doesn't know how to observe and gather facts never will be able to write a good news account.

Developing an Idea _____

Charles-Gene McDaniel was a prize winning science writer in the Chicago bureau of the Associated Press when his editor suggested that he write an article on baldness. "If I could have worked on it steadily I could have done it in three days," said McDaniel. Able to work on it only off and on while handling other assignments, McDaniel wrote the following story three years later and then waited six months before it was distributed by the AP to receive wide usage nationwide.

By C. G. McDaniel
ASSOCIATED PRESS WRITER

"The only thing that will stop falling hair is the floor."

So advises John T. Capps III, who is bald and proud of it. If you're bald or getting there, just relax and enjoy it.

"Bald is beautiful," Capps proclaims, along with about 5,500 members of Bald Headed Men of America, which includes three women and many foreign members. They range in age from 11 to 95.

And medical authorities agree. So far anyway, it is not possible to do anything to stop hair from falling out. Once it has, the baldies have the option of buying something to cover it up or—in some cases—having a hair transplant.

Otherwise, the nostrums advertised in magazines and newspapers as baldness cures do not serve any purpose other than to enrich the seller, they say.

Capps, 38, of Dunn, N.C., founded Bald Headed Men of America in 1973. Why? "I felt like bald headed men needed a little moral support," he says.

"If you don't have it, flaunt it," is one of the organization's mottoes.

"One thing about baldness is it's neat," says Capps, who apparently has the agreement of some well known public figures, such as actors Yul Brynner of "The King and I" and Telly Savalas of television's "Kojak" fame.

The list also includes singer-composer Isaac Hayes, comedian Don Rickles and football players Y. A. Tittle, formerly of the New York Giants, and Otis Sistrunk of the Oakland Raiders.

Members of Capps' organization include former President Gerald Ford, Sen. Henry Jackson, D-Wash., and sportscaster Joe Garagiola.

They're in the tradition of Julius Caesar, Socrates and Shakespeare, among other great onionheads of history.

And it's getting to be chic among some high-fashion men to have a chrome dome to go with their disco duds.

Capps said in a telephone interview that for years Madison Avenue advertisers have projected an image of how they wanted people to look and people have followed their line.

But, "skin is in," says Capps, a marketing specialist, political campaign advertiser and publisher of "The Donkey Tale Newsletter."

He comforts those who lament their plate pates with, "The Lord is just, the Lord is fair. He gave some brains and others hair."

Capps' automobile license in North Carolina is BALD 1 and the address of his organization is P.O. Box BALD.

While Capps and his fellow club members are not ashamed of their egg-heads, and in fact enjoy them, it would seem that millions of others have a problem coping with their depleted pelts.

The Department of Commerce reports that $48 million worth of "hair goods" were imported in 1976. And that was before markup—which may run as high as 400 percent. An additional $3 million worth—wholesale—is being produced annually in the United States.

The yellow pages of telephone directories have pages of advertisements aimed largely at men promoting hair transplants, hairpieces, fusion, weaving and other hair replacement techniques which remain mysterious in the context of the claims.

Cranium rugs, made from natural or synthetic hair, may cost from $15 to several hundred dollars, and that's just for starters. Then there's the upkeep and the need to replace them about every three years.

Millions of dollars more are spent on hair transplants and for dubious baldness remedies, such as special light treatments and salves.

Dr. Edward Krull, chairman of the dermatology department at Henry Ford Hospital in Detroit, says of the charlatanism, "Wherever we have problems that don't have solutions, there are always going to be people moving into that area."

There is no practical way, say he and other medical authorities, to grow new hair in bald spots other than hair transplants. Once it is gone, it is gone.

Dermatologists generally agree that the major causes of baldness are age, heredity and hormones.

Hair is dead tissue, Krull points out, and there is nothing that can be put on the scalp to make it grow once it has stopped. Routine dandruff won't cause the hair to fall out, Krull says, advising that the shampoo that works best and costs the least is the one to use to take care of dandruff.

But for many people, hair transplants are available. This procedure, which should always be done by a qualified physician, involves transplanting plugs of hair from the back of the neck to bald parts of the scalp.

Care must be exercised so that the hair is transplanted so that it will grow in the proper direction and will look natural once it has grown out in a few months.

An estimated one million persons have undergone this procedure, which is usually done in a doctor's office under local anesthetic.

The cost varies from about $5 to $35 a plug and 100 to 500 plugs may be required, depending upon the degree of baldness.

Another type of hair replacement has proved to be not only unsuccessful but to result in serious complications and permanent scarring. This is the implantation of synthetic fibers in the scalp.

A recent study published in the Journal of the American Medical Association reported that in 20 patients seen at one clinic in Cleveland, nearly all of the implanted fibers had fallen out by 10 weeks. The physicians also reported that the patients suffered from facial swelling, infection, scarring, permanent hair loss and other complications.

These implants cost $1,500 to $3,500 and, the physicians said, often were performed by technicians with physicians only briefly in attendance.

Other techniques, not without their problems, involve hair weaving, or braiding remaining hairs to keep the hairpiece from falling off, and suturing of the hairpiece.

But for those who don't want the bother or expense, Utah's bald Sen. Jake Garn offers this reassurance, "God has made very few perfect heads. The rest of them he covered with hair."

McDaniel's first step in researching the article was to consult his personal file on dermatology. He found only a few items of little help. So he phoned Frank W. Chappell Jr., science news editor for the American Medical Association. From him he received a package of material, the important item turning out to be an old clipping from *Time* magazine on John T. Capps III.

To obtain Capps' address McDaniel contacted the Chicago Public Library where a friendly helper consulted a reference book on organizations. What the reporter learned during a couple of long-distance calls is indicated in several parts of the story.

From the library reference book McDaniel also learned of the American Academy of Facial, Plastic and Reconstructive Surgery and of the American Association of Dermatology headquartered in New York. From the public relations counsel of the latter organization he learned of Dr. Edward Krull of Detroit, whose contributions to McDaniel's project are apparent in the article. The New York source also referred McDaniel to a Dr. Stough of Hot Springs, Ark., who had just returned from a conference on transplants held in Lucerne, Switzerland. What McDaniel wrote as a result of his telephone interview with that authority, however, was edited out of his story, which was reduced in size about one-third.

McDaniel learned of the Department of Commerce report from a Chicago *Sun-Times* news story. As the story indicates, he consulted the yellow pages in the telephone directory to discover that reputable surgeons do not advertise there. He considered it a safe guess that millions of dollars are spent on the items that are listed. Also he based such statements as "medical authorities agree," "dermatologists generally agree" and "an estimated one million persons have undergone" a kind of hair transplant, on the basis of his interviews with Drs. Krull and Stough and his perusal of the reports, and articles obtained from Chappell. He mentioned some historical and contemporary baldies of whom he knew. It was not an assignment to cause him to lose hair himself, but it illustrates how even a simple situation feature story requires painstaking inquiries of several persons and references.

6

Choosing the Lead

In 1977, Roy Peter Clark was a young member of the Auburn University English Department. Then he met Eugene Patterson, editor of the St. Petersburg *Times,* generally regarded as one of the better newspapers in the United States.

Here is what happened next, according to an article Clark wrote in the Feb. 28, 1978, issue of the magazine of the American Society of Newspaper Editors:

Gene Patterson plucked me out of a snug English department office last June and plunked me into the middle of the St. Petersburg *Times* newsroom. He then described what was to become my year's labors in the newspaper business: "I want you to learn all about this business. I want you to improve the quality of the writing here at the *Times*. And I want you to find ways by which any newspaper can improve its writing." Then, his jaw set with determination, he went on vacation.

Thus abandoned in the newsroom, I had no choice but to meet reporters and editors on their own terms. I accompanied reporters to dull courtroom trials and duller county commission meetings. I watched them write three stories in an hour. I sat in the press box during a Tampa Bay Buccaneer loss (until early December a tautology), and I marvelled as our sportswriters banged out lines of able prose under an oppressive deadline. I worked for a month on the copydesk, absorbing the experience of editors as they gave muscles to flabby prose.

I learned a few valuable lessons right away: that newspaper writing is better than most academic writing, that a newspaper contains individuals of widely varying abilities, that few agree on what constitutes "good" newspaper writing, that newspaper writers have fragile egos and that reporters and editors love to blame each other for the weaknesses in newspaper writing. . . .

Clark spent time talking about writing with staff writers at the paper. In an internal newsletter, he critiqued writing in the paper, doing far more praising of what he liked than condemning of what he did not like. In private talks in the newsroom, he would make casual-sounding suggestions as to how a writer might improve his work. He sometimes would formally interview a staff reporter who had done a particularly good piece of work, publishing the text of the interview in his in-house newsletter, called "The Wind Bag." The focus of the interviews was on how the writer had conceived, developed and written the story. His basic ideas were:

—To get people on the paper talking and thinking about writing.
—To praise the good in all writers' work.
—To make clear that good writing is difficult both to do and to define.
—To avoid getting discussion about writing bogged down in editors pontificating about rules of grammar.

Clark offered a simple set of 10 style points, which he urged writers to use as a checklist for evaluating their stories. His points were:

1. Use active verbs.
2. Keep subjects close to verbs.
3. Avoid unreadably long sentences.
4. Cut out needless words.
5. Seek alternatives to cliches.
6. Use verb tenses consistently.
7. Strengthen transitions.
8. Use quotations to enrich prose.
9. Think about structure: beginning, middle and end of story.
10. Avoid cluttering leads with needless attribution, confusing statistics or bureaucratic names and titles.

Lead Writing Controversy _____

Interest in what Clark was doing quickly spread around the nation's news-papers. Clark became something of a guru of the movement to improve newswriting. "He had a profound effect on our writers," said Patterson in a 1981 interview with David Shaw, media critic of the Los Angeles *Times*. Thomas Winship, then editor of the Boston *Globe,* hired a writing coach for his own paper. Winship told Shaw a coach was not necessary for the best writers on a staff and probably would not help the worst writers much. "But it helps all those in the middle if they want to be helped," Winship said. "If a writing coach can really help just two writers on your staff, he's more than earned his pay." Other papers joined the movement. Soon Clark was conducting writing seminars at the St. Petersburg papers' Modern Media Institute (later re-named The Poynter Institute), a training school for journalists from all over the country.

Among Clark's enthusiasms were nontraditional leads, leads that broke the pattern of the inverted pyramid formula of newswriting. By 1982 some disenchantment had set in among editors and others over what some writers around the country were doing with their stories once freed from the stylistic rules of the inverted pyramid. The disenchantment surfaced in an article called "Jell-o Journalism: Why Reporters Have Gone Soft in Their Leads." The article appeared in the April 1982 issue of the *Washington Journalism Review.* It was written by Gerald Lanson and Mitchell Stephens, directors of journalism programs at New York University. These opening sentences of their article summarized their complaint: "Sometimes the news seems to be the last thing on a reporter's mind. Consider this lead paragraph from a front-page story, January 29, in the Miami *Herald:* 'Tequesta, Fla.—A storm was gathering around Cynthia Marie Weinberg.' Some storm. Cynthia Marie Weinberg was dead, as readers who persevered until the fifth paragraph found out. It was the *Herald*'s first account of the apparent suicide the previous afternoon of the estranged wife of Abscam's star witness, Mel Weinberg."

Patterson and Winship, who only a few years earlier had been praising the movement launched by Clark, jumped ship in the Lanson-Stephens article. "Our readers must think we've lost our minds when we print some of that stuff," Patterson was quoted as saying. Winship said that he had ordered his staff to limit the number of articles dressed up with colorful writing. Patterson added: "I have a very low impatience threshhold when it comes to a leisurely takeoff for a story. I want to know what a story is going to say, and I don't want to have to track down through a long anecdote to find out." Lanson and Stephens, citing example after example of leads where the main news element was delayed for many paragraphs, often not appearing until the portion of the story that was continued on another page, boiled down their criticism this way: "No one is arguing that every newspaper story should start with the bare facts—who, what, where, when and why. New features, analysis pieces and long take-outs, frequently call for carefully crafted delayed leads . . . but only if the delay is not excruciatingly long."

Later in 1982, in an article in the October issue of *WJR*, Clark struck back, conceding that the news element should not be ignored in leads.

Nevertheless, accompanying his piece arguing with Lanson and Stephens, Clark offered a new list of tips for lead writing. Clark's new list said leads should be kept short and, if the news in leads was delayed, the story should purposefully provide readers with elements of drama, foreshadowing and suspense building. Suggestions of the hard-news aspect of the story should be woven into the delayed lead, he counseled.

Seldom in modern American journalism has there been such a well-publicized, fiercely argued exchange over the art of writing leads for a news story. The prominent clash was healthy. It underlined a point that this book long has made: There is no single way to write any news story. Given the same set of facts, equally competent writers will compose accounts that read differently. An impartial judge might find it impossible to choose the best with any degree of certainty.

Consider, for example, these two possible leads for a story about the trial a few years ago of six Nazis and Ku Klux Klansmen on charges of murdering five members of the Communist Workers Party during a CWP rally against the Klan in Greensboro, N.C. A traditional, straight news lead for a weekend story might read.

> GREENSBORO, N.C.—Defense and prosecuting attorneys agree that it may take months to try six Nazis and Ku Klux Klansmen here on charges that they murdered five members of the Communist Workers Party during an anti-Klan rally.

That lead would be perfectly functional for a long story bringing readers up to date on the situation regarding the case. There is nothing wrong with it. But others might prefer the lead that Charles Madigan wrote on his front-page Chicago *Tribune* story:

> GREENSBORO, N.C.—The last verse of "The Old Rugged Cross" echoed across the North Carolina hills, and the last flaming pieces of burlap wrapped round the cross sputtered out in the darkness.
>
> It was a fitting blasphemy to end a "Hitlerfest" on a farm near the rural North Carolina town of McGee's Crossroads. The 50 persons who attended came to honor six men they called "Christian soldiers."
>
> That was last spring. The passions of the moment have calmed, broken down into the rituals and details of a criminal court, where six Nazis and Ku Klux Klansmen are standing trial on murder charges.
>
> They are accused in the deaths of five members of the Communist Workers Party [CWP], who were gunned down during a "Death to the Klan!" rally they were staging in a black area of Greensboro last Nov. 3.
>
> The nation viewed some of the aftermath of that incident at the Democratic National Convention, where CWP members, including two widows of victims of the Nov. 3 violence, staged protests, including a demonstration during President Carter's acceptance speech Thursday night.
>
> The trial itself is packed with potential flashpoints. Several witnesses have admitted they were hypnotized to recall the incidents they saw on Nov. 3. Also, it has been learned that a federal agent and a local police informant

were working within the Klan and Nazi organizations shortly before the incidents.

Security is heavy on the third floor of the modern Guilford County courthouse, where Superior Court Judge James Long has ordered daily searches and has kept the potentially explosive trial under tight control. . . .

Madigan does not get to the immediate news element of his story—the newspeg—until the third paragraph, much later than the writer of the more conventional preceding lead on the same event did. That might be too late for a reader in a hurry, wanting to get the gist of the story quickly and move on to other items. But Madigan's lead is much more interesting, much more visual, much more compelling. Its language captures the mood of the time and place in a way the more traditional lead does not. For a thoughtful reader willing to take time to try to understand the setting and context of important events of the day, Madigan's lead might seem better.

So it is, in lead writing as in so much else in reporting. The reporter's interpretations are crucial, unavoidable and often controversial. There are many ways to perceive, develop and write a news story, and no one can prove that one way is right, the other wrong. As we have seen, even leading newspaper editors such as Eugene Patterson and Thomas Winship can end up second-guessing if not contradicting themselves. A. M. Rosenthal, the top editor at the New York *Times,* for example, was critical in the early 1980s of the growing number of delayed, descriptive leads in daily newspapers. Yet as a reporter for the *Times,* among Rosenthal's most justifiably admired leads was this one, written to begin a *Times* Sunday magazine story about his visits to concentration camps in Poland in 1958, a piece in which he said there was no news to report:

> The most terrible thing of all, somehow, was that at Brzezinka the sun was bright and warm, the rows of graceful poplars were lovely to look upon and the grass near the gates the children played.
>
> It all seemed frighteningly wrong, as in a nightmare, that at Brzezinka the sun should ever shine or that there should be light and greenness and the sound of young laughter. It would be fitting if at Brzezinka the sun never shone and the grass withered, because this is a place of unutterable terror.

Thus, as you read through this chapter and consider the possibilities available to you in choosing leads for stories, remember that while there are conventions that can help you learn to make choices, there is no avoiding making the choices and no guarantee that everyone, or anyone, will agree with the choices you make. Ultimately, the interpretation you choose to put into the stories you are reporting is your interpretation—a reflection of your mind and spirit—and you will have to live with it. So will your readers.

The News Peg

No matter how the lead is written that part of it that contains the kernel or more of news that is the story's excuse for being is called the *news peg.*

It is a matter of editorial judgment what angle or phase of the total information available should receive emphasis. It is not enough that the first part of a story answer as many of the questions Who? What? When? Where? Why? and How? as the story demands be answered. These elements must be arranged to give proper emphasis to those most important.

News Values

Disregarding considerations of policy as a determinant of news judgment, newspapers and other media of communication, despite their differences, have similar criteria by which to determine the potential newsworthiness of the thousands or millions of occurrences from which they make their selection daily. Psychologically these criteria may be superficial or erroneous, but they have been tested by years of experience and, rightly or wrongly, are in vogue in all but a negligible number of newsrooms.

Differing in arrangement, nomenclature and emphasis, the main determinants of news values, textbook writers and editors in the main agree, are these:

1. Timeliness.
2. Proximity.
3. Prominence.
4. Consequence.
5. Human interest.

Timeliness

Familiar to every journalist of the past half century is the axiom that "nothing is so dead as yesterday's newspaper." Today, possibly, should be added "or the radio or television newscast of an hour ago." Certainly the increased speed by which news is transmitted has stimulated all who are engaged in the communications business to obtain and stress "latest developments first." The rule is always to bring a story up-to-date as much as possible before going to press or on the air and, if at all possible, to avoid using "yesterday" except in early morning reports.

This "last minute" effect often can be obtained by omitting the "when" from the lead, as in the following:

> A Circuit Court judge has given the owners of a slum tenement 60 days to repair their building or face losing the property to the city.
> The action was taken Thursday by Judge Ernest L. Eberholtz in a case involving the five-story brick building at 2122 W. Ashberry St.

Proximity

Wars and revolutions, political, economic and other crises no matter where they occur have expanded the home-town newspaper reader's interests. As a consequence, within a generation the old newsroom rule "It takes a very important foreign story to crowd out a fairly important local story" no longer holds true.

Nevertheless, most events occurring within the territory of a newspaper's circulation are still of greater interest than similar events outside that area. A $50,000 fire in Keokuk will get a bigger play in a Keokuk paper than a $100,000 fire in Baton Rouge. People still want to know what is going on in their communities. As metropolitan newspapers have felt the necessity to print more national and international news, there has been an increase in the number of community and suburban papers devoted primarily to local coverage and to special pages and supplements in the big city press.

Not only do people like to read of happenings in their vicinity of which they have no previous knowledge, but also, perhaps especially, do they look for accounts of events with which they are familiar. They like to see their own names in print and to read what the paper has to say concerning situations about which they already know something. When people expect that their name, or the name of those they know well, is to appear in the newspaper, they look first of all for the item containing it. They are eager to read the newspaper's account of a meeting that they have attended, an accident that they have seen or an athletic contest at which they have been present. Logically, the contrary should be true: They should read first that which they do not already know. But they don't always do that, and editors know that they don't. This being so, newspapers try to please as many readers as possible. If editors think that there is any chance of an appreciable number of readers being interested in an item, no matter how trivial it may be, they print the item, space permitting.

This statement contradicts the supercilious attitude that it is only rural folk who delight in gossip. Just the opposite is true. We do not read in a New York paper that Mary Taylor is spending the weekend with relatives in New Haven merely because not enough people are acquainted with Miss Taylor. Those who do know her are interested in the item of her visit; if the name happens to be Elizabeth Taylor there is a strong possibility that the item will be published. There is no gossip about celebrities too trivial for publication in a metropolitan newspaper. No city reader has any right to laugh at readers of country weeklies who are interested to learn that Henry Jones has painted his barn red.

Writers should play up the local as well as the latest angles of stories. For instance,

> Robert A. Brown Post No. 89 of the American Legion will be represented at the tenth annual convention of the state American Legion Monday, Tuesday and Wednesday at Neillsville, by a delegation of approximately 50 members, including 35 members of the fife and drum corps.

This is better than

> The tenth annual convention of American Legion posts of the state will be held Monday, Tuesday and Wednesday at Neillsville. The local post. . . .

Newspapers rewrite or supplement the stories of press associations, correspondents and press releases, which carry general leads, such as the second, in order to meet the interests of local readers. They localize national stories, as illustrated by the following:

The nationwide airline strike is having little or no effect on air mail service in Lincoln, Postmaster Kenneth Lewis said.

He said that sufficient flights are available on nonstruck lines to ship air mail cargo from Lincoln.

Problems, however, are occurring at the national transportation centers such as Denver, Kansas City and Omaha. National air mail deliveries are being delayed as much as 24 hours.

Mail has been moving on airlines not affected by the strike and most of them have put on extra flights. But, William J. Hartigan, assistant U.S. postmaster general, reported that the emergency scheduling cannot be maintained and some of the extra flights will be canceled.

Military mail for servicemen in Southeast Asia and in Europe has been proceeding on an almost normal basis because all airlines have maintained their military contracts. [Lincoln (Neb.) *Journal*]

Prominence

All men and women may be created equal, but some grow up to be more newsworthy than others. This may be because of the positions they hold, because of their entertainment value or because they have behaved so unusually in the past that they have created interest in whatever else they may do.

What is true of persons also is true of places and organizations. All other elements being equal, a newsworthy event, such as a fire or crime, is more important if it occurs in one's home town. The reader, however, does not have the same interest in all other places. Such large population centers as New York, Chicago and Los Angeles rate ahead of most small cities and towns. Among the latter, however, there are some considered more newsworthy than others, often because they have become associated with a particular kind of news. Among such places are Reno, Las Vegas, Hollywood, Tiajuana and Monte Carlo.

To the home-town editor, news of all potential subscribers is important, and he tries to use the names of as many of them as space permits. Newspapers often print long lists of delegates to conventions, guests at weddings and social events, committee memberships and so forth. Reporters are instructed to obtain as many names as possible and are cautioned to get complete names and their correct spellings. Last names seldom are enough. News media should use a person's name as its owner uses it in business and society generally. Sometimes a telephone book or city directory may give a full name whereas the person uses one or more initials or even a nickname. The only safe way is to ask the person. The reporter must never take chances with the spellings of names. Is it Kern or Curran, Smith or Smythe, Reilly or Riley, Meyers or Myers, Pew or Pugh, Cole or Kole? The rule is this: take nothing for granted, don't guess.

If a widely known person figures in a news event, that fact may become the feature of a story, as in the following:

> Sen. Lyle G. Fitzhugh and six other persons were injured Tuesday night when a row of temporary bleacher seats collapsed during the Milltown-Rushville basketball game.

Consequence

Not only the prominence of persons, places and things mentioned in news stories originating outside the community which a newspaper serves causes them to be published in place of local news; an equal or perhaps more vital factor is the importance of the item.

To illustrate: News from Washington, D.C. is front-page copy in Chicago and San Francisco not primarily because it contains the widely known names of a senator or cabinet member, but because the issues with which those figures are connected vitally concern the best interests of readers all over the country. Every American citizen is directly affected by an important piece of legislation before Congress. National or state political news often is more important than local political news. In a nuclear age one-world-mindedness is a necessity.

Stories concerning changes in the weather or fashions, and stories of epidemics and pestilences, are important because the immediate community may be affected indirectly if not directly. A coal strike in a distant state may lead to a local shortage of fuel; a new model of automobile will be on sale locally within a short space of time; an important scientific discovery may change a reader's way of thinking on a metaphysical problem. The interest in such stories is very personal and very real.

In addition to localizing nationally important stories, newspapers emphasize the consequence of news by seeking the *tomorrow* angle on strictly local stories. This device serves to make the item seem timely and to point up significance. Emphasis is on results rather than causes, on explaining what the present continuing or probable future effect will be.

> The cost of riding city busses in Lincoln is about to increase. The Nebraska State Railway Commission reported Thursday it has approved the application of Lincoln City Lines for a 5-cent-per-fare rate hike, effective Aug. 1.
>
> The change will boost the adult fare from 45 to 50 cents, and the fare for children under 12 from 25 to 30 cents.

Human Interest

Interest in human beings as such, and in events because they concern men and women in situations that might confront anyone else, is called *human interest.*

It is human interest, interest in the lives and welfare of others and in the well-being and progress of mankind as a whole, that causes us to read, with interest and sympathy, of loss of life and property in communities far removed from our own. When an earthquake destroys homes and takes lives in southern Italy or in Japan, there is little likelihood of our being affected directly, except perhaps as we are asked to contribute to the Red Cross relief fund; but we are interested in learning of such "acts of God" because other human beings like ourselves are involved.

It is this personal appeal which editors mean when they say that an item of news has reader interest even though it may not possess any of the other elements of news value: timeliness, proximity, prominence and consequence.

Strictly speaking, all reader interest is human interest. Because readers differ in their occupational, recreational and other interests, some news that has a *personal appeal* to one reader fails to interest another. Any reader, however, no matter how cynical or self-centered, has some *sympathetic interest* in the lives and well-being of other humans. This interest includes both extremes of the pathetic and humorous in everyday life, whatever causes a reader to feel sorry for or to laugh with or at some other fellow being.

Interest in accounts of disasters involving loss of life and property is sympathetic. There may be other elements of interest in stories of fires, wrecks, accidents and other catastrophes; but when individuals are mentioned in unfortunate situations, there also is sympathetic interest. Sickness, near death, suffering of any kind, loss of wealth and the like create attitudes of sympathy in readers.

At the other extreme, ludicrous accounts of typical men and women touch a sympathetic vein also. Americans like to laugh and are amused at almost anything in any way incongruous. In most humorous stories there is someone who suffers some inconvenience, but this does not detract from the humor of the situation any more than does knowledge of possible injury to a person who has slipped on a banana peel and fallen suffice to suppress the smile which comes to one's lips.

Such incidents also involve *unusualness*. People everywhere, and perhaps Americans in particular, love thrills and anything with an "-est" to it. Unusual people, quaint and picturesque places, exciting adventures, all appeal to us. And when we cannot meet those individuals, see those places, experience romance ourselves, we like to read of them all the more. We take vicarious pleasure from stories of adventure and romance.

Once news of new theories and discoveries in the field of science was considered unusual. In the present nuclear age the element of surprise has disappeared, but the interest in *progress* continues. Likewise, unfortunately, the element of reader interest which probably outweighs all others—that in *combat*—also continues. Critical examination of the lists of "biggest" news stories of any year indicates that there is no other single element of reader interest that is present more frequently. Americans, it must be, like a good fight and consider life as a whole to be a struggle. The element of combat is found most prominently in stories of athletic contests, crime, politics, adventure, disaster and heroism. Man against man or man against nature always draws a big crowd, which usually roots for the underdog.

If there is *suspense* in the story of combat, or any other story for that matter, the interest is heightened. Frequently, the attention of an entire nation is centered upon a single news event, as in the case of a mine disaster when rescuers work frantically to save human lives. Illness, especially of a prominent person or from an unusual cause, may be reported so as to emphasize the element of suspense. There is suspense in political campaigns, in law cases and in athletic contests.

The beginning reporter must learn to recognize the human interest possibilities of stories and to brighten up a story by giving it the twist that turns a drab yarn into a bright one without, of course, exaggeration or distortion.

Basic Lead Elements

The *who* or the *what* usually is the feature of a short one-incident (simple) news story. It often is difficult to determine which is more important, as most news concerns people and what they do. For instance, in the following short item many readers will be interested primarily in the young man mentioned as a friend or acquaintance. Others, however, will be interested chiefly because of the extent to which the local schools will be affected by the news. When the news is about a definite person the name usually comes first, as

> Peter L. Clay has resigned his position as instructor in history in the local high school to accept a teaching fellowship in history at Booster College.

The Who

The *who* is unmistakably the feature in the following story:

> George L. Rose has been elected ninth vice-president of the American Council of Civil Service Employees.

Often the interest in the *who* comes from the kind of person involved judged by his occupation, religion, sex, age and so on, or by the circumstances in which he figures in the particular story, or from the number of persons involved, as

> A private watchman shot a suspected burglar Tuesday when he and two companions resisted arrest.

The indefinite *who* is used increasingly as cities become larger and persons in the news are known to fewer other persons in proportion to the population as a whole. The names are introduced in the second paragraph.

The What

The *what* is more important than the *who* when the circumstance would be significant no matter who the persons involved, as

One man was shot and another was beaten today in an outbreak of violence as strikers tried to prevent operation of the Johnson-Smith Corp.

A youth who went beserk with a butcher knife was captured and held by police tonight as a suspect in two recent murders in Milltown.

Press associations usually write their stories in this way, as names may not mean anything outside the immediate vicinity in which the event occurred. The writer of a news story always must decide which is more important, the name or the event.

Often a *what* lead begins with the *who* as an easier rhetorical method or to emphasize authority. Note in the following example that, although the *who* comes first, the *what* is more important:

President Joseph E. Jennings today announced that the County Board is able to pay off current expenditures as they arise, despite the fact that it has retired $568,910 in outstanding debts since he assumed office three years ago.

In the following example the *what* is unmistakably predominant:

Vandalism against cars was reported in Southside Milltown Friday.
Vice squad detectives began an investigation after auto windshields and windows were reported smashed on Haberkorn Road, Lakeside Drive, Alcott Drive and Norton Road, SW.

In action stories readers usually are interested in results rather than causes, as

Two infant brothers perished and three firemen attempting a dramatic rescue of them were injured Monday in a blaze at 3142 N. Patzin St.

The Why

Sometimes, however, it is the cause rather than the result that is the feature of the story, as

Trying to pass another car while traveling at high speed brought serious injury to two men Friday night when their automobile overturned on Washington Boulevard at Potter Avenue.

Taxpayers want to know the reasons for the actions of public officials.

In order to save money and to allow men to spend New Year's Day with their families, the Sanitation Department, in its early planning, has decided to cut back sharply on its force for tonight's midnight-to-8 a.m. shift, leaving only a thin force of 188 workers on duty.

The Where

In advance stories of meetings, speeches, athletic events, etc., the *where* must be very definite. Room numbers, street addresses, and so forth, should be given. In local stories, it is not always necessary to mention the name of the city or a street address. The immediate community is understood, as

> Eight testing lanes on which motorists must submit their automobiles and trucks to examination for safe driving qualifications will be opened Monday.

The *where* may be the featurized element:

> In her 400-year-old ancestral home, the only daughter of an English general recently became the wife of a gypsy, who worked as a handyman on the estate.

In each of the following examples, the *where* definitely was the feature, although, in the second example, the *when* rhetorically came first:

> A tract of approximately 30 acres at Forest Boulevard and Kerwood Avenue, assessed at $900,000, has been sold by Herschel Steel, represented by the Wray-Graw Co., to John L. Finch.

> Beginning today, parking will be permitted in the Underground Lakeside Exhibition Hall of Citizen's Hall by patrons of events at the hall and the Civic Auditorium, at a rate of $5 per car.

When a place is more familiar than the names of those associated with it, the following style may be used:

> The operator of a candy store at 717 S. Ninth St. pleaded guilty Monday in U.S. District Court of the purchase, possession, and sale of 5 ounces of heroin.
> He is Andrew Solberg, 41, of 141 W. Oak St., who was arrested by narcotics agents last month.

The When

About the same may be said of the *when* as of the *where*. It ordinarily is included inconspicuously in the lead, as

> Fur thieves hit two Milltown stores early Wednesday and got away with a total loot estimated at $230,000.

Frequently the *when* may be left until the second paragraph, as

> Commissioner William Wheat has appointed a seven-man hospital committee to look into the situation surrounding construction of a county-wide hospital for pay patients.
> The members were appointed at a Monday afternoon session with the commissioner.

Such omission of the *when* from the first paragraph is common practice with press associations, especially when preparing news of one day for use in the morning newspapers the following day.
The *when* may be a matter of "continuous action," as

A couple of hearty oldsters who defied the wilderness for ten days on a can of beans, a bit of jelly and a small packet of powdered milk are recovering from exhaustion and hunger today in Milltown Hospital.

The *when* may be the featured element, as

Midnight tonight is the deadline for 1985 automobile license plates and vehicles in use after 12:01 Thursday must carry 1986 plates, the Bureau of Motor Vehicles reminded automobile owners today.

A type of *when* lead is the "duration of time" lead, as

After deliberating five hours Friday night, a Superior Court jury returned a verdict of guilty in the steel purchase fraud trial of four Gruner County highway employees.

A similar type of *when* lead is the "since when" lead, as

After being gone for two weeks, Duke, a wistful looking Collie-Spitz hybrid, decided he liked his old home better and trudged 40 miles to return to the residence of his former owner, Humane Officer Thompson Meredith.

The How

By definition the *how* means details to explain how something occurred. Consequently, when the feature unmistakably consists in such details, care must be exercised to avoid wordiness:

Frederick Bascom managed to drive off an Alberto Expressway ramp Monday in Evergreen, tear a tree completely out of the ground, knock a corner off a garage two blocks away, bounce off a car and come out of the whole incident without a scratch and with only one traffic charge.

Sports stories frequently are given *how* leads:

Fritz Tech used seven pass interceptions to frustrate the Ironton Academy attack and converted one of them into a one-yard scoring plunge by Peter Baldwin for the winning touchdown Saturday in a 28–27 win over the Eagles.

Rhetorical Devices _____

The Summary Statement

Most new leads are mere summary statements consisting of simple sentences or of compound or complex sentences with the principal clauses first. Many examples given so far in this chapter illustrate how the feature of a story can be emphasized by means of such simple straightforward writing. Observe, in addition, the following example:

A 23-year-old woman was fatally injured early Friday morning after a car in which she was riding went out of control and slammed into a mailbox and a light post. Rene Fudala of 524 E. 24th St. died at Milltown Hospital at 4:20 a.m.

Conditional Clauses

Often, however, it is difficult to get the feature into a main clause. This is so when the feature is present in addition to the main news idea that the writer must include in his lead. Features to be found in accompanying circumstances, conditions, coincidences in the *when* and *where* and so on often can best be played up by beginning the lead with a complex or complex-compound sentence with the conditional clause first.

In the following examples note how the conditional clause contains the feature, whereas the main idea, which is the excuse for the story, still is in the main clause.

Because Paul Gregg, a 17-year-old high school student, was caught as a stowaway and locked in the infirmary of the liner *Justice,* he started to burn the ship to seek his freedom, he admitted to steamship authorities here today.

This emphasizes the feature much more than would inversion of the clause order, as

Paul Gregg, a 17-year-old high school student, today admitted to steamship authorities here that he set fire to the liner *Justice* to obtain his freedom after being caught as a stowaway and locked in the infirmary.

The Substantive Clause

The substantive clause usually takes the form of a "that" clause which has been much overworked by news writers because it is easy to write and is consequently taboo in many offices. Occasionally the substantive is forceful, as in these rather awkward leads:

That the present legislative appropriation must be doubled if minimum essentials are to be provided welfare recipients, is the warning contained in the monthly report made today by Harold G. Todd, local administrator, for the State Department of Public Welfare.

Return to the pioneer days, when youths in their early teens could assemble a muzzle-loader and pick off game 50 yards away, was sought in a bill before the state legislature today.

Phrases

Participial, prepositional and gerund phrases and absolute constructions also may be used to emphasize a feature when it happens to be one of the minor *w*'s or *h.* In such constructions, the main clause contains the *who* and *what,* one of which is modified by the phrase.

Inverted sentence structure may be used to identify (tie-back) the news with previous news (see Chapter 9) and to identify persons, places and events. Use of phrases and of the absolute construction for different purposes is illustrated in the following examples:

WHEN

After a three-hour search by police and relatives, James Fillmore, 30, his wife and four children who had been missing since Saturday, were found early today in a friend's home.

WHERE

Beside the Ring River, which he made famous in song and verse, the body of Feodor Vladik today was buried with only a handful of close relatives present.

WHY

Delayed somewhat by recent hurricane alerts, work to complete Harris Civil Defense Headquarters in the basement of the Carnegie Free Library was pressed anew last week.

HOW

Citing a permissive 1867 ordinance which never has been repealed, Henry Bucher today won the right to raise geese in his backyard at 10 Cherry Lane.

TIE-BACK

Disregarding three previous failures, Grace Slawson, 21-year-old grocery clerk, Friday will attempt to set a record for swimming across Lake Malthusia.

Care must be taken to avoid what Roy Copperud calls "linguistic smog," illustrated by the following example by Howard C. Heyn in an article, "A Newsman's View: Writing With Precision," in the 1970 _Montana Journalism Review:_

Two firemen fought their way into the smoke-filled building where a boy was trapped on the second floor and died of asphyxiation.

To make it clear who died the phrasing had to be converted to a direct approach in this manner:

Two firemen were asphyxiated while trying to rescue a boy trapped on the second floor of the smoke-filled building.

The Quotation Lead

In reporting speeches, public statements and the like, it is almost always better to epitomize the feature in the reporter's own words rather than by means of a direct quotation.

Weak

"A sharp decrease in maternal mortality, medical progress, and greater economic prosperity have enabled welfare agencies to solve most of their problems except that of the emotionally disturbed child," Horace V. Updike, Council of Social Welfare director, said Saturday.

Better

The emotionally disturbed child is the "No. 1 problem" facing welfare agencies today, Horace V. Updike, Council of Social Welfare director, said Saturday.

In news stories that are not accounts of speeches or documents, however, it sometimes is effective to begin with a direct quotation, as in the following examples:

"In this country, as in yours, we take a rather dim view of serious infractions of this kind," Provincial Judge P. J. Bolsby said today to a 22-year-old New York City man charged with assaulting a police officer while trying to gatecrash Saturday's rock festival at the Canadian National Exhibition.

[Toronto *Globe-Mail*]

The Question Lead

Ordinarily the reporter should answer, not ask, questions in his news stories. To do otherwise merely delays telling the news, as in the case of a lead beginning. "What causes delinquency?" followed by a summary of a new idea advanced by some authority. It would be much better to start: "Failure of teenagers to obtain jobs causes them to become delinquent in the opinion of . . ."

Sometimes, however, it may be possible to obtain interest by means of a question lead, as

Baltimore, Aug. 7 (AP)—Could one man in one night at one bar on The Block, Baltimore's strip-tease row, run up a bill of $1,900? Or $1,349.50? Or $1,722.11 at three clubs?

The Baltimore Liquor Board, investigating complaints from credit card holders about the bills they found on their vouchers, had its doubts. . . .

The Staccato Lead

When the time element—either fast action or the intervals separating a series of related events—is to be emphasized, the staccato lead occasionally suffices. It consists in a series of phrases, punctuated either by periods or dashes and usually is a form of descriptive lead. The style suggests the tone of the story, its feeling.

By Timothy McNulty
CHICAGO TRIBUNE PRESS SERVICE

Ft. Worth—An oil multimillionaire . . . his beautiful but straying wife . . . her murdered lover . . . a lawyer named "Racehorse" . . . the oilman's faithful mistress . . . the mysterious "man in black" in the woman's wig . . . a young girl killed . . . a murder-for-hire revenge plot secretly videotaped . . . the "carnival" trial . . . a secluded and bloodstained mansion . . .

It all may sound like dust-jacket blurbs from a racy new novel, but these are the elements of the strange double case against T. Cullen Davis, which is still unfolding on a backdrop of Texas wealth and society.

The Explosive Lead

Similar to the staccato lead but consisting of more grammatically complete phrases, the explosive lead is especially useful for feature articles. It can, however, be used for straight news stories as well.

A fellowship wooded retreat, freeing the human mind, communal living, Renaissance songs, sensitivity training—they're all there in the next six weeks of the Near North Unitarian Universalist Fellowship.

The Dialogue Lead

It is difficult, if not impossible, to begin a serious news story of an important event with dialogue. Minor court stories, with strong human interest, and occasionally stories of a more significant nature, however, can be handled effectively by means of a dialogue lead, as

"Wouldn't it be terrible," asked Hazel Muller, 22, of 1864 E. Payne Ave. "if I got locked in that record vault and couldn't get out?"

"Ho, ho," replied Thomas Keyes, production manager of the Majestic Foundry Co. at 146 E. Belmont Ave., where Miss Muller is a secretary, "It couldn't happen."

But it DID happen Tuesday and it WAS terrible.

Here's a play-by-play account. . . .

Purposeful Leads _____

The Punch Lead

Since World War II, the punch lead has grown in popularity and on some newspapers is used for almost any kind of story, not just stories of presumed extra newsworthiness. It has been called the "blind" lead because of its emphasis on situations rather than specific persons and details. It is a form of writing easily open to misuse (1) in stories whose importance is thereby exaggerated and (2) by being excessively indefinite or "empty." An example of the latter is "Politics has a different look in Congress today," a sentence which tells exactly nothing. Paragraphs two and three of a well-written story with a punch lead should supply definite details:

A policeman has been suspended on charges that he deserted his school-crossing post.

Placed on indefinite suspension by Police Chief Patrick C. O'Brien Tuesday was Albert Murchison, 27, of 885 W. Strong Ave., attached to the Vickers Station, 1412 E. Vickers Ave.

Lieut. Ira Walters of the Vickers district said a routine check at noon Monday disclosed that Murchison was absent from his post at Bristol and Sacramento roads.

The Astonisher Lead

Beginning writers are discouraged in the use of superlatives and expressions of opinion. When deserved, however, superlatives can be used, as in this example:

> For the first time since 1963, the Chicago Bears are the champions of professional football, having won the most super victory in Super Bowl history in defeating the New England Patriots 46-10 Sunday.

The Contrast Lead

Sometimes the feature of a news story consists in the contrast between the immediate and a former situation or between the event at hand and another of which, for any of a number of reasons, it is a reminder. Note that the news peg is retained in the following lead, though not so definitely, the emphasis being upon the unusual situation:

> Behind the same walnut desk which he used to dust 25 years ago as an office boy, Virgil F. Stimson Monday received congratulations upon becoming president of Andalia Trucking Co.

The Descriptive Lead

The feature or key to the spirit of a story may be in its setting, in the physical appearance of some person or object involved or in an unusual phase of the action with which it deals. In such cases, a graphic or descriptive lead may be the most effective to give the tone or feeling necessary to proper understanding and appreciation. Before he can describe, the reporter must know how to observe; the best descriptive leads are written by eyewitnesses. To be avoided are superfluous and inapplicable adjectives, extraneous matter serving no purpose except, perhaps, to prove the writer's possession of an extensive vocabulary of trite and hackneyed expressions—clichés. The following lead to an important story avoids these hazards:

> For more than a minute today the sun hung over central Minnesota like a twinkling, slate-blue Christmas ornament as the moon moved between it and the earth.
>
> In the awesome half-light that covered the area, hundreds of scientists and thousands of other persons had a perfect view of the total solar eclipse.
>
> [New York *Times*]

The Figurative Lead

Triteness must be avoided in the use of metaphors, similes and other figures of speech, either in the lead or in any other part of a news story. The following lead was a winner in a Best Lead contest at the San Angelo (Tex.) *Standard-Times*. It described a potential flood.

Cold, dirty water lapped and licked at Pecos Tuesday night like a patient cat toying with a cornered mouse.

The Epigram Lead

The tone or moral of a story also may be emphasized by means of an epigram lead, in the writing of which bromides and platitudes must be avoided. The epigram is a concise and pointed expression, usually witty. The epigram lead may be either a familiar saying or a moral applicable to the story at hand, as

Silence can be golden in more ways than one, Shortstop Tommy Jacobs of the Maroons has discovered.

After striking out three times against Bristol Aug. 12, Jacobs complained to his manager, Bucky Johnson, that he had been the victim of several debatable calls by the umpire.

"The trouble with you," said Johnson, "is that you spend so much time turning around to squawk that you're not ready to hit the ball. Just for the fun of it, forget to turn around and look at the umpire for any reason and concentrate on hitting the ball."

Tommy followed the advice today and hit three home runs and a triple.

The Literary Allusion Lead

The writer with a normal background of knowledge in literature or history will have frequent chances to use it to advantage. Care must be taken to limit references to fictional or historical characters and to literary passages familiar to the average reader. The following example illustrates how it is possible effectively to make use of one's general knowledge to improve his writing:

By Ralph Blumenthal

A desire named streetcars is growing—a desire for the return of one of America's oldest forms of urban public transportation.   [New York _Times_]

More Than One Feature _____

So far, only stories containing simple features relatively easy to pick even though related to important events have been considered. Not infrequently, an item of news presents so many angles that the rhetorical devices described in this chapter are inadequate. There are several ways out of this difficulty.

Separate Stories

The easiest way is to write more than one story. When there are sidelights or interviews of opinion or features connected with a news event, the assignment usually is split between two or more reporters. Some repetition usually occurs but is not discouraged; in fact, in some cases it is encouraged, and a paper may run several stories of the same event written by different reporters.

The Crowded Lead

When the various elements of interest are of nearly equal value, a number of facts may be crowded into a single lead, as

By Diane Amann

Stagnant air, overcrowded halls, inadequate toilet facilities, and jacked-up food prices at the International Amphitheatre, 43d and Halsted streets, infuriated many people taking their nursing board examinations there Tuesday and Wednesday. [Chicago *Daily Tribune*]

Succeeding paragraphs naturally would take up each item mentioned in the lead, providing full details.

The "Shirttail" Method

To avoid crowded and vague leads, one item deemed the most important can be played up. Paragraphs containing mention of other items then can be introduced by such expressions as "In other actions the City Council . . ." or "In a similar accident . . ." and so forth.

Ald. Val G. Grauer (17th Ward) has been elected chairman of the powerful Finance Committee of the City Council.

Other standing committee chairmen, named at last night's board meeting, follow. . . .

The board also voted to continue for one year its contract with the Republic Light Company for street lighting. . . .

In other actions, the board referred a proposed new ordinance regulating business licenses to the Finance Committee and rejected a request by Front Street property owners that all-night parking be permitted in the 400 block.

Wall Street Journal Formula

One of the most currently popular types of leads is what has become known among journalists as the *Wall Street Journal* formula. It is a variation of the delayed lead, usually involving some form of specific example in the opening paragraphs, followed by a paragraph stating the larger theme illustrated by the examples (the thematic paragraph is called the *nut graf*.) The specific example is designed to draw readers into a story about a larger theme. When done well, the example used to illustrate the larger theme is chosen only after the reporter has explored many possible examples. Otherwise, there is no guarantee that the example said to reflect the general theme really exemplifies anything. Here is an example of a lead of this kind. Many other examples of the *Wall Street Journal* formula style of lead can be found throughout the book.

By Dennis Farney

Pawhuska, Okla.—West of here the land shakes off the threadbare vestiges of the forest like a discarded overcoat. Then the tallgrass prairie begins.

It is a green-blue immensity, stark and spare beneath an empty sky. A world of barbed-wire fences and lonely windmills; of thunderheads that boil up in the shimmering heat; of grasses and wildflowers in profusion. Indian-grass and big bluestem, prairie coneflower and blazing star, compass plant and black-eyed Susan, swirling in the wind.

This, said Walt Whitman, is "North America's characteristic landscape." Now Oklahomans are hotly debating whether to put 50,000 acres of it, recently private land, into the National Parks system. At issue is a kind of ghost landscape, one that all but vanished before most living Americans were born. . . . *[Wall Street Journal]*

The 1-2-3-4 Lead

After a short summary statement of the situation constituting the news, the different features can be emphasized by tabulation and numbering, as

The wishes of Mayor Louis T. Tupper were ignored by the newly elected City Council in several votes at its organizing meeting Friday night. Most importantly the Council did the following:

1. Elected Ald. Val G. Grauer (17th ward), political rival of the mayor's, chairman of the powerful Finance Committee.

2. Referred a proposed new ordinance regulating business licenses to Ald. Grauer's committee. The mayor has called the new ordinance unnecessary.

3. Continued for one year the contract with the Republic Light Co. for street lighting. The mayor opposed the renewal in campaign speeches last month.

4. Rejected a property owners' petition for all-night parking in the 400 block on Front Street, which the mayor had approved.

The preceding lead, of course, is interpretative. It plays up the significance of the council's actions rather then merely reporting them deadpan. It does not editorialize for or against the council's insurgency, and the treatment probably could be adversely criticized only if it could be shown that every council action was taken despite rather than because of any attitude toward Mayor Tupper.

The article as written does not say the four actions indicated hostility by the board toward the mayor. Nevertheless, there is no mistaking the fact that such an impression is given. If, at a subsequent meeting, the board were to vote in favor of a number of measures sponsored by the mayor, the facts as they existed after the earlier meeting would have to be reexamined. If, however, the facts as stated in the first story are accurate, the reporter could not be accused of coloring the article. Certainly readers were given background information whereby it would be possible for them to draw conclusions, whereas a strictly factual account of the actions of the City Council, without attempt at any perspective, might have created a wrong impression.

It cannot be pointed out too often that essential for this kind of interpretative reporting is knowledge. Without it, the newsgatherer will consider as new something that is very old and will have news sources "revealing" and "disclosing" information that is common knowledge among a wide circle of readers.

In other words, you can't play up a feature unless you have educated yourself enough to identify it. Interpretative reporters, to interpret, must have diligently done their homework.

7

Journalistic Style

The late Red Smith wrote mostly about sports. His prose was admired for its lean, crisp, precise qualities. He once said: Writing is easy. You just sit down at your typewriter and wait until a drop of blood oozes from your forehead.

James Kilpatrick is a syndicated columnist. His prose also pleases many people, including some who think his political point of view is too conservative. In an article in the October 1984 issue of the *Washington Journalism Review,* Kilpatrick said, in effect, that too little blood is flowing in the newsrooms of America:

> To read almost any American daily today is to conclude that copy editors have vanished as completely from our city rooms as the ivory-billed woodpecker has vanished from the southern woodlands. . . .
> Those marvelous VDT screens are garden plots that grow words in glorious profusion, with the result that a crop of prose is harvested before it matures. I say it's spinach, and I say the hell with it.

You may be tempted to skip this chapter. Reading about the rules of grammer and the characteristics of style bores many otherwise dutiful folks.

Some even get drowsy reading their own copy, and, thus, as Kilpatrick laments, do not get around to editing their own stuff. That's the attitude of "the hell with it." It is a decidedly unhealthy attitude for those who plan to feed at the trough of words. So, even if this chapter seems to you like a helping of spinach, dig in. It's a snack that will be good for you.

Today's recognizable journalistic style evolved during the past century. It is economical and suited to the needs of the medium. Its characteristics include:

1. Compact, usually short, sentences, every word selected and placed for maximum effect.
2. Short, terse paragraphs.
3. Conciseness, directness and simplicity, through elimination of super-fluous words, phrases and clauses and through proper emphasis.
4. Factualness, without editorial opinion, puffs and boosts, unwise su-perlatives, adjectives, nouns or other dogmatic words.
5. Strong verbs and nouns preferred to trite, hackneyed and obsolete words and expressions.
6. Observance of the rules of good grammatical and word usage.

Conciseness _____

The objective of effective journalistic writing should be to avoid cumber-someness without becoming choppy or repetitious through the excessive use of referents.

Superfluous Details

Relaxing of the rule that all of the five *w's* and *h* must be included in the first paragraph of a news story generally achieves the objective of un-cluttering the lead.

Cluttered

Clifford Britt, 38, 1459 Grove St. and another passenger on an eastbound Mitchell Boulevard bus were injured about 8 a.m. today when the bus collided with a westbound bus at Mitchell Boulevard and Perkins Street.

Scores of other passengers en route to work who filled both vehicles were heavily jostled and shaken up as the two buses came together, according to police, who also said another man was injured but disappeared from the scene of the accident.

Britt was taken to Municipal Hospital with lacerations and abrasions on the head and hands.

Uncluttered

Two men were injured when two buses collided at Mitchell Boulevard and Perkins Street about 8 a.m. today.

One of the injured men was Clifford Britt, 38, 1459 Grove St. Police said another man was injured but disappeared from the scene of the accident.

Britt suffered cuts and bruises on the head and hands. He was taken to Municipal Hospital.

Both buses were filled with passengers on the way to work.

Superfluous Words

The articles *the, a* and *an* often can be eliminated, as

WEAK: The Booster students who heard the talk—
BETTER: Booster students who heard the—
WEAK: It is for the men who make good.
BETTER: It is for men who make good.

Sentences may be shortened and made more forceful by making verbs more direct, as

WEAK: The committee arrived at a conclusion.
BETTER: The committee concluded.
WEAK: The society held a discussion on the matter.
BETTER: The society discussed the matter.
WEAK: They did away with the old building.
BETTER: They razed the old building.

In their *The Art of Editing* (Macmillan, 1972) Floyd Baskette and Jack Sissors list 48 "pet" circumlocutions that can be reduced to save 100 words:

A good part of (much)
A little less than (almost)
Accidentally stumbled (stumbled)
As a general rule (usually)
At the present time (now)
At the rear of (behind)
Bouquet of flowers (bouquet)
Basic fundamentals (fundamentals)
Commuted back and forth (commuted)
Concentrated his efforts on (concentrated on)
Continued on (continued)
Disclosed for the first time (disclosed)
Drew to a close (ended)
Due to the fact that (because)
Easter Sunday (Easter)
Entered a bid of (bid)
Estimated at about (estimated at)
Filled to capacity (filled)
Gave its approval (approved)
Grand total (total)
Hot water heater (water heater)
In the not too distant future (eventually)
In the immediate vicinity (near)

Invited guests (guests)
Jewish rabbi (rabbi)
Kept under surveillance (watched)
Long chronic illness (chronic illness)
Made arrangements (arranged)
Made an arrest (arrested)
Mental telepathy (telepathy)
Officiated at the ceremony (officiated)
New recruit (recruit)
Soothing balm (balm)
Once in a great while (rarely)
Paid a visit (visited)
Personal friendship (friendship)
Present incumbent (incumbent)
Private industry (industry)
Promoted to the rank of (promoted to)
Put in his appearance (appeared)
Reached an agreement (agreed)
Referred back (referred)
Rough estimate (estimate)
Strangled to death (strangled)
Tendered his resignation (resigned)
Voiced objections (objected)
Went up in flames (burned)
With the exception of (except)

Don't waste words in giving dates, as

WEAK: The Chemical society will meet on Saturday.
BETTER: The Chemical society will meet Saturday.
WEAK: The meeting will be held this coming Friday.
BETTER: The meeting will be held Friday.
WEAK: The meeting was held at 12 o'clock noon.
BETTER: The meeting was held at noon.

Sometimes a series of related facts can be presented in *series* form, in chronological order, as a word saver. Robert G. Martin cites the following example:

He was born in Russia, reared in Austria, graduated in 1914 from the University of Vienna, and then served throughout World War I as an Austrian artillery officer on the Italian and Russian fronts.

Erling H. Erlandson, correctly warns against misuse of this style, as "Born in Tennessee, he served on the Los Angeles Board of Education from 1935 to 1941." Wrote Erlandson: "When two unrelated facts are jammed together, it may be tight writing but it's also faulty subordination."

Superfluous Phrases

WEAK: The meeting was held for the purpose of discussing the matter.
BETTER: The meeting was held to discuss the matter.
WEAK: We met at the corner of Spring and High streets.
BETTER: We met at Spring and High streets.

What someone who makes this mistake means is "intersection," where there are four corners, not just one.

WEAK: We reached him by the use of telephone.
BETTER: We reached him by telephone.
WEAK: The color of the cart was red.
BETTER: The cart was red.
WEAK: He will be here for a period of three weeks.
BETTER: He will be here for three weeks.

Often a strong verb, adjective, adverb or possessive form can be substituted for a phrase.

WEAK: A baby with brown eyes.
BETTER: A brown-eyed baby.
WEAK: The arguments of Brown.
BETTER: Brown's arguments.
WEAK: They assembled with little commotion.
BETTER: They assembled quietly.
WEAK: The howitzer went off with a boom.
BETTER: The howitzer boomed.

Before emulating the last preceding example, the writer must be certain that he has not distorted meaning. There is great temptation to use shorter action verbs that create a feeling of excitement not justified by the facts of the story.

Superfluous Clauses

WEAK: All citizens who are interested should attend.
BETTER: All interested citizens should attend.
WEAK: He will speak at the meeting, which will be held Monday.
BETTER: He will speak at the meeting Monday.
WEAK: John Farrell, who is secretary of the Engineers' club, will attend.
BETTER: John Farrell, secretary of the Engineers' club, will be there.

Sometimes, though, clauses make possible word-processing interpolations.

Even though he lost both sets, 8-6 and 9-7, he outscored Segman in earned points, 46-43, and his passing shots, often executed while he was running full tilt, were effective.

Redundancies

The Minnesota Newspaper Association prepared the following list of redundancies.

absolutely necessary	enclosed you will find	postpone until later
advance planning	exactly identical	reasonable and fair
ask the question	fair and just	redo again
assemble together	fall down	refer back
at a later day	first and foremost	refuse and decline
attached hereto	friend of mine	right and proper
at the present time	gathered together	rise up
canceled out	honest truth	rules and regulations
city of Chicago	important essentials	send in
close proximity	necessary require-	small in size
consensus of opinion	ments	still remain
carbon copy	open up	temporarily suspended
continue on	other alternative	totally unnecessary
cooperate together	patently obvious	true facts
each and every	plain and simple	various and sundry

Others are "general consensus" and "new record."

Simplicity

Simplicity is obtained in large part by avoiding pretentious words when simple ones would do better. Usually

about is better than *with reference to*
agreement is better than *concordance*
although is better than *despite the fact that*
before is better than *prior to*
body is better than *remains*
buried is better than *interred*
burned is better than *destroyed by fire*
city people is better then *urban people*
clear is better than *obvious*
coffin is better than *casket*
danger is better than *precariousness*
died is better than *passed away* or *succumbed*
dog is better than *canine*

farming is better than *agriculture*
fear is better than *apprehension*
fire is better than *conflagration*
forced is better than *compelled*
funeral is better than *obsequies*
horse is better than *domesticated quadruped*
if is better than *in the event of*
leg is better than *limb*
man is better than *gentleman*
marriage is better than *nuptials*
meeting is better than *rendezvous*
money is better than *lucre*
nearness is better than *contiguity*
since is better than *inasmuch as*
theft is better than *larcency*
understand is better than *comprehend*
well-paying is better than *lucrative*

When two words are synonyms, brevity can be obtained by using the shorter, as

after for *following*
ask for *request*
buy for *purchase*
car for *automobile*

expect for *anticipate*
get for *obtain*
try for *attempt*
use for *utilize*

Passive and Active Voice

The active voice usually is more emphatic than the passive. The passive should be used, however, when warranted by the importance of the grammatical object of a sentence. In the following sentences, for example, the passive voice is preferable to the active:

Henry Binger has been appointed chairman of the County Republican campaign committee.

Earl Kromer, prominent local merchant, was killed instantly early today when a bolt of lightning struck his home, 34 E. Wilson St.

Increased rates for the Middletown Municipal Water Works were ordered by the Public Service Commission in an order issued Thursday.

In other cases the feature can better be played up by use of the active voice, as

WEAK: The accident was witnessed by ten boys.
BETTER: Ten boys witnessed the accident.

WEAK: The report was received by the mayor.
BETTER: The mayor received the report.
WEAK: The keynote address was delivered by Governor Furman.
BETTER: Governor Furman delivered the keynote address.

Proper Emphasis

Vagueness and indefiniteness are avoided, and clarity is obtained, by placing important ideas at the beginnings of sentences. Also by playing up the action, significance, result or feature of the paragraph or story, by avoiding vague and indefinite words and by eliminating superfluous details, words, phrases and clauses.

VAGUE: Some 50 persons were present.
BETTER: Fifty-one attended.
WORDY: People of Chester will be asked to contribute $4,000 to the National Red Cross campaign to relieve suffering in the drought area of the United States, according to announcements made today by John Doe, local chairman.
CONCISE: Chester's quota in the National Red Cross campaign for drought relief is $4,000, John Doe, local chairman, said today.
WEAK: When asked what he thought of the compromise plan of unemployment relief, Senator Sapo today said that—
DEFINITE: Senator Sapo today condemned the compromise plan for unemployment relief as demagogic, unconstitutional and inadequate.
WEAK: The purpose of the Student Council meeting at 7 p.m. Monday in Swift Hall is to discuss the proposal to limit student activities.
BETTER: The Student Council will discuss limitation of student activities at 7 p.m. Monday in the Swift Hall.

Avoiding Banality

The day of the grammatical purist is gone. Contemporary authorities recognize that language makes dictionaries and not vice versa. Many words in common use today were once frowned upon as slang or vulgarisms. Every year prominent writers invent new words or discover archaic ones that meet with popular acceptance. The fault of many writers as regards word choice is not so much selection of what might be called undignified words but tactless use of bromides, platitudes, and clichés. Some examples follow.

Figures of Speech

The following figures of speech should be avoided because they have been overused and often misused:

a checkered career	blessing in disguise
acid test	busy as a bee
alike as peas in a pod	clutches of the law
ax to grind	cool as a cucumber

dull as dishwater
eyes bigger than his stomach
flow like water
hail of bullet
hangs in the balance
heart of the business district
honest as the day is long
in the limelight
innocent as a newborn babe
late hours of the night
loomed like sentinels
met his Waterloo
never rains but it pours
nipped in the bud
picture of health
pillar of the community
police combing the city
pretty as a picture
rains cats and dogs

round into shape
sea of upturned faces
silver lining
slow as molasses in January
smell a rat
sober as a judge
something the cat dragged in
spread like a house afire
stormy session
the crying need
the great beyond
the wings of disaster
threw a monkey wrench into
to swing the pendulum
watery grave
went by the boards
white as a sheet
won his spurs
worked like Trojans

Bromides; Clichés; Platitudes

Generally considered too trite or hackneyed for effective use are the following:

all-out effort
almost fatally injured
any way, shape or
    form
as luck would have it
augurs well
bated breath
beaming smile
better half
bids fair
bigger and better
blushing bride
bright and shiny
broad daylight
burly lineman
coin a phrase
departed this life
doing as well as can
    be expected
doomed to disappoint-
    ment
dull thud
each and every
early on
easy prey
fair maidens

favor with a selec-
    tion
few and far between
hale and hearty
head over heels
hectic
he-man
host of friends
in the offing
internal fury
laid to rest
last but not least
last sad rites
leering ghost
light fantastic toe
loomed on the hori-
    zon
making it a whole
    new ball game
many and various
method in his mad-
    ness
music hath charms,
    etc.
no uncertain terms
order out of chaos

point with pride
powder keg
present day and gen-
    eration
received an ovation
red-blooded
resting comfortably
scintillating
sigh of relief
signs of the times
smashed to smither-
    eens
sparkling eyes
take a hard look
thick and fast
threw his hat into
    the ring
trend of public senti-
    ment
variety is the spice of
    life
view with alarm
vital stake
weather permitting
wild and woolly

Journalese

Newspapers have not contributed so much as one might expect to the development of new words, but they have helped exhaust the effectiveness of a large number through indiscriminate repetition. Among these are the following:

blunt instrument	grilled by police	rush
bolt from a clear sky	gruesome find	sleuths
brutal crime	gumshoes	smoke-filled room
brutally murdered	hot seat	smoking revolver
cannon fodder	infuriated mob	solon
cheered to the echo	man hunt	speculation is rife
cops	moron	swoop down
crime wave	mystery surrounds	thug
cynosure of all eyes	news leaked out	usually reliable sources
death car	police drag nets	war clouds
fatal noose	political pot boiling	while thousands cheer
feeling ran high	probe	whirlwind tour
fishing troubled waters	quiz	will be staged
focus attention		

At any time there are words and expressions that are popular and that are used by many who don't fully understand their meaning. Among recent examples are viable, bottom line, scam, *deja vu,* ripoff, syndrome, do your thing, macho, let it all hang out, name of the game, panic button, bite the bullet, get the show on the road, and get the act together.

Gobbledygook

Wallace Carroll, when editor and publisher of the Winston-Salem *Journal Sentinel,* described the difficulty the newsgatherer encounters in trying to write with clarity about what news sources say.

Do you want to be recognized as an authority on reading in the public schools? Then you have only to write like this:

"Perhaps the task of developing proper motivation is best seen, at least in a nutshell, as limiting the manipulation of extrinsic factors to that of keeping homeostatic need and exteroceptive drive low, in favor of facilitating basic information processing to maximize accurate anticipation of reality."

Do you want to become a professor of the behavioral sciences in a great university? Then you simply need to express yourself in this way:

"If the correlation of intrinsic competency to actual numerical representation is definitely high, then the thoroughly objective conclusion may inexpugnably be reached that the scholastic derivations and outgrowths will attain a pattern of unified superiority."

Do you want to become the chief of a government bureau? Then learn to write and talk like this:

"The Board's new regulatory goal is to create a supervisory environment conducive and stimulative to industry adaptation to its fundamentally altered markets. We will give you the options to restructure both sides of your statement of condition, but the decision-making and the long-range planning function is management's . . . We will look to you for input of information which we shall rely on in making our decisions."

Or do you want to become an expert on business management and go around lecturing to leaders of industry? You can if you will learn to talk like this:

"The focus of concentration rests upon objectives which are, in turn, centered around the knowledge and customer areas, so that a sophisticated awareness of those areas can serve as an entrepreneurial filter to screen what is relevant from what is irrelevant to future commitments."

This bastardization of our mother tongue is really a disaster for all of us in the news business. The English language is our bread and butter, but when ground glass is mixed with the flour and grit with the butter, our customers are likely to lose their appetite for what we serve them.

The best exposure of the superficiality of pseudo-intellectual gobbledy-gook is *Social Sciences as Sorcery* by Stanislav Andreski.

Academic Obscurity.

Because of the growing evidence of the functional illiteracy of many high school graduates, there is an increasing demand for a return to the basics, meaning the traditional 3 r's—reading, 'riting and 'rithmetic. The behavioral scientists who have been in the majority in schools of education and teachers colleges are in retreat with their arguments that training in sensitivity, social responsibility, creativity, and the like are more important than more rigorous, disciplined course content. Of the professional exponents of obscurity the *Wall Street Journal* has editorialized:

> Complexity and obscurity have professional value—they are the academic equivalents of apprenticeship rules in the building trades. They exclude the outsiders, keep down the competition, preserve the image of a privileged or priestly class. The man who makes things clear is a scab. He is criticized less for his clarity than for his treachery.

In the New York *Times* column entitled "Why Profs Can't Write," Donald Holden wrote, "Book publishers know that most professors are bad writers. The professor's grammar, spelling and punctuation are usually passable but his prose is apt to be pretentious, unclear and chaotic." Holden wrote that "dissertationese is the language that professors use to disguise self-contempt with pomposity." In her *America Revisited* Pulitzer prize-winner Frances FitzGerald documents Holden's charge as regards American history books intended for high school use during the past century.

In his "Light Refractions" column in *Saturday Review,* Thomas H. Middleton frequently berated the behavioral scientists. He was especially aghast at the endorsement by the National Council of Teachers of English of the viewpoint expressed by Leonard Bloomfield: "Writing is not language but merely a way of recording language by means of visible marks." Middleton sarcastically commented: "Shakespeare, Milton, Pope, Melville, Jefferson, Twain and so on and on are no longer part of the English language. The English language is now the rap session."

A good summary of the situation is *What's Happening to American English* by Arn and Charlene Tibbetts. The viewpoint of the downgraders of grammer and writing is presented in Stanley Berne's *Future Language* and Arlene Zekowski's *Image Breaking Images*. The authors, professors of English at East New Mexico University, want a new grammarless language. According to Berne, "Grammar and spelling are the property of a once privileged minority class imposing its order on a willing majority anxious to rise out of its own supposed ignorance and vulgarity."

Another crusader against the belief held by many English teachers today that it is unimportant for students to learn to spell and write grammatically is Richard Mitchell, professor of English at Glassboro State College. He is the author of *Less Than Words Can Say*. He scoffs at sociologists and educators who say "individualized learning station" when they mean "desk." It is impossible to conceive how newspapers or other periodicals could adopt the antigrammarian viewpoint or, in fact, publish anything for anyone who does. The behavioral scientists, however, have infiltrated schools of journalism where the Ph.D. communicologists, often with little or no professional journalistic experience, write articles for *Journalism Quarterly,* the publication of the Association for Education in Journalism and Mass Communications. In the October 1979 *Quill,* Creed C. Black, publisher of the Lexington (Ky.) *Leader,* wrote about *Journalism Quarterly,* "I must confess that I found little there I could understand, much less apply." He quoted the following from a *Journalism Quarterly* article:

> We hope to accomplish two aims in this paper. We intend to explore the use of collective behavior conceptualizations in the press, focusing on the New York *Times.* We intend to test the specific hypothesis that there is a direct relationship between the reported presence of a control agency at a collective behavior event and the attribution of spontaneity, out-of-the-ordinary nature, depersonalization of participants, violence, emotionality, and the use of unit terms of reference. This hypothesis (more accurately, this set of hypotheses) will be tested by using the Spearman rank-order correlation.

In the Winter 1976 issue of *Masthead,* publication of the National Conference of Editorial Writers, Jake Highton, formerly chairman of the Department of Journalism at Wayne State University, asked, "Does Anyone at *Journalism Quarterly* Speak English?" and explained his quandary by quoting from a dozen scholarly articles in the magazine, a typical excerpt being the following:

> Overall differentiation among the six-party performance groups by the seven factors was significant (Wilks-Lamba $= 0.857$) five roots extracted 100 per cent of the variance, but only the first root was significant (Chi square $= 35.7 p < .001.$)

Highton despaired and returned to professional newspaper work. So did another experienced reporter when he attended an Association for Education in Journalism convention and received the abstract of a paper, "Subject Abilities to the Metric MDS; Effects of Varying the Criterion Plan." The abstract began:

This study addresses the problem of selecting a criterion pair to present to subjects in a metric MDS task and, more importantly, the subject's ability to reliably use that standard to describe or characterize their conceptions of a given set of elements. It was hypothesized that: (1) The structure produced by a criterion pair involving the extremes from the concept domain will be statistically identical to the structure produced by providing the same scale base with no concept anchors; (2) As the distance between the criterion pair is increased the resulting judgments of distances among concepts will increase but the pattern of interrelationships will remain the same; (3) A criterion pair that is closer together in the space will produce a larger structure than using the extreme pair, yet the concept interrelationships will remain the same.

Not all journalism educators write that way. Too many do. If you want to become a good writer, do not imitate them.

Readability Formulas _____

Shortly after World War II the two major press associations and several magazines and newspapers experimented with readability formulas that stressed brevity—shorter words, shorter sentences, and shorter paragraphs—in the belief that thereby the average American, who had only a ninth-grade education, would find the result easier to read and comprehend.

The formulas grew out of studies of several researchers, most important of whom where Rudolf Flesch of New York University and Robert Gunning, director of Readable News Reports of Columbus, Ohio. Following the recommendations of the former, the Associated press reduced its average lead sentence length from 27 to 23 words and its average word sentence length from 1.74 to 1.55 syllables. Upon the advice of the latter, the United Press simplified its writing style so as to be suitable for readers with 11.7 years of education, whereas formerly it presumably was writing for those who had gone to school 16.7 years.

Flesch's formula allegedly estimated "reading ease" and "human interest." The former was measured by the average length of words and sentences—the shorter, the easier to read, 1.5 syllables and an average sentence length of 19 words being considered best for newspapers. Human interest was measured by the percentage of "personal words" and "personal sentences." Flesch said 6 per cent of the former and 12 per cent of the latter made for good newspaper reading.

Gunning considered three factors: (1) sentence pattern, difficulty beginning when the average number of words per sentence exceeded twenty; (2) Fog Index, a measure of complex or abstract words as "rendezvous" for "meeting," "undoubtedly" for "no doubt," etc.; (3) human interest—the frequent use of names of people, referents to those names and other human interest words.

As an Associated Press Managing Editors association committee once reported: "The virtue of the Flesch experiment is that it *has* made writers think more of their writing."

The same, of course, could be said of the Gunning and several other formulas.

Brevity does not necessarily equate with clarity. A short word can be as vague as a long one, and a short sentence can be a misleading as a book. Using the syllable-length standard advanced by Flesch, such words as _beautiful, patriotism, vacation, prearrange, improbable, candlestick, brace-let, watermelon_ and other familiar ones would be considered difficult whereas use of _ohm, joule, watt, erg, baize, arn, tweak, volt_ and _tort_ would contribute to a high readability score.

Different from either the Flesch or Gunning system, in that it takes account of the reader's probable familiarity with words, is the system devised by Prof. Edgar Dale and Mrs. Jeanne S. Chall of the Bureau of Education Research of Ohio State University. The Dale-Chall system takes into account average sentence length but also uses a list of 3,000 words familiar to fourthgraders.

Dr. Dale discounts the value of counting affixes, suffixes and prefixes, as advocated by Flesch, by declaring that no two skilled judges ever get the same count. He also rejects Flesch's personal referent principle and is fond of citing a quotation from Koffka's _Principles of Gestalt Psychology_ which contains personal pronouns equal to 5.8 per cent as follows:

> In the first case, real moving objects present in the field, the shift of the retinal pattern leads to behavioral motion of objects, whether I fixate a non-moving object or follow a moving one with my regard; in the second case, when my eyes roam stationary objects, such a shift will not have this result. . . .

That would be considered very readable by both the Flesch and Gunning systems.

Proper names, other critics of these formulas have pointed out, do not necessarily lead to greater understanding unless the reader knows the persons mentioned and understands the references to them. "He was as mad as Hamlet," for instance, is about as readable as you can get; but, if the reader never has heard of Hamlet, its meaning is lost on him.

In recent years there have been several studies that show at least 21 million Americans, perhaps as many as 57 million, over the age of 16 are functionally illiterate. In addition there are about 1 million who cannot read or write at all. According to the United States Office of Education, 20 per cent of adult Americans have trouble coping with such necessary skills as shopping or getting a driver's license. In addition 19.7 per cent of Americans over 16 "function only with difficulty" and another 33.9 per cent are "functional but not proficient."

Two of the most sensible books of advice on writing are _The Elements of Style_ by Will Strunk and E. B. White and _On Writing Well_ by William Zinsser. Buy them. Study them. Apply them to your writing.

Semantics

Despite its length, the following sentence probably would be considered readable by the readability experts:

Many boys and girls are working at too young an age, for too long hours, too late at night, in dangerous and other undesirable conditions.

A general semanticist, however, would be quick to point out that no matter how clear the sentence may be, the information it conveys is vague and biased. How many is "many"? When you say "boys and girls" do you mean little children, such as used to work in sweatshops, or do you mean teenagers? What determines when one is too young to deliver newspapers, work as a fast-food clerk, fill supermarket shelves, wash cars or work on a lathe? How long is "too long" and how late is "too late"? What is a "dangerous" condition? Especially, what are "other undesirable" conditions?

No experienced newsgatherer would fail to ask these questions if such a statement were made during the course of an interview. Often, however, such "glittering generalities," as the Institute for Propaganda Analysis (1937–1942) would have called them, appear in publicity releases and in public addresses, especially by politicians. They need amplification to convey important meaning to others, and it will be a happy day when editors toss them into the wastebasket unless it is possible to obtain such amplification.

On assignment, the interpretative reporter must be sharp enough to ask the proper questions to clarify vague statements and define "virtue" or "smear" words. Often, if not always, this requires more than the usual amount of knowledge on the reporter's part regarding the field of interest. In other words, the more reporters know about a subject, the better able they are to interview someone regarding it. All the readability formulas and other aids to good writing cannot substitute for thorough fact gathering.

"Pin the source down" should be the newsgatherer's first rule. If sources talk about "progress," reporters should ask them what they mean by the term and for the facts and figures that justify its use. If sources interviewed mention "special circumstances," they should be asked what they mean by "circumstances" and what makes them "special" and to give specific examples of what they are talking about. Why? For example? Explain what you mean by that? Would you please illustrate? All those questions are excellent ones. Use them often.

Unfamiliar Words

If the words an interviewee uses are specific but nevertheless unfamiliar, the reporter should overcome any sheepishness and ask for a little elementary shop talk about his subject. Otherwise, the reporter might neglect to inquire deeply enough into the potential facts of the story at hand. Lacking such an opportunity for "depth" reporting, the reporter should consult dictionaries, encyclopedias and other reference works.

If reporters have to ask or look up the meaning of an expression, they can be fairly certain that a goodly number of their readers will need explanation of it. Perhaps they can even avoid use of the unfamiliar word in their stories. They can, for instance, say, "Union A is attempting to persuade members of Union B to change their membership from B to A." Then they can explain, "This is called 'raiding' in labor circles." Or, if they use "raiding" in their principal statement, they can define it, perhaps in an italicized parenthetical insert.

"Jurisdictional strike," "mass picketing" and "secondary boycott" are among the other terms in a story of a labor dispute that may need explanation. In weather stories it probably is wise to make clear the difference between hurricanes, tornadoes, cyclones and just plain gales or wind storms. Few readers probably remember what a nautical knot is or a French kilometer or an English mile. With the world becoming more complex daily and the areas of specializing growing, the need for such explanatory journalism is increasing. Thorough reporting is the best safeguard against the misuse of words.

Connotations

"The workers _won_ a wage boost" has one connotation. "The workers _were given_ a wage boost" has quite another. Only painstaking reporting can determine which is correct in any particular case. There should be no laziness or carelessness when the public interest is involved, as it usually is in stories pertaining to labor relations, government activities and the like.

Perhaps news sources condemn government "interference" when they mean they oppose government "regulation" in a particular area. Such words are loaded. Reportorial questioning should lead to specific details rather than vague charges or mere name calling. If loaded words are used from some necessity, they probably should be included in quotation marks or some explanatory matter should be added to indicate the alternative words for the same thought.

Newspapers propagandize if they use the labels of those with whom they agree editorially to describe pending legislation or situations. Examples of such editorializing would be "slave labor bill" for a measure regulating the mobility of the labor force in time of emergency, "dictator bill" for a proposal to increase the power of an executive, "goon" for labor union pickets and the like. It makes a great deal of difference whether you write

crop subsidy _or_ farm dictatorship
foreign _or_ international
labor organizer _or_ labor agitator
nonstriker _or_ loyal worker
picketing _or_ mass picketing
a company's earnings declined 36 per cent _or_ they plunged to that extent
regulation _or_ regimentation
UAW chieftain _or_ UAW boss
open shop _or_ right to work
bombing _or_ air support
affirmative action _or_ reverse discrimination

mandatory busing *or* assignment for racial balance
right to life *or* right to choose
right to work *or* closed (or open) shop
liberate *or* change governments
tax law change *or* tax relief

George Orwell's essay, "The Politics of the English Language," is a classic discussion of how words become weapons of power.

Evaluative Words

In quite a different category are attempts to improve the reader's understanding by the use of qualifying adjectives, other parts of speech and expressions. Even some editors who have been outspoken in adverse criticism of interpretative reporting have for years allowed and encouraged their reporters to write "One of America's *leading composers* will play his own compositions," "The two *top contenders* for the championship will meet in the first round," "An *unusual* workshop class in creative writing for talented children will be organized," "The court will hear arguments on the *complex, controversial and crucial questions*" and the like.

There is no denying that such expressions involve judgment and, to be socially responsible, the judgment must be based on adequate information. When sportswriters, for instance, write that the outcome of a contest was "a stunning upset," they must know that leaders in the sports world and fans expected it to be different. Reporters should not use superlatives without investigating to determine whether they are justified: "most devastating fire," "largest audience," "longest report," "rare appearance." Nor should they call every gruesome murder "the crime of the century" or assert that something is "unparalleled in human history" or "the greatest outrage ever recorded" unless they have done considerable scholarly research to verify their contentions.

Nouns

When, however, can you call a disturbance a "panic" or "riot"? When can you use such words as "catastrophe," "fiasco," "disaster," "climax," "zenith" or "debacle"? All you can say is that such terms should be used judiciously. To make common use of them would be to make them meaningless when they are truly needed.

What, therefore, is judicious use? Experienced reporters who have covered many similar stories have a basis for comparison, and their experience usually is better than that of most everyone else, especially those with selfish motives for hoping reporters use this word instead of that. Competent reporting and integrity are more likely to give readers correct information than are writing formulas and communication theories.

Adjectives

When is a woman pretty or a man handsome? Since the development of photography, reporters have become more cautious about indiscriminate use of such descriptive adjectives. Because there is no similar restraining influence in other areas the best that can be done is to advise caution in the use of such words as the following:

brave	ferocious	popular
brilliant	gigantic	remarkable
clever	happy-go-lucky	successful
cowardly	huge	tasteful
eloquent	illimitable	unpatriotic
enjoyable	impressive	valiant
exciting	nice	widely known

Verbs

Verbs must be exact. If news sources answer "yes" to a reporter's question, it is not always proper to say they "admitted" something. When officials make an announcement, they cannot be said to have "revealed" or "disclosed" something unless the matter previously had been kept secret intentionally. "Charge" is a strong word implying an accusation which the news source might have had no intention of making. "Claim" suggests that someone is trying to correct a wrong impression or stretching the truth.

Because few words are exact synonyms for each other, a good dictionary or thesaurus is a better companion for the writer seeking to impart correct information than Gunning's formula to determine the Fog Index. The practice of intentionally using a strong synonym for maximum visceral effect on readers instead of the word that comes closer to stating the situation correctly cannot be condoned.

Here is a list of verbs that the reporter should be hesitant about using:

allege	laugh	sneer
beg	object	squeak
confess	plead	threaten
flee	prowl	urge
grimace	roar	whine
implore	shout	whisper
insult	sneak	yell

Verbs precisely chosen, though, drive a sentence. In 1980, Washington Post reporter Henry Allen told an Inland Daily Newspaper Association writing seminar: "I like to write sentences people can dance to, and verbs put the boogy into sentences."

Adverbs

A properly placed adverb can change the entire meaning of a news story. Consider the potential power of the following:

accidentally	facetiously	jokingly
angrily	grimly	laughingly
boastfully	immodestly	mockingly
calmly	inadvertently	seriously
carelessly	intentionally	stupidly
casually	ironically	viciously

Correct Usage

It is presumed that the student has completed a course in English grammar and composition and, therefore, knows the basics of good English. Although some reputable writers still split their infinitives without losing effect, few misuse "lay" and "lie," get "don't" and "doesn't" twisted, misplace "only" or use "like" when they mean "as if" or become confused over the difference between "its" and "it's." If students of this book are deficient in knowledge of grammar, they should try to correct that shortcoming. Reporters who cannot make their subjects and predicates agree and who can't spell ordinary words don't last long.

In every newspaper office some rules of grammar, word usage and punctuation are emphasized more than others. Most good newspapers issue style sheets or style books for the guidance of new staff members. Pay attention to them.

Grammatical Faults

Many years of correcting journalism students' papers have convinced the writers of this book that the following are among the most common grammatical errors about which aspiring reporters need caution.

WRONG: Neither the mayor nor the city clerk are willing to talk.
RIGHT: Neither the mayor nor the city clerk is willing to talk.
WRONG: The Chamber of Commerce will begin their annual membership drive Monday.
RIGHT: The Chamber of Commerce will begin its annual membership drive Monday.
WRONG: Howard is not as tall as Harold.
RIGHT: Howard is not so tall as Harold.
WRONG: He gave it to John and I.
RIGHT: He gave it to John and me.
WRONG: Less than 35 percent of the group favor the idea.
RIGHT: Fewer than 35 percent of the group favor the idea.

Parts of Speech

To obtain originality of expression, writers (not all of them journalists) sometimes change the part of speech of a word. In many cases the dictionaries have caught up with popular usage. For instance, it is proper to say "chair a meeting," "jail a prisoner," "hospitalize a sick person" or "table a resolution." Even such words as "alibi," "probe," "host" and "torpedo," to whose use as verbs objection often is heard, are listed as such. President Kennedy used "finalize" as a verb and the practice of inventing verb forms of nouns is widespread; thus we say "victimize," "contact," and the like indiscriminately.

In view of the dynamic character of the language, one hesitates to become crotchety when a newspaper columnist says someone "week-ended" or "house-guested" another. In recent years such words as "babysit" and "moonlight" have come into common usage as verbs. Use of "-wise" as a suffix (businesswise, timewise, bookwise, saleswise) still is regarded as somewhat flippant, however expressive.

Usually it is left to special writers who sign their stories, sports writers and feature writers to invent unusual word usages. Authors of formal stories are more conservative and wait until the dictionaries have sanctioned an innovation before using it casually. When Webster's *Third New International Dictionary* appeared, however, many writers criticized it for allegedly going too far in legitimatizing new usages. Among the leading liberal authorities in this field is Roy Copperud, who writes a column for *Editor & Publisher*. Another was the late Prof. Bergen Evans of Northwestern University, who coauthored *A Dictionary of Contemporary American Usage* with Cornelia Evans. Defenders of the Webster dictionary pointed out that in 1800 such words as "banjo," "hominy" and "possum" were considered too slangy for its edition that year. On the other hand, there is Edwin Newman who argues powerfully in *Strictly Speaking* and *A Civil Tongue* against too much license, especially by journalists.

Troublesome Words

No matter what the viewpoint regarding definitions, there can be no disagreement that words should be used to convey the meaning intended by their employers. Caution, therefore, is advisable in deviating from standard usages.

The following are some words and expressions that often cause difficulty:

Above. Should not be used for *over* or *more than.*

Accord. Do not use in the sense of *award. Give* is better.

Act. A single incident. An *action* consists of several acts.

Actual facts. All facts are actual.

Administer. Used with reference to medicine, governments or oaths. Blows are not *administered,* but *dealt.*

Adopt. Not synonymous with *decide* or *assume.*

Affect; effect. Affect means to have an influence on; *effect* means to cause, to produce, to result in.

Aggravate. Means to *increase;* not synonymous with *irritate.*

Aggregate. Not synonymous with *total.*

Allege. Not synonymous with *assert.* Say the *alleged* crime, but "He *said* he is innocent."

Allow; permit. The former means *not to forbid;* the latter means *to grant leave.*

Allude. Do not confuse with *refer* or *elude.*

Almost; nearly. Almost regards the ending of an act, *nearly* the beginning.

Alternative. Indicates a choice of two things. Incorrect to speak of *two alternatives* or *one alternative.*

Among. Use when more than two is meant; for two only, use *between.*

Annual. Don't write *first annual.* It's not annual yet.

Antecedents. Do not use in the sense of *ancestors, forefathers, history* or *origin.*

A number of. Indefinite. Specify.

Anxious. Implies worry. Not synonymous with *eager,* which implies anticipation or desire.

Anyone or none. Use in speaking of more than two. *Either* and *neither* are used when speaking of only two. All take singular verbs.

Appears, looks, smells, seems, etc. Take an adjective complement.

As the result of an operation. Avoid this expression. Usually incorrect and libelous.

Audience. An *audience* hears, *spectators* see.

Autopsy. An *autopsy* is *performed,* not *held.*

Averse; adverse. The former is an adjective meaning *opposed to;* the latter is an adjective meaning *bad.*

Avocation. A man's pleasure, while *vocation* is his business or profession.

Awful. Means to *fill with awe;* not synonymous with *very* or *extremely.*

Balance. Not synonymous with *rest* or *remainder.*

Banquet. Only a few meals are worth the name. Use *dinner* or *supper.*

Because. Better than *due* in "They fought because of a misunderstanding."

Beside; besides. The first means *by the side of;* the second, *in addition to.*

Bloc. Don't confuse with *block.*

By. Use instead of *with* in such sentences as "The effect was gained by colored lights."

Call attention. Do not use it for *direct attention.*

Canon; cannon. The former is a *law;* the latter is a large *gun.*

Canvas; canvass. The former is a *cloth;* the latter means to *solicit.*

Capitol. The building is the *capitol;* the city is the *capital.*

Casualty. Should not be confused with *disaster, accident, mishap.*

Childish. Not synonymous with *childlike.*

Chinese. Don't use *Chinaman.*

Claim. A transitive verb. One may "claim a dog" but not that "Boston is larger than Portland."

Cold facts (or statistics). When is a fact hot?

Collide. To collide both objects must be in motion.

Commence. Usually *begin* or *start* is better.

Compared with. Use *compared with* in speaking of two things coming under the same classification; use *compared to* if the classes are different.

Completely destroyed. Redundant.

Comprise. Do not use for *compose.*

Confess. A man confesses a crime to the police, but he does not confess to a crime. Don't say *self-confessed.*

Conscious. Not synonymous with *aware.*

Consensus. Don't say *consensus of opinion;* simply say *consensus.*

Consequence. Sometimes misused in the sense of "importance" and "of moment," as "They are all persons of consequence" (importance); "A matter of no consequence" (moment).

Consist in. Distinguish between *consists in* and *consists of.*

Consummation. Look up in the dictionary. Do not use in reference to marriage.

Continual; continuous. That is -*al* which either is always going on or recurs at short intervals and never comes (or is regarded as never coming) to an end. That is -*ous* in which no break occurs between the beginning and the end.

Convene. Delegates, not a convention, *convene.*

Correspondent; co-respondent. The former *communicates in writing;* the latter *answers jointly* with another.

Council; counsel. The former is a *meeting for deliberation.* The latter is *advice* or *one who gives advice.*

Couple. Used only when two things are joined, not of separate things. Use *of* with it.

Crime. Do not confuse with *sin* or *vice. Crime* is a violation of the law of the state; *vice* refers to a violation of moral law; *sin* is a violation of religious law.

Cultured. Don't use for *cultivated.*

Cyclone. Distinguish from *hurricane, typhoon, tornado, gale* and *storm.*

Dangerously. Not *dangerously* but *critically* or *alarmingly* ill.

Data. Plural. *Datum* is singular.

Date from. Not *date back to.*

Depot. Don't use for *station.* A *depot* is a storehouse for freight or supplies; railway passengers arrive at a *station.*

Die of. Not *die from.*

Different from. Not *different than.*

Dimensions; proportions. The former pertains to *magnitude;* the latter to *form.*

Divide. Don't say, "The money was divided between Smith, Jones and Brown." Use *among* when more than two are concerned.

Dove. Should not be used for *dived.*

Drops dead. Falls dead is what is meant.

Drown. Don't say *was drowned* unless it was murder; just say *drowned.*

During. Do not confuse with *in. During* answers the question "How long?" *In* answers the question "When? At what time?" as "We were in Princeton *during* the winter"; "We received the letter *in* the morning."

Each other; one another. The former pertains to *two;* the latter to *three* or *more.*

Either; neither. Use when speaking of two only.

Elicit. Means to "draw out against the will."

Emigrant. Do not confuse with *immigrant.* An *emigrant* leaves, and an *immigrant* comes in.

Envelop; envelope. The former means *to surround;* the latter is a *covering* or *wrapper.*

Event. Do not confuse with *incident, affair, occurrence* or *happening.*

Experiment. Don't say *try* an experiment. Experiments are *made.*

Fail. To *fail* one must try. Usually what is meant is *did not.*

Fakir; faker. The former is an Oriental ascetic; the latter is a deceiver or cheat.

Farther. Denotes distance; *further* denotes time.

Final; finale. The former means *last;* the latter is a *concluding act* or *number.*

Fliers; flyers. The former are *aviators;* the latter are *handbills.*

Flout; flaunt. The former means to *scoff or mock;* the latter means *to make ostentatious display.*

Frankenstein. He was the monster's maker, not the monster itself.

From. A person dies *of,* not *from,* a disease.

Graduate, as a verb. Colleges *graduate;* students are *graduated.*

Gun. Don't confuse with *revolver* and *pistol.*

Had. Implies volition. Don't say, "Had his arm cut off."

Head up. The *up* is superfluous.

Healthy. A person is *healthy,* but climate is *healthful* and food *wholesome.*

Heart failure. Everyone dies of heart failure. There are several *heart diseases.*

Hectic. "Hectic flush" is the feverish blush of consumption. Not to be used in the sense of *excited, impassioned, intense, rapturous, uncontrolled* or *wild,* except when a jocosity is intended.

High. Distinguish from *large.*

Hoi polloi. "The many." Do not use "the" before it.

Hold. Use advisedly. The Supreme Court *holds* a law constitutional, but one *asserts* that one man is a better boxer than another.

Hung. A criminal is *hanged.* Clothes are *hung* on a line.

Inaugurate. Does not mean *begin.*

Incumbent. It is redundant to write *present incumbent.*

Indorse. Not synonymous with *approve.*

Infer; imply. The former means *to deduce;* the latter *to signify.*

Initial. A man may sign his initial, but he does not make an *initial payment.* He makes the *first payment.*

Innumerable. Not synonymous with *endless.*

Invited guests. Most guests are invited; omit the adjective.

Last. Not synonymous with *latest* or *past.*

Leave. Don't confuse with *let.*

Leaves a widow. Impossible. He leaves a *wife.*

Lectern. A reading desk; a *podium* is a small platform.

Less. Use *less* money for *fewer* coins.

Like. The slogan "Winstons taste good like a cigaret should" has helped make the use of "like" legitimate as a substitute for "as."

Literally. Often the exact opposite, *figuratively,* is meant.

Locate. A building is *located* when its site is picked; thereafter it is *situated.* A person is *found,* not *located.*

Majority. The lead over *all* others; a plurality is a lead over *one* other.

Marshal; Marshall. The former is a title; the latter a proper name.

Mathematics. Singular.

Media is plural; *medium* is singular.

Memorandum. Singular. *Memoranda,* plural.

Mend. You *mend* a dress but *repair* a street.

Minister. Distinguish between *minister,* a term used in Protestant churches, and *priest,* used in Catholic churches. Every *preacher* is not a *pastor;* a *pastor* has a church, a *minister* may not.

Musical; musicale. The former means *rhythmic;* the latter is a *recital* or *concert.*

Name after. The correct form is *name for.*

Near accident. There is no such thing.

Née. Give only last name, "Mrs. Helen Keunzel, née Bauman."

Nice. Means *exact,* not *agreeable* or *pleasant.*

Notorious. Different from *famous.*

Old adages. There are no *new adages.*

Oral; verbal. The former emphasizes use of the mouth; the latter applies to either spoken or written words.

Over. Not the same as *more than.*

Partly completed. Has no meaning. The words are contradictory.

Past. Not synonymous with *last.*

People. Refers to population. Do not confuse with *persons.*

Per cent. Do not say "large per cent" when you mean "large proportion."

Point out. Use when something is true or clear; is not synonymous with *assert.*

Politics. Singular.

Practically. Not synonymous with *virtually.* Different from *almost.*

Principle. Always a noun. *Principal* is generally an adjective.

Prone on the back. Impossible. The word means "lying on the face." *Supine* is "lying on the back."

Provided. Not *providing* he will go.

Public. Singular.

Quite. Means *fully* or *wholly.* Do not, for example, write "He is *quite* wealthy," but "He is *rather* wealthy."

Raised. Animals are *raised;* children are *reared.*

Render. You *render* lard or a judgment, but you *sing* a song.

Secure. Means *to make fast.* Don't use it for *obtain, procure* or *acquire.*

Sensation; emotion. The former is *physical;* the latter is *mental.*

Ship. Cattle are *shipped* but corpses are *sent.*

Since. Not synonymous with *because.*

So. Use in a negative comparison instead of *as.*

Someone, somebody, etc. Take singular verbs.

Suicide. Do not use as a verb.

Sustain. Injuries are not *sustained* but *received* or *suffered.*

To the nth. An unspecified number, not necessarily infinite or large. Do not use for *to the utmost possible extent.*

Transpire. Means to *emerge from secrecy into knowledge, to become gradually known.* Not to be used in the senses of *happen, occur,* etc.; must not be followed by an infinitive.

Treble; triple. The former means *three times;* the latter means *three kinds.*

True facts. Facts never are false.

Try and. Use *try to.*

Unique. Its adverbs are *absolutely, almost, in some respects, nearly, perhaps, quite, really* and *surely.* It does not admit of comparison. There are no degrees of uniqueness. It means *alone of its kind. Different* means *out of the ordinary.*

Unknown; unidentified. The former means *not recognizable by* anyone; the latter means *not yet recognized.*

Various. Not synonymous with *different.*

Vender; vendor. The former is a *seller;* the latter is a legal term.

Want; wish. The former means *need* and *desire;* the latter means only *desire.*

We. Don't use the editorial *we.* Name the paper.

Well-known. Usually *widely known* is meant.

Whether. Do not use for *if.* Don't add *or not.*

While. Means *at the same time;* not synonymous with *although.*

Widow. Never use *widow woman.*

The Writer as Musician

For all the importance of the rules of grammar, we should not forget that writing is ultimately an act of individual expression, an art. Language and its rules are what the instrument and the score are to a musician. The music is not in the piano nor is it in the notes that are played on the piano. It is not only the pianist's technique, but also the pianist's interpretation that shapes the song we hear.

Roy Peter Clark, the first and most active of the modern newspaper writing coaches, has interviewed many good journalistic writers. Of them he said in a February 1985 *Washington Journalism Review* article: "Clarity is the explanatory journalist's Grail. The quest to achieve it is more than an occupational disposition. It is a form of vision, a way of looking at complex issues that is analogous to a great mountain climber viewing a mighty cliff."

Henry Allen of the Washington *Post* offered this advice to journalistic writers at a University of Illinois seminar: "Always be aware you're running a magic show—creating an illusion—when you're writing. Be responsible about it and keep in mind that you're not telling THE TRUTH. Good writing is a dangerous commodity. It creates a kind of reality for readers. You can make people believe things."

That writers possess such powers as Henry Allen suggested is perhaps why Jack Cappon of the Associated Press once defined good writing as the art of the second thought.

PART
III

Perspectives

The primary purpose of a daily newspaper is admittedly not the cultivation of letters but the presentation of news, but I believe that very few of us rightly estimate the educative value of the modern newspaper, and when we talk of the education of journalists we are talking of the education of perhaps the only professors under whom enormous numbers of our modern reading public study. We must not be tempted to regard our profession solely as an industry and not as an art. To write and to write well is an art. It is true that by overstressing the technical side of education you would not deprive journalism of its literary merit.

—E.F. LAWSON, editor, *Telegraph,* London, England

We (reporters), who think we have adoring children and dogs, want to be loved and appreciated by everyone, friend and foe alike. We want our mistakes to be seen as inconsequential stumbles along the road to justice, beauty and a better world for all.

Alas, they hate us. Just because we are nosy, irreverent, powerful and careless.

Good! That's the way it should be. The press can take care of itself. It is, and should be, just another one of the great interests seeking attention, credibility and acclaim to gain policy and economic rewards. If prime ministers and presidents, and companies, armies and navies, occasionally kick our butts or sneer in our nosy faces, that just serves to remind us of whom we should be watching even more carefully.

—RICHARD REEVES, reporter and syndicated columnist

CHAPTER
8

Keeping Up-to-Date

There is nothing so short, sometimes, as a newspaper reader's attention span. That important point too often is forgotten by reporters and news-writers caught up in a story and working against deadline pressures. The point was driven home again in the results of a survey by two researchers at the University of Maryland, John Robinson and Mark Levy. In an October 1983 article in the *Washington Journalism Review,* they reported on a survey they conducted of more than 500 newspapers readers. "Our survey showed," they said, "how quickly Americans picked up on stories with a 'human interest' angle, but how difficult it is for the press to convey successfully the gist of complicated, technical and important stories. . . . Our general conclusion is that while the public is often better informed on news stories than we give them credit for, not enough news is getting through. Even when important news does get through, it is often confusing and confused."

Identification

The obligation of the newspaper adequately to identify persons, groups, places and events in straight news stories is recognized in any efficient newsroom. The rule is never to presume that the reader has seen yesterday's story.

It is seldom that the name of a person is mentioned in a news story without some identification. Even the occupant of the White House is given his title, and other persons mentioned frequently in the news are identified by their news past or importance. Ordinary persons may be identified in several ways. The most common methods of identification include the following:

1. Address	9. Achievement
2. Occupation	10. Life span
3. Age	11. Reputation
4. Title	12. Relationship
5. Nicknames	13. Marital status
6. Race, nationality	14. Sex
7. War record	15. Occasion
8. News past	

Address. "Where do you live?" is one of the first questions asked anyone from whom information is desired. The address in a news story locates a person and the reader does not have to ask, "I wonder if that is the Newton Blue who lives in the next block?" Readers are interested in news pertaining to persons residing in their own or in a familiar neighborhood, even though not personally acquainted with them.

Great care must be taken to get correct addresses. Stop and underline that last sentence. Memorize it. Act on what it says. It is very important. Ignoring it could cause much grief for you and for others. Libel suits have been brought by persons with names similar to those of others mentioned in news stories. Rare cases have been reported of two persons by the same name living at the same address. It is important to ascertain whether it is "street," "avenue," "place," "boulevard," "terrace" and so on, as there may be both a Ridge Avenue and a Ridge Terrace. Whether it is East, North, West or South also must be mentioned.

Emmett Dedmon, when executive editor of the Chicago *Sun-Times,* modified what he called "a journalistic shibboleth of long standing" with the following memorandum:

> The Sun-Times does not wish, as a matter of policy, to cause undue hardship or to invade the personal privacy of persons who are in the news through no fault of their own.
>
> While it is usually necessary to identify persons with their home address in a city as large as Chicago, The Sun-Times will refrain from doing so when good judgment would indicate such identification unnecessary or undesirable.
>
> In general the rule is: Don't use the address if it is secondary to the main point in the story, or if the address does not add to the identification of the individual.
>
> In all instances good judgment and clarity will be the criteria.
>
> Following are a few examples of situations where an address is not necessary:

—John Smith is held up in his drug store. Use the address of the drug store but not his home address.

—Mary Smith is posed in a weather picture.

—Richard Rowe is a witness in a crime trial. His connection with the case is sufficient identification.

—Five girls are arrested for prostitution at 1976 N. Dearborn St. The Dearborn Street address is sufficient.

—John Doe, a printer, found the body, called police, gave the alarm, identified the suspect etc. As long as he is identified in some way the home address is not necessary.

—A police officer captures a bandit. His station or section is sufficient identification.

These examples are not meant to be a complete list but should give enough of an idea to explain the general rule. There are of course countless other situations which will have to be evaluated as they arise.

Occupation. "What do you do?" also is high up in the list of questions asked when data are being sought about a person. Readers may wonder if H. R. Snow, 1516 S. Chestnut St., is the carpenter by that name who worked on their new garage.

Donald C. Sorenson, 51, Edwardstown, district representative for the Common Laborers Union, Monday was sentenced to a two-year jail term and fined $1,500 for income tax evasion.

The occupation of a person mentioned in the news may be the feature, as

A butcher today used his knowledge of animal anatomy to save the life of his hunting dog, Romeo, accidentally caught in a bear trap.

Age. It is customary to give the age of a person who is involved in a lawsuit or who is the victim of an accident. Otherwise, unless age has importance in the story, it may be omitted. Many persons do not like to have their ages known but readers are eager to find out how old popular heroes and heroines are.

William Murphy, 16-year-old Greenwich High School junior, today identified John Pratt, 21-year-old unemployed construction worker, as the armed bandit who robbed him of his clothing and $15 in cash Sunday night on West Totze Ave., police said.

Age frequently is the feature, as

An 18-year-old girl will marry a 73-year-old man on Saturday because, she said, "our common religious beliefs are of far more importance than the disparity in our ages."

Title. When people have a title by which they are known, the news writer should use it. A short title is better placed before a name; a long title should be placed after a name, as

> City Clerk George Johannsen will deliver the commencement address at 10 a.m. Monday at Craven Junior High School.
>
> James R. Wesley, commissioner of public works, will represent the city tonight at. . . .

Nicknames. Nicknames seldom are used without first names; rather, they are inserted between the first name or initials and the surname. In sports stories and in feature articles, nicknames may be used alone. Often persons prominent in the news are better known by their nicknames than by their real names, as "Tip" O'Neill, "Dolly" Parton, "Sugar Ray" Leonard etc. When such nicknames become widely familiar, the quotation marks usually are omitted. It is a common practice with some newspapers to invent nicknames for persons mentioned in the news, frequently in crime stories. In doing so, care must be exercised so that the connotation given the nickname is not prejudicial to the proper administration of justice or otherwise socially harmful. Even so, such details are more appropriate in personality sketches than in straight news stories.

> William "Wee Willie" Swayne, pint-sized killer-bandit of the 1940s, died Wednesday evening in the Stateville prison hospital. Death was attributed to a liver infection.
> The baby-faced killer, who got his nickname because he was only 5 feet 3 inches tall, was serving a life sentence for the slaying in 1947 of Hilltown's police chief.

Race, nationality. Deciding when to pass copy containing "black," "Puerto Rican," "Polish-born," "of German descent," and similar identifications has caused many an editor many a headache. Members of racial and nationality minority groups understandably object to persistent use of such identifications in crime stories, especially in headlines: "Black Rapist Sought," "Italian Gangster Shot." When someone is in the limelight—a politician, athlete or entertainer—fans are eager to learn every picayunish fact regarding the celebrity including ancestry; certainly no injustice is intended when such details are given. For some people, as musicians and artists, a foreign background may be considered an asset.

It was only after World War II that a majority of newspapers capitalized *Negro.* For a period in the '60s some black leaders preferred to be called "colored," to emphasize the idea that differences are only skin-deep. Then recently militants promoted the slogan "black is beautiful" to stress pride in color. Black is now the term most preferred. A minority of others, however, prefer *Afro-American.*

During the past few decades there has been a great increase in the mainland population of former residents of Puerto Rico, Mexico and other Spanish-speaking areas. Although many are victims of economic and social discrimination, in some respects they enjoy advantages never provided earlier immigrants from Poland, Italy, Greece and other European nations. There are bilingual schools in many cities, Spanish columns in newspapers, Spanish programs on radio and television.

Because of minority group members' desire to retain their identity it is not surprising that newspapers use identifications such as Hispanic, Latino, Puerto Rican and Chicano. The same is true of blacks and many other ethic groups.

Alfred M. Bowler Friday became the first black to be elected to public office in Calhoun County since Reconstruction Days.

War record. Under pressure from veterans' organizations, most newspapers have ceased identifying veterans as such in crime stories. Often, however, veteran status is a legitimate, even necessary identification. It may, in fact, be the feature.

Thomas Thomas, a former paratrooper, just couldn't get his training out of his head. He was sleeping in the apartment of a friend when he awoke and jumped out of a third floor window. He landed on a roof a few feet below the window sill. He was not hurt, and he explained that he had dreamed he was back in the army and had been given an order to jump.

News past. After having once appeared in the news in connection with an important event, some people continue to be potentially more newsworthy than others. Should they become "copy" again, their former exploits are a means of identification.

Miss Jane Boynton, 41, winner of several beauty contests 20 years ago, today filed a $15,000 suit against Dr. N. O. Holten, charging that his plastic surgery "disfigured her for life."

Leon L. Desmond, star witness in the Fox-Delaney murder case four years ago, today was appointed chief deputy inspector of Raymond County by Sheriff L. L. Tyler.

Achievement. The achievement of one's early life may be his identification in later life or after death, as

Dr. Hal Foster, first Kansas City physician and surgeon to specialize in the treatment of eye, ear, nose and throat, died at 6 a.m. today at his home at the Brookside Hotel. He was 88 years old.

Life span. Sometimes it is pertinent to identify a person in relation to the historical events or changes that have occurred during his lifetime, especially as they relate to the news at hand.

Harry Thom, who joined the U.S. Internal Revenue Service staff 58 years ago, when relatively few persons paid income taxes, and stayed long enough to see virtually everyone pay, will retire Saturday.

Reputation. When identifying a person by means of reputation, it is necessary to be careful that the reputation is deserved. It is possible for a newspaper to make or break people by referring to them constantly as the foremost authority on a certain subject, or as a mere pretender or charlatan.

> James (Jimmy) Eder, reputedly the wealthiest and most successful jockey in the history of the Latin American turf, Tuesday was named defendant in a suit for divorce or separate maintenance in Superior Court by Mrs. Ruth Eder.

Relationship. A person's news importance may depend upon the prominence of a relative or friend. How much the families of persons important in public life or in the news of the day should be written up and photographed is another problem for debate by a class in newspaper ethics. Relationship may be used as identification even when the members of the family referred to are not of particular importance. Minors often are identified by parentage.

Legitimate use of relationship in identification is illustrated in the following examples:

> Maj. James R. Garfield, II, training officer of the 107th Armored Cavalry Regiment, Ohio National Guard, and great-grandson of James Abram Garfield, 20th President of the United States, is taking summer training at Fort Knox. [Louisville *Courier-Journal*]

> Robert Campbell MacCombie Auld, 80, a descendant of Robert Burns and an authority on the Scottish poet's life and Scottish history, died today after a five weeks' illness.

A different kind of identification by relationship is illustrated by the following example:

> A 30-year-old father of five was stabbed to death Saturday night in a dispute on the street near his home in the Porterfield section of Avon. The victim was identified as. . . .

Marital status. Many newspapers have accepted the feminists' viewpoint that it is unequal treatment to distinguish between single and married women without doing the same for men. The title Ms. is in widespread use, as is the practice of using only last names after a first mention in accordance with how a person wants to be known. Alternatives would be Miss for an unmarried woman, Mrs. for one using her husband's name and Ms. for those who retain their birth names after marriage.

Sex. One of the most controversial issues of language in our time is the question of how to refer to women. Styles differ widely among newspapers. Standard usage of titles until recently was to use "Mr." for men, "Mrs." for married women and "Miss" for unmarried women on first reference. After the first reference, "Mr." was dropped for men, but the titles of "Mrs." and "Miss" were retained for women on subsequent references.

Many modern feminists protested that distinction as sexist. They proposed using instead "Ms." for both married and unmarried women as an equivalent for "Mr." for men. These feminists suggested alternatively that all titles be dropped on second and later references so as to treat men and women equally, although that sometimes created a problem for writers in distinguishing between people of the same surname when men and women were mentioned in a single story.

There is a similar problem in the use of pronouns. Traditional practice had been to use the masculine "he" or "him" in cases where the reference was to all people, both male and female. Feminists objected to that masculine superior rule. They suggested more neutral usage, which can be achieved by using "they" or "them" instead of "he" or "him" in such situations. More recently, as an alternative to "they," many feminists have argued for using "s/he", which some writers and readers find awkward.

Most newspapers today properly are striving for non-sexist language in their news columns and are trying to achieve it in a way that makes for clarity and lack of awkwardness in prose. No one has yet found a way to accomplish both of these objectives in a manner that pleases all those interested in language issues.

Occasion. A person's part in a news story must be explained no matter how else he is identified.

> Prince Otto of Norway, who is on a two-month study tour of the United States, will visit Chicago Oct. 12–13.

> A mother, burned in a school bus-gasoline trailer crash which killed 31 persons Aug. 14, 1977, won a $30,000 out-of-court settlement Monday.

Picking the Identification

The proper method by which to identify a person must be decided in every case. The appropriate identification should be sought in the case of a person with a number of achievements or a considerable news past, as

> Harold Bank, president of the senior class, today announced committees for class day.
> Harold "Bud" Bank, football captain, will not be a candidate for the basketball team this winter.

The Associated Press Managing Editors once debated the propriety of identifying former New York Governor Thomas E. Dewey as "a two-time failure as a Republican presidential candidate" years after his candidacies and in stories that did not deal with national politics. The consensus was that in many instances recalling that part of Dewey's "news past" was poor journalism. The same arguments applied to Adlai Stevenson II.

Sometimes the occasion calls for special identifications for prominent persons, identifications that would be inappropriate at most other times.

> Cleveland, July 25—(AP)—Federal Judge Paul Jones, once a football player himself, will hear injunction suits against Bobby Freeman and Jack Locklear, who jumped contracts with a Canadian pro team to join the Cleveland Browns.
>   [Baltimore *Sun*]

Double Identification

Sometimes, especially in obituary stories, more than one identification may be crowded into the lead, as

James Miller, retired chairman of the board of Miller & Co., wholesale drug concern, and a crusader for government reform, better education for blacks and many other humanitarian causes, died Friday night at his home, 620 Park Ave., after a long illness.

Synonyms

It is impossible, however, to use more than two or three identifications without making the lead awkward. One way out of this difficulty is to use the points of identification as synonyms for the person's name after the name itself has been used once. In this way, nicknames, reputation, news past, various titles and so on can be brought in and repetition of the name or of personal pronouns avoided, as

Former Alderman Guy L. Millard today charged that the local Fair Employment Practices Commission is failing to perform its functions.

Chief backer of the commission when he was a member of the City Council, Millard now believes the agency's work is being sabotaged. The 78-year-old president of the Royal Dye Works said he has personally interviewed 20 local workers who had sought the commission's help in vain.

Identification as the Feature

When the achievement, reputation, occasion or news past by which a person may be identified seems more important or better known than the person's name, the identification should precede the name, as

Murray, Ky., July 28—(AP)—The man who wrote the official history of General Dwight Eisenhower's unified European command will deliver the commencement address at Murray State College's summer exercises next Friday.

He is Dr. Forrest C. Pogue, commissioned by President Eisenhower to write a history of his World War II record, "Supreme Command."

Indefinite "Who"

When the *what* of the story is more important than the *who,* the identification may be featured, names being delayed until the second paragraph, as

A 32-year-old Congregational minister has been named director of Youth Inc., a new nondenominational religious research agency.

The Rev. Ernest S. Ernst, minister of the Westchester Community Church since 1973, will take over direction of the agency in January at Boone, Iowa.

When Unfair

Experts in the field object to use of "former mental patient" even when accurate. They contend its use is as unfair as it would have been to refer to St. Paul as "a former persecutor of Christians" or to Gandhi as "a former convict" or to Thomas Jefferson as "a former slaveholder." In some instances, such as obituaries, many people have similar reservations about mentioning criminal records, although writing about the death of Al Capone would have been difficult without mentioning something about his criminal background.

To be avoided is any attempt to correlate appearance with personality or character. Fads and fashion change. From the Revolutionary War to the Civil War, all American presidents (Washington through Buchanan) were clean shaven. From the Civil War to World War I every president (Lincoln through Taft with the exception of McKinley) had a beard and/or mustache. From World War I to the present all of the presidents (Wilson through Reagan) again have been clean shaven. This should be sobering evidence when it is attempted to classify people by appearance. No personality traits scale, including ones based on bodily characteristics, ever has stood the test of scientific scrutiny.

Organizations

Organizations as well as persons must be identified adequately:

BY TYPE
Directors of the Monument Builders of America, Inc., a national association of retail monument dealers, today praised the refurbished Statue of Liberty.

BY PURPOSE
Milltown's Transit Authority, set up to bring order out of the city's long existent transportation deficiencies, has ended a year of operation with a record of what some say is substantial accomplishments but others contend is inadequate.

The eight-man board held its first meeting Jan. 29, 1981, in offices at 35 Elm St., beginning operations with the backing of a $2 million fund made up of two equal contributions from the city and state, joint sponsors of the enterprise.

As a municipal authority, it has the power, fixed by state law, to acquire and operate transportation lines in and around Milltown.

BY ACHIEVEMENT
The Alameda County Fair, which has been called America's "jockey incubator", has a record number of apprentices participating in its 12-day race meeting, which opened today.

BY REPUTATION
The Milltown Associates, which for 23 years promoted city beautification, will disband Jan. 1.

In stories related to important public issues—controversial matters—brief identification of an organization usually is not enough. The interpretative reporter may have to write a parenthetical paragraph, sidebar or full-length feature to provide proper understanding of what is involved. Readers cannot judge the true nature of a group by a high-sounding title. Typical situations in which full-length identification of an organization may be necessary include the following:

1. When the name resembles closely that of another group whose outlook is different. Example: the National Council of the Churches of Christ in the United States of America and the American Council of Christian Churches.
2. When a powerful group takes a stand on a public issue or a pending piece of legislation. In such cases it may be wise to point out whether the immediate action is consistent with previous activities by the same group. It may be possible to throw light on any selfish motives by revealing the business or other connections of the group's leadership or the general nature of its membership.
3. When a new group is organized, especially when its aims are expressed in semantically vague terms or it seems interested in only a single measure or matter of public interest. In such cases it may be a "front" organization for some other older interest group. Identification of the leadership may cast more light on the organization's real purposes than a quotation from its charter or constitution.
4. When an organization is involved in an act of force or violence. In such cases it may be necessary to seek reasons for the group's very existence in the social, economic or political conditions that brought it into being. Care must be taken not to place the blame for any disturbance on the victims of it rather than on its perpetrators, regardless of the prestige factor involved.

Places

Places must be identified when they are not widely known or when significant or the feature of the story, as

> Purchase of the 1600 block on Palmer Road for a new junior high school was announced today by the Board of Education. Twenty-three private dwellings, almost all of them condemned by the Department of Health, now occupy the site.

A place's news past or its proximity to another place previously in the news may be the best identification; often it is the feature:

> Within a few feet of the spot where once grew the elm under which George Washington accepted command of the Continental Army, 25 Boston University students Tuesday organized the Army of American Liberation. Its purpose is to "wage incessant warfare against forces which are destroying American democracy."

Places, as individuals, have reputations that may be used to identify them, as

> Sauk City, Minn., the "Gopher Prairie" of the native son Sinclair Lewis' "Main Street . . ."
> Reno, Nev., divorce capital of the United States . . .
> Tarrytown, near which Rip Van Winkle allegedly took his long nap . . .

Events

Events may be identified and explained

1. By their significance (the occasion).
2. By their importance in relation to other events (comprehensive leads and stories).
3. By relating them to the "atmosphere" in the light of which they must be understood (the situation).
4. By their probable consequence (prediction).
5. By definite reference to preceding events to which they are related (tie-backs).
6. By the coincidence between them and other events.

Occasions

Circumstances of a news event—purpose, importance, significance and so forth—must be made clear, as

> The most crippling airline strike in the nation's history entered its 16th day Saturday and continued to strand travelers, disrupt tours and snag air freight service.   [Lincoln (Neb.) *Journal*]

Often the feature of the story may be found in the purpose or importance of the occasion that is the subject of the story, as

> Fort Washakie, Wyo.—(UP)—An age-old tradition was broken here when an Indian woman with white blood in her veins became a "chief" of the Arapahoe tribe.

The comparison between the immediate event and preceding similar events may be pointed out, either in the lead paragraph or shortly thereafter, as

> For the first time in memory, neither political party has a contest for any office in Crow County in the April 8 primary election.

Comprehensive Leads and Stories

The comprehensive lead is correlative and explanatory. Used in straight news writing, it is not opinionated, however, because it deals with the incontrovertible.

One kind of comprehensive lead attempts to interpret the immediate news in the light of previous events, as

> Six more witnesses Friday were called before the federal grand jury investigating the distribution of juke boxes in Farwell Township.

> Further evidence that the voters of this city may have elected a "reform" administration last month was provided by today's order by Mayor L. O. Oliver closing all massage parlors that are in violation of municipal health ordinances.

A comprehensive lead emphasizes situations. When several stories related to the same general news event are received, they may be combined into one story and a general roundup or comprehensive lead be written. This type of lead is suitable particularly for election stories, stories of disasters, and weather stories. Facts on which a comprehensive lead and story of this sort are written usually are gathered by more than one reporter or correspondent.

Atmosphere

In these days of fast communication, new ideas, movements, slang expressions and so forth spread rapidly.

Evidently encouraged by the success of similar organizations in scores of other nearby cities, more than 200 owners have organized to prevent spraying of elm trees.

Predictions

The significance of an event may be explained by pointing out the probable consequences or likely "next steps."

The City Council's Select Crime Commission starts five days of public hearings Wednesday—probably the last hearings the panel will hold, according to Chairman Robert Wilson.

The Tie-Back

The tie-back is the part of the lead of a story that shows the relation between the immediate news and some previous news event. In the following examples, the tie-backs are in italics:

Miss Colista Connor, 20, reputed heiress to a $500,000 fortune, *who disappeared mysteriously a week ago and returned Wednesday night to explain she was "on vacation,"* was gone again today.

Five hundred and fifty-two *additional* influenza cases were quarantined in Will County today, *a slight increase over Thursday's figures,* while six deaths were recorded from flu and 14 more from pneumonia.

The Follow-Up _____

Much of the news in any edition of a newspaper is related in some way to other news. It usually takes more than a single article to tell any story. After the first account has appeared, there usually are new developments.

Ability to sense phases of a news story that must be investigated further (followed up) is a valuable asset to a reporter or editor.

The Second-Day Story

The second-day story of any event may include (1) new information not available when the first story was written, (2) causes and motives not included in the first story, (3) more recent developments, results and consequences since the first story and (4) opinions regarding the event.

Latest developments always are emphasized in follow-up stories, and the use of a tie-back is a rigid rule. Never should the writer of a news story presume that a reader has seen the previous story or stories. Just as each installment of a serial story is prefaced by a brief summary of what has gone before, so each news story related to a single event has a short reference to previous news stories.

The tie-back usually is inserted in the lead in the form of a phrase or dependent clause, but any grammatical device may be used; sometimes the tie-back is delayed until the second paragraph.

New Information

A 44-year-old Ardmore woman who was found unconscious on Coulter Street near Sibley Avenue, a block from her home, was in serious condition at Bryn Mawr Hospital today while police searched for an unidentified man believed to have attacked her without motive.   [Philadelphia *Daily News*]

Cause—Motive

Four firemen who perished in a flaming back-draft that surged through the Backstage Night Club early Tuesday morning died while fighting a fire which was deliberately, criminally set.

That flat charge came from Fire Marshal Frank Kelly, chief of the San Francisco fire prevention and investigation bureau.

"The fire was not accidental," Chief Kelly declared following more than 24 hours of investigation. . . .   [San Francisco *Chronicle*]

New Development

By Frank Ryan
UNITED PRESS INTERNATIONAL

Rep. James Lewis (R-West Bend)—convicted of lying to a grand jury about a bizarre laser gun scheme—was sentenced to six months in prison Wednesday.

U.S. Judge James E. Doyle said Lewis—who also will surrender his seat in the Legislature—had to go to prison "to send the words to others" the penalty for lying under oath will be severe.

Opinion

Angry parents today charged city transit authority officials with neglect in the crossing death of an 8-year-old boy.

A system whereby one man controls two crossings at Flournoy and Lexington at Long endangers the lives of children in three schools, the parents declared.

Donald Kieft, 5227 W. Lexington Ave., was crushed to death Monday when he attempted to cross the tracks at Flournoy on a bicycle.

The crossings are protected by gates. So many trains traveling at a high rate of speed pass the intersections in the residential district that the lone gateman keeps the gates lowered even when trains are not approaching. . . .

Featurizing the Follow-up

An important news story breaks too fast to permit investigation of its feature possibilities. By a later edition or the next day, however, the features are developed either in a rewritten story, or in supplementary stories (sidebars). If reporters find themselves stuck without new facts, they may simply retell the story in feature style:

Laramie Boomerang

A freak accident was investigated early this morning when an automobile belonging to Ralph Conwell, 803 E. Flint St., crashed into a parked pickup belonging to C. H. Melvin, 657 N. Eighth St., and then crashed into the front of the Melvin home.

Police said apparently the Conwells were starting on a trip and after taking the car out of his garage, Mr. Conwell got out of the car to check if the garage was locked and the lights were out inside.

The car started creeping forward headed west on Flint. Mrs. Conwell, who was in the car and had on a safety belt, attempted to halt the car by applying the foot brake and inadvertently applied pressure to the accelerator.

The car surged forward hitting the curb and climbing it at the corner of Flint and Eighth and then headed north, striking glancingly on the outside of the Melvin pickup, also headed north, which was parked next to the curb, knocking the pickup up onto the curb.

The Conwell car continued and jumped the curb to the right and came to a stop after uprooting a large lilac bush and smashing into the front of the Melvin home.

The impact of the car was just beneath the window of the bedroom where Mr. and Mrs. Melvin were sleeping. Although the wall was driven in about ten inches from the impact, the window pane remained intact.

Police said there were no injuries reported to them.

Laramie Bulletin

It was 4 a.m. Tuesday.

Mr. and Mrs. Ralph Conwell were parked in front of their home ready to leave for a vacation at their ranch near Daniel, Wyo.

Conwell started the car. Mrs. Conwell was secure in a new safety belt next to the driver's seat.

Conwell remembered he left the garage door open and left the car to close it.

The car began rolling.

Mrs. Conwell struggled to get out of her "secure" position, gave up the idea and reached for the steering wheel and the brake.

She got the wheel, but hit the accelerator with her foot.

Around the corner she went, her husband running after her, the horn honking.

The car struck a parked ton truck, threw it 40 feet, jumped the curb, hit a 25-year-old lilac bush, threw it several feet, and smashed into the bedroom of Conwell's next door neighbors—Mr. and Mrs. C. H. Melvin.

Said Mrs. Conwell:

"It was the safety belt that saved me. You can never tell when an accident is going to happen."

Said Mrs. Melvin: "I thought it was a drunken driver."

Said Mr. Melvin: "My mother-in-law planted that bush here 25 years ago. I never thought it'd save our lives."

Mr. Conwell wasn't available for comment—he went back to the ranch, leaving his wife behind.

Second-Day Comment

Whenever the president delivers an important message, the Supreme Court hands down a significant decision, a new scientific discovery is announced or any one of a number of unusual events occurs, newspapers and press associations scour the country to obtain opinions from persons qualified to comment cogently. In such stories exaggeration must be avoided, as in the following piece in which generalizations were limited to the principals who are mentioned specifically.

By Brian Sullivan
AP SCIENCE WRITER

Linus Pauling's claims for Vitamin C as a powerful weapon against the common cold have resulted in a spurt of sales at many of the nation's drugstores. But in the scientific community, with a notable exception, the response has been more subdued.

At Herzog's Drugstore in Buffalo, N.Y., pharmacist Howard Carpenter said sales had at least quadrupled. He said the store has put bottles of Vitamin C into a basket adorned with Pauling's picture.

Many scientists remain generally skeptical, however. Some refused to be drawn into the matter at all, and others were cautious. A Baylor University Medical School virus-cold researcher said Pauling's ideas are based on an uncontrolled experiment.

Another warned against continued, mass dosage without investigating it first.

The exception is Dr. Albert Szent-Gyorgyi of the Marine Biological Laboratory at Falmouth, Mass., who won the 1937 Nobel Prize in medicine for isolating Vitamin C in 1928. . . .

Localization

A news item originating in a faraway place often has a local "angle," or it may cause readers to ask, "Could it happen here?"

Local parents need have no fear that babies in local hospitals will become confused and cause another Pittman-Garner baby mix-up a generation or so hence.

So thorough is the identification system employed in this community's three hospitals that their authorities consider mixups like Madeline Louise Garner-Pittman's in Georgia last month an impossibility.

Although many hospitals throughout the country supplement foot and palm printing as an added precaution, adequate supervision is the only real safeguard, in the opinion of H. James Baxter, superintendent of General Hospital since 1980. . . .

Reminiscences

Similarly, readers may ask, "Has anything like that ever happened before?" Good reporters draw parallels between the present and the past and relate anecdotes brought to mind by the immediate news item.

By Zay N. Smith

If there is a hall of infamy for murderers, John Wayne Gacy, killer of 33 men and boys, has found his place: No one in U.S. history has been convicted in as many deaths.

But others have tried for the distinction—and may have killed more.

One was Herman Webster Mudgett. He came to live at 63rd and Wallace in Chicago in 1883. Police searched his three-story home 10 years later and found torture chambers, vats of acid and a pit of lime.

Mudgett would woo women, gain their property and then take them on a house tour. He confessed to the murders of 47. He was suspected in the disappearace of as many as 200—all visitors to the Chicago World's Fair of 1893.

Mudgett was known as a pleasant enough neighbor. He took 15 minutes to die on the gallows.

Johann Adolph Hoch, another Chicagoan, was less forthright. He lived as bigamist at the turn of the century. He was accused in the deaths of as many as 50 wives. He told police he had married "too many unhealthy women."

The list grows crowded after that:

- Bella Sorenson Gunness was the most efficient murderess in U.S. history. She lived on an Indiana farm in the early 1900s. She butchered hogs—and boyfriends. She would drug their coffee, bash in their heads, dissect them and bury them in the barnyard. The number came to at least 16—possibly as many as 28.
- Elmer Wayne Henley Jr. and David Brooks made money on the side by procuring boys for Dean Corll of Houston. Each of the boys was worth $200. At least 27 were molested, mutilated and murdered. Henley shot Corll dead at an acrylic-sniffing party. Henley and Brooks were convicted in the murders.
- Juan Corona was convicted in the murders of 25 migrant laborers. All were mutilated with a machete and buried in California orchards or along a riverbed. Corona's conviction was overturned because of incompetence of counsel and he awaits a new trial.
- Herbert Mullin was voted most likely to succeed by his 1965 high school class. He learned about LSD in San Francisco after that and succeeded in killing three women, four men and six boys in northern California in 1973. He said he was trying to prevent an earthquake.

Howard Unruh walked out on a Camden, N.J., street one day in 1949 and shot 13 people dead.

Charles Whitman climbed a tower at the University of Texas in 1966 and killed 16 with a high-powered rifle. That was the same year Richard Speck stabbed eight student nurses to death on Chicago's Southeast Side. Then came Charles Manson and his California murder cult. Then came "Son of Sam"— David Berkowitz—who murdered six in New York City.

And then came Gacy.   [Chicago *Sun-Times*]

The Running Story

Good newspapers try to follow up stories as long as there are new angles or developments to investigate or until reader interest lags. Each succeeding story is written to bring the situation up to date.

In case of a flood, war, important court trial or political contest (to mention only a few of the possibilities), daily, almost hourly, stories are written to give the latest developments. A murder story frequently occupies the front page for weeks.

Note how the following story developed day by day, as shown by three successive leads from the Kansas City *Star:*

> About 124,000 women here today are being given the opportunity to state whether they desire to serve as jurors. The ballots should be returned to the Jackson County courthouse by June 10.

> Eighty-six ballots on jury service for women had been received this afternoon at the jury commission office in the Jackson County courthouse. Twenty-nine indicated a desire to serve on juries here. Fifty-seven declined to serve.

> The number of women desiring jury service was increasing this afternoon when 314 of the 1,440 ballots received by the jury commission indicated that more than one in four women responding to the poll were willing to be jurors. The remaining 1,136 do not desire to serve on Jackson County juries other than federal.

The Revived Story

Days, weeks or months later a reporter may be assigned to find out "what ever happened to so-and-so" or regarding "such-and-such."

By B. J. McFarland
PORTLAND, ORE. (UPI)

What happened to D. B. Cooper, history's first and only successful parachuting sky bandit?

Where is he and where did he stash the cash?

Three years ago on Thanksgiving Eve Cooper boarded a Northwest Orient Airlines flight in Portland for a short hop to Seattle.

The plane wasn't off the ground five minutes when it all started.

Cooper, threatening to set off an explosive, demanded and got $200,000 in $20 bills delivered, along with three parachutes, to the plane in Seattle.

After allowing the passengers to get off, he ordered the crew to fly the 727 to Reno, following a course down western Washington and Oregon before cutting across the mountains. Somewhere en route he bailed out the tail exit.

It set off a chain of similar skyjackings that changed the face of air travel.

But only Cooper beat the law at taking the money and jumping. The law still is looking for him.

"The case is an active one, not only here but throughout the United States," said Julius Mattson, agent in charge of the Portland FBI office.

"We're still getting leads," he said, "but not quite as heavy as we were. The case still is in the public mind and when the public thinks of it, it also thinks of us.

"There really has been no substantive development. The work now is mostly eliminating possibilities, proving or disproving tips.

"Not one of the $20 bills has turned up."

Cooper apparently strapped the money to his body for the jump. A theory that he may have fallen into Lake Merwin east of Woodland in southwest Washington about 30 miles north of Portland could not be proved following an exhaustive search by the FBI and Army troops from Ft. Lewis, Wash.

[Pittsburgh *Press*]

Investigations

Often follow-up assignments are simply for satisfying curiosity, but minor disclosures from follow-up investigations may produce more significant information. Newspapers frequently keep after someone, particularly a public official, to correct an evil brought to light by some news event.

By William Clements

Last year a team of Sun-Times reporters and photographers took an in-depth look at nearly 100 of the city's neighborhood parks.

They found the parks beaten up, abused, misused, neglected and rejected. Scores of once-proud parks and playgrounds were engulfed in litter and broken equipment, beset by rowdies, rife with graffiti and riddled with fear.

Today, over-all conditions haven't changed much.

This despite the addition of sorely needed maintenance crews and recreation workers to the hardest hit and most neglected of the parks.

Sun-Times photographers returned recently to find out what improvements the Chicago Park District has made at several sites spotlighted in last year's series. They found that:

- The arching, once beautiful, boathouse at Humboldt Park is still marred with graffiti, broken sidewalks and battered benches. The park's meandering lagoon is cluttered with cans, broken bottles and discarded fence railings. The walkway behind its famous garden is still broken and messy.
- The basin of Garfield Park's unique lily pond, once a quiet haven for West Siders seeking an interlude from some of the harsher realities of city life, remains pockmarked, crushed and unusable. The boathouse roof, an architectural treasure, is a wreck.
- Outdoor washroom facilities, such as those in Garfield and Douglas parks, remain boarded up and broken, posing major security problems for park users.
- Many benches in nearly all of the large inland parks, including Columbus, Washington, Douglas, Ogden and Garfield, are broken and unusable.

The Park District says that as the summer progresses, needed repairs will be made. The fact remains, however, that not much has changed during the past year in the 7,289-acre system which employs 4,300 and spends more than $160 million annually. . . .

[Chicago *Sun-Times*]

The Resurrected Story

Sometimes a mystery is years in the solving, or a new fact is discovered which casts new light on some historical event or personage. In writing such a story the "tie-back" rule must be observed, although the lead seldom is adequate to supply all of the "resurrected" facts that must be told. For instance, if a criminal who has long evaded capture is arrested, the story may include a recapitulation of his crime and may even be accompanied by pictures and diagrams taken or made at the time of its commission. Later, when the person is brought to trial, the story may be repeated, and again if the criminal is put to death legally.

In every news office there are notations of stories which are said to be "hanging fire," and which may break at any time. Verdicts are withheld, a committee delays its report, there is a postponement in the filing of a suit, or an important person does not make an announcement of which he has hinted.

> North Manchester, July 4.—Midnight lights burned by a Dr. Elies Ohmart prior to 1885 were explained here when Tom Richarson came across an ancient, handwritten record book in the attic of the John W. Ulrey home, which he recently purchased.
>
> The book contained notes of scientific inventions including a telephone patented by Bell in 1876, an electric arc lamp, the separation of aluminum from clay, a mechanical table of logarithms and an electric sign board. . . .
>
> [Fort Wayne (Ind.) *News-Sentinel*]

Rewrite

The day of the newspaper scoop on some major event is largely gone. In the first place, except in a small and dwindling number of large cities, there is no competitor for the one surviving daily newspaper to scoop. Furthermore, the important day-by-day news of the world is gathered mostly by two press associations (Associated Press and United Press International) and transmitted simultaneously to all subscribers. Most important, radio and television have made it impossible for any periodical to be first with such news.

Newspapers and magazines amplify, explain and interpret the news sometimes shortly after its occurrence, but, often, weeks, months or years later when new information becomes available or the passage of time gives new perspective. Newspapers today often are competitors of magazines in the attempt to obtain first rights to the memoirs of persons able to cast new light on old events.

The Nature of Rewrite

Within newspaper offices the title rewriter now is used to designate a person who remains in the office taking news over the telephone, mostly from the paper's own reporters. There persists, however, a considerable amount of rewriting in the old sense; "borrowed," with little or no attempt to obtain additional facts, from other printed sources. That is especially so in recent years in the handling of celebrity gossip items—"soft news"—that has become a prominent part of most newspapers.

Such sources include press releases, community newspapers, trade journals, house organs, public and private reports and announcements, newsletters intended for special interest groups and out-of-town newspapers.

Some papers run a column of news briefs or oddities from the day's wire report. Stories in the earlier editions of one's own newspaper may be rewritten for later editions, when new facts are obtained or to clarify the story.

Usually, the rewrite person attempts to compose an item that will read as though it had been written up on original information. In the attempt to play up a new fresh angle the writer must avoid killing a good lead and burying an undoubted feature. Awareness of the extent to which radio and television have taken the edge off some of the news may lead to this error unless there is conscious effort to avoid it.

Picking the Feature

Rewrite persons should obey the rules of good news writing which, among other things, means that the lead of the story should play up the feature of the item. The difficulty is obvious when it is realized that this feature probably already was played up in the original story. The poorer the first story, the easier the task of the rewrite person who must do more than merely restate or reword the original lead.

Rewrite persons, with no facts in addition to those of the original story, therefore, ask themselves such questions, as these:

1. Did the writer play up the real feature of the story or is it buried some place in the article?
2. Is there another feature of equal or almost equal importance as the one which the writer used that might be played up?
3. Can I make my story read like a follow-up story by emphasizing the latest developments mentioned in the first story, or by suggesting the next probable consequence?
4. Can I write a comprehensive lead that will interpret this item of news in the light of other news?
5. Is there any other news today with which I can combine this story?
6. In the case of stories appearing in publications outside of the immediate community, is there a local angle that can be played up?

Getting the news accurately into readers' minds and keeping it there requires careful attention to the mechanics of clear writing. It also demands vigorous efforts to bring the reader up to date on fresh aspects of the story as the story evolves. It requires stories that contain human elements and vivid scene setting to bring the substance alive and to give it nuance and context. It requires intelligence, artistry and the ability to interpret and reinterpret, again and again. Reporters trying to make an important ongoing story clear never should be content with the last set of answers they got to their questions. They should be looking for better, fresher questions, for more up-to-date interpretations.

CHAPTER

9

Giving It Substance

A. Completing the Account
1. *Factual Background*
2. *Eyewitness Accounts*
3. *Sidebars*
4. *Team Reporting*
5. *Localization*

B. Interpretations
1. *How Reporters Interpret*
2. *Causes and Motives*
3. *Significance*

4. *Analysis*
5. *Comparisons*
6. *Forecasts*

C. Impressionistic Reporting

D. Providing Perspective
1. *Résumés*
2. *Surveys*
3. *Situations and Trends*
4. *The Human Aspect of Issues, Trends*

Experienced reporters who develop specialties often become recognized experts. They write not only authoritative newspaper articles but magazine pieces and books as well. Their vast amount of background knowledge enables them to give meaning to current happenings. More than that, they become critics in their fields and can warn and forecast and even give advice to policy leaders, including heads of state. They may have a powerful effect upon public opinion.

Later journalistic success is determined by early experience. Nobody, that is, is catapulted into a top position of prestige and influence without having served a long apprenticeship to learn mature work habits and attitudes. Local reporting provides the first and best opportunity for the development of such essential traits as thoroughness, accuracy and resourcefulness. The aspirant for future fame and fortune as an interpretative reporter and writer begins by becoming a superior gatherer of so-called straight news to be handled as objectively as possible. In addition future interpretative experts get around more than their competitors, digging deeper for often neglected facts that provide understanding and perspective. Such newsgatherers ask regarding every assignment:

1. What happened? That is, what *really* happened—the complete story, not just the end results of a series of incidents.

2. Why (or how) did it happen? That is, what is the explanation?
3. What does it mean?
4. What next? In the light of today's news, what may be expected to happen tomorrow?
5. What's beneath the surface? What are the trends, ideologies, situations and so on, of which one should be aware so that an overt news incident will make sense? What is the historical background?
6. What are its human aspects? How can the realities beneath the surface be brought to life for readers?

The reporter seeks answers to those questions from as many varied knowledgable sources as time allows.

Completing the Account _____

Factual Background

When an event of major significance occurs, because of the mass of detailed information involved and from lack of time and space, first news stories may be in the straight news-writing tradition, leaving the more extensive interpretation for another edition or day. If, however, the reporter has an adequate knowledge and understanding of preceding events related to the one at hand, even the first story, prepared in haste, will have greater substance.

The best reporters will recall the history of a bill or ordinance and of previous attempts to promote similar legislation. They know whether lawmakers are behaving consistently, the identity of individuals and groups in support or opposition and other facts that enable readers to come to a better understanding of the immediate occurrence.

Eyewitness Accounts

To supplement the formal stories, it is common practice to ask victims of disasters (train wrecks, floods, fires) to relate their personal experiences. Often, such accounts are ghostwritten or are printed under the by-lines of the principals "as told to" some staff writer. Reporters themselves write eyewitness accounts of important scenes they have witnessed. Such stories are more informal than straight news accounts and usually provide graphic word pictures of what happened.

By William Michelmore

Dead workers were hanging from a safety ladder, and other workers frantically tore open their shirts in a desperate struggle to breath and then "dropped dead like flies."

That was how rescue squads described the grisly scene Friday night after a carbon monoxide leak at the Jones & Laughlin Steel Co. plant in East Chicago, Ind.

Six employees, including three foremen, died from inhaling the gas. . . .

[Chicago *Tribune*]

Photojournalism, including motion pictures and television, has not yet made written descriptions obsolete. Nor is it likely to do so for some time, if for no other reason than that cameramen are not always present at news events when we need to answer the question "What did it look like?" in order to present a complete account. Before reporters can describe well, they must be able to observe. Careful observation means noting features that escape the untrained spectator. A bizarre vocabulary containing innumerable adjectives is not essential. The reader, in fact, will "see" best what the writer is describing if the words are familiar. Ambiguous qualitative adjectives such as "handsome" or "delicate" should be omitted, and figures of speech, historical and literary allusions and other rhetorical devices must be readily understandable. Concrete, specific details, particularly those of the sights, sounds, smells, tastes and touches of the scene being depicted, are what bring such stories alive.

In selecting anecdotes to relate and persons to describe, caution must be exercised so that they are either important in their own right or typical of a general situation. Otherwise a distorted impression can be created. A typical situation in which this might occur is a mine cave-in or flood or similar disaster. At the scene, probably accompanying rescue workers, the reporter is attempting to describe the reaction of victims and others so the reader can get the "feel" of the story. It must be realized that one sobbing woman does not constitute a hysterical mob. The reader must be able to depend upon the integrity of the reporter.

Sidebars

When an important news events occurs, reporters often use sidebars to round out the complete account. A sidebar deals with phases of a story as a whole that conceivably could be included in the main account but not without either lengthening it too much or sacrificing some details. For example, when an office building in Chicago's Loop exploded, among the anecdotal sidebars were the following: (1) 105,000 square feet of new glass being rushed to city to replace show-window glass broken; (2) analysis of city ordinances covering gas leakage which allegedly caused the blast; (3) description of army of glaziers at work in area; (4) police pass system to admit workers employed in area; (5) refusal of pass to a window washer, obviously because there were no windows left to wash; (6) symposium of eyewitness accounts; (7) narrow escape of nearby elevated tower operator; (8) instructions on how to enter area; (9) Red Cross activities; (10) list of buildings whose windows were blown out.

When the news relates to a scheduled event, several reporters may be assigned to cover different angles. One reporter, for instance, may stay close to the wife of a visiting celebrity; at the same time, another reporter may concentrate on the crowd, noting its size and nature, ever watchful for unusual personalities and incidents. Others may observe the behavior of the police, marshals, secret-service men and the like, or they may interview members of the party of either the guest or the host or both. Someone else, who might not even need to be present, can compare the occasion with similar ones in the past.

Team Reporting

The page 1 streamer headline of the Los Angeles *Times* was DAY OF DISASTER and the two-line head read "Quake Leaves 42 Dead, 1,000 Hurt; Periled Dam Forces 40,000 to Flee." A picture and an area map occupied about one-third of the page. There were two inside pages devoted entirely to pictures and there were enough other scattered pictures to total the equivalent of a third page. The main account began in the right-hand column on page 1 and jumped for about the equivalent of a full page on inside pages. The headlines of 26 other stories related to the disaster suggest their contents and consequently the extent of the coverage. William Thomas, subsequently promoted from metropolitan editor to editor, who directed the operation, said it was perhaps "the closest we have come to accomplishing" the objective of bringing "some of our interpretative and analytical techniques to the spot news story."

Virtually all of the stories were finished within six hours of the quake. The headlines: (1) 39 Still Missing in Hospital Ruins; (2) Reservoir Dwarfs Old One in Baldwin Hills [there was fear that it might give way]; (3) First a Rumble, Then Houses Catch Fire, Glass Shatters [an eyewitness impressionist account]; (4) Reagan Favors Gas Tax Rise to Repair Streets; (5) Antelope Valley Cut Off as Bridge Collapses; (6) Shock Stronger Than One That Hit Long Beach; (7) New Skyscrapers Ride It Out, Damage Slight; (8) Disaster Planning Brings Quick Aid; (9) Olive View Hospital Termed Total Loss; (10) City Schools Will Stay Closed Today; (11) Some Guard Units Activated for Duty; (12) Partial Death List Gives Scant Details; (13) Beagle Was the Alarm for Sleeper [terrified dog jumped on bed]; (14) Sea Bubbles Off Malibu Most of Day; (15) Phone, Water, Electric, Gas Services Disrupted; (16) It Was A-Test to Las Vegas; (17) Little Quake Insurance in Effect, Broker Says; (18) Quake Talks Delayed by the Quake [relates to meeting of Structural Engineering Association on subject of laws on earthquake safety]; (19) 7 Emergency Shelters Open to Quake Victims; (20) Special Loans to Be Offered; (21) Homeless Offered Vacant VA Houses; (22) Expert Tells What to Do in a Quake; (23) Care Urged in Drinking Water Use; (24) Quake Interferes with Apollo Lines [Apollo 14 was homeward bound]; (25) Eclipse Lineup Linked to Quake by Scientist; (26) Hundreds of Aftershocks.

Thomas reminisced concerning the experience,

> One editor was in charge: I, along with considerable help from two assistants. Any complex coverage has to be directed by one person or it becomes incoherent.
>
> From there, you play it by ear. You send out to cover all conceivable action, which really is not difficult, and everything stems from this. A guy at the shattered hospital comments that it seemed a long time before help came, and that gets you to thinking about the disaster warning setup. Did it work and how well and exactly how? A report comes in that the injured are going to such a place, and as you send a team there you wonder how the evacuation process was planned and did it do the job, etc. A reporter wonders how much of the damage is covered by insurance, and you say, "That's a good idea" and you assign a man to that aspect.

As you're doing all this, you are listing your areas of coverage and deciding how to break them into dovetailing stories. Here is where our earthquake coverage differed from, say, our Watts riot coverage. The same thing was done during Watts but, instead of interpretative pieces, as we did on the riots, we assigned them for immediate publication.

Several things made this possible. First and most important is a staff who can do it. You could never do this under the old rewrite setup, where there are eight guys suitable mainly for leg work for every one who is a competent writer. We did away with the rewrite concept almost entirely some time ago, and for some years I have hired only writers. So everybody can communicate his own findings, which gives us several desirable things; greater authenticity, greater speed, better and more believable stories all around, a happier staff.

Was it organized, you asked, or random? You'd have to say it was organized in a random manner, or random in an organized manner, whichever you like best. In other words, the story was unfolding as the interpretative package was being put together so it certainly was random to that extent.

But there are certain procedures which experience dictates will bring the best results in such situations (i.e., keeping a number of the best writers in the office to handle the complex interpretative stories you know will develop, even though the temptation is to fire them out into the general area; putting the guys strongest on action reporting into those situations, the guys best on reflective stories into those, etc.). This isn't very clear, but to this extent—and to the extent that you retain a very clear idea where everybody is and what he can be expected to contribute—it is an organized procedure.

I guess you try to be organized to deal effectively with random happenings.

Another outstanding example of teamwork by the Los Angeles *Times* news staff occurred May 25, 1979, when American Airlines Flight 191 crashed shortly after take-off from Chicago's O'Hare field. Most of the 273 killed in the United States' worst commercial aviation disaster were homebound Los Angeles residents or delegates to the American Booksellers Association convention being held in L.A. Dennis A. Britton, editor in charge of that coverage, tells how his staff went into action:

We first heard of the DC-10 crash from one of our Midwest Bureau correspondents who was monitoring a Bearcat Scanner in the Chicago office. He alerted us about half-an-hour before the wires carried the first bulletin. Our second correspondent was out of Chicago and unreachable. So we first sent Bob Secter of the Chicago office to the scene. We then got a Washington Bureau reporter in the air (about an hour after the crash). We talked to every section of the paper here to determine if any other reporters were in the area. We located a sports reporter covering the Angels for us and sent him to headquarters at O'Hare.

While all of this was going on we located a reporter in our lifestyle section who was a multiengine-rated pilot and got him started calling safety experts. Our Business/Financial staff had already made contact with McDonnell-Douglas.

Within two hours of the crash we dispatched a reporter from our Denver office and one from Washington to go to Oklahoma City where the FAA keeps all flight records on all planes which fly in the United States. From this we hoped to determine if the DC-10 had experienced earlier safety problems and how its safety record stacked up against other jumbo jets.

We assigned three editors—two in Los Angeles and one in Washington—to begin monitoring and handling all DC-10 stories.

We kept about five reporters full time on the crash for three days and covered the standard air disaster stories. We then, however, assembled a team of 10 reporters under an assistant national editor (James O. Bell) and set out to find everything we could about the DC-10, how it was certified and its record. We spent hundreds of dollars on computer runs at the FAA facility in Oklahoma City and at Arizona State University's crash study unit. We were forced to file Freedom of Information requests to get public information from the FAA (we *just* got our third of five batches of material March 13, 1980). Over three months we wrote more than a dozen stories. We disbanded the team as a formal entity after three months but three reporters continue to process the FOIA material. We envision more stories, some of which will detail how the manufacturer and the FAA combine sometimes to short-circuit the certification process.

I'm proud to say that we were ahead of most national publications on the DC-10 crash coverage and ahead of all on aftermath coverage.

The day following the crash the Los Angeles *Times* devoted nine columns to stories of the disaster. Coverage in the Chicago papers was, of course, even greater. Here is how the *Tribune* explained its coverage effort:

> The *Tribune* news staff bolted into action even as the black smoke billowed toward the sky.
>
> The ensuing hours would see 41 reporters and writers, 19 photographers, and five artists, along with dozens of copy editors, graphics experts, caption writers, assignment editors, news editors and supervisors putting together the tragic story of the worst aviation disaster in American history.
>
> The responsibility for coordinating the entire operation fell to William Jones, a former Pulitzer Prize winning reporter, city editor, and managing editor-news. Just an hour before the crash a story was written for the Saturday paper announcing his promotion to managing editor.
>
> Jones immediately huddled with Maxwell McCrohon, newly-named editor of the *Tribune,* and John Wagoner, news editor, to advise them what was in the works and what to expect.
>
> "We had a series of news conferences as our coverage developed," Jones said. "In all, it was a magnificent effort by the city desk. It was really a city desk operation."
>
> "Damn near the whole financial and feature departments volunteered," said Bernard Judge, city editor. "If I had needed 60 people to cover the crash I had them. At least 20 reporters not from our staff, including one columnist, were standing by to help."
>
> The final deadline for copy to the composing room for the Green Streak replate was only minutes away when the plane went down.
>
> The replate was held up for 25 minutes while reporters in the office telephoned various sources and relayed their information to a rewrite man, who was able to make a 10-inch-long story for the day's final edition.
>
> Then, with a 4:45 p.m. copy deadline, the rewriteman, working closely with an assistant city editor who was coordinating information from the scene, rewrote and polished his original story for the Saturday Midwest edition—first of the next day's run.
>
> Within the next six hours the entire story was wrapped up. *Tribune* readers

picked up their morning papers Saturday to read: Worst U.S. Crash; 272 die at O'Hare.

The main story on page one was accompanied by a picture, the entire width of the page, of the crash scene with sticks marking spots were bodies had been located. There was also a page one overview story under the headline: 'There was rain of fire falling.'

A page one box listed related stories inside:

A chaplain describing the scene as "Too hot for anything but the last rites"; a report on confusion at the plane's Los Angeles destination; a sidebar on the history of the DC-10; a list of previous air disasters; and a story on other major plane crashes in Chicago.

There was also a full page of photos including an aerial view of the crash site; a story with graphics on the DC-10's statistics and seating arrangements; a sidebar on celebrities aboard the fatal flight; a vivid description of the task of trying to match bits and pieces of flesh; a sidebar on a streetcar crash that killed 34 in Chicago on the same date 29 years earlier; more photos; and a passenger list.

The Sunday paper, which had a 9:25 a.m. Saturday copy deadline for its first edition, picked up from there, starting with a front page strip of exclusive color photos of the DC-10 going down and crashing.

Also on page one was the main story on the investigation into the cause of the crash; an airline pilot's description of the crash; a hospital interview with a man injured on the ground when the plane hit; and a box describing inside stories and where to find them.

First word of the crash reached the city desk simultaneously from police reporter Philip Wattley, who heard a fire chief calmly request crash vehicles via the emergency radio, and from photo assignment editor William Kelly, who was monitoring police and fire calls in the office.

Wattley next used a police line to contact airport security officials who confirmed, "We've got a big one down here!"

On receiving the initial call from Wattley, Associate city editor Donald Agrella and day city editor Sheila Wolfe began dispatching reporters to the scene. Agrella notified day news editor Maz Saxinger of the crash, and alerted Judge.

"I figured we'd need at least 10 people on the way, not counting people to hospitals," Judge said. "You've got to move a drove of people to the scene, the morgue, the hospitals. Most of the good stories come from hospitals if there are survivors."

After determining who had already been sent out, Judge began to assign specific reporters and writers to various aspects of the story. On learning there were no survivors, reporters on the way to hospitals were diverted to the scene, the airport, and airline offices.

"Two-way radios were very helpful here," he said. "We're going to get more of them."

While reporters raced to the scene in the midst of the evening traffic rush, others in the office talked by phone to O'Hare tower, police, fire dispatchers, airline officials, and witnesses in the area.

"Agrella and I sat down and cut a schedule of the stories we expected to have for the Saturday editions," Judge said. "Wolfe was assigned to work solely with Dave Schneidman, the rewrite man doing the main story. William Sluis, assistant night city editor, was put in charge of everything else."

Working with Stephen Lough, national editor, Judge arranged to have Los Angeles correspondent Michael Coakley at the LA airport to talk with friends and relatives waiting in vain for the plane to arrive. David Young, transportation editor, who was aboard a private rail car en-route from Fremont, Neb., was rushed home with the help of rail officials.

Kelly, on the photo desk, meanwhile was sending photographers to the scene, diverting men from other assignments, and calling night workers to come in early. Assistant photo assignment editor James O'Leary kept abreast of developments by monitoring police and fire calls, and lined up a helicopter for aerial photos.

Picture editor Richard Leslie and chief photographer Anthony Berardi Jr. coordinated photo operations.

Enroute to the crash scene photographer Karen Engstrom was redirected to the American Airlines terminal to look for friends and relatives of passengers.

It was there she encountered Michael Laughlin, a free-lance photographer, who had made color shots of the ill-fated plane as it went down. Engstrom out-talked and out-bid competing news media and obtained the photos exclusively for the *Tribune*. She arranged to have the films processed under the watchful eyes of a Federal Bureau of Investigation agent who had taken official possession of them.

At the same time the city desk and photo desks were mobilizing into action, the graphics department began to prepare visual coverage of the disaster.

After discussions between graphics editor Howard Finberg, Gus Hartoonian, graphics art director, and Anton Majeri, his assistant, the Art Department staff was put on stand-by status.

Finberg and graphics coordinator Susan Popson worked with artists, photographers and reporters to prepare a location map; graphics of the plane; a drawing of the engine that fell off; and a sequential graphic of the aircraft's takeoff from runway to crash.

"There must have been a dozen conversations with the art directors about the shape of the graphics, who would do them, when they would be done, and who would come in the next day," Finberg said.

McCrohon, Jones, Judge, Berardi, Hartoonian, and Joseph Leonard, editor, editorial operations, worked through to 3 a.m. to assure that all Saturday stories were cleared and everything was organized for the Sunday editions. Jones came back in early Saturday to supervise the Sunday operation.

"It was a relatively uncomplicated disaster to cover," Judge said afterward. "Everyone was dead. There were no human errors involved. The engine fell off, the plane crashed, and there were no survivors."

Reporters returning from the scene said there was no "feeling of disaster" usually encountered in such tragedies. "There was no identifiable carnage," said Judge. "No looting. Just a field of debris."

The Chicago *Sun-Times* used 28 reporters, ten photographers, two news editors, 12 copy editors, three picture editors, six graphic experts, eight free-lance reporters and two free-lance photographers. For its coverage the paper received a National Headliners Club award. Intensive daily coverage of the disaster and its aftermath continued for more than two weeks before it began to taper off.

In similar critical situations, smaller newspapers respond in the same way as their larger contemporaries. Dale A. Davenport, city editor of the

Harrisburg (Pa.) *Evening News* tells how his paper handled the radiation leakage at the nuclear plant on nearby Three Mile Island:

I learned of an accident involving "some sort of cloud of something" from my Capitol Hill reporter, who got a telephoned tip at home about 8:50 a.m. March 28, 1979, from a colleague who said: "I'm not really interested in this, but your city desk might be since it looks like (just) a local story."

I was fortunate to have three reporters on the staff who at one time or another had covered Three Mile Island nuclear doings, so I assigned one of them to check the tip. Within 10 minutes she had verified that radiation had escaped and that Civil Defense (which now calls itself Pennsylvania Emergency Management Agency) had declared an alert.

I immediately assigned another two reporters to travel to Middletown, one to the TMI observation center where Metropolitan Edison Co. was keeping the press, the other to cover whatever man-in-the-street reaction he could get in Middletown. He later interviewed the mayor and filed a story for the noon edition.

I sent another reporter to the western river bank town of Goldsboro across the river from TMI and he and a reporter from our York bureau covered the story from the York County angle, i.e., what officials and civilians on that side of the river were doing. I also assigned two photographers, one to TMI observation center, which is across the road from the bridge and main entrance to the plant, the other to Goldsboro.

The woman who checked the tip, Mary O. Bradley, remained on the telephone and, working with what notes she gathered from telephone conversations and initial Associated Press reports and a statement phoned in by a Capitol Hill reporter from the lieutenant governor, compiled a story for the first edition, with a closing time of 10:15 a.m. By 10:45 a.m., that edition was on the street.

Within about 20 minutes, she had updated that story and we replaced the front page for the remainder of our 17,000 first edition run. By that time, reporters were filing their first stories from the field and another reporter in the city room, who had been assigned to assist in telephone contacts, also was contributing to the lead story.

By noon, I had compiled and/or edited three sidebar stories and the lead story, which by that time carried three bylines and, in an italic notation at the end, credited three others. Various editors and suburban bureau chiefs also worked on aspects of the story.

Within minutes, by about 12:30 p.m. we filed the fourth lead. In all, 10 reporters contributed facts for it, it was written by two of them and merged electronically into one story by me.

Of course, in succeeding days, all my eight reporters, and those eight assigned to the various bureaus, covered TMI for The Evening News. For about a week, it was virtually the only local story. Decisions about what sidebars were developed were made on a spot basis and in many instances were the ideas of reporters. I turned all my routine duties over to my assistant city editor and supervised solely the TMI story.

On succeeding days, primary assignments were to the TMI observation center for press briefings and Met-Ed and the Nuclear Regulatory Commission (these later were moved to a community building in Middletown), to the state Civil Defense command post, and to the communities surrounding the plant, where human interest sidebars were always available.

Localization

The effects of some news events are felt at considerable distances. Without mention of some of the repercussions, the original story is not complete. For instance, whenever the president of the United States or some other leader of government makes an important announcement, there are reverberations on Capitol Hill, where congressional leaders abandon or alter old tactics or institute new ones. The stock market may be influenced by mere rumor. A Supreme Court decision may affect governmental practices and legal procedures in the states and cities.

In all such and similar cases, the reader wants to know, "How will this affect me?" That is the perspective from which the interpretative reporter should approach his task. In that spirit, the Evanston (Ill.) *Review* figured out the average cost for every man, woman, and child in Illinois of a newly announced federal budget. Similarly, when the United States Supreme Court upheld the blue laws of some Eastern states, the United Press International bureau in Topeka compiled a list of laws still on the books in Kansas regulating behavior on the Sabbath. The Baltimore *Sun* used a similar story to explain how a Supreme Court decision regarding motion-picture censorship would affect Baltimore and Maryland. When Sen. George McGovern revealed in March 1971 that the Vietnam War had caused 920,028 deaths, the Chicago *Daily News* figured out that "If all those killed in the Vietnam war had lived in the same U.S. city, only seven other American cities would be larger."

Many a newspaper has investigated to determine how long the local supply of coal or steel or some other commodity would last in the event a strike continued affecting the faraway source of supply. How a new federal or state law will affect the community specifically, probably always should be explained by the public-spirited local press.

There are, of course, a pro and a con regarding every public issue. Good reporters seek to understand and convey as many varied perspectives as possible. The ethical newspaper considers itself a public forum for the airing of diverse opinions. The obligation, however, is not just to those who wish to express themselves, but primarily to readers so that they can be fully informed. When a new curfew law for adolescents is under consideration, for instance, the paper should seek out persons who are in positions to have intelligent opinions on the subject. This is not the inquiring-reporter technique, which often results in obtaining uninformed and unrepresentative viewpoints. Rather, it is a search for the best informed opinions.

Interpretations _____

It decidedly is not true that "what you don't know won't hurt you." On the contrary, in a democracy it is essential that everyone have access to as many facts as possible in order to form proper judgments and influence public affairs. For almost a century, however, there has been increasing recognition that mere reporting of objective facts is not sufficient to serve the informational needs of a self-governing people. The result: interpretative reporting.

How Reporters Interpret

In gathering information about a news event, the reporter seeks answers to the *who, what, where, when, why* and *how* of whatever happened. Of these, the first four are basic to virtually any account. Offhand, it might be held that not all stories have a *why* or *how* element important enough to engage much of the newsgatherer's attention. Actually, exactly the contrary is the case. In delving into the *what* of most stories, the reporter really is asking "why?" even though the answers he receives may become part of the *what*. The beginning journalist should be aware that doing a thorough job of interviewing for what may seem to be a minor or simple story is training for more penetrating assignments in the future. The skilled reporter develops an attitude or frame of mind toward the job.

To illustrate:

> Police arrested Carter Davis, 14, son of Mr. and Mrs. George Davis, 4513 W. Coral St.

Why?

> Because he used a knife to stab his eighth-grade teacher at Tyler Junior High School, 1216 N. Marshall St. She is Mrs. Vivian Heller, 48, 5141 W. Falconer Ave.

Why did he do it?

> The assault occured just after she had told the boy that he would fail his course in English.

But other teenagers fail in their school work without committing violence against their teachers. *Why is this boy different?* The Behavior Clinic psychiatrist is examining him now in an attempt to find out. While waiting for the report, further facts can be obtained: the circumstances and sequences of the events, the victim's condition, police activities and so forth. Questioning of school authorities reveals Carter's academic and deportment records. Classmates tell of his behavior toward and reputation with his peers, expressing either surprise or the opposite as regards the immediate situation.

Further clues as to the answer to the *why* are obtained by a visit to Carter's home and neighborhood, by talks with parents and other relatives, neighbors and friends and recreational and other workers with whom the boy has had contact.

The reporter is able to ask penetrating questions to a considerable extent because of his knowledge of modern thinking in the fields of psychology, social psychology, psychiatry and sociology. Not too many decades ago he would have presumed, with most everyone else, that there was a dichotomy of good boys and bad boys, determined largely by the individual's exercise of free will. Back then, a more lenient attitude would have been to consider the social misfit a victim of some sort of demoniacal possession. In any case, harshness of punishment was the only known corrective. Police operated on the "catch 'em and kill 'em" philosophy and were goaded on by journalists who reflected the indignation of most of their readers whenever a particularly heinous example of misbehavior occurred.

Within a generation, the attitude of a majority of enforcement officers, judges, educators, journalists and others has changed. Today it is recognized that there are more complex influences working in and on a boy who commits an act like Carter's. Psychiatrists still are reluctant to discuss cases with newsgatherers until they have made their formal reports to whatever public authorities are involved. In the meantime, reporters should refrain from making medical diagnoses on the basis of their own investigations. They can, however, publicize such pertinent facts as that a misbehaving child comes from an underprivileged, broken slum home, or from a wealthy family where everything was lavished upon him except the most important ingredient of all—parental attention.

Why do some youngsters reared in the same neighborhood "go bad" whereas others do not? The answer concerns the behavior clinician who may conclude that the boy who does not act in accordance with group standards is the problem child rather than others who "go along" with the gang in committing antisocial acts. Human motivation is an extremely complex subject for scientific research, with multitudinous influences in and out of the home and other primary institutions affecting different children differently. The journalist should be warned against acceptance of "panacea" explanations such as broken homes, poverty, slum environments and especially television, comic books, the movies and so forth as providing easy answers to explain intricate situations. Especially must all journalists not panic when "law and order" advocates seek a return to the philosophers of the Middle Ages.

Even if a reasonably clear picture emerges as regards an individual case, the probing reporter can continue to ask "why?" at several different levels of inquiry. If social statistics indicate that there are correlations between various factors, as slum conditions, racial, religious or nationality backgrounds, economic status and so forth, for understanding it is necessary to ask "why?" as regards each item. What are the cause-and-effect relationships? And how to explain the type of behavior that results? Why violence instead of suicide or something else? Because of the extreme frustration or sense of insecurity in the individual from whatever cause—an organic or biological reflex? Or because violence is an accepted or admired form of behavior in a group whose respect is desired? Or because there is violence in other aspects of the environment, including the international scene? These are matters that concern many different specialists in the social sciences whose erudition and research the newsgatherer cannot hope to duplicate. The reporter, however, can solicit their information, assistance and advice.

It would be impossible or at least superfluous to attempt extensive probing into the broader aspects of every incident such as the hypothetical one of Carter Davis. Space will not permit usage of exhaustive analyses of every vagrant, mugger, tough juvenile, prostitute or others of society's "problem children." There is no beat to compare with police, however, to provide an opportunity to begin cultivation of a querying attitude toward life. When the time comes to attempt to fathom the causes of a depression, war or major issue of any kind, the experienced newsgatherer utilizes the habits of mind learned while a young reporter. If reporters don't take advantage of the opportunities provided early in their careers their grandchildren will be visiting them in the same pressroom where they started.

Lester Markel of the New York *Times* was a leader among newspaper editors in developing modern interpretative reporting. Here is his definition of the concept and his case for its utility:

> Interpretation, as I see it, is the deeper sense of the news. It places a particular event in the larger flow of events. It is the color, the atmosphere, the human element that give meaning to a fact. It is, in short, setting, sequence, and, above all, significance.
>
> There is a vast difference between interpretation and opinion. And the distinction is of the utmost importance. Three elements, not two, are involved in this debate; first, news; second, interpretation; third, opinion. To take a primitive example:
>
> To say that Senator McThing is investigating the teaching of Patagonian in the school is news.
>
> To explain why Senator McThing is carrying on this investigation is interpretation.
>
> To remark that Senator McThing should be ashamed of himself is opinion.
>
> Interpretation is an objective judgment based on background knowledge of a situation, appraisal of an event. Editorial judgment, on the other hand, is a subjective judgment; it may include an appraisal of the facts but there is an additional and distinctive element, namely, emotional impact.
>
> Opinion should be confined, almost religiously, to the editorial page; interpretation is an essential part of the news. This is vital and it cannot have too much emphasis.
>
> I see no difference between "interpretation," and "background." Of course, part of interpretation may be the setting out of some antecedent facts—and this many editors consider "background" as distinguished from "interpretation." But interpretation is much more than shirttail material; it is in addition to the presentation of the pertinent facts, present and past, an effort to assay the meaning of those facts.

Causes and Motives

In search of the news behind the news, the probing reporter keeps on asking "why?" Official proclamations and carefully prepared press releases may conceal causes and motives that preceded the spot or "end result" news of the moment. So the interpretative reporter digs beneath the surface.

Sometimes it is possible to conjecture. For instance, if a mayor and corporation counsel have disagreed frequently in public, the reasons for the latter's impending resignation would seem to be obvious. Too often, however, newspaper columnists and others, acting on rumors and tips from "persons close to" or "usually reliable sources," may be wrong. If, for instance, the mayor and corporation counsel announce after a conference that they have settled their differences and, in fact, now "see eye to eye," only a naïve journalist would accept the announcement on its face value. To obtain the "real lowdown," however, may be difficult or impossible. Perhaps the counsel threatened to make a public statement that would be embarrassing to the mayor. Perhaps he agreed to "go along" on some current matter in exchange for a promise of political support at some future date. Perhaps the mayor indicated he would withdraw some patronage from the counsel's followers. The possibilities are many. The responsible journalist should be careful not to give currency to gossip, rumor and surmise.

Once a large company with plants in several cities announced it intended to close its factory in City A and shift operations to City B. The announcement included a strong statement of regret by management, praise for City A and the like, but explained that it had become necessary to retrench, operate closer to its supply of raw materials, and avoid the necessity of investing in costly new machinery. This sounded reasonable but an experienced reporter "smelled a rat" and started snooping. Before long he learned that months earlier the company had negotiated a contract with a union local in City B at a wage rate much lower than that which prevailed in City A. The City B union accepted the deal as it would mean jobs for several thousand unemployed members. Further probing revealed that this act was considered by City A unionists to be a "sellout" and was part of the campaign of a certain national labor leader to increase his strength. The City B union consisted mainly of his followers whereas those in City A belonged to a rival faction within the national organization. Facts such as these are necessary for a proper understanding of the news. The free press has been called a watchdog on government. It can perform no more worthwhile function than to scrutinize carefully everything that affects the public interest.

Significance

Referring a proposal to a legislative committee may mean either that its enactment into law is being accelerated or that it is being killed. Good reporters try to find out which and inform their readers. The same for all other acts of all branches of government. Readers are able to understand the significance of parliamentary and diplomatic maneuvering, but it must be pointed out to them by someone who keeps close check.

When a convicted person is sentenced to a long term of imprisonment, it is customary to point out the minimum time to be served before being eligible for release on parole. When a deadline passes for filing or withdrawing a petition, it should be pointed out what thereby becomes possible or impossible. If a diplomat attends one function and boycotts another, there may or may not be significant repercussions. In some cases, in other words, it is not difficult to explain consequences objectively. In others, a certain amount of guesswork may be necessary, in which case the rule of caution must be invoked.

Analysis

Long and/or complicated documents, including ordinances, and statutes, must be analyzed so that they can be understood. This often is merely a job of tedious objective reporting to explain what now is forbidden, allowed or required and who will be affected in what way. Often the analyst will discover ramifications and repercussions that escaped even the lawmakers.

Speeches by important persons are analyzed almost immediately by journalists and later by scholars. What the speaker emphasizes, the number of times a particular matter is mentioned and omissions are noted. Qualitative judgment enters into evaluating the importance of gestures, facial expressions, tone of voice, pauses in delivery and the like and also in estimating the reaction of a visible audience. It is not difficult to note the amount and duration of applause, of course, but the intangibles are so many that great restraint is needed by the reporter. The audience, for instance, may be easily identifiable as partisan to begin with. Nevertheless, how it reacts is part of the complete coverage. Sometimes explanation is needed for proper analysis. This is often true of crime records. Changes in the frequency of certain types of offenses may be seasonal. The population complexion of areas may change during a reporting period. Police departments have been known to alter their methods of reporting, often with the intention of making the results seem better than they should. An example would be to list automobiles as missing instead of stolen.

Below is an excerpt of a story illustrating analysis of a major issue:

By Bob Kuttner
THE WASHINGTON POST

If one had to pick the political myth of the decade, the leading candidate could easily be what lay behind "the great tax revolt of 1978."

Business conservatives, muttering about government spending and ending up as the biggest beneficiaries of Proposition 13 and its clones, have managed to convince people that taxpayers were rebelling against growth in public outlays. But the real problem, it turns out, was that businesses were already getting too big a tax break, that property taxes increasingly were being shifted *away* from them and onto homeowners.

Though the idea might give a Howard Jarvis apoplexy, in reality the tax revolt of 1978 was created largely by business tax relief at the expense of homeowners.

Consider what happened in California, incubator of the revolt. Taxes on homes there increased about 110 percent between 1975 and 1978—while business assessments rose only 26 percent. By 1978, when Proposition 13 was ratified, single-family homeowners were carrying about 44 percent of California's property tax load; five years earlier they had paid only 32 percent. Small wonder that California homeowners were angry, especially since their excessive share of tax payments was contributing indirectly to a massive state budget surplus.

Why has the tax revolt been misunderstood, continuing to provide pressure for reduced government spending? . . . .

Comparisons

As with crime statistics and taxes, so with the budgets of public and private bodies, achievements of athletes, votes received by candidates and numerous other matters, the reader wants to know how the present compares with the past. Is something more or less, higher or lower, better or worse? Answers to such questions must be given with all possible influencing factors considered so as not to be deceptive. It would, for instance, be misleading to cite an expenditure as twice that for a comparable item some time in the past without taking into consideration changes in the value of the dollar, population increases, changing needs and demands and so forth.

Political party platforms can be compared with each other and with those of previous years. Faced with a vexatious local problem, public officials and newspapers may send representatives to other communities to study what steps were taken there by way of solution. Whenever a disaster of importance occurs, it is common journalistic practice to prepare sidebars, often in the form of charts or tabulations, to show how the immediate catastrophe compares in intensity with others of the past.

Older people are prone to draw historical parallels, to feel that some contemporary event is "just like" one they recall from years before; they feel they have "lived through this before," possibly when they observe a widespread practice that they consider undesirable, as excessive installment buying, stock market speculation, real estate booms and the like. The fact that history teaches many valuable lessons cannot be denied, but what may seem to be history repeating itself may not be that at all. Numerous cities previously tried to abandon services that today are orthodox, as parking meters, traffic signals, one-way streets and off-street parking, to mention only examples in one area. Increasing populations and automobile ownership created new conditions for which new remedies no longer were premature.

Reform movements come and go in many communities. One reason for their failure to last often is the tendency of many supporters to become lackadaisical after the immediate first objective has been attained. History does prove that eternal vigilance is a prerequisite for a properly functioning democracy.

Forecasts

Giving a news story a "tomorrow" angle often is a form of interpretation. After analysis of an action by the city council, reporters can predict new employment, building, policy activities and the like. They can see "trouble ahead" for certain groups as the result of a sweeping court decision and business advantages to others. A drastic price cut by one retail establishment usually results in a price war among competitors. Tightening child labor laws may have the immediate effect of throwing a certain number of minors out of work.

When it comes to predicting beyond the immediate effect, as that unemployed juveniles will become delinquent, the reporter may be merely speculating. One should draw on expert opinion and historical example and still be slow about making deductions. The death of a prominent figure may or may not clear the way toward a reconciliation between disputing factions, lead to a struggle for succession to a position of power or destroy the chances for achieving a certain goal. The expert can point out the possibilities but should not forget that some pundits have lost the confidence of their audiences by excessive smugness, which the future exposed as such.

Unfortunately most people do not take seriously warnings of imminent danger unless precautionary actions are taken. After the race riots following the murder of Dr. Martin Luther King, several newspapers in cities where the disorders occurred produced clippings of articles published over a period of several years exposing conditions destined to foment trouble.

Yet many who ask, "Why didn't the papers warn us?" call the press sensational when it does expose misdeeds and conditions needing attention.

Impressionistic Reporting ————————————————————————

To Tom Wolfe, the saturation reporting in which the New Journalists engaged involved "a depth of reporting and an attention to the most minute facts and details that most newspapermen, even the most experienced, never dreamed of." Fully a generation earlier Thomas Sanction pleaded for "gestalt journalism," which he defined as "journalism which seeks the whole truth in any given field of politics, deeming the whole truth, or even the mere effort to discover it, greater and qualitatively different than piecemeal, selective reporting of the parts—gestalt journalism in this sense describes only what serious reporters have tried to do since writing began."

Sanction cited several news situations when "my on-the-scene notes contained, as a reporter's notes invariably do, more of the total mood and meaning . . . came closer to its 'gestalt' than their ultimate rewriting would ever have done."

Still earlier, Newbold Noyes Jr. advocated "impressionistic reporting" by which he meant attempts by skilled and impartial reporters to create in the reader the same feeling about an important event as the reporter had as an eyewitness of it. This, of course, was something quite different than the strictly objective reporting that had been advocated by his grandfather, Frank Noyes, one of the founders of the Associated Press.

It is because of the risk that personal bias will distort the reporter's effort that some editors still are cautious about granting their expert reporters too much leeway. As a result, as the late Elmer Davis put it, "Objectivity often leans over backward so far that it makes the news business merely a transmission belt for pretentious phonies."

Warren J. Brier gave scores of examples of good impressionistic journalism in an article, "The Lively Language of the Pros: A Glimpse at their Technique," in the 1963 *Montana Journalism Review*. Typical was the following from a UPI story about the Adolf Eichmann trial:

> Hausner, a small, hawk-faced, baldheaded man in a black legal gown, faced the defendant with both hands on his hips. An angry flush appeared on Eichmann's ashen-grey cheeks as the prosecutor pressed his attack.

A nerve in Eichmann's jaw twitched and he licked his lips nervously between questions. His voice rose angrily as he answered some of the more pointed questions.

Wallace Carroll recalled a complaint the New York *Times* received after it included the following in its account of a United States Supreme Court decision: "In a passionate and despairing dissent, Justice Hugo Black rejected the majority opinion." According to a dissatisfied reader, who identified himself as a former newspaperman, "passionate" and "despairing" are "editorial words and you can't use them in a news story." According to Carroll, who was responsible, his "betters" on the *Times* commented, "We agree." Nevertheless, Carroll responded as follows:

It is possible that this alumnus of the A.P. in Seattle has a better "feel" for the story than we had in Washington. But before I cleared the offending passage, I read Justice Black's dissent—all 18,000 words of it. And what impressed me from beginning to end was the passionate and despairing tone. And because passion and despair are seldom encountered in a judicial opinion, I thought this was news and worthy of noting in the *Times*.

In the cases cited, typical of what happens almost daily in any newsroom, the reporters were present as eyewitnesses, with no preconceived opinions, no causes to promote, intent on subduing their personal prejudices. So they acted as impartial critical experts. Admittedly there never will exist the completely emotionless reporter, editor or reader, but in the instances cited any bias was unconscious and deliberate efforts were made to avoid it. All anybody can do is his best to be neutral, fair and thorough.

William Braden, an expert on the subject he had investigated exhaustively, began the first of two articles for the Chicago *Sun-Times* as follows:

Cook County Jail is not so bad as recent publicity has made it out to be.
It is much, much worse.
Even now, only a few people know how bad it really is.
It is evil. It is unjust. It is dangerous.
Those who know describe it as a cultural sink, a breeding ground for next summer's riots—and a deadly weapon aimed at the heart of the community.

After several more paragraphs of editorial conclusions, Braden began to produce his painstakingly gathered evidence.

There are two essential factors relating to the jail and its inmates.
1. The jail (as a building) was designed for the short-term incarceration of the most vicious and dangerous sort of criminals.
2. The vast majority of inmates do not fit that classification.

It is in the public interest to have scholarly minded journalists like Braden on the job, protecting the public interest by investigating such places as the jail. It would be utterly absurd to insist that a man of his caliber should not state his opinions after he has done his prowling in the public interest.

A type of impressionistic reporting more within the realm of the possible for the ordinary small city reporter is represented by the following example:

By Cal Turner

Elizabethtown—Dick Gregory is still at it. Swift, sharp and close to the bone, he cuts the U.S. into little pieces, tidies up its heart and puts it back together, and his listeners love it.

Appearing at Elizabethtown College yesterday, he held a press conference before taking the podium. In a style ranging from instant indignation to a beguiling placidity, he shot down questions from the old and weary, the young at heart and those with no cause but to sit and listen. The acid sometimes dripped.

Coming off a long fast which had as target the nation's anemic attempt to snuff out the narcotics traffic, he stroked a bearded jaw, rolled his eyes, gestured extravagantly and pictured doomsday just around the corner.

"The country is sick," he said. "Nothing will change it until its people learn how to deal with human problems on a human level. Why today, the automobile is more important than the youth."

If the tune sounded antique, the mood he wrought wore long after the conference ended. Calling himself, a "social doctor," he looks at America's ills with a venomous glee.

"I don't like to go into my predictions of the past," he said. "And I don't like to place myself as a prophet." Lacing his thin fingers together, it was here that he ripped into the CIA (Central Intelligence Agency).

"There's a good chance of this country being overthrown by the CIA within the next 18 months," he snapped, his eyes riding to the edge of their sockets. "And if they don't do it, you may see one of the damnedest blood baths the world has ever seen within the next five years."

Digging deeper, he emphasized this was possible because the American people just don't believe it can happen.

"The CIA doesn't have to answer to nobody," he said. "Not even the President. We just don't believe it can happen, yet the CIA goes all around the world, creating incidents, toppling governments. Why, they called off those trials about Vietnam (the massacres). They tap our phones. If America doesn't awaken, then you're going to see what this all will lead to."

Just back from Tokyo, the final lap on a world trip, Gregory said he had looked long and hard at the problems of poverty on a global scale. . . .

[Harrisburg (Pa.) *Evening News*]

Providing Perspective _____

News does not consist only in specific incidents that can be written up with clearcut inclusion of all of the five *w*'s. Ideas are news. So are ideologies, trends of thought, psychological situations and similar intangibles. It is not highbrow to believe that it would be a better world if more newspaper readers were aware of social, political, economic and other stresses and strains that often must be written about without definite news pegs. The "think piece" is a comparatively old journalistic device, but its use constantly is being broadened to include areas previously reserved for research scholars.

As Robert E. Garst, then assistant managing editor of the New York *Times,* wrote in *Nieman Reports:*

> Too much of past reporting has dealt only with the surface facts—the spot news—and too rarely has dug into reasons for them.
>
> A race riot, a prison outbreak, a bad slum condition—even a murder—has a social background, deeply rooted perhaps in the customs, traditions, and economic conditions of a region or community; but it is there and discoverable. It's the newspaper's job, it seems to me, to discover it. Only with that knowledge can a remedy be found for many of the ills that affect us.

Résumés

News weeklies, monthly digest magazines and weekly newspaper news reviews got their start during the depression years and appealed to persons in all walks of life who sought understanding in the midst of confusion. They have continued as an adjunct to quick spot-news reporting to provide recapitulations or résumés of series of fast-happening events. Few occurrences are treated as isolated happenings but as related to other events preceding and following them.

In addition to weekly news reviews, newspapers use "wrap-up" articles on running stories such as legislative assemblies, court trials, political campaigns and the like. In such stories, the expert reporter treats the events of a number of days, usually a week, as constituting material for a single story. Readers' memories are refreshed and relationships are pointed out. Often a condensed chronological recapitulation of the news is sufficient. In other cases, more elaborate interpretation is added. This week, the observant reviewer may write, a certain objective came closer to realization because of this or that train of events. Defense strategy, another may explain, became clearer as cross-examination of prosecution witnesses continued in a court trial. A public official took two steps forward and one backward under observation by a knowledgeable journalist. And so on, all in the attempt to round up the events of a period into a comprehensive single story with proper perspective.

At the end of any session of the state legislature, a résumé of its activities is a journalistic must. Annual or semiannual appraisals of the handling of his official acts by a public official are in the same category. Reporters often take a second look at the cumulative record about every part of which they have previously composed separate accounts.

Surveys

When similar news occurs in a number of places, a journalistic medium may conduct a survey to find out what the overall situation happens to be. Perhaps attempts to enact similar legislation were made in a number of states, in which case a compilation of the results is significant. Let disaster of any kind occur in one place and a follow-up survey reveals how widespread are conditions believed to have been its cause.

Newspapers have conducted surveys to determine the death rates on transcontinental highways, the outcomes of referenda on school bond issues, the use of prison labor on private projects, the attitude of condemned prisoners toward capital punishment, the extent of racial and religious discrimination in housing, schooling and job opportunities, the increase in the ownership of yachts, and on many and many other matters. Some of the material, though not quite so up-to-the-minute, might have been obtained from public and private research agencies.

In drawing conclusions from any kind of data, the press must avoid the error that professional researchers and pollsters also must avoid, that of inadequacy or lack of representativeness of the sample. It is incorrect to write, "Public opinion today here is this or that" unless one has exhaustively questioned persons in all walks of life, something it is rarely possible for a newspaperman to do. Even an impressive group of interviewees within a given area may not be typical. There is no field in which unanimity exists among experts. Quoting officials and group leaders is good journalism but ordinary people involved in an issue, problem or trend also should be contacted.

Situations and Trends

A city editor, getting the idea from an article on the subject in a national magazine, assigned a reporter to "find out how much moonlighting there is in this community." Other editors have sought the answers to such questions as "What do we do for the mentally retarded in our town?" "What about juvenile delinquency among girls?" "Are there any independent grocers left?" "What's happening to our wildlife?"

Often such assignments result in feature articles concerning little-known persons or groups. In other cases, there may be forthcoming broader expositions of current situations to which reporters turn their attention. The result is a better acquaintance with all aspects of the life of the community and possibly an arousal of civic interest in improvement where needed.

Reporters should start on an assignment of this sort with adequate preparation, which should include not merely examination of the publication's own clipping files but also the reading of books, magazine articles and other material to acquaint themselves with the aspects of the situation that they should bear in mind during the fact finding. When the reporter encounters someone with views contrary to those usually considered orthodox, it is best to avoid altercation. Instead, the reporter should tactfully request the news source to comment upon the views of "the other side" as generally understood.

Fortified with information from a number of other places, the perceptive reporter may conclude that under study is not just a local phenomenon but part of a widespread trend. Farmers on the fringe of suburban areas, for instance, may be keeping land out of cultivation in expectation of selling their property to urban developers. Redlining by moneylending institutions, sit-in demonstrations, sympathetic picketing, streaking by college students, fads in games, dress, music and the like may be national or international in extent. The locally written feature can stress home-town manifestations but would be inadequate if it did not mention the broader aspects.

Ora Spaid did a perceptive job for the Louisville *Courier-Journal* when he investigated post-basketball game fights between rival gangs of high school boys. The following extracts, approximately the middle third of the first of three articles, indicate how Spaid tackled the assignment writing as the careful reporter and specialist-expert that he is, having been a social worker before he turned to journalism:

ATHLETICS

One of those not-new conditions is overemphasis of athletics.

A high-school basketball game has become an orgy of emotionalism closely resembling a voodoo ritual. Big crowds pack into small gyms. Drums pound a savage throb, and pretty little girls whip up frenzied partisan spirit that doesn't let up even when play begins.

Sportsmanship is usually evident—as in the exchange of "Hello" yells at the beginning. But it breaks down easily, as when a player from the other team steps to the line for a crucial free throw and the crowd jeers and shouts to distract him.

Coaches talk of the "home-court advantage"—the fact that the crowd is so partisan you can't expect a fair contest.

EMOTIONS STIRRED

Emotional pitch is built before the game in school-wide "pep assemblies," a practice that teachers consider "a necessary evil." A psychology teacher says pointedly that pep assemblies "are a real study in mass psychology sometimes."

The question is: Where does school spirit leave off and hysteria begin?

The concept of high-school sports for participation long ago lost out to the necessity of winning. Coaches build the equivalent of farm systems to produce material for winning teams. A coach becomes as much a victim of "ratings" as a television show; there's a tendency to enlarge the point spread over a defeated opponent to gain a higher rating.

Utterly lost is the grace of losing. High-school girls weep as if death had descended when their teams lose. Fathers grumble about ineffective coaches.

But gainsaying overemphasis of athletics is not enough. Why are athletics overemphasized?

It's a result, some say, of "urbanization." The exodus of people from the cities of recent decades and attendant flight to the suburbs produces a lonely-in-the-crowd society.

It also produces the big school, a factor that men like Richard Van Hoose, superintendent of Jefferson County schools, and Sam V. Noe, his counterpart in Louisville schools, hold as the root cause of many problems.

THE BIG SCHOOL

Today's suburban high school of 2,500 or more students is almost what yesterday's college was.

Let Earl Duncan, principal of the 2,600-student Waggener High School, tell of some of the problems.

"In a school of 2,600, only 12 boys can play basketball, but certainly a lot more would like to," he said. "Only five youngsters can be elected to offices in a graduating class of 350. Think how many that leaves out."

It's a case of being lost in a big school.

A bright boy in a big suburban school came home last week with failing grades. He told his mother, "I'm not good at sports; I'm not in the band; I can't get on the school paper. I've just lost all interest in school."

Most young people don't lose interest—they plunge. If they can't find something they can participate in actively, they participate vicariously. The school is something they can belong to, something to "give them identity," as the psychologists say. So they become rabid fans, fanatic followers.

MAY BOIL OVER

But nonparticipation isn't too satisfying; there's not much opportunity to blow off steam, unless in violent rooting. And it's always possible that this pent-up steam may boil over into violence, particularly if there is some way to rationalize it, like defending the school's honor or avenging a lost game.

Big schools build up tension in ways other than pep assemblies—subtler ways, often overlooked.

Principal Duncan points out that when you have only one gymnasium and it is given over to varsity teams, there is no place for other youngsters to play. To "make the best use of facilities," in gym periods or after school, the play must be scheduled and organized. Regimentation is another word for it—constant supervision, no opportunity to just horse around.

Drop in at one of these big schools at noon hour and you will see long lines of students in the cafeteria. The sheer impossibility of feeding all students at once means they eat in shifts. And mark this: lunch hour lasts only 20 minutes. Not only that, but by the time a student gets his food, he may have only 10 minutes to eat it. Of necessity, he must "bolt his food" or miss his next class.

DIFFERENCE IS GREAT

Compare this with the paper-sack days when pupils brought their lunches, ate leisurely and spent the rest of a long lunch hour dozing under a tree or breaking the tension of long hours at a desk in a make-up ball game.

This means that today's school children put in a 7-hour day with little let-up, seldom released from supervision. Even recess is now a matter of "supervised play," and in some schools, children are given a grade for lunchroom conduct.

Then there is homework. There always has been homework, but it seems to a lot of students that teachers are trying to close up the missile gap with Russia by the sheer bulk of homework they assign. The youngsters respond, not by learning from homework, but merely by "getting it done."

Getting it done means more hours under supervision, this time from a Mom or Dad anxious to see a good report card.

All this adds up to this: youngsters today are under greater tension than ever before but have less opportunity to dissipate it.

The foregoing was written by an expert, which many journalists become after considerable experience in covering a specialized type of news. Ora Spaid wrote from the perspective of his personal values, as all writers inevitably do. Modern newspapers are, among other things, an attempt to provide a mirror for society. It is a mirror with cracks, but without reporters' attempts to interpret as they see things, reality would be even more distorted.

The Human Aspect of Issues, Trends

Interpretative reporting need not be antiseptic. It should not be. Issues, trends and problems are important because they involve people and affect people. Whenever possible, the good interpretative reporter should not only tell readers that, but also show them. That approach can clarify an issue or trend and drive it more powerfully into a reader's mind than any other single thing a reporter can do. Good interpretative reporting is based on the ancient art of storytelling. Good reporters must care about other human beings not just in the mass, but as individuals, precious because of their humanity. The following excerpt from a story by an unidentified Associated Press reporter has that quality. It appeared Oct. 12, 1980, in the Chicago *Tribune*. It is about a large social, economic and political problem. It is about a tragic trend, a tragic situation. Its power to stick in the reader's mind, though, comes from the humanity of the writer's individual perspective toward the plight of other very real individual human beings.

Bloomington, Ill. (AP)—Something terrible was happening to Mary White's children, one by one.

Danny was the first. That was 14 years ago and he was only 2.

"I noticed he started holding his hands over his ears like he couldn't stand noise," she said. "Then George started acting the same way."

Mrs. White took the boys to a doctor, who diagnosed them as retarded. Social agencies said they had behavioral problems. School officials told her the boys were hyperactive and undisciplined.

"It was a nightmare," she said. "I kept saying something's wrong, something's medically wrong with my boys. You could see it by looking at them, but people acted like I should be quiet."

Paul was next, then Michael. Her children were running around the house, slamming into walls, screaming at things that were invisible. . . .

Then, in August, a routine screening of welfare mothers by the McLean County Health Department found out what was wrong. The children had lead poisoning.

Subsequent testing revealed that eight of Frank and Mary White's 13 children had dangerously high levels of lead in their blood. At least four—Danny, George, Paul, and Michael—were damaged irreversibly. In 14 years, they had never been tested for lead poisoning.

The family has lived in old houses painted with lead-based paint since moving here from Chicago 17 years ago. The children chewed on the woodwork or ate paint chipping from walls, and one by one they poisoned themselves.

Ben Boyd, county health director, called it "a terrible tragedy". . . .

"I tend to blame the agency system," Boyd said. "Somehow when the children were seen, nobody asked the question why." . . . .

Local health officials say the White case has assured that future problems will be spotted more quickly. But for Mrs. White, it is too late. Her children are damaged permanently, and she cannot understand why it took so long to find out what was wrong.

"They were born smart," she said. "It's like they were in their own little world now, like if you rang a bell they'd come out again."

As she talked, a low, steady moan intruded from the next room where the boys were, rocking back and forth on the floor, staring blankly at the television.

Danny, 16, was louder than the others, and after awhile his moaning rose to a kind of howl, then into a long, shuddering scream.

His brothers, rocking absently, paid no attention at all.

Investigative Reporting

All reporting is investigative because newsgatherers seek facts. Jay Jensen, the now retired former long-time head of the University of Illinois journalism department, once said that investigative reporting is "just old fashioned traditional exposé stuff, uncovering what is being covered up, revealing what is being hidden, nailing down lies that have been told, etc." Accurate as this definition is, it does not convey the intrigue and excitement felt by many would-be journalists who saw the motion picture, "All the President's Men" in which Dustin Hoffman and Robert Redford played the parts of Carl Bernstein and Robert Woodward, Washington *Post* reporters who exposed many of the scandals connected with the Watergate burglary.

Still, Robert Greene, two-time Pulitzer prize-winner for investigative work for *Newsday,* says simply that investigative reporting is "uncovering something somebody wants to keep a secret." Similarly, David Anderson and Peter Benjaminson, Detroit *Free Press* investigative reporters, say in their book, *Investigative Reporting,* "Investigative reporting is simply the reporting of concealed information."

This calmer approach to investigative reporting marks the mood of the '80s, welcome in some respects, but disturbing in others.

On college campuses fewer journalism students and student newspapers seem interested in exposing corruption, inefficiency or blatant hypocrisy in the operation of public and private institutions. The glamorous style of Woodward and Bernstein and other investigative reporters of the '70s is no longer a model for many in the generation of journalists in the making.

In an August 1984 Washington *Post* story on investigative reporting, Eleanor Randolph concluded that "Watergate fever" had subsided in the mainstream press as well. She found that editors instead are worried that such reporting can harm innocent people and provoke a backlash against newspapers. Greene told her he shared some of that sentiment. "When something becomes trendy," he said, "trends can breed excess." There was a similar feeling at the 1985 national conference of Investigative Reporters and Editors (IRE). "Investigative reporting stood out (in the late 1960s and early 1970s) much more than it would now," Jack Davis told a writer covering the meeting for *Editor and Publisher* magazine. Davis, who directs investigative reporting for the Chicago *Tribune,* said, "We're putting a lot less flash and self-promotion of the paper into investigative stories."

Still, citizens have a right to hope that checking the excesses of investigative reporting, quieting its tone and worrying about reader backlash does not again turn the American press into what Carl Lindstrom once called "a shaggy dog that wants to play." The need for good investigative reporting is at least as great as ever.

The Investigative Reporter

The late Paul N. Williams, who won a Pulitzer prize for exposing the financial dealings of Boys Town, wrote in his posthumously published book, *Investigative Reporting and Editing,* "Investigative reporting is an intellectual process. It is a business of gathering and sorting ideas and facts, building patterns, analyzing options and making decisions based on logic rather than emotion—including the decision to say no at any of several stages."

Another investigative reporter, Clark R. Mollenhoff, was for more than a quarter-century chief of the Washington bureau of the Des Moines *Register* and *Tribune* during which time he won a Pulitzer prize. According to Mollenhoff, "Investigative reporting is a precarious profession. For the most part it is hours, days and sometimes weeks of tedious work in combing records. It is endless interviews with people who really don't want to talk, the running out of endless leads; the frustration of having most leads end as dry holes or, worse yet, with inconclusive results; and the impenetrable stonewalling of responsible officialdom."

Nevertheless, for all the tedium Mollenhoff said: "We are the communication line that is vital to final government accountability to the public. We should all do our utmost to make certain that the life line of democracy is not cluttered with irresponsible debris or superficial froth."

Mollenhoff's book, *Investigative Reporting,* was published in 1980 by Macmillan.

Any newspaper with standing in its community is constantly being importuned to "look into" this or that, which usually means to uncover facts that it allegedly is in the public interest to be known but that someone is attempting to conceal. Annoying and time-consuming as it may become to observe the rule, it is unsafe to ignore tipsters, no matter how unreliable or crackpot they may seem to be. Maybe the police officer whose neighbor cannot understand how he is able to afford an expensive car *did* inherit a large sum of money, or the officer's affluence may be the clue to a scandal.

Before undertaking the "tedious and discouraging work," which Brit Hume in *Inside Story* says investigative reporting is, much of the time, it is smart to evaluate the motives of the tipster. Disgruntled employees or colleagues, past or present, may be merely satisfying grudges, but they may not be. And the same goes for divorced wives or husbands. The same public records to be consulted in tracing the background of a principal in a scandal can be used to discover the motivation and perhaps the probable credibility of a news source. Certainly it is almost always unwise for a reporter to confront someone against whom a charge has been made before making a thorough check of all angles involved. After the records have been exhausted, the first interviewing usually should be of those on the periphery of the story. The target of any investigation ordinarily should be the very last interviewee. By that time the reporter should be thoroughly prepared and know exactly what missing links he is after.

Actually the investigative reporter is like any other kind of reporter, only more so. More inquisitive, more skeptical, more resourceful and imaginative in knowing where to look for facts, more ingenious in circumventing obstacles, more indefatigable in the pursuit of facts and able to endure drudgery and discouragement. Investigative reporters seldom play detective in the sense of shadowing persons but they do not naïvely accept explanations. Thus, they are confronted with many situations that test their integrity.

Crusading—Muckraking _____

Present-day investigative reporters are carrying on a journalistic tradition that did not begin with the Bernstein-Woodward sleuthing or with many other post-World War II exploits including the uncovering of facts about the My Lai massacre, which won a Pulitzer prize for Seymour Hersh, then with the Dispatch News Service, and Jack Anderson's Pulitzer prize-winning exposure of official Washington's hypocrisy during the Pakistani–Indian War.

The Era of the Muckrakers, according to the history books, was the first two decades of the century when a small coterie of magazine article writers exposed corruption in business and government.

Outstanding examples of their work were *The Shame of the Cities,* by Lincoln Steffens; *The Jungle,* a novel about Chicago's stockyards by Upton Sinclair, which led to the first pure food and drug act; Ida Tarbell's history of the Standard Oil Co. and many magazine series and books by Ray Stannard Baker, David Graham Phillips, Charles Edward Russell and others.

Although President Theodore Roosevelt considered muckraking an opprobrious term when he adapted it from John Bunyan's *Pilgrim's Progress* to apply to enterprising journalists, the first decade of the twentieth century is today regarded as a "golden period" of public service journalism. Unquestionably the achievements of the press in exposing the Watergate and related scandals and American atrocities in Vietnam will be remembered similarly. Although the so-called Pentagon Papers were not the work of investigative reporters, their editing and publishing was an historic event as for the first time in American history the federal government attempted to suppress an important news story. By successfully taking the issue to the Supreme Court the New York *Times* won a Pulitzer prize.

With many other exposés to his credit, Jack Anderson ranks with Ralph Nader as an outstanding contemporary crusader. Nader won a $425,000 court judgment against General Motors, which hired private investigators to harass him after his iconoclastic *Unsafe at Any Speed* was published. Nader is the only muckraker ever to institutionalize himself. His organizations include Center for the Study of Responsive Law, Public Interest Research Group, Corporate Accountability Study, Public Citizen Inc. and many others. Anderson and Nader along with many other outstanding investigative journalists of our time are the subjects of a fine book on this type of reporting, *The New Muckrakers,* by Leonard Downie Jr., a top Washington *Post* editor.

As the number of papers with investigative reporters grew, in 1976 the Investigative Reporters and Editors was organized. More than 300, double the number expected, attended the first convention in Indianapolis. By 1980 the membership had reached 1,200 and a resource center had been established at the University of Missouri with a full-time staff large enough to publish what has become a quarterly, called *The IRE Journal.* The organization also issues reports and conducts workshops in all parts of the country. Impetus to the development of Investigative Reporters and Editors was the Arizona Project in which 23 members engaged in a four months' investigation of land frauds in Arizona. There Don Bolles, investigative reporter for the Phoenix *Republic,* had been murdered after he was lured to a restaurant, presumably to obtain information, and a bomb was placed in his car which blew up. Bob Greene of *Newsday* headed the project that produced a series of 23 articles that was syndicated to papers all over the country. Students can join IRE, receive its publication and attend its meetings at reduced rates. The IRE mailing address is: IRE, P. O. Box 838, Columbia, Mo., 65205. Steve Weinberg is the IRE staff director.

Situation Features _____

The editor who tells a reporter to "look into this" usually acts on a tip or a hunch. Often the information needed is easily obtainable and there is no hint of criminal behavior. Nevertheless, facts important for the public to know are revealed, and the opportunity to cover such assignments is excellent training for the reporter who aspires to be a competent investigative reporter. Under a byline the reporter, an expert as a result of thorough fact finding, expresses opinions together with reasons for them. Here are some examples:

Pictures of border markets and boxed lists of prices of necessary grocery items on both sides of the U.S.–Mexican border accompanied a roundup article that began as follows:

By Bill Greer
ASSOCIATED PRESS

A penny-wise consumer who does his grocery shopping on both sides of the border can make substantial savings in his monthly grocery bill, according to an Associated Press check of grocery prices here and across the border.

But there are some hazards.

For example, avocados are cheaper across the border. But the seed cannot be transported into the United States.

However, once those, and similar, peculiarities are mastered, there are bargains to be had. For this comparison, the Associated Press chose a supermarket in El Paso and its counterpart, the super mercado, across the Rio Grande at Juarez. Both were in fashionable neighborhoods.

Marketing and promotional gimmicks pushing small items were used at both stores. The Mexican super mercado perhaps held a slight edge in the sales technique.

In both stores, film, candy and razor blades were displayed near the cash registers to entice last-minute purchases.

The Mexican grocers place a real temptation at the check counter—a wooden barrel filled with ice chunks and quarts of near-freezing beer.

The mercado designers had parents in mind when they planned the lily-lined, tree-filled park on two sides of the building. Children play while parents spend. The only alternative to basket-riding, display-threatening children on the U.S. side is the parking lot.

Shopping center parking lots in the United States occasionally are sites of violence. Not so often at the mercado where an armed guard watches customers and cars. . . .   [San Antonio *Express News*]

The author of the following piece, the opening of which is printed here, could have gotten the idea for his investigation from a citizen's complaint or his own observations at the courthouse:

By James Warren

Whether you've fallen into a pothole or been shot by a police officer, suing the city is a shocking odyssey. You may win—perhaps even win big—but prepare to wait as long as *four years* to get your money.

Crane operator Robert Dils waited so long for the $246,524 a judge granted him he died waiting. Now his widow has joined thousands of frustrated Chicagoans to whom the city owes $14.8 million in judgments, and who'll be lucky to collect before the *next* election for mayor.

Lawyers here call the situation a farce, and fiscal officials in other cities laugh. But the snail-like way the city pays off is no joke and leads many to try desperately to sell their judgments for cash to brokers at discounts reaching a whopping 20 per cent. . . .   [Chicago *Sun-Times*]

In chapters 14–24 of this book there are many more illustrations of situation and trend reporting that involves enterprising investigation by interpretative reporters.

Exposés

Explaining how his paper won six consecutive Pulitzer prizes, a Philadelphia *Inquirer* investigative reporter said. "We get 95 per cent of it from public records." So, a primary requisite is to know what and where the records related to the subject matter of the assignment are and the nature of their contents.

Home Health Care

It was by looking up the law and studying health department records that the Milwaukee *Journal*'s Margo Huston turned an apparently routine assignment into a Pulitzer prize. Seeking material on "alternatives to nursing homes for the elderly," she consulted the telephone book yellow pages to obtain the names of 12 private agencies offering service in the home.

Huston was horror-stricken by the case histories she read in the welfare department books. She visited the homes of a number of the clients, which made her feel sicker. The 12 agencies admitted they were unlicensed, so the reporter consulted the state statute book in the paper's morgue. She looked under the headings "health care," "elderly," "home care," "day care" and anything else she could think of until she found a ten-year-old law that required licensing of all profit-making health care institutions.

Next Huston went to the Wisconsin Legislative Reference Library and the Administrative Code, a public record. It detailed the qualifications employees of home care agencies should have and how such institutions were to be inspected and regulated.

On a visit to the Department of Health the reporter overheard a caseworker mention the effort to test a new law by which a person could be hospitalized against his or her will. The caseworker refused to tell the patient's name so Huston went to the County Building where the corporation counsel handling the case identified the patient. A judge refused to hear the case seeking a court order, saying that otherwise civil liberties would be violated. Huston recognized the patient's name as that of an old woman whom she had visited in her squalid home. By the time she made another visit the old woman had died in a hospital where she finally went of her own volition.

As a result of the interest aroused by Huston's articles, an ombudsman program for elderly persons either in or out of nursing homes was established in connection with the Mt. Sinai Hospital Center and several private agencies improved their services. Huston received a number of calls from persons who said they had been inspired to provide better care for their parents.

Boys Town

Few if any other investigative exposés caused a greater nationwide stir than the series on the financial status of Boys Town for which the *Sunpapers* of Omaha won a Pulitzer prize for special local reporting. Founded by the Rev. Edward J. Flanagan in 1918, Boys Town, on a farm ten miles west of Omaha, was made famous by a motion picture starring Spencer Tracy and Mickey Rooney in 1938. Paul N. Williams, managing editor of the *Sunpapers,* a group of weeklies, wondered what the return was from the large-scale fund raising drives every Christmas and Easter season. Officials refused to talk, so Williams consulted the records.

Because Boys Town was incorporated as a village, it had to file condensed annual municipal budgets and brief reports of operations. Because it was a non-profit corporation, it had to file brief reports, a list of officers, and copies of its articles of incorporation. Because Boys Town operated an educational system it had to be accredited by the state of Nebraska and North Central Association, which requires reports of school enrollment, curricula staffing levels, and compliance with health and safety rules. So it was ascertained that Boys Town had fewer than 700 students, not the presumed 1,000 plus.

As a licensed child care operation Boys Town had to file other routine reports with the State Welfare Department. Since Boys Town owned land there had to be records of deeds and mortgages, taxes and prices. The land records indicated that, at the very least, Boys Town property in Douglas County was worth $8.4 million.

For publicity reasons, Boys Town was a U.S. post office, which meant it had to file certain minimal public reports with the postmaster general. When the local postmaster refused to talk, Williams obtained the cooperation of his congressman to learn that from 30 to 50 million letters were mailed annually from the Boys Town post office. Then Williams conferred with some private fund raisers, who declared that such sizable mailings could not be justified unless they brought in at least $10 million. The National Information Bureau, a confidential advisory service for large donors, told Williams that it was impossible for it to reply to inquiries because Boys Town provided inadequate data.

Most officials of the Child Welfare League of America and local and regional experts in child development and child delinquency told Williams that Boys Town's large single-institution approach was not best for the kind of problem children being served.

The climax of the *Sunpapers'* investigation was Form 990 filed with the Internal Revenue System under the Tax Reform Act of 1970, of which Williams had not previously known. The 94-page report showed that Boys Town's net worth was $191,401,421, increasing at the rate of about $17 million annually. Confronted with these figures, officers and members of the board of directors had no explanation. The money-raising mailings were canceled for a few years. By 1980 Boys Town's net worth was $256 million and the student body had declined to 398. Centers for the study and treatment of speech and hearing defects and for a study of youth development were established with an endowment of $30 million, and other plans to expand activities were considered.

Public Records _____

The importance of easily available public records to the investigative reporter was explained by Patrick Riordan of the Miami *Herald* in the May–June 1979 Issue of *IRE Journal*. With the permission of the publication and the author, the article, "Getting the Background Fast," follows:

By Patrick Riordan
MIAMI HERALD

You're methodically researching your project on the ridiculously expensive new monorail the county wants to build at the new zoo when your editor starts flailing his arms and hollering at you.

The police desk has an update on a bust at a disco last night. It turns out they found in the back room 20 kilos of cocaine, 10 bales of marijuana and 100,000 quaaludes. A Colombian citizen was among those arrested.

The cops are cooperating with the Drug Enforcement Administration, not with you. They're giving out nothing beyond the arrest sheets.

There are a hundred unanswered questions: Who owns the disco? What else does he own—land, buildings, cars, boats, airplanes? What's his economic background? Has he ever been accused of a crime? Does he use corporations to hide behind? Is there a limited partnership involved? Who are its investors? How much did they invest? Who's in business with this guy?

Public records will answer every one of those questions in a few hours.

Let's suppose the cops are really playing hard-to-get and won't even tell you the name of the owner. You can still find it.

You have the address of the disco from the arrest sheet (or the phone book.) You go to the office of the tax collector, or the office where deeds are kept on file, and ask a clerk to help you convert the street address into a legal description of the property. In an urban area that'll be a block number and one or more lot numbers in a particular subdivision.

For example, suppose the disco is located at 3000 Coral Boulevard in Miami. Either by asking a clerk or using the county real estate atlas yourself, you find that 3000 Coral Boulevard is in Miami Urban Estates subdivision, and that your particular address is Lots 5, 6 and 7 of Block 5.

With that information you can find the owner in one of two ways:

The easy way, if your county keeps abstract books, tract indexes or a property index, is to look up the book or microfilm reel for your subdivision. In that book, you flip pages or unreel film until you come to Block 5. Then go to the very last entry under Block 5 and work backward. The first entry you come to for Lots 5, 6 and 7 is the most recent. It reflects the current owner.

The other way, if you don't have abstract books for each subdivision, is to work through the tax roll. You may need to convert the legal description into a folio number, composed of the block and lot numbers, a code number for the subdivision and municipality, and other code numbers for section, range and township—terms you'll encounter more often when you're researching rural acreage.

Each piece of property in your county has a unique folio number. Once you've got someone to show you how to determine it, go to the tax roll and look it up. It shows who's paying the taxes.

USUALLY THE OWNER

About 99 percent of the time that's the owner. (In Florida and Illinois, you may have a hidden land trust with a trustee paying the taxes. Lotsa luck.)

No matter how you get the name of the apparent owner, it's a good idea to double check. Go to the office where the deeds are kept. It's the recorder's office in some states. the register of deeds, the clerk's office or the official records office in others.

Ask for the grantor-grantee index (also known as the official records index, the deed index or the index to real estate transfers.)

In our case, the current owner appears to be something called Taca Corp. To find its deed to the disco property, look up Taca Corp. in the grantee index.

There's a reference to Book 289, Page 34 in the index next to Taca Corp.

Go find Deed Book 289 on the shelf or in a microfilm drawer. Turn to page 34 and you've got the deed.

Taca Corp., it says, acquired title to the property from Rodolfo Hernandez, a name that's vaguely familiar.

The corporation owes $50,000 on the property to first Smugglers' Bank and Trust Co.

That's its first mortgage.

It also owes another $375,000 to Hernandez, payable in quarterly installments over 10 years. That's the purchase money second mortgage.

You find out how much it owes by checking in the deed book a few pages before and after the deed for a mortgage. They're usually filed with the deed, but not always. Look in the index to mortgages under Taca Corp. to be sure.

From the deed and mortgages, you now know precisely what property was bought and sold (from the legal description), who bought it and who sold it, and who's financing it.

You can also figure out how much it cost.

The amount isn't spelled out directly, but it's indicated clearly by the amount of documentary tax paid to record the deed. Sometimes called the recordation fee, this tax corresponds mathematically to the value of the transaction.

In Florida, for example, $3 worth of stamps must be attached to the deed for every $1,000 of value. On a $100,000 transaction, there would be $300 worth of stamps.

In the District of Columbia, where the tax is one percent of the value of the transaction, the amount is shown by an imprint, not actual stamps. A $100,000 transaction costs $1,000 to record.

In other jurisdictions the tax rate varies. Find out what yours is from the county office that records deeds and charges the tax, or look up your state law.

After computing the indicated value of the transaction, you note in the index to deeds (the grantor-grantee index) that Taca Corp. seems to have several other deeds on file. But before proceeding, you decide to learn a little more about Taca.

The courthouse office where occupational licenses are kept sheds little light on the subject. Taca holds the local business license in its corporate name.

You could check the utilities office to see who pays the water and electricity bills, but you decide to pass for the moment.

You call the Secretary of State's office to ask for the corporate information office. They'll give you a lot of information on the phone, and send you more by mail.

Always ask for current officers and directors, including their addresses; the corporate address (also called the registered address); the name of the registered agent; the nature of the business the corporation engages in; and whether they're up-to-date on their franchise tax.

Also ask for the date of incorporation. If you're persuasive enough, you can sometimes get someone to go find the original articles of incorporation.

From that you can get the incorporators (the people who formed the corporation), the name of the attorney who handled the paperwork, the name of the notary public who notarized the corporate charter, and sometimes a more detailed statement of the business in which the corporation engages.

In this case, one name jumps out at you: It's Rodolfo Hernandez, the guy who sold the disco to Taca.

He turns out to be the president of Taca, its registered agent and one of its incorporators three years ago when it was formed.

His lawyer, a well-known criminal defense attorney, is corporate secretary (a little out of his line.)

Before you get off the phone, you call another agency in the capital, the Uniform Commercial Code office.

That's where people file evidence of secured debts, such as car or boat loans, or business loans backed up by accounts receivable, inventory or fixtures.

Taca, it develops, owes a restaurant supply company on its kitchen and bar facilities at the disco, but that's all.

You call the nearest office of the Alcohol Beverage Commission or the Division of Beverage, or whichever agency licenses bars in your state.

The agency will have in its files a complete list of all owners of the disco if it has a liquor license.

Since the owner is Taca, this gives you a list of stockholders. There's only one: Hernandez.

A picture is emerging.

The disco where the cops found the dope has a complicated corporate structure, but only one man behind it all. The man receives large sums in the form of mortgage payments.

It could be a clever scheme to rip off the business and go bankrupt.

Or it might be Hernandez' way of establishing a large, on-the-record taxable income for IRS' consumption, in order to conceal his real income from smuggling.

Back to the deed books.

Those other transactions involving Taca now become much more interesting than they were before. You get copies of all deeds involving the company and your paper reimburses you. (If it doesn't, deduct it on your income tax return and look for another job.)

With each deed the pattern grows stronger:

In your county alone, Taca owns 50 acres near the new free trade zone, a key parcel next to the seaport, two old downtown hotels in the path of a new convention center, three condominium apartments and the disco where the drugs were found.

You extend your research. The Uniform Commercial Code office didn't have any record of loans on cars, airplanes or boats. Maybe that's because he paid cash for his smuggling equipment.

You call the state motor vehicle records office in the capital and explain the general nature of the inquiry.

A state employee looks up Taca and Hernandez.

He owns a new Seville in his own name with no lien on it. He paid cash. And Taca owns three big, straight-body trucks and a Jeep, all free and clear.

The Department of Natural Resources (or the agency that licenses boats in your state) looks in their files for Taca and Hernandez and discovers three Donzi speedboats, each capable of outrunning anything owned by the U.S. Customs Service.

Finally, the state motor vehicle office, or the state Department of Transportation, depending on where you live, looks up Hernandez and Taca.

The corporation, it seems, owns two aircraft, a plush, radar-equipped Piper Seneca, suitable for spotting ships at sea; and a Convair 220, capable of hauling 10,000-pound payloads.

Taca begins to look like a smuggling conglomerate.

En route to the office, you check the court clerk's office. You look up Taca in the index to see if anyone ever sued it. There's only one case: a slip-and-fall on the dance floor, settled out of court.

You look up Hernandez and find a divorce file. Not much you don't already know, except in the property settlement there's a reference to Taca Investors Ltd.

You double back to the deeds office and look up Taca Investors Ltd., kicking yourself for missing it the first time.

You find three deeds and limited partnership declaration.

CANAL FOR SMUGGLERS

According to the deed the partnership owns an apartment building, rural acreage that includes a landing strip, and some oceanfront land with a canal leading to a privately maintained channel where smugglers have been arrested before.

Best of all, the declaration of partnership lists Hernandez, his lawyer and a city councilman as limited partners.

The general partner is our friend Taca.

According to the declaration, each investor put up one-third of the investment. But only the general partner, the corporation, can be held financially accountable. And its liability is limited by the state corporation laws.

One last stop at the criminal courts building confirms what you thought you remembered: Nine years ago, Hernandez was convicted of selling 600 pounds of marijuana and a kilo of cocaine to an undercover cop.

He's got a record as a dealer, he's tied to a public official, he owns boats, planes, trucks, a landing strip and a secluded harbor, and his criminal defense attorney is his business partner.

You put it all together and call a friendly cop. You tell him what you have. He trades you a little information in return:

Hernandez is about to be arrested, along with five of his lieutenants. He asks you to hold the story out of the first edition until Hernandez is popped.

You spend the time polishing the writing.

Everything you have is tied to a public record. Everything is demonstrably true, documented and libel-proof.

This illustration is not entirely fanciful. A similar story—minus the limited partnership—was done last year by a Miami Herald reporter. It was not done on deadline, but it could have been: All the information was gathered in a single day.

Any good reporter could have done it, with a solid knowledge of public records. The problem is finding out what they are and where they are.

There are ways to learn:

- Ask questions of anybody who'll talk to you. Ask other reporters. Ask clerks in courthouses. Ask people on the phone. Find out what they have and how it can help you. And remember: Any piece of paper in the possession of any public employee is a public record unless proven otherwise in court.
- Call the IRE Resource Center at 314-882-2042.
- Get a copy of *Real Estate Law* by Robert Kratovil (Englewood Cliffs, N.J., Prentice Hall, 1974). It's a clearly written summary of the kinds of trans- actions on file, what the deeds look like and why they're public.
- Get a copy of Harry J. Murphy's *Where's What* (New York: Warner Books, 1976). It's a recently declassified CIA manual subtitled "Sources of infor- mation for federal investigators."
- Keep up with Congressional hearing records, particularly those involving agencies that touch on your area. They provide factual data submitted under oath. Their witness lists give you the names of experts on a particular agency or subject. Be sure to get any supplemental reports published after the hear- ings. Often they contain written responses to embarrassing questions a wit- ness wasn't prepared to answer on the stand.
- Get to know which federal agencies are most active in your area. And get to know your local state-level officials. Sometimes, when city hall wants to cover up a report, there's another copy floating around in a state or federal agency.

If your county's federal job training program is a laughing-stock and the county manager is skirting the public records law, ask for copies of all his correspondence with the Department of Labor under the federal Freedom of Information Act. If he's mis-spending highway funds, get information from the state. And if the city landfill is polluting the river, get the story from records of the state environmental agency.

Records are no substitute for shoe leather or sources. To make your story come alive, you ultimately have to talk to real people on the record. But know- ing how to run the records comprehensively can help you ask better questions.

Useful References

The news sources, individual and records, utilized by the hero of Rior- dan's piece totaled 15. Every issue of *IRE Journal* contains lists of sources for a wide variety of topics. Williams devoted ten pages to enumeration of records—local, school, county, state and federal. Anderson and Ben- jaminson list 35 most important public and private records: audit and con- sultants' reports; birth records; business records, including dba (doing busi- ness as) reports; campaign contributions and expenditures records; charity records, including police and firemen's benefit funds, which may be thinly disguised protection rackets; chattel mortgage records, which may contain clues to how low-paid public servants make big purchases, and interest- free deposits of public funds in banks in which public officials have an interest; city directories; city license bureaus; the *Congressional Record;* criss-cross telephone directories with listings by street addresses rather than alphabetically by names; death records; expense account vouchers; finan- cial information from Dun & Bradstreet and similar agencies; government directories especially the *U.S. Government Manual;* gun registrations; in- come-tax records; legal newspapers; legal notices; marriage records; mili- tary records; museum records of tax-free contributions; newspaper libraries; payroll records; private organization records; professional trade and business directories; religious directories; school directories; Securities and Exchange records; state regulatory records; telephone records; trade publications; vanity directories; vehicle registrations; voting records to obtain full name, address and possibly mother's maiden name; welfare records.

To which might be added voter registration records; immigration records; divorce court proceedings; probate court proceedings and wills; federal tax courts; driver's license registrations; building permits; board of equalization reports.

The IRE maintains elaborate, carefully indexed files of thousands of investigative stories, which can be helpful to those working on an investigative project.

The August 1985 issue of the *Washington Journalism Review* contained an especially useful introductory article to investigative reporting. Called "The Paper Trail: How to Dig Into Documents," it provides details about a wide range of reporting resources and information about exactly how to find them.

Securities and Exchange Commission

Even though a story may be almost entirely of local interest, it may be necessary to consult Washington sources for information. If so, the Washington Researchers, an information service which works under contract with individual clients, believes most important are Securities and Exchange Commission reports on the 12,000 publicly owned corporations—the heavyweights even though 90 per cent of all businesses are privately owned. Most important Securities and Exchange Commission form is K-10, filed annually. It describes a company's business, number of employees, gross profits, net income or loss, changes in security or indebtedness, any bankruptcy or receivership proceedings, any major disposition of assets, balance sheets and total assets. Also listed are major lawsuits affecting the interest of stockholders.

Other important SEC forms include these: 10-Q, a quarterly report, which updates 10-K and also analyzes changes in company revenues and expenses compared with previous periods; 8-K, filed whenever a publicly held company undergoes a change in control, files for bankruptcy or receivership or changes of accountants; 13-D, submitted whenever a person or business acquires more than 5 per cent of the securities of a company listed on the stock exchange or one that is worth more than $1 million and has at least 500 stockholders; 14-D1, filed whenever a company covered by 13-D receives a purchase order from another company. The offer, principals, including broker and past dealings between the two companies, are described.

By consulting Forms 13-D and 14D-L, the Des Moines *Register* was able to explain the phenomenon of an obscure scrap-metal owner whose heavy trading the paper had learned about through the SEC's *Official Summary*, a monthly publication that outlines the trading of stocks and bonds by directors, officers and heavy stockholders. On the other hand, the Gannett News Service had to ask 38 SEC employees for help before learning that the agency has little authority over religious organizations. Gannett nevertheless won a Pulitzer prize for its series on the financial dealings of the Pauline Fathers.

For information about privately owned companies it is necessary to consult state agencies, most of which have adopted the Uniform Commercial Code, which requires disclosure of corporate debts. This code makes available names and addresses of parties involved, property used as collateral and the maturity dates of debts.

The Food and Beverages Department of the American Federation of Labor-Congress of Industrial Organizations (AFL-CIO), has published the useful *Manual of Corporate Investigation.*

Other Federal Agencies

Three of the most important of the thousands of other federal agencies are the Federal Trade Commission, the Food and Drug Administration and the Internal Revenue Service. The FTC has the broadest authority of all agencies over domestic business practices and its decisions have nationwide effects. Its responsibility is to protect the public from anti-competitive and deceptive business practices. Its trade regulation rules have the force of law. The records of its enforcement activities are kept in its Public Reference Branch. For a fee, industry indexes and reports for individual companies can be obtained from the National Technical Information Service. The Bureau of Consumer Protection issues a quarterly *BCP Matters* sheet. The Transaction Status Sheet is updated daily. The annual Corporate Pattern Report provides information on partnerships, associations and other relations between corporations. *The Quarterly Financial Report* contains aggregate statistics on the state of the economy.

The FDA collects information in seven areas: foods, cosmetics, human drugs, animal drugs and feeds, medical devices, biologies and electronic radiological products. Its Establishment Inspection Forms and Analytical Laboratory Worksheets, obtain evaluations of how food-producing industries comply with the agency's "tolerable filth levels." Because the huge agency operates through 40 divisions it is a difficult journalistic assignment. Reporters often learn of important news about it from congressional hearings. Sometimes they use the Freedom of Information Act to obtain information.

Income-tax returns are confidential and it is futile for a reporter or anyone else to try to learn what they contain. Exceptions are the 990-PF and 990-AR forms, which private tax-exempt foundations must file with the IRS. It is easier to obtain access to them from the Foundation Center of the Library of Congress than from the reticent IRS. That was how the Omaha *Sunpapers* learned the financial status of Boys Town. Doug Longhini of WLS-TV also learned that funds raised to benefit widows and orphans were instead used for the Chicago Fire Department's marching band. The returns of the Richard Nixon Foundation confirmed a payment of $21,000 to Donald Nixon as a consultant on where the Nixon Library should be located.

In June 1984 *Chicago Lawyer* published a 20-page supplement called

"Freedom of Information Guide." It provides detailed information about how to use local, state and federal FOI laws. It also includes sample request letters, addresses of public bodies and texts of applicable laws. Copies are available by mail for $2 each from *Chicago Lawyer,* 343 S. Dearborn St., Chicago, Ill. 60604.

Playing Detective _____

If for no other reason than fear of being fired or arrested, the investigative reporter does not trespass, eavesdrop, wiretap, intercept mail or perform other illegal acts. Nevertheless, some of the techniques of a professional detective may be handy.

Newsday reporters, for instance, counted the number of garbage pickups in a certain district and compared it with the number specified in a city contract. The result was the revelation that a garbage collection firm had cheated taxpayers of about $5 million.

Robert Greene of the same newspaper suggests watching for variances in zoning permits. Otherwise, he surmises, an attractive parking space for 150 cars may deteriorate into a rundown space for 40 cars.

City hall reporters know that only enough funds should be deposited in no-interest accounts. When such accounts become too large, the suspicion arises that a politician or politician's friend may benefit.

Sometimes the names on documents such as contracts or titles to property are suspiciously unfamiliar. They may be the names of relatives or associates of the real parties involved. Or they may be fictitious. Probate, divorce, bankruptcy and other court records may provide clues. Maybe the principal has used his mother's maiden name.

An *Oregon Journal* reporter decided to read the city charter and amazed himself and his readers by discovering a secret $7,000 fund for use of the city council and mayor.

Beat reporters should be on constant alert to detect situations that the public interest requires be investigated, such as contract specifications written to favor a single bidder, contracts issued without competitive bids or to high instead of low bidders. Police reporters should take note of hearings at which motions to suppress evidence are made, because the nature of the evidence may provide clues to criminal behavior, possibly involving law-enforcement officers. The reporter also should know when prisoners are mistreated. In a Massachusetts case police testified that a retarded, black man, unable to read or write, had signed a confession. Police usually consider a case closed when an arrest has been made but the reporter's interest must continue.

A link between the Hell's Angels, a motorcycle gang, and organized crime was proved by the San Jose *Mercury-News,* which checked the security for a $1 million bail bond for a gang's leader accused of bombing a drug-enforcement officer. The paper discovered that it was property owned by three Angels, who also were among the owners of a catering service most of whose competitors had been forced out of business by bombings and other acts of terrorism.

Here are a few suggestions from experienced investigative reporters:

If a competitor or court official becomes curious while you are going through records, confuse him or her by turning your attention to other records in which you really have no interest.

If it is desired to check the stories of two principals against each other, solicit the aid of a colleague to make simultaneous calls to ask identical questions of the suspects.

Emulate the Michigan City, Ind., reporter who took plans and specifications for an extensive, expansive sewer project to an engineer outside the county for an opinion. It saved Michigan City an estimated $1½ million. The Indiana Association of Cities and Towns also examined a proposed budget and advised that if the proposed pay raises were granted the city would be bankrupt in three years.

Practice what is being called precision journalism, which means making your own charts to indicate trends. One such examination of IRS reports showed a growing practice of auditing the returns of taxpayers in lower-income brackets much more often than those in higher brackets.

Verify everything. Before you publish a story, give the other side a chance to deny or comment on what you have found. That procedure protects you against a possibly serious mistake and against charges of unfairness, either of which can undermine the credibility of your articles.

Masquerading _____

When the Chicago _Sun-Times_ failed to win a Pulitzer prize for its Mirage series, the debate intensified in journalistic circles as to how far the press should go in practicing deception. The Mirage was a tavern, which the paper bought. It was operated by two investigative reporters and a representative of the Better Government Association. Hidden photographers took pictures to provide documentary proof, and the experiment exposed the systematic corruption that plagues businesses through shakedowns and payoffs. Despite the plaudits and other prizes that the investigative reporters, Pamela Zekman and Zay N. Smith, received, the majority of the Pulitzer Prize Board considered the project unethical, possibly entrapment.

Contemporary deceptive journalistic techniques are not the crude practices of yesteryear when reporters posed as coroners and police, eavesdropped, stole pictures and manufactured information to induce news sources to talk. Modern techniques are more refined and more effective. For instance, the Minneapolis _Star_ sent a 76-year-old woman whose hearing was unimpaired to a number of hearing aid shops where salesmen invariably tried to get her to make a purchase. Similar stunts are performed to catch dishonest repairmen of automobiles, television sets and other commodities.

Journalistic patients have received widely different diagnoses of imaginary illnesses from a variety of doctors.

Hal Bernstein of Jack Anderson's organization worked on the Alaska pipeline to expose faulty piping. At another time he posed as a bum and worked in a migrant camp. Gordon Chaplin of the Baltimore *Sun* posed as a Philadelphia attorney interested in purchasing Spiro Agnew's house, the value of which had tripled as a result of so-called security improvements at public expense. When the vice president succeeded in killing the story it appeared in *More* and Chaplin went to work for the Washington *Post*.

A San Francisco *Examiner* reporter once enrolled in a high school class to try to discover why students are so uneducated. Several papers have exposed incompetency, laxity or bribery on the part of examiners at drivers' testing stations. They also have exposed the existence of racial discrimination in housing by sending black and white reporters, separately, to ask for referrals from real estate agents.

There is no universal answer to the question of what is ethical when gathering information without the source's knowing the reporter's identity. Many reporters have kept their jobs after walking into meetings where they didn't belong, sometimes dressed so as not to be conspicuous. Few editors object to consumer reporters patronizing restaurants and stores without introducing themselves. There are considerable differences of opinion, however, as regards almost any other kind of masquerading. A majority of editors doubtless do not condone deliberate lying on a reporter's part.

Evaluating the Effort

Investigative reporters and editors sometimes are disappointed, even disgusted, because quick reforms do not result from their efforts. They also risk cynicism when they enumerate all of the other exposés that could and should be made. Perhaps most discouraging to public-spirited journalists are the polls that reveal public distrust and dislike of them and support for repressive measures by government.

Without police or judicial powers all the journalist can do is direct attention to shortcomings. The press could not compel Boys Town to make better use of less money nor to desist in large-scale fund-raising campaigns. Nor could it stop Stefan Cardinal Wyszynski, backed by Pope John Paul II, from restoring the Rev. Michael Zembrzinski as director of the Order of St. Paul the First Hermit, commonly called the Pauline Fathers, at Doylestown, Pa., even after the Gannett News Service won a Pulitzer prize for exposing the financial mess there.

The Miami *Herald* won only a partial victory when the Florida state legislature recognized that the medical profession could not police itself and stripped the Board of Medical Examiners of its power to investigate and prosecute doctors and gave the authority to the Department of Consumer Protection and Professional Regulation. However, the medical board retained the power to decide how or whether a doctor found guilty should be punished.

There have been unfortunate examples of public employees exposed by the press as incompetent or corrupt who have been removed from one job only to be quietly hired for another with the same political sponsorship.

On the other hand, investigative reporters and editors can find satisfaction in the fact that as a result of the 125 stories that Bill Voelker wrote over a 29-month period for the New Orleans *Times-Picayune,* the state commissioner of administration in charge of computer operations was removed from his position, two computer firm officials were indicted by a federal grand jury and the FBI, SEC and IRS all investigated charges of illegal racketeering, mail and wire fraud and perjury.

Of the Pulitzer prize-winning investigation of the recruitment and killing in boot camp of a retarded Marine, Joe Murray, editor of the Lufkin (Tex.) *News* wrote, "Before it was over there would be Congressional investigations and hearings and inquiries by the president of the United States. The secretary of the Navy would get involved personally. There would be court martials and there would be trials. More importantly there would be reform. Before it was over, no less than the commandant of the Marine Corps would say that 1976 was a year of change for the U.S. Marines because of Lynn McClure. And because of that the Marine Corps was getting well. So I guess, in the best sense, that was what it was all about. Finding something that was wrong and doing something to change it."

Stories in the Sedalia, Mo., *Democrat-Capitol* were confirmed by a grand jury report that a teenaged inmate in the county jail had been "subjected to abuse, torture, assault and deviate sexual intercourse over a period of about a week." The jury, however, included a strange and sour note that the incident "had become a media event," and that the daily had acted irresponsibly.

There was a happier ending to the five months' investigation by WLS-TV, Chicago, and the Chicago Better Government Association into the death of an old woman in a Chicago area nursing home. Needed for corroboration of the rumor that Alma Weny died because there was no oxygen to save her was the nurse in attendance; she had moved to another nursing home so a BGA attorney obtained employment there. The project almost collapsed when she took pictures of patients illegally tied in wheelchairs. When someone approached her she quickly wrapped her Minox camera in a Milky Way candy wrapper and hid it behind her back. There it was seen by another person who said, "Oh I see you like Milky Ways too," so the spy-nurse, Barbara Klien, offered a real bar of which she had a supply in anticipation of just such a situation.

The project also seemed to be failing until the very last day of Klien's employment when a case similar to that which caused Alma Weny's death occurred and, almost unbelievably, the same nurse was on duty. From her Klein obtained the verification needed.

The final episode of this investigation occurred when Douglas Longhini, a WLS reporter, impersonated an investor interested in purchasing nursing homes. To the fictitious purchaser and Peter Karl, WLS investigative reporter, the management director confessed to income-tax fraud. By frequenting Skid Row the reporters also found another elderly woman who had been taken for more than $40,000.

On the first anniversary of The Mirage exposé, Pamela Zekman and Zay N. Smith, the Chicago *Sun-Times* reporters who posed as barmaid and waiter, summarized the aftermath: "more than a dozen government employees fired, Mayor orders updated safety codes, IRS probes tax fraud, state cracks down on license fraud, probers zero in on liquor and beer distributors, firemen prohibited from selling tickets on city time."

As the *Sun-Times* competitor, the Chicago *Tribune* says on its editorial page every day:

> The newspaper is an institution developed by modern civilization to present the news of the day, to foster commerce and industry, to inform and lead public opinion, and to furnish that check upon government which no constitution has ever been able to provide.

General Assignments (which every reporter should be able to cover)

HELP WANTED

In the first edition of his *Pennsylvania Gazette,* Benjamin Franklin wrote that to be successful an editor should be qualified with an extensive acquaintance with language, a great easiness and command of writing and relating things, clearly and intelligently, and in a few words, he should be able to speak of war both on land and sea, be well acquainted with geography, with the history of the time, with the several interests of princes and states, the secrets of courts and the manners and customs of all nations. Men thus accomplished are very rare in this remote part of the world.

11

Persons and Personalities

Names—people—make news and the journalistic rule, "as many names as possible in every edition" holds, in large as well as small places. Metropolitan papers are no longer able to publicize the comings and goings of most of their readers but they do their best to satisfy everyone's curiosity as regards celebrities. Gossip columns, specializing in trivia and alleged "inside dope," multiply. A generation ago Walter Winchell scandalized many with his "blessed event" and similar personal news, while Louella Parsons and Hedda Hopper possessed the ability to make or break glamorous motion-picture stars. Today *People, National Enquirer* and their competitors provide vicarious thrills for millions of frustrated hero-worshipers and are besieged by press agents seeking mention of their clients. Mainstream daily newspapers increasingly carry gossip columns and celebrity tidbits, too.

Gossip Is News

Community and suburban weeklies and dailies thrive on the inability of the large metropolitan papers to provide news of the routine happenings in their circulation areas. They cover not only news of governmental bodies and public and private organizations but also personal items, which never have ceased to be the backbone of the rural weekly. Typical of the one-paragraph personals that small city reporters may obtain just by "hanging around," by telephone conversations with friends or by opening their mail are the following:

> Mrs. Edwin P. Morrow of Washington, D.C., is visiting at the home of her son, Charles R. Morrow, 636 Sherman Ave. Mrs. Morrow is the widow of the late Edwin P. Morrow, former governor of Kentucky.

> Miss Eva Rathbone entertained her fellow members in the Puella Sunday school class of First Presbyterian Church at dinner Friday night at her home, 133 N. Prairie Ave. During the evening, the women worked on patch quilts to be distributed by the Women's Missionary Society of the church.

Home Town Personals

Contemporary reporters do not have to frequent railroad and bus stations, hotel lobbies, clubrooms, floral shops and delicatessen shops or stop acquaintances on street corners to obtain such news. Mostly it is contributed, and the editor altogether too often has to tone down banality and editorializing. Wielding too heavy a pencil, however, might destroy charming originality. For example, the homely informality of the following examples makes the paper more welcome in the family circle and to former residents of the communities who subscribe to their old home-town papers by mail.

> Happy birthday to Aunt Helen Krese of Grand Rapids, Michigan, and Janice Minner.
> Edith Bland, Opal Becker and Martha Narup visited Helen Nord and Irene Hayn Tuesday afternoon. Sorry to report that Irene is having trouble with her leg and is on crutches.
> Kathy Wallendorf and Little Gus and Opal Becker visited George and Edith Bland Thursday afternoon.
> Happy anniversary to Mr. and Mrs. Henry Bland of Brighton.
> [Calhoun (Hardin, Ill.) *News*]

> Son Leslie shared cukes, squash and zucchini with us. Grandson Dana up on his cycle with a pretty little blonde he introduced to me. She, Mary Drews, dare say we'd be happy to welcome in the Torsey Tribe.
> Via the grapevine, a party has purchased 1,000 acres in New Hampton. It's to be stripped and cut up into house lots. If true, why the secrecy? Doc didn't guess there was a hunk that big to go on the block. At that rate, will Old New Hampton be a city soon? If so, who will be our first mayor?
> Two big loghaulers with more logs from Sky Pond came thru our yard stripping apples from our Porter, Wealthy plus cider trees. These trucks bear Colebrook names.
> Maurice S. biked up. An orange rig up with backhoe for ditch-digging and tipping out stones. [Plymouth (N.H.) *Record-Citizen*]

Such informality has a limit, even in the smallest of towns, as illustrated by the following:

The new band leader, Don Walters, put his Hubbard group through its paces last Saturday and again Tuesday and Wednesday of this week. The youngsters are all eager and ready to go to Iowa City this coming Saturday and do themselves and their community proud. Everything points to a good chance for them to come through with shining colors. The group expects to leave town about 7 o'clock in the morning so as to give the performers time to get some of the kinks from riding out of their system.

So let's cheer them on with three big rahs. All right, here we go—rah! Rah! RAH!

On the other hand, the rural or suburban correspondent with an undeveloped nose for news may write as a brief what should have been a longer news or feature story. The properly written personal really is a news lead. As such, it is good if it fulfills the requirements of a good lead and bad if it doesn't. Note how the following barren brevities might have been made more nearly complete and interesting while still remaining brevities:

Insufficient	**Insufficient**
A. L. Scobey, 1434 Ellis St., has returned from a two-week trip to San Francisco.	Mr. and Mrs. Edward L. Parkhouse, 683 Pulliam Ave. entertained 16 guests Monday night at a theater party.
Sufficient	**Sufficient**
A. L. Scobey, 1434 Ellis St., returned today from San Francisco with the prize given the delegate traveling the farthest distance to attend the annual convention of the Fraternal Order of Leopards there last week. Mr. Scobey represented the local Leopards lodge of which he is commander. The prize was a traveling bag.	To celebrate their 25th wedding anniversary, Mr. and Mrs. Edward L. Parkhouse, 683 Pulliam Ave., entertained 16 guests Monday night at a theater party. Formerly it was believed the Parkhouses had been married only 15 years, but they chose this belated occasion to reveal that they had been secretly wed for ten years before making an announcement.

It easily can be imagined how either of these, especially the second, could have been expanded into a much longer story with considerable reader interest. Unfortunately, it is not presumptuous to imagine a beginning reporter's getting no more than the original items cited. State or county editors often despair because of the inability of rural correspondents to sense news values. Young reporters may be able to pick important names out of hotel registers but some may miss the fact that the out-of-town visitor listed inconspicuously among those "in town for the day" is negotiating with the directors of a bank for its purchase, consulting with Chamber of Commerce officials about the establishment of a new industry or applying for a position in the local schools or for the pastorate of a local church. The fault obviously is under-reporting.

Big City Snoops

There is hardly a large city daily that does not have more than a single gossip columnist. Today the same paper may have a half dozen or more of them. One of the most popular was The Ear of the Washington *Star,* later the Washington *Post,* from whose contents the following extracts are typical:

TUBED UP

We all wondered what on earth happened to Barbara Howar, when she fled for the Big Apple this year. (Remember? Those ghastly gossips all nattered and nudged about how chummy she and Ham Jordan were getting. Then bingo, she was gone.) Ear's proud to announce that she's been beavering away on a pilot for public teevee up there. It's called "Watching T.V." Barb's co-toiler on it is marvelous Marvin Titman. (Marvy Marv, as we all call him, is the tube critic for clever little *Newsday.*) This all sounded *tres originale* to Ear, which is looking for a Chic New Watching Posture. But no. On the show, Barb and Marv just sit around and dish things like "Networks used sleaze to up the gross network figures. *And gross it is.*" Ear is kind of impressed, and kind of gloomy, and kind of thinking of living on the floor *anyway.*

FINEST HOUR

A Great Moment in Anglo-American Friendship, darlings: The British Embassy's freshly-knighted defense attaché, Air Marshal Sir Roy Austen-Smith, with his Lady, purred through the White House gate for the great Maggie Thatcher Dinner Monday night, superb in their glossy black Jaguar. Well, *almost* superb: A bump in the paving at the gate knocked the Jag's low-slung exhaust system off. Britain's pride jerked under the great white portico dragging pipes, grating hideously and honking deafening razberries through the smashed muffler. The Secret Service blanched. The Knight and his Lady gallantly swept out and swept in, heads high. Ashen White Housers trundled off the Machine and patched it up with chewing gum and wire. Cost of repairs on the Jag, later: $1,500. "Worth every penny. They were *just* like the Few. The Show Went On," sighed an Anglophile, eyes moist as warm ale. Ear salutes Sir Roy. He's used to it, of course.

FINEST FLOWER

Ear's glum to catch wind of the Carl Bernstein-Nora Ephron split, so soon after Nora produced wee Max, the Divine Duo's second son. Carl's *finally* fallen in true *amour* with Another, he's telling pals. He really feels *awful* about his timing. Ah yes.

FINEST FLIER

Ear hears that Clare Crawford, a hotshot *People* maggie scribe, has some charming pix of herself with Zbig Brzezinski. He's *very* tightly zipped and buttoned throughout. So, of course, is Ear.

Family/Living _____

When New York newspapers near the end of the last century began printing the guest lists of parties attended by members of the so-called 400, they made journalistic history. At first this "invasion of privacy" was resented, but through "leaks" and gate-crashing the news continued to be obtained. Today the problem of most society editors is not how to get news but how to satisfy everyone wanting "nice" notices on the page. The problem is without solution and today the society page as such generally has disappeared in all but some very small papers. The original and enduring appeal of the page had been two-fold (1) to the vanity of those considered important enough to receive mention, (2) to the curiosity of all others regarding the glamorous way of life of their social superiors. As the scope of a paper's coverage and circulation widened, those who argued that these values are fictitious and the whole concept undemocratic have prevailed.

For several years the successor to the society page was a woman's page, which played up club news, columns and features on marriage and parenthood, possibly also cooking and household repairs. Feminists objected to this innovation, which editors also found it difficult to develop. The formula for a satisfactory substitute for the society and/or woman's page has not yet developed. Most popular of the current experiments is a family/living page or section. Adolph Bremer, editor of the Winona (Minn.) *Daily News,* described it as follows:

As for contents of *Family/Living,* we have retained engagements and weddings, although sharply reducing the space for them. The picture size in both instances is down and the text for the wedding is confined to a cutline. We have continued a club (mostly women's) calendar and have expanded the listings insofar as practical to eliminate an accompanying advance headlined story. We added an Arts/Platform weekly calendar, expanded artistic reviews, concentrated most club meeting reports of a routine nature to a roundup, and reduced photos of club officers, with an exception of two, to a 5-pica pic of president. We've kept the best seller list of books and added a local column, "Books and Such," which is more (or less?) than a book review column. Dear Abby and the horoscope go on. The main changes have been in getting more controversial stuff on the pages, as opposed to the puffy society stuff. This Sunday we're doing the abortion thing, a mighty hot topic here with about half of the city population Catholic. We've done quite a bit with marital and personality problems, sexual abuse, rape and the new "in" stuff that interest women (most of them anyhow) more than the spring fashions. To the outsider the Family/Living pages may not seem revolutionary, but the evolution has been drastic and it is continuing. We did experiment with local shopping comparisons (food), but we found comparative pricing full of hazards and we discontinued without advertising pressure. We do have a syndicated consumer column. Give us a bigger newshole in this area and we'd do more of a controversial nature within staff limitations, and utilize more of the good stuff from AP, NYTNS and CST. Except for Sunday we don't have the big holes to fill in this area. And frankly on Sunday we're loaded with columns although we do insist on one open or nearly open page.

On larger papers the impact of the effort to seek an alternative to the old women's page has been much greater, opening editors' eyes to all sorts of story possibilities and approaches to news reporting and writing that once were neglected.

The Style section of the Washington *Post* has been particularly innovative in that respect during the past two decades. Some of its best work has been collected in an excellent anthology, entitled *Writing in Style.* The book includes a discussion of the Style section's philosophy and ground rules. It is important reading about an influential new area of interpretative reporting.

Such sections, stimulated by the feminist movement, have opened the entire newspaper to new kinds of questions to explore about American social and economic institutions and to a more down-to-earth, human way of seeking answers to them. In the summer of 1985, for example, the Chicago *Sun-Times* ran on its general newspages a series of articles about Chicago schools, called "Room 247." The following page one introduction to the series from Aug. 25, 1985, captures its flavor:

> According to the "code" on Chicago's mean streets, most of the 31 kids who sat through summer school in Senn High School's Room 247 these past two months were not supposed to be there. After all, hot weather was meant to inspire hot times, not homework.
>
> So what if these teens, most of them from poor families, had each flunked at least two courses last year. By the "code's" accounting, they'd simply say the hell with it, jive on down the line, and eventually be swallowed up in Chicago's 49 percent dropout rate.
>
> But something was different about these kids. They stood their ground, spit in the "code's" eye, and grabbed at one of the last second chances many of them may ever get.
>
> For three hours a day, five days a week, for eight weeks, they made speeches, read books, took vocabulary quizzes and recited poetry in a junior-level speech class.
>
> Like the more than 5,000 Chicago public high school students attending the system's first tuition-free summer school in six years, the comeback kids of Room 247 showed they're not willing to give up and drop out.
>
> Some will make it to graduation day. Some won't. But on this end-of-summer day, at least, they can all say they tried.

The competing Chicago *Tribune* also is doing more human oriented, ongoing reporting about Chicago school students of a sort that was pioneered on the new family living pages that replaced the old women's and society pages. Here is an example in the form of a story excerpt from the *Tribune*'s main local news page on June 9, 1985. The story was written by Jean Davidson:

> When Farragut High School senior Jeanette Thomas heads for U.S. history class, her 5-year-old son goes to preschool with the children of other Farragut students.
>
> "I like having him here so I can visit during my free periods," said Thomas, who also has a 2-year-old daughter. "We really need the day care because so many kids are having babies."
>
> Pregnant girls and teenage mothers can be found in most Chicago public high school classrooms and, increasingly, behind grammar school desks as well.
>
> Circumscribed though their futures may be, those who return to the classroom and graduate from high school are the lucky ones. An estimated half of all pregnant girls in Chicago drop out of school, sending themselves and often their offspring into a cycle of failure, dependence and poverty.

Another example of how family/living stories have burst onto main newspages with a human angle is this page one story opening in the July

28, 1985, St. Petersburg *Times*. The story was written by Mark Travis and Laurie Holliman.

> One June morning last year, a St. Petersburg foster mother found a 5-day-old girl in her crib, apparently dead. The foster mother did not call paramedics for at least an hour.
>
> In September 1984 in Tampa, a 5-year-old boy fell into his foster family's algae-filled swimming pool. His foster mother checked the pool but couldn't find him. It was only when her teen-age son swept a pole through the murky water that they discovered the boy.
>
> Four-month-old Corey Greer died in a crib in his foster mother's over-crowded Treasure Island home one week ago. The monitor that could have warned of trouble was in a closet. The baby was buried Saturday.
>
> Fourteen children in the state's foster care system have died in the last 16 months, according to the Florida Department of Health and Rehabilitative Services (HRS). Two more deaths that occurred even earlier weren't reported until that period.
>
> That means children in the system are dying at a rate of nearly one a month. While some of these deaths don't appear to be anyone's fault, others might have been prevented. And together, the deaths raise questions that the people in charge can't answer. . . .

Personal News

Though downplayed these days, the traditional items of society news still have a place. The Louisville *Courier-Journal* explains its policy, which is fairly typical among newspapers of its type, to readers this way:

> We don't like to disappoint our readers in their moments of pride and happiness. To be sure that we don't have to disappoint you when you want to publish your engagement, wedding or anniversary announcement, here is what you need to know:
>
> ENGAGEMENTS
> It can take up to two months to get your engagement announced in the newspaper. We recommend sending in announcements (with or without photographs) no later than six weeks before you want the announcement published.
>
> Engagement announcements received less than four weeks before the wedding date will be returned to the sender unpublished.
>
> Photographs should be wallet size or larger. A five-by-seven glossy photograph will reproduce best in the newspaper. Although a color photograph may be submitted, it will not reproduce as well as a black and white. Photos will be returned, if a stamped, self-addressed envelope is enclosed.
>
> WEDDINGS
> Information about the wedding ceremony must be in our office not later than two weeks before the wedding date. The announcement is published in the first Sunday newspaper after the wedding.
>
> Any announcements received after that deadline will be run in an abbrevi-

ated form in a later Sunday edition. Information about a wedding more than one month old will not be used.

We do not use photographs with these announcements.

ANNIVERSARIES

Accent publishes announcements of the following anniversaries: 50th, 55th, 60th, 65th and above.

If you wish to have the announcement run on a Sunday before the anniversary celebration, we must have that information in our hands at least two weeks before the celebration.

Information for anniversaries that involve no celebration or for which the celebration has already taken place will not be published if the event is more than one month old.

We do not use photographs with these announcements either.

PROCEDURE

We have simple forms for all three announcements. You can get them by writing Accent, The Courier-Journal, Louisville, Ky. 40202, or by calling 582-4667 in Louisville.

All the announcements are published as a free service of the newspaper.

Stories are written by formula:

Mr. and Mrs. Charles J. Graf of Jeffersonville, Ind., announce the engagement of their daughter, Stacie Joe Graf, and Robert M. Eyster III, Louisville, son of Mr. and Mrs. Robert M. Eyster Jr. of Salem, Ohio. Miss Graf attended Indiana University Southeast and Western Reserve . . .   [Louisville *Courier-Journal*]

Linda Darnall of rural Atlanta and Martin England of Stanford were married at 7 p.m. Saturday at Armington Christian Church. A reception followed at the church.

The newlyweds will live in rural Armington.

The bride, a daughter of Mr. and Mrs. Dale Darnall of rural Atlanta, graduated from Olympia High School. She is employed by Illinois Agricultural Association.

The bridegroom is a son of James England of McLean and Mrs. Enid England of Stanford. He is also a graduate of Olympia High School and is employed by Thermo in Armington.   [Bloomington (Ill.) *Pantagraph*]

Mr. and Mrs. Lawrence A. Mitchell Sr., Gallipolis, Ohio, celebrated their 50th wedding anniversary Aug. 19 in Gallipolis.

Mitchell married the former Melva Cornell Sept. 22, 1929, in Winfield, W. Va.

They are the parents of Nancy James, Norman and Donna Sanders, all of Gallipolis; Fred of Roswell, Ga., Maxine of Buffalo, W. Va., Ray of Pomeroy, Ohio, and Lawrence Jr. of Milan, Mich. The couple has 15 grandchildren and one great-grandchild.

Mitchell is a farmer and is retired from Gallipolis Locks and Dam.

[Columbus (Ohio) *Dispatch*]

Formula writing is space saving and makes it easier to refuse requests that stories be written in a certain way. Many hostesses would like to have their affairs reported as the most successful of the season. The copy desk must be alert to eliminate adjectives such as "gorgeous," "radiant" and so forth to describe guests and/or decorations. Anyone who handles social items also must be wary to check news sources, since there are pranksters who think it very funny to announce the engagement, marriage, parenthood or divorce of a friend or foe.

Weddings

Backbone of the local page where news of social events is displayed is the wedding story. Some papers usually and all occasionally deviate from formula as in the following from the Freeport (Ill.) *Journal-Standard.*

> Lori Ann Fluegel and Daniel Karl Hepler were united in matrimony on Nov. 17 at Trinity United Methodist Church.
>
> Arrangements of white and lavender carnations with wheat and heather and seven-branched candelabra adorned the church as the Rev. Karl Hepler, father of the bridegroom, and the Rev. Thomas Howard officiated at the double-ring ceremony. Bill Robbins provided the piano accompaniment as Mark Anderson sang the solos.
>
> Mr. and Mrs. Robert Fluegel, 4584 Route 20 West, are the parents of the bride. The bridegroom is the son of the Rev. and Mrs. Karl Hepler, 1133 S. Maple Ave.
>
> The bride carried a cascade bouquet of sterling silver roses, stephanotis and Jack Frost roses accented with ivory angel lace. She wore an ivory satin crepe gown with a blouson bodice and drawstring neckline with a self-ruffled collar. A cummerbund accented the waistline. The full raglan sleeves were gathered into a button cuff. Clusters of ivory Elegance carnations and babies'-breath were worn in her hair.
>
> Serving the bride was Carole Holey. She was attired in a satin knit gown with a fitted tucked bodice and Sweetheart neckline with long puffed sleeves. She held a nosegay of ivory Elegance carnations tipped with lavender and babies-breath. She wore a halo of similar flowers in her hair.
>
> Doug Weiner and Brian Olson assisted the bridegroom.
>
> The reception was held in Fellowship Hall.

Information for such stories usually is obtained by means of blanks sent to prospective brides after the city hall reporter has reported that marriage licenses have been applied for. In most states there is a short waiting period between application and issuance of licenses. A sample wedding blank follows:

WEDDING REPORT

Full name of bride _____

Address of bride _____

Full names of bride's parents or guardians _____

Address of bride's parents _____

Full name of bridegroom _____

Address of bridegroom _____

Full names of bridegroom's parents _____

Address of bridegroom's parents _____

Date of wedding _____ Time _____

Place of ceremony _____

Who will perform ceremony? _____

Will bride wear a gown or suit? _____ Describe _____

_____

Will she wear a veil? _____ Is it an heirloom? _____

Describe the veil _____

Will she carry a prayer book? _____

Will she carry or wear flowers? _____ Describe _____

_____

Who will give the bride away? (name, address and relationship) _____

_____

Name of maid or matron of honor and relationship _____

Describe her gown and flowers _____

Names and addresses of bridesmaids _____

_____

Describe their gowns and flowers _____

Ribbon, ring or flower bearers _____

Describe their gowns and flowers _____

Name and address of best man _____

Groomsmen _____

Ushers _____

Will ceremony be formal or informal? _____

Musicians _____

Musical selections:

   Before ceremony _____

   As bridal party enters _____

   During ceremony _____

   As bridal party leaves _____

Order in which bridal party will enter _____

_____

Decorations (color scheme and how carried out; significance) _____

_____

Number of invitations sent out _____ Probable attendance _____

Will a reception follow? _____ Where? _____

How many will attend reception? _____

Decorations _____

Hostesses:

In parlor _____

In dining room _____

Will breakfast, luncheon or dinner be served? _____ Where? _____

Will couple take a trip? _____ Where? _____ When? _____

When and where will couple be at home? _____

Bridegroom's occupation and business address _____

Occupation of the bride _____

Bridegroom's education and degrees _____

Bridegroom's fraternal connections _____

Bride's education and degrees _____

Bride's sorority connections _____

Bridegroom's military record: service, rank, area in which served and duration,

citations, unusual experiences, etc. _____

_____

Bride's military record _____

Guests from away, names, initials and addresses _____

_____

Other information _____

_____

Picking the Feature

Whoever writes wedding stories welcomes any possible feature with which to lead the account. Possible features to give depth to the account include

1. *The romance.* The manner of meeting or the length of the engagement if unusual. Sometimes childhood sweethearts are united after years of separation. Or there may be an Evangeline or Enoch Arden complication. Ordinarily, unless the bride is a widow, the fact of any previous marriage is omitted. Exceptions to this rule are persons prominent in the news, especially motion picture actors and actresses. In their cases it is common practice to write: "It is her third marriage and his fourth."

2. *The place.* Perhaps some relative of either party was married in the same church. Maybe an outdoor ceremony is performed on the spot where the betrothal took place. Sometimes a couple selects an unusual site for its nuptials, as an airplane or beneath the water in diving suits. Wedding ceremonies have been performed in hospitals, prisons and by long-distance telephone or radio.

3. *The date or hour.* It may be the anniversary of the engagement. Perhaps the bride's mother or some other relative was married on the same date. In an effort to make its wedding the first of the year or month, a couple may be married shortly after midnight.

4. *Bride's costume.* Often a bride wears her mother's dress or veil or

some other family heirloom. There is an old superstition that a bride should always wear something old and something new, something borrowed and something blue; many modern brides adhere to this, and some article of a bride's costume may be unusual.

5. *Relationship.* If the scions of two old and prominent families are married, their family connections may constitute the feature. If either is descended from Revolutionary or Colonial ancestry that fact should be played up.

The feature, of course, may be found in any one of a number of other elements. Perhaps the bridegroom wears a military uniform or the bride cuts the wedding cake with her husband's sword. Maybe the minister is a relative. The attendants may be sorority sisters or representatives of some organization. Whatever it is, the society editor tries to find it and to feature it—anything to drive off the monotony of the stereotyped wedding lead.

Style

The trite and hackneyed style of the "country" wedding story must be avoided. To this end, avoid use of such expressions as "blushing bride," "plighted their troth," "holy wedlock," "linked in matrimony." The word "nuptials" should not be overworked.

The easiest lead sentence is the straightforward: "A and B were married—." For variety, other possibilities include

—exchanged (spoke) nuptial (marriage) vows.
Miss A became the bride of B—.
Miss A was married to B—.
First church was the scene of the marriage of—.
A simple ceremony united in marriage Miss A and B—.
The marriage of A and B took place—.
—attended the nuptials of A and B.
Nuptial vows were spoken by A and B—.
The marriage of A and B was solemnized—.
Chaplain C read the service which joined A and B in marriage—.
Chaplain C officiated at—.

Some of these phrases may be appropriate in other parts of the story. When a page includes a half-dozen or more wedding stories, it is desirable to obtain variety. However worded, the lead of the wedding story should contain the feature, if there is one, the names of the principals with the bride's name ordinarily mentioned first and the time and place of the wedding. The principals usually are identified by addresses and parentage.

Marital Status

Seldom broken has been the journalistic taboo preventing mention of extramarital affairs of persons in public life. Congressmen have slept off drunks at their desks, newspaper publishers have received employees while in bed with mistresses, presidential romances are exposed posthumously in best-selling books.

It is becoming increasingly difficult for the press to shield public figures, however, as such behavior becomes less clandestine. Since the principals are less hypocritical and more open in their relations, it hardly makes sense for the press to protect them from public disclosure. After all, few were shocked when a leading motion picture actor at the Academy Awards gala introduced "the mother of my children," nor when a presidential candidate was reported in news pictures and stories as taking his girl friend with him on a vacation trip.

Without sensationalizing, when it is pertinent, it can and probably should be reported that what boy friend and what girl friend probably have been living together for months or years, maybe a lifetime.

Births

A real toughie is the birth notice. When a prominent woman becomes a mother the event is newsworthy. If, however, the child is born out of wedlock or from adultery, before writing the story the reporter acts wisely if he seeks advice from his superiors. Paternity suits test the mettle of journalism as well as judges, so everyone concerned usually is willing to ignore the whole business.

For the noncontroversial birth story, the reporter should obtain

1. Names and addresses of parents.
2. Time and place of birth.
3. Weight of the baby.
4. Sex of the baby.
5. The name, if chosen.

The mother's maiden name may be included if she has not been married more than a few years, if the couple is living in another city and her married name is unfamiliar locally or if she uses her birth name either professionally or generally. If the date of the marriage is mentioned, care must be taken to give it correctly. Libel suits have results from mistakes of this sort even in these liberal-minded days.

Since all parents supposedly are proud, that fact is of no news value. And it never has been proved scientifically that newly born babies bounce. A baby's rosy cheeks, lusty lungs and dimpled chin may be taken for granted. "Daughter" or "son" is better than "baby girl" or "baby boy." Do not use "cherub" or "the new arrival to bless the home" or the like.

Medical treatment of sterility has resulted in a considerable increase in multiple births so that the arrival of quintuplets is no longer the story of the year. Nevertheless, they as well as quadruplets, triplets and twins still are newsworthy. Unusual weight or size, physical deformity or the circumstances under which birth took place may elevate the event above the level of the routine birth notice, as was the case in each of the following items:

Wenatchee, Wash.—Mr. and Mrs. W. E. Robinson of Entiat Valley claim to be parents of the first baby born in an auto trailer in the Pacific northwest. A daughter, Kay, was born to them in March.

The fire department ambulance crew in charge of Lieut. Irvin Martin aided the stork early Wednesday and a baby was presented to Mrs. Callie Burns, 21, 1216 Freeman Ave. Mother and infant were then taken to the general hospital.

Some newspapers play births more prominently than others. One way is to obtain pictures of the newly born, together with short feature stories in which source of the name, brothers and sisters, date of birth or some feature angle may be emphasized. The following is a typical entry from such a column:

Even if she is a girl, the first child of Mr. and Mrs. William Clifford Richards Jr., 1415 Ashland Ave., was named for her father and is called Billie Mae. Her second name is the first name of her maternal grandmother. Weighing 8 pounds 14 ounces the addition who has made the Richards family a threesome, was born Dec. 2 at St. Paul Hospital.

Some papers, especially in the suburbs, interview newcomers to the community to introduce them to their new neighbors. Also residents who return from trips abroad or to vacation lands anywhere make good subjects for features based on their experiences and impressions. Similarly, visitors may make interesting copy.

'Canned' News

Much of the contents of the page commonly called women's or family is syndicated or provided by public relation firms representing trade associations. It often is called "canned" news in newspaper lingo. It provides advice to the lovelorn; hints on how to be pregnant, give birth and rear children; advice on how to stay happily married or to live alone and like it; also, advice on how to take care of pets and stay healthy and physically attractive and fit. Experts discuss mental health, how to garden, how to cook (with plentiful recipes provided by advertisers), take care of the hair, be stylish and fashionable. Illustrations often are provided by manufacturers, along with articles which are mostly free publicity.

A few lead paragraphs that appeared on a typical modern fashion page follow:

Fashion is on a big knit-kick this season, and the look comes up fresh and new and full of energy.

Pants have come a long way from the gardening-housework-car-pool routine. Their fashion potential along with their easy-going manner has cast them in a far more important role.

At one time if a hostess told a man "casual dress," she could generally predict what he was going to wear. But today, a man might show up in anything from velvet jeans to a suede fringed jacket.

Such commercialization of the erstwhile society page has become all too common, even in papers of otherwise high quality. Reporters should resist it and, in doing so may find some friendly ears on good editors determined to improve the credibility of their papers.

Society News

Types of Society News

The typical society page or section, now found mostly outside large metropolitan areas or in zoned sections of metro dailies, consists mainly of the following kinds of news:

Parties: birthday, reunions, anniversary, coming-out, announcement, showers, weekend, house, theater, card and miscellaneous.
Teas, luncheons, dinners, banquets, suppers, cocktail parties and picnics.
Meetings and announcements of meetings of clubs.
Receptions.
Dances and balls.
Benefits, bazaars and the like.
Personal items, if not used in another part of the paper.
Engagements and weddings.

As this list suggests, the society page or section usually is written principally for women, although men are interested in many stories of engagements, weddings, parties and personal activities. A majority of society editors are women who have social rank themselves, although many large papers have male society editors. Of whichever sex, the editor should be able to attend major social events on an equal footing with other guests, although only a few occasions require the presence of a reporter. A large majority of society page items are contributed by persons concerned or by social secretaries, either in writing or by telephone. The society editor must be ever on the alert for practical jokers sending or phoning in bogus announcements of engagements, weddings and other social events. Nothing should be used without verification. If the society editor needs pipelines, such people as chefs, florists, hairdressers and delicatessen store operators are among the best to utilize.

Elements in Society News

Most society events of any importance have elements in common which include:

Names. Host and hostess; guests of honor; members of the receiving line in order of importance; assistants to hostess in the parlor and dining room; members of committees; entertainers; musicians and their selections; prominent guests; relation of guest of honor to hostess or of assistants to either.

Decorations. Color scheme, its significance and how it was carried out; flowers, palms and ferns to make room resemble tropical garden, an outdoor scene and so on.

Refreshments. Distinguish between luncheon and tea and between supper, dinner and banquet. At receptions, always learn who poured and who served and ask if these assistants were selected for any particular reason (relatives, sorority sisters, officers of an organization).

Occasion. Is it an anniversary or an annual event? What will be done with any proceeds? Does the place have any significance?

It is difficult to achieve variety in writing similar accounts of social events. Consequently, the society editor welcomes any possible unique feature.

Personalities _____

It is sad but probably true that most people go through life without ever being considered newsworthy. At best their birth, marriage and death receive brief mention. Otherwise, unless they get into trouble, as criminal or criminal's victim, or are in an accident or innocently a part of some unusual circumstance, they are ignored by the press. If, on the other hand, they attain a position of importance whereby others are affected, they become the objects of attention.

Important Position

Newly elected or appointed public figures, executives of private businesses and others in decision-making positions are objects of interest, especially when they enter upon their new careers.

By Gary Kiefer

In their rush to serve today's job-oriented students, colleges must guard against the danger of becoming vocational schools, Ohio State University's new provost says.

W. Ann Reynolds, who took over Sept. 1 as OSU's chief academic officer, said universities are facing difficult decisions as rising costs and declining enrollments force administrators to cut back in some academic areas.

She warns that universities which make curriculum decisions solely on the basis of student interest are shirking some of the responsibility that comes with being a center for knowledge.

"There is extra pressure on us now that kids are so job-oriented," she said. The changing goals of students, she added, can be seen in their increasing interest in fields like engineering, where jobs are plentiful, and decreasing interest in liberal arts studies like languages.

"As a university, we must take a hard look at our curriculum but I think we need to protect some programs, like language studies, that are important even if they are not the most popular," she said.

Dr. Reynolds, 41, will have a lot to say about the academic decisions made at Ohio State in coming years, according to OSU President Harold Enarson, who said university officials found in her "a person of truly superior qualifications. . . ."   [Columbus (Ohio) *Dispatch*]

Prominent Citizen

Even holders of important positions can go unnoticed unless the paper runs a "Know Your Neighbor" series or something of the sort, short profiles to make readers better acquainted with persons who may affect their lives and well-being. Reader interest is heightened when the profile turns out to be a success story.

By George Vecsey

Nyack, N.Y.—Once he was a bellhop at Kutsher's resort hotel in the Catskills, a black basketball player from the ghetto carrying luggage. Today he is a heart surgeon, implanting pacemakers in some of the very same people he served as a bellhop.

Dr. Fletcher James Johnson Jr. could take all the credit, say "Look what I've done," and emphasize that he had to study in Italy and Switzerland to achieve his goal. But he describes the fact of a black surgeon working in a Hasidic-owned hospital as a victory for America, a proof that the system can work.

"My father is a Bible-reading man with a third-grade education who taught me that life is short—you only get one hand," he said. "I see myself accepted as a surgeon; I feel very good about this country. People can do it."

Dr. Johnson is willing to preach a little bit because he sees good things happening around him in Rockland County, a region of green hills and views of the Hudson River 20 miles north of New York City, divided among estates and old mostly gentile neighborhoods on the one hand and the Hasidic Jewish community of New Square on the other . . .   [New York _Times_]

Unusual Occupation

Some people are highly visible as they earn a living—bus drivers, second-hand car salesmen, department store clerks, policemen and the like. Others, belonging to smaller segments of the labor force, are obscure and often considered mysterious or the object of awe.

By Kathy Megan

On a hillside somewhere between Clendenin and Walton, Danny Dunn leaned on his freshly sharpened shovel and sighed, "There's no consideration for a man digging a grave.

"A gravedigger's job is the loneliest in the world," he said. "You're the first to get here before a funeral and the last to leave. After everyone pulls out of here in their Cadillacs and Lincolns you've still got an hour's worth of work."

Whether in rain, snow or ice, or on New Year's, Easter or birthdays, Danny, Dally and their father Leo Dunn are on call. The Mount Tyler family has eked out a harsh but thriving livelihood in country graveyards.

Leo, 73, figures he has dug 3,000 graves since childhood. For 28 years he sold vaults, the outer case for a casket, while digging graves on the side. At the age of 62, a time when most men are considering retirement, Leo quit selling vaults for a company and established his own business. Danny and Dally had brandished shovels for their dad for most of their lives but, in the last few years, turned professional.

The family digs graves in the traditional manner, no backhoes or tractors. Using picks, shovels and muscle power, and consuming quarts of Dr. Pepper, Danny and Dally dig about 15 graves a month.

"The trouble with gravedigging is that you can't plan anything," Leo said. "When we get called, there's no deciding. We have to go. . . ."

[Charleston (W.Va.) *Gazette*]

Unusual Hobby

Not all persons utilize their spare time watching low-brow television programs or reading trashy magazines. Some make avocations out of collecting coins or antiques and everything in between. Or they create things or in some other way exhibit originality and creativity. Elderly people are especially newsworthy when they make constructive use of their spare time.

By Dave Person

Kalamazoo—The warm heart of Mrs. May Leedy has led to warm hands for dozens of youngsters at Edison School during the past four years.

Each year at Christmastime the 96-year-old boxes up the mittens she has made during a long year of knitting and sends them off to the school.

There, Principal Richard Grushon distributes a pair to each of his kindergarteners at the school's annual Christmas party.

The children always appreciate the mittens, Grushon said. Some youngsters already have lost their first pair of winter mittens by Christmas and need a new pair. Others, he said, have no mittens to begin with. . . .

[Grand Rapids (Mich.) *Press*]

Reminiscences

Old people often spin stories about the good old days or recall instances of historic importance, explain why they experience *dèjá vu* as history seems to repeat itself. The reporter should avoid those who have memories only of personal experience, mostly trivial, and seek out the wise sages whose experiences and recollections can be newsworthy.

Grand Junction—Al Look stretched his legs, leaned back in his armchair, laughed and began telling another story, this one about a "flannelmouthed, tobacco-chewing, bulldozing" defense attorney who managed to discredit all six witnesses to a murder.

Look's rapid-fire, precise accounting of the story was fast, but the easy flow of descriptive adjectives explained how the lawyer did it.

If you enjoy first-person stories about Indians, cowboys, cowtowns, cows, fish, archaeology, paleontology, film-making, advertising, journalism, comic strips, the Holy Land, Alaskan dog races, politics or the economy, listen a while.

Now 86 years old, Look has helped chronicle a good bit of western Colorado history, made some himself, and currently is working a few hours a day on his next book. He has another at the publisher's for editing, a third at the printers and already has had 14 others published. . . .   [Denver *Post*]

Visiting Celebrity

After apotheosizing entertainers, political and civic leaders, athletes and others, people want to know the extent to which the celebrities remain human beings. They ask reporters and others in a position to know, "What are they really like?" When a popular hero or heroine comes to town, local reporters try to find out.

By Diane Reischel

"I was never a pretty little girl. I've got the long nose, the long face."

In other words, Nancy Sparer had the aristocratic look.

It's a persona she wears with flair in her portrayal of newspaper publisher Margaret Pynchon on CBS television's "Lou Grant."

The Emmy-winning actress stopped off in Madison this weekend to visit her son David, who is in his final year of law school at the University of Wisconsin.

A graying widow on the screen, "Mrs. Pynchon" in person is softer, less forbidding, and strawberry blonde. Yet, without question, this is a woman who could keep even the most irreverent city editor in tow.

"Mrs. Pynchon is a terrific lady. I love her," said Sparer, who goes by the stage name of Nancy Marchand.

"She's obviously quite bright. She's very brave, probably pretty lonely. She has a terrific sense of humor and a tremendous sense of responsibility."

She's also had two seasons to mellow: "Some people have said to me they find she's not quite as prickly as early on in the show."

The woman behind prickly Mrs. Pynchon is an avowed easterner. She was raised in Buffalo, educated at Carnegie Tech, and unleashed on New York City in the nascent days of television.

"Television was just starting. The war had just ended. There was a lot of creativity and energy. And there was a whole new field to explore. It was a very exciting time."

In addition to television roles in "Studio One," "Playhouse 90" and "Kraft Theater," Sparer worked in radio and on stage. She spent several seasons performing Shakespeare in Stratford, Conn. In fact, that's how she met "Lou Grant" star Ed Asner, 20 years ago.

"I hadn't seen him since," said Sparer, but she understands Asner suggested her for the Mrs. Pynchon role.

In the years immediately before she took over the mythical Los Angeles Trib, Sparer played the mother in the aborted "Upstairs, Downstairs" offshoot called "Beacon Hill." She also played a wealthy relation on the soap opera "Another World."

"Then I was on a dog of a soap opera that folded pretty quickly."

Though Sparer didn't plan to limit herself to variations on high brow themes, she says that, at least in television, "I've gotten sort of stuck with roles like that."

"I was trained for classical work, so I can portray somebody who has some kind of knowledge beyond the dime store and a pack of chewing gum. . . ."

[Madison (Wis.) *Press Connection*]

Consumerism ———————————————————————————————————————

Although there now are about 200 full-time consumer reporters, coverage of news events that consumers need to know about to get the most for their money is grossly inadequate. For a half century Consumers Union and a few similar groups have advised small memberships regarding the comparative qualities of competing articles, but neither governmental agencies nor newspapers have been aggressive in exposing poor goods.

The modern movement, slow and halting as it still is, began with the appearance of Ralph Nader's book *Unsafe at Any Speed* in 1966. Publicity given the attempt of General Motors, through detectives, to smear Nader, aided him in originating Public Citizen and several other educational and lobbying groups.

As yet Congress and state legislatures have not strengthened the protection consumers deserve. It always has been so. The first Food and Drug Act of 1906 followed the public outcry as a result of Upton Sinclair's *The Jungle,* describing unsavory conditions in Chicago Stockyards. Two attempts to strengthen that act have succeeded only by timely revelations of threats to the public health. In 1938 the Copeland bill seemed doomed to defeat until the news story broke of the deaths of a score or more persons in Tennessee from improperly tested liquid sulfanilomide. In 1960 even a much watered-down bill that resulted from long hearings by a Senate Committee headed by Sen. Estes Kefauver was facing certain defeat as a result of millions of dollars spent in lobbying by the drug industry. Then, however, the news of the threat of the baby-deforming drug thalidomide was released with pictures of infants born without limbs. The drug industry was exposed as having opposed measures to ban the drug's use in the United States.

In the '30s Stuart Chase was the most prolific of a number of journalists and other pioneers of the organized consumer movement. Chase's books included *The Tragedy of Waste* and *Men and Machines,* which warned of industrial accidents, pollution and threats to the health of urban dwellers. Arthur Kalett and F. J. Schlink wrote *100 Million Guinea Pigs,* James Rorty wrote *Our Master's Voice,* a blast at advertising; Kenneth Crawford exposed lobbies in *The Pressure Boys,* William H. Whyte Jr. wrote *The Organization Man,* and a decade later, Hillel Black of the New York *Times,* wrote *Buy Now, Pay Later.*

All of these iconoclasts, especially Chase, were red-baited and/or otherwise vilified. And then came Vance Packard with *The Hidden Persuaders* and a half dozen other blasts at the Establishment. His books include *The Waste Makers, The Status Seekers, The Pyramid Climbers, A Nation of Strangers, The Naked City* and *The People Shapers.*

The late Sidney Margolius, probably the first and certainly the most successful journalistic expert in this field, took an optimistic view, as follows:

> Consumer journalism is a young profession, the youngest branch of journalism, but already it is making a significant contribution to stemming the many deceptions and diversions that cause the massive waste we have in society today. Without the new interest of the press and often radio and sometimes TV, we probably would not have achieved the useful advances of the past 12 years such as truth-in-lending and other credit reforms on federal and state levels; the new product safety law; advances in regulations governing auto and tire safety; some reforms in food and cosmetic packaging; unit pricing and open dating of foods; the 1962 drug amendments requiring that drugs be proven efficacious as well as safe; the exposure and increasing regulation of multiple

distributor investment schemes, and many other money-wasting deceptions whether actually illegal or barely inside the law.

What consumer journalism has accomplished, however, is just a beginning to what really needs to be done, including the massive task of finding ways to curb the present galloping or at least trotting inflation.

Today steps by the Federal Trade Commission and the Food and Drug Administration to warn and protect consumers get nationwide publicity and can hardly be ignored by local newspapers. It is news from coast to coast when an automobile manufacturer recalls thousands of cars for remedial work; when saccharine is or is not declared dangerous to health; toys are banned as unsafe and so are cosmetics, detergents, candy, drugs or other processed foods. There has been improvement in labeling of foods and drugs, and advertisers have been forced to desist from making false claims. The proceedings to enforce such regulations usually are time-consuming so business is not seriously inconvenienced.

Although local newspapers print wire service accounts of charges and actions directed to improve or protect the public, with few exceptions, unfortunately, and not to their credit, they refrain from localizing the national stories. There is not much journalistic policing of retail business establishments. Most frequent crusades are directed at bait-and-switch tactics, short-weight swindles and comparative shopper's lists that show discrepancies among stores offering identical products for sale. The victims of such investigations are not generally the town's leading advertisers.

Good newspapers take consumer reporting more seriously, as reflected in the following lead to a much longer story done for the Los Angeles _Times_ by A. Kent MacDougall, son of one of this book's coauthors.

> Snack time on United Airlines' flights used to mean a sandwich, beverage and peanuts. No more. Six months ago United eliminated the peanuts, thereby saving $800,000 a year. "And that's not peanuts," a United official says.
>
> A number of airlines are saving millions by packing more passengers into the coach sections of their planes. United has reduced seat width by 1.3 inches in many planes, added one seat per row in jumbo jets and reduced the distance between rows by two inches in many smaller jets. These changes began months before the recent round of fare discounts and, unlike those decisions, have not been promoted.
>
> In putting a slight squeeze on their customers, the airlines are only doing what more and more companies in many industries are doing—reducing the quantity and even the quality of goods and services in order to cut costs, boost profits and keep prices in line.
>
> Known variously as "downsizing," packing to price and the shrinking candy bar syndrome, size reductions have a common result: the consumer gets less for his money. The hidden inflation that this constitutes doesn't show up in the government's consumer price index, but it nonetheless affects a growing list of consumer goods and services.
>
> Automobiles are shrinking at the same time that their prices are rising. Houses are built less sturdily and of lower-grade materials. Whisky has been watered. Warranties on cars, tires and television sets cover less than they used to. Wine comes in smaller bottles, newspapers in smaller formats. Paper

towels and toilet tissue contain fewer sheets per roll. And a quarter dropped in a jukebox brings forth a single song or two, compared with three songs several years ago and six generations ago. . . .

People news is important and interesting, especially if reporters frame good questions to pursue in stories. There are many important questions to ask about social structures of the community, about problems in personal and family lives, and about the millions of products and services sold in America. They all involve people. Reporters should seek out such stories.

Meetings, Conventions, Speeches

The French writer Alexis de Tocqueville, perhaps the all-time most perceptive foreign observer of American life, was amazed by the avidity with which we Americans form and belong to organizations. Almost a century and a half later we are, more than ever, a nation of joiners. Even small-town dwellers do not have to go far to find a group with similar interests, be they professional, artistic, recreational or whatever. It is impossible for any newspaper to give adequate coverage to any sizable proportion of the total number of groups seeking publicity. Those considered the most newsworthy are of the following types:

1. Those that take an active part in local, state or national political, legal or governmental affairs, as the League of Women Voters, Chamber of Commerce, Daughters of the American Revolution, American Legion.
2. Those that are interested in controversial issues or engaged in extraordinary tactics, as Common Cause, Right to Life, National Abortion Rights Action League, American Civil Liberties Union, National Organization for Women and others.
3. Those that have programs including widely known speakers, musicians, artists and so forth.
4. Those with large, nationwide memberships that hold elaborate con-

ventions annually. Of this type are most fraternal lodges, routine news of which may be ignored but whose yearly meetings are first-rate shows.

In small city dailies and community and suburban newspapers, almost any organization is newsworthy. The initiative may be left to the group to send in its notices voluntarily or the publication may follow a sounder policy of attempting to have complete coverage, especially of such organizations as the PTA, church groups, Boy Scouts, Girl Scouts, YMCA, and YWCA.

Meetings

The Preliminary Story

Every meeting is held for a purpose and this purpose should be the feature of the preliminary or advanced notice. From the secretary or some other officer of the group which is to meet, the reporter should learn the nature of important business to be discussed, of communities which will report, speakers, entertainment and so on.

Note how the second of the following leads emphasizes purpose:

WEAK: The University of Illinois Board of Trustees will hold a meeting at 7 p.m. Thursday to consider the question of whether the university should own stock in U.S. businesses operating in South Africa.

BETTER: The controversial issue of University of Illinois stock holdings in U.S. firms doing business in South Africa heads the agenda for a board of trustees meeting at 7 p.m. Thursday.

Reporters should ask if the meeting is regular or special, business or social. They should inquire if a dinner or refreshments will precede or follow, whether any entertainment—dramatic, musical or otherwise—is planned. The main attraction of the meeting may be some special program. A meeting to elect or install officers, initiate candidates, hear a particular committee report or a speaker or to celebrate an anniversary has an obvious feature from the news standpoint.

The reporter must be sure to obtain the following data:

1. *The organization.* Its exact name, and the name and number of the post or chapter. "Local Odd Fellows" is not enough; instead, write "Keystone Lodge No. 14, IOOF". That is the usual form: name of the local chapter first, then the number and finally the name or usual abbreviation of the national organization.

2. *Time and place.* In the preliminary story this information must be definite and accurate. A meeting scheduled for 8 o'clock should not be mentioned in the news story as to begin at 8:30. "Friday evening" is not enough; the exact hour should be given. Both the building and room should be given in stating the place, although neither those facts nor the hour need to be in the lead paragraph of the story.

3. *The program.* If there is a program of entertainment, reporters should obtain it in detail. They should get names of musicians and their selections, names of casts and dramatic coaches, decorations, orchestras, committees in charge. Only the highlights of a program need be mentioned, and in order of importance, rather than in the order included in the program.

Note how purpose is emphasized in the following examples:

The American Legion Auxiliary's 5th District will meet at 8 p.m. Saturday in the Community club rooms, 1600 S. Grand Ave., to hear annual reports by district chairmen and to elect delegates to the state and national conventions.

An informational meeting has been scheduled for next Monday to explain two proposed additions to the Waterloo health care scene: A group home project for the developmentally disabled, and a sophisticated piece of diagnostic equipment for a hospital.

The meeting, to be conducted by the Iowa Health Systems Agency Inc., is a preliminary step in formulating a recommendation on the projects for use by the state health department.

The state must certify a need for both projects and also must approve them before the facilities involved can receive reimbursements for procedures under Medicaid, Medicare and other programs.

The group homes are planned by Exceptional Persons Inc., which intends to build three of them at an estimated cost of $658,000.

Each of the group homes will have 12 beds. Two of the homes will be for moderately retarded adults and the third for severely physically handicapped and retarded persons.

The group homes are to be financed with industrial development revenue bonds issued by the Black Hawk County Board of Supervisors.

Also on the agenda at the meeting will be a new "nuclear imaging system" for Allen Memorial Hospital.

The machine, which will cost an estimated $135,000 will replace what has become an antiquated system of patient scanning and diagnosis.

The equipment will be purchased by the hospital with cash on hand, according to its application to the state.

The informational meeting will be at 7 p.m. in the Hurwich Room of the Waterloo Recreation and Arts Center, 225 Cedar St.   [Waterloo (Iowa) *Courier*]

The Follow-up

In the follow-up or story after the meeting has been held, the outcome, or result, should be featured, and the writer should look to the future. For instance, avoid:

Keystone Lodge No. 14, IOOF voted Friday to build a $2 million lodge hall.

Rather, emphasize the future, as follows:

Construction of a new $2 million lodge hall will begin next month after members of the Keystone Lodge No. 14 IOOF approved the project Friday.

The reporter should learn the disposition of every item of business. Some matters will be laid on the table or referred to committees. Others will be defeated outright. Some business, of course, will be concluded. If the meeting or business is important, the writer should include in the story not only the result of balloting, but also the arguments presented by both supporters and opponents of the most important measures, both those that passed and those that were defeated.

The account of a meeting that has been held never should read as the secretary's minutes. The items of business are mentioned in the order of their importance rather than chronologically as considered at the meeting. So that they can interpret them correctly, reporters should obtain the exact wordings of resolutions and also the memberships of committees. It is not necessary to mention the presiding officer unless someone other than the president or usual chairman was in charge.

Note in the following example how the writer caught the importance of the occasion, which he interpreted for readers in the lead:

> The so-called conservative element in the labor union movement won in the annual election held Wednesday night by the Milwaukee Federated Trades' Council.
>
> Herman Seide was reelected secretary by a vote of 458 to 169 over Al Benson, former sheriff and now organizer for the United Textile Workers of America.
>
> Anton Sterner, nominated to oppose J. F. Friedrick for the post of general organizer, withdrew. Friedrick was reelected by 624 votes.
>
> For secretary-treasurer, Emil Brodde was reelected with 458 to 164 for Severino Pollo. Frank Wietzke, sergeant-at-arms for more than 40 years, was reelected without opposition.
>
> In the contest between conservative and liberal slates for the nine places on the executive board, the same division was apparent. Those elected and their votes are. . . .
>
> [Milwaukee *Journal*]

Style

Expressions such as "Members are urged to attend," and "The public is cordially invited" should be avoided. If the purpose of the meeting is stated correctly, the former expression is superfluous. The latter expression is poor because of the "cordially." If an invitation is not cordial, it should not be extended.

Audiences

Sometimes, as at a public meeting, the size and behavior of the audience are an essential part of the story.

By Ralph Gifford

> More than 100 Northwest Siders who gathered at the Edgebrook Fieldhouse Friday night heard assurances from two aldermen that the city has agreed to postpone the closing of the building until April 1, and that by then a way will be found to maintain its unique status as a community center. . . .
>
> [Chicago *Northwest Side Press*]

By Dean Mayer

Relatively few industrial officials turned out Thursday for a session designed to tell them about a program requiring some plants to treat their toxic and hazardous wastes before they enter the public sewer system.

The Green Bay Metropolitan Sewerage District invited representatives from 166 area industries to a session at the Brown County Library. Not all 166 firms are likely to be affected by the pretreatment program—certain definitions remain to be set—but the MSD wanted to cover all bases.

Only about 45 industry officials showed up, with some firms represented by more than one person.

"Frankly, I was surprised," said MSD Plant Manager Thomas Cooper of the attendance. "I'm afraid we just don't have the industries' attention yet."

[Green Bay (Wis.) *Press-Gazette*]

By Nan Robertson

"How long does this jealousy period last?" said a plaintive woman's voice from the audience the other night. "Forever!" cried an answering chorus. And then everybody laughed—the kind of laughter that meant everybody understood.

The scene was a packed, emotion-charged room at the Barbizon Hotel for Women, where women outnumbered men about three to one and virtually everybody was a stepparent or about to become one.

The audience had come to hear "Making It as a Stepparent: An Open Forum" sponsored by Doubleday, the book publishing concern. A psychologist, a registered nurse, and two authors who had written new books on being a stepparent, one a novel based on personal experience, were the panelists. Three of the four were stepparents. . . .

[New York *Times*]

Conventions _____

Some organizations, such as the American Legion, National Association for the Advancement of Colored People and Americans for Democratic Action, are influential in state and national affairs. Consequently, when one of these organizations meets, what it does is of general interest. Such conventions frequently pass resolutions concerning vital political and business situations and recommend passage of certain laws by state legislatures and Congress. They even send lobbyists to state capitals and to Washington.

Conventions of other organizations that ordinarily are nonpolitical may be of widespread interest because of their large membership. Fraternal orders such as the Masons, Elks and Moose have chapters in all parts of the country, and their conventions attract thousands of delegates from all states. Church groups, businessmen's organizations, scientific and educational bodies consider matters of general interest. Frequently the first announcement of a new scientific discovery or theory is made in a paper presented at a convention of some scientific group.

Aside from the general interest that an important convention creates, there also is local interest, provided the locality is to be represented by delegates. If any local person is an officer or has a part in the program, the local interest is heightened. Many fraternal organizations hold drill team, band, drum and bugle corps and other contests at conventions, and the local chapter may compete.

The Preliminary Notice

The first story of a convention usually appears a week or two before the opening session. Almost every important organization has a secretary or publicity person who prepares notices for the press. The advanced notice emphasizes the business of the convention and the important speeches or papers to be given or read. Sometimes the nature of a report which a special committee will make is disclosed in advance.

Note in the following example of a lead on a story about an upcoming convention the emphasis on a matter of interest to general readers:

> How state government can improve schools is the main theme of the program at the convention of the Texas Federation of Women's Republican Clubs opening today at the Diplomat Hotel.

Localization of convention stories sometimes can increase their interest to general readers as this lead attempts to do:

> Mayor John Johnson will call for a doubling of the state income tax to finance education programs when he makes the keynote address today at the convention of the Texas Federation of Women's Republican Clubs.

The First-Day Story

The story that appears just before the convention begins may emphasize the purpose and main business of the meeting, or it may play up the arrival of delegates, the probable attendance and the first day's program. Often a meeting of the officers or executive committee precedes the convention proper.

Some matter related exclusively to the internal organization of the group may be of sufficient general interest to be the feature, as when a rule changing the requirements for membership, or merger with another organization, is to be debated. Frequently an internal political fight is anticipated in the election of officers or selection of the next convention city.

> The leaders of the nation's banking fraternity, 8,500 strong, are arriving for the four-day annual American Bankers Association convention.
>
> The meeting, largest since the 1920s, will focus on the perplexing problem of the banker's role in curbing, while not blighting, the boom.
>
> The program at the Conrad Hilton Hotel will also include speeches on the farm price problem and the task of building the free world's strength through NATO and the nation's strength through a strong free enterprise economy.
>
> In addition, a wide range of subjects, some of interest chiefly to bankers, others with a general scope, will be discussed.
>
> While thousands of bankers and their wives flock to a private showing of the General Motors Corp. Powerama Sunday, other bankers in 22 special com-

mittees—such as those on credit policy and federal legislation—will buckle down to work.

But the committee which may prove to be the most controversial does not meet until Monday. That is the 50-member nominating committee, representing each state.

There's no doubt, short of catastrophe, who the next president will be. He's the vice-president, Fred F. Florence, president, Republic National Bank of Dallas. He'll take over automatically from Homer J. Livingston, president, the First National Bank of Chicago.

The rub will come when a successor vice-president to Florence is named.

Observers think that for the first time in a generation there may be an open fight for control of the ABA, with the issue being state versus national banks.

The "state's righters" argue that they haven't had a president for the last seven years. Because they can't name one directly this year, their strategy is to name the vice-president who will move up to the presidency.

[Chicago *Sun-Times*]

A newspaper printed in the city entertaining a convention joins with the rest of the community in welcoming delegates. Reporters are assigned to gather side features and anecdotes unrelated to the serious business of the convention. Statistics may be included of the oldest delegate, the delegate who has come the longest distance, the delegate who has attended the most conventions, the delegate who flew to the convention by private airplane or arrived in some other unusual manner, the tallest delegate, the shortest and so forth.

The newspaper may take advantage of the opportunity to obtain feature interviews with important or picturesque delegates and speakers. At a gathering of editors of college newspapers, a reporter obtained numerous interviews regarding narcotics on campuses, a subject entirely different from the business of the convention.

The Follow-up

After a convention begins, newspapers report its progress. Important speeches and debates are reported, and the outcomes of votes watched. Minor speeches, such as the address of welcome and the response and the humorous after-dinner talks at the banquet, may be ignored by press associations and correspondents, unless someone disregards customs and selects such an occasion for an important statement. Scientific papers and speeches must be written up so as to be understandable to the average reader.

Entertainment provided for delegates and their wives, the convention parade and minor business matters pertaining only to the organization are not given much space. If the organization awards prizes of any sort, the names of the winners are desired by various outside papers whose readers are likely to be interested. Such prizes may be for the best showing in the parade, for the largest delegation, for the delegation coming the longest distance, for drill team, band, or drum and bugle corps competition, for the chapter that has increased its membership the most during the year, for the chapter that has contributed most to a certain fund and so on.

The results of the election of officers and selection of the next convention city usually are of general news interest. Papers in cities that bid for the convention or whose chapters have candidates for offices, frequently arrange for prompt coverage of elections, depending upon the importance of the convention.

Estimating Crowds

At athletic contests and other events to which admission is charged, there is no difficulty in obtaining accurate figures on total attendance. If admission is not charged, and especially when the audience or crowd is outdoors, the reporter often must make his own estimate of its size. Police usually estimate the numbers to watch a parade, take part in a demonstration or riot or similar event; but police are no more competent to do so than a trained newsgatherer. Furthermore, their bias is evident, as they underestimate attendance when they are unsympathetic with the purposes of the demonstration and overestimate it when they are sympathetic. So, of course, do newspapers, notoriously so when antiwar demonstrations were popular.

The simple process for audience or crowd estimation is to separate it into sections. That is, count the number of persons occupying a particular area. This is easy when the spectators are seated in a grandstand or auditorium, as all that is needed is to multiply the number of seats in a row by the number of rows, then subtract the apparent number of empty seats. Then cast the eye over the entire assemblage and see how many blocks of similar size there are.

•Speeches _____

The Preliminary Story

In obtaining information for a story about a speech to be given, the reporter must pay special attention to the following:

1. Adequate identification of the speaker.
2. The occasion for the speech.
3. The exact time and place.
4. The exact title of the speech.

Identification of the speaker in the lead may not be lengthy, but the body of the story should contain those facts which indicate that the person is qualified to discuss the subject. The opinions of other persons may be obtained and quoted to emphasize the speaker's ability, but the reporter should not say that "he is well qualified" or "is an authority on his subject." It is better to give an adequate account of the speaker's experience and let it speak for itself.

The speaker's name usually is more important than the subject and, therefore, should come first in the lead. Sometimes, however, the subject may be more important, but rarely is it advisable to begin with the exact title in quotation marks. Note in the second example below how the writer emphasizes the subject and at the same time the importance of the speaker:

> WEAK: "Commercial Aviation" will be the subject of a speech. . . .
> BETTER: William Downs, author of a controversial new study of the causes of major airplane crashes, will analyze commercial airline safety in a speech today. . . .

In the following example of a preliminary speech story, the lead emphasizes the speaker's name, and the body explains the importance of both speakers and the occasion.

> State Sen. Charles H. Bradfield, Rushville, will outline his views on reform of the state parole system at the monthly meeting of the Council of Social Agencies Thursday at Hotel Wolseley.
> A member of the joint legislative committee that recently recommended a complete overhauling of the existent parole system, Sen. Bradfield has been a severe critic of Gov. Herbert Crowe for his failure to make a public statement on the committee's report.
> "It was Sen. Bradfield, more than any other member, who was responsible for the recommendation that a board of lay persons be substituted for the present board," said Maurice S. Honig, president of the council, in announcing Thursday's meeting.
> The speech is scheduled for 12:15 p.m. The council's committee on legislation, of which Mrs. Arne Oswald is chairman, will report on the results of its study of the legislative committee's recommendations.

The Follow-up

After the speech has been given, the emphasis should be upon what the speaker said, rather than upon the fact that the speech was given. Never write

> Bruce Paddock, Prescott city manager, gave a lecture Thursday on "Municipal Government" to the Kiwanis club of Greensboro.

Such a lead is vague and indefinite. It is only a preliminary story lead put into the past tense. It misses the feature entirely.

The feature should be found in something that the speaker said. The reporter must follow the orthodox rule of important details first and must disregard the chronological order of a person's remarks. Good speakers do not make their most important point in the introduction. The reporter should play up the speaker's most startling or important remark, which may come at the very end of the speech. Such expressions as "The speaker continued" or "In conclusion the speaker said" do not appear in a well-written story.

Every speaker tries to make a point, and the news writer should play up the speaker's attitude toward the subject as a whole. This is not a hard-and-fast rule, however, as frequently it is better to pick for the lead some casual statement or remark that has strong local interest. In playing up an aside or incidental remark, however, care must be taken not to give a wrong impression. It is easy to misrepresent a speaker's attitude by picking a single sentence which, when printed alone, has a very different meaning from that conveyed when the sentence appears in context.

The timeliness of a speaker's remarks may determine selection of the feature. If the speaker refers to some vital public problem of the moment, the speaker's opinion regarding it may be more important than anything else said. This, of course, is contingent upon the speaker's prestige as an authority on the subject under discussion.

During political campaigns, it is difficult for a reporter who travels with a candidate to write a different story daily, because the aspirant for office gives nearly the same speech day after day, possibly hour after hour. The same difficulty is encountered in reporting public lectures by persons who speak frequently on the same subject. If the writeup of the speech is for local consumption only, the feature may be selected on its face value, provided an account of a similar speech by the same person has not been printed recently. The reporter, however, should not play up, as something new and startling, a remark that actually is "old stuff" to both speaker and audience.

As preparation for speech reporting, there is no substitute for adequate knowledge of both the speaker and the field of interest. A reporter with little or no background in science, for instance, would be completely unable to evaluate the relative importance of points made by a nuclear physicist, some of which might be of great potential general interest. An uninformed reporter in any field might write that a speaker "revealed" or "made known" something that could be found in elementary textbooks on the subject.

To localize the appeal of a speech means to play up any reference that the speaker makes to the immediate locality. Thus, if in the course of a lecture on geology, the speaker declares that the vicinity is a very fertile field for research, that remark may be the most interesting, from the standpoint of his audience, of any the speaker makes. The same speech, written up for a press association, might have an entirely different lead.

The time and place need not be stated so definitely in the follow-up as in the preliminary story, and the identification of the speaker should be brief.

The Lead

Possible rhetorical leads for a follow-up speech story include:

1. The speaker's name.
2. The title.
3. A direct quotation.
4. A summary statement of the main point or keynote.
5. The occasion or circumstances.

If there is reason for emphasizing the authority of the speaker, the story may begin with the name, as:

Chief of Police Arthur O. Shanesy today told members of the Chamber of Commerce that traffic accidents in the downtown business district are largely the fault of merchants.

Ordinarily, it is weak to begin with the speaker's name, because by so doing the importance of the content of the speech is minimized. For the same reason, the lead seldom should begin with the exact title unless it is stated in an unusual way or in a way which makes a title lead effective, as:

"America's Weakness" is her failure to realize that the frontier has disappeared, said Prof. Arnold L. Magnus of Booster College's political science department, Friday night at a Milltown Lions Club meeting.

Opinions differ regarding the direct quotation lead. Jackson S. Elliott of the Associated Press once said, "Show me a news story that begins with a direct quotation, no matter how striking it is, and I will show you how it could be improved by taking the quoted statement out of the lead and placing it in the body of the story."

Other editors condone the direct quotation lead when the intention of the writer is to play up some startling statement rather than to epitomize the speaker's general attitude. Obviously, it is seldom that a speaker summarizes the entire speech in any one sentence contained in the speech itself.

The following is a fairly good use of the direct quotation lead:

"World War III is inevitable within five years," Harold E. Paulson, profession of political science at Booster College, told the World Affairs Club Friday.

The best lead for a speech story is one that summarizes the speaker's general attitude toward the subject or gives the keynote of the speech.

Kindergarten reading is out of place in high school and college, even if the students are coping with a foreign language.

So a University of Illinois professor told his fellow teachers of French, Friday, in a national meeting in the Palmer House.

"The books we're reading with our students in the first few years of French are far below their intellectual level, and below the seriousness of things they are reading in other classrooms," declared Prof. Charles A. Knudson, head of romance language at Urbana.

"In short, in French classes we are reading tripe."

The lead may emphasize the occasion or the ovation given the speaker, the crowd or some unexpected circumstance that occurs during delivery of a speech.

A well organized group of about 50 hecklers Monday failed to persuade State Sen. Roger Parnell to discuss lie detector tests for public employees suspected of leaking information to the media.

Instead, the Republican candidate for reelection stuck to his announced topic,

"The State's Proposed Highway Program," and police evicted the troublemakers from an audience of about 500 in Masonic Hall.

The Vernon County Republican Club sponsored the meeting.

The Body

Prominent persons, as public officials, usually speak from prepared manuscripts, copies of which often are distributed to reporters before actual delivery. This enables reporters to write part or all of their account in advance. The danger of going to press prematurely is obvious, as the speaker may make last-minute changes or digress from the text.

The safe way is never to publish a speech account until word has been received that delivery actually has begun. Even in such cases, and especially if it is impossible to obey the rule of delay, it is wise to use in the first or second paragraph the identification "in a speech prepared for delivery" on such and such an occasion. This offers protection in case there are unexpected developments. If there is none, the reporter, manuscript in hand, can follow the speaker and make note of any modifications necessary in the story already written.

The second paragraph of a speech story ordinarily should amplify the lead, in the process explaining more about the occasion on which the speech was given. The rest of the body should consist of paragraphs of alternating direct and indirect quotation. The first paragraph of direct quotation well may be an elaboration of the indirect quotation lead.

If, as sometimes happens, the reporter has an advanced copy of the speech, there is no difficulty in obtaining direct quotations. Otherwise, one must develop facility in taking notes.

Reporters need to exercise their judgment in selecting the parts of a speech to quote directly. Ordinarily it is best to quote directly

1. Statements representing a strong point of view, especially if related to a newsworthy controversial matter. Often it is more forceful to use the material in indirect quotation first, possibly in the lead, as "Mayor Brinton will not be a candidate for reelection." Readers, however, like to know the exact words which a speaker used and they should be given in the body of the story even though a verbatim account appears elsewhere in the paper.
2. Uniquely worded statements, including ones that might become aphorisms or slogans, as "Lafayette, we are here," "I do not choose to run" and the like.
3. Statements of facts not generally known, perhaps in statistical terms.

Ordinarily, statements that are merely ones of evaluative opinion or that contain old or easily ascertained information can be summarized in a reporter's own words if they are newsworthy at all. It would be foolish, for instance, to quote a labor leader as saying, "Unions are the hope of America." If, however, the president of the National Association of Manufacturers were to say so, it would be a sensational news story lead.

Instead of quoting directly a statement containing an old fact, the reporter can say, "The speaker reminded the audience that white-collar workers are the most difficult to organize" or "He recalled that the governor vetoed the measure two years ago."

How often a "he said" or synonym should be inserted in the body of a speech story depends on the length of the article. In paragraphs of indirect quotation a "he said" should be used as often as needed to make it clear that the ideas expressed are those of the speaker rather than of the writer. Direct quotations should be preceded, broken or followed by a "he said" or its equivalent.

The writer should try to use the most appropriate synonym for the verb "to say." Any good dictionary of synonyms or a thesaurus includes many score. Because no two verbs have exactly the same meaning, great care must be exercised in their selection. If a speaker "roared," the interpretative reporter owes it to readers to say so. If, however, the speaker merely raised his voice normally, grave injustice can be done by a reportorial magnavox.

Substance can be given to the speech story only by the reporter who knows something about the speaker and the subject. Otherwise it is impossible to comprehend the speech as a whole, to digest it with proper emphasis or to convey the proper impression of the occasion on which it was delivered. A speech is an event, and the experienced reporter comprehends its significance. The factual material of a series of phrases in a sentence or paragraph may come from a half-dozen widely separated portions of the speech as a whole, yet be properly grouped so as to give a complete and accurate summary of the speaker's point of view.

Here is an example of a competent speech story, written by a reporter who clearly understood the issue of land use planning:

By Pat McGuire
NEWS STAFF WRITER

Land use planning in Birmingham is still in its infancy, a planning expert told members of the League of Women Voters of Greater Birmingham at a Thursday luncheon meeting.

"Most cities this size have been into planning for 35 to 40 years," said Charles Shirley, deputy executive director, Birmingham Regional Planning Commission. "We probably could have saved some of the more prominent structures around Birmingham if we had gotten started earlier."

Land use will be a major item in the U.S. Congress this year, Shirley said, adding that if the Jackson bill is approved, land planning will be required in every state. There are no federal regulations on land planning at the present time, he said.

Shirley explained the organization of the BRPC and Jim Scott, public information officer for the agency, showed slides detailing the structure of the BRPC.

The Birmingham Regional Planning Commission has no power to enforce, but may only make recommendations to municipalities on land planning, Shirley said. "Our biggest single problem is that by law we are advisors. But in most cases, regional comprehensive planning is required to receive grants."

About 80 to 85 municipalities are now participating in the BRPC program, and a citizen's advisory committee is now in the process of being organized, Shirley said.

Shelby County is the only county in the six-county region served by the commission that employs a planner, Shirley said. A primary land use plan has been developed for the Shelby County area, but has not yet been approved by the citizens, he said.

Current projects the commission hopes to get the go-ahead on include a long-range transit study; a strip mining study, to be funded by the Appalachian Regional Council; and a water quality study on the Cahaba and Warrior rivers, under a grant from the Environmental Protection Agency. "The EPA wants the local governments to agree to abide by the results of the study if they are to fund it," Shirley said. "This is where we're having our problem."

Mrs. William Williams is land use study chairman for the league and Mrs. Kenneth Bohannon is league president. [Birmingham *News*]

Capturing a Mood

Accounts of meetings, conventions, speeches and the like need not put the reader to sleep. Sometimes an interpretative reporter with a sharp eye for detail can write prose that captures the mood of such events, lifting the otherwise fairly routine affair into an evocative mini-portrait of contemporary life.

Lee Mitgang, a reporter for the Associated Press, did just that in a 1985 story about the opening of an art exhibit in New York. The story, the opening of which follows, interested many papers around the country because of the universal appeal Mitgang discerned and conveyed to readers:

New York (AP)—Sssh. Be ve-wy, ve-wy quiet. You're in the Museum of Modern Art—and it's Wabbit season.

There they all are, cheek to fuzzy jowl on that venerable Manhattan museum's wall—Picasso, Van Gogh, Degas, Yosemite Sam, Foghorn Leghorn, Daffy, Speedy, Tweety, Elmer and . . . Bugs Bunny.

It's the 50th anniversary of Warner Bros.' Looney Tunes and Merrie Melodies cartoons which combined the bite of adult satire with childlike sight gags and belly laughs as none before or since.

The museum is paying homage to these Warner Bros. cartoons, recognizing them as the art works that they truly are, in a special exhibit titled "That's NOT All, Folks!"

On hand for the show's opening Tuesday were Friz Freleng, 79, and Chuck Jones, 73—names any Bugs buff instantly recognizes as long-time animators of the whole stable of Warner Bros. characters. . . .

13

Illness, Death, Disasters

A crisis over poisoned pain reliever on store shelves. An outbreak of salmonella. Artificial hearts. AIDS. Pesticides in watermelons. Mentally ill people walking the streets. Explosions. Fatal crashes.

All those phrases and more like them are regularly part of the news in the late 20th century.

Calamity and death, health or the lack of it and disasters of either the spectacular or creeping variety are among the events of our time that preoccupy our thoughts, whether we are worrying about ourselves or considering the problems of others.

They are the stuff of the news—one of the major reasons people buy and read newspapers with so much interest despite all the other demands on their time. Thus, they are among the kinds of stories reporters often must cover and interpret.

Public Health

There is hardly a newspaper, daily or weekly, without a column, mostly syndicated, by an outstanding medical expert who is cautious about diagnosing ailments on the basis of symptoms submitted by readers. Just as they discourage self-medication by patients, so do reputable doctors deplore sensationalism by the press in handling stories of unusual illnesses or treatments, as artificial hearts, organ transplants and the like. Newspapers provide the medium whereby public health officials advise the public on such matters as threats to the purity of the water supply, possible heat prostration and the presence of epidemic diseases. Some examples:

Seventeen persons will begin the painful 24-shot series of rabies vaccine today after two baby skunks taken as "pets" died and were found to be rabid, the Payne County Health Department announced.

The exposure has been called the largest in the state since more than 50 persons were exposed last year in another part of the state.

Ray Russell, sanitarian for the county, said the 17 included nine members of a local family, a grandmother of the family, several local friends, four members of a Kay County family and two relatives of that family. Two additional persons have been identified as "possible" contacts, he said.

Cost for shots will average approximately $500 per person, Russell said. Though chance of contracting rabies in this incident is small, he said, if the disease were contracted, certain and horrible death would result.

[Stillwater (Okla.) *News-Press*]

Washington (AP)—Heavy users of saccharin or cyclamate, whether they smoke or not, significantly increase their chances of contracting bladder cancer, warns a new government report.

The National Cancer Institute report released Thursday characterizes the two controversial sweeteners as weak carcinogens that enhance the likelihood of bladder cancer.

The study was done at the request of the Food and Drug Administration, the agency that tried to ban saccharin as a food additive in 1977.

The study, the largest of its type ever conducted, was based on interviews of more than 9,000 people about their habits over a period of 15 months. It cost $1.5 million and was supposed to help resolve the controversy over the safety of saccharin. . . .

By Charles Seabrook

Georgia health officials say this winter's flu vaccine will provide protection against the three types of flu that are expected to cause most of the misery in the coming months.

The vaccine will contain protection against the A Brazil flu strain, a variant of the so-called Russian flu and the predominant strain last winter.

The A Brazil type caused outbreaks in schools, colleges and military bases in Georgia and the rest of the nation.

This coming flu season's vaccine also will contain protection against A Texas flu and B Hong Kong flu, which were not as widespread as the A Brazil strain.

According to the Georgia Immunization Unit of the Department of Human Resources, an ongoing program has been initiated targeting the 996,000 Georgians over 65 years of age and those with chronic diseases for flu vaccinations.

The chronic illness group includes those with ailments such as bronchopulmonary disease (asthma or cystic fibrosis), heart disease, renal disease, diabetes and other metabolic disorders, neuromuscular problems, malignancies and immuno-deficient disorders.

The elderly and the chronic disease sufferers are those who are considered to be at risk to the complications of flu. . . .

By Steve Smith

A stroke can be devastating.

It can alter a human mind, render a once-active person helpless and change the lives of those close to the victim.

Every year, one out of every 10 Americans falls victim to a stroke. And one out of every 10 victims dies.

In Anderson County, that translates to 1,500 persons a year suffering from strokes and 150 dying.

The American Heart Association estimated this year:

• 2,000,000 Americans will suffer strokes.

• 200,000 will die.

• 1,000,000 stroke victims will be paralyzed permanently, although 750,000 will regain some use of the paralyzed area.

• 800,000 will suffer only temporary paralysis.

The Heart Association said a stroke occurs when blood enriched with oxygen is blocked from reaching part of the brain. Strokes are caused either by a clot blocking an artery in the brain or a diseased artery bursting and flooding the surrounding brain tissue with blood.

When this happens, brain cells become damaged or die, according to the association. Depending on what part of the brain has been damaged, the result of a stroke can be death, difficulty in speaking or walking, memory loss and, almost always, paralysis of both limbs on one side of the body.

Health experts agree one of the major causes of strokes is hypertension, known as high blood pressure. If hypertension is diagnosed and brought under control, many fatal strokes can be prevented.

[Anderson (S.C.) *Independent/Daily Mail*]

Apart from matters of personal health, though, there are important stories to report about how major American institutions' practices and policies affect our well-being. Some examples:

By Alan L. Otten

Albany, N.Y.—"Family Doctor," says the sign outside the office on the 14th floor of the New York state office building.

But David Axelrod doctors a very extended family. As the state's health commissioner, he is involved with the physical well-being of more than 17.7 million New Yorkers. In the course of a 70-to-80-hour workweek, Dr. Axelrod:

—Canvasses important legislators on the possibility of limiting installation of million-dollar-plus high-tech machines in doctors' offices.

—Discusses with hospital executives whether their institutions fare better under New York's system of prospective-payment reimbursement or under the federal government's Medicare program.

—Patiently explains to irate members of a New York City delegation just why he denied their application for a neighborhood family-planning and abortion clinic.

—Studies the early results from a two-year survey of some 900 hazardous-waste sites around the state.

—Sounds out a group of religious leaders on proposed guidelines for the use of "Do Not Resuscitate" orders by doctors and hospitals.

—Questions medical-society officials about their lack of progress in dealing with alcoholic and drug-abusing doctors.

All across the country, state governments are being obliged to take ever-larger roles to hold down health-care costs, minister to the poor and elderly, assess environmental risks and wrestle with novel legal and bioethical dilemmas. . . .   [*Wall Street Journal*]

By Tom Gibbons

The advertisement selling legal services in last week's Sun-Times read simply: "Accidents including food poisoning."

That specialized ad, admits the Chicago attorney who placed it, was designed to attract victims of Illinois' salmonella epidemic—the largest salmonella food poisoning case in the nation's history.

"We're not ambulance chasers. We want the public to know we have a specialty in product liability law," explained Donald A. Shapiro, whose four-man law firm is already representing 15 or 20 suspected salmonella victims.

The advertisement highlights the keen awareness lawyers have of the potential size of the litigation stemming from the salmonella-tainted milk state officials say was sold by Jewell Co. Inc.

Already, before state health officials have even determined the exact cause of the salmonella outbreak, attorneys have filed nearly 65 lawsuits in Cook County Circuit Court. More suits have been filed in Chicago's collar counties. . . .   [Chicago *Sun Times*]

By Nancy Skelton

Angry farmers Saturday blamed the Union Carbide Co. for improperly labeling a pesticide that health officials say tainted watermelons and may have caused as many as 170 Californians to become ill.

Farmers said labeling on the pesticide aldicarb states that the insect killer will leave the soil within 100 days, yet traces were found in fields as late as six years after the last application.

"What happens to us when all this blows over? I feel slandered in a way," complained Kern County farmer Don Icardo, who said he stands to lose between $10,000 and $15,000 if the state orders him to plow under his small acreage of watermelons. "Union Carbide will just deny it or take their product off the market and we'll be left holding the bag. . . .   [Los Angeles *Times*]

By Robert E. Taylor

The Charles George Landfill belches gas and oozes cancer-causing chemicals into groundwater under condominiums in Tyngsborough, Mass. Neighbors want it carted away, but it's staying put.

Why? Because the chemicals permeate much of the 70-acre landfill at least 75 feet deep. Digging up and hauling off this huge toxic sponge could cost $1.6 billion—about what the federal government has spent on all hazardous-waste cleanups since 1980.

"Besides," says Michael Deland, regional administrator for the Environmental Protection Agency, "where the hell would you put it?"

Five years after launching its "Superfund" hazardous-waste cleanup program, the U.S. is discovering that toxic contamination is far more extensive—and fixing it is far more difficult, costly and time-consuming—than almost anyone expected. The EPA struggles to master the problem, but a growing chorus of critics believe that it must make major strategic changes or be overwhelmed by the task. . . .   [*Wall Street Journal*]

Illness _____

Although the illness story may seem to be routine, it frequently is one of the most difficult to report and write. This is because the medical profession is reluctant to give out information about the condition of patients or about its own discoveries, unusual surgical performances and the like. Physicians hold that they are duty bound to protect the privacy of those under their care, and the ethics of the profession forbid anything suggesting personal publicity. They may feel that knowledge of a patient's condition, gained through a newspaper account, would be detrimental to that patient's recovery, and they do not trust the average reporter to report medical news accurately.

Relatives of a prominent person who is ill can be persuaded to authorize the physician in charge to release periodic bulletins regarding the patient's condition, but these may be in scientific language, which must be translated. Until newspapers can employ reporters capable of handling medical news with the same understanding that baseball writers have in handling their specialty, the only safe way is to ask the doctors themselves for popular "translations," or to consult a medical dictionary. Because in many cases physicians and surgeons have gone to extremes in refusing cooperation with the press, they must share the blame for inaccuracies that occur in news concerning them. The press also has learned that attending physicians may not be entirely truthful in their discussion of the nature of an ailment when a prominent person, say a president of the United States, is involved.

Medical Successes

Certain to arouse reader interest is any account of proof of the efficiency of a new drug or surgical technique.

By Mary Ann Lehnherr

Peoria—Weighing 1 pound, 9 ounces, Ashley Breitbach could fit in the palm of your hand.

Tubes and needles prick her purplish skin, monitoring every breath and heartbeat. Her gray eyes open and then flutter shut, unaware of the miracle she is.

"God and my mom are watching out for us," Karen Brietbach said. "Mom's biggest regret was not seeing her grandchildren. But I know now she's looking over us now."

Ashley was born three months premature Dec. 7 at 1:45 p.m. in St. Francis Hospital to Karen and Daniel Brietbach, 127 Division St. At birth she weighed 1 pound, 12 ounces and measured 13 inches long. Condition: "critical."

One day after she was born, her kidneys stopped working. Something had to be done to decrease the dangerously high levels of blood potassium or she would die.

Friday between 1 and 3 a.m., as a last resort, she underwent hemodialysis. Condition: stable.

"We had few other options to offer the baby," Dr. Phillip J. Olsson said. "Her parents were anxious for us to do any treatment."

Ashley is the smallest infant to receive hemodialysis, according to Dr. Michael Mauer, professor of pediatrics and pediatric nephrology at the University of Minnesota. . . .
[Galesburg (Ill.) *Register Mail*]

By Mary Ann French

His face showed little emotion, but William J. Schroeder raised a clenched fist. Sort of a victory salute.

The crowd of onlookers outside the main entrance of Humana Hospital Audubon watched yesterday afternoon as Schroeder became the first patient to be discharged from a hospital after receiving an artificial heart. . . .
[Louisville *Courier Journal*]

Medical Law

During the past century the life expectancy of Americans has increased by more than 50 per cent. Specifically, in 1850 the average life span for white males was 38.3 years; for white females it was 40.5 years; for nonwhite males, 32.54 years and for nonwhite females, 35.04 years. In 1981 the comparable figures were: 74.2, 78.5, 64.4 and 73.0. So skilled have doctors become in keeping people alive that it is becoming necessary to go to court for permission to pull the plugs on life-supporting equipment that allows heart beats and breathing to continue after a patient otherwise would be considered dead.

According to the Uniform Brain Death Act approved by the National Conference of Commissioners on Uniform State Laws, death occurs "when there is irreversible cessation of all functions of the brain." Some relatives and religious groups refuse to accept this definition and their defiance often is newsworthy. The courtroom also may become a newsworthy battleground when medical authorities encounter parental, religious or other opposition in cases involving blood transfusions, inoculations or vaccinations, sterilization or some other controversial matter.

Because advances in medical science make it possible for doctors today to make more exact diagnoses, patients are increasingly bringing malpractice suits when a diagnosis is inaccurate. A five-year survey of 19,417 malpractice suits against doctors insured by the St. Paul Fire and Marine Insurance Company revealed that diagnostic errors accounted for 24.9 per cent of all claims. Errors in treatment, however, accounted for 49.8 per cent. St. Paul experts said that many physicians fail to keep up with new tests, equipment and drugs.

Another form of illness has become news in recent years—the long-term effects of various substances on human health. Black lung, brown lung, asbestos and dioxin victims, among others, have taken their cases public and to the courts.

Reportorial Rules

Journalists in reporting medical news must be as careful as doctors who make it. Precautions to take to reduce the likelihood of error include the following:

1. Be cautious about announcing cures for important diseases. The hopes of millions of cancer victims have been raised cruelly through newspaper publicity for discoveries that turned out to be false alarms.

2. Be certain that a newly announced discovery actually is recent. Cases have been reported of some cure or method being ballyhooed as a startling find when it has been familiar to medical men for years.

3. Go easy on accrediting dogmatic statements to any medical researcher. Few of them ever speak in positive terms. Their efforts may be directed toward a certain goal, but they are extremely cautious about claiming credit for having reached it. Often they report to their scientific brethren on the progress of work they are doing; the newspaper should not credit them with having completed something they have only begun.

4. Do not use without verification stories of miraculous cures.

5. Do not ascribe a pestilential disease to a person without absolute authority, as such a story, if untrue, is libelous.

6. Do not say a person died "from" instead of "after" an operation, as such a statement may be libelous.

7. Everyone dies of "heart failure." There are diseases of the heart and such a thing as a heart attack.

8. A person does not "entertain" a sickness; and not everyone "suffers" while under a physician's care.

9. Very seldom does a person "have his arm cut off." Rather it is cut off contrary to his plans and wishes.

10. Injuries are not "sustained" but are "received."

11. The nature of a diagnosis ordinarily should be stated unless there is weighty reason for omitting it. "Natural causes" tells little. Some wag once said that according to the press there are only two causes of death: a long or lingering illness or a short illness.

12. Scientific names of diseases may be used provided the popular names also are given.

13. Attach statements of diagnoses and of the seriousness of an epidemic to an authority.

14. Do not mention the name of a physician except in stories of the illness of a prominent individual.

15. Avoid stories of medical freaks unless authorized by a medical association. Expectant mothers can be frightened dangerously by accounts that advance public understanding little or not at all.

Mental Health _____

The fastest growing field of medical knowledge probably is that of mental health. Although the supply of competent psychiatrists still is woefully inadequate, during the past few decades the thinking of many, within and without the medical profession, has been profoundly affected by discoveries and theories regarding the motivations of human behavior.

Among those most influenced by developments in the mental health field have been journalists. They have helped expose bad conditions in many hospitals for the mentally ill and have assisted psychiatrists, social workers, probation and parole officers, educators, judges and others in enlightening the public regarding the many ramifications of the newer knowledge. In its reporting of crime, juvenile delinquency, school problems and similar matters, the press has become much more understanding and consequently more intelligent in its exercise of news judgment.

For "depth" reporting in this field, considerable specialized knowledge is necessary. A typical error of the uninformed is to confuse feeblemindedness with mental illness. The former is lack of intellect, either from birth (amentia) or as a result of brain injury in later life (dementia). The feeble-minded today are called "retarded" or "exceptional" and special schools exist for those who are educable—that is, the high-grade morons, not to be confused with lower-grade imbeciles and idiots for whom only custodial care is feasible. Under pressure from mental health authorities, newspapers generally have ceased using "moron" as a synonym for "sex pervert," which it is not.

The trend in mental health work is away from categorizing specific diseases—dementia praecox, schizophrenia, manic depression, catatonia, paranoia and the like—as long study reveals the existence of few pure types. Rather, the psychiatrist recognizes and speaks of symptoms of abnormal behavior. An outstanding book tracing the development of expert thinking is *The Vital Balance* (Viking, 1963) by Dr. Karl Menninger with Martin Mayman and Paul Pruysen, subtitled, "The Life Process in Mental Health and Illness." Long gone, of course, is belief in possession by evil spirits to be exorcised, malicious lunar influence, emotional suffering as a punishment for sin and similar unscientific and superstitious notions.

Although the teachings of Sigmund Freud, stressing the strictly behavioral aspects of mental disease, still influence modern psychiatric thinking more than those of any other scientist in the field, an increasing number of practitioners today are coming to believe that Freudian psychoanalysis is good research to determine the causes of a patient's emotional disturbance but that it falls short as a cure; that, in fact, it may merely provide a patient with a scapegoat, such as a parent, for his condition and a rationalization for not making proper effort to correct irresponsible behavior. See *Reality Therapy* (Harper & Row, 1965) by William Glasser.

Experiments continue in the search for ways to cure, or at least alleviate, symptoms through insulin, electric and other types of shock treatments, glandular extracts, tranquilizers and so forth. Newspapermen can do a great disservice by sensationalizing any results of isolated experiments. They also must be careful to distinguish between psychoses (major mental disorders whose victims lose touch with reality) and neuroses, of which most of us may be victims at times. Psychosomatic illnesses are physical disorders that have an emotional base; work toward their understanding and cure progresses but has a long way to go.

Historical examples, notably that of Nazi Germany, give credence to the assumption that large groups, perhaps entire nations even, can act insanely. Certainly there are social psychological causes for the widespread success of fads and fashions, for the popularity, especially if it is sudden, of political and other movements and for crazes of all kinds. Seemingly separate phenomena may be related because of the conditions giving rise to them. For instance, in times of insecurity and fear some people may become strong activists to promote reform or change, whereas others may become escapists.

Not every reporter can be a psychiatric expert, but there are many important stories a nonexpert reporter can and should do about mental health matters, especially those involving the human consequences of policy decisions by government agencies or private institutions.

Here is an example of the lead on a good interpretative story about hospitals' use of shock treatment:

By Mary Carmen Cupito

He had been in a catatonic stupor for four years. He stayed in bed, never reacting to the outside world, and had to be fed by a tube.

His doctor gave him five injections of a drug designed to cause seizures. After the fifth convulsion, he got out of bed, asked for breakfast, got dressed, asked how long he'd been in the hospital. He did not believe it was four years.

According to one researcher, this incident in a Hungarian hospital in 1934 was the beginning of shock treatment. Its modern form uses electricity to cause seizures, but its premise remains the same: In some psychiatric patients, a convulsion somehow leads to improved mental health.

Controversy still dogs the practice. In Berkeley, Calif., the public voted to ban electroshock entirely in 1982. After a legal challenge by psychiatrists, a judge ruled the law unconstitutional. The case is being appealed.

But despite the controversy and outright fear it has generated virtually since its inception, shock treatment has outlived its contemporaries, such as lobotomy. In fact, some psychiatrists are beginning to say shock treatment may not be used enough.

Some local hospitals are either using shock therapy now for psychiatric patients or plan to start using it soon. . . .   [St. Petersburg *Times*]

And consider this opening to a series of articles on the consequences of a state government decision to release more mentally ill patients:

By Colin Nickerson

In 1965, Massachusetts started a process that led to the revamping of the state's mental health system.

Called deinstitutionalization, the process was part of a nationwide mental health reform movement that would dramatically reduce the number of patients in state and county mental hospitals. . . .

Deinstitutionalization, as originally envisioned, was not an end but a means intended to bring about a revolution in mental health care. No longer would the mentally ill be locked up like criminals: instead, they would be sustained by a community mental health network designed to provide treatment in the least restrictive setting possible. . . .

Two decades later, that dream has gone astray—primarily because the array of support services needed by people suffering from severe forms of mental illness was never fully developed. . . .   [Boston *Globe*]

Court decisions about laws affecting the mentally ill often require interpretative reporting, too, as this opening to a longer story illustrates:

By Tom Gibbons

Mental patients in Illinois who have committed violent crimes and then been acquitted by reason of insanity are not likely, after hospital treatment, to kill again, state officials say.

The issue was raised last week in the wake of the Miguel Valdes case, in which a Criminal Court judge set Valdes free, even though Valdes' wife claimed her husband threatened to kill her.

It was a charge that could not be taken lightly since Valdes was acquitted by reason of insanity of two grisly murders in 1977 and released after spending only 3½ years in a mental hospital.

Still, state mental health and correction officials know of no cases since 1977 of a mental patient committing a violent crime after being found not guilty by reason of insanity (NGBI), then being treated at a state institution and released. . . .   [Chicago *Sun-Times*]

Obituaries _____

After a three months' strike ended, the Vancouver *Sun* printed a list, in five solid pages of agate type, of all funeral notices it could gather for the period during which publication had been suspended. It did so because that was what readers missed the most, according to Stuart Keate, publisher. Nevertheless, during the past decade or so, death notices have been processed through the classified advertising departments to which they are submitted by funeral directors. The few deaths considered newsworthy are written up by formula. What may develop as a countertrend is the addition of a Monday obituary page in the Los Angeles *Times*. Editor William F. Thomas said the page will feature the obits of the famous but also will report the deaths of "ordinary people who may not have been famous but led interesting lives." He added that the page stems from "a realization that we are not doing a proper job with obits because of time and space limitations."

Basic Elements

The size obituary people get depends upon their importance as news. Even the shortest, however, must include these basic facts:

1. Name of deceased.
2. Identification.
3. Time of death.
4. Place of death.

Two other facts really are essential for even a one- or two-sentence notice:

5. Cause of death.

6. Age of deceased.

Unless death occurs in some unusual way the name *(who)* always is the feature of an obituary. Identification in the brief notice may be by address or occupation only. No authority need be stated unless the dispatch comes from an obscure place or is third- or fourth-hand. Then "it was learned here today" or some similar statement should be used. The paper must be on guard against false rumors of a person's death started by enemies or jokesters.

In giving the age of a dead person some papers permit the form "Henry Baxter, 61, died today," whereas others object to this form on the ground that placing the age after the name indicates the present tense. Papers with this attitude prefer a phrase "at the age of 61 years" or a second sentence, "He was 61 years old."

Rutherford Regal, 414 Oates St., a City Yards employee, died at 3 a.m. today at his home following a week's illness from pneumonia. He was 43 years old.

A person's importance or the achievement by which he will longest be remembered ordinarily should be used.

By Paul L. Montgomery

Martyn Green, the British actor who set the standard in Gilbert and Sullivan interpretation for half a century, died early yesterday of a blood infection at Presbyterian Hospital in Hollywood, Calif. He was 75 years old.

[New York *Times*]

Sometimes a reporter discovers an interesting circumstance in the life of a relatively unimportant person who has died. Perhaps, for instance, the deceased was present at the assassination of a president, was a pioneer of the locality or a former millionaire or in some other way a romantic figure, as:

William Dickinson, 81, lifelong Milan resident whose grandfather laid out the village and founded and built the Presbyterian church here, died at 6 P.M. Thursday in his home on Dickson St.

James Mauris, whose restaurant at 1464 E. 57th St. has for many years been a rendezvous for faculty members and students of the University of Chicago, died suddenly of a heart attack Monday. He was 70 years old.

See Warren J. Brier's "Delicate Art of Writing Obits," in the 1964 *Montana Journalism Review,* for advice on how to write colorful obituaries with dignity.

Circumstances of Death

When a person is known to a large number of readers, the circumstance of death should be related as that is one of the first things about which a friend inquires when hearing of another's demise. Circumstances of death include:

7. Bedside scene.
8. Last words, messages and so forth.
9. Account of last illness.

In a full-length obituary, according to the formula being developed, these facts usually follow the lead.

> Allen E. Schoenlaub, 57, cashier of the First National Bank, died suddenly about 8 p.m. Tuesday at his home, 1146 Elm St., from a heart attack.
>
> He was found in the kitchen by his wife after she heard him fall while in quest of a drink of water. About a half hour before the attack, Mr. Schoenlaub complained of feeling ill. He had spent a normal day at the bank and ate dinner with his wife, son, Robert, 22 and daughter, Flora, 28, apparently in excellent health. He had had no previous heart attacks nor any other recent illness.
>
> A physician whom Mrs. Schoenlaub summoned declared death was due to coronary thrombosis and that Mr. Schoenlaub probably died instantly.
>
> In addition to his wife and two children, he is survived by a brother, Herbert, Kansas City, Mo., and a sister, Mrs. R. S. Bostrum, Chicago.
>
> Mr. Schoenlaub was connected with the First National Bank for 26 years, the last 18 of which he was cashier. He was born Jan. 30, 1925 at Ann Arbor, Mich., and was graduated from the University of Michigan in 1947. He moved here in 1956 after nine years as teller and cashier of the State Bank & Trust Co., of Dowagiac, Mich.
>
> Mr. Schoenlaub was an active member of the First Baptist Church, having been president of the Men's Club from 1971 to 1978. He also was a member of Keystone Lodge No. 14, B.P.O.E., and of Milltown Lodge No. 150 F. & A.M.
>
> Funeral arrangements have not yet been made.

Note in the above the presence of three other important elements:

10. Surviving relatives.
11. Funeral plans.
12. Biographical highlights.

Reviewing a Life

Ordinarily the body of an obituary consists mostly of an objective biographical résumé of the deceased's career. Eulogies and reminiscences may be included or run as sidebars.

If, however, the death is that of a nationally known or world-famous person, one whom history will remember, the trend is toward interpretative pieces which blend the details of death with attempts to evaluate the person's importance. The purpose is to "place" the subject in history with emphasis upon lasting contributions. The interpretative obituary is not an editorial, although it is impossible for a writer qualified to pass judgment upon the subject to avoid evaluations.

Leading advocate of this type of obituary writing was Alden Whitman, long-time obituary writer for the New York *Times* before his retirement. He has written:

> For openers, let's tell what the deceased was really like in life. If he was a saint, let us by all means say so. Or if he choir-lofted with the comely soprano, let's say that, too. If he was modest and unassuming, let's tell it. Or if he was a braggart and a bore, let's also tell that. If he was a handsome donor to charity, we should make that clear, along with the tax advantages his munificence garnered him. If he was a statesman, let the bells ring out. Or if he was a fixer who put up public buildings for the profit of his friends, let the bells clang too.

Whitman expanded on his views in a book, *The Obituary Story* (Stein & Day). A typical Whitman obituary follows:

By Alden Whitman

Alfred C. Fuller, founder and retired chairman of the Fuller Brush Company and one of the foremost promoters of door-to-door salesmanship, died yesterday in Hartford Hospital of myeloma, a bone-marrow disease. He was 88 years old and lived in nearby West Hartford.

A transplanted Nova Scotia farm boy, Mr. Fuller developed a basement brushmaking concern into a giant business, with yearly sales of more than $130 million. In the process he created the Fuller Brush Man as a fixture in American Folklore—the subject of hundreds of quips and jokes—while elaborating a system of salesmanship that spread throughout the Western world. And Mr. Fuller himself became a storybook success, a man who started out with $375 and amassed many, many millions.

The company's basic product was brushes, but over the years its salesmen's sample cases have grown to include cosmetics and household chemicals. Some products have been phased out by changing life-styles—there is no longer a brush for cleaning derbies, for example—but the concept of bringing wares directly to the consumer, chiefly the housewife, has persisted. There are now about 25,000 salesmen in the United States, Canada and Mexico, each operating as an independent dealer in a fixed territory.

Mr. Fuller owed his success to his grasp of a few key business principles. One was that a few cents worth of bristles and other inexpensive materials, plus hard work, could create a much larger market value. Another was that a politely phrased sales pitch—carefully rehearsed—could almost always break down a buyer's resistance. And a third was that salesmen, if they were sufficiently motivated, could perform wonders.

The ubiquitous Fuller Brush Man (later joined by the Fullerette) paid calls on 85 of 100 American homes. He made deliveries in Alaska by dog team; he sold a doctor who set a dealer's fractured leg; he changed a customer's tire, pulled a tooth, dressed a chicken, hung out the wash. Inevitably, he was also a film subject.

Red Skelton, the comedian, played the title role in "The Fuller Brush Man" and Lucille Ball was the heroine of "The Fuller Brush Girl." In addition, Walt Disney's big bad wolf in "Three Little Pigs" disguised himself as a Fuller Brush Man.

11TH OF 12 CHILDREN

Mr. Fuller, according to his own account, was once almost enticed by a red-haired woman. "Don't lead me into temptation," she remarked invitingly after viewing his brushes. His response, he recalled, was to say, "Madam, I'm not leading you into temptation, but delivering you from evil." The woman purchased three brushes.

In his autobiography, "A Foot in the Door," Alfred Carl Fuller recounted that he had been born on a hardscrabble farm in Berwick, Nova Scotia, Jan. 13, 1885. He was the 11th of 12 children, and grew into a tall, handsome youth. With nothing but a grammar-school education and ambition to live in a more bustling world, he left home for Boston when he was 18.

After a succession of jobs, he went to work in 1905 for the Somerville Brush and Mop Company as a salesman. Having saved $375 in a year, he decided to venture on his own and set up a workshop in the basement of his sister's home. At night he turned out twisted-wire brushes for clothes, the hands, the floor, and sold them house to house by day.

His sales approach then was little different basically from that employed today. Recalling his early experience, Mr. Fuller said:

"I started out by trying to be helpful. I would knock on the door and say, 'Good morning, madam, if there is anything wrong in your house that a good brush could fix, perhaps I could help you."

The woman bought a long-handle brush and used it immediately to get at the dust between the flanges of a radiator. "After that," Mr. Fuller went on, "I studied a housewife's needs, and we made a brush for every need."

Later Mr. Fuller perfected ways to get inside the front door. On a rainy day he wore overshoes a size too large so he could get them off quickly. He was polite—"I'll just step in for a moment." And, starting in 1915, he and his dealers gave away a vegetable brush, known as "The Handy." They cost each dealer 3 cents apiece and were presented, of course, inside the door. In a recent year 7.5 million of them were pressed into housewives' hands.

After a selling trip to Hartford early in his career, Mr. Fuller decided to set up a company there in a shed he rented for $11 a month. By 1910 he had 25 salesmen and 6 factory workers. A year later he placed a small advertisement in a national magazine and was swamped with replies from would-be salesmen.

Then and later, those who sold Fuller products were independent dealers buying at wholesale and selling at retail at a profit of about 30 percent. Their incomes varied, depending on their enterprise, but they were (and are) supercharged by company pep talks. At one time, indeed, they were gathered to sing songs, one of which was "Fuller Land; Our Fuller Land," sung to the tune of "Maryland, My Maryland." Even so, dealer turnover was high, running to as much as one-fifth of the total.

PROFITED DURING DEPRESSION

With the proliferation of Fuller Brush Men, the company's sales rose to $5-million yearly by 1920, and to $12-million in 1924. The company did poorly in the Depression year of 1932, but it bounced back to record sales of $10-million in 1937, with a net profit of $108,000. Ten years later the gross was $30-million, and it has been rising since.

Mr. Fuller who was a kindly and dignified man, even-tempered and agreeable, liked to remind visitors that the word "American terminates in I Can and Dough begins with Do." His own motto, he once said, was:

"With equal opportunity to all and due consideration for each person involved in every transaction, a business must succeed."

In his business life Mr. Fuller joined a score of organizations and clubs. Outside business, his biggest interest was the Christian Science Church, which he joined in 1921. Another concern was education—the University of Hartford, to which he contributed money, and the American School for the Deaf, of which he was a trustee.

Mr. Fuller was president of his company until 1943, when he turned the post over to his older son, Howard, and became chairman of the board, a post he held until 1968. On Howard Fuller's death in 1959, the presidency went to Avard E. Fuller, his younger brother. The company was sold to the Consolidated Foods corporation in 1968.

Mr. Fuller's first marriage was to Evelyn W. Ellis of Nova Scotia. It lasted from 1908 to 1930, when the couple was divorced. Two years later he married Mary Primrose Pelton, who survives, as does his son Avard by his first marriage. Also surviving are two brothers, Harry of Newburg, Ore., and Chester of Kentville, Nova Scotia; five grandchildren, and four great-grandchildren.

Morgue Stories

It is quite likely that Whitman's piece was written before Fuller's death, possibly months or years earlier. Most newspapers have on file biographical sketches of prominent people. It is because they once contained little else except such sketches that newspaper libraries came to be called morgues.

As the Fuller piece illustrates, the morgue story actually is an interpretative biographical sketch in which the writer attempts to evaluate the person and assign him his proper historical importance. The best source of material about the basic facts of a person's life, is, of course, the person. Because the morgue sketch is prepared during its subject's lifetime, it usually is written following an interview. Also, the writer consults previously written material about the person and makes his own impartial estimate of the highlights of the career under review. Most prominent people are willing, even eager, to cooperate in preparing morgue material, and do not consider the experience macabre.

Emphasis in writing should be upon the outstanding characteristics, achievements and activities of the person. The temptation of the young writer is to begin with the fact of a person's birth and to continue with a chronological narrative. In interviewing a person for material about himself or herself it may be convenient to have the subject narrate in such a way but, in writing, the principle to be followed is the same as in all other news writing: most important facts first. The fact of birth seldom is the most important.

When only a short bulletin of an important person's death is received in time for an edition, the morgue part of the printed story may constitute almost the entire printed story.

The Second-Day Story

The second-day story is primarily the preliminary story of the funeral. When more than a day intervenes between death and the funeral, there may be two follow-up stories.

Details to look for in the funeral arrangements include, depending on the newsworthiness of the deceased:

Time and place.
Who will officiate?
Will services be public or private?
How many will attend?
Arrangements for handling a crowd.
Names of relatives.
Names of notables who will attend.
Will any club, lodge, etc. have a part?
Organizations to attend in a body or to be represented.
Names of musicians and selections.
Who will preach a sermon or deliver a eulogy?
Pallbearers, active and honorary.
Where will burial take place?
What will be the program of the services?

In virtually every case of death, friends of the dead person are given an opportunity to view the body before the time of the funeral or, if the body is not placed on view, to visit with members of the family in a funeral establishment. Newspapers should find out when such visits can be made.

The Funeral Story

When a collection is made of the outstanding newspaper stories of history, it will include more than one account of a funeral. The story of the burial of the unknown soldier by Kirke L. Simpson of the Associated Press has become a classic, as have stories of the funerals of most of the presidents of the United States. The following is a straightforward and dignified account of a newsworthy funeral:

By Jack Jones
TIMES STAFF WRITER

A celebrity-hungry crowd of perhaps 2,000 persons surrounded a glass-walled chapel at Hillside Memorial Cemetery in Culver City Sunday to stare at the famous who came to say goodby to comedian Jack Benny, 80.

At the conclusion of the short service in which old friend George Burns broke down and in which Bob Hope called Mr. Benny a genius, many of the curious pressed forward to join the line of mourners passing the closed coffin.

The doors to the chapel finally were closed "in respect to the family" and the spectators were asked to leave. But they clung, making it difficult for entertainment stars to reach their limousines.

Comedian Burns, friend of 50 years to the violin-playing Mr. Benny (Born Benjamin Kubelsky in Waukegan, Ill.), tried to offer the first tribute, saying, "I don't know whether I'll be able to do this."

Then he murmured some words which were inaudible to those outside depending on loudspeakers. He lapsed into sobs and silence and was helped away from the microphone by Rabbi Edgar F. Magnin.

Comedian Hope was more successful in delivering his prepared eulogy, saying the famed Mr. Benny who died Thursday night of cancer of the pancreas was a "national treasure."

He said of Mr. Benny, "He was stingy to the end. He only gave us 80 years, and that wasn't enough."

Hope said that Mr. Benny was a genius who "didn't just stand on stage—he owned it."

And his tribute contained a gentle almost lighthearted joke, the salute of one comedian to another. "His first love was the violin, which proves—as Jack used to say—you always hurt the one you love."

But he noted, Mr. Benny raised large amounts of money for various causes with his violin playing.

Hope concluded with, "God keep him; enjoy him. We did—for 80 years."

Among those who reached the service as hard-pressed Culver City police cleared walking space were:

Actors Raymond Massey, Cesar Romero, Frank Sinatra, Gregory Peck, James Stewart, Edgar Bergen, Jack Lemmon, Henry Fonda, Andy Griffith, Walter Matthau. . . .

Dinah Shore, Rosalind Russell, Lucy Arnaz, Candice Bergen, and Merle Oberon were there. So were Gov. Reagan, U.S. Sen. John V. Tunney (D-Calif.), and former Sen. (and actor) George Murphy.

His fellow comedians were there: Milton Berle, Hope, Jack Carter, Morey Amsterdam, George Jessel, Groucho Marx, Danny Thomas, Johnny Carson. . . .

And, too, the every-Sunday regulars of his old radio (and TV) show gathered: bandleader Phil Harris, singer Dennis Day, Eddie (Rochester) Anderson, announcer Don Wilson and Mel Blanc.

Benny's wife Mary, who played his girlfriend on the show, arrived with their adopted daughter, Joan, and three grandchildren. But the widow had to sit in the car for a few minutes before the service when the overwhelming scent of lavish floral pieces caused her to feel faint.

At the end of the 20-minute service inside the packed 350-seat seethrough chapel, the crowd pushed in so close that police had to again clear the way so the casket could be moved to the hearse carrying Mr. Benny to private entombment up the hill.

Berle, Peck and Sinatra were among the pallbearers struggling through the onlookers, as were Benny's business manager Irving Fein, Mervyn LeRoy, director Billy Wilder, Leonard Gershe, Fred DeCordova, Hilliard Marks and Armand Deutsch.

"Can you believe this?" one dismayed spectator asked another as some in the crowd ran forward to get close to the casket, pallbearers and the family.

But another woman with a small camera was complaining, "Just as we get up to the chapel, they shut the doors." [Los Angeles *Times*]

Follow-ups

A number of other stories may grow out of that of a death. Virtually everyone who is worthy of an obituary has held some position that will have to be filled. Before a speaker of the house is buried, newspapers print stories speculating as to who will be the successor. Frequently there are changes in business organizations after the death of an executive. Smart editors read the account of an executive's death and note the organizations, business, fraternal and otherwise, in which he held an office, and assign reporters to learn how that person's place will be filled in every case.

The courthouse reporter watches for the filing of wills and follows carefully every legal step up to and including the final settlement and discharge.

The Obituary Blank

The obituary may seem an important assignment, yet it is one of the first that a young reporter receives. Most newspapers have an obituary blank for reporters who gather facts about deaths. These printed forms also are given to undertakers, who cooperate in obtaining information for newspapers. A sample blank follows:

OBITUARY REPORT

Full name _____

Residence _____

Place of death _____ Time _____

Cause of death _____

Duration of illness _____

Present at deathbed _____

Circumstances of death _____

_____

Date of birth _____ Place _____

Surviving relatives: Wife or husband _____

Parents _____ Address _____

Brothers _____ Address _____

_____ Address _____

and

Sisters _____ Address _____

_____ Address _____

Children _____ Address _____

_____ Address _____

_____ Address _____

Date of marriage _____ Place _____

Came to this country _____ Naturalized _____

Residence here since _____

Previous residence and duration _____

Last occupation _____

Previous occupations _____

Education, with degrees and dates _____

Fraternal orders, clubs, etc. _____

Distinguished service, fraternal, educational, industrial, political, etc. _____

_____

_____

_____

Church affiliations _____

War record: Division, war _____

When discharged _____ Rank _____

Honors _____

Time of funeral _____ Place _____

Who will officiate _____

Organizations to attend in a body _____

Body will lie in state: When _____ Where _____

Active pallbearers _____

_____

Honorary pallbearers _____

_____

Music _____

_____

Burial place _____

_____

Prominent floral pieces _____

_____

Attending from away _____

_____

Additional information _____

_____

_____

No blank can include every question that a reporter may want answered, and so it is better not to rely entirely upon an undertaker but to keep an eye out for details that may need following up.

Language and Style

The language of the obituary should be simple and dignified. The verb "to die" is the safest to use. No religious group can take offense at it but can interpret it to suit its own tenets. "Passed away," "passed on," "called home," "the great beyond," "gone to his reward," "the angel of death," "the grim reaper," "departed this life," and similar expressions should be avoided.

Suicides _____

In covering a suicide, the reporter seeks the same information about a person's career, funeral arrangements, when the body will lie in state and so forth, as in the case of an ordinary obituary. Elements peculiar to the suicide story, however, include:

1. The motive.
2. The method.
3. The probable circumstances leading up to the act.
4. The coroner's inquest or medical examiner's report.

The Motive

A person who commits suicide usually is despondent because of financial difficulties, ill health, marital unhappiness, a mental disorder, or a philosophic attitude of discouragement toward life in general.

If the person does not leave a letter explaining motive, the reporter must investigate whichever motives seem most probable. A person's banker or doctor, business associates and friends and relatives should be interviewed. The reporter should ask if the person made any previous attempts at suicide, ever mentioned suicide, appeared to be in good health recently, especially the day before the suicide.

When there is no apparent motive, writers should say so and should quote those whom they interviewed to that effect. Reporters should not attempt to concoct a motive and must be particularly careful not to ascribe a suicidal motive when none was present. Legally, no suicide is a suicide until so called by a coroner's jury or a medical examiner's report, depending on the system in vogue. If there is a doubt, the account of death should be qualified by a statement as "thought to be suicide."

Even when the suicidal motive is present beyond a doubt, some newspapers hesitate to use the word. The editor of a paper in a small community may attempt to protect the feelings of surviving relatives by covering up the suicidal intent. Seldom is such an attempt successful, as an unprejudiced statement of the facts surrounding death indicates either suicide or murder. Only by deliberate fabrication is it possible really to "protect" the widow and other survivors.

It is doubtful, furthermore, whether the paper does as much good as harm in "hushing up" a suicide story. Anyone who knew the dead person will become acquainted with the facts anyway, and if one encounters an effort to deceive as to what actually happened, there is a tendency to conjecture. The rumors that circulate as to the motive of a suicide usually are much more damaging to a person's reputation than the simple truth would have been. A frank newspaper account puts an end to rumors.

The Method

The method by which suicide was accomplished usually is obvious. A newspaper should not dramatize the means of a suicide or print a story that might encourage another to do the same. A poison used for a suicidal purpose should not be mentioned by name, and if suicide by any other method is prevalent, newspapers should cooperate with authorities by omitting the method.

The coroner or physician summoned to examine the body can estimate the length of time the person has been dead. Members of the family and friends can provide clues as to what actions preceded the accomplishment of the act. The reporter should try to find the person who last saw the deceased alive.

Inquests

The coroner, a county official whose duty it is to investigate cases of unusual death, usually orders an inquest into a case believed to be suicide. Sometimes this is delayed until an autopsy is performed on the body and until circumstances of the death are fully determined. The coroner's jury may determine the motive as well as the manner of death. If in doubt, it returns an open verdict.

The trend is toward replacing the coroner with a professional medical examiner attached to a police department or some other law-enforcement agencies. About half the states have adopted the medical-examiner system, in full or in part. Small counties are more likely than large population centers to retain the coroner system, but it may be required that he be a physician. Either a coroner or an examiner must determine the cause of death in cases in which an attending physician cannot sign a death certificate. Neither a coroner's jury verdict nor a medical examiner's report has any more weight in a criminal case than a grand jury cares to give it.

Accidents, Disasters _____

There always have been catastrophes: volcanic ash annihilated Pompeii; earthquake and fire destroyed San Francisco; floods killed or made homeless millions of Chinese; an iceberg sank the unsinkable *Titanic;* the Zeppelin *Hindenburg* exploded; and so on. Not until the nuclear age, however, did some disaster occur somewhere almost every day: oil slicks, poison gas released from the wreckage of railroad cars or trucks; leakage of radioactive material from nuclear plants. How some papers covered the Three Mile Island crisis and the DC-10 airplane crash was told in Chapter 9.

Part of the price that people pay for the benefits of a highly industrialized society is the danger of sudden, violent injury or death. Automobile accidents result annually in nearly 60,000 deaths and nearly two million injuries. Wrecks of common carriers—railroads, buses, trucks, airplanes, boats—are fewer but are more destructive than in the days of slower speed and less delicate mechanics. Homes, public buildings, industrial plants and mines are better protected against fire and explosions, but an undetected minor flaw may result in a catastrophe without warning. Because of lack of foresight on the part of our grandfathers, we who live in the United

States today are facing a national crisis as to how to control floods, dust storms and soil erosion, which cause tremendous losses of life and property and, some say, are turning our country into a desert. "Acts of God," such as hurricanes, tornadoes, earthquakes and cyclones, continue to occur with their same frequency, and society has not yet learned how to protect itself adequately against them. The growing journalistic, as well as general interest in the problem of protecting the environment against pollution will be considered in Chapter 22.

The magnitude of an earthquake is measured by the scale that Prof. Charles F. Richter, California Institute of Technology seismologist, invented in 1927. It compares earthquakes with each other in terms of the size of the sweeping lines seismographs use to measure the amount of ground motion. The height of the lines when correlated with the distance from the quake's epicenter, determines the Richter magnitude. Every increase of one number on the open end scale, as from 6.5 to 7.5, represents a tenfold increase in magnitude.

Elements of Interest

Although they differ from each other by types, and although no two disasters of any kind are alike from the standpoint of news interest, news events pertaining to loss of life and property have in common numerous aspects that a reporter must bear in mind. Among the possible angles that no reporter can overlook are the following:

1. Casualties (dead and injured).
   a. Number killed and injured.
   b. Number who escaped.
   c. Nature of injuries and how received.
   d. Care given injured.
   e. Disposition made of the dead.
   f. Prominence of anyone who was killed or injured or who escaped.
   g. How escape was handicapped or cut off.
2. Property damage.
   a. Estimated loss in value.
   b. Description (kind of building, etc.).
   c. Importance of property (historical significance, etc.).
   d. Other property threatened.
   e. Insurance protection.
   f. Previous disasters in vicinity.
3. Cause of disaster.
   a. Testimony of participants.
   b. Testimony of witnesses.
   c. Testimony of others: fire chief, property owner, relief workers, etc.
   d. How was accident discovered?
   e. Who sounded alarm or summoned aid?
   f. Previous intimation of danger: ship or building condemned, etc.
4. Rescue and relief work.
   a. Number engaged in rescue work, fire fighting, etc.

   b. Are any prominent persons among the relief workers?
   c. Equipment used: number of water lines, chemicals, etc.
   d. Handicaps: wind, inadequate water supply or pressure, etc.
   e. Care of destitute and homeless.
   f. How disaster was prevented from spreading: adjacent buildings soaked, counter forest fire, etc.
   g. How much property was saved? How?
   h. Heroism in rescue work.
5. Description
   a. Spread of fire, flood, hurricane, etc.
   b. Blasts and explosions.
   c. Attempts at escape and rescue.
   d. Duration.
   e. Collapsing walls, etc.
   f. Extent and color of flames.
6. Accompanying actions.
   a. Spectators: number and attitude, how controlled, etc.
   b. Unusual happenings: room or article untouched, etc.
   c. Anxiety of relatives.
   d. Looting.
7. Legal action as result.
   a. Inquests, post mortems, autopsies.
   b. Search for arsonist, hit-and-run driver, etc.
   c. Protest of insurance company.
   d. Negligence of fire fighters, police, etc.
   e. Investigation of cause.

In all stories of disaster there is human interest. In most of them, there also are suspense and a recognition of combat between man and the elements. Disaster stories, furthermore, are action stories and contain considerable details as to exactly what happened. If these details are not presented in chronological order, they at least are so arranged as to leave no doubt in the reader's mind regarding the sequence of the most important of them.

Few other types of stories offer the writer greater opportunity for descriptive writing. Although major disaster stories are illustrated, the writer does not rely upon a photograph to do the work of 1,000 or even 100 or 10 words.

Picking the Feature

No formula for writing a disaster story—or any other type of story for that matter—should be accepted as absolute. In general, however, the lead of the disaster story should follow the orthodox rule of playing up the five _w_'s, giving identification and authority and emphasizing the feature. Any one of the elements listed may be the feature of the story at hand. Regardless of what is played up, the occasion must be identified in the lead by the amount of loss, either in lives or property. The reader judges the importance of the disaster by the size of the casualty list or the number of digits after the dollar sign. When the casualty list or inventory or property is long, it is impossible to be specific in the lead. Names, however, must be high in the story. If their number is not prohibitive, they should come immediately after the lead; otherwise, they should be included in a box either within or next to the story proper. If included in the story itself, they should be followed by explanations as to how every casualty or item of damage occurred.

Precautions

Reporters must be careful not to assign blame in an automobile accident, the type of disaster story that they have most frequent occasion to write. Police reports are not adequate protection against libel in such a story as the following:

> Disregarding a traffic signal and a policeman's whistle, Alex Winser, 1421 Talcott St., crashed into an automobile driven by Miss Ruth Hazelhurst, 1191 W. Villas Ct., this morning at Third and Hamilton streets.

The following is a much safer way:

> Two automobiles, one driven by Miss Ruth Hazelhurst, 1191 W. Vilas Ct., and the other by Alex Winser, 1421 Talcott St., collided this morning at Third and Hamilton streets. Neither driver was injured.

Care must be exercised in using "crashed," "demolished," "destroyed," and other descriptive verbs. The reporter should study the definitions of such words to avoid misapplying them. The makes of automobiles should not be mentioned unless pertinent.

It must be remembered that to collide two bodies must be in motion. Thus, if a moving automobile hits one parked at the curbing, there is no collision; rather, the car in motion strikes the other.

In the attempt to make drivers more careful and thus reduce accidents, some newspapers print daily tables or charts to show the total number of accidents and casualties by comparison with the preceding year. Likewise, since a magazine campaign against automobile accidents a few years ago, newspapers have been more inclined to include frank details of such mishaps to emphasize their horror. Much more gruesome pictures also are being used than formerly.

In the belief that they are performing a public service as well as fostering both reader interest and friendship, some newspapers undisguisedly editorialize in accident stories, as:

> The danger of bicycle riding on public streets again was illustrated about 7 p.m. yesterday when Harold, 13-year-old son of Mr. and Mrs. Emil J. Bornstein, 636 E. Carbany St., was seriously injured in the 1200 block of North Chicksaw Avenue. He was struck by an automobile driven by O. S. Patrick, 802 S. Lunt Ave.

What follows is an example of an ably handled, low-key account of a neighborhood tragedy.

By Tom Rademacher

James Wilson, a hero, is dead.

The 36-year-old area resident died early Wednesday at Blodgett Memorial Medical Center's Burn Unit, less than 24 hours after he rushed repeatedly into a flaming home to rescue a family friend and her children.

Wilson was staying with Julie Ann Croff, her son and two daughters at the Croff's home at 12013 Lincoln Lake Ave. NE in Oakfield Township when a gas furnace in the single-story dwelling exploded and ignited a fire about 5 a.m. Tuesday.

Wilson led Croff, 33, and her son, Kevin, 6, to safety, then went back into the home to save Croff's 1½-year-old daughter, Christina.

He rushed back in again in an attempt to save Christina's twin sister Regina, but the heat was too intense and he was forced to exit alone, according to Kent County sheriff's deputies.

Wilson suffered second- and third-degree burns over 50 percent of his body, mostly on the head, neck, torso and arms, according to a hospital spokesman. He was admitted Tuesday in critical condition.

About 10 a.m. Wednesday, he had a cardiac arrest and died 45 minutes later, the spokesman reported.

Christina Croff remains in critical condition at the center's burn unit.

The destroyed home had no basement and the furnace was located on the main floor, adjacent to the living room, deputies said. Regina's bedroom was separated from the furnace by a thin retaining wall.

Harvard Fire Chief Dale Cole said a babysitter told Wilson and Croff when they returned home Monday night that the furnace had been making strange noises.

The couple intended to have the furnace checked by a maintenance man Tuesday morning, a deputy said.

The fire remains under investigation.

Wilson's body was taken to Marshall Funeral Home in Greenville, where services are scheduled for 11 a.m. Saturday. Burial will be at Rest Haven Memory Gardens.

He is survived by a wife, Kathleen of Greenville; three children, Gina, Denise and Scott, all at home, and parents, James and Myra Wilson of Florida.

Funeral services for Regina Croff are scheduled for Saturday at 10 a.m. at the Pierce-Pederson Funeral Home in Rockford. Burial will be in Blythfield Memory Gardens. [Grand Rapids (Mich.) *Press*]

Side Features

Any one of the elements that go to make up a complete disaster story conceivably could be played up in a sidebar: acts of heroism, miraculous escapes, rescue and relief work, coincidences, etc. It is customary to use boxes or separate stories for long tabulations of casualties or damages and for lists of previous catastrophes of a similar nature. Eyewitness accounts are provided by victims who had narrow escapes and by bystanders, rescue workers, reporters, and others. When the disaster occurs outside the circulation area of the publication, it is customary to use a sidebar or in some other way play up the names of any local persons who were involved.

Perspective

Many disasters can be prevented by such obvious precautions as straightening highways, repairing defective electrical wiring and posting warning signals. Others cannot be controlled without scientific study and analysis and action on a much broader scale. The media of communication can help the public understand why a certain type of disaster is prevalent in a community, area, state or nation by "digging deeper" than the facts related to a specific news event.

> Behind last summer's great natural catastrophe, the devastating floods in Kansas and Missouri, is a simple story. The sweeping tragedy of 44 persons killed, 500,000 persons displaced, 2,000,000 acres flooded, 45,000 houses damaged or destroyed, the teeming Kansas City gutted by water and flame, and a $2.5 billion loss is only an effect. Underlying it all is the tale of three dams that became lost in politics in Kansas and the District of Columbia, and never got built.

Sociological phenomena are interrelated. Why flood control projects are not constructed involves consideration of more than selfish political interests. The stories of the depletion of natural resources, chiefly forests and grazing lands, and of soil erosion and other bad consequences of unscientific methods of farming are intricate ones.

Slum area fires usually can be blamed on faulty building codes and/or their improper enforcement. Probing deeper, to obtain perspective, however, the interpretative reporter may discover the origin of overcrowded housing in the heavy migration of blacks, Puerto Ricans or others into areas where segregation is enforced and programs for integrating newcomers into the economic and social life of the community are inadequate. The machinations of some real estate operators to reap personal profit by playing race against race or nationality group against nationality group may be revealed. Tracing the ownership of tenement property, often concealed by "dummy" titleholders, may be enlightening and a first step toward removal of fire hazards.

At a different level, newspapers can lead the way in educating home owners and tenants in how to preserve and renovate property so as to remove hazards. The famous Baltimore Plan of urban renewal could not have succeeded without the vigorous support of the *Sunpapers*.

Those concerned with safety on the streets and highways still stress the *three E*'s: engineering, education and enforcement. Increasingly, however, researchers are paying more attention to so-called human factors. The psychology of the automobile driver is being studied with remarkable results. The causes of "accident proneness" often are deep-seated within the individual and, for proper understanding, may require study of social factors external to the individual. Only a start has been made toward understanding the interrelationships in this field. Until the '80s, newspapers did little to report the extent to which drunkenness was a factor in such a large number of traffic deaths and injuries.

The same is true of most other aspects of the problem as a whole. Too many explanations of why teenagers are more reckless drivers than adults are superficial and contradictory. Simple explanations and answers should be avoided until much more study has been completed. In the meantime, the interpretative journalist can help keep the public informed as to the status of that research.

In 1966 the book *Unsafe at Any Speed* became a best seller and its author, Ralph Nader, was a key witness at congressional hearings that resulted in legislation to compel the automobile industry to pay more attention to the safety of its products. After private detectives hired by the automobile industry failed to uncover anything with which to smear or blackmail him, Nader continued to expose many other shortcomings in the operation of the economic system and encouraged many young journalists to ask why their editors failed to give them more constructive investigative assignments.

CHAPTER
14

Police, Crime, Criminal Law

As the traditional geographic beat system has been superseded or at least supplemented by "subject matter" or "field of interest" beats, and as routine crime has come to be considered comparatively less important by editors whose scope must include the whole world, the stationary police headquarters beat has become comparatively less important. Nevertheless, if for some unimaginable reason a newspaper were compelled to remove all of its beat reporters but one, it would be the person at police headquarters who would remain at the post. This is so, not because crime news is considered so overpoweringly important, but because in addition to learning of homes that have been broken into, checks that have been forged and murders that have been committed, the police reporter usually is the first to turn in tips of accidents, attempted suicides, missing persons, rabid dogs, strikes and many other events about which newspapers carry stories.

Because the police are in close touch with more phases of everyday life than any other news source, the police beat affords excellent training for beginning reporters and, fortunately, is one which they are likely to get. In the small community, covering police means visiting the police station two or three or more times a day, visiting the scenes of the infrequent important crimes that occur, verifying and amplifying the comparatively meager reports contained on the official police blotter or bulletin and writing all police news worth mention. In a large city, covering police has meant to remain all day at headquarters or at a district station, watching the steadily growing day's report and phoning tips of the most important items (perhaps 25 per cent of the total) to the city desk. When anything happens that the paper wants more about than the beat reporter can obtain from the police bulletin or by interviewing members of the force or witnesses brought to the station, an assignment reporter is sent out; the writing is done by a rewrite person.

The life of neither the police reporter nor the average police detective resembles very closely that depicted by the comic strips and mass market paperbacks. After you see one sobbing mother, one hardboiled hooker, one repentant gunman and one of all the other types who frequent police headquarters, it is all too easy to conclude that you have seen them all. That is an understandable, but unfortunate attitude. For the people who pass through the police station are human beings and each of them represents a unique clue to some aspect of our society that is malfunctioning.

Thus, the police reporter may have to struggle against both cynicism and discouragement. A good turn at police reporting is the best hazing possible for the green graduate or aspiring author of the world's greatest novel. There are few newspersons of importance who did not take the test and pass. An attitude of detached studiousness will enable beginning reporters to make this police reporting experience what it should be: the most valuable of their entire journalistic career.

Learning the Ropes _____

The Police System

The police reporter has got to know who's who and why at headquarters or at the district station. The setups of police departments differ in details but not fundamentally. At the top is always a chief of police, superintendent of police, police commissioner or some other individual appointed either by the mayor with the approval of the lawmaking body or by a police commission so appointed. Whatever its title, this office is a political one, and its holder may have little or nothing to say about the formation of general policies. If the higher-ups decide that certain "places" are to be allowed to remain open, they remain open until the word comes from above, either as a result of public pressure or for other reasons. The same is true as regards parades, rallies and demonstrations. Under orders from their superiors, police either protect or harass participants. Whenever any change in policy is made it is, of course, the chief who fronts, making the announcements and receiving the credit; likewise, when something goes wrong the chief is the scapegoat unless it is possible to "pass the buck" down the line to some underling.

This realistic picture of how the law enforcement system operates may be disturbing to young reporters with an idealistic or reformist nature, but until the public insists on an extension of the civil service system to include heads of police departments and upon strict observance of discipline and honesty throughout the entire system, the situation will not change. The trouble is that the element in the population who might favor an improvement either is unaware of the true state of affairs or is too indolent to do anything about it. The irate citizen who fulminates against the patrolman who looks the other way for a slight consideration or because of orders from above is the same who, when he receives a ticket for parking his automobile overtime, often starts on a hunt for someone who knows someone who knows someone. Above all, the reporter must realize that for all the frustrations police officers express about the limits on their power, they have great power. They can overlook wrongdoing or act against it. They can deprive people of liberty. They have a license, under prescribed conditions, to maim or kill. They are, in those senses, powerful people.

Several excellent reports have been made by presidential commissions on crime, and it would do the beginning reporter good to take them off the shelves, where they unfortunately rest, neglected, and study them. The best include these:

> *The Challenge of Crime in a Free Society,* a report by the President's Commission on Law Enforcement and Administration of Justice, Nicholas deB. Katzenbach, chairman, February 1967.
> *The Politics of Protest,* by Jerome H. Skolnick, director of Task Force on Violent Aspects of Protest and Confrontation of the National Commission on the Causes and Prevention of Violence, 1969.
> *Report of the National Advisory Commission on Civil Disorders,* Otto Kerner, chairman, March 1968.
> *Rights in Conflict,* the Violent Confrontation of Demonstrators and Police in the Parks and Streets of Chicago During the Week of the Democratic National Convention, a report submitted by Daniel Walker to the National Commission on the Causes and Prevention of Violence, December 1968.
> *To Establish Justice and to Insure Domestic Tranquility,* final report of the National Commission on Causes and Prevention of Violence, Dr. Milton S. Eisenhower, chairman, December 1969.
> *Violence in America, Historical and Comparative Perspectives,* an official report to the National Commission on the Causes and Prevention of Violence, by Hugh Davis Graham and Ted Robert Gurr, June 1969.

Despite modern training methods, many if not most policemen adhere to the "catch 'em and lock 'em up" school of criminology. Understandably, they want every arrest they make to lead to a conviction in court. They find it difficult to accept the principle of everyone's being considered innocent until proved guilty. They chafe under court restrictions regarding the gathering of evidence that forbid entering a place or searching a suspect without a proper warrant and applaud "no knock" laws, which increase their authority. They believe some eavesdropping, wire-tapping and even entrapment to be necessary. They also want more time than the United States Supreme Court says they should have to question or "work over" a suspect before filing charges against him. Police reporters should not, while making friendships, adopt the policeman's psychology. A reporter's homework should include Karl Menninger's *The Crime of Punishment,* Estes Kefauver's *Crime In America,* and Claude Brown's *Manchild in the Promised Land.*

These books, as well as the reports cited earlier, all date from the '50s and '60s. Unfortunately there are few similarly valuable references from later years except perhaps Jessica Mitford's *Kind & Usual Punishments, The Prison Business* and Barbara Gelb's *Varnished Brass.*

Paid more poorly than would be necessary to attract a higher type of public servant, police officers off their assigned duties are pretty good people. Fraternizing with them, the reporter learns to like them. Without friends in the department the reporter is worthless, as the formal reports and notations on the police blotter are grossly inadequate in case of an important story. In such instances is it necessary to talk to the policemen assigned to the case or to the principals; to see anyone in custody of the police, of course, requires permission.

A police captain is in executive control of a station that is organized in semimilitary fashion. In small communities, the chief may assume this responsibility or there may be a captain performing the function of chief at night. In large cities, every precinct station is directed by a captain. The lieutenants usually head up the different operating divisions, such as traffic, detective and patrol. The sergeant is a "straw boss," who may have charge of a switchboard over which he directs the activities of patrolmen on beats or may take charge of a small squad of patrolmen on some errand or duty. Inspectors may have roving assignments to check up on the operations of district stations or may perform the functions described as usually assigned to lieutenants; it is largely a matter of terminology. Inspectors in the traffic division are an entirely different type, being responsible for investigating the circumstances of traffic accidents.

If there is more than one station in a community, all keep in touch with headquarters by means of some electronic system, and a central record is kept of all important cases. Police departments even in small cities have two-way radio systems to enable headquarters to talk with cruising patrolmen in police automobiles. Also increasing are bureaus of identification in which photographs, fingerprints and possibly Bertillon records are taken and kept and ballistic and chemical studies made of clues.

To check up on minor occurrences, police reporters telephone the district stations at intervals throughout the day. For the most part, however, reporters watch the blotter or bulletin on which appears promptly everything of prime importance; assignment reporters are sent to district stations when necessary. Most large police departments now have elaborate electronic reporting equipment so the reporter has prompt notice of the occurrence of a crime. It still, however, is necessary to use ingenuity to interview the arresting policemen, the detectives assigned to a case, an assistant district attorney and/or others. Mechanical recording devices do not do the fact-finding job essential for good coverage of a case.

Entirely separate from the city police is the sheriff, who is the law enforcement officer for unincorporated areas within a county. Theoretically, the sheriff can intervene in municipal criminal affairs, but actually seldom does so except when invited or when local law enforcement breaks down. When such happens, it is extremely newsworthy and someone inevitably charges "politics."

Sheriff's raids are made mostly to break up drug-peddling centers and illegal gambling establishments outside city limits. Sheriff traffic police also patrol the highways along with a limited number of state police. In states where the township unit of government persists, the law enforcement officer is the constable and the local judicial officer is the justice of the peace.

County prosecuting attorneys are called circuit or district attorneys or state's attorneys. They are elected locally but are responsible to the state attorney general in the enforcement of state law. Federal prosecutors are district attorneys; federal law enforcement officers are marshals; and federal preliminary hearings are conducted by U.S. commissioners.

What Constitutes Crime

As important to the reporter as knowing police procedure is a knowledge of what constitutes crime. A breach of the law may be either a felony or a misdemeanor. As the law differs in different states, the same offense may be a felony in one state and a misdemeanor in another; and a felony or misdemeanor in one state may not be considered a crime at all in another. A felony always is a serious offense, such as murder, whereas a misdemeanor is a minor offense such as breaking the speed law. Felonies are punishable by death or imprisonment, whereas a misdemeanor usually results in a fine or confinement in a local jail. A *capital* crime is one punishable by death; an *infamous* crime is one punishable by a prison sentence.

Crimes may be classified as follows:

1. Against the person.
    a. Simple assault: threatening, doubling the fist and the like.
    b. Aggravated assault: threat violent enough to cause flight.
    c. Battery: actually striking a person, spitting on another, etc.
    d. False imprisonment: liberty unlawfully restrained by anyone.
    e. Kidnaping: stealing away a person. (May use *abduction* for women or children.)
    f. Rape: unlawful carnal knowledge of someone forcibly detained; statutory rape occurs when the victims are minors, even though they consent.

    g. Maiming (mayhem): disabling or dismembering of the victim by an attacker.

    h. Homicide: killing when the victim dies within a year and a day.

        (1) Matricide: killing one's mother.

        (2) Patricide: killing one's father.

        (3) Fratricide: killing one's brother or sister.

        (4) Uxorcide: killing one's wife or husband.

        (5) Justifiable: in self-defense or in line of duty.

        (6) Felonious: either murder or manslaughter.

    i. Manslaughter.

        (1) Voluntary: intentionally in the heat of passion or as the result of extreme provocation.

        (2) Involuntary: unintentional but with criminal negligence.

    j. Murder

        (1) First degree: with expressed malice and premeditation.

        (2) Second degree: with no premeditation but with intent to kill or inflict injury regardless of outcome.

    k. Abortion: interfering with pregnancy except as permitted by United States Supreme Court decisions.

2. Against habitation.

    a. Burglary: entering another's dwelling with intent to commit a felony therein; often extended to include any building.

    b. Arson: malicious burning of another's real estate.

3. Against property.

    a. Larceny: taking and converting to use with felonious intent the property of another.

    b. Robbery: larceny with intimidation or violence against the person.

    c. Embezzlement: larceny by means of a breach of confidence.

    d. False pretenses: confidence games, impostures, swindles.

    e. Receiving stolen goods: for sale or concealment; recipient called "fence."

    f. Forgery: altering or falsely marking a piece of writing for private profit or deception of another.

    g. Malicious mischief: killing animals, mutilating or defacing property.

    h. Extortion: blackmail; obtaining illegal compensation to do or not to do any act.

4. Against morality and decency.

    a. Bigamy: second marriage without dissolving the first.

    b. Incest: sexual relations between persons so closely related that they are forbidden to marry.

    c. Prostitution: promiscuous indulgence in sexual relations by women for profit.

    d. Obscenity: anything offensive to a sense of sexual decency as defined by statute and court decisions.

    e. Indecency: anything outrageously disgusting.

    f. Contributing to delinquency of a minor: encouraging or permitting any waywardness in youths.

    g. Sabbath laws restricting commercial and other activities on Sundays.

5. Against the public peace.
    a. Breach of the peace. (May cover disorderly conduct and a variety of nuisances.)
    b. Affray: fighting in a public place to the terror of the public.
    c. Unlawful assembly: gathering for purpose of planning or committing illegal act.
    d. Rout: unlawful assembly that begins to move.
    e. Riot: unlawful assembly or rout that becomes tumultuous or violent.
    f. Disturbance of public assembly: interference with legal meeting.
    g. Disorderly conduct. (Statutes stipulate acts forbidden.)
    h. Forcible entry and detainer: illegal seizure or holding of property.
    i. Defamation: libel if written, slander if spoken.
    j. Concealed weapons. (May be listed as disorderly conduct.)
    k. Gaming: playing games for money or games of chance, unless they are games in which betting is allowed by law.
    l. Gambling: betting on outcomes of events over which bettors have no control.

6. Against justice and authority.
    a. Treason: breach of allegiance to country; giving enemy aid.
    b. Perjury: false testimony under oath in judicial proceedings.
    c. Bribery: attempt to influence public official in his duties.
    d. Embracery: attempt to influence a juror.
    e. Counterfeiting: making false money that is passed as genuine.
    f. Misconduct in office: extortion, breach of trust, neglect, etc.
    g. Obstructing justice: resisting arrest; refusing to aid arresting officer.
    h. Obstructing punishment: escape; prison breach.
    i. Compounding a felony: agreeing not to prosecute felon or assisting him in evading justice.
    j. Exciting litigation: stirring up lawsuits for profit; barratry; maintenance; champerty.
    k. Election laws: fraud or illegal interference with voting.
    l. Conspiracy: planning or plotting to commit crime.
    m. Contempt: improper respect for court.

7. Against public safety, health and comfort.
    a. Nuisances: annoyances.
    b. Traffic regulations.
    c. Food and drug acts.
    d. Health regulations.
    e. Safety laws for common carriers; use of explosives, etc.

The police reporter must understand these popular definitions of criminal offenses, the names of which may or may not correspond to the statutory titles, which differ somewhat by states.

Elements of Crime News _____

The Police Blotter

Despite the quantity of news emanating from police headquarters which gets into print, much more that appears on the blotter or bulletin is disregarded by the police reporter. Whereas it is possible to give feature treatment to almost everything that is reported to police, there is so much sameness in most of the routine of law enforcement that such entries on the bulletin as complaints against peddlers, small boys or dogs, notices from the police of other cities to be on the outlook for a certain person or automobile, reports of suspicious characters and lost and found articles go unheeded. The usual style is that followed by the Appleton (Wis.) *Post Crescent,* in which the following items appeared, almost verbatim, from the police bulletin:

John E. Livingston, 2400 N. Drew St., told police that his home was broken into on Thursday and $214 in cash and some small items were stolen.

Appleton police are investigating an indecent exposure complaint that occurred about 6:45 p.m. Thursday in the children's section of the Appleton Public Library. A man exposed himself to an 11-year-old girl and then left.

Janice L. McDaniel, 526 N. Rankin St., reported that her wallet with $250 in cash and personal papers was stolen from 106 W. College Ave., on Thursday.

Many newspapers generally omit names of victims and their exact addresses in order to protect them and their privacy. For example:

Forty dollars was taken April 30 from an apartment in the 1200 block of Hull Terrace.

More nearly complete records are turned in on regulation forms in all such cases, and these blanks may be consulted by police reporters. Usually, however, reporters prefer to talk to the policemen involved or with the principals. It is not safe practice to rely upon the police bulletin as authentic because policemen are notoriously bad spellers and make numerous mistakes in names and addresses.

If attempts at verification fail, the reporter should accredit the story to the police bulletin. It is presumed, of course, that the reporter knows the law of libel, which offers no protection if the story uses the expression, "police say." It is not safe to print news of an arrest until a person has been taken into custody and booked on a certain charge; then the newspaper can relate only what has happened. It is impossible to say without risk that a person is "wanted for having fled the scene of an accident." Rather, the reporter should write that the person is wanted "in connection with the accident . . ." Every item of police news should be verified before being used.

Usually for an adequate account of any item appearing on the police bulletin, more details than given there are needed.

Picking the Feature

All crime stories involve action. They relate to incidents that are potentially exciting when read about, provided the reporter has been resourceful and thorough in newsgathering. Until a case reaches court, knowledge of law is secondary to ability to observe, describe and imagine all of the angles needing investigation and the sources from which information may be obtainable. Good crime reporters, in other words, must possess some of the qualities of a good detective although the purpose is entirely different. The reporter is not out to solve the crime but to learn all that it is possible to find out about it.

Because anything can and constantly does happen, the following list of potential elements of interest in news of crime cannot possibly be complete. It is only suggestive.

1. Casualties.
   a. Lives lost or threatened.
   b. Injuries and how received.
   c. Description of any gun play or fighting.
   d. Disposition of dead and injured.
   e. Prominent names among dead and injured.
2. Property loss.
   a. Value of loss.
   b. Nature of property stolen or destroyed.
   c. Other property threatened.
3. Method of crime.
   a. How entrance was effected.
   b. Weapons or instruments used.
   c. Treatment of victims.
   d. Description of unusual circumstances.
   e. Similarity to previous crimes.
4. Cause or motive.
   a. Confessions.
   b. Statements of victims.
   c. Statement of police, witnesses and others.
   d. Threats.
5. Arrests.
   a. Names of persons arrested.
   b. Complaint or policeman making arrest.
   c. Charges entered on police blotter.
   d. Police ingenuity.
   e. Danger incurred by police.
   f. Arraignment.
6. Clues as to identity of criminals.
   a. Evidence at scene of crime.
   b. Testimony of witnesses.

      c. Statement of police.

      d. Statements of victims and others.

      e. Connection with other crimes.

   7. Search for offender.

      a. Probability of arrest.

      b. Description of missing persons.

      c. Value of clues.

      d. Contact with criminal through ransom notes, etc.

Juveniles

The first juvenile court in the United States was established in Chicago in 1899. Leader of the citizens' group that had agitated for it was Jane Addams of Hull House, where the Juvenile Protection Association was founded to lobby for better laws affecting children. One law that most states adopted forbade publication of the names of juveniles involved in crime. Even newspapers in states without such a law adhered to the policy.

Today, the pendulum is changing as a result of drastic increases in juvenile crime. In a case involving a 17-year-old girl arsonist, the Colorado Supreme Court declared that state's law unconstitutional. In doing so it cited a 1976 United States Supreme Court decision that courts cannot suppress facts about even normally secret juvenile proceedings if the facts have been made public. In that case the court overruled the Oklahoma Supreme Court, which had upheld the conviction of Oklahoma City papers for reporting a hearing for an 11-year-old boy who fatally shot a switchman.

The decisive case was that of the Charleston (W. Va.) *Gazette* and *Daily Mail,* in whose behalf 11 journalistic organizations filed *amicus* briefs in the United States Supreme Court. The papers had published the name of a 14-year-old boy arrested for fatally shooting a classmate in the presence of seven witnesses. In June 1979 the Supreme Court declared the state law unconstitutional.

Regardless of what the courts decide it is unlikely that most newspapers will abandon all restraint in publishing juvenile crime news. It is more likely that they will follow the lead of the Peru (Ind.) *Tribune* as follows:

> The *Tribune* will publish the names, ages, and addresses of all youthful offenders thirteen years of age or older provided:
>
> 1. in the opinion of the court there is no valid reason for such information to be withheld from publication
> 2. the offenses are not of an extremely minor nature
> 3. the offenders are actually charged with a specific offense.
>
> These facts will appear, along with all other pertinent facts of the case released by the proper authority.
>
> The *Tribune* will follow up with stories which tell whether or not the youth charged has been found guilty or not guilty.

Human Interest

In every community, no matter how small, there occur brushes with the law or situations reported to police which, in the hands of a skilled writer, can be made into compelling copy. In writing brevities originating on the police beat, the rewrite person is permitted considerable stylistic leeway as the emotional appeal outweighs the news interests as the following two story excerpts illustrate:

By David Dahl

Doug Friend went out drinking Friday night with his pet python Monty, and they both got thrown in the brig.

After being asked to leave a St. Patrick's Day party at a local tavern, Friend was seen walking along a street in western St. Petersburg with the snake wrapped around his neck.

A police officer arrested Friend and took Monty to a local wildlife office for safekeeping.

Police charged Friend with violating a St. Petersburg ordinance that prohibits having a "vicious" constrictor snake more than six feet in length. Monty, a brown and tan Burmese python, is 7 feet 3.

"It's a pretty snake," said St. Petersburg police officer Thomas Foster, who arrested Friend and also let Monty curl up on the dashboard of his cruiser while driving the snake to the refuge. . . .　　　　　[St. Petersburg *Times*]

By Jerry Riley

Yesterday wasn't a good day for a man who robbed the Bank of Louisville branch at 5616 Bardstown Road.

He had the money. He was out the door. An escape seemed so close.

Then he wrecked his getaway car, right in front of the bank.

A dye bomb planted in the money exploded, filling the car with smoke.

About the same time, he accidently shot himself in the foot.

Then, limping, he stole another car at gunpoint—from a passer-by who had stopped to help after his car had filled with smoke.

But he wrecked the stolen car too.

He finally found himself held at gunpoint by an alert off-duty policeman who just happened to pass by. . . .　　　　　[Louisville *Courier-Journal*]

Other Police News

Not all news originating in police headquarters has to do with pursuing criminals. Police engage in a variety of activities, many of which may be newsworthy. For instance, the missing persons bureau of any large department receives hundreds of calls weekly. Children who leave home in search of adventure, old people who wander off and spouses and parents who desert their families often are news. The first intimation that a crime has been committed also may come from a report that a certain person is missing.

New traffic rules, warnings concerning dangerous intersections, demands that householders make better disposal of their garbage and innumerable similar announcements come from police headquarters. Then there are additions to the staff, retirements, promotions, demotions, citations and administrative foul-ups within the department itself. Monthly, annual and other reports contain statistics and other information of public interest. Following are excerpts of examples of such stories:

By David Newton

"Buddy, can you spare a dime?"

That familiar refrain from street people hanging out in Williams Park may be less familiar beginning Oct. 1 if a request by the St. Petersburg police department is approved for the 1985–86 budget.

The request would increase police coverage downtown from five officers, eight hours a day, to seven officers, 14 hours a day. Panhandling by street people won't be the only thing reduced by the increased forces scooting around on golf carts, officials say.

They expect reductions in other crimes downtown, such as purse snatching and break-ins. For police purposes, downtown runs from Fifth Avenue S to Fifth Avenue N and from Ninth Street to Tampa Bay.

With the budget request, the city is trying "to achieve a sense of security in the downtown area," says City Manager Alan Harvey. The effect, Harvey says, will be to reduce purse snatchings and other crimes and to keep undesirables and panhandlers away. . . . [St. Petersburg *Times*]

By Mike Burris

Edwardsville police would get a modern, easily monitored alarm system to replace old equipment if city officials endorse a plan advocated by Director of Police Bennett W. Dickmann.

The proposal has the approval of the city's Public Safety Committee.

Dickmann, who has been interested in replacing the old system for some time, wants to have a private firm take out the old alarm panels and install a modern system. The company—instead of the Police Department—would maintain the equipment. The company also would be responsible for billing customers and collecting payment. . . . [Edwardsville (Ill.) *Intelligencer*]

By Spotlight Investigative Team

It was an idea with noble intentions, born out of the demonstrations of the 1960s that pitted police against civil rights activists, college students and Vietnam protesters. Police needed to become more sensitive to the communities they were asked to control, and the best way was college education.

In 1970, Massachusetts adopted the nation's highest pay incentives for police officers to obtain college degrees. The program, which now costs more than $12 million a year, has turned into a quick and easy way for officers to secure salary increases of up to $13,000. . . .

No one has monitored the program to ensure that the estimated $75 million expense, shared by the state and local communities in the last 15 years, has produced more capable or insightful police. In state government, the sole employee working full time on the multimillion-dollar program performs only bookkeeping tasks, collecting transcripts and reimbursement requests.

Known as the "Quinn bill" after its sponsor, former attorney general Robert H. Quinn, the Police Pay Incentive Program has become a sweetener that demands little academic sweat, making police the envy of all other public employees. "We have police captains in the city who earn more than $40,000 a year because of the Quinn bill," said Cambridge City Manager Robert W. Healy. "They don't like it when I say, 'When I'm reincarnated, I want to come back as a captain. . . . [Boston *Globe*]

Crime Statistics

Since 1930, the Federal Bureau of Investigation, in cooperation with the International Association of Chiefs of Police, has published *Uniform Crime Reports*. Great caution must be exercised in using the statistics therein contained because they are submitted voluntarily by local police departments. As the FBI itself warns, "In publishing the facts sent in by chiefs of police in different cities, the FBI does not vouch for their accuracy. They are given out as current information which may throw some light on problems of crime and criminal law enforcement."

With reference to the volume of crime—number of offenses—pressures are always present to keep the figures low," the Chicago Crime Commision warns. In addition, the same source declares, numerous known crimes never are reported, including (1) various types of sex offenses because the victims wish to avoid the embarrassment of publicity, (2) those that private citizens fail to report because of lack of confidence in the police, (3) those unreported by citizens who do not wish to become involved in extended court actions and (4) matters that are handled by private police or protective agencies.

Blacks and members of other minority groups are especially reluctant to summon policemen to their neighborhoods. This fact counterbalances, in part at least, the greater avidity with which police often arrest members of minority groups.

Whenever there seems to be an increase in crime, especially violent crime, there is likely to be a clamor, to which editors often contribute, that the size of the police force should be increased. It is to conjecture, however, how much good huge forces, even large enough to provide a bodyguard for every citizen, would accomplish inasmuch as approximately three-quarters of all homicides are committed indoors by relatives, friends or acquaintances of the victims, and the really big crime, white-collar corporate crime, is stonewalled until a congressional hearing is held.

Situation Stories

One type of interpretative writing open to police reporters is that in which they describe not one or a number of specific crimes, but a situation related to antisocial conduct or law enforcement of continuous public interest. Here are portions of such stories:

By Tom Gibbons

Violent crimes against low-income minorities are routinely downgraded to minor offenses by the state's attorney's office and Chicago Police Department, the Sun-Times has found.

The practice involves the reducing of the felony crimes of rape, stabbings and shootings to misdemeanors which carry much lighter sentences.

An examination of 400 randomly selected misdemeanor battery cases found that 47 of those cases, or nearly 12 percent, had been downgraded. And in each of the downgraded cases, the crime involved either a minority victim or assailant. In most cases both were blacks or Hispanics who lived in the city's poor neighborhoods. . . .   [Chicago *Sun-Times*]

By Andy Furillo

Officer Doran Christenson has walked the night beat in the heart of the Rampart Division, the Los Angeles Police Department's busiest, for 14 years.

His beat—the MacArthur Park area—takes him into some of the city's meanest neighborhoods in pursuit of robbers and burglars, dope dealers and prostitutes, wife beaters and car thieves.

And like most street cops in Rampart, Christenson loves his work.

"You've got to admit it," Christenson said, turning to his longtime partner, Paul Afdahl, as they raced to a shooting. "This is fun."

Christenson is one of 193 street cops in Rampart, which last year had 64,096 calls for service—more than any other division in the city—and 23,009 major crime reports, second highest in the city.

Despite the heavy action—in fact, because of it—Rampart is considered one of the best places in Los Angeles to be a street cop. No one at Rampart asks to transfer, and officers wanting in must get on a waiting list. . . .

[Los Angeles *Times*]

By Lynn Emmerman

It was to have been a routine undercover drug bust. According to the police plan, a detective posing as a gang member would buy cocaine from suspected drug dealers in the parking lot of a popular North Side restaurant. Once the transaction was complete, the police back-up team would close in and make the arrest.

But the suspects had another plan. When the undercover officer showed one of the men his $25,000 bankroll, a second man jumped out of the suspects' car waving a machine gun. He took the money, then aimed at the policeman's head and reached for the trigger.

Before he could shoot, the officers' back-up team arrived on the scene shouting, "Stop, police!" The men fled, spraying the lot with bullets. They led police on a chase and engaged in a gun battle in which one of the suspects was wounded before he was apprehended.

Several similarly harrowing scenes have been played out on Chicago area streets in the last year. Narcotics unit Cmdr. John Ryle, who described the violent encounters, believes they indicate a marked increase in drug-related robberies and murders in the Chicago area. . . .   [Chicago *Tribune*]

Criminal Procedure _____

When suspects are arrested and charged with a crime, they are taken immediately to a jail or police station where they are held pending arraignment. If the arrest is made upon the complaint of another person, the magistrate or judge already has provided the arresting officer with a *warrant,* which commands him to bring the defendant to court. Those seeking the arrest of another must affirm under oath that they have reasonable grounds for belief in the guilt of the accused. A *search warrant* permits search of a premise where there is reason to believe evidence of a crime may be found. Unless police on raids have search warrants, their testimony is worthless in court. By a *motion to suppress* the evidence the defense obtains the right to question the arresting officer as to the means by which the officer gained admittance to the place where the arrest was made. Even though the entrance was legitimate, the case still may be dismissed if *entrapment* (inducing someone to commit a crime) is proved.

Arraignment

Those persons who are arrested have a constitutional right to be brought into court promptly to be confronted with the charge against them. When that is done, they give their legal answer to the charge. If they remain mute, a not guilty plea is entered. Then the court proceeds according to its authority.

> Easton—Robert Fehnel, 29, of 1236 Bushkill St., was arraigned Thursday before District Justice David T. Reibman on a bad check charge. He was released on his own recognizance for the next term of court.
> The charge was filed by Easton National Bank and Trust Co. He was accused of having insufficient funds in his account for his $400 check which he cashed Sept. 27.   [Easton (Pa.) *Express*]

Preliminary Hearing

If the offense is one over which the inferior court does not have jurisdiction, it holds a hearing to determine whether there is enough presumption of guilt to *bind over* the case for grand jury action in the higher court. If it decides differently, it dismisses the case and frees the suspect. In such a case, either on a coroner's jury verdict or on the initiative of the prosecuting attorney, the case still can be presented to the grand jury. Persons charged with indictable offenses frequently waive preliminary hearing.

> **By John McCarroll**
> Des Moines—Merle Bennett, formerly of Brooklyn, was bound over to a federal grand jury in Des Moines Monday on charges of armed bank robbery and conspiracy stemming from the Nov. 12 robbery of the Grinnell State Bank.
> . . .   [Cedar Rapids (Iowa) *Gazette*]

Pending hearing, the suspect may be released on *bail,* usually requiring a bond of cash or security. Sometimes a person is released on a *recognizance,* which is merely a written promise to appear when wanted or forfeit a stipulated sum.

The Grand Jury

The grand jury must be distinguished from the petit jury. It does not try a case but merely investigates crimes that have been committed and decides whether there is enough evidence to warrant the expense of bringing the accused persons to trial in the circuit or district court. The grand jury hears the evidence of the prosecution only, and, on the basis of that *ex parte* (one-sided) evidence, it may indict the accused.

An *indictment* may take the form of a *true bill* in case the evidence has been submitted by the prosecuting attorney. If the jury itself gathers evidence of a crime, the indictment is called a *presentment.* A grand jury is supposed to investigate the conduct of government in the territory served by the court and to consider conditions that it thinks should be remedied by law.

In some states, accused persons may be brought to trial upon *informations* submitted by the prosecuting attorney under oath and without a grand jury investigation.

Whenever a crime has been committed and the guilty person has not been ascertained, a *John Doe hearing* is held by the grand jury in the attempt to discover the identity of the person wanted. The prosecuting attorney has the power to summon witnesses to any grand jury hearing.

Grand jury proceedings are secret, but there frequently are leaks from which the reporter benefits. It is contempt of court, however, to publish the results of a grand jury action before it is reported in court. Often, newspapers withhold information even longer so that indicted persons not in custody of police can be arrested on a *bench warrant* (or *capias*) without tipoff.

The reporter should watch (1) the number of indictments naming the same person, (2) the number of counts or charges in the same indictment, (3) the number of persons included in the same indictment. By standing outside the jury room, reporters can determine who the witnesses were and, on their past knowledge of the case, can speculate as to what testimony must have been. The law under which indictments are returned and the punishment, in case of ultimate conviction, frequently should be obtained. Some states have immunity laws to permit witnesses to testify without incriminating themselves. The power of prosecutors in determining what evidence shall be presented to a grand jury makes them important political figures. In writing the story, the reporter must use great care to accredit every statement to the true bill.

> Five police officers and six private citizens appeared before the special grand jury investigating police department activities in the jury's second consecutive meeting of the week, Tuesday night at East Side Court.
> One of the first police officers to be called was Detective Sgt. Thomas Buzalka, who remained closeted with the jury for more than an hour. While awaiting call, Buzalka chatted with Robert Hull, head of the police garage, and Patrolman R. L. Lincoln, who also appeared before the jury.
> Emerging from the jury room, Buzalka left the building hurriedly with a brief "good night" thrown over his shoulder to those awaiting their turns. . . .

> Six indictments charging five companies and 14 individuals with illegally obtaining 800,000 gallons of cane syrup were returned by the federal grand jury Monday before Judge Peter Ennis.
> The indictments followed an investigation by the Agriculture and Justice departments to determine how the companies were complying with a supplement to the federal sugar rationing order. . . .

Pleas and Motions

When someone is arraigned on an indictment, or at any time thereafter up to trial, there are numerous pleas and motions that may be made, chiefly by the defense. Those which merely seek delays are called *pleas in abate-*

ment. One such is a *challenge of the panel* (or *to the array*), which contends that the grand jurors were selected or acted improperly. A motion for a *continuance* is merely a request for a *postponement.* A *severance* may be asked so that a defendant will not have to stand trial with others named in the same indictment.

A *plea to the jurisdiction* challenges the authority of the court. A motion for a *change of venue* asks that the case be transferred to another court or locale or that a new judge be assigned to it. Motions that would stop all action are *pleas in bar.* One is a *demurrer,* which contends that even though true the acts alleged in the indictment do not indicate crime. A *plea of former jeopardy* is an assertion that the accused previously has been tried on the same charge.

The two common pleas, of course, are *guilty* and *not guilty.* A modified form of the former is *nolo contendere* by which the accused says he will not contest the charges. It is frequent after a test case when others awaiting trial realize that they have no chance to "beat the rap." It keeps the defendant's record clear of an admission but otherwise is the equivalent of a guilty plea. If any civil action is brought, this plea cannot be used against the defendant.

There is no legal plea of "innocent," but some newspapers use the word instead of "not guilty" as a precautionary measure. They fear that the "not" might get lost in the composing room, thereby committing possible libel.

The one important plea that the prosecution can make is *nolle prosequi (nol pros),* which means "do not wish to prosecute." It is made when new evidence convinces the prosecutor of the accused's innocence or when there is insufficient evidence to convict. If it occurs under any other circumstances, an alert newspaper should expose the fact.

> Circuit Attorney Franklin Moore today dismissed in Circuit Judge Harry Jamieson's court indictments against six precinct officials in the Fifteenth Precinct of the Fourth Ward, charged with fraudulent removal and secretion of ballots in the primary election, Aug. 7.
>
> The indictments were returned Nov. 3, but the cases have been continued from time to time by the defendants who said they were not ready for trial. The cases were originally assigned to Judge Charles R. Watson, but transferred to Judge Jamieson on a change of venue.
>
> The last continuance was sought Monday by the state, which said it was not ready for trial, in view of the fact that State Supreme Court had not yet acted on applications for permanent writs of prohibition to prevent the Madison grand jury from examining ballot boxes and other election records of the Fourth Ward. Moore told a Journal reporter that the records were needed to prosecute the cases.
>
> Those indicted were. . . .

Other Preliminaries

When fugitives from justice in one state are arrested in another, they may be returned to the jurisdiction where they must answer charges by *extradition.* The procedure is for the governor of the state seeking custody of such fugitives to request the governor of the state in which they are apprehended to return them. It is newsworthy when such a request is denied, as it sometimes is in such cases as that of an exconvict who has lived an exemplary life for years since a prison break. In federal courts, the equivalent of extradition is *removal* from one jurisdiction to another following hearing before a commissioner.

> A description of torture allegedly inflicted upon him in the Georgia State Penitentiary was given Tuesday by an escaped prisoner as he opened a fight against extradition proceedings to return him to that prison.
> He is Leland Brothers, 35, who was released Friday from the Stateville Penitentiary after serving a one-to-three-year sentence from Brown County for armed robbery. . . .

In both criminal and civil cases, *depositions* may be taken with court permission when there is a likelihood that a witness will be unavailable during trial. A deposition differs from an *affidavit* because it is conducted by a court appointee, both sides are notified and the rules of evidence are followed. In other words, the witness testifies under the same conditions that he would in court; the transcript of his testimony may be introduced as evidence.

Witnesses who do appear in court usually are there as the result of *subpoenas* (court orders), which either side may obtain as a matter of right. A *subpoena duces tecum* orders a witness to produce certain real evidence, usually documents and records.

Criminal Trials _____

Most criminal trials (same is true of civil trials) last only a few hours or minutes. Some, however, take days, weeks or months. The story the day before or on the day of trial may forecast its probable length, based on statements by attorneys for both sides and what the reporter knows of the probable evidence.

First Stories

The reporter should include (1) careful tie-back to the crime itself—time, place, names, events; (2) the charges as stated in the indictment; (3) the possible outcome, meaning the minimum and maximum penalties fixed by law for all of the possible verdicts in the case; (4) the probable evidence with names of witnesses and attorneys' statements, if obtainable, as to what they will attempt to establish; (5) any unusual angles, as possible difficulty in obtaining a jury—for instance, one side may be expected to favor persons of ages, occupations, religion or politics different from those favored by the other side—or maybe this is the first trial of its kind, or the first in a long time, or a new law may be applied to some part of the proceedings. The possibilities are limitless.

Picking the Jury

After the indictment has been read and the plea entered, and after any last-minute motions have been disposed of, selection of the jury begins. The jury of twelve is picked from a panel of *veniremen* prepared by the jury commission or its equivalent. They are questioned by attorneys of both sides and, if found unsatisfactory for reasons that are obvious, may be *challenged for cause*. In addition, each side has a stated number of *peremptory challenges* for which no reasons need be given; usually the defense has twice as many as the prosecution. The questioning of prospective jurors is called the *voir dire* (to speak the truth). Clues to future tactics may be obtained from the types of questions asked veniremen. If, for instance, prosecutors do not inquire whether prospective jurors are prejudiced against the death penalty, it is apparent they do not intend to ask for that punishment. If the original panel of veniremen is exhausted without a jury's being completed, additional persons are summoned; they are known as *talesmen* and in inferior courts may be brought in off the street or selected from courtroom spectators.

Opening Statements

The state leads with a statement of what it intends to prove and the nature of the evidence to be introduced. The prosecutor presents no evidence. The defense may make its reply immediately or may wait until after the prosecution's evidence has been presented.

Evidence

First witnesses for the state are called for the purpose of establishing the *corpus delicti,* or proof that a crime was committed. All testimony is given in answer to questions by attorneys. After *direct examination* by attorneys for the side calling him, a witness is subjected to *cross-examination* by attorneys for the other side. They must restrict their questions to matters about which he already has testified and they often attempt to *impeach a witness* by catching him in contradictory statements. Objections to questions frequently are made by counsel; the judge is the arbiter. Occasionally, the jury is taken from the room while arguments on the admissibility of evidence are heard. A *jury view* is the taking of a jury to the scene of a crime or any other place outside the courtroom for the purpose of observing anything pertinent to the case.

By Vanessa Shelton

Identifying persons involved in a May 20, 1978, incident at a southeast-side tavern was difficult, a Cedar Rapids police officer said today in the Linn District Court trial of Edward Williams.

However, he added, there was no mistake about Williams or his actions.

Williams and six other men were charged with rioting in connection with a brawl involving police and patrons of the L and H Lounge (formerly the Brown Derby), located at 601 12th Ave. SE.

Williams is the first of the seven to stand trial on the rioting charge. Trials were delayed while awaiting a state supreme court ruling on the constitutionality of the riot statute in Iowa's new criminal code. In its July ruling, the court held that the statute requires the prosecution to prove a person within a group actually participated in the group's violent acts.

In opening statements today, defense attorney Mike Vestle said the arrest of Williams was a mistake and that he did not participate in any violence occurring the day in question. For his trial, Williams, 26, was transported from the Iowa Men's Reformatory where he is serving a two-year term on an unrelated charge.

Cedar Rapids police officer Michael Klappholtz, testifying as the state's first witness today, said he was able to identify Williams as one of several persons outside the tavern who were "pushing and shoving" him and two other officers.

Prior to opening statements, a twelve person jury was selected. The state was expected to rest its case this afternoon. Attorneys expected the trial would last about two days.   [Cedar Rapids (Iowa) *Gazette*]

After it has presented all of its evidence, both through the testimony of witnesses and by exhibits, the state *rests*. Then the defense usually automatically makes a motion for a *directed verdict of acquittal* on the ground that the state has failed to prove its case. Most such motions are denied as automatically as they are made; when they are not, there is a news story. A *mistrial* can result in cases of gross irregularity, as an attempt to bribe a juror.

All motions having been denied, the defense presents its case, beginning with its opening statement if not already made. Direct and cross-examination proceed as before. There follow *rebuttal* witnesses by the state and frequently the recalling of witnesses by either side for further questioning.

Closing Statements

The prosecuting attorney usually has the right to go first and then to follow the attorney for the defense with a brief rebuttal; frequently she waives her right to speak twice and lets the defense go first. These final statements by attorneys are argumentative. Then the judge *charges* the jury, explaining the law in the case, the possible verdicts it can return and the meaning of each. Often the law stipulates the exact wording judges must use in at least part of their charge. Judges have little right to comment on the evidence itself but by facial expressions, gestures and verbal emphasis they often can prejudice a jury without the fact being evident in a written transcript.

Reporting Trials

In reporting trials of long duration, the reporter bases every new lead on the most important new development since the last preceding story. Factors to consider are:

1. Does some new testimony or other evidence contradict or supplement some preceding evidence?

2. Do the questions asked by defense counsel on cross-examination portend what the constructive defense case will be?
3. Is any of the evidence surprising; that is, has it been unreported in connection with either the crime itself or the trial?
4. How do the versions of what happened as presented by both sides coincide or differ?
5. Is there consistency of purpose in the types of objections raised by counsel and in the judge's rulings on them? Is the defense laying the ground for possible future appeal?

Seeking answers to these and similar questions involves an interpretative approach to the assignment. Much of the reporting "on deadline," however, is likely to be strictly factual. Often testimony can be presented in Q and A (question and answer) form if there is space; otherwise, it can be summarized briefly or the important parts quoted. The courtroom scene, including the attitudes of principals, witnesses, relatives, friends and spectators, is newsworthy, especially if there are any disturbances. In capital cases, the way the defendant acts when the verdict is announced is of interest.

By Jerry Taylor

A man whom Myles J. Connor Jr. was supposed to have killed, according to a prosecution witness, testified yesterday at Connor's murder trial in Norfolk Superior court in Dedham and denied he was stabbed and injected with a drug overdose.

Osby DePriest, a New Bedford fishermen known as Ozzie, denied the assertion made by Diane M. Wazen to federal agents six years ago that Connor had stabbed and "hot-shotted" him in her apartment in Quincy and carried him away wrapped in a sheet.

DePriest, 40, an ex-convict and former heroin addict, also testified about seeing Connor's chief accuser, Thomas Sperrazza, pull a gun on Arthur Linsky, the son of Boston police Detective Arthur Linsky, outside the Beachcomber, a Quincy nightclub, and about hiding in woods in Northampton with Sperrazza after they had robbed a nearby bank. The incidents occurred 10 or 11 years ago, DePriest said.

Connor, 42, a former rock band leader who lives in Milton, is accused of ordering the stabbing deaths of Karen T. Spinney and Susan C. Webster in Wazen's Quincy apartment in the early hours of Feb. 22, 1975, after the two 18-year-old women from Jamaica Plain had seen Sperrazza shoot and kill a man outside a tavern in Roslindale.

Wazen and Sperrazza, both 32, testified against Connor at his 1981 trial, when he was convicted of the murders, and at Connor's second trial. The state Supreme Judicial Court last August overturned the convictions, partly because Connor's lawyer was forbidden to question Wazen about criminal charges pending against her.

Sperrazza has been convicted of the Spinney-Webster murders and of killing three other people—Officer Donald A. Brown of the Boston police, in May 1974; Ralph Cirvinale, the victim in the Roslindale shooting of Feb. 21, 1975; and John F. Stokes, Jr., who took part in the Spinney-Webster murders, in June 1976 at Walpole State Prison while both were inmates. Sperrazza has been granted a new trial for the Stokes murder. He is in the federal witness protection program.

According to DePriest, Stokes also pulled a gun on young Arthur Linsky in the Beachcomber's parking lot that night in the mid-1970s. He said Connor disarmed Stokes and Sperrazza, who were both fugitives at the time.

DePriest said Stokes hid out in Northampton with him and Sperrazza after the bank holdup. . . .   [Boston *Globe*]

Verdicts

The jury leaves the courtroom and deliberates, with the foreman presiding. After the case is over, the reporter may find out, by questioning jurors, how many ballots were taken and how the vote stood every time. The length of time it takes a jury to reach unanimity is newsworthy. If no decision ever is reached, the jury is said to be *hung,* and there is a *mistrial.* Some indication of how a jury is thinking may be obtained if it returns to the courtroom to ask further instructions or to have part of the evidence read to it again. The reporter's best tipster as to what goes on in a jury room is the bailiff standing guard at the door.

The defendant must be in court when the verdict is read. If a verdict is reached late at night, it may be written and *sealed* and left with a court official, so that the jurors may leave. All, however, must be present when the envelope is opened and the verdict announced. The losing side may demand a *poll* of the jury, which requires all jurors to declare that they concur.

Sentences

Unless it is "not guilty" in a felony case, a jury's verdict is advisory only; the judge accepts or rejects it. He may grant a defense motion to *set aside* the verdict and grant a *new trial* if there have been errors that he knows would cause an appellate court to reverse the verdict and *remand* the case. A motion for *arrest of judgment* accompanies such motions to postpone sentencing.

The leeway permitted judges in pronouncing sentence is established by statute for every crime. In some cases, they may have no choice at all; convictions on a certain charge may mean an automatic sentence of a certain kind. A *suspended sentence* is one which the convicted person does not have to serve pending good behavior. It is rapidly being replaced by *probation,* which gives the convicted person limited freedom of action under the supervision of probation officials; those who violate the conditions of their probation, serve not only the original sentence but an additional one also because of the violation. Probation is most common for minors and first offenders. It should not be confused with *parole,* which is the supervised conditional release of prisoners who already have served part of their prison terms.

Those convicted on more than one count may serve several sentences *concurrently* or *consecutively.* If the former, they serve only the longest of the several sentences; if the latter, they serve the accumulated total of them all. An *indeterminate* sentence sends convicted persons to the penitentiary for "not less than" a designated number of years, and "not more than" another number of years. The exact time of release is determined by the state board of paroles. Usually prisoners are not eligible to apply for parole until after at least one-third of their sentence has been served, so judges often give maximum penalties to run consecutively to make release on parole unlikely.

Punishments

Despite the trend toward individualized treatment of lawbreakers and the substitution of theories of reformation and protection of society for theories of retaliation and expiation, the criminal law still requires that convicted persons serve at least large portions of their sentences. To carry out any sentence is to *execute* it, although the popular connotation of the word limits it to cases in which capital punishment is inflicted. The death penalty was virtually outlawed by the United States Supreme Court but it was being neglected anyway because judges and juries are reluctant to impose it. Recently the court has upheld some new state laws permitting the death penalty in certain cases. It is within the power of a governor to *commute* any sentence: that is, to reduce it, as from death to life imprisonment. A governor also can issue a *reprieve* which, however, is merely a postponement of execution. A *pardon* is a granting of freedom. If absolute, it restores civil rights. If conditional, it prescribes limits to the ex-convict's behavior. Few states as yet have adequate systems for recompensing persons proved to have been imprisoned wrongly.

BY BARRY KLEIN

Dade City—A unanimous jury recommended Saturday that Bobby Joe Long die in the electric chair despite testimony from psychiatrists that he could not stop himself from murdering an 18-year-old prostitute last year.

Long's fate now rests in the hands of Circuit Judge Ray E. Ulmer, Jr.

He can either go along with the jury's recommendation or impose a minimum 25 year prison sentence. Ulmer set sentencing for May 3.

It took the four-man, eight-woman jury only 30 minutes to settle on its recommendation. They spent all day Saturday listening to witnesses explain why the 31-year-old Long strangled Virginia Lee Johnson and left her body to rot in a Pasco County horse pasture.

"I always thought it was a good idea not to pass judgment after a long, emotional trial," Ulmer said in his office while waiting for the jury.

Long stood with his hands in his pockets as the jury filed in to the courtroom. He showed no emotion when the recommendation was announced. Throughout the day Saturday, Long showed no reaction as countless details of his life were paraded before the jury.

One psychiatrist testified Long has the emotional outlook of a 2-year-old. Another said he can kill a human being the same way most people kill a bug.

As a child, Long was amused by the suicide of a schoolmate, and as an adolescent, he slept in the same bed with his mother, the jury was told. When he grew older, he beat and choked his ex-wife.

Long's is a pathetic story.

His problems began at birth, said psychiatrist Michael Mayer, who examined the former X-ray technician shortly after he was arrested last year and charged with the murders of eight women in Hillsborough County. Long will stand trial for those murders in June.

There is a history of mental illness on both sides of his family, Mayer told the jury. Those inherited traits, he said, were complicated by a chaotic home life, and a steady series of injuries and illnesses.

His father was an alcoholic who had trouble holding a job, he said, and his mother worked as a carhop and spent most of the time out of the home. As a result, Mayer said, Long's emotional development was arrested at an early age.

"His emotional outlook on life remains that of a 2-year-old," said Mayer, a psychology professor at the University of South Florida. "He is not capable of making a moral judgment."

His parents separated when Long was 8 months old, according to his mother, Louella Long, and she and the baby moved to south Florida. Mrs. Long told the jury they moved frequently. Bobby Joe, she said, was taken care of by whoever owned the house that they happened to be staying in at the time.

At age 6, Long's jaw was disfigured in a car accident.

"Children teased him, called him bucktooth," said Mrs. Long in a soft West Virginia accent that quivered with emotion. "It upset him an awful lot."

She said he also was disturbed by a hormonal imbalance that caused his breasts to greatly enlarge around the time of puberty. Eventually, she said, he had surgery to correct the problem. . . .

On the day Long picked up Virginia Lee Johnson in Tampa and strangled her, said Mayer, the emotional turmoil inside him had changed him into "a stick of dynamite waiting to explode."

Ms. Johnson was a prostitute, Mayer said, and that was enough to "light the fuse." Police say several of the women who were murdered in Hillsborough County also were prostitutes.

"Afterwards, he was to some extent free of the emotional turmoil," Mayer said. "But eventually, the anger would build up again." [St. Petersburg *Times*]

Appeals

The appellate court system will be described in Chapter 15. Mostly, the appellate courts do not review evidence introduced in a lower court, only procedural matters. Nevertheless, the results often are newsworthy.

The Ethics of Crime News _____

No ethical problem connected with newspaper publishing has been more thoroughly discussed by both newspaper and lay persons than the treatment of crime news.

It is not so much a question of the amount of crime news but of how it is presented. Contrary to popular opinion, only a small proportion of the total offering of the average newspaper relates to lawlessness. Several sociological studies have revealed that whereas readers guess from 25 to 50 per cent of the contents of the newspaper is crime news the actual proportion is hardly 5 per cent.

A Fair Trial v a Free Press

Some newspapers, magazines, and radio and television stations have been accused of inciting to crime by glorifying and making heroes of criminals; of assisting criminals to escape by relating detailed accounts of the activities of police; of interfering with the administration of justice by emphasizing the horrible aspects of brutal crimes, by quoting prosecutors as to the severe punishment they are going to demand and by editorial comment; of causing unfair suffering on the part of the relatives and friends of principals in a criminal case; and of offending public taste by relating lurid details of crimes and scandals.

By far the most important issue today is how much pretrial publicity there should be so as not to interfere with a defendant's right to a fair trial before an impartial jury in an unprejudicial atmosphere. Several United States Supreme Court decisions and adverse criticism of the press contained in the Warren Commission report on the assassination of President John F. Kennedy renewed the debate. Law enforcement officers, although not liking the restrictions placed on them by the court, have nevertheless become cautious about discussing cases with reporters and scrupulous in obeying the rules imposed upon them as regards questioning of suspects, especially that a suspect must be warned immediately of the right to remain silent and have a lawyer. On the other hand, some newspapers toned down quite a bit after the United States Supreme Court ordered a new trial for Dr. Sam Sheppard of Cleveland on the ground that the Cleveland newspapers had made a fair trial for him impossible. Said the court in this case: "The press does not simply publish information about trials, but guards against the miscarriage of justice by subjecting the police, prosecutors and judicial processes to extensive public scrutiny and criticism." At issue, however, is how far the press should go in exercising this function without jeopardizing the rights of the defendant. Neither legal nor journalistic leaders are unanimous in their opinions on the matter.

In October 1966 the Advisory Committee on Fair Trial and Free Press of the American Bar Association, of which Massachusetts Judge Paul C. Reardon was chairman, issued a preliminary report that most newspapers felt recommended too-narrow restrictions on the press during a pretrial period. Shortly before the report appeared, the Toledo *Blade* adopted a code that other papers have emulated. It includes the following:

Before a trial begins, the Toledo papers pledge to publish only the following data:
¶ The name, age and address of the accused.
¶ How, when and where the arrest was made.
¶ The charge and the identity of the complainant.
¶ The fact that a grand jury has returned an indictment and that a trial date has been set.
The policy will be to provide detailed coverage so that information perhaps held back at the time of the arrest may be published later in the proceeding if and when it will not interfere with the judicial process.
During the progress of the case, unless very special circumstances dictate otherwise, the following types of information will not be published:

¶ Any prior criminal record of the accused.

¶ Any so-called confession the accused may have made other than the fact—if it is one—that he has made a statement to the authorities, but with no indication of the nature of the statement.

¶ Any statements by officials construed as detrimental to the accused.

¶ Any statements by lawyers either detrimental to the accused or concerning any defense that is to be made during trial.

¶ Any names of jurors selected for a particular trial.

¶ Any arguments made in court in the absence of the jury, or evidence excluded from the jury.

Other papers have publicized policy changes. The St. Louis *Post-Dispatch* no longer prints the house number of a burglary victim; nor will it report whether a burglar overlooked other valuables. The Boston *Globe* will print the name of a street on which a crime victim lives but not the house number. In common with most other papers, the New York *Times* will not print the name of a rape victim unless she wants it used in alerting the community. Many papers withhold publicity concerning telephoned bomb threats to businesses, industries and public institutions, believing that most such calls are by publicity seekers.

In January 1981 the U.S. Supreme Court unanimously ruled that it is permissible for a state to allow cameras and television coverage of trials. It did so by affirming the refusal of the Florida Supreme Court to hear a challenge to Florida's law permitting the electronic coverage of court proceedings brought by two Miami Beach policemen who blamed their convictions for burglary on the disturbing influence of photographers in the courtroom. A few states now are experimenting with allowing cameras in the courtroom.

Understanding the Criminal

Perhaps the most important adverse criticism of the press in the past was that it had not taken sufficient cognizance of modern criminological and penological thought. By advocating harshness of treatment as the only corrective, by labeling every sex offender (even before apprehended) as a moron (a scientific term meaning high-grade feeble-minded), by pointing to every paroled prisoner violating his parole as proof of the unsoundness of the parole principle, by ridiculing leading thinkers as maudlin sentimentalists, and in other ways, the media, it is charged, have been a sizable obstacle in the movement to replace a barbaric philosophy and methods of curbing antisociability with a scientific approach.

World War II awakened interest in psychiatry and acquainted millions with the fact that abnormal behavior does not necessarily result from malicious willful choice. Sociological research, furthermore, has proved that what is considered criminal in one environment may be perfectly normal in another, and that, particularly in large cities, there are communities in which the incidence of crime remains virtually constant although the racial or nationality complexion of the population changes many times. Gone is belief in born criminals, feeble-mindedness as a major cause of criminal behavior, and many other unscientific explanations. Today, psychiatry is throwing light on the peculiarities of the individual offender and sociologists are examining slums, economic status, marital relations and other social factors that breed misbehavior.

In tune with the times, few newspapers any longer consult phrenologists, handwriting experts, fortunetellers, and other quacks whenever a major crime occurs. Instead, they interview scientists and they are adding steadily to their own staffs specialists able to do more than invent "cute" headline-fitting nicknames for murderers and their victims.

CHAPTER
15

Courts, Civil Law, Appeals

Just as it is essential for a sports reporter who covers baseball to understand the rules of the game, so is it necessary for the reporter assigned to the courts to know the basic structure of American law.

Kinds of Law

Roughly, all laws can be divided into *public* and *private* (usually called *civil*), the distinction being whether the state (organized society) is a party to the litigation. The dichotomy is not exact because government can be a party to certain types of civil actions. In general, however, the distinction holds. Branches of public law include constitutional, administrative, international and criminal, with the ordinary reporter, of course, being most interested in the last.

The two major divisions of private, or civil, law are *common law* and *equity*. The former is that law which was developed through the centuries in judicial decisions in English courts, and—roughly again—it can be divided into *real* and *personal* law. Real law relates to the possession of and title to property whereas personal law relates to attempts to recover damages for injuries received, to enforce a contract, to bring about the return of property and to settle similar matters. The two major divisions of personal law relate to *contracts* and *torts* (all injuries received other than by violation of contract). Equity law, as developed in the equity (or *chancery*) courts of England, begins where common law leaves off. One does not go to equity to recover damages for injuries to self or property, but to compel someone to do or to refrain from doing something. Modern equity courts handle such matters as injunctions, foreclosures, receiverships, partitions etc.

The law administered in the courts originates either (1) in the acts of Congress, of a state legislature or of some other lawmaking body, such law being known as *statutory,* or (2) in the accumulated decisions of courts both here and in England, such law being known as *common law.* Courts adhere to the principle of *stare decisis* (let the decision stand), which means that lawyers quote at length from decisions in earlier cases in the attempt to show that the case in hand should be decided similarly. When there has been a pertinent decision by the Supreme Court of the United States or some state appellate court, the issue may seem clearcut. Usually, however, such is not the case. Either the matter at hand differs in some essential from the previously decided case, or the appellate court decision is limited in scope. Also, there may be conflicting decisions in apparently identical cases.

Young reporters should know that, despite the apparent inconsistencies in both the written *(basic)* law itself and common law decisions, and despite their ability to find citations to substantiate both or all sides of almost any argument, lawyers as a whole profess belief in the existence of absolute justice, and hold that the purpose of any court case is to find the abstract principle that applies. Such lawyers are not conscious rogues, whose main interest is to "play a game" and win a judgment for their clients at all costs. They have been trained to think in a precise specialized manner that makes it easy for them to rationalize their actions, even though to the layman the results may not seem tantamount to anything resembling common sense or justice.

The Court System _____

A knowledge of the court system of the state in which they work is essential to reporters assigned to cover the courts. If they move from one state to another reporters will discover that even the names of generally similar courts may differ. For instance, what is known as a circuit court in Indiana is called a district court in Nebraska, a superior court in Massachusetts and a supreme court in New York.

The jurisdictions of courts also differ, even between counties of different sizes within the same state. For instance, there may be a separate probate court in one county or state whereas probate matters may be handled by the circuit court or its equivalent in another place. One court may handle both civil and criminal matters or there may be different courts (*common pleas* courts are civil courts; courts of *oyer and terminer* are criminal courts). Similarly, law and equity courts may be separate or combined. The practice is growing of establishing special branches of courts to handle particular kinds of cases, and these branches may be referred to in news stories by their specialized names, such as Renters' Court, Juvenile Court, Traffic Court, Divorce Court. To the reader, it makes little or no difference that such courts really are only branches of a circuit, municipal or county court, but the reporter should know their nature.

It is particularly important that the reporter know which are *courts of record,* that is, ones that keep a permanent record of their proceedings. What happens in *courts not of record* is not privileged and the newspaper that covers them must be careful to avoid committing libel.

Differences in both *substantive law* (defines what is and is not proper behavior) and *adjective law* (defines legal rules and procedures) also provide potential snares for unwary journalists. For instance, in one state grand larceny may be defined as stealing anything worth more than $15 whereas in another state stealing anything worth less than $100 or $1,000 may be petty larceny. Since inferior courts generally can handle petty larceny cases but not grand larceny cases, the same offense committed in one jurisdiction will be tried in one type of court whereas if it happens in another jurisdiction it will be tried in a different type court. In one jurisdiction, a civil action may be considered to have begun with the filing of a complaint, whereupon the reporter is safe in reporting it; in another, however, the action is not considered to exist until the other party has been notified. Similar rules may affect all motions by attorneys and court rulings.

State bar associations—organizations of lawyers—generally publish handbooks written for lay people, including reporters. The handbooks explain fundamental aspects of the state's laws and judicial system. Reporters should obtain copies of the handbook for the state in which they are working.

Fortunately, the similarities between the 50 court systems are greater than their differences. Roughly, the typical system is as follows:

Inferior Courts

Inferior courts have the least amount of jurisdiction. Generally they can handle criminal cases involving misdemeanors for which the punishment is a fine only. Their jurisdiction in civil matters generally is limited to cases in which the amount of money does not exceed a few hundred dollars. Among the most common of such courts are the following: *justice of the peace* (townships); *police magistrates* (limited to a city or a section of a city); and *city* and *municipal* courts, which, however, in some larger places may have much greater jurisdiction.

County and Probate Courts

The jurisdiction of a county court depends upon what other state courts exist. Thus, it may be an inferior court or a court of first instance, with unlimited jurisdiction in civil and criminal matters. In other cases, it may operate mostly as a probate or juvenile court or as overseer of the election machinery and county institutions and agencies concerned with poor relief, adoptions and similar matters. Probate courts supervise the disposition of the estates of deceased persons and may also handle adoptions, sanity hearings, commitments of feeble-minded and insane persons and guardianships for minor and incompetents.

Courts of First Instance

The "backbone" courts are the circuit, superior, district, supreme or whatever they are called. In them, all kinds of civil actions may be brought and, unless there are separate criminal courts, criminal matters as well. In some states, there are separate equity, divorce and other courts, but in a large majority of states the court of original jurisdiction either has separate calendars or branches for different kinds of civil actions. The criminal court may be set up separately or may be a branch of the circuit court. It may handle all kinds of criminal matters, or there may be separate courts for felonies (as the Court of General Sessions in New York). The number of circuit or district courts in a state is dependent upon the state's size and population. A large city or county may be a circuit in itself and may be permitted a large number of judges, the exact number being established by constitution or statute. Outside of thickly populated areas, a circuit may include two, three, ten or more counties and the judges may hold court at different times in different county seats. The number of terms annually, and often their length, are established by constitution or statute.

Appellate Courts

Appellate courts do not try cases originally, but only review decisions reached by courts of jurisdiction in the first instance when defeated parties, dissatisfied with lower-court decisions, appeal to the higher courts. In smaller states, there is likely to be only one appellate court, usually called supreme, ranging in size from three to twenty-three judges, either appointed by the governor with the consent of the state legislature or elected (at large or by divisions). In larger states, there are intermediate courts of review, often called circuit courts of appeal, which, however, seldom if ever receive appeals involving constitutional or other important matters. Some of the decisions of the intermediate court may be appealed a second time to the highest appellate court, either as a matter of right or with that court's permission. The three, five, seven or more members of an intermediate appellate court may be appointed or elected, or they may be regularly elected circuit or district court judges assigned to appellate court duty by the supreme court. Appellate courts do not try cases as lower courts do; they merely pass on the arguments of attorneys in the case as presented to them in written form *(briefs)* and orally (at *hearings).* The practice is growing to permit new evidence not introduced in an original trial of a case to be presented to an appellate court, but this is not yet common practice. All appellate court decisions are by majority vote of the judges; there never is anything resembling a jury trial in an appellate court.

Federal Courts

Although the federal judicial system is growing in importance with the passage by Congress of an increasing number of laws defining as federal crimes certain offenses of which formerly only the states took cognizance, and with the establishment of additional federal court districts, the federal judicial system is outside the worries of the average small-city reporter. Anyone arrested for a federal offense is taken for arraignment to the nearest city in which a federal court is situated.

Despite the activities of the Federal Bureau of Investigation in recent years, kidnaping is not a federal offense because Congress does not believe the Supreme Court would hold constitutional a law declaring it such. The so-called Lindbergh law makes the transportation of a kidnaped person across state lines a federal offense, which, together with the federal law against sending ransom notes through the mails, allows the FBI to enter kidnaping cases.

Similar technicalities permit federal agents to participate in other criminal cases. For instance, automobile theft is not a federal crime but transporting stolen automobiles across state lines is prohibited by the Dyer act; seduction is not a federal offense but transporting a female across state lines for immoral purposes is prohibited by the Mann act. The notorious Al Capone was convicted in a federal court not for gangsterism but for failure to make a faithful federal income tax return. Law enforcement officials and others are prosecuted in federal court not for murder but for depriving a dead person of his civil liberties.

In addition to those suggested, cases commonly handled by the federal courts include (1) frauds against the federal government, including embezzlements from national banks; (2) citizenship and denaturalization cases; (3) violations of federal income tax and other revenue laws; (4) violations of post office regulations, including sending threats and other improper material through the mail, rifling mailboxes and other interferences with the mails; (5) violations of federal statutes such as the food and drug acts, antitrust act, Securities and Exchange act, Interstate Commerce act, narcotics act and Railway Labor act; (6) bankruptcy proceedings.

Officers of the Court

Officers of a circuit court or a court with similar jurisdiction are as follows: (1) The *judge* presides during trials, decides points of law, rules on the admissibility of evidence, instructs juries as to the law, pronounces final judgments and sentences, admits criminal defendants to probation. In fact, the judge *is* the court and even oral judicial orders are authoritative and violations of them constitute contempt of court. (2) The *clerk of court* receives applications and motions made formally for the record, preserves pleadings until used in a formal trial, prepares a court docket and trial calendar with the cooperation of the judge, during a trial records all motions and prepares records and orders of the judge, receives moneys paid to the court as fines, damages and judgments. (3) The *prosecuting attorney* prosecutes all civil and criminal actions in which the state is a party, defends actions brought against the county, examines all persons brought before any judge on habeas corpus, gives legal opinions to any county officer or justice of the peace and, in general, represents the constituency electing him in all legal matters. The prosecuting attorney usually is called *district attorney* or *state's attorney*. (4) The *public defender* is paid by the state to defend persons unable to afford private counsel; where no such officer exists the court often appoints a member of the local bar to serve in that capacity. (5) The *bailiff* acts as sergeant-at-arms, announces the opening of court ("Hear ye, hear ye," and so forth), keeps order in the courtroom, calls witnesses, ushers jurors from the jury room and acts as messenger. Many bailiffs really are *sheriff's deputies,* assigned to the courts. In justice of the peace courts the comparable officer is the *constable,* in federal courts it is the *marshal*. (6) The *masters, referees* and *commissioners* act as "assistant judges" in civil matters. They hear protracted testimony and make recommendations to the judge who has final authority. Masters act in *chancery* (equity) matters and referees in *common law* matters. Commissioners in state courts are appointed for particular tasks, mostly investigative; federal commissioners are examining magistrates in criminal matters. (7) The *court reporter* is not an elected official but a licensed stenographer authorized to take verbatim testimony and prepare notes in a transcript of evidence called a record. The court reporter may sell copies of his transcript to parties engaged in a trial; in cases of appeal, several copies of a transcript are necessary. (8) A *friend of the court* is a temporarily appointed adviser to the judge who serves during a particular case. The Latin translation of friend of the court, *amicus curiae* is used to designate someone, not a party to the litigation, who volunteers to advise regarding it, usually by filing a brief with the court's permission. (9) The *jury commissioners* make up a jury list or panel consisting of the names of a certain number of voters in the territory served by the court for each term of court. In smaller counties, the board of supervisors appoints the commissioners; in larger counties, the county judge does so.

Civil Law _____

Through codification and/or passage of civil practices acts, many states have simplified both substantive and adjective law. Whereas formerly it was necessary to bring parts of the same action in different courts, in the federal courts and many state courts, it now is possible to ask for both legal and equitable relief in the same action. For instance, you can ask for *damages* (legal relief) and for an *injunction* (equitable relief) to prevent continuation of the cause of injury in the same complaint.

The reporter must be warned, however, that such is not universally true. Several Atlantic seaboard states in particular still adhere to old common law and equity definitions and procedures. In those states one would not bring a simple action to set aside a contract or to force compliance with it or to recover damages because of its breach. Rather, one would bring an action in *covenant* (to recover money damages) or *debt* (to recover specific sums) or *assumpsit* (for damages if the contract was not under seal) or *detinue* (to recover specific chattels). Similarly, a damage suit (tort action) would be one in *trespass* (for money damages) or *trespass on the case* (if injuries were not the direct result of the action complained of) or *detinue* (to recover specific chattels) or *replevin* (a statutory right to recover both property and damages), or *trover* (damages in case the property is lost, destroyed or otherwise incapable of return), or *deceit* (damages for a wrong committed deceitfully).

Starting an Action

In noncode states a common law action is an *action at law* whereas a case in equity is a *suit in equity*. In federal courts and states with civil practices acts, there is just one *civil action*. To start it the *plaintiff* (who brings the action) files a *petition* (also called *declaration* or *complaint* or *statement of claim*) stating clearly the alleged cause for action and the relief the court is asked to grant. Every paragraph of the complaint is numbered and is called a *count*. When one files an *answer,* as must be done within a specified period to avoid the plaintiff's winning a *judgment by default,* the *defendant* (often called *respondent,* with any third parties mentioned as equally guilty being *co-respondents*) must admit or deny each count. In the old days, litigants could continue arguing a case on paper almost indefinitely. Under simplified procedures, the *pleadings*—as all such written arguments are called—are limited to two or three by each party.

> A judgment for $50,000 against Lang's Bar, 179 E. 3rd St., and Roger Brown, also for $50,000, was filed last week in the Winona County District Court clerk's office by Steven Meyer.
>
> Meyer claims that on Sept. 11, 1978, he and the defendant, Brown, were at Lang's Bar and at approximately 10 A.M. Brown assaulted Meyer as a direct result of Lang's selling intoxicating liquor while Brown was in an intoxicated condition.   [Winona (Minn.) *Daily News*]

Defending an Action

Defendants who have been properly served by *summons* (law) or *subpoena* (equity) must answer within a prescribed time or at least file an *appearance,* which is an acknowledgment and indication that they will answer later. When the answer is filed the reporter scans it for its contents.

To avoid answering, defendants may enter a *motion to dismiss* the action, contending that the plaintiff has no legal right to bring it. In such a motion, defendants may challenge the jurisdiction of the court or the sufficiency of the process by which they were notified of the beginning of the suit; or, most importantly, they may contend that the plaintiff has failed to state a ground for action. Under old procedures, defendants may enter a *demurrer,* which is a plea that, even if true, the facts alleged do not constitute a cause for action. They also may plead that the *statute of limitations,* which sets the time limit within which such action can be brought, has been violated.

To delay or postpone the case, defendants may resort to dilatory tactics by a *plea in abatement,* which may (1) *challenge the array*—that is, question the procedure by which the panel of veniremen (potential jurors) was selected as the case nears trial; (2) ask a *change of venue,* which is a transfer to another court or branch of the same court on the grounds that judge or jurors are prejudiced; (3) ask a *continuance,* or postponement, for any of a variety of reasons, the merits of which the judge must decide: (4) be a *motion to quash* because the summons was defective.

A special kind of answer is one in *confession and avoidance* wherein the defendants admit the facts but declare they acted within their legal rights. A *counterclaim* is an answer in which defendants not only deny liability but contend that the plaintiff is obligated to them. Counterclaims are frequent in damage cases involving automobile accidents; each driver blames the other.

When several actions related to the same incident are begun, the court may order that there be a *joinder of parties* or *joinder of causes.* On the other hand, on its own motion or that of one of the parties, the court may grant a *severance* when co-defendants make separate answers. Third parties who believe their interests are affected by the action may petition the court for permission to file an *intervening* petition to become either a plaintiff or defendant.

To understand what is going on, the reporter should be familiar with a few other types of motions: (1) a *bill of particulars* may be demanded by the defendant if the complaint is unclear or not sufficiently specific; (2) a *bill of discovery* may be asked if the defendant wishes to examine documents or other material in the plaintiff's possession; (3) either party may ask permission to submit an *interrogatory,* or set of questions, to the other to obtain necessary information; (4) scandalous, redundant, irrelevant or otherwise objectionable portions of any pleading may be eliminated if the court grants a *motion to strike.*

Civil Trials

Unless there is a *default judgment* (or *decree*) because of failure of the defendant to answer or a *summary judgment* because the answer is inadequate or a *judgment by confession* because the defendant admits the plaintiff's charges, the issue becomes joined and, upon motion of either party or the court itself, the case is placed on the trial calendar.

Most civil trials today are heard by a judge alone. In fact, it generally is necessary to make a formal request and pay a court fee at the time of filing a complaint or answer to obtain a civil trial by jury. Except for the preliminary step of selecting the jurors, theoretically the procedure is the same. The steps are as follows:

1. Opening statement by plaintiff, through his attorney, of what he expects to prove.
2. Opening statement by defendant. (Often waived.)
3. Direct examination of plaintiff's witnesses.
4. Cross-examination by defendant of plaintiff's witnesses.
5. Direct and cross-examination of defendant's witnesses.
6. Redirect or rebuttal witnesses for plaintiff.
7. Closing statements by both sides, plaintiff speaking first, then the defendant, and, finally, rebuttal by plaintiff.

In actual practice, a hearing before a judge usually is informal. With all of the principals and their attorneys and witnesses clustered about the bench, the judge may interrupt, change the usual order of procedure and take a hand at questioning. Then the judge either takes the case under *advisement* (meaning to think it over before deciding) or enters a *judgment* for either plaintiff or defendant, in a law action, or a *decree* if the case is one at equity. Even if there is a jury, it can only recommend what *damages* are to be assessed against the loser in a law action; the final decision is up to the judge and, upon motion of the losing party or on the judge's own initiative, the judge can disregard the jury's findings and enter a *judgment notwithstanding the verdict*.

Damages may be (1) *general,* meaning they are the same as might be expected to compensate anyone for the type of loss proved to have been incurred; (2) *special,* those peculiar to the particular case; (3) *nominal,* which are trifling and for the purpose of moral vindication only; or (4) *exemplary,* assessed in addition to the general or *compensatory* damages, to punish the other party.

A civil action may end in a *nonsuit* if at any time the plaintiff fails to continue; such a judgment naturally is for the defendant. So is a *dismissal,* the difference being, however, that in case of a nonsuit the plaintiff may begin another action whereas a dismissal is a final disposition of case, unless it is a *dismissal without prejudice,* which usually comes upon request of the plaintiff. A *consent* judgment is entered when the court approves an out-of-court agreement between the parties. A *declaratory* judgment, obtainable in federal courts and some state courts, is an informatory opinion in advance of any legal action; by means of it the court declares what its decision would be in the event action were brought. Its use prevents much expensive and useless litigation.

An ordinary judgment or decree is either (1) *final,* or (2) *conditional,* which means certain acts (as exchange of property) must be performed before it becomes final, or (3) *nisi* (unless), which means it becomes final after a certain lapse of time if certain forbidden acts do not occur, or (4) *interlocutory,* in which case restrictions on behavior—as against remarriage—are designated.

Enforcing Civil Law

There is no imprisonment for debt in the United States, so plaintiffs may not be much better off after they receive a judgment against a defendant than before. By applying for a *writ of execution,* the judgment creditor can force sale of the judgment debtor's property to satisfy the claim, but if debtor does not possess enough assets to meet the obligation it is often better to allow the judgment to stand as a lien against what the debtor has until the day when it is wise to enforce it. To discover a debtor's assets, a creditor may obtain a court *citation* ordering the debtor to appear in court for questioning by a referee. Failure to comply means that one may be cited for *contempt of court* which, in some cases, may be punished by imprisonment. In such cases, however, the judgment creditor usually has to pay for the debtor's keep. The inmates of "alimony row" in the county jail are contemptuous divorcees.

Either at the beginning of a suit or after a judgment has been obtained, the plaintiff may obtain a *property attachment,* placing the defendant's assets under control of the court to prevent their conversion. A *body attachment* or *execution* is a court order to arrest principals in disputes to prevent their untimely departure from its jurisdiction. A *ne exeat* decree is an order forbidding such departure. *Garnishment* proceedings are for the purpose of attaching debtors' incomes, usually their salaries, for the benefit of the creditor.

If a court becomes convinced that a supposedly closed case should be reopened, it can entertain a motion to *reinstate* a case that has been dismissed, to *set aside* a verdict, to *vacate* a judgment or to *review* a decree. A *writ of audita querela* stops execution of a judgment when new evidence is presented. A *writ of supersedeas* orders a court officer to stop execution which has not gone too far.

Many damage suits contain a *malice* count, which means that the alleged injury was committed intentionally or because of gross negligence. If the court upholds the contention, guilty defendants may be jailed if they fail to satisfy the judgment.

The following excerpts of stories illustrate how an interpretative court reporter can help inform the public regarding legal and judicial matters:

By Tom Gibbons

Sitting at a table behind piles of legal documents, the Highland Park man sifted through the papers for several minutes before pulling out a 35-page itemized bill from the attorney handling his wife's divorce.

The lawyer, who is billing for 391 hours of work and court fees, wants $50,000.

"It's staggering. They want my last penny," said the father of two who has been going through divorce proceedings in Cook County Domestic Relations Court for nearly three years.

The distraught man's legal fees already total about $85,000, which includes his own attorney costs, and before the contested divorce is settled he expects the price tag to approach $100,000.

"I worked my whole life for what we have, but at $100 an hour for an attorney fees, the dollars are ticking away," said the 53-year-old retired naval officer, who estimates his worth at $300,000.

Hoping to "find some justice," the husband of 20 years, who asked anonymity, took a step that is becoming increasingly popular—he filed a complaint against his wife's lawyer for charging excessive fees.

The Illinois Supreme Court's Attorney Registration and Disciplinary Commission refuses to acknowledge whether any charges have been filed, let alone discuss details of any other pending cases.

But although commission officials aren't talking, its annual report shows that divorce lawyers drew the second highest number of complaints last year. . . . [Chicago *Sun-Times*]

By Betty Kohlman

Rather than provide a judge, jury and a trial for every lawsuit, federal judges in Tampa have turned to arbitration as a way to reach a quick settlement in more cases.

Under a new rule, all civil lawsuits seeking damages of less than $100,000 must first be submitted to a panel of three lawyers, or arbitrators, who consider both sides and recommend who gets how much.

The parties to the lawsuit don't have to accept the recommendation, however, and they can still request a trial.

"Arbitration provides . . . an opportunity of settlement at a much earlier stage in litigation" and doesn't consume "precious judge time" needed for the criminal cases that swamp the court, says U.S. District Judge Wm. Terrell Hodges of Tampa.

The effect of arbitration, says Mary Ann Perry, arbitration deputy to the court in Tampa, is to settle cases in less than six months, the approximate time frame set by the rule, rather than the one or two years it usually takes to get through the court.

The arbitration process in federal court is less than 10 years old, having started in Pennsylvania and California.

Karen Siegel, an official of the U.S. courts administration in Washington, D.C., said her office became so interested in the program that it won a $400,000 appropriation from Congress for the 1985 fiscal year to expand it. The money goes to pay arbitrators, who get $75 a day, she said. . . .

She said all district courts were given an opportunity to try the experimental program, but of the three federal court districts in Florida, only the Middle District became the third federal court district in the country to initiate the arbitration process, Ms. Siegel said.

The purpose of the arbitration process, she said, "is to reduce court congestion. We can't keep expanding the federal court system. We've got to find alternatives. . . . [St. Petersburg *Times*]

Civil Actions _____

There are a seemingly interminable number of kinds of actions. Judges and lawyers with years of experience pore over ponderous legal tomes for hours to refresh their memories regarding many of them. Reporters cannot be expected to master the intricacies of even an appreciable number of them. If they understand the basic differences between the major types of actions and can translate the most frequently used legal language, they can get along. There are several good law dictionaries which reporters can consult when they "encounter a new one." What follow are a few suggestions concerning some of the kinds of actions that are most newsworthy.

Damage Suits

The news interest usually is in the incident giving rise to the action: an automobile accident, a surgeon's error and so forth. If so, perhaps the paper carried a story at the time, which means the account of the filing of the complaint should contain a careful tie-back. The reporter should get names and addresses of principals; the plaintiff's version of exactly what happened, all charges being carefully accredited to the complaint; the comments of the defendant on the charges; the amount of money demanded. And reporters should find out if there is a malice count.

By Gary Wisby

Pepper the German shepherd is either a gentle family pet who barks only at strangers and racoons, or a menace to neighborhood peace who should be locked up or destroyed.

There is a $4 million difference between those descriptions.

The dog's owner, William LaPietra, is suing the city of Lake Forest for that amount, charging a campaign of harassment brought on by Pepper's barking.

The federal suit stems from a neighbor's complaint that his sleep was being disturbed, but LaPietra's lawyer, William Marlatt, insists "This is not a barking dog case."

Marlatt said the civil rights of LaPietra's wife, B.J., were violated when police took her to the station at midnight Oct. 24, 1983 and asked her to post $50 bond.

The city can't legally seek bond for an offense—in this instance, "breach of the quiet"—not punishable by imprisonment, the lawyer said. "The proper procedure would be to give her a ticket," Marlatt said. "There was no need to take her to jail. . . ."

[Chicago *Sun Times*]

Divorce

Distinguish between *divorce* and *annulment,* and between *separate maintenance* and *alimony.* What are the grounds (desertion, cruelty and so forth)? Watch out for libel when reporting specific incidents cited as grievances (beatings, criminal behavior). The reporter should obtain names and addresses of both principals; dates of marriage and of separation; names and ages of children and what the bill requests regarding them; suggested disposition of property; whether alimony is requested; whether wife asks court to authorize use of her maiden name. When a case comes to hearing, testimony, of course, can be reported; state whether defendant contests case or allows decree to be obtained by default. States are slowly but steadily passing no-fault divorce laws, making the decree obtainable by mutual agreement without one party's having to state a case against the other.

Foreclosures

Those who default in payments on a mortgage stands to lose the property through foreclosure proceedings. In most states, however, they have an *equity of redemption*—a period of time in which to pay up, even though a court has awarded the property to the mortgage holder.

Evictions

The Renters' Court always is a fertile source of human interest stories. The legal name for actions to evict is *forcible entry and detainer*. During housing shortages, renters' courts are crowded. Reporters should examine the statutes of the state for sections pertaining to the rights of landlords to evict or refuse to rent to families with children or pets. They also should read up on statutes and court decisions mostly outlawing restrictive covenants whereby property owners agreed not to sell or lease to blacks, Jews or members of other minority groups or otherwise restrict the use of property.

Inadequate inspection and inability, under the statutes, of judges to assess heavy penalties mean that large city slumlords consider this court as only a minor nuisance. Reporters are handicapped by protective secrecy laws covering trusts to determine who the real culprits are when outrageous housing conditions are exposed. Urban renewal projects have caused urban center slum areas to increase and worsen as real estate interests use residential land areas for more lucrative purposes and friendly public officials offer little or no interference. Tearjerking, albeit accurate, stories can be written about unfeeling landlords and others who exploit poor and ignorant tenants. One device is to purchase tax delinquent bills so as to make evictions legal. Seldom, however, is the greedy action considered morally commendable.

Especially in Florida and Illinois where secret land trusts are allowed to conceal ownership, arson is suspected when abandoned or dilapidated buildings are destroyed by fire.

Despite supposedly protective legislation, blockbusting and redlining persist. The former is the practice of enabling a single black family to move into a white neighborhood by making the purchase price extremely low. Then the remaining white property owners are panicked into selling their property at low prices after which it is resold to blacks at a considerable profit.

Redlining is making geographical boundaries within which banks and other lending institutions do not make loans for building construction or repairs, in the belief that the neighborhood is deteriorating. Residents who continue to deposit money in such institutions complain because their deposits are used for loans outside the area and are a major factor in bringing about deterioration.

Condemnation Suits

When a new street or highway or public building is planned, the proper government agency uses its right of *eminent domain* to purchase—at a fair price—any privately owned land needed for the improvement. Property owners often resist such taking of their property or hold out for higher compensation. Public clamor may cause a change in official plans, as happened when property owners in Connecticut objected to the headquarters of the United Nations being established there. Scandals occur when some public officials use prior knowledge of governmental plans to purchase certain property. They purchase it themselves and consequently reap a profit when its value increases. The insider may not technically be a part of the spending agency but such behavior obviously is not in the public interest.

Receiverships

Creditors or stockholders of a corporation or individuals in financial difficulties may apply to an equity court for appointment of a receiver to conserve assets and rescue the business. A chancery receivership, intended to put a going concern back on its feet, must be distinguished from a receiver in bankruptcy, who is in charge of liquidating a defunct institution. Many banks, hotels, transportation companies and others continue operating under receiverships for years. Often newspapers uncover scandals regarding political favoritism in appointment of receivers or companies with which they do business. Reporters should watch the periodic reports that receivers must make to the courts appointing them.

Bankruptcy

A financial failure may file a *voluntary petition* in bankruptcy, or his creditors may file an *involuntary petition* in his case. The reporter should examine the inventory filed with the petition, to obtain total assets; total liabilities; nature of the assets (stocks, real estate, controlling interest in other companies, etc.); nature of liabilities; clues as to reasons for failure. Bankruptcy matters are handled by the federal courts. Every petition is referred to a *referee in bankruptcy,* a permanent court officer; the *trustee* is elected by the creditors and, if approved by the court, takes over the task of liquidating the assets and distributing them on a pro rata basis. Instead of dissolving a business, a company may undergo *reorganization* under a court-approved plan. Usually, some creditors are "frozen out" when such happens, and the legal jockeying between them to avoid that happening is newsworthy when the company is important. Since every action of a trustee must be approved by the court, the reporter can keep close to the situation.

Here is an excerpt from a brief, but well done bankruptcy story:

By Lorri Denise Booker

Three brothers whom Pinellas County officials have accused of dumping toxic materials near a county well field filed for protection from their creditors Thursday while they reorganize their finances.

James F. "Bobby" Martin, Charles H. Martin and William H. "Billy" Martin, filed separate petitions under Chapter 11 in federal bankruptcy court. The brothers declined to discuss the filing in detail.

"The only thing I can tell you is Pinellas County has broke me," Billy Martin, 49, said Saturday. "I just have no more funds."

The county sued the brothers in 1982, saying a borrow pit owned by Bobby Martin and a 10-acre dump near the Pinellas-Hillsborough county line threatened to pollute the nearby Eldridge-Wilde well field. Charles and Billy Martin own the dump.

Pinellas County has obtained a court order to clean up the dump and hopes to recover clean-up costs from the Martins. County officials have said the clean-up may cost about $1.5 million.

Billy Martin said he owes about $235,000 to several creditors, most of them banks. Not included in that figure, he said, is the money he has spent trying to prove there are no toxic materials at the dump site. . . .

[St. Petersburg *Times*]

Since 1960 there has been a phenomenally steady increase in personal bankruptcy petitions, about 20 times as many as in the '40s. The Consumer Bankruptcy Committee of the American Bar Association blames abuses of credit by both recipients and grantors and would tighten the laws to make such petitions more difficult to file. In this area, as in so many others, the interpretative reporter can find valuable in-depth situation and trend stories. What follows is about one-third of an excellent explanatory article in this area.

By Robert Enstad

The payoff plan was simple enough. For $84.21 a week he could pay off his creditors, maintain his standard of living, and still hold his head high as a man who pays his bills.

His financial crunch had come about easily enough. An overwhelming craving for material goods and merchants who extended him credit had pinched his wallet.

Now the man was before Richard L. Merrick, a federal bankruptcy judge in Chicago. Merrick looked at the repayment plan and then looked down from the bench at the debtor.

"I'm familiar with your plan and I think you will be able to complete it all right," the judge said.

With those few words from the judge, the man was on his way, not as an adjudicated deadbeat, but as a man given another chance to make ends meet. In bankruptcy parlance, the man had undertaken a "Chapter 13" reorganization of his debts.

Going into debt is becoming more common, less of a social stigma.

"Indebtedness has grown like a cancer," says Leonard Gesas, a veteran Chicago bankruptcy lawyer. "It is hard to find a family that has not been exposed to it."

The ominous signs of a consuming public that is charging more and saving less are all over. For example

- Consumer debt soared a record $4.45 billion in September. This year's growth in consumer debt is expected to be about 16 per cent.
- Bankruptcy filings in U.S. District Court in Chicago are expected to be up 20 per cent this year. The total of about 12,000 cases will be the highest number in recent years. Bankruptcy courts in other metropolitan areas report the same upward trend.
- For the third quarter of this year, consumers put only 4.1 per cent of their disposal income into savings, the lowest level in years. In September, withdrawals from savings accounts exceeded deposits by $200 million.

Why the changes in the way people manage their money? . . .

The rising consumer debt, which is rapidly approaching $400 billion [not counting home mortgages] has triggered concern about whether Americans are assuming more bills than they can handle. . . .

However, for a small minority the urge to "pay with plastic" and to say "charge it" leads to bankruptcy court. In the Chicago area, the chances of being in that court this year are one in 666.

A year ago, the odds were one in 800.

Part of the increase in bankruptcy filings this year has been attributed to the new Chapter 13 federal bankruptcy law. The law, which is debtor-oriented, enables the debtor and his lawyer to devise, with court approval, a plan for paying back the debts.

If all goes well, the debtor avoids liquidation of his assets and an adjudication of bankruptcy.

Chapter 13 filings are up 10 per cent in Chicago, according to court records.

"The debtors run the gamut from the very poor to very rich," says Craig Phelps, the Chapter 13 trustee in the bankruptcy court. . . . [Chicago *Tribune*]

Injunctions

Distinguish between a *preliminary restraining order,* which is issued by a judge on ex parte evidence only and without notice, and *temporary* and *permanent injunctions.* The orthodox procedure is for the court to issue a temporary order to the defendant to appear in court and "show cause" why it should not become permanent. In the meantime, the alleged offensive conduct must cease. Injunctions are used to prohibit government agencies and officials from exceeding their authority; to test the constitutionality of a law; to restrain picketing and other activities by labor unions; to restrain corporations from acts injurious to stock- or bond-holders; to compel persons to keep the peace and not interfere with the civil liberties and other rights of others; to stop and prevent nuisances; and for other purposes.

By Frank Clifford

U.S. Circuit Court of Appeals Judge Irving L. Goldberg temporarily stopped FBI agents Tuesday from seizing records of Maxwell Construction Co., a local firm under federal investigation for its multimillion dollar business dealings with the Dallas Independent School District.

Tuesday afternoon, during a seesaw struggle between government lawyers and attorneys for Maxwell to gain control of the records, U.S. District Judge Sarah T. Hughes ruled that the records must be turned over to the government and authorized FBI agents to proceed immediately to the Maxwell offices at 3722 Bowser. . . .   [Dallas *Times-Herald*]

Contracts

There follows a typical complaint:

STATE OF ILLINOIS
COUNTY OF COOK   ss

IN THE SUPERIOR COURT OF COOK COUNTY

IRIS GARDNER,
                Plaintiff
        —vs.—   NO. 42 s 10542
CHARLES W. WRIGLEY,
        Defendant

COMPLAINT AT LAW FOR
BREACH OF CONTRACT

Now comes IRIS GARDNER, plaintiff in the above entitled cause, and complains of the defendant, CHARLES W. WRIGLEY, as follows:

1. That the plaintiff was, on the 15th day of October A.D. 1937 temporarily sojourning in the City of Chicago, County of Cook and State of Illinois; and, on the date aforesaid, she was about to depart from the said city, county and state, and return to her domiciliary city and state, to-wit: St. Louis, Missouri.

2. The plaintiff had a long social acquaintance and friendship with the defendant, CHARLES W. WRIGLEY, prior to October 15, A.D. 1937, when, on the date, aforesaid, she, the plaintiff, at the special instance and request of the defendant, CHARLES W. WRIGLEY, met the defendant, CHARLES W. WRIGLEY, in his offices, located at 400 North Michigan Avenue, in the City of Chicago, County of Cook and State of Illinois, and that at the place and on the date aforesaid, plaintiff entered into a verbal agreement with the defendant, CHARLES W. WRIGLEY, the substance of which agreement is hereinafter verbatim alleged.

3. That the defendant, CHARLES W. WRIGLEY, was then, and is now, engaged in the advertising business, and was then, and is now, reputed to have considerable material wealth.

4. That the plaintiff was then, and is now a woman possessed of pulchritude, charm, and numerous other attributes and qualities to enchant, charm, and grace any person; or, in fact, any social circle.

5. That the defendant, CHARLES W. WRIGLEY, met the plaintiff, at the place and on the date aforesaid, at his special instance and request, and then and there the defendant, CHARLES W. WRIGLEY, was expressly charmed and enchanted by the plaintiff, because of plaintiff's charm, graciousness, and other womanly qualities and attributes and thereupon the defendant, CHARLES W. WRIGLEY, informed plaintiff that she was the person for whom he had been searching to assist him, socially and in his business. Whereupon, the parties entered into a verbal agreement, which, in words, figures and substance, is as follows:

a. The defendant, CHARLES W. WRIGLEY, verbally agreed with the plaintiff to pay plaintiff the sum of One Thousand Dollars ($1,000) per month, either in cash, or by letters of credit, or in any other mode or manner the plaintiff might see fit provided the said sum was paid in full to the plaintiff before the expiration of each and every month, commencing on the 1st day of November, A.D 1937, during the rest of her natural life; and the defendant, CHARLES W. WRIGLEY, further agreed, in order to protect plaintiff, in the event of predeceased plaintiff, to create a trust in the sum of Two Hundred and Fifty Thousand Dollars ($250,000.00), said trust to be evidenced by a trust agreement, the provisions of which trust agreement were to provide that the plaintiff would be entitled to receive the proceeds, rents, profits, and emoluments accruing therefrom, during the plaintiff's natural life.

b. That in consideration of the said verbal agreement, the plaintiff was to cancel her then imminent departure, as aforesaid from the City of Chicago, County of Cook and State of Illinois; and it was further agreed that the plaintiff should reside and domicile continuously in the City of Chicago, County of Cook and State of Illinois, during the natural life of the defendant, CHARLES W. WRIGLEY, in order to assist the defendant, CHARLES W. WRIGLEY, in his social activities, as the defendant might, from time to time, direct, which social activities, according to the defendant, CHARLES W. WRIGLEY, could be efficaciously performed only by the plaintiff, or by some other member of the fair sex with abilities co-equal to those possessed by the plaintiff.

c. That in pursuance of said verbal agreement, the plaintiff remained, resided and domiciled, and continues to remain, reside and domicile, in the City of Chicago, County of Cook and State of Illinois; that the defendant, CHARLES W. WRIGLEY, in pursuance of the terms of said verbal agreement, obtained or rented an apartment on behalf of the plaintiff, at the St. Clair Hotel, and paid plaintiff (in cash or by check, or paid the expenditures of the plaintiff directly to plaintiff's creditors) the stipulated consideration thereof to wit: One Thousand Dollars ($1,000.00) per month, including the rental for said apartment; and that the defendant, CHARLES W. WRIGLEY, continued to comply with the terms of said agreement until on or about the 30th day of May, A.D. 1943, on which date the defendant, CHARLES W. WRIGLEY, expressly repudiated the same, verbally informing and advising plaintiff that he would no longer continue payment thereof, in view of his reduced financial status.

6. That in pursuance of the terms of said verbal agreement, the plaintiff heretofore has exerted much effort, and expended her youth, grace and charm, to the end of ameliorating defendant's social as well as esthetic, well-being.

7. That at the time the aforesaid agreement was entered into defendant was approximately twenty (20) years plaintiff's senior.

8. That the plaintiff has performed each and every condition of her contract with the defendant, CHARLES W. WRIGLEY, whether precedent or subsequent, and she is not in default thereof.

9. That the defendant, CHARLES W. WRIGLEY, has willfully and maliciously, and without any just cause, but merely whimsically, breached the provisions of said verbal agreement.

10. That the plaintiff has sustained damages, by reason of the breach of said agreement by the defendant, CHARLES W. WRIGLEY, in the sum of Five Hundred Thousand Dollars ($500,000.00) and costs.

This is how the Chicago *Sun* handled this news:

Suit for $500,000 charging breach of contract, was filed in Superior Court yesterday against Charles W. Wrigley, 71, brother of the late William Wrigley Jr., chewing-gum magnate, by a woman who described herself as possessing "pulchritude, charm, and manner."

She is identified in the bill as Mrs. Iris Gardner, 41, of the St. Clair Hotel.

Her complaint, according to the bill, alleges that Wrigley is not paying her $1,000 a month. He agreed to do this back in 1937, she said, and kept up the payments for six years before quitting.

Wrigley, head of an outdoor advertising firm, with offices at 400 N. Michigan Ave., indignantly denied the entire alleged transaction. Reached at his home, Canterbury Ct., Wilmette, he said:

"It's an outrage to file a suit like that. The lady's husband worked for me 15 years ago.

"She never worked for me. As to the payments of $1,000 a month, why, that's crazy! Where would I get the money? She started after me just after Charlie Chaplin's trouble."

According to the bill, Wrigley, uncle of Philip K. Wrigley, owner of the Chicago Cubs, agreed to pay Mrs. Gardner $1,000 a month for life and, if he died first, leave a $250,000 trust fund to provide the income.

In return, the bill continued, Mrs. Gardner was to "assist him socially and in his business." The agreement, Mrs. Gardner said, was verbal.

Note that (1) the reporter obtained information other than that contained in the complaint, and (2) he exercised great care in ascribing every fact based on the complaint to the complaint itself, by means of such phrases as "according to the bill" and "the bill continued." It is absolutely necessary never to allow any statement in a story based on a legal document to stand by itself, even at the risk of boring repetition of references.

Extraordinary Remedies

The equitable relief provided by an injunction originated as an extraordinary remedy, but has become so common it no longer is extraordinary. Almost the same is true of *habeas corpus,* whereby a jailer is required to produce a prisoner in court to answer charges against him. Dating from Magna Charta, it is one of the great Anglo-Saxon democratic protections.

Other so-called extraordinary remedies follow.

Prohibition

Prohibition is a writ issued by a superior court to one of inferior jurisdiction commanding it to desist in handling any matter beyond its authority to consider.

Certiorari

Certiorari also is an inquiry into the behavior of a lower court after it has taken some action. Thus, it usually operates as an appeal, to bring about a review of the lower court's action in the higher court. In granting a writ of certiorari or *writ of review,* as it also is called, however, the higher court merely agrees to look into the matter. It may return the case later.

Mandamus

A *writ of mandamus* is directed by a higher court to administrative officers, corporations or an inferior court ordering some action required by law. It does not specify what the action must be—as in a case where a required appointment is overdue—but it does demand that some action be taken.

Quo Warranto

By a *quo warranto writ,* a higher court inquires into the right of a public official to hold office or of a corporation to exercise a franchise.

Probate Proceedings _____

When people die, the state supervises payment of their debts and distribution of their property. If they die *testate* (that is, if they leave a will), unless someone can prove that the contrary should be done, the court sees that its provisions are carried out. It usually appoints the *executor* named in the will to supervise settling the estate; that official, often a relative of the deceased, posts bond for about one-and-a-half times the estimated value of the estate and receives a commission when the work is done. If there is no will (deceased died *intestate*) the court appoints an *administrator.* In many states there now are public administrators. Either executor or administrator receives *letters testamentary* to authorize the work, which includes notification of beneficiaries named in a will or legal heirs if there is no will, advertising for bills against the estate, collecting money due the estate, preparing an inventory of the estate and so forth.

Filing a Will

The first step in probate proceedings is the filing of the will by whoever has it in custody or finds it. Reporters watch for such filings of wills of prominent persons recently deceased. In their case, it is news whether the estate is large or small. As a matter of fact, it usually is difficult or impossible to determine an estate's size from the will itself; it is not known with certainty until an appraisal is made months later. The first public information may come with the filing of an inheritance tax return.

> The estate of Henry B. Ritter, Milltown construction contractor, totaled $3,062,182, according to an inheritance tax return filed Thursday with the Vernon County clerk.
> Ritter, uncle of former county treasurer Herbert C. Ritter, died Dec. 19, at the age of 77. He lived at 345 W. Fullerton St.
> The estate was left in trust to the widow, Lillian, with a provision that upon her death one-half of it to go their children, Mrs. Marjorie O'Neil of 706 S. Sheridan Ave., Barton, and Henry Jr., of 12 E. Scott St.
> The federal tax on the estate was $358,659 and the state levy, $117,328.

An ingenious reporter in some cases can estimate value by determining the market value of securities or the assessor's valuations of real estate and by similar investigation. Frequently, the nature of an estate is newsworthy as a person may be revealed to be the owner of property that he was not known to possess. From the will, the beneficiaries can be determined, and often a will contains surprises. The first news story should mention when and where the will was drawn and possibly the witnesses. In small places, virtually every will is newsworthy; in larger places, only those of important persons or involving large estates receive mention.

Admitting to Probate

The reporter must not confuse filing a will and admitting a will to probate, which is done by court order upon petition of the executor or someone else. Before such a petition is granted it must be proved to be genuine and there also must be proof of heirship; usually referees supervise such routine matters. If anything happens to disturb the routine, it probably is newsworthy.

> The will of Richard W. Young, founder and chairman of the board of the Young Corp., who died March 1, at the age of 70, was admitted to probate today by County Judge Thomas Sullivan.
> The executors are Thomas B. Young and R. L. Waters. Waters declined to place an estimate on the size of the estate, but it is generally understood to be in the millions.
> The will sets up a trust fund on behalf of 11 relatives of the industrialist. The division is as follows:
> One-sixth of the estate to Thomas B. Young, now president of the Young Corp., a nephew. One-eighth to Frank Young, a nephew. One-eighth to Ruth Young Stoddard, a niece.
> One-twelfth to Louise R. White, a niece. One-twelfth to Margaret Rolnick, a niece. One-twelfth to Nancy Young, a niece. One-twelfth to Mary Sheridan, a niece. One-twelfth to Robert Carpenter, a nephew. One-twelfth to Richard Sheridan, a nephew.

One-twenty-fourth to Patricia Young, a grand-niece and one-twenty-fourth to Kent Young, a grand-nephew.

The will provides that the Young Investment Co., established by Young, may be liquidated within 12 months of his death and the assets distributed to the stockholders, this with the approval of the executors. It also provides that the entire estate shall be liquidated within 20 years and may be liquidated, if the executors approve, in ten years.

Contesting a Will

By law an interval that varies from three months to two years must elapse between the time a will is admitted to probate and a *final accounting*. During that period, suit may be brought to break the will, perhaps by a disgruntled relative who was disinherited. Common charges are that the deceased was unduly influenced when he made the will, or was not in full possession of his mental faculties. Sometimes it is charged that the will filed was not the most recent. Such suits usually are filed in courts other than that handling routine probate matters.

> Suit to contest the will of Mrs. Margaret W. Winchester, widow of Charles B. Winchester, an official of Scott & Co., in which she left most of $100,000 to friends, was filed in Circuit Court Tuesday by six relatives, including three sisters and a brother. Mrs. Winchester plunged to her death from a room in the Bacon House last July 27 at the age of 68.
>
> The suit charges she was "eccentric and peculiar" and "susceptible to influence and blandishments," and that undue influence was put upon her in making the will. Attorney G. A. Yates, co-executor under the will, who was left a $20,000 bequest, was her close financial adviser, and Attorney Allan E. Mack, also left $20,000, was his associate, the bill points out.

Rules of Evidence _____

To "feel at home," as reporters should whenever they step into any courtroom, they must understand the fundamental rules of evidence.

Nature of Evidence

Most evidence is in the form of testimony by witnesses. Other forms of evidence include objects and written material introduced as exhibits. Together they constitute the *proof* whereby it is intended to influence the court's decision. All evidence must be (1) *material*—have a direct relation to the case; (2) *relevant*—pertinent; and (3) *competent*—authoritative. Otherwise, the court will uphold an *objection* to its introduction.

Burden of Proof

In a civil action it is *preponderance of evidence* that counts; in criminal cases, the state must prove guilt *beyond any reasonable doubt*. At all times, the burden of proof rests with the side that must refute evidence that if allowed to stand, would be injurious to it.

Presumptions

The law presumes that any situation known to exist at one time continues to exist unless proof to the contrary is provided. Thus good character and impeccable behavior on the part of all citizens are presumed until disproved.

Judicial Notice

Common knowledge—such as the organization of government, size and location of cities and countries, business practices and the like—need not be proved in court. Instead, the court "takes notice" of them unless challenged for doing so.

Qualifications of Witnesses

Children, wives, husbands, insane person, felons, dependents, interested lawyers and other parties once were barred from testifying. Today, the restrictions are much lighter. Almost anyone competent at the time of trial or hearing can be a witness; the credibility to be attached to the testimony is a different matter.

Privilege

The Fifth Amendment to the Constitution of the United States protects anyone from being compelled to testify against oneself. In actual practice, refusal to testify because to do so might incriminate oneself often is a "dodge." Lawyers cannot be compelled to reveal what clients have said in confidence. Similar protection is afforded physicians and clergymen in many cases and, in several states, newspapermen.

Leading Questions

Witnesses tell their stories in response to questions by attorneys. Those questions cannot be so worded as to suggest the answers desired.

Hearsay Evidence

Witnesses can testify only to that of which they have firsthand knowledge. They cannot draw inferences from the facts. Exceptions to the rule include dying declarations, spontaneous declarations, confessions and admissions against one's interest.

Opinion Evidence

Experts must be qualified before their testimony is considered credible. An expert's opinion often is obtained by means of a *hypothetical question* in which a situation comparable to that at issue is described. Otherwise, all people are considered authorities on matters they have witnessed or on matters within the knowledge of an ordinary person.

Real Evidence

Clothing, weapons and objects of all sorts are introduced as exhibits. So are models and photographs.

Circumstantial Evidence

Correct inferences often can be drawn from evidence pertaining to people's behavior both before and after a crime is committed and from their known capacities and predilections. A great deal of the evidence in both civil and criminal cases is circumstantial rather than eyewitness accounts.

Best Evidence

Copies of documents are admissible only when there is proof that originals are unavailable. In every case, the court demands the best possible evidence regarding any point.

Appeals

Since the trial judge passes on motions for new trials, not many are granted. Only in rare cases, however, does a judge refuse to grant a dissatisfied party the right to take his case to the appellate court. In criminal matters, no appeal is possible by the state in the event of acquittal, but a convicted defendant can appeal; and in civil matters either side can do so.

The distinction between *appeal* (of civil law origin) and *writ of error* (of common law origin) is virtually nonexistent today. Where it exists, it means that in the former instance a case is removed entirely from the lower to the higher court, which then can review both the law and the evidence; a writ of error, by contrast, is an original proceeding, not a continuation of that in the lower court.

Appeals are either *as of right* or *by permission* of the upper court as the statutes designate. Common grounds on which an appeal can be made are (1) irregularity of the submission of evidence, (2) new evidence discovered since the trial ended, (3) misconduct of the jury, (4) lack of jurisdiction of the court, (5) an error by the judge in instructing the jury, (6) incompetent witnesses, (7) excessive damages allowed (in civil cases) and (8) influencing or packing of the jury by the adverse party.

A *bill of exceptions* (also called *statement of the case* or *certificate of reasonable doubt*) must set forth clearly and completely the grounds on which appeal is taken. It may be accompanied by a *brief* in which the details are made more elaborate and the case as a whole summarized although the trend is toward simplification of procedure so that only one document is necessary. Certified copies of *transcripts* and *abstracts* of lower court records also are submitted.

The party taking the appeal is known as the *appellant* or *plaintiff in error* and the other party (usually the winner in the lower court) as the *appellee* or *defendant in error*. It is good practice for reporters always to ask defeated parties in an important case whether they intend to appeal. Otherwise, the reporter first learns of such action by a *notice of appeal* filed in the appellate court. Today, such notice acts as an automatic *stay of proceedings* or *supersedeas* to hold up execution of any lower court judgment or sentence. In some jurisdictions, however, it is necessary to petition for such writs.

If the higher court's permission is necessary, whatever the court decides regarding a petition is news. If it agrees to review a case, it sets a date for *oral arguments* by attorneys. Then it takes the case *under advisement*. Every justice studies the case independently before the court meets to discuss it. After a vote is taken, the chief justice assigns one justice to prepare the *majority opinion* supporting the court's *decision*. Other members may prepare *concurring opinions* or *dissenting opinions*. Any part of a decision that deals with background not directly pertinent to the case at hand is called *obiter dictum;* it explains the mental processes by which the justices formed their opinions.

By its decision, the appellate court *upholds* or *reverses* or *modifies* the lower court's decision. A *mandate* is an order to a lower court to take any kind of action, and the upper court *remands* the case to the lower so that it can act.

Juries and Judges _____

For all the efforts over centuries to make the legal system objective and dispassionate, it remains at its core dependent on human judgments, especially of judges and juries. That elemental truth sometimes makes for good copy, as the following story excerpts illustrate:

By Ann Schottman Knol
"Jury" to many of us means old Perry Mason reruns or some faceless court body that made a decision we read about in the paper.

But for people who have been jurors, "jury" means a memory of a particular person whose life was changed by the jury verdict.

Mary Ann Rieckenberg of Jackson County cried after the jury she was on convicted a man of murder, even though she was sure the verdict was correct.

Don Daniels of De Soto is still haunted by the memory of the murder trial in which he served as juror a year ago, even though he, too, is sure the jury did the right things when it convicted the 19-year-old defendant.

Paula McCrary of Pickneyville remembers vividly how difficult it was to be one of a few jurors who couldn't agree with the majority of the jury.

If people decide not to fight a call to jury duty, it's usually not because of the pittance that's called jury fees—they only get $15 a day plus mileage from their homes.

Some people, like Mrs. Rieckenberg, serve because they're fascinated by the dynamics of the court system, and because they find it rewarding to participate.

Others, like Daniels, serve because they believe in the jury system and they know people have to be willing to serve to make the system work.

"I think of myself as an honest person and I thought, 'I will try to give an honest and unbiased opinion,'" Daniels said. "I never tried to get out of it. The way I look at it, somebody has got to do it."

The experience of handing down a verdict affects different jurors different ways.

John Sauer of Murphysboro said that when the jury on which he recently served returned a verdict of guilty of aggravated assault, he never worried about the sentence that would follow. But Daniels said during the entire week he sat as juror on a murder trial, such thoughts weighed heavy on his mind.

"I was just totally occupied with that (trial) for the whole week, and even times after that sometimes, it's all that's on your mind," Daniels said. "You think, 'What's going to happen to this person if we find him guilty?' And you think of the grief everyone else is going through because of the crime committed. . . ."   [*Southern Illinoisan*]

By Ben Bradlee, Jr.

San Francisco—Now, from the state that in recent years has given the nation both the tax revolt movement and the incumbent conservative President, comes a new right-wing cause celebre: "judicial accountability."

Next year, political observers feel, the hottest campaign in California will not be Sen. Alan Cranston's or Gov. George Deukmejian's re-election bid, but a populist movement to defeat Rose Bird, chief justice of the state Supreme Court, and three of her colleagues, who under law must stand for a retention election. Conservatives call the justices the "Gang of Four."

To her detractors, Bird is the Earl Warren of the '80s—the symbol of criminal-coddling, soft-hearted, liberal judges bent on making law, not interpreting it. Bird's supporters portray her as the victim of a band of right-wing zealots trying to undermine the independence of the judiciary and give Deukmejian a dream opportunity to pack the court with his own conservative appointees.

For years, California judges, like those in most other states, stood for re-election unopposed, and a tradition developed that a judge was on the bench for life unless he or she turned senile or was involved in a scandal. But now, Bird has become the linchpin of a growing conservative movement to remove the judiciary from its position above the fray. The New Right is promoting the notion that judges should be held accountable just as politicians are, and that if their decisions have been questionable (read: liberal or too lenient), the judges should be thrown out. . . .   [Boston *Globe*]

CHAPTER
16

Politics, Elections

One beneficial consequence of the disappearance of local competition between newspapers has been an increasing trend toward political independence on the part of surviving newspapers. It is both good business and in the public interest that the news be presented accurately, fairly and completely. Conscious of past criticisms for sometimes partisan and unbalanced coverage of political campaigns, most newspapers now attempt to give rival candidates equal treatment.

The American politician is a practical businessman or woman. What politicians sell is their public service, which the public purchases with its ballots. The politician's remuneration is employment by the electorate with all the emoluments that the position entails. As a merchant, the politician is responsive to consumer demand and, in turn, attempts to influence that demand. Independents in other lines of business have plenty of difficulty in withstanding the competition of Big Business with its holding companies, chain stores and conglomerates. Political lone wolves are virtually without hope. Any success they attain is temporary; to get far they must align with one of the two large rival organizations that, since the Civil

War, have divided the nation's political profits with very little loss to third parties.

Almost any reporter can cover routine political news: announcements of candidacies, issues and platforms, rallies, speeches, registration, electioneering, voting and results. Competence in handling such assignments is necessary preparation for expert specializing later.

More interpretative political writing consists in explaining the immediate phenomenon in terms of long-range trends, national or international. Accepting the fact that practical politicians still do not operate with any appreciable awareness of such trends, pragmatic interpretative political writing consists in identifying leaders with movements and groups—political, economic, religious, ethnic and others—and in "seeing through" motives and actions to discover their probable meaning and effect upon political fortunes.

The good interpretative reporter of politics also will dig out a politician's performance on issues and try to determine the impact of that performance on the daily lives of the many varied segments of society. The good political reporter, moreover, should cover political campaigns not just as races between candidates, but also as contests among different values, beliefs and proposed public policies.

In preparing to derive the most benefit from their experiences, political reporters should (1) know something about political philosophy; (2) be a student of public opinion, its nature and manipulation; (3) understand practical political organization and election machinery; (4) be sufficiently on the "inside" to distinguish the bunkum from the realities of political phenomena.

Political Philosophy

Plato, in describing a highly disciplined perfect state in which philosophers would be kings, Aristotle, in advocating a balanced democratic government, and political theorists ever since, have expressed points of view that the enlightened political reporter will detect in substance in the arguments of contemporary seekers for public office. Heaven forbid that the college-trained reporter should be a pedantic idealist passing judgment upon twentieth-century practical men of affairs in terms of a favorite thinker of the past. Nevertheless, historical perspective is indispensable in enabling one to make sense of modern affairs. Being conversant with the history of political thought, especially with how it has been affected by practical considerations, at least provides political reporters with the tools for making their work personally instructive.

In the writings of many contemporaries, the aspiring political reporter will find plentiful interpretative analyses of the modern scene. A superabundant amount of material concerning capitalism, communism and fascism, of course, exists. The average person may not be able to tell the difference between these and other political theories, but political writers cannot be so ignorant. They should at least know when a demagogue is incorrect in branding an opponent as socialistic or fascistic or the like.

Political writers are a potent force in educating the public regarding the pros and cons of such matters as the two-party versus multiple-party systems, permanent registration, proportionate representation and the direct primary. Nobody, however, can write on such subjects without deep understanding of them.

Political Public Opinion

Before formulating an opinion about the nature of public opinion, one must understand what is meant by each word. What is a public? And what is an opinion? Consequently, a minimum of training in sociology and psychology, or in the dual science social psychology, is essential to political writers. From a good course or textbook they will learn that few modern thinkers in the field share the faith formerly held in instincts or a group mind as the explanation of why men behave similarly. Instead, inspired by the revelations of the behaviorists, psychoanalysts, anthropologists and other specialists, they are impressed by the importance of cultural conditioning, which involves traditions, customs, myths, legends, taboos, superstitions and the like of which most people are dimly conscious if at all. One of the co-authors of this book, Curtis MacDougall, evaluated these factors in *Understanding Public Opinion.*

The politician as a psychological phenomenon was first effectively treated by Harold D. Lasswell in *Psychopathology and Politics* and by A. B. Wolfe in *Conservatism, Radicalism, and the Scientific Method.* Walter Lippmann's *Public Opinion* and *The Phantom Public* resulted from his observations as a newspaperman. Lincoln Steffens' momentous *Autobiography* was inspired similarly. There is a sizable library on modern propaganda, including political propaganda, and abundant reading material on all other phases of the subject.

Failure of the professional pollsters to predict correctly the outcome of the 1948 presidential election gave impetus to research into the motivations of voting behavior. Paul Lazarsfeld and associates at Columbia University stress the effects of group interrelationship (*The People's Choice, Voting*). Louis Bean emphasizes longtime economic trends (*How to Predict Elections*). Samuel Lubell thinks the effect of nationality and cultural background has been underestimated (*The Future of American Politics, The Revolt of the Moderates*). Angus Campbell and associates demonstrate in *The American Voter* that voting preferences are consistent with a person's total personal and cultural conditioning.

Modern politicians and their consultants are well aware of current thinking about public opinion and how to manipulate it, to the extent that many campaigns today are contests between candidates' consultants as much as the candidates themselves. A recent book, *The Rise of Political Consultants,* provides a good look at that phenomenon.

Another slant on the role of public opinion and popular political movements in U.S. elections is offered in David Brader's book, *Changing of the Guard.*

Political Organization _____

Local

Municipal political affairs in recent years generally have become dissociated from major party organizations. Candidates for mayor and other city officers run as independents but may be identified in state and national politics as members of established parties that tacitly lend them support. In smaller communities, the rival groups in a municipal campaign are more likely to cross established party lines and to be dissociated from all but strictly local issues.

Because of the supposedly nonpartisan character of municipal elections, it should be the newspaper's function properly to identify candidates by the interests of the persons or groups backing them. Local political groups may take names as the People's party, but these have little or no meaning until party members have held office and given indication of what they represent. A local candidate's backing may be racial, religious, economic, geographic or in some other way classifiable. In preparing slates of candidates, political parties try to have as many of the important elements as possible represented. Furthermore, in larger cities it is customary to run a Catholic against a Catholic, a Jew against a Jew, someone of Swedish extraction against another with similar ancestry and so on. In this way, awareness of nationality, racial and other backgrounds is kept alive as well as taken advantage of politically.

Precinct, Ward

To assist the party to power in elections involving established political parties, cities are organized by wards and their subdivisions, precincts. The lowest rung on the political organization ladder is that of precinct worker, who carries the responsibility of ringing doorbells, talking to voters, handing out campaign literature, watching at the polls and assisting voters to and from polling places. Ambitious workers are conscious of their positions between elections and "talk up" the party or some of its prominent members on all occasions; intensive work, however, is only during the few weeks or months before an election.

Precinct workers are most effective in getting votes for local candidates about whom voters know little and often care less. They are influential in determining party policies and selecting candidates for city and court clerks, assessors, recorders of deeds and other offices that dispense patronage. In general elections it is not unusual for precinct workers to ask voters who support the rival party's candidates for president, congressmen, governor and other national and state offices to split their tickets sometimes "as a favor" to help elect local candidates of the precinct worker's party. Sometimes there are deals whereby workers of different parties seek split votes for local candidates.

Procedure for selecting precinct and ward captains differs, but ordinarily both are elected by registered members of the party in the sections. It may be, however, that only the ward or township captain or chairman is elected and given the responsibility of appointing precinct captains. A precinct, created by the election board, usually contains from 500 to 2,000 voters, and it is the precinct captain's job to carry the precinct in both primary and general elections. Most precinct captains have patronage jobs that depend upon their continued satisfactory performance on election days.

Precinct workers are paid for their work during campaigns by the precinct captain, who gets the money from the ward leader, who gets it from the city or county committee, which raises part of it and gets more from the state or national committee. Original sources of the millions spent annually to assist candidates to get elected are the candidates themselves, public officeholders and others who have obtained employment with the assistance of the party, businessmen who have profited by providing goods and/or services to the party's officeholders, and interested outsiders who believe they have more to gain if a certain candidate is elected than if the opponent were to win. Some large donors, mostly potential recipients of official largess, bid for the friendship of whoever occupies an important political office and may contribute to the campaign funds of both major parties.

The precinct captain generally is credited with controlling at least 50 voters among friends and relatives, the families of those whom he has been helpful in obtaining positions on election day as judges and clerks at the polls and other recipients of political favors. Unlike the ordinary worker, the precinct captain is active between elections, obtaining minor favors for voters in his precinct, such as assistance when they run afoul of the law, financial help in case of illness or death, advice on how to obtain employment, and any other services that the strength and wealth of the organization permit.

Under any circumstances, bucking the efficiently organized party is virtually impossible; so-called reform slates result from fusions of political cliques or parties out of office at the time and with no hope of victory without each other's cooperation. The history of such fusion movements is one of temporary successes only. The primary laws in many states, furthermore, make starting a third party virtually impossible.

Most candidates for public office at the local level who receive regular party endorsement have earned the reward by hard work in the precincts. Not always, however, is this the case. Sometimes, ward committeemen become jealous of the growing popularity of a subordinate and maneuver to get the rival into a public office where that rival will be less of a personal power threat. Usually, this means a judgeship or some appointive job whose incumbent is required by the Hatch act or other laws, or by tradition, to minimize politicking.

County

County chairmen usually are elected by ward and township leaders, some or all of whom constitute the county executive committee. Not all bosses are officeholders or even party officials; they may be influential dictators who prefer to operate in the background. By whatever type of person occupied, the political boss' office is the clearing house for finances and information. Reporters may obtain tips from underlings but seldom get anything official except directly from headquarters.

"Getting next to" a political boss is not impossible, as Lincoln Steffens discovered. How to do it, however, is an individual matter dependent upon the reporter's particular personality. Just as the boss must be cautious about making promises but scrupulous about keeping them once made, so must the political reporter become resigned to learning more "off the record" than on and to not learning anything about a great deal of important party business. It is because newspapers are unable to obtain the information that they do not give more "inside dope." It is dangerous journalistically for reporters to get too close to powerful politicians personally or to become too much of an insider. The price is one of often being used by the politician journalistically and losing credibility with readers.

The newspaper reporter's task is magnified whenever television cameras are present. In such instances the interviewees, from the president down, usually dominate the occasion, having the prerogative to designate who questioners shall be. They can cut off probing reporters before reporters have a chance to put all of the questions necessary for a complete story. Political candidates are particularly astute about making the arrangements conducive to their presentation of prepared statements and controlling the entire experience.

State, National

State and national committees nominally exist continuously but are often quiescent most of the time, arousing from their lethargy about a year before an election. Most active are potential candidates who are "pulling strings" to obtain machine backing when nominating time comes around. With feigned modesty, the aspirants get some friend or group of backers to "front" for them so that the suggestion that they run for office may seem to emanate from someone other than the candidate. To reporters, the aspirant is evasive and unambitious and is so quoted by a press, which, of course, knows better.

Precampaign Activities _____

Petitions

To have one's name placed on the printed ballot as a candidate for office, a person must obtain the signatures of a certain proportion of the voters on nominating petitions that must be filed before a certain date with the proper public official—city clerk, county clerk, secretary of state and so on. Because top positions usually are given to candidates filing their papers first, candidates stand in line waiting for the hour at which it is legal to file them.

It is news both when petitions are taken out and when they are filed. The candidate's name, address, occupation, political experience and general background are included in the first story about the filing of petitions. Sometimes the candidate already has prepared a statement or platform regarding the candidacy although generally that comes later. If the candidate holds or has held public office, the story can include information about things the candidate has done as a public official in the past. In city elections, the first petition stories should contain information as to the deadlines for filing, the number of signatures needed and possibly something about the position at stake. The names of prominent signers of a petition are newsworthy. Here is an excerpt from a story on petition filing:

By Manuel Galvan

Candidates vying for election to the posts of alderman and committeeman steadily poured into Chicago and Cook County election offices Friday to beat a deadline for entering the crowded field in the March 18 special elections.

By the end of the day, 87 candidates had filed to enter the races, most waiting until late Friday to file collected signatures and petitions to get on the ballots.

"We had 50 candidates file for alderman in seven wards. That's an extremely large number," said Thomas Leach, spokesman for the Chicago Board of Election Commissioners. Thirty-seven candidates, many of whom also sought aldermanic posts, filed petitions for committeeman in the special elections.

Elections are scheduled in 7 wards, the 15th, 18th, 22d, 25th, 26th, 31st and 37th, to obey orders by a federal judge to give minorities a greater voice in selecting legislative and political representatives.

The ruling came as a result of a suit filed against the city during Mayor Jane Byrne's administration, which charged that minority communities had been broken into different wards, denying them sufficient majorities to choose their representatives.

Leach said that the late filings by so many candidates is a political maneuver designed to cut down opponents' opportunities to challenge petitions. Objections may be filed until Wednesday on any petition signatures.

The 26th Ward aldermanic race is expected to be the toughest and perhaps the most pivotal in any Chicago City Council shift of power between the majority bloc, led by Ald. Edward Vrdolyak [10th], and the minority bloc of Mayor Harold Washington's council allies.

Both the Washington and Vrdolyak forces have fielded their strongest candidates in that ward. . . .   [Chicago *Tribune*]

Registration

Eligibility to vote differs by states but some sort of registration usually is required. On certain specified days, all otherwise eligible voters (those who have resided in the state, county and precinct a sufficient length of time, have paid certain taxes, given evidence of literacy, and so forth, as the case may be) appear at their polling places to have their names recorded. Such registration may be quadrennial, annual or permanent; for municipal elections no registration at all may be necessary. Voting by affidavit also may be permitted in case a voter is unable to register on the designated dates. If there is permanent registration, the voter merely notifies election officials of a change of address.

The total number of voters registering is news. Knowing that only about 60 percent of the nation's eligible voters take the trouble to register, crusading editors often investigate abnormally large registrations. Pulitzer prizes have been won by newspapers that checked registration lists to discover "ghost" votes from empty lots, abandoned buildings and transient hotels. The following excerpt from an April 14, 1985, interpretative story by political writer Steve Neal of the Chicago *Tribune* illustrates the significance that registration statistics and laws can have on political processes:

In his midterm report, Mayor Harold Washington jovially noted that his administration had forced Chicago's regular Democratic organization to become the biggest reform outfit this side of Common Cause.

Though Washington is a reformer, he still prefers to do some things the old-fashioned way. For example, the mayor says that he's against patronage and favors the Shakman limitation on political hiring, but like other politicians he's trying to revise the guidelines to hire a few more pals.

The Mayor also has modified his views on voter re-registration, which he supported as a state legislator but now opposes. State Senate President Philip Rock [D., Oak Park], who has been Washington's closest ally among the legislative leadership, has introduced a bill that would require every Illinois voter to re-register by Jan. 1, 1987. Those who don't comply with the new law will be dropped from precinct lists. Washington isn't pleased with Rock's measure, which mayoral associates have tagged as an anti-administration bill.

For Rock, who has announced his candidacy for attorney general, election reform could be a politically appealing issue with Downstate voters, and it has also been embraced almost overnight by his friends in the Chicago Democratic organization.

It doesn't take a rocket scientist to figure out why Ald. Edward Vrdolyak [10th], chairman of the Cook County Democratic Party, and State Sen. James "Pate" Philip [R., Elmhurst], chairman of the DuPage County GOP, have become overnight champions of election reform.

Vrdolyak and Philip are interested in mandatory re-registration on the chance that it might wipe out some of the registration gains among blacks that were generated by Washington and Rev. Jesse Jackson in the last three years. Rock, though, contends that minority registration could increase with re-registration. He said that minority registration went up about 40 percent last year when Rock Island had mandatory re-registration. . . .

Primaries

With the notable exception of the national tickets every four years, most candidates for important office are chosen by party primaries instead of by convention as formerly. Any citizen may enter a primary election as a candidate for the nomination of any party. A voter, however, can participate in the primary of one party only. The names of only those candidates who have filed nominating petitions appear on the ballot, but the voter can add the name of anyone else. It is seldom, however, that a "write-in" candidate is elected.

In some states, if no candidate receives a majority, runoff primaries are held of the two or three leaders. In most states that have primary laws, a plurality in a single primary is sufficient to nominate.

If there is little contest in their own party, in most states voters may vote in the primary of another although they intend to vote for their own party candidate in the general election. In how their primary election laws are written, some states make such cross-over voting more difficult than others.

If too many voters desert it in a general election, however, the party may not receive a large enough proportion of the total vote to receive a place on the ballot at the next election. Likewise, the party voter may forfeit the right to vote in any special primary within the time limit, usually two years, during which it is possible to change party affiliation.

Presidential primaries in about half the states are for the purpose of electing delegates to the national conventions at which the candidates are nominated. Procedures differ considerably. In most cases the delegates' preferences are known and they are pledged to vote for them on at least one ballot. Some delegates, however, may be uncommitted and even if they have choices they may not be indicated on the ballots. In addition there may be "beauty" contests as they are facetiously called, allowing voters to indicate their preferences for nominees. The way the political winds are blowing often, but by no means always, can be judged by the outcomes of the early primaries or those with the largest number of delegates.

Even below the national level, however, primary election fights within a political party can make big news requiring considerable interpretation, as illustrated by this excerpt from the main front-page story of the Chicago *Sun-Times* on August 25, 1985:

By Basil Talbott Jr.

A Democratic civil war has begun, pitting powerful allies of Adlai E. Stevenson III and Attorney General Neil F. Hartigan and threatening the most wrenching realignment in city and state politics in half a century.

Within a day after Stevenson said last Wednesday that he might run for governor, long distance telephone lines sizzled as the potential Democratic challengers and their agents sought to call in political IOUs, neutralize opposition—and gossip about the prospects.

"Who would have ever thought that Adlai Stevenson could ever provide the most refreshing political news of the year?" independent strategist Don Rose mused about the possible nominee for governor, who lost to James Thompson in 1982. "You have to go back to Gov. Henry Horner in the 1930s to see anything like it. . . .

Conventions

Adoption of a direct primary law does not mean the end of state party conventions, but such conventions (or conferences) are held outside the law and for the purpose only of recommending and endorsing candidates to receive the party's nomination at a primary election. Often rival factions within a party hold separate conventions and endorse different slates.

The news writer can estimate the strength of candidates at a state or national convention by comparing the instructions given to delegates. Delegations sometimes support "favorite sons" from their localities and may deadlock a convention by refusing, after the early ballots, to change their votes to one of the leading candidates.

Knowledgeable political editors suspect deals whenever stubborn delegations suddenly change their positions. Possibly appointment to a cabinet position or judgeship or some other office has been promised someone; or support has been pledged in some future campaign. Maybe the compromise involves stands on issues to be involved in anticipated legislation.

A party convention is called to order by a temporary chairperson who gives a prepared keynote speech. Then a permanent chairperson is elected and also gives a speech. Usually the committee's recommendation for permanent chairperson is taken, but sometimes rival factions may nominate different candidates. The vote for permanent chairperson then may be an indication of how delegates will vote later on other important matters.

The group in control of a state or national committee has the advantage of obtaining a personnel to its liking. Through its committee on credentials it determines which delegates are eligible for seats, if rival delegations from the same locality claim recognition.

Vote on the platform submitted by the committee on resolutions is conducted by a roll call of delegations. After the platform is adopted, with or without amendments, the next procedure is the election of candidates. Often, several ballots are necessary for a choice. When a deadlock continues after several ballots, a "dark horse," someone not among the leaders, may be elected as a compromise candidate.

A party convention frequently is interrupted by the demonstrations of different delegations. When the time to nominate candidates arrives, the roll call begins. Every delegation either nominates someone or passes its turn or permits some other delegation, whose turn normally could come later, to use its opportunity. In addition to the principal nominating speech there may be several other speeches to second a nomination. Every speech is the signal for an outburst of enthusiasm by supporters of the candidate. Unfavorable viewers' reactions to the carnival aspects of the televised proceedings have caused the two major political parties to attempt to streamline their quadrennial conventions somewhat. The stage managers, however, may become overly conscious of what is considered prime viewing time and either slow down or hurry up activities with the nationwide television audience in mind. Thus the conventions tend to become entertainment rather than serious exercises in statesmanship.

A party *conference* is for the purpose of discussing an important matter. A party *caucus* differs from a conference because all who attend it, by their attendance, pledge themselves to support the decisions of the majority. Insurgent members may stay away from party caucuses because they do not wish to commit themselves to the support of what the majority will favor. Following are some examples of political convention coverage below the national level.

First, here is an excerpt of a story about caucuses held to elect delegates to a state political party convention. Note the interpretation included along with the basic facts:

By Chris Black

From the Oak Bluff Town Hall to the Goody Goody Cafe in Fitchburg's Ward 4, Democratic Party members gathered yesterday to elect 3500 delegates to the Democratic Issues Convention, which will rewrite the state party platform on May 18 in Springfield.

The annual rite is a form of spring training for Democratic politicians who expect to seek support at the endorsement convention for statewide office next year.

The caucuses offer an opportunity to act out ancient rivalries and force alliances.

Since the party resurrected the annual state convention with the party charter adopted in 1979, the political organization of Gov. Michael S. Dukakis has dominated state conventions.

Yesterday, "coalition" slates put together in cooperation with the Dukakis organization were reportedly winning easily in many communities. . . .

[Boston *Globe*]

This story excerpt demonstrates the interpretative concept applied to coverage of social festivities at a convention:

By Lauren Silverman

A Wisconsin delegate was looking around for a place to sit at the "Fritz Fest," former Vice President Walter Mondale's party at Ovens of Brittany Friday night. He was holding a beer in one hand, a plate of food in the other. And he was wearing a button that said "My vote is not for sale."

"My vote is not for sale," he said. "But it sure is rentable by the hour."

That typified the night. From the moment delegates arrived at the Puster Hotel to register for the State Democratic Convention, through the end of the night, the name of the game seemed to be "Win that vote." And one method was with free food, drink and hotel rooms.

At the parties Friday night, Mondale was the hands-down winner. His staff had it down to a science. There were the good-looking young people holding large signs directing people to his party at Ovens of Brittany, 770 N. Jefferson St. Once you got there, everything about it suggested that this was a winner. . . .

[Milwaukee *Journal*]

And here is the opening to a report about a state party convention, including interpretation to help the reader have perspective on the event:

By John Balzar and Keith Love

Sacramento—Gathering for the first time since the 1984 elections, California Democrats convened here this weekend to take a look at themselves and where they are heading. Many did not like what they saw.

"Today we are paying the price for ignoring the most intensely felt concerns of the American public—crime and violence, taxes and spending and education," Los Angeles County Dist. Atty. Ira Reiner told the conventioneers in the sternest lecture delivered at the gathering.

"We're getting what we've got coming to us," Reiner continued later in an interview. "The American public is not supporting us because we left them a long time ago. The only people who are talking to the American public are the Republicans."

The state Democrats remain strikingly splintered, if not controlled by no fewer than 14 single-issue caucuses, ranging from the disabled, to environmentalists, to gays, to senior citizens, to organized labor and peace caucuses. . . .

[Los Angeles *Times*]

Campaigns _____

Socially responsible coverage of a political campaign involves providing readers with as much pertinent information about candidates and issues as possible. This means more than merely reporting speeches and platforms. Significant facts that may not appear in a candidate's own biographical sketch or news releases must be published and the importance and ramifications of issues analyzed. What is ignored or soft-pedaled may be a better clue to what candidates believe than what they stress, possibly to an exaggerated extent, in public statements.

Candidates

Who the candidates are and how they differ from each other must be reported.

Sometimes that involves calling attention to an unglamorous contest getting little media attention. The Los Angeles *Times* did that in this Mar. 3, 1985, story, which began with the opening printed below, and then included short political analyses of the supporters, financing and positions on issues of each candidate:

By Victor Merina

With small klieg lights shining and a video camera rolling, the candidates for Los Angeles city controller took turns standing at a bare lectern to earnestly pitch their campaign philosophies.

But in the Occidental College classroom, only four students sat in the audience as a panel of fellow students questioned the prospective controllers on why they conveted the city's third highest elective office.

At another gathering in downtown Los Angeles, only a few reporters showed up at the City Hall steps for a news conference called by one controller candidate who said he would outline a plan to save the city $5 million.

As the would-be controller waited for more news people to appear, a reporter walked up to the group and then scurried away—after learning that he was at the wrong press conference.

The campaign for city controller—the city's chief financial officer and auditor—has become the Rodney Dangerfield of municipal elections, clamoring for respect and encountering apparent indifference. . . .

Another way to shed light on issues in a campaign is to get out where the voters are and poke around, as this Mar. 17, 1985, Chicago *Sun-Times* story excerpt illustrates:

By Andrew Herrmann

"Isn't this something?" asks an exasperated Kenneth Fisher, the village president of south suburban Dixmoor for the last four years. "I mean this is unbelievable."

If you're talking about the Dixmoor president's race, as Fisher was, the word unbelievable is not far off.

By all accounts, the race for the $900-a-year post between a white maintenance man, a black secretary and a black CTA mechanic has whipped into an ugly windstorm of burning crosses, hate mail and threatening phone calls.

And the contest may give the dingy, predominantly black, blue-collar town of 4,175 its first minority president in its 63-year history.

Unbelievable is a label that also might be affixed to the town's other problems as well.

A drive down a few of the town's curbless streets is a gloomy trip indeed.

Potholes, broken glass, unmarked streets lead past a bevy of abandoned, boarded-up houses and stores.

There is scant industry, 13 percent unemployment and, according to one resident, "rats as big as cats". . . .

The story then went on to define in detail issues differences among the candidates against the backdrop of Dixmoor's past and current problems.

Traveling with a candidate sometimes can give a reporter insight into what is really going on that otherwise would be unavailable. Consider, for example, this excerpt from a Jan. 20, 1985, Los Angeles *Times* interpretative story:

By Janet Clayton

Los Angeles Mayor Tom Bradley, in North Hollywood, had just been tugged by a supporter into a hotel conference room to speak before a group of tax accountants. A large group, aware. Likely voters.

He had not been scheduled to talk to the group, but "a politician is not likely to pass up such an opportunity, especially during an election," he said, smiling broadly as he took the podium.

After a rocky start two weeks ago, when Bradley was put on the defensive and responded snappishly to nearly every charge made by his reelection bid opponent, Councilman John Ferraro, the mayor last week returned to his more typical style of trying to stay above the fray.

But the public ebullience contrasts with some private concerns about Ferraro's challenge. Campaign officials say they are "nervous" about a potentially divisive and negative campaign that could be waged by Ferraro's campaign manager, Ron Smith, who has a reputation for no-holds-barred strategy.

Ferraro has assured Bradley that he will run a "clean and fair" campaign. Nevertheless, Bradley's political instinct is to stump, and stump hard.

During a typical day of mayoral duties and campaigning last week, Bradley passed up no opportunity to talk to nearly every type of constituent group in the city, ranging from the accountants, to travel agents, government middle managers, charity workers in the San Fernando Valley, minority bankers, to Westside homeowners. . . .

Issues

Issues cannot be described separately from candidates or their supporters, but the reporter can put the emphasis on what is at stake.

Austin, Texas (AP)—The Texas Railroad Commission—an agency that regulates so many things besides railroads that it may be the most powerful such department in the nation—has two seats up for grabs.

Commissioners John Poerner and James Nugent, both former legislators who were appointed to their posts in non-election years, are now running with all the big industry money and political backing traditionally awarded incumbents.

The challengers are a timber baron's son and a muckraking journalist who used his tabloid to criticize the cozy relationship between the commissioners and the very industries they regulate.

What attracts so much attention to the 1980 statewide races for two $45,200-a-year jobs is the commission's duties.

The three-person agency was created in 1891 to control outrageous rail freight rates. Over the years, the commission kept its name but added duties.

Now it regulates the strip mining of coal, lignite and uranium; the rates and routes for intercity buses and trucks; and the production of liquified petroleum gas such as propane and butane.

But most vitally, it sets prices and regulates production for Texas' oil and gas industry, which supplies 25 percent of all fuel consumed in the United States.

"We know a senator can debate energy policy and we've seen a governor can spill oil on our beaches, but a railroad commissioner actually sets energy prices," says Jim Hightower, 36.

Hightower, given to cowboy hats and boots, touts himself as a candidate who owns no oil wells and gets no dividend checks from "Exxon or Lone Star Gas or one of railroads."

He quit as editor of the bimonthly Texas observer to run against Nugent, who was nicknamed "Supersnake" for his maneuvers in the Texas House. . . .

Sometimes, interpretation that shows what is not being said about issues and that provides historical background for readers can illuminate an issue, or even a whole election campaign.

By Bill Boyarsky

There is a new Boys Market just a few doors down from Mayor Tom Bradley's South-Central Los Angeles campaign headquarters, in the Martin Luther King Jr. Shopping Center. On a recent Saturday, when Bradley formally opened his office, the market was busy and almost everything looked good, especially the meat section.

At first thought, there is not much connection between politics and a supermarket manager's skill at tasteful display.

But the history of urban America since the riots of the mid-1960s explains the connection and why a shopping center in Watts has a relation to the mayoral campaign between Bradley and his main challenger, Councilman John Ferraro.

The subject came up briefly in the recent debate between Ferraro and Bradley. Bradley said the shopping center was evidence of how Watts had been rebuilt during his administration. Ferraro contended that the completion of just one shopping center showed how little had been done.

Their discussion left out something important: the future of such inner-city revitalization projects now that the Reagan Administration is pushing for elimination of the financial-aid programs that support such enterprises. What was lacking in the debate—and in the entire campaign between the two—were solid ideas about the future.

Shopping centers are an important benchmark in measuring the economic health of inner-city neighborhoods, a sign of whether they have been abandoned to poverty or retain the basic amenities vital to urban life. They are also symbols of a city's commitment to its poorer sections. . . .

[Los Angeles Times]

Tactics

Politicians seeking election or reelection employ a wide variety of tactics to achieve their goal. Making those tactics clear to voters often requires reporters to use investigative and interpretative methods.

An example is this Louisville _Courier-Journal_ story of Apr. 14, 1985, a small portion of which follows:

By Leslie Scanlon

Some Louisville aldermen were furious in 1978 when a new mayor, William B. Stansbury, gave two lucrative contracts to his campaign finance chairman, John T. Fowler.

They set off a war between Stansbury and a faction of aldermen generally allied with Stansbury's predecessor, Harvey Sloane. In the end, the aldermen seized more control over the city's personal and professional service contracts, which in most cases are awarded without competitive bidding.

Fowler and Stansbury are dead now. Sloane is back in City Hall.

Now Fowler's son, John T. Fowler III, has a city contract, and so does his daughter, Marilyn Hartley, one of four attorneys working for the aldermen.

Since Sloane sought his second term as mayor in 1981, the younger Fowler has contributed at least $2,500 to Sloan's campaigns, and his sister has contributed $4,000. Between them, they also gave $1,000 to two aldermen.

When Sloane was elected, his supporters saw his administration as vastly different from Stanbury's, which hired people whom critics called "political hacks. . . ."

But in the area of discretionary contracts, it is not at all clear how different the Sloane era has been.

What is clear is that, in his second administration, Sloane has practiced traditional patronage politics. Millions of dollars of city business has gone to Sloane's campaign contributors and friends. . . .

In an interview, the mayor said he has never pressured city employees or contract-holders to give, and he has never mentioned a person's contract in asking for a contribution. . . .

Speeches

A campaign really gets under way with the first speech of the candidate. In the case of a presidential candidate this is the speech of acceptance of the nomination formerly made at a formal notification ceremony, but in recent years usually at the nominating convention. Although presidential candidates have fresh speeches for every important occasion thereafter, in the case of candidates for less important offices the opening or keynote speech may be the pattern for all others delivered during the campaign. The political reporter traveling with the candidate may be hard put to obtain a fresh angle in reporting the day's forensics, but the local news writers who hear the candidate only once are not so handicapped.

When candidates start calling each other names, hurling challenges, answering each other's arguments and raising new issues, it makes things easy for reporters. Otherwise, they may be forced to rely upon the press releases of political headquarters. If they travel with a candidate reporters tell of the crowds, the opinions of local leaders, the reception given the candidate and the like.

Most newspapers try to equalize the space given rival candidates. Often this is difficult to do. William Pride, executive news editor of the Denver *Post,* summarized the difficulty in part as follows:

> Last time around we had a congressional race (suburban) featuring staid, stodgy 3-term incumbent vs. young, sharp, interesting challenger. Problem: how to treat 'em equally. We allotted equal space and traded off reporters, following them the last two weeks. The incumbent was a shoo-in from the start, so all he did was stand at factory gates and shopping centers shaking hands. The young guy, full of ideas, uncorked a new major speech about every other day. If we give each half a column, what can we say about the first guy after we say he stood at the entrance to the supermarket all morning? If we give the second guy more space, we get squawks, pickets, etc., so there you are. (I hardly need add that the incumbent was easily re-elected.)

A related problem is how to include all of the candidates for all of the offices that will appear on the ballot. Naturally, the most important—president, governor, senator, mayor, and so forth—will receive most attention if for no other reason than the fact that the candidates will campaign more vigorously. But despite the trend to making formerly elective offices appointive voters still are asked to make a multitude of choices. They may stare at a long ballot with scores of unfamiliar names of candidates for public offices about whose duties they know little or nothing.

A traditional method is to print thumbnail sketches of all candidates shortly before election day. These include the essential facts of family background, education, occupational, civic and political experience. They seldom include statements on issues. In local elections when there is a short ballot, depth interviews can be obtained with all candidates and the written questionnaire method, soliciting answers regarding key issues, can be used effectively. Space is given the candidates' own words in reply.

Records

Gov. Alfred E. Smith of New York, Democratic presidential candidate in 1928, frequently advised, "Let's look at the record." It's a good idea for politicians, voters and journalists.

By Doug Harbrecht

Washington—A congressman votes against a controversial bill, knowing he will please a bloc of constituents and the hometown newspaper will record his vote.

The next week, in a less publicized and intense atmosphere, he turns around and votes with his party or his conscience.

Thus, he has it both ways. To one group he can say he voted for cuts in public spending, or restrictions on abortion, or foreign aid. To another, he can say he opposed such measures, and his record speaks for itself.

In Washington, it is called the "yahoo vote," the vote that plays to the right audience. Congressional leaders recognize and allow for it, as long as the chickens eventually come home to roost. Sometimes it works the other way.

The U.S. House has had 530 record votes since January, ranging from routine measures approving the previous day's record to hotly contested amendments.

But if you were to check the Congressional Record for this year, you would find that Rep. Austin Murphy, D-Mononghela, has somehow managed to vote for and against a pay increase for congressmen, for and against the Panama Canal treaties, for and against the 1980 budget resolution, for and against the Department of Education bill, and for and against raising the national debt ceiling.

Murphy, a thoughtful former state senator whose district includes Upper St. Clair, Moon, Findlay and Robinson, as well as Washington and Fayette counties, has an articulate reason for all his votes, as does every congressman who takes seriously his role as U.S. representative.

But his voting record is probably the most checkered of any area congressman and shows a broad range. . . .   [Pittsburgh *Press*]

Polls

Because of the apparently uncanny ability of television networks to predict the outcome of elections after only a small proportion of the total vote has been tabulated, newspaper editors, readers and politicians have come to place considerable confidence in polling. Political parties and candidates conduct private polls and some newspapers have their own.

It took the Gallup organization a quarter-century to recover from the 1948 fiasco when it and its rivals predicted an easy victory for Republican Thomas E. Dewey over incumbent Democrat Harry S Truman. There has been no comparable failure of any professional organization in a presidential election since that time. There have, however, been many failures in predicting the outcomes of presidential primaries and local elections.

In considering how to judge and interpret political polls, journalists should be aware of these standards adopted in 1979 by the National Council on Public Polling, a group of professional public and private pollsters. They constitute the closest thing there is to minimum ethical standards for pollsters:

1. Indicate who sponsored or paid for the survey.
2. Give the dates of interviewing.
3. Define the method of interviewing.
4. Describe the population interviewed.
5. Reveal the size of the sample.
6. Describe and give the size of any subsamples used in the analysis.
7. Release the wording of all questions.
8. Release the full results of the questions on which the conclusions are based.
9. Do not remain silent if a client publicly releases and misrepresents a poll result.

In an April 1984 article in the *Washington Journalism Review,* Associated Press reporter-writer Evans Witt offered these ten rules for journalists writing about political polls:

1. Do not overinterpret poll results.
2. Include the results of other polls, even if they cast doubt upon the latest results.
3. Always include and be aware of the sampling error.
4. Never forget the base.
5. Look at the exact wording of questions carefully.
6. Do not use non-scientific readings of public opinion for anything but entertainment value.
7. Be very, very careful when writing about polls conducted for candidates, special interest groups or political parties.
8. Never forget that polls give little hint about the depth of people's emotions or commitments.
9. Do not disguise your own interpretations as poll results.
10. Use common sense and do not fall under the spell of the numbers.

Elections ————————————————————————————————————

Election Day

The size of the vote, violence at polling places, amusing anecdotes, the circumstances under which the candidates cast their ballots, last-minute statements and predictions and methods used to get out the vote or persuade voters on their way to the polls provide news on election day before the ballots are counted.

Ordinary newsroom routine is upset on election day as regulars work overtime and extra helpers gather and compile returns. Radio and television have eliminated the newspaper election extra although editions may be set ahead to provide details, background and interpretative material that the broadcast media cannot give.

In national elections the three television networks and the two press associations sometimes pool their efforts to gather the returns rapidly. As the results come in by isolated districts they are tabulated, and the political writer prepares a trend story for the first edition. Some outcomes can be predicted comparatively early; often, in a close race, the result is in doubt until the last vote is counted. When the result is apparent, campaign committees and candidates issue statements claiming victory or conceding defeat. Losers send messages of congratulations to winners.

If an outcome is close, a loser may demand a recount. Some elections are protested by defeated candidates who charge fraud, stuffing or tampering with ballot boxes and other irregularities. All candidates are required to file statements of campaign expenditures. Investigations of alleged violations of the corrupt practices act during an election are not infrequent.

The mid-election-day story should include the number voting and a comparison with previous elections.

Candidates were being nominated in today's statewide primary elections for United States Senator and Representatives in Congress, and for some state and local offices in St. Louis and St. Louis County. In the city and county, balloting was generally light, indicating one of the smallest off-year primary votes in years.

By 4 p.m., it was estimated 61,889 ballots had been cast in the city, following 10 hours of balloting in the 784 precincts. This was 18 percent of the total registration of 343,830.

In the county, an estimated 9,936 ballots were cast by 4 p.m., nine hours after the 7 a.m. opening of the polls. The estimated vote was 7.9 percent of the 125,782 registration.

St. Louis polling places will close at 7 p.m. Those in the county will close at 8:07 p.m. with the exception of those in University City, where the closing time is 8 p.m. The hours given are daylight saving time.

Special deputy election commissioners are on duty in all precincts of the Fifth and Sixth Wards, in which a recent recanvass of the registration indicated efforts to pad the lists. Chairman Frank L. Rammacciotti of the Election Board said the deputies were stationed in the two downtown wards to guard against any election irregularities.

Ballots and registration lists for the two wards were not delivered to the polling places until early today. Rammacciotti said this was done because many of the election officials resided outside of the wards and they did not have adequate means to care for them. These were the only two wards where this was done, the ballots and voters' lists having been delivered to election officials in all other wards last night.

The special deputies in the Fifth and Sixth Wards were instructed specifically to guard against ballots being marked openly instead of in the regular voting booth, and to see that all ballots were counted by Republican and Democratic poll officials working together instead of dividing ballots for a separate tabulation by each party's officials.

City voters received two ballots at the polls, a party primary ballot and one for the two amendments to the City Charter and the proposed $4,000,000 bond issue for rubbish collection facilities, each calling for a Yes or No vote.

Proposed amendment No. 1 would permit. . . .   [St. Louis *Post-Dispatch*]

Results

When all or nearly all returns are in, so that the outcome is known, the news feature naturally is who won. The story also should emphasize (1) by how much—in total votes and proportions; (2) areas in which different candidates were strongest and weakest; (3) upsets—incumbents with long services who were defeated, candidates on a party slate who lost whereas most of the others won; (4) whether results coincide with predictions; (5) what significance the outcome is likely to have both locally and/or nationally, as the case may be; (6) statements by winners, losers and party leaders, and similar matters.

By Charles Hayslett

In a staggering display of political prowess, Sen. Herman Talmadge rolled up more than 553,000 votes to swamp Lt. Gov. Zell Miller and finally put down the most serious challenge to his three-decade dominance of Georgia politics.

Rebounding from a public bout with alcoholism, a sensational divorce and a damaging Senate probe of his personal and official finances, Talmadge swept at least 140 of Georgia's 159 counties as he polled 58 percent of the runoff votes Tuesday and nailed down the Democratic nomination to a fifth straight six-year term in the Senate.

He now faces Republican Mack Mattingly, a former GOP state chairman making his first bid for public office, in the Nov. 4 general election. . . .

[Atlanta *Journal*]

Sidebars in the same edition included the scenes in the headquarters of both winner (Roar of Crowd: Talmadge, Talmadge, Talmadge) and loser (Zell Miller: "I Feel Good About the Race I Ran"), plans of the Republican nominee and first indications of how the fall campaign would be conducted.

Post-Mortems

A great deal of post election interpretative writing is of the "I told you so" or "We should have known it" type. By analyzing the vote in different sections where the electorate is predominantly of one type—workers, members of a particular racial, national or religious group—it is possible to imagine which campaign issues or attitudes antedating the campaign were most effective. Skilled political writers analyze results in the search for trends. Often, they have to compare local with state and national results to interpret correctly.

When a new officeholder or party takes over a city hall, county building, state or national capitol, the citizenry expects that "there will be some changes made." Party platforms and campaign speeches provide clues as to what they will be, but voters have become suspicious of politicians' promises. Personality sketches and reviews of the past records of successful candidates are valuable.

The leads of next-day stories after the 1980 Georgia runoff primary follow.

By Frederick Allen

Lt. Gov. Zell Miller symbolically lost his chance at capturing Herman Talmadge's Senate seat on the afternoon of March 20, 1980, when he accepted the poisoned kiss of endorsement from Atlanta Mayor Maynard Jackson.

However, the story of Miller's punishing loss in Tuesday's runoff is considerably more complicated than the easy explanation of white backlash and antipathy for liberal ideas.

A leading factor, of course, was the tremendous political strength demonstrated by Talmadge, while Miller's own flawed strategy played a leading but misunderstood role.

With all 2,251 precincts counted Wednesday, Talmadge had 553,244 votes, or 58.5 percent, to 393,931 votes, or 41.5 percent, for Miller. Turnout in the Democratic runoff was nearly 950,000 voters, or 42.5 percent of Georgia's 2.23 million registered voters.

The main component of Talmadge's strategy was a record amount of money. He spent about $1.5 million, swamping all of his pursuers combined.

However, Talmadge also demonstrated considerable finesse, deciding early on a risky but effective advertising campaign that dealt directly with his personal problems.

Knowing he was the front-runner, he avoided direct reference to his challengers until the runoff, when he went for Miller's jugular in a series of television debates.

The senator ran a masterful "retreat" campaign—limiting potential losses of support among his traditional followers. No farmer failed to hear about Talmadge's chairmanship of the Senate Agriculture Committee, no constituent went uninformed about Talmadge's years of answering requests for help, and no Georgian was allowed to forget Talmadge's seniority.

In the runoff, Talmadge saw quickly that Miller could be shredded as a "big spender," and the debates were a showcase for the senator's abilities at making Miller sound like U.S. Sen. Edward Kennedy on a buying spree.

Talmadge also realized the potential damage from anti-Talmadge voters, so he limited his advertising in the last three weeks and relied instead on a telephone canvassing operation aimed at pinpointing his followers and spurring them back to vote again.

About the only mistake Talmadge made was misreading his own polls and thinking he would win without a runoff. It took Talmadge about three days to recover from his initial panic and realize that the numbers made him a prohibitive favorite against Miller. While his decision to debate Miller was a mild error, he recouped by winning the debates. . . .   [Atlanta *Constitution*]

By Charles Hayslett

It was in August that Zell Miller first began to crawl onto the limb that would put him to the left of his foes and ultimately collapse under him.

Answering questions at a convention of Georgia's Young Democrats, Miller said he, like the others, favored balancing the federal budget, but finally admitted that he would vote against any budget that had to be balanced on the backs of the nation's poor.

In the weeks and months ahead, Miller edged farther and farther out onto that limb, pledging to support an extension of the federal Voting Rights Act, openly accepting the support of controversial black leaders despite predictions of a white backlash and refusing to abandon his less-than-conservative positions on spending issues that would most benefit the state's black and poor.

Tuesday, Zell Miller got his reward. One out of five registered black voters cast a ballot for him.

There were many stories in Tuesday night's numbers, but none more stark than that one. While the statewide turnout was again bubbling over the 40 percent mark, Georgia's black voters were turning out at a much slower pace.

A survey of 14 black precincts in Fulton County showed the black turnout averaging only 25.9 percent. Miller got 79.1 percent of that, but the raw math of those numbers—if that trend held throughout the county—would put no more than 25,000 votes in Miller's column.

In the low income areas the story was even more dismal. Worst of all for Miller was Atlanta's precinct 4C, which has 1,929 black registered voters and 10 white registered voters. Herman Talmadge got 10 votes. Zell Miller got 109.

Late Tuesday night, while those numbers and others were rolling out of the state's computers and spelling an end to Miller's Senate hopes, Miller was on a podium at the Atlanta Stadium hotel, flanked by Maynard Jackson and a dozen other supporters, several of them black. He would not have done anything differently, he told the roomful of supporters.

"You are the future of Georgia," he said, "and history will prove us right."

"Some have the job of planting seeds, while others reap the harvest. We have planted the seeds, and in future years others will reap the harvest."

And in the cool morning hours after Tuesday's runoff, it indeed appeared that Zell Miller might never reap that harvest. The seeds he planted with his highly touted coalition of blacks, teachers and union members, raised, if nothing else, grave questions about his future in Georgia politics.

While Miller has established himself as the pre-eminent maverick-populist in Georgia politics, and won two statewide races along the way, the truth is that he has never seen competition like he faced in the Senate campaign or would face in a 1982 bid for the governor's office. . . . [Atlanta *Journal*]

Behind Scenes ————————————————————————————————

Newspapers increasingly feel it necessary to explain political processes to their voters. Interest in politics is high among some readers, but others may know less than reporters, who cover government and become knowledgeable about it, think readers do. So it is important for journalists to keep in mind the need to frequently explain how democratic processes work, both in theory and practice.

Basic Interpretation

This Jan. 22, 1985, story from the *Southern Illinoisan* in Carbondale attempts to explain for readers the fundamental matter of the laws and rules for holding municipal elections in Illinois, and to do it in a readable interpretative fashion:

By Ann Schottman Knol

Sam is trying to figure out why he has to vote for officials in his town in both a primary and general election, while his aunt sits in on a party caucus to choose candidates in her town and his cousin doesn't have an election at all this year in his town.

Election officials admit the municipal election laws are complicated, but—believe it or not—they're simpler than they used to be.

Bea Swartz of the State Board of Elections said municipal election procedures are so confusing that her office gets numerous questions about those procedures from just about anybody involved in the elections—candidates, attorneys and local and county officials.

But, she said, the election schedule is better than it used to be before counties started handling all elections in 1980. Now only five elections are held during a two-year period, instead of "many, many" each year.

Library, park, fire protection, school and township elections used to be held at different times, but now the school elections are held along with the November general election in odd-numbered years, and library, park and township elections are held in April with the municipal elections.

County handling of all elections helps make election procedure uniform throughout the state and also means polling places are the same for all elections, Ms. Swartz said.

Election laws, outlined in the Cities and Villages Act and the state election code, have evolved through many years of amendments, Ms. Swartz said. The legislature attempts each year to make election procedures simpler.

The main problem Ms. Swartz sees with the current municipal election procedure is that the consolidated primary, on Feb. 26 this year, is too close to the general election, this year on April 2.

"That makes it difficult (for election officials) to conduct all the necessary procedures between the two elections," she said.

So here's the explanation Sam needs to figure out why his relatives have different voting procedures than his municipality does.

First of all, municipalities with a commission form of government hold elections every four years and all other municipalities hold elections every two years.

That's the simple part. Trying to figure out when candidates file and whether a primary or caucus will be held is more complicated.

Candidates from nonpartisan municipalities filed for office in December, and if more than two file for each office, a municipality will hold a primary election Feb. 26, before the April 2 general election. If no more than two candidates file for each office, the municipalities are not required to hold primaries.

Elections are not partisan in commission cities and municipalities that have a council-manager form of government, where the council members are elected at large.

All other municipalities run elections by party. Candidates in party elections also can be independents or can form new political parties. If a candidate files as an independent or as a new party candidate, his or her petition to be put on the ballot must be signed by a minimum of five percent of the number of voters who voted in the last municipal official election.

Party candidates in cities and villages with population over 5,000 have to file their petitions to be put on the ballot in December, and if more than two party candidates file for an office, a Feb. 26 primary will be held before the April 2 general election. Candidates filing as independents or new party candidates file for office in January, and are not included in any primary.

Cities and villages with populations under 5,000 must caucus Jan. 10 to select candidates. That means members of the established parties in those municipalities get together and select candidates from their party. Again, independent or new party candidates are not included in the caucus—they will file their petitions to be put on the ballot in January.

Municipal parties may or may not be the traditional Democrat and Republican parties. Candidates can form their own parties and give names to those parties. If at least five percent of the voters in a municipality vote for candidates from a new party, that party becomes an established party in that municipality. However, the Democratic and Republican parties are always recognized as established parties, no matter what the vote is for Democratic and Republican candidates.

Sam, can you follow that?

Media Politics

As dependence on television for news about politics and much else has grown among many Americans, political party organizations have become relatively less important in political campaigns and the media more important. Newspapers increasingly have recognized that they have become a significant part of the political process, and the best political reporters are trying to reflect that fact in their coverage.

In an Oct. 7, 1985, story, a portion of which follows, Washington *Post* writer Paul Taylor tried to explain how incumbent U.S. senators view the importance of television to their campaigns and their efforts to shape coverage to their liking:

As a third of the nation's senators look toward the 1986 reelection battles, some also are casting nervous, cock-eyed looks back at the big winners of the last war.

Namely, a hound dog and a lizard.

The droopy-eared canine starred in campaign commercials last year that played up former Kentucky Sen. Walter D. Huddleston's absenteeism (bloodhound searches far and wide, never finds senator).

The lizard carried the attack against Illinois Sen. Charles Percy's inconsistencies (chameleon changes colors before viewers' very eyes).

As negative spots go, these were pretty tepid, but both got their men. In Huddleston's case, that was no small trick, given the 29-point lead he had enjoyed over his longshot Republican opponent, Mitch McConnell, less than two months before the election.

The Senate incumbents have taken heed and gone into a protective crouch. They are toying with schemes to keep such attack ads off the air in 1986. The happiest thing to be said about their proposals is that they're likely to go nowhere.

One bill, known as the Clean Campaign Act of 1985, would provide that any candidate for federal office referred to on the air by any stand-in (animal or human) for his opponent would be entitled to free response time. Only when the opponent has the gumption to go in front of a camera and do the dirty deed himself or herself would the provision be waived.

At its first hearing in the Senate Commerce Committee in September, the bill evoked a series of wounded laments from incumbents about the sorry state of modern campaign ethics.

"It's a sickening . . . revolting mess," Republican Sen. John C. Danforth of Missouri said of the proliferation of attack ads. "There is a revulsion at these unethical, immoral ads," said Republican Sen. Bob Packwood of Oregon. "The most disgusting development in politics in my lifetime," said Republican Sen. Barry Goldwater of Arizona. "The sleaziest new element in politics [and maybe] the most dangerous," said a statement by former Senate majority leader Howard H. Baker, Jr. . . .

Reporters sometimes even show how they are manipulated by politicians as is illustrated in a June 15, 1985, story by John Harwood, Washington correspondent for the St. Petersburg *Times*. A portion of that story follows:

Washington—No one ever said the hounds of the White House press corps can't smell a good story. So when reporters heard that an agitated President Reagan had pounded the table during a meeting with Republican congressional leaders on Nicaragua policy, they pounced.

"Was this in the middle of his presentation?" NBC correspondent Chris Wallace asked Larry Speakes, the White House spokesman.

"Did you see it?" followed ABC's Sam Donaldson.

"Did he double up his fist or did he slap the desk with his open hand?" demanded someone else.

"How many times did he hit the desk? Just once?"

"Was he pounding for emphasis," asked Gerald Boyd of the discerning New York Times, "or was it pounding out of anger?"

"Or was there a roach on the table?" wondered Bruce Drake of the New York Daily News.

The dogged questioning in this briefing in late May produced some answers. No, eyewitness Speakes said, Reagan did not whack the table "in the middle of his presentation", it occurred during "a continuing discussion" of Congress' failure to approve aid to the *contras*, the rebels fighting against the Sandinista government in Nicaragua. He used his fist and not his palm.

On the emphasis-versus-anger question, "I would say it was emphasis," Speakes added.

Dialogue of this kind is part of a twice daily ritual of Washington politics and journalism: the White House news briefing. At 9:15 and again at noon, some of the nation's most prestigious journalists take their assigned seats in the White House press room for exchanges with Speakes that are part hostile crossfire and part comic relief, if not often momentous news.

The sessions might surprise outsiders whose view of big-time journalism is shaped by the romantic legends of Watergate, with furtive meetings in underground parking garages and damaging leaks from unidentified sources.

By and large they are desultory affairs, in which Speakes offers routine announcements and tersely conveys the official administration view on a few prominent issues. Yet on many days, these may be the only scraps of news that the White House serves up. . . .

Some reporters are trying to show the difficulty politicians can have getting enough media attention to get their ideas across. Here is a portion of an Oct. 9, 1985, Washington *Post* story reporting on that aspect of American political life:

By Sandra Sugawara

Hagerstown, Md.—Outside the Always diner on Rte. 40 here, a large marquee proclaimed "Welcome Mike Barnes," while along the front of the diner Barnes' face smiles out from posters that were hanging close to the "No Shirt, No Shoes, No Service" sign.

Inside four men in flannel shirts and caps shrugged and shook their heads when asked by a reporter if they knew who Mike Barnes is.

Few people looked up from their breakfast and none of the diners talked to Barnes as he entered for his news conference, the last in the statewide series to announce that the congressional representative from Montgomery County is seeking the Democratic nomination for the U.S. Senate.

"They've got a tough task ahead of them," said Arthur Katz, owner of the Always diner, as he shook his head and laughed.

Katz, an active member of the Democratic Party in western Maryland, said few people have heard of Mike Barnes in Hagerstown, although it is less than an hour's drive from Montgomery County.

This afternoon on the Eastern Shore things were much the same. Standing on a brick walkway next to the White & Leonard office supply company in the shopping district of Salisbury, Barnes declared his candidacy to the half-dozen local reporters who appeared.

A short time later a gray-haired woman with glasses and a shopping bag walked by and stopped to inspect a campaign banner. "What's this?" she asked. A Barnes assistant enthusiastically told her, "That man's running for Senate."

"I'm Mike Barnes," he yelled out good-naturedly at the woman as she resumed walking. "Mike who?" she said quizzically.

"Mike Barnes," he repeated. "Oh, nice to meet you, Mike Barnes," she said politely, as she briskly walked out of yelling range.

At each stop across the stage, local reporters hit Barnes with the same question: How can he win when few people in those areas know him?. . . .

Political Finances

Political campaigning is becoming an increasingly costly undertaking, not just for federal offices, but even for positions of mayor and the city council in metropolitan areas and for state legislative seats. Federal law and laws of many states require disclosure of details of campaign financing. The financial records thus available to reporters can make excellent material for interpreting political trends and possible political motivational or causational factors. The excerpts below from 1985 interpretative stories on campaign finances illustrate the possibilities of such important reporting efforts:

By Paula Schwed

Washington—A record flood of money is pouring into campaign coffers on Capitol Hill, and lobbyists say the price of persuasion is rising ever higher.

With the next election still 15 months away, an unprecedented eight senators already have at least $1 million in cash on hand. Sen. Alfonse M. D'Amato (R-N.Y.), has $3.4 million in his re-election fund so far to defend himself against a possible challenge by former Democratic vice presidential nominee Geraldine A. Ferraro.

Sen. Bob Packwood (R-Ore.), has nearly $2.7 million socked away for his 1986 re-election bid.

Others in the million-dollar club, according to a study of FED figures by Common Cause, are Robert J. Dole (R-Kan.)—$1.6 million; Arlen Specter (R-Pa.)—$1.6 million; Don Nickles (R-Okla.)—$1.4 million; Paula Hawkins (R-Fla.)—$1.3 million; Mack Mattingly (R-Ga.)—$1.2 million; and Alan Cranston (D-Calif.)—$1 million.

Some of the candiates raising money in 1985 aren't even up for election next year. Sen. Pete Wilson (R-Calif.), who doesn't face election again until 1988, already has accumulated almost $1.2 million.

The unprecedented surge in money-raising documented by Common Cause indicates more lawmakers are holding numerous fund raisers at steeper prices and earlier in the election cycle than ever.

Political consultants say a good part of the increase is concentrated in the tax-writing committees of the House and Senate, where members nearly tripled the amount of political action committee contributions they received in the first six months of this year. With overhaul of the tax code pending, some lobbyists apparently believe they cannot afford to refuse an incumbent's request for money. . . . [Newhouse News Service]

By Edward Roeder

Washington—The 99th Congress has the largest collective campaign debt in history: around $18 million.

In most cases legislators have lent their own money to their campaigns or obligated themselves to obtain loans or credit for their campaigns, making them personally liable for their debts.

As a source of money for congressional elections, such campaign debts are growing faster than PACs (political action committees), direct-mail solicitations and large gifts from donors and lobbyists.

Most members of Congress elected in recent years have loaned large amounts to their own campaigns, then raised money from PACs and lobbyists to pay themselves back. . . .

"You have members going into debt and becoming obligated to PACs almost from the moment they enter Congress," said Fred Wertheimer, president of Common Cause in a telephone interview. "When those debts are personal debts, the relationship becomes even more potentially dangerous because the contributions are not just going to pay off campaign debts, they're going to the candidates themselves."

"PACs are filling the vacuum in a way that creates enormous obligations for new members of Congress before they even have a chance to start making public policy decisions," Wertheimer said.

The debts are part of a growing trend toward deficit financing of elections, particularly by wealthy nonincumbents who have not yet established relationships with the Washington lobbyists and PACs seeking to influence national policy.

Federal election law treats loans as contributions, and limits them to $2000 from each person for each campaign. The law does not limit gifts or loans from candidates to their own campaigns. . . .   [Boston *Globe*]

By Laurie Hollman and Mark Travis

Tallahassee—Florida politicians are getting more and more of their campaign money from special interests.

Consider, if you will: In 1982, money from special interests accounted for half the contributions collected by Florida legislators running for office, according to a computer analysis conducted by the St. Petersburg Times, Miami Herald and Orlando Sentinel.

Last year, special interest contributions accounted for more than 58 percent. All told, legislators got $4.1 million of the $7.1 million they raised in 1984 from special interest groups.

If this keeps up, there may come a time when the Legislature is owned lock, stock and barrel by all the doctors, lawyers, realtors, banks and other groups who paid to put lawmakers in office.

Is that anything to worry about?

You bet it is, says Deborah Hughes, executive director of the citizens' lobbying group Common Cause.

"It's very easy to raise money from special interest," she says. "And it's very easy for that to result in legislators listening to those interests.

"They're going to remember when the phosphate industry or the citrus industry or the realtors gave the $1,000. They're going to remember, and it's going to be difficult to legislate the public interest as a result."

Not so, says Harry Landrum, a lobbyist who represents realtors and insurance companies. "One thousand dollars doesn't go anywhere in a campaign anymore," he says.

All those thousands add up, of course, but Landrum isn't troubled by that either. "There's something about money that seems to make people think evil," he says. ". . . I just don't find it that bad. . . ."   [St. Petersburg *Times*]

By Robert Barnes

How much is too much for a contributor to give a candidate?

State law says $3,000 is the limit for a gift to a candidate for governor. But for some loyal supporters of the three men who have raised the most money in their campaigns for governor, $3,000 is just the beginning.

For example, take Charles Clarkson, a Jacksonville investor who is one of three finance coordinators for his town's favorite son, Democrat Steve Pajcic. Clarkson has done his part, chipping in his $3,000, and so have his wife and brother. And in addition, eight corporations of which Clarkson is an officer also have contributed the maximum $3,000. That brings the contributions to Pajcic from the Clarksons and their companies to more than $30,000.

Pajcic's aggressive fund-raising campaign has also brought in contributions from the estate of a dead man and the trust funds of two children in Tampa. But he is not the only candidate taking advantage of the state's broadly written campaign contribution laws allowing gifts from all sorts of related corporations, partnerships and trusts. . . . [St. Petersburg _Times_]

Having a voice in choosing those who will run our governments—from city to county to state and federal levels—was one of the basic issues over which the American revolution was fought. Independent elections are a right not enjoyed by much of the world, now or throughout history. Those covering politics who are tempted to treat it as nothing more than a game or a horse race should keep those facts in mind. If money is the mother's milk of politics, as one cynic has said, it also is true that politics is the life blood of freedom and of government responsive to the will of the people, subject to orderly changes of power. Thus, the job of interpreting politics is one of the highest, most demanding tasks of reporting.

CHAPTER 17

Government

As population increases and all phases of life become more complex, "closing the gap" between governed and governors becomes a major problem in a democracy. The journalistic media have a great opportunity and responsibility to stimulate interest and participation on the part of the citizenry in governmental affairs.

Journalism's first obligation is to report fully the activities of public agencies and officials. As all public issues ultimately are decided by public opinion, the duty includes presentation of the pros and cons of all important matters and expert analysis of them. In other words, interpretative reporting and writing are essential in the field of governmental affairs.

To prepare for the role of expert in this field, aspiring interpretative reporters must be thoroughly grounded in political history and theory. They must understand the nature and purpose of all governmental agencies and the political connections and motivations of public officials and their backers. No matter how public spirited or socially conscious officeholders may be, they are candidates for re-election or reappointment; they do not cease to be politicians and become statesmen suddenly the day they take office.

Interpretative reporters who specialize in governmental news make use of all of the devices of the interpretative reporter anywhere. To place an immediate occurrence in proper perspective, they may give its historical background. Even before legislators or administrators take action, they may describe the existence of a problem. When a proposal is pending, they explain its nature, the arguments pro and con and the political alignment as regards it. They describe the functions of various offices and officers and review the records of the representatives of the people.

City Government

Closest to the average newspaper and its readers is city government. The oldest and still most prevalent type of city government is the *mayor-council plan*. Members of the city council (or board of aldermen) usually are elected from wards, one or two from a ward, their terms often staggered so that half of the members always are carryovers. The mayor is elected at large. The trend is toward nonpartisan elections rather than contests between nominees of political parties. When political parties do exist at the city level they usually are not affiliated with the national parties and have names with local significance. Once elected, in some places the mayor has almost unlimited power of appointment of subordinates; in other places the legislative board exercises tight veto power.

If the city has the *commission plan,* instead of the aldermen there are two, four or six commissioners, usually elected at large, and fewer appointive officers, the duties usually performed by them being assigned to the full-time commissioners. If the city has the *city manager plan,* the important officer is not the mayor but the city manager who performs the duties, in a small city, of many appointive officers under the mayor-council plan. Under the city manager plan, the office of the mayor, if it is retained at all, may be little more than that of presiding officer at council meetings. A city manager runs a city as a general superintendent operates a business or as a superintendent of schools directs a school system. He is chosen for his expert knowledge of municipal business affairs and is not necessarily a resident of the city at the time of appointment.

Although city hall still is a beat, large city newspapers, especially, have learned that it is impossible to rely on beat men alone to cover local government. Rather, the trend is toward so-called urban affairs reporters who cover issues that overlap governmental levels, as urban renewal, public housing, civil rights and others. Otherwise, the city hall reporter is frustrated when the urban renewal director complains about federal "red tape" and bureaucracy. The "issues" reporter must have a sound background in regulations and operational procedures of state and federal governments.

Mayor

Under the mayor-council plan, which still exists in a majority of American cities, the mayor is chosen, as is a governor of a state or a president of the United States, by popular election every two or four years. A significant change has taken place in recent years, however, in that city politics has been divorced from state and national. Except in the larger cities, candidates for mayor generally do not run as Republicans, Democrats or Socialists but as independents, their backing crossing party lines.

Wealthy businessmen and industrialists who live in the suburbs provide financial support for mayors and other city officials who promote measures, as urban renewal and zoning laws, of benefit to their financial interests. Although these pillars of the Establishment cannot vote in the city, they must take an interest in what happens within the city limits because that is where they do business. In recent years staunch diehard suburbanite Republican conservatives have been the financial supporters of strong big-city Democratic political machines, the most notorious example being Chicago under the late Mayor Daley.

As the executive head of the city, the mayor is the chief news source in the city hall. Mayors should be aware of every important occurrence in all city departments, most of them headed by persons whom they have appointed with the approval of the city council. For details, the reporter should see the department heads themselves, or subordinates in closer touch with the news at hand.

As municipal affairs become more complex and the bureaucracy grows in size, reporters' access to primary news sources becomes more limited. They have to learn to circumvent press agents alias publicity directors alias public relations counsel alias public affairs vice presidents or directors of information. So they find it smart to cultivate the good will of telephone operators, receptionists and other potential tipsters.

Because mayors are called upon to take part in most important nongovernmental activities in the city, they become potent sources of miscellaneous tips. Mayors are visited by delegations of all sorts and receive letters of complaint and inquiry, they buy the first Red Cross button, proclaim special days and weeks, welcome convention delegates, attend meetings and give speeches. Strong mayors have a program for the city that they reveal in reports, messages and remarks to the city council. Usually mayors are close to certain aldermen who introduce motions, resolutions and ordinances embodying their ideas. Unable to speak on legislative matters without leaving the presiding officer's chair, the mayor who is a leader has spokesmen in the council who present the chief executive's point of view.

City Council

Councilmen or *aldermen* usually devote only part time to their official duties, possibly doing little more than attend weekly or semimonthly meetings. Committee meetings are held council night before the general session and may be closed to reporters. Chairmen of important committees, such as finance, streets and welfare are compelled to give some attention to the aldermanic duties throughout the week, at times at least, and may be interviewed in case of important news. A typical order of business for a city council meeting follows:

Roll call by the city clerk.
Minutes of the last meeting.
Communications read by the city clerk.
Standing committees (reports called for in alphabetical order.)
Special committee reports.

Call of wards (each alderman brings up any matter pertaining to his
ward that needs council or executive attention.)
Miscellaneous business, including mayoral reports.
Adjournment.

The rules for covering a city council meeting do not differ from those
that apply to any other type of meeting. Because of the importance of council meetings, however, it frequently is necessary to write two or more stories adequately to play up different matters affecting the public. It is seldom that reporters can write a story entirely from the notes taken as motions
are made and argued and matters are referred to different committees.
Usually the reporter must verify names, the wording of motions and resolutions, the outcome of votes and other matters by consulting the city clerk
or the clerk's stenographer at the end of a meeting.

In an advance story of a council meeting, the nature of business likely
to come up should be emphasized. Experienced reporters usually can anticipate the nature of debate and the lineup of votes. They also should attempt to interpret the significance and possible aftermath of any controversial matter.

By Raul Reyes

When the new expanded Houston City Council assumed office early this
year, few city observers expected a proposed sign ordinance to become the focal
point that it now is.

The proposed ordinance has caused tempers to flare and produced shouting
matches among members of council, and split council down the middle.

The ordinance, if passed, would prohibit the construction of any new so-call
off-premise signs (billboards not at the locations of the businesses they are
advertising) and effectively outlaw portable, mobile signs, and high-voltage,
"spectacular" signs. Also, within six years, existing signs would have to conform to strict height and size requirements.

The ordinance's third and final reading is scheduled for this Wednesday and
proponents on both sides of the issue will be maneuvering for any advantage.

On Wednesday a number of possibilities can occur. It is possible that sign
industry representatives will persuade council members to defeat the ordinance. Several amendments are expected to be introduced which could dilute
the ordinance. Or, a completely new version of the ordinance—some say a
weaker version—could be introduced for consideration. Still another possibility is that the entire matter could be delayed for at least a week.

[Houston *Chronicle*]

It is the responsibility of the press to explain the nature of council actions, as well as to report them.

By Brad Frevert

Contracts totaling more than $100,000 were awarded at Monday night's
Winona City Council meeting, but the council rejected all bids on two items
and ordered specifications rewritten to allow local firms another shot at the
contract.

Five contracts totaling $101,967 for equipment and supplies were awarded with little discussion by the council. But when the bids for two 72-inch mowers for the park-recreation department were reviewed the matter was no longer cut and dried.

Six bids were received on the contract for the two mowers. One mower was to include a snowblower attachment, the other a broom. Both are to have cabs. The two lowest bids were received from local firms, Feiten Implement and Winona Fire and Power Equipment Co., but the bids did not meet specifications.

Outgoing 3rd Ward Councilwoman Jan Allen said, "If we write specifications that exclude Winona bidders, it's wrong."

Park-Recreation Director Robert Welch disagreed. "If we don't write specs for equipment to do the job, we're missing the boat," he said.

The mowers from local dealers did not have a "true zero turning radius," meaning the wheels on each side operate independently. The machine could turn in its own wheel base, Welch explained, but only by using the brake on one side, which leaves a divot on grass and makes for difficult operation on ice.

The only bid that met specifications came from Edwin Johnson Co., Minnetonka, Minn.

The council voted 6–1, with At-Large Councilman James Stoltman opposing, to reject all the bids on the mowers. The only legal way the council can keep from accepting the lowest responsible bidder is to reject all bids and readvertise.

The council then voted a number of times on a motion and related amendments—splitting 4–3—with Mayor Earl Laufenburger, 1st Ward Councilwoman Susan Edel, and 4th Ward Councilman Jerry Borzyskowski voting no— to have the bids rewritten to allow for a water-cooled engine and not restrict the specifications to one brand. One of the local firms has a machine with a water-cooled engine.

Phil Feiten, owner of Feiten Implement, was in the audience but did not address the council.

Apparently the council's action will result in the specifications for the mowers being redrawn, making them broader so as to allow more than one brand of mower to fit. [Winona (Minn.) *Daily News*]

Readers should be told how governmental actions affect them.

By Bernie Peterson

Appleton homeowners will be hit with a 20% sewer user fee increase in 1980, according to a budget of more than $3 million approved Thursday by the Common Council's Finance Committee.

Similar hikes will be felt by industrial customers, as Appleton feels the impact of full-fledged operations at the sewage treatment plant, which is close to completing a $31 million renovation started in 1976.

According to Public Works Director Robert Miller, the quarterly bill for a "typical" family of four persons using 2,800 cubic feet of water will increase from $17.64 to $21.28.

He also cited three specific industries, which he did not identify by name. [Appleton (Wis.) *Post-Crescent*]

The collective effect of governmental activity is important.

By Dean Mayer

The city of Green Bay's refusal to part with a sewer interceptor could raise the dollar figure and alter the timetable for extending sanitary sewers into a portion of the town of Scott.

It could also lead to a court battle between Green Bay and the Metropolitan Sewerage District Commission following action approved at the MSD's meeting Monday.

Green Bay owns the Scott-Bayshore sewer interceptor on the city's Northeast Side along lower Green Bay and, in some portions, in the bay.

An interceptor is a sewer line that has no direct user hook-ups but serves to connect a number of sewers.

The Scott-Bayshore interceptor currently serves only Green Bay residents. But the Metropolitan Sewerage District needs to acquire it from the city to extend sanitary sewers to a portion of Scott recently annexed by the MSD.

The annexed portion affects about 240 persons, many of whom face severe sewage problems. The segment runs south from the Wequiock School area to the town limits and includes parts of the Scott-Bayshore and Wequiock drainage basins.   [Green Bay (Wis.) *Press-Gazette*]

Disgusted reporters of legislative bodies and governmental agencies at all levels—municipal, county, state and federal—sometimes write in the spirit of the following first half of a Minneapolis *Tribune* news story:

By M. Howard Gelfand

By 8 p.m., when the show begins, there isn't an empty seat in the house. And no wonder. The most popular repertory company in the suburb of Dayton never does the same show twice.

Not that the cast—the five members of the Dayton City Council—doesn't repeat its favorite lines from time to time: lines like, "Shut up," and "You're out of order," and "What was the motion?"

This week's Monday-night meeting was such a hit that after a five-hour, three-act performance, the Dayton City Council decided to continue the drama next Monday.

When the decision was made it was 1 a.m., and the council hadn't even plowed halfway through its agenda. Still, only a few in the standing-room only audience of 50 had left.

The central issue at the meeting was whether to grant a zoning variance to Dayton developer Erland Maki. Maki wants to build an addition to a development on which he already has constructed 30 houses. The problem is that since he began the development, the council passed a law prohibiting houses on lots of less than 2½ acres. He wants to build 42 more houses on lots of half-an-acre each.

The council never did decide what to do. It seems likely, though, that some sort of compromise will be reached next week.

On one side of the issue is the mayor, Mrs. Gene Nelson. (Mrs. Nelson, 50, is also the police chief, and . . . but that's another story. More of that later.) Mrs. Nelson wanted to grant the variance, and it was partly her refusal to accept a compromise that resulted in the stalemate.

On the other side of the issue—and just about every other issue—is maverick Councilman Gerald Barfuss, a junior-high school art teacher. He contends that granting the variance would be illegal and environmentally unsound. He further says that Maki is guilty of a conflict-of-interest because Maki sits on the city's planning commission.

The scene for the bi-weekly sessions in the northwestern Hennepin County community is the Dayton City Hall, a blue metal structure that houses two caterpillar trucks but no telephone.

Mrs. Nelson conducts the meetings like a stern schoolmarm, scolding audience members and Barfuss for laughing or talking out of turn.

Barfuss, 33, is her sassy pupil, the incorrigible class wit who accepts the titters of his friends as payment for the admonishments he constantly endures.

Barfuss walked out of a special hearing on the matter held by the council last month, but before he did so he outlined his case against the variance. Mrs. Nelson told him last night:

"You have prematurely presented your opinion at the hearing and unless you've had a change of heart that can stand."

"I'm a council member," he responded, "and I intend to speak."

"I'd like to hear what the other council members have to say," she said.

City Clerk

The *city clerk,* an elective officer, might be termed the city's secretary. The clerk attends council meetings and takes minutes, receives communications addressed to the city, issues licenses (dog, beach and the like), receives nominating petitions, supervises elections and preserves all city records.

Corporation Counsel

A lawyer, the *corporation counsel* is legal adviser to the city and its representative in court in major matters. In smaller communities these duties are performed by the *city attorney,* who, in larger places, is the prosecuting attorney in criminal cases: much of the work relates to minor court cases. The title may be *city solicitor.*

Public Works

The tendency is toward consolidation, under a *commissioner of public works,* of the departments of streets, water, public buildings, local improvements and the like. If the offices are not consolidated, the commissioner of public works has charge of new construction of streets, sewers and so on, whereas the *street commissioner* has the responsibility of seeing that the streets are kept clean and in repair and usually has charge of garbage collection. The *city engineer* works under the commissioner of public works.

Finances

The elected officials are usually the mayor, city clerk and city treasurer; other city officers also may be chosen by the voters but usually are appointed by the chief executive with the approval of the council. It is the duty of the *city treasurer,* of course, to collect taxes and other moneys due the city and to pay bills upon executive order. There also may be a *city auditor,* who keeps detailed records of the city's financial setup and acts as financial adviser. Also there may be a *city collector,* who is chiefly a desk clerk to take in money, and a *purchasing agent,* in charge of buying material authorized by the city council.

The financial setup of a city requires study to be understood. The reporter struggling to comprehend it has the consolation of knowing that many city officials don't know what it's all about. State law limits the taxing power of a municipality, usually by restricting the rate at which each $100 of assessed valuation of real and personal property can be taxed for each of several different purposes, such as streets, parks and libraries. The financial operations of a city furthermore are limited by state laws, restricting the city's bonding power. A city, for instance, may be allowed to issue tax anticipation warrants to only 50 or 75 per cent of the total amount which would be realized from the collection of taxes if all were paid. Financial houses that purchase these warrants, however, may not be willing to approve the issuance of as many as the law would permit.

The reporter with a good grounding in economics and commerce courses has an advantage in comprehending municipal finance, which varies widely from community to community and state to state. The reporter should not feel embarrassed to ask some city official qualified to do so—the city treasurer, auditor or chairman of the council finance committee perhaps—to give an hour's time to outline the basic principles of the system. Once reporters have mastered the essentials they will be in a position to perform a valuable public service by making every story related to city finance a lesson in an important phase of government for tax-paying readers.

Three financial stories annually are of "sure fire" interest. They are (1) announcement by the assessor of the assessed valuations of real property, (2) announcement of tax rates and (3) passage of the city budget.

The assessment story may not be an annual one, as many places have new assessments biennially or quadrennially. There invariably follow interminable appeals to the board of tax appeals by property owners seeking reductions, and there always is at least one additional news story regarding the quantity of such suits. It is in the public interest that those who pay taxes understand the procedure by which they are levied.

When one knows the valuation placed on a piece of property and the legally adopted tax rate (the amount one will have to pay for each $100 worth of assessed valuation), taxpayers can figure out their own tax bill. Taxpayers' suits to set aside a tax rate in whole or part on the basis that some item in the city budget is improper are frequent. Usual practice in such cases, and when appeals are pending from the assessor's valuations, is to pay the tax under protest. If the protest is allowed, often after an appellate court decision, refunds are made. To postpone tax collections until after all appeals are decided would be to deprive the city of revenue.

The following is an example of a journalistic attempt to explain the tax-assessment process:

By Dolores McCahill and Lillian Williams

There was bad news for some Cook County property owners Monday when the Illinois Department of Revenue authorized an almost 7 percent increase in the multiplier used to compute real estate tax bills in the county.

The multiplier, a mathematical device designed to make property taxes equal for homeowners throughout the state, was set Monday at 1.6016, compared with last year's 1.4966.

Assuming the tax rate this year was identical to the rate a year ago, the tax on a $60,000 home in Chicago would rise to $1,386 under the new multiplier, as compared with $1,295 under the old multiplier, according to the Civic Federation, a taxpayer watchdog group.

However, the federation noted, most homeowners wouldn't have to pay the increase because the first $3,000 in increased taxes would be exempted under a new state law.

The Civic Federation said the owners of industrial plants, commercial buildings and large apartment buildings wouldn't escape the tax increase.

Cook County Assessor Thomas C. Hynes immediately criticized the boost in the multiplier as too high.

"I am concerned because this decision of the Department of Revenue could result in an unwarranted and objectionable property tax increase even without any increase in assessment or tax rates," Hynes said.

However, Hynes said most homeowners would be cushioned against the higher multiplier by the so-called homeowners' exemption, which exempts up to $3,000 in increased assessed valuation from real estate taxes. Hynes sponsored the exemption when he was president of the state Senate.

Frank Coakley, executive director of the Civil Federation, criticized the multiplier increase as "excessive and unjustified."

The tax multiplier, also known as the county equalization factor, is a mathematical formula that is supposed to make property assessments equal in each of the state's 102 counties.

The 1.6016 multiplier announced Monday was higher than the tentative multiplier of 1.5917 announced earlier. The previous figure also had drawn criticism from Hynes as too high.

Barbara Moore, of the state Revenue Department, said the higher multiplier was made necessary by "a considerable number of cutbacks" in property assessments by the Cook County Board of Tax Appeals.

She said the board granted a total of $355 million in reductions from assessments made by Hynes' office.

On April 30, Hynes' office announced that total assessments in the county stood at about $15.9 billion, up 6.4 percent from the previous year.

Tax experts said it was difficult to estimate the impact of the higher multiplier on individual tax bills because of the varying rates set by taxing agencies in the many county taxing districts.

The multiplier will be applied to 1979 tax bills payable this year. Property owners already have paid the estimated first installment on the 1979 tax bills. Bills for the second installment, which will reflect final tax rates and the impact of the multiplier, will be mailed later this summer. . . .

[Chicago *Sun-Times*]

The newspaper that takes seriously the watchdog function should keep a constant eye on the assessor's office. It should insist on learning, so as to inform the public, what rules the assessor follows in so-called special cases. Too often it seems that political friends of the administration are the chief beneficiaries. In large places the Establishment is more concerned over who controls the assessor's office than it is over most other offices. This is especially true now that the old central business districts are fighting to maintain their financial supremacy over the suburban and outlying shopping centers. Provided that property is not assessed too high, urban renewal projects may make it possible for older people, potentially good spenders, to live near the old central shopping areas. Expensive high-rise apartments often replace slums where the purchasing power of the residents was negligible. Public buildings and recreational centers also attract upper- and middle-class people.

Other Offices and Boards

The police and fire departments and the courts already have been discussed and schools will be the subject of the next section. There remain the offices of the building commissioner, commissioner of health, superintendent of playgrounds and recreation, other minor officers (sealer, purchasing agent and so forth) and the numerous official and semiofficial boards and commissions.

The first requisite of the city hall reporter is to be aware of the existence of these offices and boards and of their functions. In no two communities is the setup exactly alike, although the following are generally to be found: civil service commission, zoning board, park board, board of tax appeals, liquor control, library board and planning commission. The number of land clearance commissions, urban renewal and housing authorities is increasing. So also are various types of pollution-control agencies. There may be any of the following boards or commissions: traffic safety, local improvements, recreation, health and quite a few more.

In some cities, these groups are active and newsworthy; in others they are dormant, their existence seeming to serve little purpose other than to provide the mayor with the opportunity to appoint minor political followers to prestige positions. A live chairperson, however, can make any one of the groups a vital factor in municipal affairs. The civil service commission, for instance, can cease being the rubber stamp for political appointments that it is in many places and can become a real watchdog of the merit system by insisting that all jobs that should be filled by civil service examinations be so filled, that the spirit of civil service not be defeated through repeated temporary appointments in lieu of holding examinations to fill vacancies, that too much weight not be given in the final ratings of candidates to the "intangible" qualifications as contained in the recommendations of political friends, that dismissals from city employment be for valid reasons rather than as a result of trumped-up charges and that the conduct of examinations be absolutely honest.

Most large city newspapers now have welfare beats that take reporters to a multitude of local, state and national offices engaged in operating a variety of programs. According to Lois Wille of the Chicago *Tribune,* in recent years the welfare field has become an important offshoot of political reporting. The fact that government agencies, rather than privately supported agencies, are the biggest supplier of welfare services puts welfare in the political arena and makes it a key function of governments. Says Wille: "Groups struggling to compete with an established machine have learned to use welfare services as a means of gaining political power. For example, the movement to give free medical care to the poor through 'people's health clinics' has a dual purpose: to mobilize physicians and nurses and other volunteers to give genuine service to the poor, and to organize viable political action groups in poor communities that often have no 'clout' in city hall. And, as a result, City Hall may react by trying to sabotage the clinics. Thus, we have a good political story going as well as a welfare story."

Advises Wille: "Treat welfare reporting as the big story it is. An occasional feature story about a child whose brain has been damaged because he nibbled lead-poisoned paint crumbling from tenement walls is not enough. You have to find out who owns the building, whether city officials have enforced housing codes to repair the broken walls, who, if anyone, will treat and cure the child, and who, if anyone, will fix the house so he won't get sick again." In a dramatic and informative interpretative series that ran for several months in 1985, entitled "The American Millstone," the *Tribune* examined such issues and many more affecting the underclass of poor and jobless people in Chicago. It was first-rate reporting.

Increasingly since New Deal days federal funds have become available for local projects. With the largess have come standards that states and municipalities must observe. Perhaps the most newsworthy situations resulting from conflicts over whether federal rules are being obeyed relate to charges of discrimination against minority groups regarding employment compensated for in part by money from Washington.

Urban renewal

No aspect of local government operations in the large cities has grown more in importance in recent years than slum clearance and urban renewal. Federal, state and local funds are involved and many metropolitan centers are undergoing wholesale renovations costing into the millions or billions of dollars. Whereas a generation ago the strength of a political machine was its ability to act as a welfare and relief organization—the Tammany Hall method—today municipal political leaders feel that their strength comes mostly from their ability to remake the appearance of their bailiwicks by tearing down and rebuilding. Mayors and their planning, housing and land clearance boards trot to Washington to seek approval of "workable plans," the first step in obtaining federal funds for any program. There follow an interminable number of steps, including legislative and administrative action at three levels of government, condemnation proceedings, letting of contracts, demolition, housing of dispossessed tenants, haggling over plans for buildings, streets, the location of parks, schools and the like. Civil libertarians and human relations groups often are apprehensive over the futures of blacks and members of other minority groups who are most frequently affected by slum clearance projects dubbed "people removal."

The movement of whites to the suburbs means that the proportion of nonwhites within the big city limits is becoming greater. Political as well as social and economic upheavals result. Inevitably, despite the fear of racists, little revolutionary fervor has developed among the underdog groups.

Blacks and other minorities don't want to overthrow the system; they just want to become a part of it and benefit fairly therefrom.

So intricate and important have urban renewal and economic development become that large newspapers increasingly are hiring or training reportorial specialists to keep up with those efforts. In the '80s, developers profited from a wide range of tax breaks and other subsidies granted by local, state and federal governments to encourage economic development. As this edition of *Interpretative Reporting* went to press, few newspapers anywhere had examined whether these programs were efficient or effective.

Some critics, notably Jane Jacobs in *The Death and Life of Great American Cities,* contend that such programs are destructive of small independent businesses and are a weapon used by large commercial interests in central business districts to combat the growth of suburbs and outlying shopping centers and to preserve their economic power.

Journalistic watchdogs should probe to determine the extent to which uprooting people from old neighborhoods has created new social and economic problems. Martin Anderson wrote in *The Federal Bulldozer* that during the 1950–60 period 126,000 dwelling units in good condition were destroyed to make way for urban renewal projects that resulted in public or private commercial construction. Only 28,000 new housing units were built in the same areas.

What is the quality of the new housing to which displaced persons go? Consider health, educational and other facilities. Do dislodged families merely form new slums in other localities? Is there any hope for the small businessman? What leadership is being provided and with what success by church, political, community and other groups, including aggressive self-help councils? What effects are tax breaks and subsidies to business and real estate developers actually having on people in need of jobs, better housing and physical safety?

Schools and Education

Routine coverage of school news is not too difficult. It consists of watching such items as enrollment figures, bond issues, faculty and curriculum changes, new buildings and equipment, commencement and other programs, student activities and the like. What follows is a routine story of a board of education meeting.

Stephen Construction company of Glenwood was named last week to construct a new addition to Brookwood Junior High School, school district No. 167. The board of education awarded the contract to the company in the amount of $520,918. Base bids had been received from 13 firms on the addition.

Stephen Construction company built the original school building at Longwood, board president Weldon Nygren noted.

At the board's continued meeting on Wednesday, Superintendent Louis M. Prevost announced that 1,662 pupils presently are enrolled in the district, an increase to date of 122 students. He also reported Brookwood elementary school enrollment at 630 and pointed out that grade three had class sizes of 34 and 35 students.

Anticipated additional enrollments during the course of the present school year, due to construction of 62 more homes in the district, will require an additional mobile unit to house the students, Prevost said. He was authorized by the board to obtain bids for the additional unit to alleviate crowded conditions in the third grades.

The board discussed participation in the building program for trainable mentally handicapped of the South Cook County Education cooperative (SPEED), and endorsed the joint-agreement program. A resolution was adopted specifying that District 167 shall bear a share of the program's cost not to exceed the yield of tax levy of two percent for five years.

In other actions, the board directed Prevost to obtain a bid from Horace Mann before deciding an award of insurance coverage for all school district employes, awarded a contract for $425 to Lustig Construction company to install a window in the Longwood school kitchen and authorized purchase of 18 desks from Lowrey-McDonnel Co. for Brookwood Junior High School.

Raymond Brejcha reported that life safety construction work at Brookwood elementary school was "essentially complete."

The board also approved the hiring of personnel. Approval was granted for the employment of Mrs. Karolyn Margerum as an elementary librarian at $7,800 per year, for the hiring of a full time library clerk at Brookwood elementary school to assist the librarian and for the payment of $400 to Mrs. Janet Dart to supervise girls' extra-curricular physical education activities.

The board approved a motion to support a memorial fund drive by the PTA to be conducted in tribute to Mrs. Lucile Barron. Mrs. Barron, who taught in District 167 for more than 17 years, died September 5.

In final action, the board appointed Kappel, Barton Herr and John Dougherty to represent the school district at a meeting of the Chicago Heights planning commission. [Park Forest (Ill.) *Star*]

Helping citizens—more than 50 percent of whose local tax dollars go to maintain the public schools—understand what's going on educationally is a different matter. When the children of World War II veterans began reaching school age in the '50s, there was hardly a school district in the United States which did not find it necessary to expand its educational facilities. Nevertheless, in many places there persisted grave shortages in buildings, classrooms, equipment and teachers. By the mid '70s the war babies were graduated and many communities faced with financial problems considered closing some schools and firing some teachers. Protests by parents and others made many school board meetings much livelier than ever before.

As the total tax burden—federal, state and local—grew during the cold war period and the Vietnam War, taxpayers became reluctant to approve school bond issues and little progress was made toward obtaining financial aid from the federal government. Whereas formerly school elections aroused only meager interest, by the mid '60s exactly the opposite came to be the case in many places. Many voters, furthermore, voted against proposed bond issues or proposals to raise the tax rate as a protest against heavy taxation, most of it federal income tax, about which ordinary people lack the opportunity to express themselves directly at the polls. So they vote against any and all taxes presented to them, regardless of their own immediate best interests. The result was a decline in the quality of schools, especially in ghetto areas, and in the quality of people entering the teaching profession. Concern over the consequences of those efforts led in the mid-'80s to new education reform proposals and renewed interest by newspapers in the quality of schools in their communities. Whether the reform impetus and newspaper interest will last was an open question as this book went to press.

In addition to the basic problem of finances, other educational issues have become controversial and, consequently, newsworthy.

Integration

In the '50's the entire world knew, from news reports and pictures, of the violence connected with attempts to implement the United States Supreme Court decision that racial segregation must end in schools. In the '70s the nation's image as the citadel of democracy suffered again when violence flared in the aftermath of court orders that school children be bussed to foster integration.

In the interim there were incessant court battles and incidents to make the international headlines, as the goals of equality still eluded millions. School segregation exists in many places as a result of housing segregation. Some bond issues for the construction of new schools were defeated in the suburbs to discourage the migration of blacks and other minorities.

Most newspapers are moderate or liberal in their attitude toward the school integration issue and generally strive for strict objectivity in reporting news of the controversy. Most agree that the quality of education in ghetto schools must be vastly improved. Aroused black parents have brought pressure resulting in some benefits to all students as a result of abolition of so-called tracking systems whereby children are assigned to classes on the basis of intelligence and other tests now generally discredited. But in the late '70s and '80s, politicians responded to public pressure and backed off tough enforcement of integration laws and court decisions. While many Southern school districts were less segregated, in most large Northern cities, school segregation was worse than ever.

Religion

Public taxpayers' assistant to parochial schools became a political issue in the '70s and '80s as the schools, mostly Roman Catholic, pleaded inability to continue to exist without it and exerted pressure on Congress, state legislatures and delegates to constitutional conventions to find ways to circumvent the constitutional separation of church and state.

The parochial school crisis followed a considerable increase in their number and enrollment in the '50s and early '60s, the period of war babies. As the need for public assistance grew, traditional Catholic opposition to bond issues to support public schools diminished, and promotion of shared-time plans—whereby parochial school students take some studies in public schools—grew. Catholics also became candidates for public school boards, causing bitter campaigns in some places.

The Catholics' argument is that their children should benefit from free bus transportation and similar services and that such assistance is "child aid" and not "church aid." Catholics have traditionally fought federal aid to education programs in Congress because their schools were not included on an equal basis. The Catholic church is very secretive about its finances and wealth.

In opposition, the crying need of public schools for more funds, especially in the ghettoes and rural areas, is argued; the contention is advanced that two school systems, both financed by public funds, obviously cost more than a single system and are likely to be inferior. Furthermore, it is argued that the religious education presumably provided parochial school students is outdated and the existence of the dual system is divisive and undemocratic.

Leading the opposition to parochiaid is Americans United for Separation of Church and State, which publishes the magazine *Church and State,* and lobbies. It applauded the United States Supreme Court decisions that forbade use of school property for released-time religious instruction and outlawed prescribed prayers and bible readings in the public schools. Bound to become an increasingly crucial issue are the tax exemptions for church-owned real estate not used for religious purposes. Not only the parochial schools but municipalities are in a financial bind, and more than 50 per cent of the potentially taxable land in many of them is tax exempt.

Delinquency

From one standpoint, the history of public school education in America could be written to show how, step by step, the schools have assumed responsibilities formerly considered the prerogative of the home, factory or other institutions. Most broadening of the curriculum has resulted from outside pressure, including statues requiring the teaching of American history, the dangers of drug abuse, automobile driving and the like. As a consequence, the students' choices are limited, especially if they are among the increasing number who seek to meet college entrance requirements. Were it not for compulsory attendance laws, the already serious dropout problem would be greater. Problem children are generally ones in revolt against regimentation, real or imagined. In the huge high schools of today, potentially disturbed adolescents develop intense feelings of frustration. Despite physical education and intramural athletic programs, participation in varsity sports is limited to an increasingly smaller proportion of the student body. The same is true of other school activities, with opportunities to become officers or star performers restricted to small numbers of young people. In several large cities, post-athletic contest riots between fans representing rival schools have become serious. The emphasis that rooting alumni insist colleges and universities place on sports, especially football, sets a nationwide pattern. Exposures of widespread professional gambling activities, which include attempts, successful and otherwise, to bribe players, occur frequently.

Maintaining discipline has become a major problem at all levels. Teachers and pupils alike are the frequent victims of violence, and police and security guards sometimes are necessary to preserve order and protect property. Teachers often blame indifferent parents, who in turn say the schools are too permissive and should straighten out any disturbed youngsters.

Even if the schools solved all the problems suggested in this section, of course, the problem of juvenile delinquency would continue to exist because its social and economic causes are mostly outside, not inside, the school walls.

Exceptional Children

Counselors, psychologists, psychiatrists and other advisers deal with individual problems of disturbed and other children. Special classes or instructions exist for physically handicapped children—the deaf, dumb, blind, crippled and mentally retarded—and the gifted child is attracting more and more attention. Opinions differ as to whether children should be grouped according to potential ability, usually determined by intelligence or other tests, or achievement. On the one hand, the consciousness of being labeled superior, medium or inferior is considered disturbing to some children who will have to compete in a world of unequals. On the other hand, it is contended that fast learners are held back if instruction has to be kept at the level of the slowest. The pros and cons of this matter have been debated by educators and parents for a number of years in many parts of the country.

Standardized Teaching

Related to this issue is the controversy over the extent to which instruction should be standardized in the interest of reducing teaching burdens. Under the influence of teachers colleges during the past generation, testing of many kinds—intelligence, aptitude, achievement and so forth—has developed considerably. The results are used for placement of students in classes in the grades and high schools and by colleges and universities to determine admissions. Criticism is growing that if improperly used these tests result in "giving a student a number" at an early age and prejudice teachers' attitudes toward actual classroom work. Also, and more seriously, it is contended that the tests do not measure a student's ability to organize his thoughts, his total understanding of a topic, imagination, ingenuity or originality. Devised for fast grading by machines, the tests require the student merely to put an x after which of three of four answers to a question is correct. University professors, especially in the professional schools such as engineering, law and medicine, complain that students are coming to lack the ability to express themselves and that automatized teaching makes for conformist robots. Teaching machines, airborne television programs and the like ease the teacher problem, but often stultify initiative and creativeness.

Impetus to the "back to fundamentals" movement has come about because of growing evidence, noted by employers and others, that Johnny really can't read, or spell or compose a grammatical sentence; and that, furthermore, he has little or no knowledge of history, geography or contemporary social, economic and political problems. The protests have led to the abandonment of many fads that originated in the teachers colleges: Dick and Jane, gestalt reading, no alphabet, no syllables, New Math, and programmed learning by lesson plans mechanized by commercial companies.

Academic Freedom

There is hardly an American community that has not had a "case" involving a teacher with allegedly heretical ideas, a reading list that someone does not like or a textbook or magazine under attack by a patriotic or other pressure group. The best way to keep abreast of developments is by reading the *Newsletter on Intellectual Freedom* of the American Library Association. The situation unquestionably has made teaching less attractive to many young men and women and has contributed to the development of the strong administrator type of school superintendent. As in all other aspects of contemporary complex society, rules and regulations and forms and reports have multiplied in the school system. Teachers often complain that they are left too little time to teach and that they have increasingly less to say about the determination of educational policy. In huge school systems, not only pupils but teachers as well run the risk of becoming merely numbers.

County Government _____

The county building is what ordinarily is known as the courthouse because the county court is the most important room in it. The same building probably also contains the circuit court and possibly the municipal court, if there is one, and the court of a police magistrate or justice of the peace. There also are other offices of county officials.

County Board

Corresponding to the city council (or *board of aldermen*) of a city is the *county board,* sometimes called *board of commissioners* or *board of supervisors,* which is the governing body of a county. Its president (or chairman) may either be elected by the voters or be selected by the board members who are elected by townships or at large. In smaller places, the board may meet infrequently, as bimonthly or semiannually; in large places it meets almost as frequently as the city council. Its powers are limited because the county is primarily an agent of the state in collecting taxes, enforcing laws, recording documents, constructing and maintaining highways, providing poor relief, administering rural schools, supervising nominations and elections, guarding public health and performing other similar functions. These duties are the responsibility of the elective county officers. Here is an example of routine same-day coverage of a county board meeting:

By Roland Krekeler

The Linn County Board of Supervisors decided today to negotiate for a contract with Associated Engineers of Cedar Rapids for remodeling of the courthouse.

Supervisors Ken Schriner and Joe Rinas voted for the attempt to work out a contract with the company, which was one of several that were interviewed by the board recently. Supervisor Jean Oxley did not vote on the matter.

There was no discussion on the motion, and Mrs. Oxley did not explain her failure to vote, saying simply that she would "pass."

The supervisors plan to remodel the courthouse to provide more court space after most of the county administrative offices move to the Courthouse South, the former Penick and Ford administrative building, later this year.

Federal revenue sharing funds totaling about $1.2 million are to be spent on the remodeling over a period of several years. Purchase and remodeling of the former Penick and Ford building also is being financed with $1.1 million in revenue sharing funds.

In other action, the board:

- Received a notice from Teamsters Local 238 that a majority of persons doing administrative assistant work for the county had voted to designate the union as their bargaining representative with the county. A total of eight persons were listed in the category.

Teamsters business representative Bob Schorg said a petition has been filed with the Iowa Public Employees Relations Board to set up the bargaining unit and asked the supervisors to sign a stipulation about the makeup of the unit.

However, Assistant County Attorney Glenn Johnson advised the board that the employees appear to be confidential employees and would thus not be allowed to organize for bargaining under state law.

Schorg said that matter would be taken up by the state board.

- Gave permission for Bob Jeter of 1635 Park Towne Lane NE to set up a two-chair shoeshine stand under the shelter for bus riders at the west edge of the Witwer Building at Second Avenue and Third Street SE.

The supervisors set a 90-day limit on the endeavor, saying they wanted to review the matter since only handicapped persons and the city previously had been allowed to use space in that area.

- Officially declared that the $1 million Squaw Creek Lake bond issue last Tuesday had failed to get the 60 percent approval required. A canvass of the election showed the official vote to be 4,574 in favor and 3,485 against. The unofficial figures on election night were 4,571 in favor and 3,485 against.

Accepted with regret the resignation of Beth Reed of Cedar Rapids from the Health Center Board. She submitted her resignation for health reasons.

[Cedar Rapids (Iowa) *Gazette*]

County Clerk

Secretary of the county board, the *county clerk* also issues licenses (wedding, hunting and the like), accepts nominating papers, supervises the printing of ballots, receives election returns and keeps county records. If there is not a separate elective officer, *a register of deeds,* the clerk also records articles of incorporation, receives applications for corporation charters and keeps all other records and documents of private transactions. It is to the county clerk one writes for a copy of a birth certificate or to prove ownership of a piece of property.

Duties of the *sheriff, prosecuting attorney* and *coroner* and the operation of the county court have already been explained. The sheriff usually has an office in the county jail and the coroner may be a practicing physician or undertaker with a private office.

The *county treasurer* is an agent of the state who collects taxes that are forwarded to the state capital. The treasurer pays county employees out of funds reallocated to the county from the state and meets other obligations in similar fashion. The *county assessor* assesses the value of property in the county, prepares maps to show real estate ownership and reports his/her findings to the state.

The *county highway commissioner, county engineer, county surveyor, county superintendent of schools, county health officer, county agricultural agent* and other county officials perform duties suggested by their titles.

With the population explosion into the suburbs, county government has had to pay more attention to unincorporated areas because they inevitably are involved in problems related to water supply, transportation, recreation, policing and the like. Counties also operate poor farms, homes for the aged, jails, general hospitals, special hospitals for the tubercular, mentally ill and others, nursing homes and other institutions that cities and states also maintain. The awarding of contracts must be watched carefully as well as the quality of service performed. Illegal operations, as gambling, banned from the cities, may flourish in nearby areas.

Interpretative reporters may goad public officials to take action at the same time they enlighten readers regarding a governmental function.

By Len Kholos

Erie County commissioners' refusal to enter into regional planning with the city is not only hampering efforts to attract new industry, it is actually costing Erie taxpayers extra thousands of dollars.

In an interview with The Erie Dispatch last week, J. Cal Callahan, of Morris Knowles Inc., disclosed that the federal government is willing to pay half the cost of developing a workable program when more than one community is involved.

"The federal government feels that regional planning is the only sensible vehicle for progress, not only to promote orderly growth of an area but to prevent mistakes that will be costly in future years," Callahan said.

How is refusal of the county leaders to cooperate costing Erie taxpayers money?

Before the government will forward funds for redevelopment, whether it be for industrial or residential purposes, the communities involved must prepare a workable program.

Erie has already spent $5,000 and has contracted to spend $25,000 more to prepare this program in order to become eligible for federal planning money.

Assuming that the cost of work within the city would cost the same amount in a regional planning setup, the federal government would then have paid $15,000 plus half the costs incurred outside the city limits.

Can the individual communities in the county do anything to protect their own futures?

County Solicitor Jacob Held has told county commissioners that they cannot spend any money for planning. This came as a surprise to local government observers.

Held may also claim that the boroughs and townships are not allowed to spend money to plan for themselves.

On the other hand, the government will pay half the costs of preparing a workable program for communities of less than 25,000 population or, if they join in the city's planning efforts, half of the cost of the joint project.

We have explained why the federal government wants communities to have a workable program before it will forward funds for redevelopment. Now, here is what a workable program includes:

1. Sound local housing and health codes, enforced; an end to tolerating illegal, degrading, unhealthy substandard structures and areas.

2. A general master plan for community development, an end to haphazard planning and growth, a road map for the future.

3. Basic analysis of neighborhoods and the kind of treatment needed, an inventory of blighted and threatened areas upon which a plan of treatment to stop blight in its tracks can be developed.

4. An effective administrative organization to run the program, coordinated activity toward a common purpose by all offices and arms of the local government.

5. Financial capacity to carry out the program, utilizing local revenues and resources to build a better community for the future instead of continuing to pay heavily for past mistakes.

6. Rehousing of displaced families; expanding the supply of good housing for all income groups, through new construction and rehabilitation, so that families paying premium prices for slums can be rehoused.

7. Full-fledged, community-wide citizen participation and support, public demand for a better community and public backing for the steps needed to get it. [Erie *Dispatch*]

State, Federal Governments

Unless beginning reporters work in one of the 50 state capitals, they have little contact with state governmental offices. If a reporter is ambitious to become the state capital correspondent for a metropolitan newspaper as a possible step toward a similar position in Washington D.C., covering the city hall and local politics provides excellent training.

Although the reporter does not attend legislative sessions or visit the offices of state officers, some member of the editorial staff of the small city newspaper follows what is happening at the state capital as the local community is certain to be affected. City officials, civic organizations and other individuals and groups discuss state governmental matters and make known their opinions to their representatives in the legislature. Often it is necessary to obtain passage of a state law before it is possible for the city council to take some desired action; the corporation counsel may write such laws, which members of the legislature from the district introduce and push to adoption.

Local newspapers use, often by rewriting to play up the local angle, press releases from state offices. State representatives may write weekly newsletters to summarize legislative activities. Press associations in state capitals handle special queries from newspaper clients regarding matters of special interest. Only larger papers, however, usually are willing to maintain bureaus in the capitals, either while the legislatures are in session or at any other time. Such assignments almost invariably go to reporters with experience covering local politics and government. They can educate their paper's readership regarding the realities of lawmaking, as in the following example:

By Pete Plastrik

Lansing—The art of pork barreling, as practiced by lawmakers with the approach of Christmas, is to get the most fat with the least blood and fuss.

In a flurry of last-minute deals, lawmakers carved plenty—grants costing from $5,000 to $10 million each—out of the state budget.

Little political blood was shed. Rather than battling over who got what, lawmakers simply shoved something for just about everyone into the $770-million grants-and-transfers bill.

"We're going to give the governor a busy time with his pen (vetoing items)," quipped Rep. Dominic J. Jacobetti, D-Negaunee. Jacobetti is chairman of the House Appropriations Committee and the legislator in charge of "stuffing the stocking."

The bill had to be passed because 80 percent of the spending was the state's revenue-sharing program for local governments. That made it an easy target for pork barreling, adding on special projects for the ride through the Legislature and to the governor's desk. Biggest add-on was an estimated $40-million package for the City of Detroit.

Then came other projects, a way to deliver "goodies" to non-Detroit lawmakers and to get their votes, which were needed to approve the package.

This year, the Muskegon area almost was knocked out of the bill because Jacobetti was miffed with Sen. Phil Arthurhultz, R-Whitehall.

Jacobetti tried to squelch an $800,000 grant to build a dock at Whitehall, even though it also would go to a Democratic representative's district.

He said he had been offended by remarks belittling his power that were attributed to Arthurhultz.

"I don't like the senator from that area," Jacobetti barked before relenting.

He also was bristling over being forced to strip projects for his Upper Peninsular district from the bill because of adverse publicity.

"I'm a dammed fool for what I did. Look at what you guys put into the bill," he snapped at other lawmakers.

Then Jacobetti slipped $75,000 into the bill for study of an Olympic training site at Northern Michigan University in Marquette.

He planted $250,000 for what was called the "Sturgeon River Sloughs Wetlands Development" project.

Lawmakers and staff aides weren't sure what that project is. It would help create a sanctuary for geese on state-owned land, suggested an aide.

But Jacobetti had the answer. It went back to a $250,000 grant to build a cultural-recreation center in Pelkie which he had been forced to remove from the bill earlier: "They didn't like the name Pelkie so I changed it," he said.

The buck-grabbing didn't stop with Jacobetti.

Sen. Bill S. Huffman, D-Madison Heights, squeezed a $4-million item into the bill to buy computer terminals for the state's lottery.

Outside lawmakers plugged in $25,000 for a rape-crisis center in Saginaw; $10,000 for a halfway house for female convicts in Grand Rapids; $1 million for the Gerald R. Ford Museum; $150,000 to build a waterline across the Muskegon River; and more.

When the bill was before the legislature, little opposition surfaced.

[Saginaw (Mich.) *News*]

Of the major divisions of the federal government only one has a peacetime representative in even the smallest city or town. That is the Postal Service, which in 1970 replaced the Post Office Department, which had existed since colonial days. In moderate-sized cities, at least for a few days before April 15, representatives of the Internal Revenue Service of the Department of the Treasury may be there to assist taxpayers in making the filing deadline.

With the exceptions noted, the federal government as a local news source in a small city hardly exists. However, the lives of American citizens are more and more affected by it. Whereas the press associations and special column writers from Washington must be relied on for interpretations of major current events in the national capital, intelligent handling of much local news requires an understanding of national political issues and events.

Even in small towns, for example, a wide range of federal policies affect the elderly, the poor, farmers, small businessmen, bankers and consumers. Transportation, whether by highway, air or rail to anywhere else in the state or country is affected by the federal government. So are many other aspects of the lives of Americans, wherever they live.

State governments, of which local governments are legal creatures, have similar effects on our lives.

In cities of even medium size, and especially in the nation's great metropolitan areas, what federal and state governments do or do not do has enormous impact on people's lives and pocketbooks. Among other things, that is why interest groups of all kinds spend so much time lobbying state and federal officials and contributing so much money on the campaigns of candidates for elected statewide and federal offices. In the next chapters of this book on business, labor and agriculture, there is extended discussion of the web of connections among government, politics, money and how those connections affect citizens' pocketbooks. There are also many examples of good interpretative reporting of the intersection of politics, government and economics in our society. Be sure to take the contents of those chapters into account in thinking about how you want to do political and governmental reporting.

Case Studies

There are many ways that reporters for local newspapers can do good interpretative reporting on local, state and federal governments. Earlier in this chapter we mentioned the job that Chicago *Tribune* reporters did in 1985 examining why such a large, permanent and growing underclass of poor and jobless people is trapped in that city's ghettos. Other good examples of ambitious investigative and interpretative reporting can be found in newspaper's large and not-so-large all around the country. Just a few of them in 1985 were:

—A series of long articles that appeared in February, 1985 in the Dallas *Morning News,* showing in graphic detail the causes and consequences of the fact that much of the nation's federally subsidized public housing for the poor and elderly remain segregated, in violation of the federal government's own laws. The series was entitled "Separate and Unequal: Subsidized Housing in America" and won a Pulitzer Prize for the *Morning News.*

—The Boston *Globe* in June ran a special series of articles called "City Services: Does Boston Deliver?" Done by a team of reporters, the series found that Boston police rank in the lower third of crime solving among major U.S. cities; that almost 40 percent of the city's streets have faults that are hazardous to safe driving; that citizens give high marks to city fire protection, garbage collection and street lighting; that the city's parks and playgrounds are poorly maintained and that city government has no way to determine systematically how well it is doing at delivering services.

—During the summer, the *Southern Illinoisan* in Carbondale, a newspaper of only 30,000 circulation and with a relatively small staff of reporters to cover a large region, did an impressive series of interpretative articles on the penitentiary at Marion, the new Alcatraz of the federal penal system.

—In October, the Baltimore *Sun* did a long, one-article piece exploring the city's school system, examining the question "Are Tests a Valid Measure of School Quality?" Reporters discovered some possibly fatal flaws in school reform efforts as well as some important problems in Baltimore schools.

—In the spring, the St. Petersburg *Times* in Florida did its annual series of humanized interpretative articles about issues that would confront the state legislature in its coming annual session. The series cast considerable light on trends, problems and human living conditions. It put pressure on state lawmakers to do more than just cater to the special interest groups lobbying them.

—The Los Angeles *Times,* as did many other newspapers in the country, carried a series of articles on the growing numbers of homeless people. The series showed that economic recovery was leaving many people behind, that public health and mental health policies were ill serving millions of people. The articles examined the causes and human consequences of those shortcomings of government policies.

Such reporting goes beyond the routine coverage of press releases, news conferences and government meetings. It happens because reporters are intelligent enough, compassionate enough and energetic enough to dig for causes and for human consequences, to inquire about how government is working, whom it is serving well or poorly and why it is doing what it is doing. Such stories are done best by reporters who have read documents and talked to public officials, but who also are in close touch with ordinary people of widely varying backgrounds and stations in life.

For all the criticisms of the media from scholarly or other perspectives, many of them justified, many reporters are doing truly first-rate, intelligent, sensitive and perceptive reporting of government at the local, state and federal levels.

SPECIALIZED REPORTING (requiring particular knowledge and expertise)

There's uncertainty about the economic future and, as one result, there's pressure to stop covering negative things like pollution and hazards of the workplace. Many editors and publishers are yielding to years of hammering by corporate executives who insist the press is prejudiced.

BEN BAGDIKIAN, media critic, journalist and journalism professor

We all (religion writers) have one problem: except for some religious insiders who want us to be a daily theological journal, readers don't want more serious stuff in newspapers and weekly magazines—their attention spans aren't that long.

KENNETH BRIGGS, religion writer, New York *Times*

CHAPTER

18

Business, Finance

Business and financial news became a major growth area of American journalism in the '80s. Business sections of most metropolitan newspapers expanded in size. Business staffs were enlarged. New sources of advertising revenues opened up.

Some of the impetus for this new reporting focus of daily newspapers came from the rapid rise of the business oriented *Wall Street Journal* to its place as the largest-circulation daily newspaper in the United States. More prodding came when the nation's largest newspaper chain, Gannett, introduced *USA Today,* its national daily, with a large section devoted to business and financial news displayed with flashy modern graphics that took advantage of the potential of modern color printing processes.

Instrumental in the boom, too, was the challenge of specialized weekly and monthly business and financial publications at the national level. Magazines such as *Business Week* and *Fortune* were supplementing the daily *Wall Street Journal*'s reporting and winning growing numbers of readers and ad dollars at the national level. Television coverage, especially on cable systems, increased.

Whereas a generation ago ability to read a financial ticker tape, bank statement and annual report of a corporation was about all that was required, today's business or financial page reporter must be able to explain as well as report what goes on in this field. Several developments have made almost nonexistent the strictly local business news story. Among these have been the growth of retail chain stores that are parts of nationwide operations or conglomerates, the mushrooming of shopping centers serving more than one community, the specialization of factory production so that few products any more are manufactured all in one plant, the growth of dependency of small industries upon large ones for subcontracts and of large industries upon the federal government for orders, the increase in foreign trade and investments, multinational corporations, government aid to underdeveloped countries and other similar trends, which add up to this: what happens almost anywhere else in the world today can affect the prosperity of the small town or the large city, neither of which is any longer self-sufficient economically as it may have been in grandfather's day.

Reader interest is heightened when economic conditions affect a person's standard of living. The journalist should be expected to provide accurate information regarding the extent of a recession or inflation and analysis of important factors affecting employment, wages, prices and the like, together with the opinions of experts.

As 'Pro's' See Challenges

For a working newsperson's insight into the recent major changes in business reporting, listen to what William H. Wylie, business editor of the Pittsburgh *Press,* had to say about developments at his paper in a 1985 letter to a coauthor of this book:

Virtually every metropolitan newspaper and even some small dailies that didn't bother with business coverage before have beefed up their staffs . . . our paper has tripled the size of the financial staff. We are still a modest group of nine in the finance department, but we have our own copy desk with a staff of three and six writers, including myself. Not so long ago, I had to do it all with very little help. More important, we have emphasized quality in hiring people, insisting on several years of experience in financial coverage. This is paying off with more in-depth stories that attempt to satisfy the readers' thirst for business news.

As is the custom of most of our peers, the *Press* publishes a special financial section called Marketplace on Tuesdays. We focus on trend stories and backgrounds that are designed to appeal to consumers. The objective is to attract readers who normally do not read the finance pages.

Recently, I did a story about the strong dollar, an economic phenomenon of our time. Because there are so many people traveling abroad, we ran the story in the general news section rather than on the finance pages. Five years ago, we might not have attempted a story like this because of the time involved.

We are using a lot more charts and graphics. *USA Today* has something to do with this. Sometimes a good chart tells the story, but it can be overdone.

Suddenly, no story is complete without the opinion of two or three security analysts. While this does tend to provide balance—and it can be a useful practice—one should be careful in soliciting outside opinion. Some so-called experts aren't all they're supposed to be. One steel company chairman (Dave

Roderick at U.S. Steel) told me it bothers him to read what some Wall Street analysts have to say about his business when he knows they never sold a ton of steel in their lives. I'm not opposed to seeking outside opinion, in fact I think it's a good idea, but one should make certain of the expertise involved.

Use of anonymous sources is another touchy issue. We always try to get people to go on the record, but face it, if somebody is likely to get fired for talking, he'll clam up tighter than a drum. So you have to go off the record. But isn't it better to know the truth so you can approach the story properly? The main thing is to *know* the source and whether he is authoritative. It's one thing for a fired employee to take his wrath out on an employer. That's a matter that requires *double* and *triple* confirmation. But it's another thing for a director of a corporation to tell you the firm is going to file for Chapter 11 bankruptcy. . . . It's a matter of having confidence in your sources. If they have to be protected, so be it.

Tiring though it may be, poring over Securities and Exchange Commission filings can be rewarding. Business executives may lie to the public but the SEC has a way of making them tell the truth, even about subjects they'd prefer not to discuss. Recently, a large McKeesport-based discount chain was purchased by a Connecticut retail firm. The day the deal was sealed, the chairman of the buying firm said the merger wouldn't have any effect on employment at the acquired company. Well, you know that isn't the way mergers work. And sure enough, several weeks later in a filing with the SEC, the buyer revealed plans to close 130 stores of the chain being purchased.

Because stories are longer, we put a lot of work into our business roundup. The idea is to increase our story count. Some developments of the day are reduced to a single sentence, but at least the reader gets a bulletin. One person spends two or three hours going through the wires and local news to make sure we don't miss anything.

Ever since we launched our Marketplace section two years ago, we have been using the question-and-answer interview. We interview an authority on a particular subject and let him put the story across in his own words. It is an effective way of dealing with complicated subjects. And the readers seem to like it.

Reporting well about business and economics, however, is no easy matter, even with the increasing interest of readers in such reporting. It requires considerable expertise, energetic digging and a sensitive interpretative touch. The stakes can be high, as is revealed in the following excerpt from an article in the January-February 1983 issue of *Columbia Journalism Review* by Phillip L. Zweig. Zweig is the reporter who revealed and covered the financial troubles of a big Oklahoma City bank, Penn Square, for *American Banker* magazine.

Writing about troubled banks is like performing a high-wire balancing act: lean too far in one direction, and the reporter can cause a run on the bank, precipitating a failure that might not have occurred otherwise and opening himself to lawsuits. Lean too far in the other direction, however, and he runs the risk of misleading depositors, investors, and other "outsiders" whose only reliable source of information about the bank may be a journalistic account.

Banks are unique among business or organizations in that their existence depends totally on public trust and confidence. Consequently, there is considerably less media speculation about the health of specific banks than about airlines, steel companies, or other industrial or service firms. Indeed, the laws in some states make it illegal for anyone to speculate publicly on the condition of a banking institution, although there is debate about the constitutionality of such statutes.

So, in reporting on Penn Square, I was constantly aware of the dual dangers of being overly restrained or overly critical. Of course, it was impossible for me to know for sure last spring just how bad things were. The subject was so sensitive that few of the more than seventy-five bankers, directors, regulators, auditors, analysts, and other sources I interviewed (in addition to the bank's senior officers) were willing to speak on the record. Indeed, it was difficult to get some of them to talk even on background. Thus I felt I had to be more skeptical in evaluating the evidence they gave me on Penn Square's lending and management transgressions than I would have been if they had been willing to speak on the record.

Business and financial reporting, like all reporting, involves a reporter's subjectivity and interpretations. And because of the powerful, pervasive influence of business on American values due to the enormous economic and political power of American businesses, the more such reporting is done, the more controversy is likely to swirl around the interpretations of the human beings doing the reporting. Such controversy swelled in the '80s with the boom in business and financial reporting. It reached into the political arena, which is not surprising because politics in good measure is a process of dividing the wealth of the nation.

Business _____

Despite the trend toward localization of as much as possible of what appears on the business-financial pages, there is no business beat as such. That is, the reporter's day is not spent making regular stops comparable to those that other newsgatherers make at police headquarters, city hall and so on. Rather, covering a story for the business page means mostly investigating a tip or following up an idea, and every assignment may require making contacts with an entirely different set of news sources. Thus, the business page reporter must be fully conversant with the public and private agencies from which information of all kinds can be obtained.

Typical examples of how the business reporter obtains information would be the following: a railroad shipping clerk knew that a company that was close-mouthed was on the decline because its shippings had fallen off; a city assessor provided information on plans for a major shopping center with which the reporter confronted the developer who persuaded him to postpone publication in exchange for a promise of an exclusive story eventually; a department store official had an informed guess on the sales volume of a statewide chain that did not disclose sales or earnings; a paragraph in a routine quarterly report of a company indicated a major change in marketing plans; a union official confirmed rumors of a reduction in a plant's production as indicated by the laying off of a large number of employees. Frequently, a business reporter can persuade a company to talk even though it at first declares, "We don't want to say anything for competitive reasons," by pointing out that the reporter can dig out the information needed from Dun & Bradstreet reports or from other sources available to competitors as well as everyone else.

Even in the case of a routine story, the explanation may be the feature.

Routine News

Publicity departments of businesses, industries, trade organizations and governmental agencies voluntarily supply the bulk of the routine news in this field: new advertising campaigns; new products; stock sales; production figures; expansion programs; comments on pending legislation, court decisions or other events affecting business; big orders received; reports on dollar sales; new models; personnel changes in partnerships, corporation officials, managerial appointments, promotions, and the like; new building or other expansion plans; moves to new locations; public shows and exhibits.

Trade associations and institutes make reports covering entire industries monthly, quarterly, semiannually and annually. The weekly reports on department store sales have been taken over by the Commerce Department from the Federal Reserve banks and are regarded as a "holy index" even though they do not include suburban stores or discount houses. Federal Reserve bank monthly reports are an index to the state of the overall economy and usually include profiles of particular industries. Some university business schools issue composite weekly reports on department store sales using percentages instead of dollars. For instance, the University of Pittsburgh School of Business issues a composite weekly report on sales of three major department stores. Sales are listed for the preceding week, for the preceding four weeks, for Jan. 1 to date and for how they compare with similar periods of the previous years. There is a breakdown of downtown and suburban sales along with the total metropolitan percentages.

The monthly Federal Reserve index of industrial production gives information regarding the outputs of mines, mills and so on. Also up-to-date are the reports put out by some state agencies—for example, the _Illinois Business Review,_ a monthly summary published by the Bureau of Economic and Business Research of the College of Commerce of the University of Illinois. Its summaries are made public from two to six weeks after the data are gathered whereas government figures may be two or three months old. Similar first-rate reports are put out in Indiana and Texas, among other states.

Other good overall business and economic indicators are monthly and weekly reports on carloadings; reports of shipments of folding paper cartons; reports on shipments of collapsible metal tubes; weekly Edison Electric Institute reports on electrical production and percentage changes. Gross national product reports (dollar values of all goods and services produced) are widely used.

Monthly employment reports are economic indicators. The Pittsburgh office of the U.S. Employment Bureau, for example, covers the four-county metropolitan area. Although the figures are a month to six weeks late, they suggest how the local economy is doing. Included is the unemployment rate, the number of people looking for work, new filings for benefits, size of the local work force and a breakdown of employment in industries with a comparison to the same month in earlier years.

Because so much of this news originates or at least is announced in New York or Washington, it first reaches local newspaper offices throughout the country via press association financial wires. The business page editor must be highly selective and naturally considers the particular interests of the readers in the paper's circulation area. It is easy to clutter a page with indiscriminate use of commodity market reports—livestock market prices, dairy, poultry, produce, grains, prices of various futures, dividends and earning tables and the like.

Localization

Famine in India, an earthquake in Japan, revolution in Venezuela or the peaceful overthrow of a government anywhere can affect local business conditions. This it may do directly if an industry sells or buys abroad, or indirectly if anyone with whom it does business is directly affected.

Local opinion should be sought whenever important new legislation is proposed, introduced, passed or tested in the courts. Always the desideratum should be "How will this affect us locally?" The same is true of work stoppages from strikes or for other reasons. If the commodity is coal, oil, steel or some other basic that is used locally by manufacturers or the public, estimates of stockpiles should be obtained.

An excellent example of enterprising interpretative business reporting appeared in the Hattiesburg (Miss.) *American* in 1984. Frank Sutherland, managing editor of the 25,000-circulation paper, was intrigued by a suggestion of a World Bank official that even small newspapers without a foreign correspondent could do significant reporting about poorer nations' impact on the economics of American communities. Sutherland and the official, John Maxwell Hamilton, a former foreign correspondent, decided to see if the suggestion indeed was workable. The newspaper's staff was put to work on the subject. The result was a five-day, front-page series with sidebars. The series showed that Hattiesburg was directly affected economically by Third World countries' fates in more ways than most of its residents believed. In an article in the March 1985 *Quill* magazine in which they explained how the series was executed, Sutherland and Hamilton concluded that, "Whatever its cost, on-the-spot foreign correspondence is essential to understanding the world. Local reporting on the Third World, however, can critically complement those reports by illuminating for Americans why foreign events really do make a difference at home— why foreign news is, after all, news."

National trends and forces also influence a newspaper's local communities. Good interpretative reporting can illuminate the impact for local readers, as was illustrated in this Sept. 15, 1985, Boston *Globe* story by Peter Mancusi, the beginning of which follows:

The Great Escape, a Weymouth nightclub and restaurant, no longer has liquor liability insurance to protect it from lawsuits. The owners decided the coverage was too expensive.

Rilla Stuart, who runs a daycare service for five children in her Brighton home, is also without liability insurance. Her policy, like those of hundreds of other day-care providers across the state, has been canceled by the company.

For Environmental Solutions of Waltham, one of a dozen or so Massachusetts companies that specialize in the removal of asbestos and other toxic substances, the picture is just as bleak. The firm's liability coverage is drying up, along with a portion of its business.

Tomorrow, the general liability policy for the town of Randolph, which has been covered by the same company for 10 years and has paid more than $1 million in premiums over that time, expires. The firm has refused to renew the insurance.

The list goes on and on. A broad range of businesses and professions, many municipalities and some states are having trouble buying the liability policies that are vital to the stability of their operations and their financial well-being.

Besides covering claims for bodily injury and damages caused by products or practices, these policies pay the costs of defending and settling lawsuits. Without them, many businesses and enterprises are open to potentially crippling suits.

The nationwide insurance crisis is a byproduct of recent record losses of the property and casualty industry and, insurance executives say, of a legal system that has made it easier than ever to win huge damage awards. . . .

Trends

Ways of doing business—from the executive suite to the factory floor—have been changing rapidly in American life in the '80s. And the impact is felt in the lives of most newspaper readers in many ways, from what they do on the job to whether they or their friends, neighbors and customers have jobs or much money to spend.

The *Wall Street Journal*'s front page in-depth interpretative pieces are masterful at reporting such trends. Here is an example, the opening portion of a Jan. 12, 1983, *Journal* article by Mary Bralove:

It's 7:30 a.m. Do you know where your chief executive is?

Managers at Thermo Electron Corp., Banco Internacional de Colombia and Northwest Industries Inc. strongly suspect that at their companies, the boss is already pecking away at a computer terminal to monitor the business and, they fear, to check up on them. Depending on their boss's style, they are beneficiaries or victims of a new wrinkle in computer technology—executive information systems.

These systems, also called decision support systems, allow an executive to bypass the usual intelligence channels and quickly discover for himself how his company or industry is faring. Depending on the system's complexity and his own needs, a boss unfazed by computers can call up information as detailed as the name of a bank officer who authorized a specific loan and as general as total corporate sales.

To most people, the ability to control what the chief executive officer sees and to influence how he sees it is power. Staff people who collect, interpret and analyze executive information therefore tend to be very powerful. So are operating executives who set plans, budgets, and strategies. Executive information systems change all that.

"If you believe information is power, anytime you change the information flow you change the power structure," says John Rockart, the director of the Sloan School of Management's Center for Information Systems Research. "The CEO is potentially in a much more powerful situation. The question is how he uses it. The good guys use it with knowledge of human effects."

Put more bluntly, these systems scare the daylights out of subordinates. If the chief executive has direct access to information, staff groups and data-processing managers fear that their influence will wane, and operating heads fear a loss of autonomy, as well as microscopic scrutiny by headquarters. . . .

In today's interpretative journalism it is not just the *Wall Street Journal* that is making front-page news out of economic and business trends. Consider these portions of stories from two of the nation's most prominent general interest newspapers. They illustrate how interpretative reporting of business and economics trends is being used to inform all readers, not just those who play the stock market:

By Michael Schrage

With tones of frustration and bitterness, Robert Noyce accuses Japan of cheating its way to dominance in the semiconductor industry that he helped to create:

"There is no doubt in my mind that dumping has occurred," he said. "The prices that have been quoted are far below production costs. Clearly, there is a case of predatory pricing."

Noyce, co-inventor of the integrated circuit—the silicon chips that have spearheaded technological revolution in the information age—has an ominous view of Japan's trade practices:

"We have to recognize that this is a crisis situation. . . . The Japanese problem is far bigger than even OPEC [the Organization of Petroleum Exporting Countries] was. The dimensions of this thing are simply horrendous. I don't think people realize how big the dimensions are, and it's getting worse. . . .

Noyce's complaints against the Japanese highlight the new and harsh anti-Japan stance the U.S. semiconductor companies have taken as they've sunk deep into the industry's worst depression. Semiconductor executives in California's Silicon Valley privately wonder if their industry's survival is at stake. . . .

In August, the Semiconductor Industry Association slashed its 1985 U.S. chip market revenue estimate to $8.7 billion—fully 25 percent lower than last year's sales level of $11.6 billion. The previous estimate was a 20 percent cut.

Capacity utilization plummeted below 70 percent—the lowest rate ever measured by the SIA. Semiconductor orders for June through August fell 55 percent to $466.2 million from about $1 billion a year earlier.

What's worse, as the SIA and industry analysts have pointed out, is that semiconductor demand has plummeted even though the general economy is relatively healthy—a major deviation from historic industry patterns.

The problem is not just Japanese competition but an array of underlying forces that threaten the industry. . . .   [Washington *Post*]

By Charles Stein

In the electronics business, forecasts can change as quickly as technology. Just a few months ago the slowdown in sales plaguing high-tech industry was being described as a glich, a short-term problem that would correct itself by summer. With summer almost here, many companies have already written off 1985 as a lost cause. Uncertainty has replaced optimism in their crystal balls.

"We no longer think this is just a hiccup," said Stephen Roach, an economist with Morgan, Stanley in New York.

In part, the industry is a victim of some basic economic problems over which it has no control—a drop in capital spending and a persistently strong U.S. dollar.

At the same time, there is a feeling that some of high-tech's troubles are of the industry's own making. Certain key markets—especially personal computers and computer-aided design equipment—have become over-crowded, making a shakeout inevitable. And some customers have concluded that the industry has promised more than it has delivered.

"Past performance has fallen woefully short of expectations," said Nicholas Pagon, an analyst with Butcher & Singer, a Philadelphia investment house.

Perhaps most troubling is the growing perception that the problems will not disappear quickly. Analysts say that for the forseeable future the industry may have to learn to live with growth rates well below the spectacular pace of the last two years. The number of companies will probably shrink, they say. And small, young companies may find the going tougher. . . .   [Boston *Globe*]

Keeping readers up-to-date on business and economic trends is important even for the smaller papers, as this example from the Dec. 29, 1985, edition of the 30,000-circulation *Southern Illinoisan* in Carbondale demonstrates:

By Jim Ludwick

The New Year will bring economic improvement to Illinois, but the gains will be modest for communities grappling with serious problems that are far from solved.

Economists and business leaders expect low inflation, relatively low interest rates and good corporate profits that will help the state while fueling national recovery. But they also warn any progress will be painfully slow for Southern Illinois and areas like it, as well as for the state's farmers.

Illinois problems stem from foreign competition, a strong dollar that hurts exports and a reduction in heavy manufacturing. Downstaters should expect only glacial progress, and high unemployment could continue statewide for five to 10 years, experts contend.

They also predict:

Coal industry unemployment will remain at about 25 percent in Illinois. "We're sort of on a treadmill," says Taylor Pensoneau of the Illinois Coal Association "I do not foresee any long-range forward movement until we have some kind of compromise on acid rain and related issues limiting the market.

The planned Chrysler-Mitsubishi plant at Bloomington will provide opportunities for suppliers. But Southern Illinois and other sectors cannot count on this to fill empty plants. Some industrial sections could indefinitely remain the modern-day equivalent of ghost towns.

Houses should be easier to buy and sell next year because of the lowest mortgage rates since the 1970s. Lenders are offering adjustable-rate loans at slightly less than 10 percent. More typical are mortgages at 11 percent or 12 percent. Further reduction is expected in the first half of 1986.

Stores expect consumer spending to increase steadily. In most of Illinois, spending increased faster than the rate of inflation during 1985. Even in the hardest-hit section for retailers—northwestern Illinois—consumer spending matched inflation and Wal-Mart, a major chain of department stores, began building new outlets.

Farm problems may be bottoming out, but as many as 5 percent of the state's farmers could go broke in 1986. "Any public figure would be looking at it through rose-colored glasses if he didn't agree with that," says Larry Werries, director of the Department of Agriculture. In the most trouble are those who borrowed to buy land between 1975 and 1981, Werries says.

Small business operators will reconsider growth plans amid fear consumers may be nearing credit limits. Most will stand pat during the first quarter, predicts Donald Hughes of the National Federation of Independent Business. "Small business owners are slowing their own borrowing, cutting back on capital spending and trying to trim their inventories," he says.

Even more certain is that economic development will be central to next year's race for governor. Democratic candidate Adlai Stevenson will remind voters he unsuccessfully campaigned four years ago on promises it would be his top priority.

"Industry has been galloping out of this state during Thompson's years as governor," says Stevenson press secretary Robert Benjamin, arguing Thompson lacks the needed vision. "He is supposed to be the focus of leadership in this state. He is supposed to inspire people."

But Thompson repeatedly boasts of his economic record, contending he has improved the state's job recruitment and has helped resolve statewide labor issues.

Michael Woelffer, director of the Department of Commerce and Community Affairs, says the state is helping develop new businesses, retrain workers, lure and retain companies. He also cites Build Illinois public-works legislation that will help rebuild roads and sewers needed for commerce.

"Something everybody has to realize is our economy is going through a slow transition. I don't think there is any short-term solution."

He adds legislative changes in recent years have made the business climate "competitive with any other state." That, he says, should halt the job exodus.

Others stress lawmakers will face still more business-climate issues. Among them are the costs of liability and unemployment insurance.

Finance _____

Until they broadened their scope to include business news, most newspaper financial pages contained little more than listings of transactions on the New York and/or other stock exchanges. Such charts still are used and every editor must exercise judgment as to what items to include in the limited amount of space available. The editor does so by editing the listings transmitted by the press associations or obtained from local brokerage houses to include those securities in which local readers have the greatest interest, because they are those of outstanding nationally known companies or of companies that have plants or do business in the community. This news has potential widespread interest as is indicated by a 1983 New York Stock Exchange survey. The survey showed that about 42 million Americans owned individual stocks or stock mutual funds in U.S. corporations.

Stock Exchanges

Elementary is ability to read stock quotations. A typical line as follows:

High	Low	Stocks Div.	Sales in 100's	High	Low	Close	Net Change
$26\frac{7}{8}$	$18\frac{5}{8}$	Jeff. 1	278	$20\frac{3}{4}$	$19\frac{1}{8}$	20	$-1\frac{1}{4}$

This means that the highest price for which one share of Jefferson company stock sold during the current year was $26⅞ and the lowest price was $18⅝ per share. The "1" means that the stock paid $1 per share in dividends last year. This day, 27,800 shares were sold on the exchange, at prices which ranged from $20¾ to $19⅛ per share. The last day's sale was for $20, which was $1¼ less than the closing sale the preceding day.

This is the raw material on the basis of which the financial reporter describes the "ups" and "downs" of the market. Because most stock trading takes place in New York, what happens on the New York Stock Exchange is, of course, of primary importance. There is also the American Stock Exchange, which in 1984 had about only one-twentieth the annual volume of trading in stock shares as the New York Stock Exchange. Others are the Midwest Stock Exchange in Chicago and numerous smaller exchanges in different cities throughout the country. Before a corporation's securities can be listed on an exchange, it must register under the Securities and Exchange act of 1934, which means it must meet minimum standards of financial soundness. Then its application must be approved by the exchange's board of governors. This act does not guarantee the value of the stock but, because of the double scrutiny by federal government and exchange, listed stocks generally are considered more secure. Over-the-counter sales, however, are large, too. Such stocks, although registered with the SEC, are not listed on any exchange, so the transactions in them are conducted between brokers on behalf of their clients, away from the formal setting of a trading floor. For each OTC company there are a number of brokerage firms that act as market-makers to execute trades in its stock. The salesmen are supervised by their own self-regulatory agency, the National Association of Securities Dealers, which provides information to the press, as does the National Quotation bureau. The National Association of Securities Dealers Automated Quotations reported turnover volume of 15.1 billion shares in 1984. The NASDAQ has a computerized network of traders dealing in about 4,000 OTC companies, to provide an "instant market" for any issue on a list. OTC stocks remain a risky investment.

The advantages of a stock exchange are said to be (1) to provide financial facilities for the convenient transaction of business, (2) to maintain high standards of commercial honor and integrity and (3) to promote just and equitable principles of trade and business. This is decidedly not to say, however, that most other trading is unethical, dangerous or otherwise undesirable. As a matter of fact, the extent to which what happens on the large exchanges actually reflects the state of the nation's financial health is a matter of considerable dispute. Certain it is that the exchanges respond emotionally to political and other news and the prices of particular securities may fluctuate widely within a matter of hours or minutes. Some skeptics say that a great deal of what goes on is just dignified or aristo-cratic gambling.

Seeking Explanations

Whatever the truth may be, financial reporters have the responsibility to seek reasons for important fluctuations. They are aided in the first instance by the Dow Jones & Co. ticker-tape news service, which continuously transmits selected stock quotations, late news on the grain, meat and foreign markets, sometimes baseball scores and top national and international news. Its most important function is reporting business news of all kinds and its averages of what stocks are doing in accumulated major categories—industrials, railroads, utilities—are widely accepted as indices of the financial market as a whole. The purpose of the Dow Jones averages—industrial, railroad and utility—is "to give a general rather than precise idea of the fluctuation in the securities markets and to provide a basis of historical continuity of security price movements."

Of the stock averages compiled by Dow Jones, the industrial average is the one investors most carefully scrutinize. It is made up of the stock prices of 30 industrial corporations, generally regarded as "blue chips."

The average goes back to Jan. 2, 1897, when Dow Jones began publication of the daily average closing prices of 12 active stocks. This continued until 1916 when the list was increased to 20. This list was expanded to 30 in 1928.

The stocks in the average now and then are changed to stay modern. Otherwise, the average today might have a buggy whip manufacturer among its components. Substitutions also are made when a stock becomes too inactive or its price is too low.

In recent years there has been a great increase in stock market trading by institutional investors, such as pension funds, profit-sharing plans, unions, religious groups, insurance companies, banks, governments, universities, mutual funds etc. Institutions overshadow the individual investor on Wall Street. Institutions are by far the most active traders.

Because institutions buy and sell large blocks of stocks, they have a tremendous impact on prices. At the same time, because of the size of their trades, they lack the flexibility of an individual. This inhibits their ability to move quickly. Sometimes their holdings of a given stock are so large that they get locked in. This was apparent in the recession of '75 when bank trust departments suffered huge losses in the value of their portfolios as stock prices tumbled.

Case Study in Interpreting Stock Market

Sharp changes in the buying and selling of stocks and bonds can become major news, requiring considerable interpretation so as to make the stories comprehensible to readers who do not follow the markets closely, yet also satisfying to the reader with more intense interest and detailed knowledge.

One such day was Jan. 9, 1986, when the Dow Jones industrial average dropped more than it ever had before in its history. In smaller communities where there were no major financial institutions, stories about the drop did not generally get as prominent display as they did in larger cities. But in such large cities as New York and Chicago, the plunge in the Dow Jones average was big news indeed, receiving prominent display on the front pages of newspapers in stories aimed at the general reader with even more detailed interpretative reporting on the business pages to supplement the front page coverage.

Following are two stories that show the considerable degree of interpretation required to make the stories aimed at general readers understandable. To do such stories without interpretation and have them be understandable to the reader who is not a financial expert would be impossible. But even with the interpretation by skilled, knowledgeable writers, the stories still may not be fully clear to the ordinary reader. That is no small matter, because the state of the economy at the time was of great interest to all Americans. It is important to their decisions in regard to their family budget. It is central to most public policy debates and political campaigns from the municipal and county to the state and federal levels.

Here is how the Chicago _Sun-Times_ wrote its lead story on page one:

> After months of buoyant optimism that pushed the stock market to one record high after another, a selling frenzy described by one analyst as a "panic" hit Wall Street yesterday in late trading.
>
> The Dow Jones Industrial Average plummeted 39.10 points—most of it in the last hour—for its biggest one-day drop in history.
>
> "In the last half-hour, there was a selling panic," Chicago analyst Jim Oberweis of Oberwies Securities said.
>
> The Dow retreated from an advance that carried the market to record highs Tuesday. The index surpassed the previous record point drop of 38.33 points on Oct. 28, 1929.
>
> In percentage terms, however, the slide came nowhere near the proportions of the 1929 stock market crash that preceded the Great Depression. Yesterday's drop amounted to 2.5 percent of the DOW, while the single-day loss in 1929 was nearly 13 percent.
>
> Investors started the day enthusiastic over Tuesday's showing. But amid the general enthusiasm, howls of dismay were heard from traders who had bid up Pennzoil shares Tuesday on false rumors that Texaco would acquire the company. Pennzoil, which jumped 19¾ Tuesday, fell back 8½ to 74½ yesterday.
>
> "Disappointment about the interest rate outlook" triggered the broad decline, said David Hale of Chicago's Kemper Financial Services. "It was the bond market that pulled the stock market down."
>
> Accelerating the sell-off, said Salomon Bros. chief economist Henry Kaufman, known on Wall Street as Dr. Doom, was the fact that the Federal Reserve Board was unlikely to make a further cut in the "discount rate" that banks are charged for borrowing federal funds. Rumors of another interest rate cut had fueled the market in recent weeks.

While Chicago has a major stock exchange and is home to some of the nation's largest, most powerful industries and financial institutions, a smaller proportion of the Chicago _Sun-Times_ readers than of some other metropolitan newspapers are deeply knowledgeable about the stock market. That sense of the newspaper's audience probably indicates why the *Sun-Times* main story on the Dow Jones decline is written with a minimum of detail and jargon as well as concisely.

By contrast, consider the story that appeared on page one in the New York *Times*. The *Times* operates in the city that is the financial center of the world. The paper has a national as well as local audience. To some extent, it competes not just against the other daily newspapers in the New York metropolitan area, but also with the *Wall Street Journal*. Moreover, a much greater proportion of its readers than those of the Chicago *Sun-Times* have a detailed knowledge of the workings and language of the financial markets. Thus, the New York *Times* front page story, an excerpt of which follows, was longer and interpreted differently than did the counterpart piece carried by the *Sun-Times* in Chicago:

A sudden shift in Wall Street's thinking about interest rates sent a shock wave through the stock market yesterday that lowered the Dow Jones industrial average by 39 points, its biggest fall ever. . . .

Traders said the Government's release of unemployment data for December—which showed that the national jobless rate had dipped to 6.8 percent and that 320,000 more Americans were employed—jarred the credit markets and precipitated a sharp rise in rates. When interest rates rise, stock prices tend to decline. . . .

The drop in equities may have also reflected worries that the approval yesterday by the Federal Reserve of restrictions on "junk bonds" may dampen corporate takeovers. Such bonds, which are below investment grade, are a popular financing device in many buyouts. . . .

Ironically, it was the gain in jobs, an indication that the United States economy was becoming more robust, that bothered investors. December's rise of 320,000 in employed Americans compared with an increase of just 180,000 in November.

Seeing the employment numbers, analysts decided that the economy was too strong for the Federal Reserve to be prompted into lowering interest rates further. Under current conditions, the central bank may be reluctant to bring borrowing costs any lower, fearing that the economy might become overstimulated and inflation could result. . . .

More than half of the Dow's loss came in the final hour. At that time, traders said the price of stock index futures, a means for betting on the general movement of the stock market rather than on individual stocks, became so cheap that they attracted hordes of professional buyers.

Those buyers, engaging in a complex strategy, sold stocks, especially blue chips. This second half of an arbitrage process, which has been occurring with more regularity over the last year, has in the past resulted in some of the widest price swings on the stock market. . . .

It is instructive about the challenges facing economics reporters to consider not only the relatively obvious differences in the approach of the stories in the Chicago and New York newspapers, but also to analyze the similarities.

The writers for both papers felt compelled to try to explain the causes of what had happened and to consider some of the consequences. That probably was because it was obvious that readers, whose lives already had been buffeted by the sometimes harsh economic forces of the '80s, would want to understand what was going on in that January of 1986. The writers also were surely aware that most readers would have some kind of recollection of the 1929 stock market crash, and therefore wonder if they were living through a repeat of it. Further, the writers had to consider the kinds of effects a panic resulting from that recollection could have on the financial situation nationally, including on savings institutions, and, thus, to be cautious in interpreting what had happened on Wall Street the day before.

The writers also had to consider what they could assume most readers would know about economic terms and what needed explaining. Even the New York *Times,* for example, knowing that its readers were more economically literate than those of most papers, felt compelled to explain such terms as junk bonds and stock index futures and to attempt to explain in a sentence the workings of the Federal Reserve Bank.

Furthermore, the writers for each paper had to face up to the problem of using language that could be understood by readers without expertise, yet would not be so generalized as to make more expert readers feel as if they were not getting a detailed enough explanation.

Such are the challenges facing those reporters trying to interpret financial events in the United States, where such stories sometimes are vitally important to the entire society, including people who are not insiders, yet from which the insiders need and want to learn more than the less expert reader might to able to understand. It is a problem not only in financial reporting, but also in business reporting, which we considered in the previous section of this chapter and in reporting of labor, agriculture, science, the environment and religion, which will be examined in ensuing chapters. And it is a challenge particularly for those trying to do general assignment reporting about government, politics and the legal system, because those institutions of democracy and representative government increasingly are dealing with issues of economics, science, technology and religion that vitally affect all our lives. The challenges are further complicated by the fact that widely disparate interests are at stake, both private and public, and there are intense philosophical and moral differences of opinion as to how to resolve competing differences of opinions. Reporters cannot avoid interpreting if they are to make clear the news they are reporting. But their interpretations are bound to be challenged as unfair or biased by those who have personal stakes in the clash of interests going on in our society now, as it has since before the nation's birth.

Historical Overview ──

To understand the challenges facing contemporary business reporters, it is important to recall the historical context. Today's reporting is practiced against the backdrop of a long, tangled historical record, which reporters ignore at their peril.

Prelude to the '80s

Throughout American history, information about business and economics has been crucial to many people and linked to political issues.

The American revolution was fought in the name of a concept of human liberty deriving from the rights leading spokesmen of the rebellion claimed to find in natural laws. But many of the grievances were economic in origin, linked to the economic self interests of influential, wealthy colonists. After the revolution was solidified, debate sharpened in America over many economic issues that were rooted in regional social structures and political priorities. Eventually, it took a bloody civil war to prevent the secession of the Southern states, whose leaders feared that their economic system with its roots in slavery would be obliterated by Northern control of the federal government.

That war was followed by 75 years of great technological advances in American society, the rise of giant industries and large cities, waves of immigration, increasing control of local business by national financiers, a movement of population from farms to cities and a long struggle by exploited workers to unionize and to humanize their working conditions. It was an exciting, dramatic time, marked by great fortunes made by a few, the growth of a professional middle class and also by great suffering and poverty among millions. The economic changes and their human consequences quickly became part of the nation's political agenda, in small communities and large cities, in state legislatures and in Washington. "The business of the United States is business," said President Calvin Coolidge in the '20s, when the country seemed to have reached the height of prosperity.

Then came the Great Depression of the '30s when the bottom fell out of the boom, when hope for a time seemed, like prosperity, a thing of the past and when social, economic and political revolution seemed to many close at hand.

For the next 50 years, the national government grew in power, gradually doing more and more to regulate the economy and set the rules for relations between business ownership and workers, between consumers and small investors. State and local governments also assumed more of a regulatory role in relation to business owners. The political debate became not so much whether government should simply subsidize business without regulating it, but rather which level of government should enact what kind of regulations to subsidize and protect whom. The Great Depression, however, was not fully ended until World War II. After the war the United States enjoyed a brief two decades as a prosperous, but psychologically insecure arbiter of global affairs, presiding over the break-up of the old colonial empires as it expanded its nuclear arsenal, but worrying all the while about the challenges to its economy and values from the Soviet Union and China.

Yet despite the controversial Vietnam conflict, which reflected the American fear of the Soviet Union and China, it turned out that the greatest challenge to American economic supremacy and stability came from other places abroad.

In the '70s, the oil-producing nations of the Mideast and Africa were able to disrupt the U.S. economy, increasingly dependent on oil imports, in pursuit of their own economic and political goals. Japan and West Germany, among America's military adversaries in World War II and its diplomatic allies afterward, developed particularly strong modern economies that challenged the United States not only for global markets, but increasingly for markets on the soil of the United States, much as American corporations were more intensively converting themselves to multinational corporations operating decisively in many other nations' economies, often with the cooperation of American foreign policy, military and national security agency decision makers.

Enter the '80s

That is the history and state of affairs that set the stage for the issues with which today's business and financial reporters as well as their political counterparts are grappling in the '80s.

Since 1976 both major national political parties have been struggling for a new mix of policies that will appeal to voters, serve the interests of American corporations abroad, make the nation somehow feel secure in a world where many nations possess nuclear weapons capable of causing once undreamed-of devastation, meet foreign competition in markets that were once unchallenged American preserves, create jobs for Americans able to work and pay the bills for the social welfare programs vital to decent lives for so many Americans. Democratic President Jimmy Carter won the presidency in 1976 probably largely because of many Americans' revulsion to the whole mix of events that became known as Watergate. But by the end of his presidency in 1980, double-digit inflation and the new economic threats from the Middle East to America's supremacy abroad had changed American concerns again.

Republican Ronald Reagan, projecting supreme self-confidence, won power with promises to set the American economy right again. A Democratically controlled Congress went along with most of his programs, which promptly hurtled the nation into its worst economic difficulties since the Great Depression. But a mild and geographically spotty recovery began just in time for his run for a second term, which he won by the widest margin in America history, causing the Democrats to question even harder their economic policies and to search for new ones. As Reagan became more and more a lame duck president, Republicans, too, began arguing anew over their party's economic policies.

The Media Role

After the dramatic days of the muckrakers of early twentieth-century journalism, American daily newspapers tended to cover business and financial news mainly on jargon-laden business pages, depending on news releases and occasionally puffy profiles on business leaders, relying largely on deadly dull government statistical reports about various economic indicators. Television, the main source of news today for most Americans, had even more trouble with economic news covered that way, because that kind of news did not lend itself to easy understanding or to easy-to-obtain visuals. So long as the economy was doing well, most people had little interest in trying to penetrate the media fog surrounding economic and financial news. And the media for the most part showed little interest in making such news more relevant, more interesting or more compelling.

Vietnam, Watergate and the troubled Middle East became the focus of the most heavily played breaking and in-depth reporting of the '60s and the early '70s. The focus did not shift to economic news until the oil-producing nations began to raise prices during the '70s. The effects spread quickly through the economy, affecting businesses and consumers alike, sending inflation soaring into double digits, accompanied by rising economic competition across a global front from the industrial accomplishments of several revived Western European and Asian economies. Many suspected that the multinational oil companies were manipulating prices for their own benefit. The suspicion quickly spread to the policies of other major international and national companies, who increasingly were closing plants, laying off workers and resisting wage-hike demands.

All of this created a great deal more interest among readers in reporting about economic, business and financial matters. It also produced much more critical reporting than business executives were accustomed to receiving. The critical reporting was stimulated in part by politicians trying to figure out how to make economic policy and in part by those politicians blaming major corporations for what had gone wrong.

As the critical reporting about business increased, businesses saw that to defend themselves and present their point of view, they would have to respond to reporters' questions of a kind that had seldom if ever been asked in modern times. Many of the executives felt threatened and abused by the questions reporters were asking, sometimes perhaps because the reporters' questions were all too incisive, but sometimes because the questions were from reporters without much understanding of the complexities of modern economics, business and finance as well as inexperienced in dealing with stories about corporations and their activities.

But if there were frustrations for businessmen and for publishers, there were frustrations for reporters, too. Open-meeting laws did not provide access to the basic decisions of businesses or labor unions as they did to governmental bodies. While government officials could keep few kinds of documents secret from reporters unless they could stretch the interpretation of national security (which many of them did), businessmen could and did keep many important documents secret in the name of protecting themselves from their competitors. What's more, business was a vast new beat for the nation's reporters, most of whom worked for newspapers already hard-pressed to gather and edit all the news they were covering before the business-news boom hit. Nor was it easy to pry more money out of publishers to add reporters to newspaper staffs, because publishers were worried about how to finance the changeover to an entirely new production process of composing and printing their papers as well as about how to protect themselves against a new kind of competition for readers' time and advertisers' money. Few reporters or editors, moreover, had much experience in covering, understanding or writing clearly about economic, business and financial news in the new ways because there had been so little reporting of such news in the recent past. They had educated themselves mainly about other things. It was time consuming to dig out information about business and finance, and difficult to write it clearly for general audiences. Key business decision makers, unlike politicians, had no built-in incentive to talk to reporters. Many of those executives were far less comfortable with reporters, providing few good, concise quotes of the kind that make for audience interest and understanding.

Perhaps most crucial, businessmen were supported in their point of view and public image by huge advertising campaigns in all the media. Those ads portrayed corporations, their products and their employees in the most psychologically positive ways that modern marketing experts could devise. Corporations thus had a propaganda apparatus behind them and their policies, an apparatus with powerful influence on public mind-sets. They had an independent access to reporters' audiences. It was the kind of apparatus American politicians dream of, but that few except perhaps the president can command. Modern corporate advertising for decades had skillfully used the powerful advertising medium of television in ways to make consuming the products and services of large corporations almost a national religion. While readers suspected corporations, those readers also were the target of lavishly financed efforts to condition them to adore corporations and corporate products. A reporter's story pointing out something not so nice about a corporate leader's policy can be perceived by readers as David casting a stone at Goliath, but also as saying the reader's church is doing nasty and unpleasant things. And so readers are torn, frustrated and confused, too.

Current Controversies _____

The criticisms of modern business reporting can be fleshed out by examining the point of view of some of the participants in the heated controversies surrounding it. Implicit in these views are practical guidelines for doing effective business reporting in modern journalism.

Consider, for example, the view of Jane Bryant Quinn, who writes a nationally syndicated personal-finance column for newspapers around the country as well as reporting on business issues for network television and national magazines. Responding to criticisms of President Reagan and the business community that too much reporting about economic issues is negative, she told a _Washington Journalism Review_ writer in 1982: "I would guess that if Mr. Reagan's policy were working better, the reporting would not be so negative. I mean, what does he want me to write? That he's balanced the budget. Is it negative reporting to write that he hasn't balanced the budget when he said he was going to . . . There are all kinds of economics reporters taking all kinds of angles. The press is simply reporting what is out there. What is out there is a vastly unbalanced budget, very high real interest rates, increased business bankruptcies and a lot of people are scared as hell."

It is one thing for a writer to disagree sharply with a president of the United States. It is something else again for a newspaper publisher, editor or reporter to feel the wrath of readers and advertisers close to home, where the criticism, if widespread enough, can take a toll on circulation and anger advertisers whose dollars contribute to the profits and pay the newspaper's bills as well as reporters' salaries.

In May 1984, for example, *Editor & Publisher* magazine reported that a five-part series in the Fort Worth *Star-Telegram,* which publishes in the highly competitive Fort Worth-Dallas area, led hundreds of readers to cancel their subscriptions in the midst of a wave of angry phone calls and letters to the editor. The series detailed design flaws in a helicopter rotor manufactured by a large employer in the newspaper's circulation area. The design flaw, the series maintained, had resulted in the deaths of more than 200 servicemen in helicopter accidents related to the design flaw. The company's public relations director did not dispute the accuracy of the series, but rather argued that the reporter's interpretation was too sensational. The company did not deliberately make the design error, he said, and had alerted the army of it as soon as it was discovered, suggesting how the flaw easily could be remedied. Mail ran 10-1 against the series, many readers contending that the stories, even if true, should not have been published because they would create among readers an antibusiness, anticommunity sentiment. One union representing 600 employees of the firm asked members to cancel subscriptions. The stories should have blamed the army, some angry residents said. The reporter said the army blamed the company. The publisher supported his reporter. The reporter said, "We wrote a story because we saw in autopsy reports that people were dying for 'unknown reasons' from a machine that's built in our circulation area."

Such criticisms of business reporting are frequent where newspapers go beyond routine stories written largely from businesses' press releases. The Des Moines *Register,* for example, has heard considerable grousing from powerful business executives in Iowa for its practice of seeking out and publishing information about the compensation paid to those executives. The statewide newspaper, a frequent Pulitzer prize winner and regarded as one of the best newspapers in the nation, went to great pains to explain the workings of its agribusiness-related economy for readers with aggressive, thorough interpretative reporting. Business executives claimed their salaries were their own business and that publication of them would negatively influence their wage bargaining with employees.

Despite such outcries against business reporting that goes beyond press releases, recent studies show that such reporting still is not typical of the bulk of business and financial news. In 1981, for example, a unit of the J. Walter Thomson advertising agency conducted a survey of business editors located in the nation's 100 largest markets. The responses indicated that on the larger newspapers press releases from businesses seldom were used as anything more than tips that might be explored independently by reporters. On smaller papers, the survey said, editors indicated they relied much more heavily on the use of press releases from businesses to fill their business pages.

A more comprehensive, systematic study by A. Kent MacDougall, staff writer for the Los Angeles *Times* and son of one of this book's coauthors, reached a similar conclusion. His study, first published in the *Times* and later as a book entitled "90 Seconds to Tell It All," solicited and examined complaints about business reporting from scores of major corporations and business associations. Those complaints then were matched against press and television coverage of business. Among his findings were that much of the negative business news found in the media was initiated by government agencies in the course of their enforcement of laws affecting businesses. That news was the result of reporters covering government, not of investigative reporting about business launched by reporters themselves. He concluded that the toughest, most independently conceived reporting of negative news about corporations is to be found not in newspapers and magazines or on radio and television, but rather in books, many of them done by independent writers such as Rachel Carson, Jessica Mitford and Ralph Nader. Corporations can live with such reporting, he speculated, because books have relatively small circulation. Corporations are more concerned, he argued, when negative news about them gets on network television, although he found that there is little economic news of any kind, relatively speaking, on either network or local TV news shows. Newspapers have a higher portion of negative than positive business news on their front pages, he found, but he also discovered that business and financial sections contain much more positive or neutral than negative news.

MacDougall cautioned businessmen to resign themselves to an increasingly public interest in what they do given the extent to which what they do depends on their own extensive efforts to influence government policies and given the impact of what they do on the lives of every American. He also aptly warned that journalists need to be sure that their skepticism about business does not turn into cynicism. A newspaper's reputation for fairness, he said, is an even more precious asset than its reputation for completeness.

Toward Better Coverage _____

So, if higher quality economics and business reporting is to get done, how is it going to happen? How can the reporters of today and tomorrow do a more thorough, more fair, more compassionate kind of reporting? How can they do more reporting that serves not only those who are prospering under our economic system, but also those still trapped in poverty and unemployment? How can they do more reporting that protects the capacity of business to compete, but that also protects the public health and safety and the natural environment upon which all life, human and otherwise, depends? Especially given the rapid spread of technology in all its forms across the globe, the question, put in those ways, is no easy one.

A healthy starting point would be for reporters, businessmen, government officials and citizens to ask questions from a larger frame of reference, to consider more than the immediate pressures on them in the daily decisions they make. The fruits of modern science and technology, distributed by businesses, have created the basis for what prosperity and convenience there is in our lives and, for those of who can afford such things, it is considerable prosperity and convenience. But the fruits can have bitter, sometimes deadly aftereffects. We are learning that from such events as the near disaster at the Three Mile Island nuclear power plant, the actual disasters at Love Canal, Cape Canaveral, Bhopal and Chernobyl, from the diseases of black lung and brown lung, from such phenomena as acid rain and a threatened ozone layer, from dead lakes and polluted skies, from a food chain laden with substances whose long term effects on human life, human bodies and human minds we know little. In dealing with that science and technology, we need to learn, all of us, a little skepticism and a lot of humility, if we wish to protect not just the future of generations living today, but the future of the species and the planet.

The Business Viewpoint

In an unprecedented outpouring of criticism about the work of reporters in recent years, the American business community has called for more informed and balanced reporting of business and economic news. It has launched its own campaign of advertising and education on behalf of that cause.

Through foundations it has helped in the establishment of programs in business-journalism education at the Columbia University Graduate School of Journalism and at the University of Missouri, among others. It has organized a variety of mid-career workshops and educational programs. It has done so on the not misplaced assumption that economics and business issues should get more attention in coverage of political campaigns and of the work of politicians elected to government offices at local, state and national levels.

Reporters would be foolish not to take advantage of all these and other opportunities, about which more information can be obtained from writing to such business-sponsored organizations as the Institute for Applied Economics at 370 Lexington Ave. in New York City or The Media Institute at 3017 M St. in Washington, D.C.

Young people preparing for careers in business and financial journalism should heed carefully the criticism of today's economic reporting. They should avoid cynicism about business. They should take advantage of every opportunity to improve their educational background about the complex events they will report, perhaps through journalism courses or majors in business journalism, perhaps by going on to get an advanced degree in business or economics, certainly by trying to keep abreast of the main business publications and books available from any reasonably good library. Such efforts are essential on a continuing basis for anyone who wants to interpret the important, complicated subject matter with which today's reporters deal.

Would-be reporters should do those things, however, in an independent, skeptical manner, with an eye toward neither shining nor dimming the image of big business, but rather toward giving newspaper readers and citizens the information they need to make their decisions about all the many varied matters relating to the role of business institutions in our society. There are ways they can do that beyond those suggested by today's many vociferous spokesmen for the business point of view.

Other Viewpoints

Let's consider some of those alternative possibilities.

Jerry Heaster, business and financial editor of the Kansas City (Mo.) *Star,* is a former president of the American Society of Business and Economics Writers. In the April 1984 issue of *The Editor's Exchange,* a publication of the American Society of Newspaper Editors, Heaster said that the key to improved business and economics reporting is "attracting good people and encouraging them to dedicate a good portion of their careers to learning this very difficult specialty." Good salaries and specialized training are essential to such an effort, he said. Among his other sensible suggestions were:

—Aim for coverage with wide appeal. Don't sacrifice the interests of average consumers, savers and investors to coverage of routine business details.

—Regard business and financial journalism as economics journalism. Cover the political aspects of economic issues because, among other reasons, government spending at city, state and national levels consumes 40 percent of the gross national product.

—Emphasize substance over style. Making a section graphically attractive should be a matter of concern, but visual slickness is no substitute for reporters covering economic stories in ways relevant and intelligible to readers.

—Don't just report economic developments, but put them in perspective through analysis and even commentary.

—Encourage editors to consider putting the most important economics stories done locally in the general news section, including on page one, rather than burying them in the business and financial section, where they may escape the attention of many general readers.

Other good advice different from the sort given by spokesmen for the business community was offered by liberal economist Lester Thurow, a Massachusetts Institute of Technology professor who also writes a column for *Newsweek* magazine. In a *Washington Journalism Review* article, Thurow said that there should be more in-depth reporting of the long-term economic trends reflected in statistics. In his view, there is, for example, too much reporting of day-to-day stock-price fluctuations and not enough reporting on the larger forces shaping the fluctuation trends over much longer time periods. Similarly, he argued, too much economic news reporting focuses on what is happening to public policies in Washington and to the financial markets in New York, and not enough on what is happening to the industrial economy elsewhere and why it is happening. Thurow closed with a plea for more interpretation in business reporting. He put his case this way: "There is the problem of establishing appropriate background to help readers and viewers understand the significance of various news events. How many readers of articles containing the monthly release of unemployment figures know that in May only 4.0 million out of the 10.5 million unemployed workers were receiving unemployment insurance? Not many. How many readers of the various articles confidently citing the fraction of the GNP devoted to defense in the Soviet Union know the great uncertainty that actually surrounds that number? Probably very few. How can a reader judge the public policy significance of such numbers without that crucial information?"

It is concern for such a larger perspective rather than just making businesses look good, concern that news about economics is understandable not just to specialists but also the general reader, who also is a citizen, that leads such publications as the *Wall Street Journal* to want their reporters above all to be good researchers and good writers. A front page headline in *Journal*'s 1983 Educational Edition, which explained how the paper works, asserted: "Writing a Good Story Counts More than a Degree in Economics." The *Journal* wants reporters who can go beyond press releases and statistics. It wants reporters who can dig out news that public relations departments may not want reported, understand it, write it clearly and put it into perspective so that readers also can understand it. And it wants reporters who can do that more quickly than the average economics professor works.

Here's a down-to-earth human example of the *Journal*'s approach in action:

Paul Ingrassia, a former colleague of one of the coauthors of this book, was up against a stern reporting challenge in early 1985 when the savings-and-loan industry of Ohio suddenly was teetering on the brink of collapse as the result of originally little noticed business events in Florida. Ingrassia, then the *Journal*'s Cleveland bureau chief (he was promoted later to head of the Detroit bureau), told a reporting class at the University of Illinois subsequently about the quick response his staff had to make. Ingrassia conceded that the story had originally caught him off guard, that he had not realized, even after nearly 10 years of covering business and financial news, how fast events could move in such a story. He said it gave him a new appreciation for the accounts of the Great Depression he had read as a student, but never had really experienced firsthand. Nevertheless, Ingrassia and his staff quickly got on top of the story and within a week were able to pull together, with the help of other Journal staffers around the country, a story explaining what had happened, the causes, the political and governmental responses and the implications. The story ran for several columns in the *Journal*. Ingrassia admitted that it was not a perfect job, only the best that some reasonably knowledgeable people could do at the time with the help of the *Journal*'s far-flung reporting and editing network.

How do journalists such as Ingrassia learn to do such reporting and writing as well as they do? How do they prepare themselves for work that requires a keen traditional news instinct, scholarly insights and analytical capacities, the ability to write clear, interesting prose about complex, not always inherently exciting subjects and to do it all with deadline pressures hanging over their heads?

There are many backgrounds from which good business reporters emerge, but among the best is the path Ingrassia followed. He got a good liberal arts and sciences education at the University of Illinois during his under-graduate years. Seventy-five percent of his course work was in those fields. The rest of his undergraduate education was in public-affairs journalism courses, some taught by scholars who had studied and thought carefully about the role of the media in society, often in ways critical of media per-formance. But most of his journalism coursework focused on accurate, clear reporting and newswriting, in courses taught by teachers who themselves were experienced journalists with high expectations for the craft. Those teachers required students to do a lot of journalism under tight deadline pressure and judged students' work by high standards. In addition, Ingrassia did considerable work for the *Daily Illini,* the campus newspaper.

When he graduated, Ingrassia didn't immediately gather up his clips, his grade-point average and go showing them off along with his credentials as a former *Daily Illini* editor-in-chief, all of which probably would have landed him a job. Instead, he studied for a master's degree in labor and industrial relations at the University of Wisconsin at Madison, aiming not to become a specialist in that field, but rather to become a more knowl-edgeable, more thoughtful journalist.

Then, rather than seeking a job at a major metropolitan daily, he took a position with a group of downstate Illinois newspapers well regarded for both breaking news and interpretative coverage of state issues, trends and problems. He paid his dues there for more than two years, polishing his skills as a reporter and writer and learning how government works before applying to the *Wall Street Journal.* By then, he had developed a good background knowledge not only of economics, but also of the problems of reporting in the confusion of the real world of politics and of daily journal-ism. He had obtained a mature feel for what good editors expect of report-ers and of what general readers need if they are to understand the affairs of their time.

Ingrassia kept learning as a reporter in the *Journal's* Chicago bureau. Eventually he was promoted to bureau chief in Cleveland and then in De-troit. He retains his enthusiasm for the challenges of journalism, both of the breaking news and in-depth variety. He keeps striving to do reporting himself and to improve his own writing even as he now supervises other reporters. And he keeps working to further educate himself across a wide range of public affairs issues, both by reading and doing reporting out in the real world beyond his office.

Covering Politics of Economics

Improved economics reporting will require a clear understanding of the historical conjunction of political and economic issues in American life. That understanding too often is neglected. A 142-page study of press cov-erage of economic issues in the 1980 presidential campaign, for example, found serious inadequacies. The study was done at American University under the direction of Nick Kotz, an adjunct faculty member of the school's National Center for Business and Economic Communications and a prize-winning reporter himself. Said Kotz: "Too often, we found, the story is covered as if it were a fire, a ball game or just another speech at the National Press Club." The report itself said that "political reporters cover what the candidates say and the mechanics of politics; economic reporters cover what the economic experts say and the mechanics of the economy." Too often, the report added, the two specialists end up neglecting to relate the findings of the political reporters to those of the economics reporters, despite the fact that the interrelationships are increasingly important for readers and voters to understand.

In his 1982 campaign for governor of Illinois, Adlai Stevenson had observations similar to Kotz's. Stevenson offered a series of complex economic-position papers as the basis of his campaign, but in a state deep in recession, found little media interest in them. Instead, Stevenson charged, reporters seemed more interested in his opponent's implications that the Stevensonian personality was wimpish. There was little prominent media reporting of Stevenson's economic proposals and what there was did not get played nearly as prominently as the horse-race aspects of the campaign, which Stevenson lost by only 5,000 votes.

What About the Poor?

Another shortcoming of today's economics reporting was pointed out forcefully in 1985 by Thomas Winship, then the only recently retired long-time editor of the Boston *Globe*. Winship's criticism struck to the heart of the segregation of economics and political news practiced by too many newspapers, both large and small, in the United States. Speaking to the National Association of Black Journalists annual meeting in Baltimore, Winship said, "The time has come for a new generation of social concern and activism in journalism. And it is my fervent hope that black reporters and editors will be in the vanguard of it." Winship made clear that he was not urging editorials posing as news coverage, but rather "covering more stories of more social importance." He said he is rooting for "more urgent, more constant attention to our people in deep trouble, and for less superficial, show-biz reporting." He contended that "the biggest domestic time-bomb story of the decade is going uncovered." "You know what it is," he added. "It is the worsening plight of the underclass—black, Hispanic and white—in our large cities. None of us have grasped the full dimensions of this crisis. This bottom strata of society is worse off today than it was in the wake of the civil rights movement, and all the affirmative action programs allowed only the present middle class minorities to walk through the doors to a better life . . . The leadership of our public and private institutions is damn near as lily white and male as it was after the first show of concern 20 years ago. We simply are not examining with adequate vigor the broad rising problems of the poor, much less exploring avenues of possible solution."

Winship would not have found much consolation in a lecture delivered earlier that year by Mervin Aubespin, then president of the National Association of Black Journalists and a veteran reporter and editor for the Louisville *Courier Journal.* Speaking to journalism students at the University of Illinois, Aubespin pointed out that there still are far fewer minority reporters and editors in American journalism than their proportion in the populations of the nation or of most metropolitan areas. Progress in recruiting such journalists, moreover, has levelled off, Aubespin said. The doors are open, but not many newspapers are doing enough to get more minority would-be journalists prepared to appear at those doors, he charged. Aubespin also had some friendly criticism of today's journalism students, the reporters of tomorrow. He said that from his frequent travels to journalism schools around the country in recent years, he had found students to be smarter and better prepared than those of previous generations. But he said that they were preoccupied with being career successes and showed few signs of social conscience, few signs of heart for the poor, few signs of outrage that many Americans still were without the reality of equal economic opportunities. He said he was speaking not just of white students, but also of minority students.

Winship and Aubespin, in short, like the American University study and the complaints of candidate Stevenson, were conceding that interpretation is an inevitable part of all reporting, including the reporting of the economy and business, whether at the national, state or local level. And they were saying that the problem may not be one of too much unfair reporting of business, but of narrow range and shallow depth of interpretative reporting about business and the economy.

And so, the effective interpretative reporter of economic issues of the future will need not just to prepare himself or herself with knowledge about technical matters of corporate life, financial markets and conservative economic theory. Such reporters also will need to learn about the life of those who are not sharing in the goodies, about the literature of the dispossessed and about theories of political economy and social justice from the left of the political and academic spectrum.

Tips on Preparing Yourself

To meet the challenge of the kind of broad-gauged economics reporting American society needs, the beginning reporter should study economics, American business and labor history, sociology, political science and philosophy. For those planning to specialize in business or financial reporting, graduate study in business or economics is something to consider seriously.

Meanwhile, many economists of both the right and the left are writing good books that offer informative, understandable analyses of economic issues as well as proposals for dealing with those issues. Those books are readily available in public libraries. Journals of political opinion also offer good reporting and commentary on economic issues. Among them are *National Review, Human Events, Commentary, The New Republic, The Nation, The Progressive* and *In These Times.* Keep in mind, though, that economists and economics journalists all have their own value systems and philosophies, and that writings by those who are called economics experts are no more objective or less subjective than those of other journalists.

A good overview of the contemporary business journalism scene, containing a concise bibliography of books that can add to understanding of business and finance institutions, is Don Gussow's, *The New Business Journalism* (Harcourt, Brace, Jovanovich, 1984). The book includes a guide, including addresses, to universities offering courses in business journalism.

A textbook-like volume on business and economics journalism with much useful basic information about the workings of American corporate and financial institutions is *Reporting on Business and the Economy,* edited by L. M. Kohlmeir (Prentice-Hall, 1981).

Useful in understanding many business concepts and terms and for learning to analyze the workings and finances of major American corporations is a clearly written booklet available from offices of Merrill Lynch Pierce Fenner & Smith, a nationwide brokerage firm, called *How to Read a Financial Report.*

Exceptionally helpful in educating yourself about business and financial institutions is the *Manual of Corporate Investigation: Building Profiles of Public and Private Companies.* It was first published in 1978, then revised in 1981 by the Food and Beverage Trades Department of the American Federation of Labor-Congress of Industrial Organizations. The booklet contains an extensive guide of how to research almost any economics issue—national, state or local. It includes a thorough, easy-to-understand glossary of economic terms. It can be obtained by writing the AFL-CIO, or asking your library to obtain a copy.

The August 1985 issue of *Washington Journalism Review* devoted almost half of its contents to an excellent listing of many important business news sources. The issue also carried several articles on how reporters can add to their knowledge and background for the long-term as well as more quickly find specific facts they need about business and financial matters.

For access to reporting and research with a more muckraking slant than is normally provided by such more well known business publications as the *Wall Street Journal, Business Week* and *Fortune,* there is *Multinational Monitor,* one of Ralph Nader's publications. Its address is P.O. Box 19405, Washington, D.C. 20036.

As examples of thoughtful, introspective reporting about the effects of economic policies on poor people, three excellent books are James Agee's classic, *Let Us Now Praise Famous Men,* and the more recent, *I Hear Them Calling My Name,* by Chet Fuller and *All the Lonely People* by Robert Hamburger.

Probably the most helpful government source of information about American companies is the Securities and Exchange Commission. All companies that meet requirements for selling their stock to the public file detailed reports with the SEC. The most basic of these documents is called a 10-K annual report, which often has more information in it than the annual reports companies send to stockholders. This information is available to the general public. The SEC address is SEC, Public Reference Room,

500 N. Capitol St., Washington D.C. 20549. The phone number is 202-523-5506.

For historical background on Wall Street, corporate finance and the SEC, Joel Seligman's *The Transformation of Wall Street* is excellent.

Finally, a 300-page paperback, *How to Find Information About Companies,* published by Washington Researchers (918 16th St. N.W., Washington, D.C. 20006) has much practical information helpful in doing economics writing. It includes advice on how to read the 10-K statements available from the SEC.

Economics reporting is complicated and requires a good deal of technical knowledge. Information is not always easy to come by or interpret. But with the help of sources like those cited in this chapter and determination to learn, even nonspecialists can do more good economics reporting and understand more than they might think they can. The secret is not to be daunted by the jargon or the unfamiliar terrain, but rather to be determined to find out what you want to know and not to be afraid to ask questions until you understand.

Economics issues are not just the territory of the folks on the business staff. Indeed, it is impossible to cover government, politics or other aspects of a community adequately even on a general basis without finding good written and human sources on business and economics issues and using those sources so thoroughly that you eventually begin to feel comfortable with them.

19

Labor

As the previous chapter discussed, there is a boom in business news coverage in American journalism. But for whatever reasons, labor reporting is not getting the same attention from newspaper people. And, while business officials appear to have scored some points in their calls for a more sympathetic coverage of their enterprises, other voices calling for better coverage of both ordinary working men and women and the unemployed have had much less effect on contemporary newspaper reporting.

Concerned Critics

In the March-April 1984 edition of the *Columbia Journalism Review*, Michael Hoyt observed in an overview on labor reporting in the United States that, "While business coverage is on the rise, labor journalism is declining in quantity and quality." After a detailed review of trends in labor journalism, he concluded: "Business journalism is a growth industry these days, and the public's economic sophistication has gained. But too much of this expanded coverage of the struggle for profit leaves out labor's perspective. The balance is off. To correct it will take more reporting on work, more economics and the human touch."

The nation's major journals of media studies and the publications of various journalism organizations, however, contain fewer such criticisms and less worrying about coverage of labor than they do about coverage of business. Seldom do you read the kind of critique offered by Thomas Littlewood, head of the journalism department at the University of Illinois and a reporter before that for more than two decades for the Chicago *Sun-Times*. In the August 1981 edition of *Illinois Issues* magazine, Littlewood detailed the stereotypes that Illinois print and broadcast reporters had conveyed in their stories of a labor union rally held that summer in Springfield, the state capital. After the rally, Gov. James Thompson invited the unionists to the lawn of his executive mansion for a speech. He served beer in kegs. The workers were rallying to protect themselves from anti-labor bills, including some that were aimed at reducing workman's compensation and unemployment compensation benefits in a state suffering through its biggest recession since the '30s. Littlewood wrote of the coverage:

> This typecasting of trade unionists as beer guzzling slobs who can't talk right is typical of news media that are generally indifferent to routine news of labor relations. "The press made light of it," remarked state AFL-CIO president Robert Gibson. "They made it look like the only reason we came down here was to drink the governor's beer."
>
> If there is an anti-union bias in some Illinois newspapers, it should come as no surprise. This year for the first time the board of the Illinois Press Association, representing Illinois newspapers, ordered its lobbyists to work against unemployment and worker's compensation benefits "that the IPA said are sapping the economic vitality of our state and undermining the confidence of business people." IPA President William Schroeder, publisher of the Grayslake *Times* and other Lakeland newspapers, blamed the "union dominated General Assembly" for the benefit abuses. He urged fellow editors and publishers to use "both your support and 'press power' in the legislative battle." Heretofore the IPA confined its legislative interests to matters directly affecting newspaper operations.
>
> Not many of the bigger papers can afford to be blatantly anti-labor in the news columns, though. The problem is more subtle than that. All reporters approach their assignments with certain pictures in their heads. They know their editors have pictures in *their* heads, too, and that the story is more likely to land on page one if it doesn't jar these preconceived images too severely. Besides, not many of today's college educated journalists know very many blue-collar workers anymore. The opportunities for misunderstanding are everywhere.

In a letter to the editor in the Oct. 27, 1979 issue of *Editor & Publisher* magazine, reprinted here with the permission of that trade journal of American daily newspapers, journalism professor Howard Ziff of the University of Massachusetts, put the phenomena that Hoyt and Littlewood were discussing in a larger cultural, historical context. Young, would-be reporters of business, labor and political news should think deeply about what Ziff had to say because he is discussing nothing less than the forces that shape the kind of questions journalists will ask or not ask in their reporting, and thus the kind of answers they will report or not report to readers and citizens.

Ziff, a former reporter and city editor for the Chicago *Daily News,* wrote:

> I have no hard statistics in front of me but I'd like to suggest that the most important change taking place in American journalism, and in journalism here in Massachusetts is a very human one. . . .

A little history might put this into perspective. In the period after the Civil War, the nature of newspaper work changed. Industrialization hit the press and with it the technical possibility for mass circulation newspapers, the amassing of mass circulation audiences in the big cities, and the financial resources of mass circulation through advertising. The new ad revenues came through the revolution in marketing, the birth of department stores, chain stores, regional and national trademarks, and the decline in do-it and grow-it yourself self-sufficiency among the consumers.

The press became industrialized. And below the top-level editorial job, journalists began to become a city-room working class. By the turn-of-the-century, newspapering was widely thought of as something not a gentleman would go into. It was no longer a lower-level doorway to literature, it was a lower-level white-collar job. There were exceptions, of course. But, reporters were being increasingly drawn from the upward-bound, mobile sons and daughters of the Irish, Jewish, Swedish and other immigrants. Or migrants from the American countryside, or the South, who crowded to the big, industrial cities of the North. Thus, the great reporters of two decades ago, the ones I looked up to and tried to emulate as a young man were men like Meyer Berger of the New York *Times* or Ed Lahey of the Chicago *Daily News*. If I remember correctly Berger's father was an immigrant tailor, and Lahey's a railroad brakeman.

Things began to change around the second world war—thanks to the romance of war correspondency, the growing strength of the reporters' union that had improved working conditions and pay in the city room, and the widening public perception of the power of mass media which lent prestige to media jobs. In the past decade, however, even more college-trained sons and daughters of the middle class have gone into journalism—thanks to their perception of the impact of the reporter on shaping national history in Viet Nam or Watergate. And the idea that here was a job where you would get something done and have some influence. Of course, broadcast executives and publishers have welcomed this development. Clearly a better educated, higher-toned kind of person was entering the city room. I would like, however, to sound a note of caution. The earlier generation of reporters had something which the new, college-trained one lacked. They simply were closer to everyday life, as it is lived in the street, the farms, the ghettos and the barrios.

They had to cross over from the other side of the tracks and the really good ones never forgot that.

As a journalism professor I'm responsible for helping produce the new, better educated crop of journalists. But I often worry that my students have a touch of class, at the expense of losing the common touch.

What Hoyt, Littlewood and Ziff all are driving at, in one way or another, is the possibility that the boom in business reporting and the changing backgrounds of reporters in modern journalism may, for all the contrary complaints from the business community, be skewing American economics reporting to unbalanced interpretations and blind spots in question asking. They fear that much economic reporting is not so much probusiness or antilabor as insensitive to the blue-collar workers, lower-paid white collar workers and the poor. The possibility should give pause to editors and reporters genuinely concerned about the credibility of the American press and its capacity to give society all the information it needs to act on the many issues of economics that come together at the junction of economics reporting with political and governmental reporting.

Labor History ——

The history of the American labor movement is as much that of a struggle of different ideologies for supremacy within the ranks of labor itself as it is that of a fight between capital and labor for a share of the national wealth and income. In its early stages, organized labor was handicapped because of its control by leaders of foreign birth or influence and by native-born intellectuals who lacked experience as workers and were discredited further because of their known unorthodoxy in other fields.

In the middle half of the nineteenth century, labor was too prone to espouse every new economic or political theory that offered a possible step upward on the economic scale. Agrarianism, idealistic cooperative plans, greenbackism, the single tax, free silver and syndicalism were among the ideologies with sizable followings within the ranks of labor. Until the American Federation of Labor emerged as powerful under the leadership of Samuel Gompers late in the nineteenth century, organized labor hardly was an important permanent factor in American economic and political life.

The AFL's triumph over the Knights of Labor represented a victory for the craft union as opposed to industrial unionism, of the "aristocracy of labor" idea over the "one big union" idea. Gompers and his followers believed in working within the existent capitalisitc system, seeking through unions of craftsmen organized horizontally throughout industry as a whole to obtain the maximum benefits for the workers. The Knights of Labor had admitted unskilled as well as skilled workers.

Craft unionism remained dominant until 1936, when, under the leadership of John L. Lewis, the Committee (later called Congress) for Industrial Organization began to organize many large basic industries, such as mining, automobile and steel, in which large masses of unskilled workers were not eligible for membership in craft unions. CIO unions were industrial or vertical unions because membership in them was all-inclusive within a given plant in which there might conceivably be numerous craft unions.

In December 1955 the two big organizations reunited as the AFL-CIO, but today many old units of each, at all levels from international to local, still operate with virtually unchanged autonomy. Also still independent are the railway brotherhoods and a number of other large groups, as the miners, automobile workers and teamsters and several mavericks that were expelled as leftwing by the CIO in 1949.

In mid-1985, only about 17 percent of the entire labor force belonged to unions. Little progress ever has been made among white-collar (professional) workers whose proportion of the total labor force continues to grow with the expanding service industries and as mechanical automation reduces the ranks of the blue-collar workers.

In the United States, with its rugged indivualistic frontier tradition and its democratic open-class social system, there never has developed strong class consciousness at any social or economic level. Despite considerable demagoguery to the contrary, socialistic and communistic ideas never have attracted any appreciable number of rank-and-file working people. There is no political labor party as in many other parts of the world, and organized political activity by labor always has been condemned by the rest of the populace. Because of the absence of class consciousness as a welding force, there has developed a strong type of labor leader in the United States. Whoever happens to be the leading labor figure at any time is bound to be considered a "public enemy" by antilaborites. Regardless of the justice involved, this has been true of such widely different labor leaders as Samuel Gompers, Eugene V. Debs, John L. Lewis, Sidney Hillman, Walter Reuther, James Petrillo, Harry Bridges and James Hoffa.

Because organized labor never has enjoyed the confidence of an appreciable proportion of the American people, it has been faced with the problem of avoiding mistakes that are more costly to it than similar ones are to any other segment of the population.

Labor Laws

The National Labor Relations (Wagner) Act of 1935 was called labor's Magna Charta because it gave federal protection to the right to organize and bargain collectively and to maintain closed shops. It was mostly under its protection that the CIO became established in the mass production industries, using the Gandhi-inspired sit-down strike strategy. The Taft-Hartley Act of 1947 and the Landrum-Griffin Act of 1959 considerably weakened the basic law from the standpoint of labor. Among other things, the former outlawed jurisdictional strikes (one union against another), secondary boycotts, strikes for union recognition and the closed shop except by majority vote of eligible employees. It also stipulated penalties for breaches of contract and boycotts by unions, forbade union contributions and expenditures for political purposes, forbade the services of the National Labor Relations Board to unions that had not registered financial information and filed anticommunist affidavits for all its officers, allowed employers greater freedom to campaign against unionization of workers and gave the federal government the power to use injunctions to compel an eighty-day "cooling-off" period before a strike could be called.

The Labor-Management Reporting and Disclosures Act (Landrum-Griffin) of 1959 was aimed at racketeering labor officials. Among other things it required annual reports from all unions, gave the FBI power to enter cases of suspected violations, forbade "hot cargo" pacts in which a trucker, for example, refused to handle cargo from another trucker if the union labeled it forbidden, outlawed extortion or blackmail publicity, outlawed "sweetheart" contracts between unscrupulous employers and labor leaders and provided for secret ballots in union elections, machinery for ousting crooked union officials and a ban against arbitrary raising of union dues or assessments without a secret ballot vote of the members.

In the '50s, several states adopted "right-to-work" laws. These were a misnomer for open shop as they guaranteed nobody a job and were intended to forbid closed union shops under any circumstance. In its behalf, organized labor increased agitation for the guaranteed annual wage, shorter work week and strengthening or recovery of old protections as maintenance of membership clauses, seniority rights, check-off systems for the collection of dues, pensions, longer vacations, profit-sharing plans and the like.

Covering Labor Disputes

Newspaper headlines naturally emphasize conflict, especially when it leads to strikes and lockouts. It is easy to overlook the fact that the overwhelming majority of labor-management affairs are conducted harmoniously and that there are numerous companies and even entire industries in which there has been little or no trouble for decades or longer. Labor leaders have traditionally charged that when matters do come to a point of conflict, the press underplays its side of the story. During the day-to-day account of a strike, the issues causing it often become lost because of the emphasis given incidents of violence, hotheaded statements by leaders and human interest accounts.

Any major or protracted shutdown in any part of the American economy today would be catastrophic throughout the entire economy, so interrelated have all parts of it become. How to preserve the dignity and freedom to work or not to work guaranteed all Americans in the Thirteenth Amendment to the Constitution and at the same time protect the general population from the repercussions of a strike or lockout is a major social political issue. Through its Mediation and Conciliation Service, the federal government investigates and provides leadership in bringing about peaceful settlements of most disputes. During periods of comparatively full production of high prosperity, as during a cold war with huge government expenditures to keep industry going, its successes far outnumber its failures. Organized labor has been a leading supporter of American foreign policy, and local unions prod employers to be diligent in seeking government contracts to maintain full employment. If such a condition continues, organized labor may be expected to devote more of its energy to worker education programs and to plans to assist workers to participate in community affairs.

The main obstacle to such activities continues to be the matter of racial integration. AFL unions were discriminatory against blacks and the unskilled foreign born. The CIO forbade such discrimination, but unions must share with management the blame for the slowness with which blacks and members of other minority groups obtain equal job opportunities, are upgraded and are given seniority rights, not to mention managerial positions.

In covering many aspects of labor news, the reporter should consider the public interest as paramount.

Aside from the same reader interest that exists regarding the activities of any large organization, in the cases of unions there is the additional public interest as regards their control and policies.

By Andrew Ross

Concord—After working for months without a salary contract, some of the 1,500 central county employees of Chevron USA are shaking their fists in anger—not at management, but at the union.

It's the union of Oil, Chemical and Atomic Workers, which has been representing workers in Concord, Walnut Creek and other West Coast cities since May of this year.

Six months and 28 negotiating sessions later, the effectiveness of OCAW is being questioned by workers in Contra Costa County.

The employees complain that they haven't had a pay increase for 18 months and inflation is quickly catching up with them.

The company has offered an 8 percent wage increase retroactive to February of this year, but the union repeatedly has turned down the offer because of dissatisfaction over contract language pertaining to items such as grievance procedures and merit raises.

"From what we've seen, we're happy with the company offer," said Mike Hicks, a head computer operator at the Chevron accounting center in Concord. The Pittsburg resident said his feelings are representative of a majority of workers locally.

But Bob Boudreau, the international representative for the OCAW, dismisses their complaints.

"The company has been playing games in Concord," he said. "Since becoming the bargaining agent, I haven't had a chance to talk to the these people."

"They (the company) sit them down and tell them what they want to tell them," he added. "They have a captive audience."

Ironically, though, local employees say they are being held captive by the union. Employees like Mike Hicks don't belong to the OCAW, but the union does represent them at the bargaining table.

Boudreau won't say how many of the 2,700 hundred Chevron employees he represents belong to OCAW. He says it's a significant number, but concedes "the degree of organization here is not as high as everywhere else. . . ."

[Contra Costa *Times*]

The press also must keep an eye on the corruption that unfortunately has infested some unions or union locals, including penetration by organized crime. This kind of reporting is illustrated in the following lead to a much longer May 22, 1985, story by Stanley Penn in the *Wall Street Journal,* a paper that, despite its business orientation, often carries important interpretative reporting about labor:

Federal agents who recorded the conversation say the voice is that of Frank Manzo, whom they identify as the overseer of the Lucchese organized crime family's interests at Kennedy International Airport.

He is talking with associates about an air-freight operator who has been unwilling to pay money to avoid labor trouble. "I don't think he knows in his heart," says the man identified as Mr. Manzo, "that we run the airport."

Rule they do, federal prosecutors say. For five years now, lawyers and investigators in a federal organized-crime strike force have been trying to break the mob's grip on the thriving air-freight business at the nation's biggest air-cargo terminal. Some 200 air-freight companies last year handled cargo valued at more than $50 billion at the airport. Moving the cargo to and from the airport requires truckers. Where there are truckers, there is the Teamsters union. And the federal agents assert, where there are Teamsters at Kennedy, there are mobsters.

Kennedy Airport has become a classic example of collusion between organized crime and a powerful union to put the squeeze on business. The cost is ultimately borne by all businessmen who ship by air—and by their customers. . . .

Even wildcat strikes are not spontaneous but the culmination of incidents to which workers object. A sharp labor reporter has inklings of increasing discontent long before there is overt action. It usually is in the public interest to acquaint readers of impending trouble.

One of the Black Hawk County Health Department employees active in a movement to oust Rita Burbridge, county health director, from her job has been fired by Mrs. Burbridge.

The discharge of Karen Blonigan, a public health nurse, occurred the same day the County Board of Supervisors received notice that the employees have taken steps to form a union.

Mrs. Burbridge's attorney, David Nagle, Tuesday denied Ms. Blonigan's claim she was fired because she was helping to line up support for a union. Instead, he said it had to do with the health director's "obligation to maintain an ongoing department."

Nagle refused to be more specific and Mrs. Burbridge declined comment.

[Waterloo (Iowa) *Courier*]

Too often strikes or lockouts occur to the inconvenience of the public. Too often the issues in the dispute are not clear and frequently if the strike continues for a protracted period, the issues are forgotten.

By Ted Schafers

As at least five construction sites in St. Louis were padlocked Friday, contractors accused union officials of the striking equipment operators of demanding "pure and simple featherbedding" to make work for themselves "at the expense of other AFL-CIO building trade unions."

And "the real long-term issue," said Edward L. Calcaterra, president of the Associated General Contractors of St. Louis, "is the survival of the AFL-CIO unions and contractors."

Negotiations entered the 51st day Friday.

It was the strongest management statement issued since the beginning of the strike, which has idled nearly 10,000 union building tradesmen in St. Louis and the eastern half of Missouri. It came as federal mediator Beryl Carlew announced that a tentative agreement had been reached early Friday between the Associated Contractors of Missouri, an outstate organization, and Local 513 of the International Union of Operating Engineers. The agreement involves mainly road construction.

Among the five St. Louis projects on which construction work was halted were the $20 million, 22-story addition to the Marriott's Pavilion Hotel downtown, a visitor's center for Missouri Botanical Gardens, and hospital additions to St. Luke's West, Incarnate World and St. Mary's Medical Center.

"It simply is no longer feasible to work the other trades," said Tom Dollar, senior vice president of construction for McCarthy Brothers Constructions, whose contracts are involved.

The latest agreement is similar to that reached last weekend with Fred Weber, Inc., also a road builder. If accepted by both parties, it could open road jobs to as many as 1,000 members of Local 513 outstate. Carlew emphasized the agreement will not become operative until both the union and management groups ratify it, and said he expected that to begin next week.

Union officials could not be reached for comment Friday.

The Globe-Democrat learned the latest agreement provides for a wage increase of $4.15 an hour spread over three years on work in St. Charles, Jefferson, Franklin, Lincoln and Warren counties, with $4.30 more for equipment operators employed in surrounding outstate counties. . . .

[St. Louis *Globe-Democrat*]

When management balks at union demands, a strike is always a potential threat. State and federal conciliators may step in to attempt mediation; one side may offer to arbitrate. In all such cases, the reporter should seek the versions of both union and management as to the issues: what the union asks and what management offers. This involves comparing the new conditions sought with existing ones. A résumé of the past history of relations between the particular company and the union may suggest the possibility of peaceful settlement in the current situation.

By Edward Peeks

Chances are that members of the United Mine Workers will ratify the latest contract offer by a sound majority vote, although the contract will be weighed and found wanting by many miners.

For one thing, pension and health care benefits fall short of demands, despite improvement over benefits in the previous offer turned down by the UMW membership.

For another, a demand for the right to strike fell early by the wayside in the course of bargaining between negotiators for the UMW and the Bituminous Coal Operators Association.

The UMW Constitutional Convention at Cincinnati in 1976 voted overwhelmingly for a right to strike clause in the new contract now up for ratification. Miners spoke of the clause as a means of tightening up the grievance machinery that had become an object of anger and a trigger of wildcat strikes.

Arnold Miller and other top UMW officials favored such a clause. They saw it as a way of controlling unauthorized work stoppages and confining them to the mine where a labor dispute arose. A strike would be authorized at the source of the dispute upon majority vote of the UMW local after other measures had failed. The strike, in the framework of the grievance machinery, was regarded as a last resort by Miller and other proponents.

Moreover, it was looked upon, from the standpoint of the union, as a way to curb roving pickets and to stop miners from genuflecting at the sight of every picket or picket line. It was meant to strengthen UMW local leadership and make members themselves more responsible for stability in the workplace.

But coal operators wouldn't or couldn't buy the limited right to strike. Some held that there was nothing in the history of the UMW that argued for the right to strike as a measure against wildcats in the coalfields.

The 1974 contract, operators say, offered UMW members one of the best grievance procedures in the country, but miners wouldn't abide by it. All too often if they didn't like an arbitrator's decision, members of a local would go on a wildcat strike and spread it across the coalfields.

In addition, from the view of operators, miners take umbrage when they are hauled in court for violation of the union contract. They defy court orders and some miners even have the gall to try to deny an operator his constitutional right to go to court in a labor contract dispute.

Against this backdrop of labor-management relations, the new UMW contract has nothing that promises to forestall wildcat strikes in the coalfields.

Nevertheless, the new BCOA offer makes improvements in pension and health care benefits over the two previous offers found unacceptable by the union.

[Charleston (W. Va) *Gazette*]

Unless it is a "wildcat," a strike is preceded by a strike vote of the membership. This vote may be taken long in advance of the actual walkout and may consist in authorizing the officers to use their own discretion. In states with "cooling off" periods it may be necessary to file notices of intention to strike weeks or months in advance. One result of such laws may be that a union keeps an industry under almost perpetual notice, as was the case frequently under the wartime Smith-Connally act.

After a strike begins, the reporter describes factually what happens: (1) how many members of what unions walk out, when and where; (2) what is the status of picketing—number engaged, location and activities; (3) police handling of the situation and comment by both union and management on the handling; (4) violence or threats of violence; (5) the effect upon the public because of curtailed production or services; (6) efforts to settle the strike. A fair treatment of labor disputes requires constant contact with both sides and equal space to comments.

William Eaton, who handled labor news for the United Press International in Washington for many years, gives the following advice:

The reporter starting on the labor beat needs a certain persistence to overcome (1) the mild paranoia of most labor leaders toward the commercial press, and (2) the timidity of most management spokesmen in dealing with the nosey newspaperman. A new labor reporter also should:

Walk a picket line—and listen.

Find a friend on each side of the bargaining table and not neglect the mediators, either.

Be cautious about predictions on the length of strikes and the imminence of settlements.

Learn to wait for hours outside a bargaining room and eat cold hamburgers at 3 o'clock in the morning.

Keep the faith with the rank-and-file.

Never violate a trust.

Beyond Strike Reporting _____

Truly good interpretative reporting of labor also includes stories besides those about labor disputes and labor unions. Quality interpretative reporting should deal with such things as how the economy is doing at generating jobs for people as well as profits for stockholders, labor issues in the political arena, management practices affecting labor and the world of work itself, including the situations of the unorganized and the unemployed.

Providing Substance with Human Touch

Sensitive, intelligent interpretative reporting of the relationship between the economy and working people is one of the major challenges facing today's reporters. The first requirement of such reporting is substance, but the substance can be given the human touch by a reporter willing to do careful legwork, willing to try to understand the problems of people outside the realm of cushy offices, willing to take risks. An interesting example of such a story is this 1980 report in the New York *Times* by William Serrin. Here is the story Serrin wrote on a steel town down on its luck, reprinted with permission of the *Times*. It is a good example of interpretative reporting with a human touch:

McDonald, Ohio, Nov. 1—High, high in the black night, the football tumbled, and then it began to fall, and so it had begun, the game that was so important to the stout-hearted McDonald players, to students, to parents, the game that was the most important thing of all on this Friday night, in October, in Ohio.

They have not changed, these shining fall nights of youth when the playing fields are alight, the fans cheer, and the bands play.

The young men still wear their jerseys to school on game day. They still sit dourly at the pep rallies, and the pep bands play and the girls watch the players and the players know the girls are watching them. The hard-eyed coaches still exhort their men not to quit, to do their best. The girls still curl their hair just so, and they smell so fresh. And the bandsmen high-step down the field, and their tassels, in school colors, bounce on their white shiny boots.

Friday night is high school football night for much of America.

But there was something special about this contest. Here in the Mahoning River Valley in northeast Ohio, the steel works, McDonald Mill, is closed, a victim of cheap steel from abroad or of mismanagement by American companies, depending on the observer's ideology.

In McDonald, where the mill provided a living for many people, life is uncertain. For some it is frightening. The McDonald High School football team, 35 young men seeking a perfect 10-0 season, has given the town something good; it has, says the school principal, James Bodnar, helped hold the town together.

In this fall, Andrew Golubic, the high school football coach, has the most important job in town. His pay as teacher and coach is $18,000 a year, far less than he could make in industry. But this job is what he wants to do, and in a town like this, all eyes are on him.

Northeast Ohio is a splendidly storied place. Fearless Indians roamed these hills, the pioneers clambered through the black forests in the razorback ridges to the east, emerged under these hills and built compact, charming villages like those they had left hundreds of miles behind in New England.

But steel changed this area of Ohio. Using ores from the Great Lake states, the area, in the last part of the 19th century and the first part of this century, became the "Ruhr Valley of America," as old history books say.

In 1916 the industrialist, Andrew Carnegie, built McDonald Mill, then one of the most modern in the world. The houses, most of which were also built by the Carnegie Company, were fine stout houses. Residents today recall how when the company would dump hot slag, the whole northern sky would burn a fiery red, and how, after fresh snowfalls, boys and girls would trudge with their sleds up Pennsylvania Avenue and slide deliriously for what seemed like miles, all the way to the clag crusher at the river bottom.

Today, the Mahoning Valley is hardly a Ruhr. Thousands of jobs have been lost. Several of the McDonald football players have fathers who have lost steel jobs. An industrial battle is being waged as workers attempt to take over McDonald Mill, but U.S. Steel Company, which owns the plant, says this is impractical.

But this town is surviving, as precarious as its financial situation may be. And throughout the fall, the football team, the apple of the town's eye, has helped it survive.

Football, which the school has played since 1925, has taken minds off troubled finances. It has brought recollections of the town's fine football customs, of fine seasons in years past, of how families have stayed in McDonald through generations.

Fathers of sons on the football team today played from McDonald High School. Bart Domitrovich's father. George Grant's father. Andrew Golubic, the coach, played for McDonald High School. His father, Andrew Golubic, Sr., was McDonald coach in the 1940's and 1950's.

It has not been an easy time for Mr. Golubic and for the McDonald High School football team.

Two years ago, Mr. Golubic's first year, the team lost nine games and tied one. The players were embarrassed. But Mr. Golubic instituted a weightlifting program and his players gained strength. Last year, the team won nine games and lost one. And this year the team and many townsmen were pointing toward a perfect season.

Other McDonald teams had gone undefeated, including the 1946 team, under Mr. Golubic's father. But in 1980, the team wished to do what only one other McDonald team had done, the 1974 team, go undefeated and untied through 10 games.

In August, during grueling twice-a-day practices, many team members had cut their hair, getting Mohawk haircuts or cutting the block letter "M" on the side of their heads, to raise team spirit. They asked Mr. Golubic if he would cut his hair. He said he would if the team achieved an undefeated, untied season.

The opening game, in August, was a cakewalk, 41–8 over Dalton. Then one by one, the teams fell. Pynatuning Valley. Mathews. Mineral Ridge. It had a close victory over Springfield, 22–14, then defeated Jackson-Milton, and Lowellville. It won a stirring, last minute victory, 21–20, over South Range. Then a week ago it handily defeated Western Reserve.

Now, the last game of the season, it faced Columbiana, a rural town about 25 miles south whose team had won only three games. But Friday afternoon, walking back from a church service he had attended with his players, the gold leaves that had fallen from the sugar maple trees scraping beneath his feet, Mr. Golubic said he was fearful of each team; if you are not fearful, he said, you could lose the game.

A pep rally Friday afternoon was a joyous affair. The school has a terrific band, and it played with wild exuberance the fight song, which someone recognized as the "Notre Dame Victory March." A spirited contest was held to see which grade could cheer the loudest. Mr. Golubic asked the students to "raise the roof out there and let these people from Columbiana know what spirit is all about."

This was parents night, and, shortly before the 7:30 kickoff, McDonald players, resplendent in white and midnight blue uniforms, and cheerleaders lined up and down the field. The band formed two lines at midfield and each young man, the cheerleaders as well, walked across to his parents and then walking with them moved through the line the bandsmen had formed. Each player or cheerleader gave his mother a single red rose.

Then, just after the public address announcer exhorted the McDonald residents to vote on Tuesday for the six-mill school levy, to help make up more than $150,000 the system will lose because of the closing of McDonald Mill, the football that had soared through the sky tumbled into the arms of George Grant, a fleet backfield man. He moved to his left, cut through the right side of the Columbiana men and moved some 60 yards down field.

A couple of hours later, hours punctuated by skyrockets marking McDonald scores, the town had its unbeaten untied season. The score was 43–16.

Players, cheerleaders, bandsmen, McDonald team followers—all were delirious. Players and cheerleaders gathered around Mr. Golubic, in front of the home bleachers. One by one, the young men and women snipped the locks of Mr. Golubic's hair. When the cutting was finished, Mr. Golubic looked like his players, a burrhead.

The dressing room was riotous. The players hooped and hollered, like, it seemed, the Indians who roamed these hills two centuries ago. One by one the coaches were carried into the showers. Soda pop was sprayed about, as though it were champagne.

Finally, one by one or in groups, the players left. The lights had been turned out on the field. The coaches had changed their sodden clothes. In the darkness of the field, so alive with light and noise not long before, the constellations were visible in the northern sky. Dogs barked from the river bottom, in the area of McDonald Mill.

Some players were heading for Bart Domitrovich's house. Joe Pearson said he was going out with a girl from Columbiana.

Many of the young men and women were seniors, so never again would they know the sweetness of these fall nights. There seemed something else, too. Despite the desperate times that face many people in this valley, that face this town, happiness had been achieved. Copyright © 1980/86 by The New York Times Company. Reprinted by permission.

What William Serrin was doing in that story was establishing a larger cultural and historical context for the pressures millions of American families and thousands of American communities were feeling from international and national economic forces. He was translating the statistics and the hard news stories into flesh and blood, joy and tears. In the context of economics and labor reporting, he was reporting the human condition as he saw and felt it as a human being. He had gotten out of the boardrooms, the offices of politicians, union officials and bureaucrats and away from his telephone, to cover an important story at the human level, interpreting a slice of humanity from his own human perspective. Serrin's story, you'll note, fits no standard formula for reporting, except that it combines good research and careful observation of detail, that it establishes setting, significance and context and that it employs a deft command of the power and gentleness of language and of the literary devices that give language its life and majesty.

It is a misnomer to call such reporting "new journalism." In fact, such reporting has roots that go back to the journal-keeping that was the original journalism before anyone even had thought of the modern concept of "news."

The Case for Better Labor Reporting

It is the shame of modern American journalism that there is not more sensitive, penetrating and humane reporting of the world of ordinary workers or of those who want to work to balance the increased reporting of the problems of American businesses.

The labor story is a significant one. Consider the excerpt below from the interpretative story filed for Labor Day 1985 from Washington by Pete Yost, a staff writer of the Associated Press. It reflects the panic that was setting in many parts of America where blue collar workers were being forced to accept lower wages because other jobless people were ready to take their jobs. Recession was cutting into the prosperity many unions and workers had struggled hard to attain. Wrote Yost:

> Labor Day 1985 finds American union leaders struggling to halt the draining away of their rank and file and surrendering on many fronts to employers' demands for concessions.
>
> Pay raises for union workers have lagged behind non-union wage increases for nearly two years. And the switch recently has been occurring across the board, in the service sector of the economy as well as in economically depressed, heavily unionized manufacturing industries hard hit by foreign imports.
>
> "Unions simply don't have the leverage," says Mark A. de Bernardo, manager of labor law at the U.S. Chamber of Commerce. "The card they hold is no longer trump."
>
> "Organized labor is down to 17 or 18 percent of the work force; they've got far fewer guns there than in the past," says Richard Freeman, an economics professor at Harvard University. "Some of the younger union leaders would like to punch back, but it's clear the opportunity isn't there. They don't have the power to impose their will on the other side."
>
> Labor's great hope of a year ago, electing a Democratic president, was dashed in a 49-state landslide for Ronald Reagan. Major strikes, labor's ultimate weapon, totalled just 18 in the first six months of this year, reflecting a downward trend that began in 1979, when there were 235 for the year. . . .
>
> Deregulation, foreign competition, the 1981–82 recession, a conservative president and a huge pool of non-union, unemployed workers willing to be strikebreakers have cleared the way for concessions. And labor has paid a heavy price when it tried to buck the trend. . . .

The failure to report economics from the point of view of the workplace as well as the corporate headquarters offices can have many negative effects on the larger society.

For example, it may lead to not detecting dangers workers face, dangers that can take employees' lives and make their families dependent on the government. Just one of thousands of such examples that occur each year can be seen if you read this lead to a story in the Apr. 26, 1985, Chicago *Tribune* with such considerations in mind:

> Firefighters and rescue workers early Saturday recovered the body of a third
> victim of an explosion and fire in a Pilsen neighborhood factory.
>
> The bodies of two men were recovered from the factory Friday and the body
> of the third man was recovered Saturday morning from the Tool and Engi-
> neering Co. factory, 1720 S. Peoria St. Fourteen people were injured in the
> gas leak.
>
> The explosion, which officials said may have been caused by a natural gas
> leak, occurred at about 7 p.m. Friday in the complex of three connected build-
> ings on Peoria Street between 16th and 18th streets. Fire department spokes-
> man Donald Walpole said some employees reported smelling natural gas be-
> fore the explosion. People as far as a mile away reported feeling the blast. . . .

Another consequence of that noninvestigative approach to labor reporting was illustrated in a story that appeared in the Chicago *Tribune* the
same day as the account of the Pilsen factory explosion. The second story,
written by Casey Bukro, the paper's environment writer, began this way:

> With two high-priority federal Superfund sites and 10 others under consid-
> eration for emergency clean-up, Waukegan is shaping up as the toxic waste
> hot spot of Illinois.

The effort to clean up such waste dump sites will cost at least $1 billion,
an official told Bukro. And the costs, to say nothing of the human tragedy,
no doubt would be much larger if you include the health care bills of people
dependent on water supplies in places like Waukegan. There are many
reasons for America's belated discovery of a hazardous waste crisis, reflected in microcosm at Waukegan, and it should be sobering for journalists of today and tomorrow to consider that among them may be a failure
on the part of American reporters to ask more critical questions about
business policy, to ask questions about workers' safety and to cultivate
more sources among the ordinary blue collar workers who could have revealed what was going on in plants using chemicals.

A similar journalistic and social phenomenon may be developing in respect to the high-tech industries. In the early '80s economics reporters
throughout the country reported the rise of high-tech industries in largely
glowing terms, asking few critical questions about whether high-tech was
a fundamentally sound direction for the American economy to take, or
whether it was being oversold as a basic long-term solution to some of
America's economic problems. Our extensive research files for this section
of *Interpretative Reporting* bulge with such stories, including thick wads of
them from some of the newspapers that pride themselves with doing the
best economics reporting. Cautions of leaders of old-line trade unions representing workers in declining smokestack industries got much less attention from the economics reporters of many newspapers. Few critical questions were asked by economics reporters about huge tax breaks and public
tax subsidies that were lavished on new high-tech firms. Then, in the heart
of New England high-tech country, appeared this lead to an Aug. 1, 1985,
page one story in the Boston *Globe* by Jane Meridith Adams:

> Tracy Green remembers, with the poignancy of the newly disenchanted, how
> urgently she wanted a career in the high technology industry two years ago.

"I was doing temporary work then and I told the agency, 'If you have a job at Computervision, even if it's washing rugs, get me in.'"

Her determination worked; she joined the marketing department at Computervision Corp. Last April, on what came to be called Black Tuesday at the Bedford Company, she was one of 950 workers laid off. Along with her job, Green lost her faith in the high tech mystique.

"It was sort of assumed that if you had a college degree and you were trying to get a career going that would have some growth in the long term, you'd go into high tech," Green recalls. "Now I tell people, 'If you don't have a technical background, don't look to high tech as the promised land.'"

More than 5,000 Massachusetts high-tech workers have lost their jobs since the beginning of 1985. With their jobs, for some, went a piece of personal mythology: that the high tech dream—a great future in a growing industry—would remain unmarred.

The dream is being diminished in high-tech centers across the country. . . .

To avoid being an accomplice in such shattered dreams, to help Americans to assist their society in solving its human problems of the workplace and of the larger economy, newspaper reporters should remain skeptical. They should give as much attention to the point of view of union officials, ordinary workers and the jobless as they do business spokespeople in framing questions and forming interpretations.

Agriculture

A. Bridging the Gap
B. The Rural Population

C. The Social Effect
D. Political Power

The University of Illinois at Urbana-Champaign, where one of the coauthors of this book teaches, is located in the heart of some of America's richest farmland, only a few interstate miles from medium sized cities that are home for some of the nation's most powerful agricultural associations and from two giant, Fortune-500 agribusiness companies' headquarters. A healthy portion of the state's prosperity hinges on companies that manufacture products and provide services important to farmers.

Yet it is commonplace for University of Illinois students, including journalism students, to respond to questions about agriculture on current events quizzes with answers such as: "How could you expect me to know that? I'm not a farmer." That the students, most of them from the Chicago suburbs, located not far from rich farmland, are not farmers is clear from their poor knowledge of almost anything related to farming.

One young woman, for example, a few years ago was assigned by a journalism teacher to do a story on farming. After poking around in the university library to do some reading on the subject, her deadline was approaching. In a panic, she buttonholed another professor in a corridor and said, "I have a problem. I need to find farmers to interview and I don't know how to do it."

The professor, thinking he would be a bit sarcastic, asked her if she had a car. She said she did. The professor said, "Fine. Get it, pull it up in front of this building, pick a direction and drive that way. Pretty soon you will be out of the city. You will see fields and scattered among those fields you will see houses. Get off the highway and drive on a side road. When you get to a house, stop, get out and go up and knock on the door. The person who answers will be a farmer or a relative of a farmer. Introduce yourself, be friendly and ask questions you have from your reading. You will be interviewing a farmer. You can interview a lot of farmers that way."

The student, rather than being put off by the sarcasm, was gushingly grateful: "Thank you, professor. Thank you. You've saved me."

That incident is one measure of how far today's urban generations have lost touch with the people and processes who bring the food to our tables. It is a cultural gap of monumental dimensions and one potentially devastating to our society, which depends on farms not only for food at reasonable prices but also for exports to keep the nation's vast balance of trade deficit from getting even larger.

It is a gap so severe that in September 1985 when many Midwestern farmers had their backs against the wall, it required country and western singer Willie Nelson to organize a FarmAid concert featuring famous rock singers at the University of Illinois to call national attention, including that of the media, to the little noticed but highly important financial crisis among many American farmers.

All of that suggests that American newspapers and their reporters need to do a great deal to improve reporting of the agriculture story.

Bridging the Gap

Metropolitan daily newspapers often have neglected the rural, farm or agricultural sector. Generally such papers rely on the press associations to cover Washington and state capital developments regarding farm legislation. Some press releases from agricultural organizations are rewritten to stress local angles and, especially in smaller places, columns written by local county agents are sometimes run. By comparison with the treatment given business and/or labor, this coverage is meager. As a result the press is accused of neglecting its responsibility by ignoring changes that have occurred in farming. "Too many daily papers run farm news as if it were a running battle between farmers and the secretary of agriculture or between farmers and town people—or between farmers themselves," according to former Secretary of Agriculture Orville Freeman.

The irony is that while metropolitan newspapers and their readers consider themselves cosmopolitan, they are out of touch with the continuing importance of agriculture in American life and the many important forces nationally and internationally affecting agriculture. But farm country newspapers and their readers—supposedly provincial—are aware of those national and international forces and are working hard to educate others about them. The metros would do well to ask more and better questions about agriculture and its vital place in our society. Farmers and farm organizations are willing to help in such understanding, to provide insights if only some reporters will come and ask questions.

Consider, for example, these excerpts from three stories by reporter Kay Shipman, published in the _Register Mail,_ a daily newspaper in the small central Illinois city of Galesburg, which gave Carl Sandburg to the world, and whose farm neighbors also help supply the nation and world with food. In one story, she reported:

Gilson—Todd and Shawn Smith of Chicago weren't quite sure they wanted to hold a couple of squealing piglets.

Shawn, 9, even held his ears before he and his 12-year old brother gingerly petted the squirming animals while their parents watched.

"This is the most hogs I've seen in my whole life, I think," said the boys' mother, Lucy.

The Smiths, of Chicago, spent the weekend learning about life on the farm. As part of the Illinois Farm Bureau Farm and City Days, they stayed with Ken and Lorri Walker of near Gilson.

Twenty-eight city families will stay with farm families over two weekends in July and one in August.

For Carroll Smith, a job trainer with the Chicago Metropolitan YMCA, and his wife, a graphic artist with World Book Encyclopedia, it was a chance to show their sons real farm life.

"I think the first place they saw farm animals was in a zoo," Mrs. Smith said. "That's when I first realized if you don't make an effort, children in an urban area aren't exposed to farm life."

In Ms. Shipman's other stories, excerpts from which follow, it becomes clear that life on the farm these days is not exactly the way it is portrayed on television's "Hee Haw." America's farmers are in many ways a wonder of the world to sophisticated people abroad, even if many sophisticated metropolitan papers and many sophisticated young reporters in the United States think there are few interpretative stories worth telling about American agriculture or American farmers for city and suburban readers. Here is reporter Shipman, filing again with a Gilson dateline for the *Register Mail:*

Gilson—U.S. Secretary of Agriculture John Block defended the payment-in-kind program, saying that the government will recover half of the $21 billion program expense and reduce farm program costs.

"Let's get the record straight," Block said during a press conference on his farm Saturday. . . .

The secretary conducted on-the-farm diplomacy when agricultural ministers of 20 countries toured the Block farm. . . .

The visitors said they learned more about the food they import and gained a better understanding of U.S. farm problems. . . .

Ms. Shipman, this time from Altona:

Altona—Japanese agriculture officials viewed Rollie Main's farm, near here, through camera lenses.

Recording every detail—from an anhydrous ammonia wagon to computer print-out sheets—the 15-member group toured Main's grain farm Tuesday as part of a study mission of United States agriculture. . . .

"I've never seen such big equipment," said Makoto Yui, assistant manager of the international research department of Sumitono Banking and Trust Co. . . .

"Every farm in the U.S. has management," Yui added. Japanese farmers do not quite have that type of management. . . .

It is risky for the United States to depend on city dwellers visiting American farms to have an understanding of modern agriculture. And it seems downright provincial of American urban daily newspapers and their reporters to provide little coverage of agriculture when visitors are coming from other lands to try to understand U.S. farm realities and issues.

One exception to that pattern of scant major metropolitan newspaper attention to agriculture is the work of Andrew Malcolm in the Chicago bureau of the New York *Times*. Malcolm has done intelligent, sensitive reporting on Midwestern farm issues and life. His 1986 book, *Final Harvest*, is a sensitive yet penetrating examination of the life of modern farmers. Another excellent piece of interpretative reporting on agriculture is Mark Kramer's book, *Three Farms*.

The Rural Population _____

Whereas in colonial days 90 per cent of the population was rural, today about 2 per cent is, down from 18 per cent at the end of World War II. American farm units reached their all-time peak of 6,500,000 in 1935. In 1983 there were only 2,370,000 units, approximately half of them marginal and not needed to supply the nation's food needs. The small independent farmer is almost nonexistent today. Since 1945 an average of 330,000 farmers have gone out of business annually. Agriculture has become Big Business, very big. The top 35 so-called farmers have larger incomes than the bottom 350,000.

"Every day 12 square miles of American farmlands vanish forever," according to Peter J. Ognibene. "Where crops, barns and silos once stood, roads, subdivisions and shopping centers have sprouted. In the past decade we have lost farmlands equivalent to the combined areas of Vermont, New Hampshire, Massachusetts, Rhode Island, Connecticut, New Jersey and Delaware. Today we still have 24 million acres in reserve—currently unfarmed land that could be brought under cultivation within a short time. If the present rate of loss continues, however, that reserve will evaporate by 1990."

According to the Council on Environmental Quality, since 1935 "100 million acres have been degraded to the point where they cannot be cultivated, and on another 100 million acres more than 50 per cent of the topsoil has been lost."

There are good stories to be found in rural America, stories with compelling human interest. They are stories that could help urban Americans and the politicians they choose to represent them in state legislatures and in Congress better understand the importance of U.S. agriculture to the nation and the world.

Sometimes they are buried in publications that newspaper reporters should be aware of but are not, such as those telling of agricultural research at land-grant institutions like the University of Illinois. There, the faculty newspaper, for example, told in June 1985 how scientists have developed new strains of soybeans that may reduce the cost of animal feed and give a substantial edge to American soybean producers on the world market. "What's going on in American higher education important to agriculture, to farmers, to consumers and to America's ability to compete in international trade?" is just one of many questions that should be on the minds of good economics reporters. If such questions do not get asked by reporters, Americans are going to be without important information they need.

There are other story possibilities, such as the page one piece that Timothy McNulty filed in April 1985 for the Chicago *Tribune*, detailing the impact, not all of it positive, that came to the small Kansas river town as a result of the opening of its first McDonald's restaurant. Or the February 1985 story by Christopher Drew of the same newspaper that told of the fear bred in a small Iowa town by a bank failure in the community that threatened to put many long-time farmers out of business and cause ripples of financial trouble that might spread to America's cities.

Louisville *Courier Journal* business writer Frederic Biddle found a significant story that appeared in his paper on Jan. 20, 1985. His story began this way:

> The U.S. Justice Department's foreclosure suit filed Friday against Big River Electric Corp. may produce effects greater than the utility's 72,000 Western Kentucky customers will ever feel, utility-industry officials say.
> Across the country, executives of rural electric cooperatives, which, like Big River, have borrowed vast sums of federal money to finance electrical generators, express fears that they also will be dealt with harshly by a government itself steeped in debt. . . .

The Decatur (Ill.) *Herald and Review* in February 1984 unearthed a good investigative story when it learned that some officials of the Illinois Farm Home Administration had built up their own land holdings while supposedly helping other officials compete financially for available property. In the process, the paper revealed to its urban readers how some aspects of federal agricultural programs operate differently than intended.

In May 1985 the *Wall Street Journal* carried a good in-depth report on the struggle of migrant workers to survive on Texas farms after entering the United States illegally, a story that revealed a good deal not only about American agricultural policy, but also about immigration policy and the workings of minimum wage laws. It was a story as gripping in its own way as John Steinbeck's classic novel *Grapes of Wrath*.

In *The New Yorker* magazine, E. J. Kahn during 1985 wrote a fascinating series on various grains, entitled "The Staff of Life."

For reporters who ask probing questions and are willing to dig in the interpretative spirit, there are interesting agricultural stories to tell, stories important for Americans to read.

The Social Effect

The stories add up, eventually producing patterns that good interpretative reporters, if they have done their homework, can explain to urban readers in clear, compelling terms.

Consider Larry Green's Feb. 24, 1985, report for the Los Angeles *Times* date-lined Corydon, Iowa, and headlined "Harvest of Heartbreak—Debts Could End Family Farm Era":

In the cold courthouse square, near the stone monument dedicated to the dead of three wars, the Wayne County Sheriff sold Wendell and Max Tuttle's farm last Wednesday.

It took little more than 11 minutes to complete the foreclosure sale. Neighbors and clergy, almost 500 of them, crowded the courthouse steps to watch, standing motionless in silent requiem.

The week before, 225 miles north of there, in Dinsdale, Scott and Judy Breakenridge bundled up in near-zero weather to see their livestock and the tools of their trade auctioned off—cows, bulls, tractors, plows, wagons and planters, rakes and pitchforks, pliers, fencing, bins of nuts and bolts. It took seven hours.

"Sixty years of farming! Sixty years! It's our heritage being sold," Scott Breakenridge said. "I'm dead. The auctioneer is just trying to put the corpse away."

The Audubon County sheriff came to Elmer and Pat Steffes' farm two weeks ago at dawn with a procession of trucks and an army of deputies from neighboring counties. He left near dusk with the family's livelihood—repossessing the sheep and hogs they raised and the machines and tools they used to work the land.

"He took everything that wasn't frozen down," Pat Steffes said.

But the repossessed animals and equipment will not pay the Steffes' debts. The farm will go next.

"We're grieving," Elmer Steffes said.

These Corn Belt farm families have been swept up in the great collapse of America's rural economy since the Great Depression. Nationwide, as many as 200,000 full-time commercial farmers could join them before the year is over. And this is only the beginning.

"The stress will become more intense before it eases," said Marvin Duncan, Kansas City Federal Reserve Bank vice president. . . .

Green's story goes on to detail the causes and larger consequences of developments "down on the farm" for the lives of these families, their neighbors, the state of Iowa, the American economy and the U.S. position in the world. It is a story of importance far beyond the farm, even as it is an intensely dramatic story. Such stories are there in rural America, but getting them will require sensitive, intelligent reporters asking penetrating questions and willing to piece together isolated answers into a comprehensive whole for readers and citizens in metropolitan areas.

Political Power _____

Several United States Supreme Court decisions in the '60s led to considerable changes in the rural-urban balance of political power. States have had to reapportion congressional and legislative districts in accordance with the equal representation rule: one voter, one vote. Previously, through gerrymandering and refusal of the rural-dominated legislatures to reapportion, the farm areas were represented way out of proportion to their population strength. For instance, a Georgia farmer's vote was 62 times more effective than that of a Georgia city voter. A typical situation existed in Michigan where an upper peninsula congressman represented 177,431 persons whereas a Detroit congressman spoke for 802,994.

Logrolling by members of the Farm Bloc, representative of noncompetitive agricultural interests as cotton and cattle, wheat and vegetables, no longer is so effective with total rural representation reduced. No drastic changes have occurred yet; but as the power structure is altered by deaths and elections, metropolitan areas should find it easier to obtain needed laws from state legislatures and possibly will be able to rely less heavily on Washington. The farm lobbies should become less active. The Big Three of such lobbies are the American Farm Bureau of over three million members, generally sympathetic to the larger and wealthier farm owners; the National Farmers Union with about 300,000 members, a gadfly New Deal-born organization of small and independent farmers; and the National Grange, whose 700,000 members regard it mostly as a social group instead of as a militant political force as it was when it began shortly after the Civil War. There is also the National Farmers Organization with almost 200,000 members, which has aspects of both a cooperative and a labor union. Formed in 1955 in Iowa, it has engaged in several holding actions (keeping a commodity off the market) and in 1979 from $650 to $750 million worth of farm products were marketed through the organization, which acted as agent for blocks of production.

Today's federal agricultural policy is still substantially the same as that established in early New Deal days by Henry A. Wallace and associates. The essential feature is to keep farm income high by payments to farmers for participation in the Soil Conservation program whereby part of their acreage is kept idle and by loans through the Commodity Credit Corporation secured by products that can be forfeited in case the market price stays low.

These and similar efforts are geared to what is called parity, the relationship between the well-being of the farmer and nonfarm population using the period 1910–14 as the base. Devised years ago by the American Farm Bureau, it has been called a statistical monstrosity, and the Bureau in recent years has favored reduction or elimination of federal farm supports. The small independent farmers, however, insist that the present policy is necessary for their continued existence, even though the large corporate farms admittedly benefit more from it and do not need it to survive. Ceilings on federal governmental subsidies to big producers are favored increasingly by urban-suburban members of Congress, who now outnumber their rural area colleagues.

Critics of the present policy correctly point out that it is handicapped in achieving its aims because it still is based on acreage rather than productivity. Today an hour of farm labor produces five times as much as it did a generation ago and crop production by acres is up about 75 per cent. All of this has been accomplished by the technological revolution that began in the late nineteenth century with the threshing machine, reaper and similar machines and by the experimental work of the land-grant agricultural colleges, which have made higher education an essential for farming today. Contemporary farming is Big Business and expensive. The family farm is becoming obsolete. Whether that occurs purely by default depends greatly on whether more newspaper reporters decide to tell the story.

21

Religion

A. Modern Liberalism
B. The Conservative Reaction
C. Cults
D. Church and Politics

E. Religious Group Pressure
F. Church News
G. Reportorial Qualifications

Less than a generation ago a standard Friday or Saturday feature in almost any daily newspaper was a column or page of church notices, listing the times of Sunday services and possibly sermon subjects and announcements of meetings of church organizations throughout the week to come. Today, this Saturday ghetto, as it came to be called by church editors, has disappeared from all except some small dailies and community and suburban weeklies. Newsworthy events involving churches and churchmen, such as appointment or installation of a new pastor, dedication of a new building, a public concert or lecture or the like, are reported throughout the regular news sections on any day of the week.

This desegregation of church news is a consequence of one of the most important changes in journalistic news practices in recent or perhaps all times. It involves a shift of interest from church news to news of religion, including religious ideologies and controversies. Abandoned is the traditional hush-hush policy as regards religious conflict and supercaution to avoid giving the slightest offense to anyone, the longtime policy that had as its commendable purpose the avoidance of ill will and conflict. As Gustavus W. Myers detailed in *A History of Bigotry in the United States* (Random House, 1943), religious intolerance has been severe throughout American history, with virtually every one of the 300 or so denominations that exist in this country having suffered from some sort of discrimination at one time or another. On the whole, however, freedom of religion and separation of church and state, as guaranteed by the Constitution, have worked well for two centuries and nobody, least of all the press, has wanted to stir up trouble.

Modern Liberalism ————————————————————————————————

The abandoning of taboos against anything but gingerly handling of matters involving religious differences does not mean journalistic incitement to bitter divisiveness. Quite the contrary, for the first time normal reporting techniques are being applied to religious news with the intent of transmitting information "across the closed borders of denominational differences and thus making for better mutual understanding," in the words of George Cornell, Associated Press religion editor. To quote him further:

> Since religious education is denominationally segregated for the average person, and since prevailing practice in this country has kept the subject out of the public school classroom, most people have been left largely uninformed or misinformed about each other's religion, and dependent mostly on hearsay or backfence supposition. This has caused one of the deep social sores in America's religiously heterogeneous makeup, and informative reporting across the compartmentalized lines has helped and is helping to make for fuller all-around understanding. And this is one of the values in the information business. Now that the ecumenical movement has exploded all over the map, it is extending the process.

The new reporting of religion in the same way other stories are handled can put great pressures on reporters and editors, though. And it can lead to considerable controversy. That was dramatically illustrated in 1981 when the Chicago *Sun-Times,* employing its traditional investigative techniques, broke a series of controversial articles about the then cardinal of the nation's largest Catholic diocese. Celeste Huenergard told the story in an account in the Sept. 19, 1981, issue of *Editor & Publisher* magazine, a portion of which follows, reprinted with the permission of *E&P:*

By Celeste Huenergard

By 10:45 p.m. on September 9, the story that would jar Chicago's slumbering legal, religious and political sectors for months to come was about to be put to bed. Minutes later, the presses rolled and the news that Cardinal John P. Cody was under federal grand jury investigation screamed across the Chicago *Sun-Times* five-star edition in 96-point Spartan.

That the *Sun-Times* was investigating the controversial religious figure was common knowledge for months.

A favorite topic at local media watering holes, the investigation also had been the target of a lengthy and fiery assault by the *Chicago Catholic,* the diocesan weekly newspaper, which accused the *Sun-Times* of seeking, "circulation profit in anti-Catholicism" and threatening the "right of Catholics to worship as they choose."

Gannett News Service, the *Wall Street Journal* and the Chicago *Tribune* all admitted to having assigned reporters at one time or another to check out the rumors that seemed to follow the cardinal from one post to another.

Carlton Sherwood, a reporter for *Gannett News Service* and a Pulitzer winner for an investigative series on the Roman Catholic Pauline Fathers, began work on the Cody story about the same time the *Sun-Times* did.

Sherwood contacted the Chicago U.S. attorney's office the Tuesday morning before the *Sun-Times* unleashed its findings, seeking confirmation of basically the same facts the daily had uncovered.

"I expected the guy at the U.S. attorney's office to fall on the floor after I told him what I had and confirmed it. What he did was fall on the floor and then set up an appointment for me on Thursday," Sherwood said.

When asked if the Gannett reporter's query may have pushed the *Sun-Times* to break the story in its Thursday editions instead of its more widely-read Sunday product, *Sun-Times* executive vice president and editor Ralph Otwell merely said, "We decided to go with it . . . because key pieces of information had been confirmed." He would not elaborate on which pieces.

Sherwood found out five hours before the *Sun-Times* hit the streets that it was going to break the news the federal grand jury was investigating whether or not Cody had illegally diverted as much as $1 million in tax-exempt church funds to a life-long friend, Helen Dolan Wilson.

Sherwood spent most of those hours waking up his editors, trying to convince them to go with the story that he too had been working on for 18 months.

"The story here is not Cody but that Janet Cooke has killed sources for investigative reporters," Sherwood said in a recent interview. "My editors just wouldn't buy it (Cody) even though I told them the names of some of my sources and they were golden."

The Chicago *Tribune,* which could not be reached for comment, announced in an editorial on Sunday that "various news organizations including this one, pursued the rumors about Cody but found nothing substantial enough to warrant publication. But the Chicago *Sun-Times,* which has often been the target of attacks by the Cody-controlled diocesan newspaper, decided to publish and as a result finds itself in the role of the accuser." The editorial then called on the cardinal to break his silence and explain the accusations reported by the *Sun-Times.* . . .

The three-man reporting team, religion editor Roy Larson, and reporters, William Clements and Gene Mustain, kept their notes and drafts under lock and key on a separate magnetic tape. Meetings with Otwell were held outside the newsroom and the identities of all anonymous sources were revealed to at least one editor. No one on the newsdesk was involved in the story until a few hours before it went to press Wednesday night. . . .

Otwell said it was probably the most sensitive story he had ever worked on. . . .

The single event which, more than any other, caused the revolution in the journalistic treatment of religious news was the Second Vatican Council, from 1962 to 1965. The 2,300 Roman Catholic bishops were revealed to have sharp differences on a multitude of matters, both theological and social, thus dispelling the myth of unanimity among the leaders of a supposedly monolithic medieval institution. Although Pope John XXIII died in 1963, the liberal reformist spirit that he espoused grew, and among the revered ancient practices that were modified was secrecy of deliberations. Perspicacious newsmen explained that most of the supposed new positions, as collegiality, had been debated for decades in scholarly journals, largely in Latin, and the council merely affirmed a consensus that had developed and in some cases, as the role of bishops, represented the unfinished agenda of Vatican Council I in 1870. Commenting on the continued debates, Edward B. "Ted" Fiske of the New York *Times* declared:

Some future council will have to ratify a new consensus. The difference is that while the last debate was carried on in private, the current one is going on under the glare of publicity and the media in fact become factors in the consensus that will emerge. Many Catholic bishops, among others, will not accept this and still cling to the idea that responsible deliberations can be carried on in secret. This, however, will have to change and already is. Witness the new policies of financial disclosures, semiopen bishops' meetings, conferences, etc.

It is estimated that because of disagreement with the Vatican II reforms, 45,000 American nuns left the convents and 10,000 American priests resigned. Other nuns and priests have been active in civic affairs, visible in the streets with civil rights and antiwar demonstrators. Until John Paul II forbade it in 1980, some ran for public office, several successfully. They also now participate in ecumenical movements with Protestants and Jews and openly debate each other regarding such issues as divorce, abortion and birth control, despite the Vatican's oft-repeated conservatism. For years the Vatican tolerated the heretical teachings of the Swiss Prof. Hans Kung, who challenged the infallibility of the church on matters of faith. Finally, in May 1980, Kung was barred as a Catholic theologian.

It is not only Roman Catholics who are questioning long-established creeds, dogmas and taboos. Disputes between traditionalists and reformers are considered newsworthy, as the following illustrates.

It's OK for Lutherans to have sex.

It's also OK to mention it.

That's the word from the Church Council of the American Lutheran Church (ALC), which recently recommended positive attitudes toward human sexuality.

"We reject the view that sexual behavior in and of itself is evil, lustful, unmentionable, a duty to be done, a burden to be born," said a statement adopted by the council and recommended to the ALC convention next October.

"We repent for the fact that Christians so often have taught such false views. We do not, however, accept the view that sexual intercourse or sexual satisfaction is the highest or noblest goal in human life."

Nor does it mean wild nights on the town.

"Scriptures set the standard of a lifetime monogamous marriage of one man and one woman, and that sexual intercourse reaches its greatest potential only within the committed trust relationship of marriage," said the document, prepared by ALC's Office of Research and Analysis.

The report also rejects homosexuality as proper Christian behavior.

The Lutherans said sexuality includes "all that we are as human beings—biologically, psychologically, culturally, socially and spiritually." They said birth control could "enhance" sexual enjoyment but criticized "willful abortion."

[Detroit *News*]

The Conservative Reaction _____

Gallup pollsters say 47 per cent of all Americans have been "born again" and evangelical Christians in the United States now total about 45 million.

Bruce Buursma, religion editor, traced the development of the Video Church in the Chicago *Tribune* for Dec. 7, 1980. Thirty years ago the only important religious leader to use television was the Roman Catholic Bishop Fulton J. Sheen. Then came the evangelist William Franklin "Billy" Graham. Since then, according to Buursma, television "has changed the face of American church life forever."

Cults

Commenting on the more than 600 members of the People's Church who committed suicide at the command of the Rev. Jim Jones in Guyana, Aryeh Neier wrote:

> We find them interesting not because we think they were freaks but because we think they may be representative of a great many other Americans who would welcome the opportunity to dedicate themselves to a cause. The power that Jim Jones achieved over them did not emanate from him. It came, we think, from their desire to endow him with qualities deserving of the sacrifices they were prepared to make.

Events in the Middle East, mainly Iran and Saudi Arabia, indicate that Islam as well as Christianity is undergoing a reactionary religious reformation. In the United States there has been a proliferation of new movements or cults, which appeal mostly to youth. These phenomena are not strange. Similar ones have occurred throughout history during times of insecurity and fear of the future. During these times many people turn to the supernatural for comfort. Prior to the current trend to adopt new religious movements, American young people tried activism, participating in political activities and liberal movements such as those promulgating civil rights and peace. Often discouraging failure resulted from their efforts. Therefore, many who had been unsuccessful in attempting to reform the world, rejected it. And when the rotten world was still there after their revolt they found solace in fanatical movements that promised peace of mind on earth and salvation in the beyond. Bewildered parents have gone to court and have hired kidnappers to deprogram their sons and daughters. Belatedly, interpretative journalists have attempted to make the strange new cults understandable in terms of their recruits.

Church and Politics

The timid role of the Roman Catholic church in Mussolini's Italy and Hitler's Germany has been criticized by several historians who correctly point out that the wartime and post-wartime power of the Vatican was a matter of widespread alarm, assuaged only by the Vatican's strong anticommunist policies, and regardless of the ironic fact that outside the Soviet Union—

in such nations as Italy, Hungary, Poland and others—the majority of Communists are also Catholics. Postwar fears grew as the American Catholic church became the principal financial support of the worldwide Catholic missionary efforts and contributed heavily to other causes operated from headquarters in Rome. So great was the Protestant protest that President Truman had to abandon plans to name an ambassador to the Vatican. The first Catholic president, John F. Kennedy, helped diminish anti-Catholic fears, especially because of his disagreement with church leaders regarding federal aid to parochial schools and other measures that might infringe upon the traditional principle of separation of church and state.

Nevertheless, it is a historical fact that religious peace up to the immediate past was more apparent than real. For more than a century, religious controversy was at a minimum because the United States was predominantly a Protestant nation. Split into almost 300 sects, Protestants could proselyte each other but, except for the Know Nothings just before the Civil War and the Ku Klux Klan immediately afterward, few felt great alarm over Roman Catholicism. In the late 20th century, however, the two major divisions of Christianity are pulling even. The best available figures indicate that between the two campaigns, 1928 and 1960, in which Catholics were nominees for the presidency, the American Roman Catholic population increased from 19,000,000 to 40,000,000. By 1985 it had reached 52.5 million or 22 per cent of the entire population, 60.1 per cent of which belonged to some religious body.

Because the Republicans were entrenched among the upper economic classes, during the second half of the nineteenth century the Democrats made strong appeals to the immigrants who came in waves and settled in the large urban centers to do the most menial work. The social welfare services, developed by Tammany Hall in New York and by other urban Democratic organizations, resulted in the recruitment of most of these new citizens into the Democratic party. They were predominantly from southern Europe and were Roman Catholics. Today, their grandchildren run the city governments of many large cities in the United States, although the exodus of the older white elements to the suburbs is increasing the importance of the urban black voter and has resulted in the election of several black mayors. The relationship that exists between parishioners and their church is suggested by the appellation usually given the local Catholic archdiocese office. It is Powerhouse, and its opposition to any important public issue jeopardizes its success. Public health commissioners do well to clear promotional matter related to venereal diseases, birth control and some other matters so as not to risk public chastisement. The hierarchy is concerned over assignment of judges to such courts as Juvenile, Divorce, Domestic Relations and Family, and with the attitudes of social welfare workers, hospital administrators and the like.

During the 1980 and 1984 campaigns several fundamentalist religious groups were active in support of Ronald Reagan for president and helped defeat several liberal senators. The most vigorous group was Moral Majority organized by the Rev. Jerry Falwell, described as a rightist vigilante group. There also were the National Conservative Political Action committee and the Life Amendment Political Action Committee. The last named was especially adamant in its opposition to members of Congress who opposed an anti-abortion amendment or legislation. Although these groups may not have been as influential as they claimed to be, they frightened the American Civil Liberties Union, the Union of American Hebrew Congregations and other liberal groups into launching campaigns to counter the growth of fundamental religious and other right wing organizations.

The politicking is not decreasing. Consider these two excerpts of major stories from Chicago newspapers, the first printed in January 1985 the second in May of the same year:

By William Hines

Washington—Twelve years after the Supreme Court's controversial Roe vs. Wade and Doe vs. Bolton decisions, anti-abortion forces are on the march with a new drum major at their head. Last week, for the first time, a sitting president took the opportunity to address in glowing terms an assemblage of Right-to-Life proponents on the occasion of their annual lobbying effort and to meet with their leaders in the White House.

President Reagan's opposition to legalized abortion is long-standing and well-known. But throughout his first term he kept a distance between himself and the Right-to-Lifers on the anniversary of the Supreme Court abortion ruling.

Not so this year. He told a horde of shivering anti-abortion zealots, "I feel a great sense of solidarity with you," and spoke of the issue as "ours" rather than "yours."

He even went so far as seemingly to express support for a flat ban on abortion, causing White House staffers to explain hastily that he still favors abortion as a life-saving measure for the woman.

There has probably not been since the nation-splitting issue of slavery, a question so diverse as abortion and apparently so unamenable to compromise. Of all the "single issues" that bedevil the life of office-seeking (or office-holding) politicians, this one is unquestionably the hottest.

The opposing sides in this battle have difficulty even in agreeing how to disagree about abortion. Though Roman Catholic and fundamentalist Protestant groups are closely identified with anti-abortion fight, one of their leaders—Dr. Wanda Franz of the National Right-to-Life Committee—said last week, "It is not a religious matter."

But Frederica Hodges, of the Religious Coalition for Abortion Rights, countered that "it is an individual decision before God and only the person making it has that responsibility."

On one silent point they do agree: that the abortion issue is a civil rights matter. But, whose civil rights? Franze says the right of the unborn child to its life is paramount; Hodges says the right of a woman to control of her own body must be preserved. . . .   [Chicago *Sun-Times*]

By Bruce Buursma

Washington—To listen to the lamentations of the television preachers on the religious Right, the Congress is a demonic den of "secular humanism" and decadent liberalism.

On the other hand, there are those who complain with equal vigor that the House and Senate—particularly on the Republican side—have been powerfully influenced by resurgent fundamentalist Christianity, posing a perhaps unprecedented threat of civil liberties and democracy itself.

The battle for the slippery soul of Capitol Hill waged with high-tech weapons of electronic evangelism and tons of often histrionic direct-mail appeals, has intensified since President Reagan's re-election in anticipation of next year's congressional elections and the 1988 presidential campaign. . . .

[Chicago *Tribune*]

Religious Group Pressure

At all levels of government, the activities of religious groups interested in censoring motion pictures, plays, magazines, books and the like are opposed by civil libertarians, most strongly represented by the American Civil Liberties Union. A generation ago it was Protestant groups that were most active, censoring books in Boston and fostering laws forbidding the teaching of Darwinism in the South. More recently Catholic groups, as the Legion of Decency and the National Organization for Decent Literature, brought pressure on motion-picture theaters, libraries and bookstores and advocated the establishment of official censorship boards. Today, in a period of comparative freedom in the arts, religious groups concentrate on encouraging good works rather than condemning poor productions. The Broadcasting and Film Commission of the National Council of Churches (Protestant) and the National Catholic Office of Motion Pictures still comment on films but motion-picture critics are not intimidated by them as they were once. Instead, they pay attention to the Motion Picture Association of America reviews and ratings. Pressure from numerous groups is growing to restrict the showing of pornographic films, especially when juveniles are involved. The revival of Sunday blue laws, forbidding certain commercial operations, as the sale of used automobiles, is more economic than religious in origin. Such groups as the Jews and Seventh Day Adventists, however, are in opposition for religious reasons. Differences in religious viewpoints certainly are paramount in legislative and public discussion of many matters, as dissemination of birth control information, abolition of anti-abortion laws, easier divorce laws, elimination of restrictions on adoptions by parents with religious backgrounds different from those of the children involved and many more. Growing journalistic practice is to cover such news on its merits, identifying adversaries but emphasizing issues.

The schools probably are the battleground for more religious controversies than any other institution. In the late '40s the United States Supreme Court ruled that school properties cannot be used for religious instruction but that so-called released-time programs, whereby children are excused from school to go elsewhere for religious instruction, are legal. Originally supported by Protestants who feared the effect of the decline in Sunday School attendance, released-time programs now are also approved by Catholics especially in areas where there are no parochial schools. Jews are unalterably opposed. Still to be tested in the United States Supreme Court are shared-time programs whereby parochial school students take some of their work in public schools.

Although the state and federal governments already contribute considerable sums to local boards of education, through such programs as those which provide hot lunches and through the National Defense act and similar legislation, "federal aid to education" is a controversial phrase whenever a bill is before Congress to provide large-scale federal expenditures for school building construction, teachers' salaries or other services. Many Catholics oppose such federal aid unless it is provided parochial as well as public schools and have succeeded in blocking several proposals, even when they were endorsed by the nation's first Roman Catholic president. Catholics argue that free transportation for parochial school students and similar benefits are proper governmental expenditures as they are made to benefit children rather than churches. Under President Johnson's War on Poverty programs such grants multiplied, but not without protest from such organizations as Americans United for Separation of Church and State. That group also has attacked sales or gifts of public property to religious institutions and much tax exemption of church-owned property, especially that not used for strictly religious purposes.

United States Supreme Court decisions declaring that neither the federal nor a state government must pay for abortions by welfare recipients were hailed as a victory by the Right-to-Live proponents. The fundamentalists, both Catholic and Protestant, also are pleased with the progress they are making in persuading public schools and colleges to teach "scientific creationism" as well as the conventional Darwinian evolutionary theory. The Scientific Creationists believe that God created the world in seven days as related in *Genesis*. Presumably this viewpoint was discredited during the 1925 Scopes trial in Dayton, Tenn., when Clarence Darrow cross-examined William Jennings Bryan.

United States Supreme Court decisions outlawing a New York Regents Prayer and compulsory Bible reading in public schools have been followed by attempts, so far unsuccessful, to amend the United States Constitution to permit such practices. Leader of movements to extend prohibitions of religious influences has been Dr. Madalyn Murray O'Hair, founder and head of the Society of Separationists and the American Atheists. Atheists oppose chaplains in Congress and the military establishments, would remove "under God" from the pledge of allegiance to the flag and strike "in God we trust" from coins. They also, of course, oppose laws restricting their right to hold public office or testify in court.

Church News

Although church pages have disappeared from most large and many small daily newspapers, they still are to be found in small dailies and weeklies. They usually specialize in announcements of Sunday observances to come but also publicize special events and meetings of church organizations.

Handling all of this routine church news is time-consuming and easy to the extent that church authorities cooperate in preparing material adequately and on time. Personal acquaintanceships between reporter and news sources are important so that ill will does not result from mistaken ideas regarding deadlines and space limitations.

An important consequence of the broadened journalistic interest in religion news is consideration of theological issues and other aspects of religion news even when there is no specific news peg.

Such stories can make exceptionally interesting and informative articles for readers whose interest in religion may be limited or narrow.

An example was a well-written interesting five-part series that ran in January 1983 in the Charlotte (N.C.) *News,* prominently displayed at the top of the front page. Here is the opening of that series, which detailed what life is like inside an abbey:

By Terry Mattingly
©1983, Charlotte News

Belmont—Five minutes before services the bells ring out from the tower in the church at Belmont Abbey. On the second and third floors of the monastery, the monks filter out into the halls. The doors to their rooms open and close in a series of quiet thuds.

Dressed in black robes, the monks walk through the arches along the long halls of the building's closed section, called the cloister. The old floorboards creak under the gray carpet that runs down the center of the polished-wood hall. Few words are spoken as the monks walk past religious paintings and statues.

Sometimes as the monks gather, the windows along the hall are dark; at other times, they are bright with sunlight. Almost any time of day or night, a visitor to the abbey can encounter individual monks walking along the tree-lined paths around the monastery, lost in thought. In lives dedicated to prayer and meditation, the clock often plays a minor role.

The monks congregate four times a day, every day—at 7 a.m. for morning prayer, at 11:30 a.m. for community Mass, at 5:30 p.m. for a service of scripture and prayer called the Office of Reading and 7 p.m. for a sung vespers service.

It doesn't matter if there are two people or 200 people in the sanctuary: The monks believe they have a devine calling to perform acts of worship for an audience that is always present—God and the saints.

Unlike many monks, however, the monks of Belmont Abbey do not live in a monastery hidden in the hills or in a remote rural area.

The windows in the monastery halls look out on the Belmont Abbey College campus, nestled in pine trees off Interstate 85 in the eastern Gaston County textile mill town of Belmont. On most days, students can be seen walking from dormitory to library, from library to classroom.

The students walk to class; the monks walk to Mass. The two patterns exist side by side and times cross. Still, the monastery remains in a separate world.

"I think most people just think that we're a school. That's what they always say, 'That school out there at Belmont.' Some people realize that it's a Catholic school and that there are a lot of priests out here. But, I think that very few people realize many of the teachers at the college are monks and that the monastery is even here," said Father Anselm Biggs, a monk who teaches history at the college.

Belmont Abbey is a Benedictine monastery. The monks who live there are not part of an "order," in the usual sense of the word. Each Benedictine community is a separate institution. It raises its own funds and is under the direction of its own elected leader, an abbot. Belmont Abbey is part of a loose federation of U.S. Benedictine monasteries and is also part of the worldwide Confederation of Monks.

Although Benedictine communities have existed for centuries in Europe, they arrived rather late in North America. The first Benedictine monastery in the United States, Saint Vincent Archabbey in Latrobe, Pa., was founded in 1846 as an offshoot of an abbey in Germany. Belmont Abbey was established as an independent priory in 1876 and was made an abbey in 1884. (A priory is a religious house that ranks just below an abbey). . . .

Another variation is the story that, instead of using a microscope as reporter Mattingly did, looks at trends in religion with a telescope, as does this excerpt from the first of a two-part series on American Catholicism. The article appeared in the May 19, 1985, issue of the Los Angeles *Times:*

By Russell Chandler

For most of their history in America, Roman Catholics have looked to the Old World for roots, to the Pope for unquestioned authority and to their priests to run the parishes.

Today, few of the faithful take it for granted that Father knows best.

Since the Second Vatican Council, which stretched from 1962 to 1965, American Catholicism has become a pluralistic church in a pluralistic society. Gone is the image of a church tethered to European immigrant communities.

But if the winds of change from Vatican II stirred Catholics to enter the mainstream of American society, they also blew in a gale of new challenges and a confusing cross-current: ambiguity about authority, and uncertainty over benefits.

The slogan *Roma locutta, cuasa finita* ("Rome has spoken; that settles the matter") has in the minds of many been relaxed to "Rome has spoken; now we'll see what we think about the matter."

"It is one church but there are many manifestations of it on the American continent," says a new study of American Catholic parishes. "Sometimes the response to Vatican II is precisely what has given new life to a parish; sometimes it is the factor that has torn the parish asunder."

By most accounts, the Roman Catholic Church in America is healthy. With 52.5 million members—nearly one of every four Americans—it is the largest and fastest-growing religious body in the country. This growth has been fueled by the fact that Latinos, the fastest-growing ethnic group in the nation, now account for nearly a third of the U.S. Catholic population—as many as 17 million, according to church and census officials.

But like other mainstream religions, the church is also facing a host of issues that raise questions about its ability to adapt to these changing times. . . .

Such reporting can take a longer historical view, too, as did a Boston *Globe* series that ran in February 1985, entitled "Jews in a New World." The first article in the series was called "Becoming Bostonians" and began this way on the paper's front page:

By Ross Gelbspan and Muriel Cohen

After the Jews moved from Judea through Canaan to Babylon, from Rome to Alexandria and Iberia, through Champagne and Hamburg, London, Kiev and Krakow some came to Boston.

Here, they re-created that Diaspora through the neighborhoods and suburbs of Boston. At times they found themselves divided by national and ideological differences; often they were buffeted by the sometimes subtle, sometimes violent antagonism of gentile Boston.

Groping through a succession of identities, the Jewish community earned the animosity and the admiration of other Bostonians and proved to share some of their characteristics: the shrewdness and frugality of the Yankee traders; the intellectual adventurousness of the New England transcendentalists; the self-protecting clannishness of their Irish and Italian co-immigrants; the low public profile and private bigotries of the Brahmins; the passion for social justice of newer black Bostonians, which later soured into mutual fear and distrust.

Arriving in the second half of the 19th century, they found a society as bewildering as it was promising. The community was divided and tribalized along class and ethnic lines. At the same time, Boston was the nation's fourth largest industrial center, its textile-based economy employing thousands of immigrants. And, to the history-conscious Jews, this was also the Boston central to the creation of the first nation built on the ideals of equal justice, institutionalized democracy and universal freedom.

There emerged from this mix a highly energized community which, while warring with itself and constantly redefining its relations with other Bostonians, created a prolific and diverse set of institutions and gained wealth and prominence far out of proportion to its numbers. . . .

Church news is put to the same test as all other news: the extent of its appeal. Thus, an item of interest to only one congregation seldom is used unless it involves something innovative. Comings and goings of pastors and rabbis are news in the same way that changes in business and industry leadership are news. Churches long have been involved in social and welfare work, operating charities, hospitals and other institutions, which often are newsworthy. Even such news is more valuable if related to outside issues and interests. The leadership provided civil rights, antiwar and other groups by church leaders such as Martin Luther King in Alabama, Father James Groppi in Milwaukee, the Berrigan brothers and others made plenty of front-page news.

Reportorial Qualifications _____

According to the late Richard Cardinal Cushing of Boston, "It is not too much to suppose that the time is coming when we will expect the religious news reporter to have attended, for some time at least, a school of theology or divinity or religion; that he is in simple terms an expert in his own work."

Quite obviously Cardinal Cushing believed that a journalist with training in any religion would be able to report fairly news of other denominations. Editors are coming to be of the same opinion. Edward B. "Ted" Fiske, long-time religion editor of the New York *Times,* was a Presbyterian minister, Roy Larson of the Chicago *Sun-Times* was a Methodist minister, William B. MacKaye of the Washington *Post* had a year at General Theological Seminary and other religion news writers similarly have had specialized training. All leading publications are represented among the 100 plus members of the Religious Newswriters' Association, formed in 1945. The object of its newsletters is to advance professional standards in the secular press.

The Religious News Service was established in 1933 as an independently managed agency of the National Conference of Christians and Jews. It provides daily news reports and various features and a photo service for an estimated 800 news outlets. Subscribers include the religious press of all denominations, various church agencies and major secular media. It is served by a network of stringer correspondents in the United States and abroad.

There are also the Catholic Press Association, which operates the National Catholic News Service, and the Associated Church Press for Protestants. Since 1953 there has existed the James Supple award given annually by the Religion Newswriters Association for excellence in reporting religious news in the secular press. The award was named in honor of James Supple of the Chicago *Sun,* who was killed in an air crash in 1950 while en route to Korea. Since 1970 there also has been an award memorializing the late Harold Schachern, religion editor of the Detroit *News.* It is given for editing a church page or religion section in the secular press. In 1974 the Louis Cassels award was created in honor of the late UPI religion writer. It is for papers with circulations under 50,000.

George Cornell, religion editor of the Associated Press, believes that modern readers are much better educated and informed so that they recognize words related to science and technology—as radiation, astronaut, genealogy and electrocardiograph—but are stumped when it comes to such elementary religious terms as atonement, apostolic succession, mystical body, presbyter and justification of faith. It is the responsibility of the specialist religion writer to promote public enlightenment.

A *Christianity Today* survey resulted in replies from 180 religion news reporters for the secular media out of 460 who were queried. Of them 146 said they hold church or synagogue membership; 107 said they are active in local congregations and 25 are active in a larger unit of their denomination.

CHAPTER
22

Science, Technology

A. The Contemporary Challenge
B. Newsgathering Problems
C. The Newspaper's Responsibility
D. Energy and the Environment

E. Definitions
F. Nuclear Age Hazards
G. Space Exploration
H. Reportorial Qualifications

Humanity's progress at any stage throughout history can be calculated in good measure by the extent to which scientific discoveries made known what previously as unknown and old, ignorant and superstitious explanations of the origin and nature of life on this planet and in the universe were abandoned.

Long-lived beliefs, myths, and legends do not disappear quickly. Many heretics, both before and since Copernicus and Galileo, have been vilified, persecuted, punished and killed by those whose faith they have shaken. Even today, more than 300 years later, there is a Flat Earth Society with a growing membership that believes news accounts and photographs of astronauts on the moon were fabricated. And, despite the victory Clarence Darrow supposedly won over William Jennings Bryan in 1925 in the Scopes' trial at Dayton, Tennessee, there is considerable organized pressure to forbid the teaching of Darwinian evolution in the schools or at least to offset it with the creationist theory in Genesis.

Considering the extent of their knowledge, primitives were rational when they invented a multitude of gods, devils, angels, ghosts, leprechauns, trolls, witches, fairies and other supernatural forces to explain the sun's diurnal movement across the sky, life and death, day and night, the powerful invisible wind, the seasons and other phenomena.

The Contemporary Challenge

Contemporary journalists are not so easily excused for their contributions to the perpetuation of ignorance and superstition through daily horoscopes

455

and sympathetic treatment of astrology, clairvoyance, fortune telling, faith healing, extrasensory perception (ESP), witchcraft, spiritualism, haunted houses, miraculous escapes, premonitions, reincarnation, prophecies by professional psychics and soothsayers, UFOs, Loch Ness and other sea monsters, Big Foot, the Abominable Snowman and other animal freaks, good- and bad-luck charms and spells and similar sensational or hysterical news features.

The tangible evidence of applied science, however, are not so easily disregarded as the philosophical and ethical implications of scientific knowledge. Since World War II, no matter what the effect on their preconceptions, few have been able to ignore (1) the threats to the environment from polluted air and water, hazardous waste and depletion of natural resources in an overpopulated world, (2) atomic and nuclear energy problems and (3) space exploration.

Ours is called an Age of Science. In view of the stubborn refusal of many to accept the deeper implications of reality, the present world more properly should be called an Age of Technology. Today the average person tinkers with an automobile and household electrical appliances, takes motion pictures, dreams of owning his or her own airplane and uses scientific or technical language unknown just a few years ago. The Jules Verne science fiction novels of great-grandfather's day and the Tom Swift and Boy Aviators yarns that commanded grandfather's attention are old stuff to modern youth.

Actually there is no such thing as Science. Rather, there are sciences, scores of them, man-made categorizations for convenience in studying and utilizing knowledge. A generation ago high schools offered courses in physics, chemistry and biology, and that was presumed to about cover the field. Today it takes three solid pages just for the table of contents of *A Guide to Science Reading* (Signet Science Library), compiled and edited by Hilary T. Deason of the American Association for the Advancement of Science. Take one of the shortest main sections, "Earth Sciences." Listed are History of Geology, Geophysics, Oceanography-Physical, Meteorology and Paleontology. So specialized is knowledge becoming that the experts, who know more and more about less and less, find it difficult to converse with each other, even in closely related fields.

Newsgathering Problems _____

As the awful power of applied science to make the planet uninhabitable became apparent, the absolute necessity for everyone's understanding something of the implications of scientific progress (?) became recognized.

Even before the atom bomb and spaceships, newspapers had awakened to their social responsibility as regards science. The remarkable improvement, in completeness of coverage, in accuracy and clarity of writing and, in general, in social purpose, followed years of misunderstanding and consequent inadequate cooperation between scientific writers and scientists. Out of the namecalling came a mutual decision to get together in a common program to protect the public against false science and to assist it in obtaining the maximum benefit from what the experimental laboratories and the scholars' studies are revealing daily, almost hourly.

By assigning to scientific news reporters with sufficient training to talk the language of those whom they must interview, newspapers have broken down much of the reluctance of inventors, medical personnel and theoretical scientists to give information to the press. Whatever hesitancy to cooperate remains results from several factors: fear of being considered a publicity seeker, fear of revealing the nature of an experiment before absolute proof has been obtained, a feeling that one's fellow scientists deserve to hear of a new scientific fact or theory for the first time at a learned gathering, fear of being misquoted, doubt of the reporter's ability to translate a technical matter into popular terms, fear that improper emphasis will be given to sensational, unimportant aspects of a news item.

On the other hand, partly through the pressure of well-intentioned journalists, many leading scientists have come to realize the value to them of sharing their findings with the public, of their social obligation to do so and of the sincerity of a vast majority of present-day journalists attempting to do a completely honest and creditable job. Scientists and writers cooperate to combat quacks.

Dr. Irvine H. Page described the lingering doubts of many medical men. After expressing shock because of a television offer of $50,000 to a patient for exclusive rights to broadcast his heart transplant operation, Dr. Page wrote:

> There are two aspects of reporting. The one concerns publicity after a discovery is reasonably established and reported in a scientific publication; the other concerns the precipitate announcement to the press of the discovery of a new procedure, especially one of magnitude, before it has been adequately tested. An example of the first was the discovery of insulin and its use in diabetes. The most recent example of the other is the artificial heart.

Only by adherence to the highest ethical principles can editors and reporters retain the confidence of public-spirited scientists in all fields. It is unrealistic to condemn the press for sensationalizing science when so much science news cannot be described by any word other than sensational. To be guarded against is the faker or publicity seeker. A century and a half ago the New York *Sun* could get away with its hoax concerning life on the moon because of public ignorance. Today such a hoax would succeed for exactly the opposite reason: because the "impossible" has happened so many times there is nobody willing to doubt anything. If the astronauts had declared the dark side of the moon, never visible to earthlings, is inhabited, they would have been believed. The same is true of virtually any item of science fiction posing as fact. In some regards science has made people more, not less, gullible and credulous.

At the same time there must be caution so as not to uphold orthodox scientists who are as adamant as religious fundamentalists in resisting new ideas destructive of some of their own pet theories and systems of thought. Scientists can be as fanatical and narrow-minded as defenders of the faith, no matter what. A classic example was provided by the threat of several of America's leading astronomers to boycott all Macmillan textbooks unless the company discontinued publication of *Worlds in Collision* by Immanuel Velikovsky. Similar violent opposition also was shown the same author's other books, all published by Doubleday, which has no textbook department. They are *Ages in Chaos, Earth in Upheaval* and *Oedipus and Akhnaton.* More than a decade later many of Velikovsky's theories were validated by Mariner and other space flights.

Journalists also must be mindful of the depth and breadth of the revolt within the organized ranks of scientists by peace-minded and socially conscious, mostly younger, persons who object to the extent to which their older colleagues have cooperated with the military-industrial establishment in promoting the war effort, mainly by the development of weapons inimical to the continuation of life on this planet. Newsgatherers must realize that in great part they are dealing with businessmen, that few pure scientists have kept their purity. Rather, they seek to make discoveries of value to their commercial or military employers, or to the images and general fund-raising capacities of universities for whom they work.

In view of the attention now given atomic energy, other energy sources, space exploration, pollution control and other recent scientific topics, it is difficult to recall that newspapers of the past virtually ignored Robert Fulton, Charles Darwin, Samuel F. B. Morse and the Wright brothers.

The Newspaper's Responsibility _____

In the stories of sufferers from virulent diseases who have been given pathetic false hope because of premature announcements of new cures, of lives and fortunes that have been lost because of misplaced confidence in inventions, and of persecution and injustice resulting from unscientific superstition is implied the social responsibility of the newspaper as regards scientific news. Likewise, for that matter, is implied the duty that the reputable scientist has not only to maintain proper caution himself but to discipline his fellows as well.

What scientists deplore is reporting that they consider "shallow, inept and totally lacking in scope and understanding," to use the phraseology which Dr. Jonathan Karas of the Lowell Technological Institute applied to the radio and television handling of the first manned Soviet orbital space flight.

Scientists are appalled when some journalist refers indiscriminately to a new scientific announcement as a "major breakthrough" or "major advance" or "a key to life." They deplore journalistic playing up and exaggerating the significance of a medical or scientific contribution.

A point the scientists have conceded, in the face of evidence, is that dramatizing an item of scientific news does not destroy its educational value. Austin H. Clark, eminent biologist, for instance, once confessed that he would not object to a newspaper article beginning

Those unfeeling mothers who leave their babies on the doorsteps of prosperous people's houses have their counterparts among the birds. . . .

as a popular translation of a scientific paper in which he might declare

Most cuckoos, the honey-guides of Africa, the weaver finches, some hangnests, our cow birds, the rice-grackle, a South American duck, and, according to recent information, one of the paradise birds, lay their eggs in nests of the other birds which hatch these eggs and raise the young.

Most people, including readers and editors, live in the here-and-now. Much science news, however, is important because of what it portends for the future. Casey Bukro explained the plight of the environment reporter, which is what he is for the Chicago *Tribune:*

In the old days, stories were more obvious. A murder, a fire, or financial ruin. These obviously are stories. But is the snail darter a story? Especially in Chicago? A radioactive leak at a nuclear power plant? The ozone content of the air on any given day? Polychlorinated biphenyls (PCB) in Lake Michigan?

These are matters of degree and long-range impact. A newspaper editor wants to know what is happening NOW! They don't want to hear about something that MIGHT happen 10 or 20 years from now, which is the incubation period for some cancers. It all sounds pretty iffy, and that turns off an editor.

But one thing both environment and energy have in common is the danger of long-range consequences. Some of the problems are fairly immediate, like gasoline lines or the polluted Cuyahoga river in Cleveland. Those are obvious stories. But a major part of both beats deals with things off in the future. And in both beats, there are no obvious answers. . . .

Journalism has thrived on single-dimension stories, writing about a single event, in a single time, in a single place.

Now we're into multi-dimensional journalism. Our environmental impact statements require alternative choices. What is the best spot for a nuclear power plant? Is there a better spot? Would it be better to build a coal-burning plant? What are the advantages in fuel? The advantages in pollution control? The advantages in waste disposal? Relative costs? Impact on neighboring communities? Public sentiment? Is the utility economically able to support the project? How much power is expected? Do future power demand projections justify building another power plant? What does it mean to electric bills?

And so on. We are getting into a lot of detail in these stories. We once called it in-depth reporting. That's becoming more routine.

The following thoughtful observations on the reportorial hazards in this field were made by Jerry Ackerman, environment/energy editor of the Boston *Globe:*

As with most everything, the environment is a subject area which is often better developed by feel. Geography, politics, events, economics and personalities pretty well decide what is important for the moment and what is not. Water-diversion in the sense of the perennial war among the Colorado River states is certainly of only peripheral interest in the East. Similarly, offshore oil drilling and the issues that surround it will find little interest, among either lay readers or opinion shapers, until it is a clear and present danger close to home. The Boston Globe wouldn't have agreed to send me to Mexico for the Bay of Campeche blowout in 1979 had it not been a harbinger for future petroleum development being planned on Georges Bank. Timing is a crucial determinant of what should be done, too—except in the Rockies, coverage of the environmental questions surrounding oil-shale would have been premature and probably lost before the nation's energy awareness was heightened in 1973.

On the other hand, there is an array of environmental issues with universal appeal and implications—national parks, national land policies, endangered species, air pollution, the threat of a carbon-dioxide "greenhouse" effect, melting polar ice caps are among the obvious ones. A caveat is in order, though: I am reluctant to write in much depth on any of these without being able to do some first-hand, on-the-spot reporting. While the ivory-tower view is tempting, all too often it is likely to be erroneous, with oversimplification the greatest pitfall. The issues are seldom as clean-cut as they seem from afar. Thus I don't think I could have written well on the snail-darter controversy without having visited the Tellico Dam and talking with the principals—managers at the TVA, environmentalists at the University of Tennessee—in more relaxed circumstances than the best alternative, telephone interviews, would have allowed.

The biggest problem facing a conscientious environmental reporter is the far-flung field that demands coverage. To keep one's sanity, the reporter must pick and choose what he'll be doing, and shove all the rest to the back of the desk. . . .

Yet the environmental reporter must also be in a position to swing into new areas on a moment's notice. The first alert, all too often, is an emergency one. Contamination in the wells. A chemical accident. A harbor suddenly polluted. An oil well run amok. A nuclear power plant shut down for other than obviously routine reasons. In a sense, it was sinful that so few journalists in America were prepared to ask the right questions about nuclear safety when the Three Mile Island balloon went up. . . .

And there's simple observation. Not every new real estate development is going to be worth a full-scale environmental story, of course. But each bulldozer, smokestack or oil tanker you see around you is likely up to little good from an environmental point of view. It's up to you to decide if a little good reporting might not be in the public interest.

Journalism professors Michael Ryan of Temple University and James W. Tankard Jr. of the University of Texas studied "Problem Areas in Science News Reporting, Writing and Editing" and made these recommendations:

1. Science reporters, like reporters in other areas (such as government), should dig for information beyond the publicity handout.
2. Science reporters should use journal articles and published reports to verify and improve the accuracy of their stories. They should not rely solely on interviews with scientists.
3. Science reporters should resist the temptation to exaggerate or oversimplify in a lead sentence for the purpose of attracting reader interest; many scientists report that "catchy" leads distort their findings.
4. Science reporters should pay particular attention to quoting sources accurately and in context. This may be more important in science than in other areas of news because of the care with which scientists use language.
5. Science reporters should be cautious in introducing lay terminology that

the scientist himself did not actually use. Scientists often object to such terminology and find it inaccurate.

6. Science reporters should be wary of interpreting a scientist's technical conclusions, as scientists often think such interpretations are misleading.

7. Science reporters should avoid the temptation to sensationalize information about science. As one responding scientist pointed out, progress in science is slow and often does not make "good copy."

8. Science reporters should avoid using the words "cure" and "breakthrough" unless the scientist himself approves the use of the words in describing his work.

9. Science reporters should consider giving information sources an opportunity to review articles or parts of articles for accuracy before publication. Such a review can be done with the reporter still making the final editorial decision, and it might help prevent serious inaccuracies.

10. Headline writers should resist the temptation to put simplistic, cute, or "scare" headlines on science stories.

11. Make-up editors should be aware that the practice of cutting news stories from the bottom to fit available space may not apply very well to science stories, as science articles often need to be reported completely to make sense.

12. Finally, scientists themselves should accept their share of the responsibility for accurate communication of science information to the public. In the words of one of the responding scientists, they should learn to "think about their work [in] a simple and adequate manner that the layman can understand."

But there are other perils for the science writers. Those were suggested in the following three paragraphs of Gloria Cooper's review in the July–August 1985 *Columbia Journalism Review* of a recent study of science reporting. The study was entitled "Science and the Media: The Boundaries of Truth." That study was done by Jay Winsten and appeared in the spring 1985 issue of *Health Affairs* magazine. Here is what Cooper had to say about Winsten's study:

One science reporter confesses that he almost has to hype a story if he expects it ever to see the light of day. Another denies exaggeration, but concedes the need to stretch her stories to some precariously permissible edge of truth. A third complains about the constant push from desk editors to cut the qualifers out. And as if internal pressures are not enough, there is the further certain knowledge that, however resolved one may be not to overstate a given story, one's colleagues at other news organizations are at that very same moment giving that very same story everything they've got.

But the operative standards of competitive journalism are not the only forces at work in distorting science news, according to this report on what is justifiably billed by its publisher as a landmark study on the relationship between science and the press. Conducted by a scientist/science writer (Winsten, who directs the Office of Policy Information at Harvard's School of Public Health, holds a doctorate in molecular biology, and devotes considerable time to freelance writing for such publications as the *Wall Street Journal* and the New York *Times*), and based on lengthy interviews with twenty-seven senior science reporters and editors around the country, the study traces many of the excesses of science reporting to the scientific community itself.

Indiscriminate use of press conferences by academic medical centers competing for publicity; self-aggrandizing claims of individual researchers competing for investors; professionally orchestrated public relations campaigns by practitioners competing for patients—no wonder so many of the journalists Winsten talked to feel "manipulated," "victimized," "horrified," and "inundated" by the deluge of science information pouring their way. Indeed, the author warns, the rapidly rising flood—one science writer notes that he gets four to five hundred pieces of mail a week, more than any other reporter in the newsroom—threatens to seriously alienate the very journalists it is trying so hard to impress. . . .

The modern reporter of scientific events and issues, in short, needs to remain skeptical about the motives of those dispensing scientific information.

Rae Goodell, who teaches science writing at the Massachusetts Institute of Technology, has a Ph.D. and has written a book called *The Visible Scientists,* underlined that point in a specific way in a piece she wrote for the November–December 1980 issue of the *Columbia Journalism Review.* Her article was entitled "The Gene Craze." It was a critique of reporting about one of the new frontiers of science and the American economy—genetic engineering. In her piece, she observed:

> One of the most startling transformations in genetic engineering has occurred not in the laboratory, however, but in the news media: a press that spent much of the 1970s dwelling at length on the drawbacks of genetic research now heralds its breakthrough and benefits almost as if the 1970s had never happened. Genetic engineering has become a media celebration, a rags-to-riches story on the titillating theme of the merger of "life" and big business. . . .
>
> Between hypothetical benefits and imaginary monsters, there seems to be no room in most recombinant DNA coverage for questions of occupational hazards, environmental impact, public regulation. Although by no means all reporters take this Pollyanna approach, the general effect is anachronistic, a throwback to the gee-whiz, science saves 1960s before the press learned that technological advances have side effects. The nuclear industry may have its Three Mile Islands, and the chemical industry its Love Canals, but the genetics industry is somehow different, foolproof. . . .

Some prominent scientists and journalists interested in science journalism have banded together in the Council for the Advancement of Science Writing, Inc. The organization has a variety of print and video materials available to help those interested in learning to do better science reporting. It also has sponsored workshops and likely will do more of them in the future. In 1985 the president of the organization was Barbara J. Culliton of *Science* magazine. The executive director was William J. Cromie. For more information, you can write to Cromie at 618 N. Elmwood, Oak Park, Ill. 60302 or call him at 312–383–0820.

Energy and the Environment _____

For many Americans the first warning of a national energy shortage came Nov. 9, 1965, when the lights flickered out in New York City and 30 million people in eight Northeastern states were plunged into darkness. The next day they heard the term "energy crisis" for the first time.

Many heard about an "environmental crisis" for the first time a few years later, Jan. 28, 1969, when an offshore oil well blew out off the Pacific coast. The million-gallon oil spill that followed fouled the harbor and beaches at Santa Barbara, Calif., killed thousands of shore birds and marine creatures, and alerted the nation to the dangers of a polluted environment.

It was some time after these two headline events—the New York black-out and the California blowout—that the American press began to realize how the energy and environmental crises are interwoven: It is impossible to produce energy without some degradation of the environment—the land, the water, or the air—and so there is a constant conflict between our demand for energy and our desire for a clean environment.

After the landmark National Environmental Policy Act was signed into law by President Nixon on New Year's Day, 1970, and millions of Americans demonstrated against air and water pollution in the first national observance of Earth Day, Apr. 22, 1970, many newspapers established energy/environmental beats and assigned reporters to cover the conflict on a full-time basis.

Reporters on that beat are covering what might be called the Survival Story—man's effort to provide enough energy for the ever-growing human race without degrading the planet to the point where it is uninhabitable. The beat has produced a plethora of big, long-running stories—the passage by Congress of laws setting national clean air and water quality standards, regulating stripmining and the disposal of toxic wastes, protecting wild and scenic rivers and endangered species of wildlife and the eight-year fight over the Alaska Pipeline, which threatened the delicate ecological balance of the 49th state.

It has also produced many local stories that quickly became important national news stories, such as the discovery in 1978 of birth defects in families living along the infamous Love Canal in upstate New York and the near-disaster at a nuclear power plant on Three Mile Island, near Harrisburg, Pa., in 1979.

To keep the Survival Story in perspective, the environmental movement did not begin with the publication of Rachel Carson's *Silent Spring* in 1962 or with Earth Day in 1970. Rather, a part of the modern conservation movement began early in this century under such leaders as Theodore Roosevelt and Gifford Pinchot, the first head of the U.S. Forest Service. Most early conservationists were hunters and outdoorsmen who perceived that in nature "everything is connected" and thus became interested in the wise use and management of all natural resources.

Many of the old-line conservation organizations, such as the National Wildlife Federation, the National Audubon Society, and the Izaak Walton League, still have a special interest in wildlife. NWF, the nation's biggest nongovernment, nonprofit conservation group, was founded at a 1936 conference called by Franklin D. Roosevelt "to bring together all interested organizations, agencies and individuals in behalf of restoration of land, water, forests, and wildlife resources." Now it can call upon 4.1 million members and supporters in 50 states to bring pressure to bear on the White House or Congress, not just on wildlife issues, but for a stricter strip-mine law, tougher requirements for nuclear waste disposal, or more solar energy research.

When such groups as the NWF, the Audubons, and the "Ikes" join forces with the Sierra Club, the Wilderness Society, Friends of the Earth, the Natural Resources Defense Council, and other smaller specialized groups in a lawsuit or lobbying effort, they comprise a potent force—though they are not so formidable, financially, as the National Association of Manufacturers, the U.S. Chamber of Commerce, and others who are often aligned against them.

The Conservation Directory, listing more than 11,000 officials of approximately 1,700 conservation groups and government agencies, is an indispensable reference tool. It is published by the National Wildlife Federation, 1412 16th St. NW, Washington, DC 20036.

Definitions _____

Among the important terms with which the energy/environment reporter must become familiar are the following:

Accelerator. A device that increases the speed (and thus the energy) of charged particles such as electrons and protons.

Alpha ray. The nucleus of the helium atom, consisting of two protons and two neutrons. Emitted from certain heavier nuclei as radiation.

Atom. The smallest unit of a chemical element, approximately 1/100,000,000 inch in size, consisting of a nucleus surrounded by electrons.

Background radiation. Radiation from natural sources (cosmic rays, rocks and from minerals inside the body). Normal background radiation for Americans is about 100 to 200 millirems per year, with the higher figure occurring at higher altitudes.

Baryon. A type of strongly interacting particle. The baryon family includes the proton, neutron and those other particles whose eventual decay products include the proton. Baryons are composed of 3-quark combinations.

Base gas. Gas that cannot be extracted from gas storage reservoirs.

Beta ray. An electron or positron emitted when weak interaction causes a nucleus to decay. The neutron, for example, decays into a proton, an electron (beta ray), and an antineutrino.

Boiling water reactor (BWR). A reactor in which water, used as both coolant and moderator, is allowed to boil in the core. The resulting steam is used directly to drive a turbine.

British thermal unit (BTU). The quantity of heat necessary to raise the temperature of one pound of water one degree Fahrenheit.

Bubble chamber. A particle detector in which the paths of charged particles are revealed by a trail of bubbles produced by the particles as they traverse a superheated liquid. Hydrogen, deuterium, helium, neon, propane and freon liquids have been used for this purpose.

Catalyst. A substance that increases the rate of a chemical reaction without being consumed in the process.

Charm. The distinguishing characteristic of the fourth type of quark, also called the *c-quark*. Each *quark* is characterized by a number of properties including familiar ones like mass and electric charge and less familiar ones, which were arbitrarily given names like *charm* and *strangeness.*

Cladding. The outer jacket of nuclear fuel rods. It prevents corrosion of the fuel by the coolant and the release of fission products into the coolant. The most common cladding material is a zirconium alloy.

Condenser. Apparatus in which steam that turns the turbines is cooled and condensed to liquid state for return to steam generator.

Control rod. A rod, plate or tube containing a material such as cadmium, boron etc. used to control the power of a nuclear reactor. By absorbing neutrons, a control rod prevents the neutrons from causing further fission.

Cooling ponds. An artificial lake into which the heated cooling water from a power plant is pumped and from which cooler water is extracted to resupply the cooling loop.

Cooling tower. A tower designed to aid in the cooling of the water used to condense the steam after it leaves the turbine of a power plant.

Core. The central portion of a nuclear reactor containing the fuel elements.

Crude oil. Oil as it is recovered from oil wells.

Cyclotron. In this type of accelerator, magnets cause particles to travel in circular orbits and to pass repeatedly through a constant-frequency alternating electric field, which adds a small amount of energy each time the particles travel through it. In these low-energy machines, the time for a particle to make one orbit is constant.

Deuterium. Heavy hydrogen, the nucleus of which contains one proton and one neutron.

Electromagnetism. A long-range force associated with the electric and magnetic properties of particles. This force appears to be intermediate in strength between the weak and strong force. The carrier of the electromagnetic force is the *photon.*

Electron. An elementary particle with a unit negative electrical charge and a mass 1/1840 that of the proton. Electrons surround an atom's positively charged nucleus and determine the atom's chemical properties. Electrons are members of the *lepton* family.

Electron volt. The amount of energy of motion acquired by an electron accelerated by an electric potential of one volt: MeV = million electron volts; BeV = billion electron volts: TeV = trillion electron volts.

Fast-breeder reactor. A reactor that operates with fast neutrons and produces more fissionable material than it consumes.

Fission. A process in which the nucleus of a heavy atom such as uranium splits into two small nuclei, with the release of energy.

Fuel rods. Long hollow rods, usually of a zirconium alloy, into which are packed thimble-sized pellets of uranium.

Fusion. A process in which two light nuclei are joined or fused together to make a heavier nucleus, with the release of energy.

Gamma rays. Penetrating electromagnetic radiation emitted in radioactive decay, similar to radiation produced by X-rays.

Gravity. The weakest of the four basic forces and the one responsible for the weight of matter and the motion of the stars and planets.

Half-life. Term used to describe the time rate at which radioactive materials decay into stable elements.

Helium. A light colorless nonflammable gaseous element found primarily in natural gases.

Hydrocarbon. An organic compound containing only hydrogen and carbon commonly found in petroleum, natural gas, and coal.

Ion. An atom or molecule that has lost or gained one or more electrons and therefore becomes electrically charged.

Isotope. One of two or more atoms with the same atomic number (the same chemical element) but with different atomic weights because of a difference in the number of neutrons.

J. A particle made of a *c-quark* (see *Charm*) and an *anti-c-quark*. It is also called the *psi particle* and is three times as massive as the proton.

Kilowatt hour (KWH). The amount of electrical energy involved with a one-thousand watt demand over a period of one hour. One kilowatt hour is equivalent to 3,412 BTU of heat energy.

Melt-down. The overheating of a reactor core, usually as a result of loss of coolant, to the extent that uranium melts through the metal cladding on the fuel rods. It is believed in extreme cases that heat in the core could become so intense that the core would melt through the reactor vessel and down through the concrete floor of the containment vessel.

Methane. A gaseous compound (CH_4) that is the primary constituent of natural gas.

Millirem. A measure of radiation. A millirem is one-thousandth of a *rem* (Roentgen), the basic measure of radiation. A chest X-ray exposes a person to between 20 and 30 millirems.

Molecule. A unit of matter made up of two or more atoms.

Nuclear reactor. The device in which a fission chain reaction can be initiated, maintained and controlled. Heat from the fission process is used to turn generators for production of electricity.

Neutron. An uncharged baryon with mass slightly greater than that of the proton. The neutron is a strongly interacting particle and a constituent of all atomic nuclei, except hydrogen. An isolated neutron decays through the weak interaction to a proton, electron and antineutrino with a lifetime of about 1,000 seconds.

Nucleus. The central core of an atom, made up of neutrons and protons held together by the strong force.

Particle. A small piece of matter. An elementary particle is a particle so small that it cannot be further divided—it is a fundamental constituent of matter. *Quarks* and *leptons* now appear to be the only elementary particles, but the term is often used in referring to any of the subnuclear particles.

Particle detector. A device used to detect particles that pass through it.

Photon. A quantum or pulse of electromagnetic energy. A unique massless particle that carries the electromagnetic force.

Positron. The antiparticle of the electron.

Pressurizer. Vessel designed to control pressure level in the reactor vessel and main coolant system.

Pressurized water reactor. The most common type of commercial nuclear reactor in the United States. Coolant in the primary loop is kept under pressure to prevent its boiling. TMI Units 1 and 2 are pressurized water reactors.

Primary loop. The loop through which the reactor coolant circulates. Coolant is heated in the reactor and then pumped under pressure to the steam generator, where it heats water in the secondary loop (see below) into steam that turns the turbines.

Propane. A hydrocarbon that exists under normal pressures and temperatures as a liquid; however, it gasifies easily and for many purposes it is an excellent substitute for natural gas. The main source of propane is from the refining of crude oil.

Proton. A baryon with a single positive unit of electric charge and a mass approximately 1,840 times that of the electron. It is the nucleus of the hydrogen atom and a constituent of all atomic nuclei.

Psi. A particle made of a *c-quark* (see *Charm*) and an *antiquark* and three times as heavy as the proton. It is also called the *J particle*.

Radioactivity. The spontaneous decay or disintegration of an unstable atomic nucleus, usually accompanied by the emission of ionizing radiation.

Reactor vessel. Steel-walled (8–10 inches thick) container housing the nuclear reactor fuel core and control rods.

Refinery. An industrial plant that processes crude oil and manufactures refined petroleum products (i.e., gasoline, wax, fuel oil).

Relief valve. Device designed to reduce excess pressure in the primary loop.

Solar cell. A device, usually made of silicon, that converts sunlight into electrical energy.

Secondary loop. The loop through which water circulates from steam generators to turbines, then through condenser and back through the steam generator.

Solar energy. The energy produced by the fusion reaction occurring on the sun, which reaches the earth as radiant energy.

Thermonuclear reaction. A reaction in which very high temperatures allow the fusion of two light nuclei to form the nucleus of a heavier atom, releasing a large amount of energy.

Thermodynamics. The physics (science) of the relationship between heat and other forms of energy.

Turbine. The device that converts heat energy into electrical.

Upsilon. A particle believed to be made up of a *b-quark* and an *anti-b-quark*. It is approximately ten times as massive as the proton.

Volatile. Vaporizing readily at a very low temperature.

Waste (radioactive). Equipment and materials from nuclear operations that are radioactive and for which there is no further use.

Watt. An electrical unit of power or work equal to one ampere flowing under pressure of one volt. Approximately 746 watts are equivalent to one horsepower.

X-rays. Photons produced when atoms in states of high energy decay to states of lower energy.

Nuclear Age Hazards _____

William Laurence, then New York *Times* science editor, was in the air over Nagasaki when the second atomic bomb was dropped on Japan in August 1945. He had been privy to the secret experimentations at Oak Ridge, Tenn., Los Alamos, N.M., and other places and had the confidence of both the military and scientific authorities. By now it is known to every schoolboy that there is no secret regarding how nuclear energy is released. The atomic armaments race was over the technological details of the destructive weapon, and the speed with which the Soviet Union produced its own bomb proved that the scientists who opposed secrecy were correct.

From the start the tremendous scientific breakthrough, for which basic credit goes to Albert Einstein, has served the purposes of politicians and militarists more than it has private industry or the common man. It was a shocker when the Nobel prize-winning Englishman P. M. R. Blackett published his *Fear, War and the Bomb* in 1948 and revealed that the strategic purpose of bombing Hiroshima was to try to keep the Russians from honoring their Yalta Conference pledge to enter the war; the bomb's use was unnecessary in order to defeat the Japanese. Since then many others, including former Secretary of State James F. Byrnes, have confirmed the Blackett revelation. A foreign journalist, Robert Jungk, wrote two books to depict the awfulness that the atomic age already had produced. They are *Brighter Than 10,000 Stars* and *The Future Is Already Here*. John Hersey's book *Hiroshima* is a classic piece of humanized interpretative reporting on the effects of nuclear war.

During the past quarter century there have been many incidents to worry people not about what an enemy might do but about what we have done to ourselves. Japanese fishermen were contaminated by fallout from American tests of nuclear bombs in the South Pacific. As radioactive materials from American, Russian, British and other atmospheric tests began raining onto farmlands and waterways, President Kennedy negotiated a treaty with the Soviets to restrict further testing to underground. Because the injurious effects of contamination may not show up for generations, widepread frustration has replaced mere alarm. Revelations of improper disposal of waste materials, frequent leakages of poison gases and chemicals in transit by rail, sea, air or road have caused large areas to be cleared by civilians for hours, days or weeks.

The difficulties reporters encountered in covering the Three Mile Island nuclear plant disaster were described in Chapter 9. Similar obstacles are met with when flocks of sheep die mysteriously in Utah near testing grounds. When Lake Erie and other waterways become contaminated by industrial waste, the water is unfit for drinking, bathing or fishing. A widely publicized case that caused Americans to lose further confidence in the federal government was the pollution of the Love Canal at Niagara Falls. The following is part of a story relating an aspect of the situation.

By William Hines

Washington—The possibility that a dangerous poison gas used in World War I may be included in the devil's brew of chemicals dumped into the Love Canal was raised last week in a report made public by the New York Legislature.

The report, which casts doubt on the truth of Army denials of earlier charges of illicit dumping, could seriously weaken the federal government's efforts to stick the Hooker Chemical Co. with financial responsibility for the nation's worst toxic waste crisis to date.

The poisonous gas is phosgene (also known as carbonyl chloride), which Webster's dictionary defines as "a severe respiratory irritant [whose] deadliness is increased by the fact that serious symptoms appear only after some hours following the exposure."

The report, released Thursday at the New York state capital of Albany, challenged statements made by the Army two years ago when it absolved itself of earlier charges of illegally dumping toxic chemicals in the abandoned canal in Niagara Falls, N.Y.

Faced with the challenge from Albany, the Army late last week said it would analyze the report "for new evidence and then make a decision as to whether to reopen the [1978] investigation."

In 1978, the Army stated that it did not produce phosgene in the Niagara area during or after World War II. The new report says that declassified documents from the War Production Board dated 1943 show "that phosgene was being manufactured under the direction of the Army with a coordinating officer by the name of Maj. Willard."

The Army's 1978 disclaimer may have been a quibble. "Phosgene was being produced at the Niagara Chlorine Plancor in Lockport and Hooker Electrochemical Co.," the report says. "The [Army] Chemical Warfare Service was receiving phosgene from both locations to meet their requirements."

One of these "requirements," the World War II documents indicate, was to supply this chemical to the Soviet government, apparently under the lend-lease arrangements in force at the time.

Phosgene was not used in combat in World War II, but it was stockpiled, and troops undergoing combat training learned about it and other chemical-warfare agents and how to defend against them.

The declassified documents "indicate extremely dangerous chemical substances were being produced in the area of the Love Canal, substances dangerous to personnel," the Albany legislative task force report added.

Also, according to the documents, phosgene was being shipped in unorthodox ways in Army vehicles to get around safety regulations of the Interstate Commerce Commission. . . .   [Chicago *Sun-Times*]

The following article from across the continent relates other ways in which shortsighted citizens and governments injure themselves.

By Charles Gay

Salmon spawning grounds are being ruined, creeks are spilling over their banks during heavy rains, and streams are turning into open storm sewers.

The question is, "How can King and Snohomish County governments reverse the trend and how much are people willing to pay to save their creeks?"

The public will get a chance to speak on the subject Thursday night at a hearing of the Snohomish Subregional Council to the Puget Sound Council of Governments.

The subregional council will be considering recommendations on how to solve stormwater problems and manage streams and lakes at the hearing, which begins at 7:30 in the first floor hearings room of the SnoCo Administration Building in Everett.

"We've got a lot of small streams that are dying, and no one seems to care," said Tom Murdoch of the Snohomish County Surface Water Management Program. "People just don't know what's there."

Murdoch is interested in the creeks and streams that flow down from Snohomish County through King County to empty into rivers like the Sammamish and eventually into Lake Washington.

He insists that citizens have to act now to save the creeks and the salmon that live in them.

The planner said development activities in the two neighboring counties are killing the creeks. The more land that is cleared, the more streamside vegetation is stripped. Banks erode, and in the winter, creeks turn into flood channels.

Silt flows into creekbeds where it settles and eventually kills salmon eggs. "There's salmon going to McAleer Creek (in Lake Forest Park), but that's sad, because it's so silted up," Murdoch said. "They'll dig a hole and lay their eggs, but the eggs won't survive."

"And once you rid the streamside of vegetation, you lose the insects that live there, so there's no food when the fish do hatch, anyway." . . .

[Bothell (Wash) *Northshore Citizen*]

In all parts of the country there are newspapers that are expending considerable effort to expose conditions about which citizens should be demanding that public officials act. Among the leaders is the Chicago *Tribune,* whose environment editor, Casey Bukro, wrote the following stories of which the first few paragraphs follow:

A torrent of potentially dangerous wastes pours out of Illinois industries each year—3.8 million metric tons by official estimates—enough to fill a tankcar train 123 miles long.

That puts Illinois in a second-place tie with Ohio among the nation's top hazardous waste producers, at a time when careless toxic waste disposal is considered the country's biggest environmental problem.

To make matters worse, at least a dozen states send more than 500,000 tons of industrial wastes to Illinois each year for disposal. About the same amount is sent by Illinois to other states.

This bewildering pattern of hazardous waste shipments around the country explains, in part, why state and federal officials don't know where those millions of tons of wastes produced by Illinois oil refineries, steel mills, and chemical plants are going. . . .

The rolling fields around south suburban Crete seem an unlikely place for an environmental mystery that has Illinois officials searching for answers to:
• What killed 16 horses at Rita Battenhauser's stable?
• What is causing Mike Brown and his wife, Mary, to have blurred vision, headaches, and feelings of disorientation?
• Is any of this related to Crete Metals Co., a scavenger operation that sent

billowing clouds of black smoke over the countryside while burning electrical cable and film to recover copper, silver, and other metals? The burning was stopped by a court injunction April 1.

No one knows if there is any connection between Crete Metals and the unexplained sickness and animal deaths that have stricken this area about 35 miles south of downtown Chicago. Crete Metals contends that any problems caused by the plant must have occurred before it took the plant over last fall. . . .

Space Exploration ─────────────────────────────

The debate over how much and what next in the space exploration program also has been more political and financial than scientific, much to the disgust of many journalists as well as scientists. Too often it has seemed that the launchings at Cape Canaveral were conducted in a circus atmosphere. Hundreds of journalists seated in bleachers had less opportunity to observe details than television watchers. The reporter has had to be alert to distinguish between a publicity or political propaganda stunt and a genuinely important event; and the science writer's task has been made difficult by extravagant announcements of innovations in several governmental programs, space and missiles prominently. The idea altogether too often has been to beat the Russians regardless of need or value of the venture. Government-imposed secrecy has, of course, been the biggest handicap of all to adequate coverage. That became clear after the Challenger spaceship exploded during launch in January 1986, killing the astronauts aboard, including a civilian school teacher. Postcrash investigations revealed serious management problems in the space program that journalists had not detected. Many journalists and scholars fear that secrecy will increase greatly if President Reagan wins approval for his "Strategic Defense Initiative," otherwise known as "Star Wars," which would take the nuclear arms race into outer space.

News of early space explorations caused considerable excitement. Consternation is a better word to describe the reaction of hawkish Americans when the Russians launched the first sputnik well ahead of our first rocket. Since the moon flights, the reception has been calmer as many nations are responsible for millions of tons of hardware circling the earth or flying on to explore Mars and other planets. The use of satellites in space has greatly increased the speed of transmission of news reports and pictures of events occurring anywhere on earth.

The basic authority for writers in the space exploration field is the *Dictionary of Technical Terms for Aerospace Use,* National Aeronautics and Space Administration SP-7, 1965. What follows is a condensed version of the glossary attached to the press kit for Apollo X.

Ablating materials. Special heat-dissipating materials on the surface of a spacecraft that vaporize during reentry.

Accelerometer. An instrument to sense accelerative forces and convert them into corresponding electrical quantities usually for controlling, measuring, indicating or recording purposes.

Adapter skirt. A flange or extension of a stage or section that provides a ready means of fitting another stage or section to it.

Antipode. Point on surface of planet exactly 180 degrees opposite from reciprocal point on a line projected through center of body. In Apollo usage, antipode refers to a line from the center of the Moon through the center of the Earth and projected to the Earth surface on the opposite side. The antipode crosses the mid-Pacific recovery line along the 165th meridian of longitude once every 24 hours.

Apocynthion. Point at which object in lunar orbit is farthest from the lunar surface—object having been launched from body other than Moon. (*Cynthia,* Roman goddess of Moon.)

Apogee. The point at which a moon or artifical satellite in its orbit is farthest from Earth.

Apolune. Point at which object launched from the Moon into lunar orbit is farthest from lunar surface, e.g.: ascent stage of lunar module after staging into lunar orbit following lunar landing.

Attitude. The position of an aerospace vehicle as determined by the inclination of its axes to some frame of reference; for Apollo, an inertial, space-fixed reference is used.

Burnout. The point when combustion ceases in a rocket engine.

Canard. A short, stubby winglike element affixed to the launch escape tower to provide CM blunt end forward aerodynamic capture during an abort.

Celestial guidance. The guidance of a vehicle by reference to celestial bodies.

Cislunar. Adjective referring to space between Earth and the Moon, or between Earth and Moon's orbit.

Closed loop. Automatic control units linked together with a process to form an endless chain.

Deboost. A retrograde maneuver which lowers either perigree or apogee of an orbiting spacecraft. Not to be confused with deorbit.

Declination. Angular measurement of a body above or below celestial equator, measured north or south along the body's hour circle. Corresponds to Earth surface latitude.

Delta V. Velocity change.

Down-link. The part of a communication system that receives, processes and displays data from a spacecraft.

Entry corridor. The final flight path of the spacecraft before and during Earth reentry.

Ephemeris. Orbital measurements (apogee, perigee, inclination, period, etc.) of one celestial body in relation to another at given times. In spaceflight, the orbital measurements of a spacecraft relative to the celestial body about which it orbited.

Escape velocity. The speed a body must attain to overcome a gravitational field, such as that of Earth; the velocity of escape at the Earth's surface is 36,700 feet-per-second.

Fairing. A piece, part of structure having a smooth, streamlined outline, used to cover a nonstreamlined object or to smooth a junction.

Fuel cell. An electrochemical generator in which the chemical energy from the reaction of oxygen and a fuel is converted directly into electricity.

g or g force. Force exerted upon an object by gravity or by reaction to acceleration or deceleration, as in a change of direction: one g is the measure of force required to accelerate a body at the rate of 32.16 feet-per-second.

Inertial guidance. Guidance by means of the measurement and integration of acceleration from on board the spacecraft. A sophisticated automatic navigation system using gyroscopic devices, accelerometers, etc., for high-speed vehicles. It absorbs and interprets such data as speed, position, etc., and automatically adjusts the vehicle to a predetermined flight path. Essentially, it knows where it's going and where it is by knowing where it came from and how it got there. It does not give out any radio frequency signal so it cannot be detected by radar or jammed.

Injection. The process of boosting a spacecraft into a calculated trajectory.

Insertion. The process of boosting a spacecraft into an orbit around the Earth or other celestial body.

Multiplexing. The simultaneous transmission of two or more signals within a single channel. The three basic methods of multiplexing involve the separation of signals by time division, frequency division and phase division.

Optical navigation. Navigation by sight, as opposed to inertial methods, using stars or other visible objects as reference.

Oxidizer. In a rocket propellant, a substance such as liquid oxygen or nitrogen tetroxide which supports combusion of the fuel.

Penumbra. Semi-dark portion of a shadow in which light is partly cut off, e.g.: surface of Moon or Earth away from Sun where the disc of the Sun is only partly obscured.

Pericynthion. Point nearest Moon of object in lunar orbit—object having been launched from body other than Moon.

Perigee. Point at which a Moon or an artificial satellite in its orbit is closest to the Earth.

Perilune. The point at which a satellite (e.g.: a spacecraft) in its orbit is closest to the Moon. Differs from pericynthion in that the orbit is Moon-originated.

Reentry. The return of a spacecraft that reenters the atmosphere after flight above it.

Retrorocket. A rocket that gives thrust in a direction opposite to the direction of the object's motion.

S-band. A radiofrequency band of 1,550 to 5,200 megahertz.

Selenographic. Adjective relating to physical geography of Moon. Specifically, positions on lunar surface as measured in latitude from lunar equator and in longitude from a reference lunar meridian.

Sideral. Adjective relating to measurement of time, position or angle in relation to the celestial sphere and the vernal equinox.

State vector. Ground-generated spacecraft position, velocity and timing information uplinked to the spacecraft computer for crew use as a navigational reference.

Terminator. Separation line between lighted and dark portions of celestial body which is not self luminous.

Umbra. Darkest part of a shadow in which light is completely absent, e.g.: surface of Moon or Earth away from Sun where the disc of the Sun is completely obscured.

Up-link data. Information fed by radio signal from the ground to a spacecraft.

Yaw. Angular displacement of a space vehicle about its vertical (Z) axis.

Reportorial Qualifications _____

It would be utterly impossible for anyone, including both journalists and scientists themselves, to be expert in more than one or a few of the multitudinous branches into which scientific knowledge is separated. What scientists of all kinds have in common is a belief in the importance of science and the scientific spirit of open-minded inquiry, which survives despite any prostitution to business or military interests by many scientists.

Science reporters must know enough about the fundamental sciences, physical and organic, to be able to converse with professional scientists. If they are well grounded in any scientific field, they will find it easier to grasp meanings in other fields. They must win the respect and confidence of the scholars they interview by their knowledge and attitude. They must overcome the risk of acting as apologist for scientists.

The public interest is the prime consideration of the science reporter as it should be of any responsible journalist. This means critical analysis of scientific proposals and it may mean warning and shocking readers.

In 1934 the National Association of Science Writers was founded under the leadership of David Dietz, who in 1921 was employed by Scripps-Howard to become the nation's first science writer. At present the association, with a membership of about 950, publishes a bimonthly *Newsletter,* which provides a forum for the discussion of problems of scientific newsgathering. There also exist the Council for the Advancement of Science Writing, mentioned earlier in this chapter, and the American Medical Writers Association.

Already there is accelerating realization of the high moral sense that both scientists and science writers must develop. Today it is not what next but to what end shall we use what we already know or are on the verge of finding out. In *Harper*'s for March 1975 Horace Freeland Judson, writing mostly on molecular biology, asks, "What are we afraid of?" The opportunity and/or obligation of the science writer is made clear as Judson becomes specific:

We are now into the third or fourth cycle of alarms about all this; the subject is intrinsically sensational, as can be seen from the examples that recur. What do you think, then, of choosing the sex of your children-to-be? Of growing human embryos outside the body and experimenting with them? Of genetic screening, to skim the trash out of the gene pool by determining who shall be permitted to breed? Of cloning, or the multiplication of large numbers of genetically identical individuals—what one entirely serious writer has described as the "asexual reproduction of 10,000 Mao Tse-tungs?" Of genetic engineering, or the creation of posthuman creatures with new or magnified bodily or mental strengths—what another serious writer has called "parahumans, or 'modified men' . . . . chimeras (part animal) or cyborg-androids (part prosthetes)"?

The late Arthur Snider, a long-time science reporter for Chicago newspapers, noted that "the content of newspaper science writing has shifted to ethical and social science stories. Questions such as these arise: When is a patient dead? Shall genetics be used to make a super race? Shall a substitute mother carry the fertilized egg of another woman to term? Who shall get the kidney?"

The following are extracts from a statement directed to potential science writers by Casey Bukro, environment editor of the Chicago _Tribune:_

> Look at what they did to Lake Erie.
> Look at what they did to the air in Los Angeles.
> Look at what they did to the American bison.
> If you're not moved by these classic examples of America's indifference to the destruction of the earth and life upon it, then you're not cut out to be an environmental writer. . . .
> Resist. Ask why these things happen. Don't settle for fuzzy answers. Don't shrug and say you can't fight city hall. Don't let them snow you. There are answers somewhere. Find them.
> The cornerstone of the environmental beat is questioning and testing so-called conventional wisdom: That growth is good, that more is better, that biggest is best, for example.
> The environmental beat had a part in exploring national policies that put economic values above human values. The need for this kind of exploration will go on. But you've got to be ready for it. . . .
> Environmental reporting needs a modern generation of Renaissance men and women without tunnel vision who can understand complexities, who can see how many subtle forces move gargantuan issues like strings on a puppet. . . .
> Accuracy is not served by publishing raw lists of facts and figures and two opposing viewpoints. Environmental reporters will be asked to explain "what it means." In doing this, environmental reporters—whatever their label—have a chance to forge a link between our ancient natural world and our modern technological society.
> Some experts believe we'll avoid environmental blunders in the future by getting doctors, lawyers, sociologists, engineers, city planners, and others to rule on the consequences and benefits of urban development projects.
> Prepare for that day so you'll know what they're all talking about and pull it all together.

And Bukro, the veteran expert, has this advice for the beginner who wants to follow in his footsteps.

As for how to prepare. I'd still be a journalism student. You still have to be able to report and write. I'd take some courses in natural resources, urban affairs, economic reporting. I'd spend some time at a wire service to pick up some practice in writing fast and clearly.

I'd get some basic reporting skills, like police reporting. Then move on to specialize. I can't help but feel that extra attention must be given these days to writing skills. Technical writing is almost self-defeating if it is not conveyed in an understandable way. The more complex the issues, the more readable the writing must be. People have to be drawn in by stories that catch their eye and hold their attention. It has to be interesting. You can't expect the reader to stay with it if the reading is painfully dull.

Now, when do I get to be the expert? I'm an expert first and foremost when I know the right questions to ask, and when I know where to go to ask them. When I come to the interview with sufficient knowledge and training to be able to pass all the elementary stuff, and get on with an interview that will keep the interviewee as interested as the reader. You get the best out of a source when he's interested, not just plodding through some basics. If I were to interview Einstein today, I'd know a heck of a lot about his theories even before going into the interview.

This is where journalists earn the contempt of scientists. They know when we have not done our homework. Conversely, they know when we have done our homework and are not trying to write another trite piece.

Being an expert does not mean I get a chance to shoot my mouth off every-time I write a piece. The old rules of objective writing still apply when doing a piece for the news section.

One of my old editors at City News Bureau would say: "Don't tell me what you think; tell me what you know." A reporter or a specialist still must report facts for the news section.

My status as an expert becomes more obvious when I write a series, or when I do an op-ed piece allowing me to give some opinion, or when doing a signed column. In those, I can comment on issues reported in the news, or even give some behind-the-scenes insight. But the news itself still must come unadulterated with opinion, and reflect all sides of the issue.

I must explain patiently that the news stories do not reflect my own views, but that signed columns are a bit different. Even so, I am mainly a reporter of events. I am not a columnist. I am not an editorial writer. Being a specialist does not mean I am free to write my opinions. It places a very special obligation on me to somehow bridge a gap between the old-time reporter, who only gave facts, to a new kind of reporter that gives the facts and tries to explain what they mean. But explaining what they mean often means another round of reporting or two, talking to experts, who in turn explain what they mean. I have to put that all together by way of detecting significant developments, asking the right questions, and writing it clearly.

To which should be added the comments of Jerry Ackerman, who became environment/energy editor (technically ecology specialist) of the Boston *Globe* in 1975 after ten years as a general reporter and small town editor.

It took me two years just to get a feel for what the principle issue is. Not surprisingly it's money.

But wrapped into this is all sorts of consciousness-raising trickery and chicanery not only on the side of developers (nuclear, oilfield, housing, highway, whatever) but those who grind axes against them (environmentalists of all colorations). More than anything, a writer on these subjects has to understand the sciences and economics behind things which have impact on the environment.

This doesn't mean the writer must also be a working chemist, physicist, economist or financier. But a firm grasp of the principles is essential as a guide to asking the right questions.

Politics naturally follows but the arguments therein are all built on the various ways available to massage hard data to suit one's own purposes. A good reporter in this field, as any other, needs to stoke up with a wealth of information whose principal purpose is only to sort out the crap as the stories come along. It often is necessary to report the discrepancies on one's own authority—something that can be done only if the writer is confident he understands the issue to at least the same depth as the bullshit artists who deal out the position papers.

An illustration of what such understanding can tell me:

Texaco currently advertises (in *Newsweek, Time,* and elsewhere) that it's one company that is Doing Something about developing oil shale, and we all should be patriotically proud.

Bullshit.

Texaco has purchased rights to use a microwave oil-extraction process developed by Raytheon which has yet to be tested outside a laboratory. It worked there, but that doesn't mean it will function efficiently in a large-scale deployment.

What's more, it hasn't yet locked up the leases on land that it proposes to mine out in northeastern Utah. There is absolutely nothing going on there, according to my Western sources.

Beyond this Texaco isn't going to do too much until it can be sure it pays. Texaco folks will be right in the pack when and if Washington makes tax credits available for oil-shale development. And they'll also be at the door with the others when and if the Energy Mobilization Board gets around to choosing "priority" projects to avoid sapping national capital resources. In that contest Texaco will be competing with about eight other big oil operators—each with its own pet technology and self-styled claim to fame.

Needless to say, it helps to be a curmudgeon in looking at all these shenanigans.

CHAPTER

23

Weather

A. Elements of Interest
B. The Local Summary
C. Interpretations

D. Forecasts
E. Definitions

With maps, charts, illustrations and other devices, serious and "happy talk" television announcers often calling themselves expert meteorologists have made the weather into a major journalistic interest. Newspapers continue soberly to correct the record but all journalistic soothsayers get their information from the same source, the National Weather Service of the National Oceanic and Atmosphere Administration, a part of the Department of Commerce. That agency was long known simply as the Weather Bureau. If, as is often the case in small places, there is no local representative of the Service to provide official information, the newspaper obtains the most reliable data available from other sources. Possibly a college or high school can provide it; if compelled to rely upon its own resources, the newspaper at least can make certain that its thermometer is properly set up. As any conversationalist knows, the weather is interesting even when there are no hurricanes, floods or droughts. Since people lived in caves their life has been dependent to a large extent upon the behavior of the elements: the machine or power age has not reduced their dependency in this respect. In fact, in many aspects of life, it has increased the dependency, as delicate machines may require certain atmospheric conditions for proper operation.

Elements of Interest

It is not necessary to read a newspaper to know that it is abnormally hot or cold or that there has been a thunderstorm, but the reader does expect a newspaper to supply authentic statistics about the weather, the widespread consequences of any unusual climatic condition and predictions as to a change in the situation. *USA Today,* the Gannett newpapers chain's

478

flashy national daily, has stimulated the use of detailed, colorful weather pages in many U.S. newspapers during the '80s.

As newspapers have escalated their routine weather coverage to include intricate details about weather conditions almost everywhere and as television has expanded its use of gizmos for the weather portions of the evening news shows, weather journalism at times has gone beyond the line of news into pandering excess. Boston *Globe* columnist David B. Wilson unloaded his frustrations with the more frivolous aspects of the weather news boom in this Feb. 17, 1985, column:

> Once upon a time, a long time ago, before the tube began to make boobs of sensible people, there was something called the Weather Report.
> It was heard at the end of hourly radio news programs and found ordinarily in the upper right-hand corner of the front page. It used to say things like:
> "Fair and warmer."
> Dull.
> But the old-fashioned Weather Report had its advantages. It didn't take long. It was terse and unequivocal, even if frequently wrong. You knew where to find it and what it was trying to say.
> Meteorology, after all, is light entertainment masquerading as pseudo-science. At best, it ranks in credibility somewhere near astrology, phrenology and the analysis of entrails. . . .
> Instead of the Weather Report, America now has The Weather, which is quite another kettle of bouillabaise, a soporific exercise in disinformation during which the "meteorologist" makes a point of not getting to the point.
> It is trash news, pseudo-news, non-news, glitzy junk, consisting largely of laborious flirtation between the female anchor and the weather person, who was hired because he is what high school sophomore girls called "cute". . . .
> The Weather is Gresham's Law news, cheap currency driving out dear.
> The Weather is popular because weather is simple. There are only about six kinds—fair, cloudy, warmer, colder, rain and snow, plus a few subspecies. The audience is familiar with the subject. Weather does not perplex the dull of wit with big words or abstractions. . . .
> Real news is expensive, requiring astute news directors, reporters who can talk and know what they're talking about, skilled camera crews, aircraft, vehicles and some familiarity with the community and its history. . . .

Still, to meet this reader demand, newspapers print weather reports and forecasts daily. The maximum and minimum temperatures for the preceding twenty-four hours and the next day's forecast frequently are printed on the first page with detailed hourly readings, reports from other cities, wind velocity, rainfall and other details on an inside page. If the weather becomes unusual in any way, a full-length news story is written.

When the weather becomes extreme, the reporter should seek information including the following:

1. Statistics and explanation.
   a. Maximum and minimum for day.
   b. Hourly readings.
   c. Comparison with other days during the season.

      d. Comparison with all-time records for the same date, month and season.

      e. Comparison with situations in other localities.

      f. Humidity, wind velocity, etc.

      g. Predictions: when relief expected.

      h. Official description of nature of phenomenon.

2. Casualties.

      a. Illness and death directly caused by the weather.

          (1) Heat prostrations.

          (2) Freezing.

          (3) Lightning.

          (4) Tornadoes, cyclones and hurricanes.

          (5) Floods.

          (6) Sleet and hail.

      b. Injuries and deaths of which the weather was a contributing cause.

          (1) Drownings.

          (2) Spoiled food.

          (3) Accidents from slippery pavements, snow, wind etc.

          (4) Fires.

          (5) Heart disease from heat exhaustion or exertion.

3. Property damage.

      a. Telephone and telegraph wires.

      b. Water craft sunk.

      c. Bridges and highways, pavements buckling.

      d. Farm buildings and animals.

      e. Automobiles, buses and other public conveyances.

4. Interference with ordinary life.

      a. Transportation.

          (1) Railroads.

          (2) Buslines.

          (3) Airlines.

          (4) Highways and bridges.

          (5) Private automobiles.

      b. Communication.

          (1) Mail service.

          (2) Telephone.

          (3) Telegraph.

          (4) Cable.

          (5) Radio.

          (6) Stoppage of food and other supplies.

      c. Public utilities.

          (1) Electric lights.

          (2) Gas pressure.

          (3) Water supply.

          (4) Fuel shortage.

5. Methods of seeking relief.

      a. Increased demands on water supply.

      b. Bathing beaches and parks.

     c. Trips.

     d. Sale of fans.

     e. Children cooled by hydrants, hoses etc.

6. Methods of handling situation.

     a. Police activity.

     b. Volunteer groups: Boy Scouts, Legionnaires etc.

     c. Red Cross, Civil Defense and other relief agencies.

     d. Use of ashes and other materials.

     e. Public warnings on driving, diet, etc.

7. Freaks.

     a. Narrow escapes.

     b. Undamaged property surrounded by desolation.

     c. Unusual accidents.

The Local Summary

Because the weather affects every reader, no matter what unusual features are included or how the story is written, the reporter must include as many of the preceding elements as are pertinent. Emphasis should be on the effects of an unusual weather condition—casualties, damage, disrupted service—and on the basic statistics such as temperature, inches of rain or snowfall and wind velocity.

The following portions of three stories from the main local page of the Apr. 7, 1985, edition of the St. Petersburg *Times* show how spot news reporting, interpretation, backgrounding and sprightly writing can be combined into significant, informative reporting about the weather:

By David Dahl and Diane Rado

A fast-moving thunderstorm dumped more than an inch of rain on the thirsty Suncoast Saturday, but it was hardly enough.

Even with the healthy dose of rain, water officials said the area still needs three or four more such storms to replenish supplies diminished by an eight-month dry spell.

"We need about 10 inches total to break the drought," said Bill Courser, a spokesman for the Southwest Florida Water Management District.

That means restrictions on lawn sprinkling and car washing will continue in eight counties along Florida's West Coast. The restrictions were imposed last week to ease the strain on water supplies. Officials except Saturday's rain to ease the situation a bit, because now yards won't need to be watered for another day or two.

How dry is it? The last good rain along the Suncoast was March 22nd. Before that, a few drops fell March 16th and 17th. Before that, February 14th.

"When we're in a dry spell, a rain or two doesn't help much," explained Chuck Eggleton, a forecaster for the National Weather Service in Ruskin.

For today, forecasters predict scattered thundershowers, although they likely won't be as dense or violent as Saturday's. Temperatures should reach the lower 80s under partly cloudy skies. Forecasters predicted a "slim chance" of rain for Monday, with temperatures in the 70s. . . .

By David Ballingrud

Florida has *lots* of water. It's one of the wettest areas in the Western Hemisphere.

Lakes, rivers, springs, swamps and marshes are abundant. Annual rainfall is between 50 and 60 inches. The underground aquifer, experts say, contains more water than all five of the Great Lakes combined.

Even in Pinellas County, which now pipes in almost all of its water from neighboring counties, there is plenty of water underground.

So why, when there is so much water, do we keep coming up short?

Explosive growth and too little rain have put great pressure on water supplies, but there's more to it than that.

Bad luck and a pinch of salt, for instance.

Major rivers enter the northern part of the state from the Appalachian Mountains. One of them, the Apalachicola, "could conceivably supply the domestic needs of the entire state," according to a report by the Florida Conservation Foundation.

But the Apalachicola makes a slow turn to the right in the Florida Panhandle, and exits into the Gulf of Mexico. The Suwannee does the same a little farther south.

In the central part of the state, five major rivers begin in or near the Green Swamp. But they, too, quickly run to the sea. "The Withlacoochee exits at Citrus County; the Hillsborough exits in Tampa Bay; the Peach empties into the Gulf; the Kissimmee flows into Lake Okeechobee, and the Oklawaha flows north, eventually into the Atlantic," says Bob Bryant of the Southwest Florida Water Management District.

That leaves most of the central and all of the south portions of Florida dependent on the underground supply and on enough rainfall to recharge it.

And that's what is missing, as the two driest months of the year begin. . . .

St. Petersburg Times Staff Writer

The Pinellas County Sheriff's Department has been flooded with calls from residents seeking information about the water restrictions imposed last week.

"Our switchboards are being swamped with such important calls as, 'Can we sprinkle?' " a sheriff's dispatcher said Saturday. "We get 100 calls a day."

Lt. Mike Brown, a department spokesman, said most callers seek information about when they can water. Others call to report neighbors breaking the rules. Others call to complain and to try to get themselves exempted from the rules.

Brown said no citations have been issued yet. "We want everybody to be properly informed," he said. "If (it's a violator's) first time, we try to work with them."

On Tuesday the Pinellas County Commission imposed mandatory water restrictions on about 156,000 country residents and on 19 cities that rely on county water.

No daytime sprinkling is permitted, and night-time sprinkling is allowed only from midnight to 7 a.m. and 9 p.m. to midnight.

Residents whose home addresses end in even numbers can water on even-numbered days. Those whose home addresses end in odd-numbers can water on odd-numbered days.

Phones at the sheriffs department in Hillsborough County, where water restrictions are also in effect, have been tied up with water-related inquiries this week as well. In St. Petersburg, police say they haven't gotten too many water calls because residents have become familiar with the restrictions.

"We're just waiting for the rain so everyone will stop calling," a dispatcher said Saturday morning.

Interpretations _____

Public curiosity concerning unusual weather conditions is a form of scientific interest. To satisfy it, the communication media cannot be expected to define every meteorological term as it appears in a news account, as many of the most common must be used almost daily. When occasion seems to demand, however, parenthetical inserts, sidebars and longer feature articles can be used, mostly for the benefit of middle-aged readers who went to junior high school before its curriculum was enriched by elementary instruction in this field.

After many decades of stubborn refusal to popularize its vocabulary, the National Weather Service has relented in recent years. It takes cognizance of popular usage now by permitting such phrases as "unusually fine weather" and "clear and bright" in its forecasts.

Explanations of natural phenomena can be given in scientifically accurate but easily understood language.

By Cathie Huddle

It sounds like the roar of a freight train and the sky turns green.

That's a fair description of a tornado striking, according to Orval Jurgena of the National Weather Service office in Lincoln.

Each year tornadoes add an ugly twist to spring in Nebraska and it's that time of year again. Time to get ready, time for some facts.

The sky turns green as sunlight reflects from the hail that often falls to the Northeast of a tornado, Jurgena said.

He dispelled a myth—that there is always a deathlike silence before the twister hits. That isn't always the case, he said. When a cold front passes through, the strong south winds drop before the north winds set in sometimes causing the "quiet before the storm."

One dictionary's "tornado" definition is "a violently whirling column of air extending downward from a cumulonimbus cloud . . . almost always seen as a rapidly rotating, slender, funnel-shaped cloud that usually destroys everything along its narrow path."

Between 1974 and 1978, 246 tornadoes touched down in Nebraska, killing four persons and injuring 195, according to a recent report.

Nebraska had more tornadoes than any of the other eight states in the central southwestern region during that time, according to a report from the U.S. Commerce Department's National Oceanic and Atmospheric Adminstration.

Tornadoes form where air masses of contrasting temperature and moisture clash, often creating severe thunderstorms that produce high winds, hail and torrential rainfall. About 5 percent of all thunderstorms produce tornadoes and scientists are not sure what triggers them, according to NOAA.

Tornadoes are usually easy to identify by the familiar funnel, which drops from its apparent cloud overhead like a dark rope or elephant trunk. Larger storms, however, may appear as a general black mass from the sky to the ground.

There is almost complete devastation wherever a tornado touches ground. The winds, which can exceed 200 mph, can roll cars end over end, flatten mobile homes and lift the roof from a house before smashing its walls to splinters. They also bring a lethal barrage of flying mud, sticks, rocks and other debris, including glass from shattered windows. . . .

[Lincoln (Neb.) *Sunday Journal and Star*]

Forecasts _____

Important decisions such as whether to take an umbrella to work, postpone a trip, or cancel an outdoor picnic depend on weather conditions and make expert forecasting important. Not even the best forecasters, however, can guarantee the accuracy of any prediction, which makes life more uncertain but perhaps more interesting.

By Chris Satullo

They weren't denying they'd blown one, but the free spirits at the National Weather Service station didn't sound very penitent today.

"What can I tell you? We goofed," said weather specialist Ed Karpinski about the 4 to 6 inches of snow that fell Wednesday morning with no warning. "Actually, I don't feel bad at all. I just got back from vacation today. If you want to talk to the guy who really messed up, I'll get him."

The mistake, Karpinski said, was that the weather service thought a low pressure system would pass farther north than it did. When the pocket dipped south, the snow came, causing dozens of minor traffic accidents, catching most road departments unawares and cutting into school attendance.

Karpinski ventured a forecast calling for partly sunny skies and warmer temperatures Friday followed by highs in the 40s over the weekend. . . .

[Easton (Pa.) *Express*]

Some forecasts are in the form of warnings, thus performing a valuable public service if people will heed the warnings, which they do not always do, even when the warnings are graphic. Consider these two stories, which ran side-by-side in the Feb. 24, 1985, Los Angeles *Times*:

By T. W. McGarry

A $350,000 hillside home, dumped off its foundation by a mysterious earth movement, slid down a steep slope in the Los Feliz district with six people trapped inside Saturday afternoon and crumpled into the street, injuring a 63-year-old woman and her granddaughter.

City officials ordered six nearby homes evacuated until a geologist could determine whether they were also in danger. Inhabitants of four were allowed to return later Saturday night.

The collapse began about 2:30 p.m. when the hillside behind the house at 3583 Amesbury Road began sliding toward the street, said John Mirhij, 77, who was in the house with his wife, three grandchildren and a maid.

"It was like an avalanche," said a neighbor, Joan Watt. "It started with a couple of little rocks off the back of the hill, then all of sudden, va-voom, and the hill just folded up. It was a miracle they got out alive."

The slide burst through a retaining wall and dirt and large rocks cascaded into the rear of the house.

"Everything was coming down into the house like an earthquake," Mirhij said. Walls parted from the roof and "we could see the sky," he said.

Floors and walls tilting at many angles kept him from moving, he said.

"The floor was full of broken glass," he said. "My wife tried to escape through the door, but everything fell on her. She was held up by all of the things falling on her," which cut her face, he said. . . .

By Jan Klunder

Cary Black returned to her beachfront Malibu apartment four days ago and spotted a cryptic sign on the front door that declared her home was "UN-SAFE" and should not be entered.

"I thought the monster from the deep lagoon was in there," Black recalled Saturday.

But no, it was just another of the little inconveniences that Malibu residents have learned to tolerate. The hillside across Pacific Coast Highway was cracking and threatening to crash down on her home.

No big thing.

"Everyone says living in Malibu is like playing Russian roulette," said Black, who pays $1,700 a month for a three-bedroom apartment. "You take a certain amount of risk living here."

Despite warnings from geologists that a major rock slide is imminent in the 20400 block of Pacific Coast Highway, only two of 16 families ordered Wednesday by Los Angeles County officials to evacuate had left their homes by Saturday. . . .

Definitions _____

To write understandable weather accounts, the reporter must know the meaning of the most important meteorological terms. The following list was prepared especially for this chapter by J. R. Fulks, who served for many years in the Chicago office of the United States National Weather Service, and William M. L. Briggs, meteorologist in the forecast office of the National Weather Service in Chicago.

Barometer. An instrument for measuring atmospheric pressure. There are two types. In one, the mercurial barometer, pressure is measured as the height (commonly expressed in the United States in inches) to which the atmosphere will lift mercury in a vacuum. An average height of the barometer at sea level is about 29.9 inches, and in the lowest several thousand feet one inch less for each thousand feet above sea level. The other type of barometer is the aneroid which measures air pressure by the expansion or contraction of one or more metal vacuum cells. Pressure is also measured in millimeters of mercury, but the international unit used by meteorological services is the millibar (1 millibar equals 1000 dynes; 30 inches of mercury equals 1015.92 millibars). An airplane altimeter is a high-precision aneroid barometer.

Blizzard. Strong wind accompanied by blowing snow. The National Weather Service uses this term for winds greater than 35 mph, and visibilities less than ¼ mile. The snow may be either falling or may be picked up from the ground by the wind.

Ceiling. An aviation term used in the United States to designate the height above ground of the lowest opaque cloud layer which covers more than half the sky.

Contrail. The name of a cloud which forms behind high-flying aircraft.

Cyclone. Same as a *low*. The term *cyclone* refers to its system of rotating winds. It is a moving storm, usually accompanied by rain or snow.

Degree days. The number of degrees that the day's mean temperature is above or below 65° F. Heating degree days are the number of degrees the day's mean temperature is below 65° F. These are totaled monthly and seasonally to obtain a measure of heating needs. Cooling degree days are the number of degrees the day's mean temperature is above 65°; they indicate air conditioning needs.

Dew point. The temperature to which air must be cooled for fog to form. It is an index of the amount of moisture in the air.

Fog. A condition of lowered visibility caused by minute water droplets suspended in the air. It is a cloud resting on the ground.

Forecasts, weather. Statements of expected weather, prepared by specially trained professional meteorologists. They are based on weather data collected rapidly over a large portion of the world. To obtain the most probable expected weather, the forecaster uses prognostic computations made by the electronic computer, considers other physical and statistical factors and applies judgment based on long experience. Specific forecasts are generally for periods of one to three days at the most, but the National Weather Service issues both five-day and monthly forecasts of *average* conditions. Weather forecasts are of many types, such as public, aviation, marine, agricultural and forest-fire weather. The National Weather Service also prepares and issues flood forecasts, watches and warnings.

Front. A boundary between two different air masses, one colder than the other. A *cold front* moves towards the warmer air, a *warm front* toward the colder air. When a cold front overtakes a warm front, they form an *occluded* front.

Frost. A deposit of ice crystals on outside objects caused by condensation of moisture from the atmosphere on clear cold nights. Killing frost is defined as the first frost of autumn sufficient to kill essentially all vegetation in the area.

High. An area of high barometric pressure, usually several hundred to a thousand miles or more in diameter. In the Northern Hemisphere, winds blow clockwise about a high center. The approach of a high generally means improving weather—the ending of rain or snow, then clearing, colder and finally somewhat warmer as a result of sunshine. The weather in highs, like lows, varies from one high to another and will differ depending on where the center passes. A slow-moving high may cause fog, and often accumulation of air pollution, in and near its center.

Humidity. A general term applying to any of various measures of the amount of moisture in the atmosphere. See _Relative humidity_.

Hurricane. The name applied in the Caribbean Region, Gulf of Mexico, North Atlantic and eastern North Pacific (off Mexico) to a tropical cyclone in which the strongest winds are 75 miles per hour or greater. The same type of storm in the western Pacific is called a typhoon.

Inversion. An increase of temperature with height, in contrast to a normal decrease with height. Inversions at or near the ground trap pollutants by preventing the upward dispersion.

Jet stream. A line or band of maximum wind speeds high in the atmosphere, generally somewhere between 30,000 and 40,000 feet. The speeds are often in excess of 100 mph.

Lake breeze. A relatively cool breeze which frequently blows, on warm afternoons, from a cool lake onto adjacent warmer land. It may extend less than a mile or as much as several miles inland.

Lake effect. A general term which applies to any effect of a lake on weather. Near the shores of the Great Lakes a sometimes spectacular effect is that of heavy snowfall over a small area (perhaps a county). It is caused by moisture-laden air in winter moving from the lake onto the land, the air having been originally very cold, probably much below 0° F, before it moved onto the lake.

Local storm. Any storm of small scale, such as a thunderstorm. _Severe local storms_ are those likely to cause damage, including severe thunderstorms, damaging hail and tornadoes.

Low. An area of low barometric pressure usually a few hundred miles in diameter. In the Northern Hemisphere, winds blow counterclockwise around a low center. Typically, the approach of a low means worsening weather—increasing cloudiness and finally rain or snow, but the pattern of weather varies for different lows and will be different depending on how far away the center actually passes. The low may affect weather up to several hundred miles from its center. Usually, as a low approaches, the weather becomes warmer, then colder as the low passes; this is typical of a low that passes to the north, but there may be little or no warmer weather if the low passes to the south.

Mean temperature. The average temperature over any specified period of time, such as a day, month or year. The United States National Weather Service uses the average of the lowest and highest temperature of each day as the mean temperature—an approximation that is very close to the true mean.

Mist. A condition intermediate between fog and haze—a thin fog. Also, in the United States, often applied to drizzle (fine rain).

Precipitation. Water droplets or frozen water particles falling to the ground. It includes rain, drizzle, freezing rain, freezing drizzle, snow, snow pellets, snow grains, hail, ice pellets (in the United States, sleet) and ice needles. The term _precipitation_ is applied also to total measured depth of precipitation for which purpose any frozen form is first melted.

Precipitation probability. In the United States National Weather Service forecasts, the probability that .01 inch or more of precipitation will fall at any one point in the forecast area during the specified time period, usually 12 hours.

Relative humidity. A commonly used measure of atmospheric humidity. It is the percentage of moisture actually in the air compared to the amount it would hold if completely saturated at the given temperature. High humidity contributes to human discomfort at high temperatures but only slightly so if at all at low temperatures. Indoor relative humidity is sometimes applied to the relative humidity which outside air will have when heated to indoor temperature (usually taken as 72°F).

Shower. A rain of short duration, such as with a thunderstorm. Typically, showers begin abruptly and the intensity of precipitation varies considerably. There may be many separate showers on a day of showery weather. The term is also used with other than rain, for example, *snow shower* or *sleet shower.*

Sleet. In the United States frozen rain drops, but in Great Britain a mixture of rain and snow.

Smog. A contraction of the words "smoke" and "fog." It is, however, applied commonly in large cities or industrial areas when the pollutants may include other types in addition to smoke and fog.

Squall. A strong wind which begins suddenly and lasts a matter of minutes—somewhat longer than a gust. Also, especially in nautical usage, a sudden strong wind and an accompanying cloud mass that may produce precipitation, thunder and lightning. A *squall line* is a line or band of active thunderstorms.

Storm. A general term that may mean a cyclone, thunderstorm, wind storm, dust storm, snow storm, hail storm, tornado, hurricane or the like.

Storm warning. Can be a warning of any type of storm, but is applied more specifically to warnings for mariners. Marine storm warnings are of four types. *Small Craft* (less than 39 mph), *Gale* (39–54 mph), *Storm* (55–73 mph) and *Hurricane* (74 mph and greater). On the Great Lakes, the term *Small Craft Advisory* is used instead of *Small Craft Warning,* and *Storm* is used for any speed above 54 mph (*Hurricane* is not used). The figures refer to wind speeds.

Temperature-humidity index. A measure of human discomfort in warm weather. It takes into account the effect of both temperature and humidity. The THI is found by adding the dry bulb temperature and the wet bulb temperature, multiplying this sum by 0.4 and adding 15. With a THI of 70, nearly everyone feels comfortable; at 75, at least half the people become uncomfortable; at 79 or higher, nearly everyone is uncomfortable. Fewer people, however, are uncomfortable if there is a good breeze.

Thundershower. A thunderstorm accompanied by rain.

Tornado. A small, violently rotating storm, commonly a few hundred yards in diameter. It accompanies a thunderstorm, but only a very few thunderstorms have tornadoes. Direction of rotation is usually the same as that of a Low, and the strongest winds range generally 100 to 300 mph. In addition to wind effect, some damage to structures is caused by low atmospheric pressure in the tornado center which causes buildings to collapse outward.

Water vapor. Water in gaseous form. The atmosphere always contains some water vapor, but the amount varies greatly. In hot humid conditions, it sometimes constitutes as much as 2 per cent (by weight) of the air. At low temperature, the amount is much less. Water vapor is invisible, but when it condenses it forms water droplets that become visible as clouds or fog.

Watch. A bulletin issued by the United States National Weather Service to alert the public to conditions which may require issuance of later warnings. The warnings, when issued, are generally for smaller areas and give more specific locations and times.

Wind direction. The direction *from* which wind blows.

CHAPTER 24

Entertainment

When they are not working to earn a living, Americans engage in a variety of activities for self-improvement, relaxation or pleasure. In their enjoyment of hobbies and games and other diversions they are either active participants or spectators. In either capacity they have easy access to a quantity of printed material written by journalistic experts to enhance their enjoyment. Newspaper columns and special-interest magazines appeal to the home gardener, interior decorator, pet owner, collector of stamps, coins, antiques or objects of art, players of games such as chess and bridge, theatre-goers, movie buffs and rock music enthusiasts. They also cater to hunters, fishermen, campers, hikers, yachtsmen, canoeists, swimmers, joggers, golfers, tennis enthusiasts, bowlers, bird-watchers, tourists, nature-lovers and others. In the '80s, entertainment news of a mind-boggling variety has been getting more coverage and more space in newspapers of all kinds. Items range from calendars of coming events to reviews to investigative reporting.

Sports

Greatest journalistic attention is paid to professional sports. This means that sports pages contain mostly free publicity for commercial enterprises, including college football and basketball, which have become businesses themselves. Several newspapers have attempted to reduce the attention paid professional sports but reader complaints invariably have resulted in a reversal of policy. Some technically amateur sports activities, as college football and other athletic contests, are actually huge financial ventures that cannot be ignored. Small city papers can pay more attention than the metropolitan press to high school and other really amateur events. The increase in sports activities for girls and women has created new readers for the sports page. Even in smaller communities, however, it is impossible to give equal treatment to intramural or sandlot athletics.

Most newspaper sports pages now carry several full pages daily of detailed results, personnel changes and betting odds for both major and minor sports. The appetite of the fans for such information seems insatiable.

The Sports Reporter

High value is put upon the experience gained in writing sports, generally for two reasons: (1) only the critics and reviewers have anywhere near comparable freedom as to both what they say and the manner of saying it, and (2) there is no audience more critical than that consisting of sports fans who demand of a writer absolute accuracy and soundness of critical judgment.

Knowledge of the fine points of a game, which comes from having played it oneself, increases a person's interest in the skill of experts at the sport. Baseball became established as the national sport at a time when it was the most common sandlot pastime; in later years, the boys who played it relived vicariously the thrills of their adolescence through the achievements of Babe Ruth, Ted Williams, Willie Mays and others. Today, with young and old enjoying golf, tennis, bowling, swimming and other sports, interest in professional experts in these fields is growing. This means that there are more readers who like to second-guess the umpire—and the reporter.

Remaining Cool

Everyone who attends an athletic event does so in quest of pleasure—that is, everyone except the sports reporters. This does not mean that sports reporters do not enjoy their work; it does mean that they cannot permit their enthusiasm to approach that which the fan displays. The press box should not be a cheering section because its inhabitants have all they can do to follow closely what is happening so as to explain the difficult plays and decisions for fans who were too busy spurring on alma mater to notice exactly what happened. It is pleasant for reporters to view sports events from the best seats but they never should assume the carefree attitude of the casual fan.

Following Plays

From his or her superior vantage point, the sports reporter should be expected to observe accurately. In many sports, the action is so fast that spectators cannot always follow it. The news story should let the bleach-erite know what kind of pitch went for a home run or should tell the fans who sat in the cheap seats how the knockout blow was struck. At major sports events, the work of sportswriters is facilitated by the assistance of an official scorer who decides whether a hit or an error is to be scored. There also will be statisticians to prepare details in addition to those going into the official score book. At minor events, however, reporters usually have to compile most of their own statistics. If, in addition to a general story of an event, a play-by-play account is desired, customary practice is to assign two reporters. An indispensable part of any featured sports story is a summary or box score, as the particular sport requires, which is run separately or at the end of the story proper. To the fan, the summary or box score is a complete account in itself.

Knowing the Rules

The sports fan not only attends contests but also receives considerable pleasure from discussing the past performances and future chances of play-ers and teams. A favorite pastime is to second-guess the coach or manager and to pass judgments upon the abilities of referees and umpires. Just as popular among fans is criticism of the write-ups of sports reporters. In other words, the sports writer should know the game just as well as do players and officials. It is inconceivable that a reporter not understand the rules of the game to be covered. Writers of business news can make mistakes that only economists recognize; sports writers produce copy for readers who think they know as much as the reporter knows.

Knowing the Records

To keep up with what is expected, the sports reporter not only must understand the rule book but also must know the record book containing the statistics of what players and teams have done in the past. Otherwise, the reporter will not know whether a particular achievement is unusual. The sports expert whose mind is a storehouse of information regarding the history of sports is in a position to enrich copy considerably.

Talking the Language

A New York sports writer of a generation ago, Charles Dryden, is given credit for having been first to introduce on the sports page an informality and originality of language that would scandalize readers if found in the regular news sections. The credit for genius due Dryden has been dimmed because of the banal depths to which thousands of imitators, consciously or unconsciously, have sunk since then. Stanley Walker, longtime New York *Herald Tribune* city editor, wrote: "If it is true, and it appears to be, that Dryden was the father of whimsical baseball reporting, then the man has a great deal to answer for. He may have freed some reporters and afforded them the chance to do their gorgeous word-painting with a bold and lavish hand, but for every one he liberated he set demons to work in the brains of a dozen others—demons which made American sports writing the most horrendous mess of gibberish ever set before the eyes of a reader."

Writing Sports News

One advantage the sports writer has over the reporter who specializes in political, governmental, business, scientific or any other type of news: the rules are definite and, despite occasional minor changes, remain the same year after year in all parts of the country. This situation, which contributes to the ease of sports reporting, also may lead to monotony. It is the belief of many successful writers that the opportunity to develop an individual writing style, which sports reporting affords more than any other kind of newspaper work, exists up to a certain point only, after which the sports reporter should do the more serious writing for which earlier work has provided training.

On the other hand, however, there are scores of first-rate sports writers whose copy seems just as fresh as ever after years of writing. Outstanding was the late Walter (Red) Smith, whose syndicated column originated with the New York _Herald Tribune_ and survived the paper. Tom Boswell of the Washington _Post_ and Roger Angell of _The New Yorker_ are two fine stylists still at work.

In reporting amateur or local sports, the sports reporter almost invariably supports the home team. Any criticism of local heroes is constructive and usually is consistent with what a large number of fans believe. The tendency to "build up" local players may be overdone to the detriment of both the players and writer when performances do not square with predictions. Sports writers should have a friendly attitude and make it clear that they, as well as the readers, want the home team to win. On the other hand, journalists should not act as a virtual public relations counsel for coaches or managers who may wish to use a reporter to send up deceptive trial balloons to confuse opponents, or to promote their own interests. The dangers of excessive boosterism in sports reporting have been made clear in recent years with court exposes of extensive drug abuse in professional and amateur sports, with widespread disgust at fixed games and violations of recruiting rules and with economic and physical exploitation of many athletes. A new generation of sports reporters is using investigative techniques to cover the economics, sociology, and politics of the sports beat. That is a development long overdue.

Although all contests of a particular sport are played according to the same rules, the major news interest of an individual game might be any one of a number of potential elements. In determining the feature of a game, the sports reporter considers the following:

1. Significance.
   a. Is a championship at stake?
   b. Effect of the result on the all-time records of the contestants.
   c. Effect of the result on the season's records of the contestants.
   d. Are the contestants old rivals?
   e. Are they resuming relations after a long period?
   f. Will the outcome suggest either contestant's probable strength against future opponents?
2. Probable outcome.
   a. Relative weight and experience of contestants.

      b. Ability as demonstrated against other opponents, especially common ones.

      c. Improvement during the season.

      d. New plays, tactics and so forth.

      e. New players, return of injured players, strength of substitutes and so forth.

      f. Former contests between the two contestants.

      g. Weather conditions favorable to either contestant.

      h. Lack of practice, injuries and other handicaps.

      i. Tradition of not being able to win away from home.

      j. Recent record, slumps, and so forth.

  3. How victory was won.

      a. The winning play, if score was close.

      b. The style of play of both winner and loser.

      c. Costly errors and mistakes of judgment.

      d. Spurts that overcame opponent's lead.

  4. Important plays.

      a. How each score was made.

      b. Spectacular catches, strokes, and so forth.

      c. The result of "hunches."

      d. Penalties, fouls, and so forth.

      e. Disputed decisions of umpire and referee.

  5. Individual records, stars, and so forth.

      a. Records broken.

      b. High scores.

      c. Players who "delivered" in pinches.

      d. Teamwork.

      e. Players not up to usual form.

  6. Injuries.

  7. The occasion or crowd.

      a. Size of crowd; a record?

      b. An annual event?

      c. Enthusiasm, riots, demonstrations, and so forth.

  8. The weather.

      a. Condition of track or playing field.

      b. Effect of heat or cold.

      c. Effect of sun on fielders, and so forth.

      d. Which side was more handicapped? Why?

      e. Delays because of rain, and so forth.

  9. Box score, summary and statistics.

Reviewing and Criticism _____

If college-trained reporters are not ambitious to become foreign correspondents or sports columnists, they are likely to want to be critics—motion picture, dramatic, musical, literary or art. Unfortunately for the youngster with talent that might lead to success in such writing, the average small newspaper offers inadequate opportunities for either experience or editorial guidance. As a result, many—including some of the best that the schools of journalism turn out—redirect their energies into other channels.

This section is intended both for the few who create opportunities for themselves, perhaps by developing a column of motion picture or book criticism in addition to their other work, and for the regular staff members who draw the assignments to cover the annual high school play, the local art club's exhibits, the occasional Broadway cast that makes a one-night stop and the home talent Gilbert and Sullivan light opera.

The Reporter-Critic

Essayists

The lure of critical reviewing probably is the opportunity it seems to offer for self-expression. The great critics, including Matthew Arnold, Stuart Sherman and George Bernard Shaw, also were creative artists and social philosophers. In addition to explaining to their readers how some muralist, playwright or composer regarded life, they chronicled their own reactions.

To prevent "spouting off" too much on the basis of only textbook knowledge and classroom discussions, it is perhaps fortunate that beginning reporters are hampered in their critical writing. To become a competent critic one must first serve an apprenticeship as a reviewer. When beginners cover a dramatic, musical or any other kind of aesthetic event, they do well to accept the assignment as one in straight news reporting. That is, while they are learning.

The purpose of the average member of a small-town audience at a motion picture, play or concert is pleasure seeking. A safe guide for newcomers in reviewing, therefore, is the reaction of audiences; it supplies an element of news interest of which the critic always should take cognizance. What got applause? What evoked laughs? Regardless of what reporters think of the audience's taste, to make a fair report of the occasion they should mention what indisputably were its high points from the standpoint of those for whom it was presented.

This advice is not tantamount to condoning the practice of building a review upon fatuous sentences or short paragraphs lauding every performer, but it is intended as a brake for those who might be tempted to use a night at the opera merely as an inspiration for an essay upon the fallacies of hedonism as demonstrated by _Faust_ or a dissertation on the evidence regarding Hamlet's insanity.

The following is an example of a straightforward, objective report:

By Elaine Markoutsas

Christmas trees and lights. Candy canes. Sleigh bells. Angels. Reindeer. Santa Claus.

It wouldn't be Christmas without them. And it wouldn't be Christmas without "The Nutcracker," which opened Thursday night for 24 performances [thru Jan. 4] at the Arie Crown Theater.

The classic late 19th-century ballet, set to the superb Tchaikovsky score and updated by Ruth Page, has become a tradition in Chicago, juxtaposed with other important works of art. Some make it an annual addition to their holiday fare. Others, present company included, are dazzled by the event as first-time-first-nighters. It's for everybody, and you don't have to know a thing about ballet or music to enjoy it. [Chicago *Tribune*]

Formulas

The critic with a bias is as dangerous as the political or labor reporter whose prejudices forbid interpreting fairly the activities or viewpoints of more than one side in a controversy. In criticism, application of a formula as to what an artistic form should be often results in conclusions as grotesque as condemning a cow for not being a horse.

An example of a critic with a formula is one who believes art should exist for art's sake only and that no artistic form ever should be utilized for propagandistic purposes. As a result, if the hero of a modern picture or play happens to be identified with a particular racial, nationality, economic or other type of group, the critic is likely stupidly to condemn the entire production as propaganda, even though it be an honest and perhaps brilliant attempt to describe sympathetically a certain segment of life.

Even worse than the opponent of propaganda is the exponent of it who is sympathetic only when a certain theory is promulgated by the particular art form under review. Such critics dismiss books, plays or other artistic creations with (to them) derisive adjectives, as "romantic" or "too realistic," with a condescension that, in the small community at least, cannot but brand them as supercilious or, as the critics' critics may put it, "half-baked highbrows."

Critics with a formula are bound to be mostly negative, carping and constantly dissatisfied. Because a Hollywood production does not square with their conception of what the Old Globe players would have done, they see no good in the result. Regretting that some artistic hero did not execute the idea, they are likely to make absurd comparisons between what is and what might have been.

The essence of competent reviewing of any kind is understanding an artist's purpose so as to interpret it to others. Any art form—painting, drama, the novel, music—is a medium of communication. No artistic creation should be condemned merely because of inability to understand its language, although those who hold that the artist should use a vocabulary that it is possible for others to learn have a valid point.

The duty of the reviewer or critic, in addition to that of describing a piece of art or an artistic event, should be to assist readers in an understanding of the artist's motives, to enhance their enjoyment of it. This obligation is prerequisite to that of passing expert judgment upon the artist's success in an undertaking; the role of evaluator is one that critic-reporters should postpone until they have reached maturity in artistic understanding, and not even then if the public consists largely of lay persons. The greatest service the newspaper that gives space to artistic news can perform for both artists and spectators or auditors is to interpret the former to the latter. The educational background that such service requires easily may be imagined.

The writer of the following example attempted to explain motives without passing judgment:

By Bob Rohrer

The political side of America's struggle for independence receives engrossing and frequently amusing treatment in the Broadway musical play "1776," now being performed with patriotic gusto by the road show company at the Atlanta Civic Center.

The plot covers the last months of the second Continental Congress in Philadelphia, which—after considerable political maneuvering—approved the Declaration of Independence as war raged between Colonial and British troops.

Authors Peter Stone and Sherman Edwards have skillfully blended a wealth of historical detail—much of it humorous—with imaginative dialogue and warm-blooded, affectionate parodies of the men who supported and opposed independence.

The production itself moves vigorously; the staccato pacing of the deftly-handled ensemble scenes alternates effectively with strategically placed slower interludes, and the surging action never backs over itself.

There are quite a few fine individual performances. Particularly outstanding are the efforts of Don Perkins, who is convincingly choleric as the irascible John Adams; Paul Tripp, who turns in a wry performance of an earthy Benjamin Franklin; Reid Shelton, who livens the production with an explosively uninhibited portrayal of the unabashedly egotistical Richard Henry Lee of the Virginia Lees, and Larry Small, who is effective in a small part as a courier who sings a moving antiwar ballad—just about the only memorable musical number in the show.   [Atlanta *Constitution*]

Reviewing

The difference between reviewing and criticism has been implied in the discussions under both previous headings. No matter how critical they may become with experience and expert judgment, art critics should not overlook their duty to supply the answer to the question "What is it like?" to the reader who has not read the book, attended the play or viewed the exhibit in question.

Is it a book about Russia or about how to raise puppies? A farce or a tragedy? A painting in imitation of Cézanne or one suggestive of Norman Rockwell? Readers who must select the books they read, the motion pictures, plays and musical events they attend, expect the newspaper to tell them the answers. Readers want, furthermore, an honest, fair statement, not an advertiser's blurb; and they do not want their pleasure spoiled by being told too much. That is, if the success of the playwright or novelist depends upon an unusual plot incident, it is unfair to both artist and audience for the writer to reveal its nature. How to convey an adequate impression of the nature of an artistic creation without spoiling one's fun demands only that quality known as common sense.

WOMAN OF VIOLENCE. By Geula Cohen. Translated by Hillel Halkin. 275 pp. New York: Holt, Rinehart and Winston, $5.95

Reviewed by Emily C. McDonald

"Woman of Violence" is the story of Geula Cohen and the life she led as a member of the notorious Stern Gang—which fought for the liberation of Palestine from the British. The gang—also known as the Lechi—was composed not only of terrorists, but also of idealists.

Geula Cohen was no exception.

She left her comfortable family life while still a student to join the freedom fight. First she tried the sanctioned organization—Betar. Then she turned to the more revolutionary Estel. Still not satisfied, she finally let herself be "recruited" into the Lechi.

From that day on her life changed completely. She went underground and rarely emerged from hiding except under cover of night. Geula learned to fight, to hide, to recruit, and—perhaps most important of all—to put dreams and ideals into action.

Finally, Geula became one of the "voices" on the Hebrew underground radio. Her voice brought news and inspiration to thousands of Jews eagerly awaiting news of the freedom fighters.

Although her work was dangerous, she never feared the danger. Her family was under surveillance, her friends were captured and put to death—still she went on with her broadcasts.

Then she too was captured. Through the Lechi underground, however, her escape was planned and finally brought about. She immediately returned to work.

Geula's memoirs end on the eve of Independence Day, 1948. Her active work in the Lechi ended then, too. She watched the celebrating but couldn't take part in it. The independence gained was not the Lechi ideal. As she put it:

"But I would remain outside. An ancient, heady melody that had started long ago would continue to resound far beyond these voices and frontiers."

[Nashville *Banner*]

Criticism

To pass judgment on the merits of a book, play, painting, musical number, motion picture or any other attempt at art demands expert judgment. To be an expert, one must have a specialist's education and training. This does not mean necessarily that newspaper critics must be able to produce masterpieces to be qualified to pass judgment on the efforts of another, but it does mean that they must have a thoroughgoing understanding of the field they write about.

It is not peculiar that supposedly expert critics often do not agree. Neither do political theorists, economists or scientists. A difference of opinion among specialists, however, is based upon sound principles whereas philistines have as their premises only stereotypes.

Critics who win the respect of readers usually are those who have proved their ability to report an artistic event correctly and to review fairly the nature of a piece of art. If they can observe correctly and interpret with understanding, they also may be trusted as artistic "tipsters." If they lack either of the other qualities, however, their starred selections will be ignored.

These, then, are the three responsibilities of the finished critic, which the ambitious beginner would do well to master one at a time in order (1) to describe objectively an artistic object or event, (2) to explain what the artist intends it to convey and (3) to pass expert judgment on the artist's success in achieving his purpose.

Note in the following example how the writer, although passing critical judgments, remained aware of his role as reporter:

By Albert Goldberg
TIMES STAFF WRITER

The differences in technique among dancers qualified to be principals in such an organization as the Bolshoi Ballet are generally so minute as to defy anything except pedantic expert analysis.

But the differences in personalities can be enormous and readily apparent, and it was this factor, with six changes of cast in the leading roles, that made the Bolshoi's second performance of "Don Quixote" in Shrine Auditorium Thursday night a much livelier and more convincing affair than the one of the previous evening.

Type casting is not ordinarily one of the basic principles of ballet, but it was utilized to maximum advantage by placing Ekaterina Maximova and Vladimir Vasiliev in the roles of Kitri and Basil the Barber. Seldom has a couple—they are Mr. and Mrs. in private life—been better matched in every respect than this irresistible pair of handsome youngsters.

Naturally they capitalize on their youth and beauty, but their skills go far beyond the physical aspects. Though quite different in other respects, Miss Maximova has something of the radiance of Margot Fonteyn. She lights up the stage with her petite, mischievous sparkle, and she dances with a buoyancy that completely reflects her personality. . . .

It is characteristic of the ensemble principle on which the Bolshoi operates that Natalia Bessmertnova, the troupe's third-ranking ballerina, should turn up unannounced in the comparatively minor part of the Queen of the Driads. Though brief, she made its opportunities count with a serene elegance of style and technique that aroused anticipation of more extended roles.

Alexander Lavreniuk took over the Toreador with a welcome addition of refinement and aloofness, and Rimma Kerelskaya, the Queen of the Driads on opening night, injected more variety and less routine into the street dancer. Maya Samokhalova, the previous street dancer, did the first variation of the last act, but we'll have to take that on faith.   [Los Angeles *Times*]

Handling the Assignment

Two factors that reviewers and critics must bear in mind are these: (1) Are those upon whose work they are to pass judgment professionals or amateurs? (2) Is the performance (dramatic or musical), production, presentation or object of art an original creation or a copy or imitation?

It is unfair to judge an amateur by professional standards. The home talent cast usually gets as much fun out of rehearsing and acting as do the relatives and friends who witness the result. Generally, amateur events should be reported factually with the audience's reactions as the guide.

Whereas Broadway first-nighters are as interested in the work of a playwright as in the excellence of actors, when the local dramatic club puts on something by Oscar Wilde or Somerset Maugham, it is stupid to place the emphasis in the review upon the familiar plot or problem with which the dramatist was concerned. Rather, it is the acting and staging that should command attention.

The broader the critics' backgrounds, the better able they are to make comparisons between immediate and past events. If they have seen several actresses play the same part, they can explain the differences in interpretations. When a motion picture is adapted from a novel, short story or stage play, they can point out the changes made in plot and artistic emphasis. The same orchestra under different conductors behaves differently in rendering the same musical masterpiece; two authors handling the same subject may have little in common as to either method or conclusions.

The following was a clever handling of the home-town performance of a familiar play.

By Elaine Cloud Goller
P-C ARTS WRITER

The *Pajama Game* has some tops—and some bottoms.

Dress rehearsal Tuesday night of Jonesborough Repertory Theater's current production had some wrinkles, but for the most part, provided a delightful musical evening that stirs mid-1950's memories of Doris Day.

The story line of *Pajama Game,* based on Richard Bissell's novel *Seven-and-a-Half Cents,* is a familiar boy-meets-girl, girl-rejects-boy, boy-gets-girl plot. Although it may hail from 25 years ago, the situation is one that we in 1980 can all identify with.

Management versus labor—the employees want a 7½-cent raise, but the boss isn't about to negotiate. (Sound familiar?)

Sid, the handsome new superintendent in the Sleeptight Pajama factory finds himself to be the third fellow in a year in his position. But it is easily understood. The boss, Mr. Hasler, hassles everybody over every little thing. (What makes this man so mean?)

Sid's fancy has been caught by Babe, the leader of the factory grievance committee. She is concerned about the conflict of interests—her love life, or the issue of the raise—and denies the taunts of the other girls by declaring that "I'm Not at All in Love." Which of course isn't at all true.

The pairing of efficiency expert Vernon Hines, with Hasler's prim bookkeeper Gladys creates a very funny couple. Secretary Mable, who sees and understands all in a matronly cupid's role, tries to illustrate to Hines that he is far too quick to jump to green-eyed conclusions in a comic softshoe duet, "I'll Never Be Jealous Again."

Considering himself the greatest lover of all time is the sex-crazed, daffy factory workers' union "Pres"—who appropriately works in ladies pants. He flirts with every skirt. One unwilling victim of his attentions is Gladys in his hilarious comeon, "Her Is."

By far the singing star of the heavily scored play is the crooning Sid, in such songs as "A New Town is a Blue Town," "There Once Was a Man," and the heart-rendering "Hey There." Perhaps due to the first night before an audience, Babe had some difficulty with some of her songs, although there were moments when her almost operatic voice was evident.

Chorus singers of note include Anita Irvin, Barbra Dawson and Frank Stith.

But the chorus in general seemed unsure of itself, especially in the opening number "Hurry Up," a difficult vocal counterpoint, granted, but practicing the words and timing would go a long way to improve the song.

There were some wonderful bits of comic activity, although some of the members of the large cast appeared nervous about little mistakes. They need reminding *anything* is likely to go wrong on stage, and learn to improvise and go on as if nothing had happened. There seemed a bit too much standing around awkwardly, exchanging glances that said "I don't know what to do," slowing the flow of action drastically. (For heaven's sakes, don't look at your feet!) Stage business is not the sole property of leading characters, it is an art to be practiced by everyone. Discovering a character's personality and then projecting it to the audience without disrupting the action is just as important (if not more so) for those who have few lines.

On the other hand chorus singing and dancing in "Hernando's Hideaway" was a spiffy production, as was the sizzling "Steam Heat." Choreography by Sheila B. Cox added much to the show.

The use of a small jazz combo has promise, but again, a little more rehearsal with the entire cast seemed necessary.

Among the minor problems Tuesday were an unfinished set and a short-handed stage crew. Perhaps the most obvious technical problem was with lighting—which was later explained to have been due to last minute rewiring that caused a blackout when lights should have come up. Panic-city in the control booth, but all was quickly returned to normal.

Then of course, the garage adjacent to the theater was once again inhabited by an inconsiderate neighbor playing a radio and racing an engine during the performance.

But despite the difficulties (many of which will undoubtedly be corrected—after all, it _was_ a rehearsal), the play is rousing, happy-ending family entertainment, and lots of comedy and familiar songs to brighten an audience.

[Johnson City (Tenn.) _Press-Chronicle_]

Motion Pictures

There are few places large enough to support a newspaper that do not also have a motion-picture theater. For the assistance of small-town editors, motion-picture producers issue publicity material descriptive of their films and performers. Obviously, however, much to be preferred is the locally written review or criticism composed from the standpoint of the audience rather than that of the advertiser; fearlessness is a quality without which motion-picture reviewing is likely to be jejune.

By Janet I. Martineau
NEWS ENTERTAINMENT EDITOR

"Kramer vs. Kramer" is, quite simply, one of the best movies in a year which started out with a whimper and is closing with a bang.

A nicely crafted script, which never allows pathos to overshadow humanity and laughs; sensitive direction and virtuoso acting on the part of three of our brightest actors give the movie its strength. Who could ask for more?

Well, there's the cinematography—capturing the ins and outs of life in New York City. And then there's Justin Henry, the child who in the end pits Kramer vs. Kramer. Picked out of a New York school, with absolutely no acting experience, he is a charmer—and a charmer without resorting to constant tears like his counterpart did in the sudser "The Champ."

In the storyline we view the lives of Ted and Joanna Kramer (Dustin Hoffman and Meryl Streep). On the surface they seem happily married, and he is a highly successful advertising agency artist (too successful, perhaps).

On the eve of winning a big promotion, his wife of eight years states simply she is leaving him—and her child—to find herself.

What follows is a lovely story of a father finally learning to know and ap-

preciate his son—the hard way. His career begins to take second place to PTA
meetings and doctor appointments, making his boss nervous. His whole life is
changed around, but he copes.

And, then, she comes back, announcing she wants the child now.

To writer-director Robert Benton's credit, and to the credit of Hoffman and
Miss Streep, there are no clear-cut good guys and bad guys in this film. There
are only grays.   [Saginaw (Mich.) *News*]

The Stage

What has been said about the motion picture applies also to the legitimate stage. If the play is a much-acted one, reviewers should not devote
any appreciable amount of space to relating the story of the plot or to
describing the general motive. Rather, they should perform the difficult
task of distinguishing between the acting and the actor's role and should
consider stage management and direction. Obviously, to criticize effectively the critic should have some acquaintance with the technique of play
production.

If the play is a new production, the critic rightfully evaluates the playwright's success in achieving his purpose. Is there proper congruity in settings, costumes, language and plot? Is the action logical or is the happy
ending arrived at by a series of unnatural coincidences? Are exits and en-
trances merely artificial devices to get characters on and off the stage?

If the production deals with a problem, is it met squarely or is it falsely
simplified? Are the characters truly representative of the types they portray or are they superficial or caricatures? Is the play propaganda? If it
points a moral, is the playwright sincere or naïve or bigoted? Is anything
risqué just smut for smut's sake or is it essential for dramatic completeness?

These are just a few of the questions critics ask themselves. For whatever conclusions they reach, they should give sound reasons.

Truly great dramatic critics have been students of life as well as of the
drama. "Ideally," according to Norman Nadel, critic for the old New York
World-Telegram, "the theater critic should be a Renaissance man," meaning one "with a knowledge of architecture, sculpture, painting, music, government, history, philosophy and other liberal arts subjects." Nadel suggested that college students finish their four-year course with a good classical
and historical background so as "to have perspective and to understand
the art form in relation to the world as it exists." He urged a knowledge of
philosophy because "people turn to a play to express a philosophical question," and a knowledge of history of the theater and playwriting "to recognize a play's originality and importance and to acquire an intellectual
appreciation of the play form."

Walter Kerr, long with the New York *Herald Tribune* and then the New
York *Times,* has said a drama critic must have an extensive background
in dramatic literature on a broad humanistic base. John Mason Brown felt
that critics should be able to "feel, touch and have sight of the world." He
advised students aspiring to be drama critics to get a thorough knowledge
of history. Richard Watts of the New York *Post* emphasized the value of
studying the English language as well.

Entertainment Places

Today the form of entertainment closest to the old-time vaudeville program is found in night clubs, arenas, hotels, summer resorts and similar places. Performers appear solo, delivering monologues, making music, dancing, engaging in pantomime or even acrobatic and other circus-type acts. The skill of the performer is what's at stake and that occupies the attention of the critic-reviewer more than perhaps anywhere else in the entertainment or artistic world today.

Marty Allen has the body of a Japanese wrestler gone to seed, the face of a troll and a hairdo inspired by a Brillo pad.

But he comes across beautifully in his act at the Holiday House, where he is substituting for Joan Rivers, whose week-long engagement was canceled at the Monroeville supper club.

Allen mixes up his fast-paced act well. One moment he bombards the audience with one-liners (his delivery is so good that you laugh even at jokes you've heard before); at another moment he might be doing a character sketch, like "Johnny Money," a hilarious spoof on Johnny Cash. He also does an interesting pantomime routine about an aging clown and hoofs it up in a finale about the sights and sounds of New York City.

Assisting Allen is Colleen Kincaid, who sings while he takes costume breaks, and she comes across well.

A fine singer, she also is an excellent dancer (she's a former member of the Golddiggers) and has not only an engaging stage presence but also an engaging physical presence.

Allen does one number with Kincaid called "Hey Big Spender" from "Sweet Charity." In this bit Allen is in drag, wearing platinum blonde wig, red silk shift and rhinestone earrings. He camps it up heavily looking like an aging hooker who would have trouble turning on a lightbulb.

Allen, a Pittsburgher, localizes some of his jokes and each area reference is met with guffaws. Also drawing a big response is a segment in which a bewigged and bejeweled Allen does a betwitching satire of Elvis Presley.

[Mike Kalina in Pittsburgh _Post-Gazette_]

Radio and Television

Newspaper criticism of television still is experimental. No orthodox formula has become widespread. Much of the columnar material is anecdotal or program announcements. The job of critically commenting on any appreciable amount of what is presented viewers is staggering. Celebrity interviews regularly make news for the news pages. The critic generally concentrates on dramatic performances, as in the following first-rate example:

By Robert C. Marsh

Are you sure you saw the new Lyric Opera version of Gounod's "Faust"?

Don't answer until you have had a second look at the telecast, which WTTW (Channel 11) will air (with stereo sound on WFMT) at 7:30 p.m. Wednesday. This "Faust" was a controversial stage production but it makes an extremely effective TV show.

Why? The camera gives you a different perspective on the work than was possible in the theater. In the Opera House, Pier Luigi Samaritani's settings dominated the stage. On the tube, for most of the evening the stage does not exist. You are tightly focused on the singers. Their facial expressions have a vitality and impact impossible in the Opera House (unless you carry a telescope), and the costumes become more important. (Faust's is silly but most of the others are good.)

Some of the moments that seemed odd in the theater are powerful here; for example, the spinning rose window in the church scene becomes, by a superimposed image, a symbol of Marguerite's anguish. The final scene is softened just enough that the angelic chorus can be taken impressionistically rather than as an illustration from a Sunday school tract. On the other hand, the descent of Faust and Mephistophiles into hell on stage elevators is rather pale. We expect better special effects on the tube. . . .   [Chicago *Sun-Times*]

Books

The first task of the editor of a book review page is one of selection of those few of the 25,000 or more new titles published annually that are to receive mention. Harry Hanson, veteran newspaper and magazine book reviewer, said:

> The daily book review lifts a book from an overtowering mass of printed material and makes it an integral part of life. It often becomes news of the first order. Between the covers of all these volumes there may be an authoritative voice touching on our vital problems, and if this is true, that voice certainly deserves a hearing. The book reviewer's job, it seems to me, is to sort this flood of titles, find the one that fits in the day's news, and then write about it as news.

That the first duty of the writer about books is to assist readers to select those they wish to read also was the viewpoint of another leading reviewer, Joseph Wood Krutch, who said:

> The best review is not the one which is trying to be something else. It is not an independent essay on the subject of the book in hand and not an aesthetic discourse upon one of the literary genres. The best book review is the best review of the book in question, and the better it is the closer it sticks to its ostensible subject. . . . However penetrating a piece of writing may be, it is not a good review if it leaves the reader wondering what the book itself is like as a whole or it is concerned with only some aspects of the book's quality.

As to the style of book reviewing or criticizing, there is no formula. The writer is free to use virtually any method he chooses, the only test being the effectiveness of the style used. Somewhere in the review or criticism the writer should be expected to classify the book as to type—fiction, philosophy, biography—to describe its contents, communicate something of its quality and pass judgment upon it.

A temptation that even seasoned reviewers sometimes do not resist is to use the writing as opportunity for personal therapy, with the result that seems sophomorically sophisticated or pseudo-intellectual. Take, for instance, the first paragraphs of Godfrey Hodgson's review of *The Glory and the Dream* by William Manchester in the Washington *Post*:

When this Brobdingnagian work first thumped on my desk for review, I took note of its bulk and of the inflated rhetoric of the title, and my first impulse was to dismiss it as the ultimate *Guiness Book of Records* champion nonbook.

I would count its pages, I said to myself, and I did. There are 1302 of them. That is not counting end pages, forematter, acknowledgments, bibliography, copyright acknowledgments, and index.

All of which it is provided with so lavishly that one might suppose that it is as scholarly as the *Monumenta Germaniae Historica,* which it is not. At something over 500 words to the page, that is more than two-thirds of a million words.

Next I thought I would weigh it on the kitchen scales. And that, too, I did, though it proved harder than I imagined since the chic little brass weights that I gave my wife for Christmas a few years ago only go up to two pounds avoirdupois, and Manchester is out of that division. As far as I was able to determine with the help of a pound of beans and a can of grapefruit sections, however, *The Glory and the Dream* tips the scales at around three pounds, eight ounces.

And then, I supposed, I would write a savage little review, commenting on the economics of book publishing, and ending, perhaps, "A book, however, this is not."

And yet I was wrong. It is even rather a good book of its kind, so long as one does not expect too much from it.

Another standard method is to relate the current volume to earlier works by the same author, as John Brooks did when he reviewed the Manchester book in the Chicago *Tribune:*

William Manchester is famous for *The Death of a President,* the "Kennedy book" of the 1966 headlines remembered less for its hair-raising account of the assassination of John F. Kennedy than for the prepublication objections to it by the fallen President's relatives and friends. Among his other books are *The Arms of Krupp* and a novel of much merit, *The City of Anger.*

Now he has written an enormous (1,300 page) popular history of the United States over four recent decades. Thru the sheer nerve of his undertaking and the dogged persistence of his execution of it, he almost batters the reader's critical faculties into submission and brings him to a helpless nod of assent. Almost, but not quite.

Prominent among the pitfalls of popular history-writing are the following:

(1) Drawing instant mood-pictures of past years with the help of phrases like "It was a time of . . ." and "It was that kind of year."

(2) Evoking instant nostalgia by writing down old song titles.

(3) Sounding like *Time* magazine.

(4) Sounding like Dos Passos in *"U.S.A."*

(5) Contriving corny melodrama by withholding a famous name until the end of an anecdote ("And that man's name was. . . .")

(6) Trying to convey a sense of destiny by faking detailed knowledge of the playpen days of people later to be famous ("Fifteen-year-old John F. Kennedy heard the long, plaintive wail of the steam whistle at the Choate School in Wallingford, Conn.").

A more scholarly approach is to compare a new book to others dealing with the same subject, as illustrated by the following from what John P. Roche wrote for *Saturday Review:*

Historical chronicles come in different styles, perspectives, and sizes. Frederick Lewis Allen, for example, utilized the principle of parsimony in his *Only Yesterday*. He made no effort to cover everything, but he did write a book. Cabell Phillips, in his *1929–1939: From the Crash to the Blitz,* drew extensively on *The New York Times* (the volume is one in a series called *The New York Times* Chronicle of American Life), but the result is far more than a scissors-and-paste job; reading it, one gets the distinct impression of a mind at work, of priorities established and maintained. Then, of course, there are specialized works, such as Irving Bernstein's *The Lean Years,* which view American life through the prism of the working class.

Now comes William Manchester with an immense narrative history of the United States 1932 to 1972. I began reading it with great interest, because the time frame is precisely the span of my political consciousness. This could be the story of my generation. Unfortunately it is not. By the time I emerged from the seemingly interminable 1,300 pages, I was convinced that Manchester had simply taken a vacuum cleaner to his task and swept up every bit for information, meaningful and trivial, and had never sat down to sort out the wheat from the chaff.

How different experts can react differently is illustrated by the following examples. The first is by Alfred Kazin, author of *Bright Book of Life: American Novelists and Storytellers from Hemingway to Mailer:*

This fluent, likeable, can't-put-it-down narrative history of America from the Bonus Army to Watergate is popular history in our special tradition of literary merchandising. It is all about the audience that will read it. Mr. Manchester is a steadier and more reliable source on American vicissitudes than photograph books, Theodore H. White, Time and Life, Frederick Lewis Allen, The New York Times Op-Ed page, Norman Mailer, Betty Friedan, Peanuts, et al. But his real virtue is not just that he is a dependable fact man with an eye for the unexpected fact and that he tells his story with all the ease of a practiced rewrite man who has been inspired by Dos Passos. He is really obsessed by the American audience, the great American consensus, the mass, the popular mind itself. He is confident that there is an all-present character called the American people and that he can describe 40 years of simultaneous experience. He identifies with this character and makes you believe that your whole life has been lived inside it. Reading Manchester, you run with the Bonus Army, lift up your chin like Roosevelt, put up the flag at Iwo Jima, and nervously dismiss MacArthur. You are against Communism *and* the Cold War. You participate!

Manchester is always thinking about *you,* you who are reading him, you who read history and can afford 20 dollars for a book. This book is your life.

By contrast, Curtis MacDougall, one of the co-authors of this book, who also wrote *Hoaxes* and *Gideon's Army, the Story of the Progressive Party of 1948* wrote the following for syndication by Field Enterprises:

Just about everything that happened for 30 years—in politics, diplomacy, education, science, labor-management relations, public health, the arts, entertainment, fads and fashions, civil rights, civil liberties, law, sports and all else—receives at least brief mention in this 1,397 page narrative.

There are some editorial jibes, such as that Elvis Presley was lewd and vulgar, Lyndon Johnson "characteristically said one thing while believing the exact opposite," the Prince Rainier-Grace Kelly wedding was an M-G-M press agent's dream. Typical of longer evaluative comments are:

"He (Eisenhower)) was a backslapper; Nixon was a brooder. In economics and political ethics the general was a fundamentalist. The senator was a relativist, an opportunist, and a fatalist," and "by 1961 the space race no longer had any bearing on national security . . . or on the pursuit of knowledge."

Mostly, the tome is objective reporting of what appeared on the front pages. William Manchester has no inside dope, no behind-the-scenes facts, no skeletons dragged out of closets. He makes no sociological interpretation of the era as a whole, notes no trends nor relationships between the multitudinous events he summarizes. Without historical perspective, he merely records the "what" and leaves the "why" to abler scholars.

Music

Reporters who are timid about covering a musical event because they lack technical training in music at least have the consolation that by far a majority of their readers, both those who attended the event under review and those who didn't, know no more than they do. The superior musical review, of course, is written for both the professor of music and the music-lover. The qualities demanded of the music critic were summarized as follows by the late Lawrence Gilman, long music critic for the New York *Herald Tribune:*

> The best music critic is a good newspaperman. Of course, he must know music, deeply and thoroughly and exactly; he must know what he is talking about. But the first and indispensable requirement of any article written for a newspaper, no matter on what subject is that it must be readable—it must be interesting as well as clearly intelligible to the lay reader of average education. A professional musician might be able to write a competent, technical account of a composition or a musical performance. But his review would probably be interesting only to other musicians.
>
> The chief aim of a newspaper critic must be to interest the general reader. And if he can interest those readers who have not heard the performance, as well as those who have, he is entitled to call it a day. Quite apart from its value as a report and estimate of a musical performance, his criticism must be able to stand alone as an interesting, readable story.

It is the musician in whom music critics primarily are interested, because only occasionally, even in the large cities, are they required to pass judgment upon a new symphony, opera or other musical creation. Thus, if the audience includes musically trained auditors, they may well take a cue from audience reactions as to the merits of the performance. If woefully lacking in musical training, the critic can make the entire story descriptive of the audience or the personalities of the musicians.

By Donal Henahan

When Alexander ran out of worlds to conquer, he could think of nothing better to do than to sit down and cry. But Leontyne Price, who has enough musical conquests to her credit to satisfy most sopranos and then some, took a more constructive approach Tuesday night at Carnegie Hall: she sang the "Liebestod" with the Chicago Symphony Orchestra.

Miss Price, as you must know, is one of this era's premier singers, but until now she has not ventured into the weightiest Wagnerian repertory. She built her opera career mostly in moderately heavy roles such as Leonora and Aïda, and has gone so far as Turandot in the area that the Italians designate as lirico spinto, the hinge between the purely lyric and the truly dramatic voices.

But, under the baton of Sir Georg Solti, that tested and proven Wagnerian, Miss Price did what all the greatest artists do: she took a chance. Whether at age 53 there is an Isolde in her future would be risky to say right now, but it can be safely stated that her performance of the famous aria "Mild und leise" from "Tristan und Isolde" carried the day. The audience, its appetite whetted by a suffocatingly evocative reading of the Prelude by the Chicago, gave Miss Price the kind of ovation that most sopranos only get in their reveries. If the Metropolitan Opera chose to announce her as Isolde tomorrow you may be sure seats would go at black-market prices. Miss Price, incidentally, has just completed a recording on which she sings the "Liebestod," and it is entirely possible that she intends to let the matter drop.

Certainly, the voice on this night was splendidly used and wisely husbanded, in the manner most Isoldes learn early if they are to survive. It never did quite become the flood of tone that a Wagnerian soprano of the Nilsson or Farrell type can produce with such seeming lack of strain. Miss Price's more slender soprano could, however, ride the crest of orchestral sound quite thrillingly, and almost invariably did. And there was an ecstatic excitement to it all that probably even benefited from one's consciousness of the effort involved. What would the Love-Death be, after all, without struggle?

[New York *Times*]

The Dance

Whereas music is written with complete directions by the composer to guide the virtuoso, and whereas rules for the playwright, novelist, painter and sculptor may be found in textbooks, no way as yet has been devised to score the movements that characterize what, historical evidence proves, was one of the first if not the original form of art. Motion-picture recording may prove the way out for future teachers of the dance who wish to convey the qualities of the work of a Rudolph Nureyev or a Martha Graham.

The medium of the dance is motion, but motion may be either abstract or pantomimic, rhythmic or natural. Folk dancing, being pantomimic, reflects the customs of the people participating in it. Natural dancing consists in such normal movements as running, walking, skipping and leaping without studied posing. What is called the German school of dancing emphasizes strength, endurance and precision of movement. The ballet is rhythmic and repetitious. Greek or classical dancing, revived after World War I by the late Isadora Duncan, is symbolic and involves the entire body, not just the head, arms and legs. Miss Duncan considered her art interpretative of poetry, music, the movements of nature and of moods and emotions; as such, it defied analysis.

To review a dancing entertainment with any intelligence, the reporter must understand the principles superficially sketched in the preceding two paragraphs. A sympathetic attitude perhaps is more essential than in reviewing any other form of art, if for no other reason than that it is the form with which the average person has the least everyday contact.

By Anna Kisselgoff

A major premiere by Martha Graham is a major theatrical event by any standard, and the premiere of the new "Judith" by the Martha Graham Dance Company Tuesday night at the Metropolitan Opera House was no exception.

There were two stunning moments. The first was spellbinding in its immediacy. Applause broke out and a cry of "fabulous" rang out from the public as the curtains parted. They revealed two works of art—the two sculptures by Isamu Noguchi that make up the set. Beautiful in form but also the counterpart of Miss Graham's genius in functioning on several levels, they suggest many things at once. Smooth and curved, the first piece implies an abstraction of a lyre. The second piece, constructed in the image of a spit and a sawhorse, is clearly reminiscent of an animal.

Of course, these are phallic symbols—true to the tradition of Noguchi-Graham collaborations in the past. This "Judith" is about sex, and Miss Graham is no stranger to eroticism. Yet she takes her story—the seduction and murder of the Assyrian tyrant Holofernes by the biblical heroine Judith—into a larger, abstract plane. The male and female principles embodied in Noguchi's sculpture find their reflection in the two protagonists: Judith, as danced by Peggy Lyman and Holofernes, portrayed by Tim Wengerd.

Miss Lyman, under Miss Graham's direction, is responsible for the second stunning moment. This is the minute in which she takes off the black widow's robe and begins to attire herself alluringly to seduce Holofernes. Halston's costumes, based on Miss Graham's original ideas, offer a flash of brilliant expressive colors here. Miss Lyman removes the black and gold veil in which she has been wrapped. Covered from head to toe, dressed according to our ideas of Jewish heroines of antiquity, she sheds her stance of modesty and determination suddenly in favor of a contemporary frankness.

As she emerges by her lyre, shoulders and arms bare in a red leotard top with a purple skirt, her entire demeanor changes. She sits, legs apart, back up, hand to thigh. If she is not brazen, she embodies a state of sexual forwardness. And, when like a queen going to her execution, she covers her torso with gold snake-coiled jewelry, the change is total.

This transformation was so complete and so extraordinary that one was compelled to go back to the original tale of Judith—who is not a strictly biblical heroine in that her story is contained in the books of the Apocrypha. The corresponding passage, referring to the Jews' reaction, reads as follows: "And when they saw her, that her countenance was altered and her apparel was changed, they wondered at her beauty greatly."

Miss Graham, as choreographer, and Miss Lyman as the dancer, have arrived at the truth of this image—of exterior and moral transformation—so powerfully that their accomplishment goes beyond translation of a literary idea. It is difficult to believe that Miss Lyman, as the woman resolved to free her besieged people, was the same dancer who opened the work. It was a transformation explained by the way Miss Lyman modified the way she held her body—a magnificent example of Miss Graham's use of the body as an expressive instrument. . . . [New York *Times*]

The Fine Arts

The camera was, to a large extent, the cause of the contemporary "war" in the field of painting that has had repercussions among the sculptors and architects as well. Dadaism, futurism, surrealism and other 20th-century "schools" of art are revolts against the formal, and a popular explanation given laymen is that the day of a portrait painter is gone and with it a theory as to the purpose of art. It is argued that the role of the 20th-century artist is to communicate an idea or an emotion; the extremes to which some go in upsetting tradition is dumbfounding to laymen. In the works of such painters as Grant Wood and Thomas Benton, so-called regional artists, is found an abandonment of the photographic purpose, but the models still are recognizable. Some abstract art has as many interpretations as there are interpreters.

Peter Schjeldahl epitomized recent trends as follows:

> The 1960's in American abstract painting was a period of conscientious esthetic and technical pure research, remarkable for its tireless experimentation with hard-edged stripes, disks and polygons of solid color. The avant-garde of a decade ago, having thrived during the abstract Expressionist 50's on seemingly slapdash procedures followed in an intellectual climate of romantic assertiveness and big ideas, took with a sort of cool, evangelical passion to the new use of T-squares and masking tape, and began to couch its self-advertisement in impeccable dry, quasi-scientific language.

How to combine reporting and expert critical analysis is demonstrated in the following:

By Hilton Kramer

The rose is a venerable subject in the history of painting but there are no roses to be found in this history quite like those that appear in the paintings of Bert Carpenter, whose one-man show is now installed at the Zabriskie Gallery, 699 Madison Avenue at 63rd Street.

For Mr. Carpenter, while lavishing a familiar lyricism on the realization of this conventional subject, manages to transform it into something quite different—the materials of "heroic" painting.

Mr. Carpenter projects his imagery of roses on a monumental scale, making of each petal, leaf and stem a weighty architectural member. The roses in his paintings are giant roses, monument roses—roses that carry the humble dimensions of nature into the realm of pictorial fantasy. And yet, he effects this magical change in scale without sacrificing anything of the "realism" of his depictions. These roses, as large as the head of man, retain all their tender luminosity.

As a sheer technical feat, the exhibition is remarkable. But it is also extremely interesting as virtuoso painting. Mr. Carpenter has adopted something of Alex Katz's pictorial strategy in enlarging his subjects to more than life-size, and the particular "cropping" he employs seems to owe something to Philip Pearlstein's painting—Mr. Carpenter often cuts off the tops and bottoms of his roses the way Mr. Pearlstein crops his views of naked models. But whatever he may have borrowed in the realm of formal ideas, Mr. Carpenter's pictures establish a presence all his own. He is an interesting and powerful painter.   [New York *Times*]

Current tendencies in painting, sculpture and architecture are not new. The history of art reveals that throughout the centuries every conceivable theory has been employed, at least experimentally. Likewise, the search for a definition of art is as old as artistic criticism; upon the answer to the question depends largely the nature of what an artist produces.

Through reading and fraternizing with artistic people reporters can become educated in the meaning of art to the different "schools," the work of whose representatives they are called upon to review. In no other field is the responsibility for interpreting artists to their public greater than in that of the manual arts. In fact, such interpretation is about all there is to this kind of criticism.

Probing on Entertainment Beats _____

On the entertainment beat, in addition to the short items of gossip and the profiles that, along with reviews or game reports, have been the staple of coverage, there is a lot more in-depth interpretative reporting these days. Investigation and explanation now are much more a requirement for reporters working in this area of journalism.

Here are just a few examples of that trend, illustrated by leads of what were much longer sports page stories:

By Mike Tierney

Some know him by his given name, Don. Others call him by his nickname, Duck. He likes either one.

For one notorious year in Canada, he was addressed by his younger brother's name Greg. It's a name Donald "Duck" Williams wishes he'd never heard.

This case of altered identity drove William's resuscitated basketball career down a dead-end road and a Canadian college that once was comparable to UCLA toward a scandal resulting in a one-year suspension of its program. . . .   [St. Petersburg *Times*]

By Jody Homer

Carbondale—It's difficult to know whom to believe these days at Southern Illinois University, where a sad saga has been slowly unraveling. Sad because of the reputations it has tarnished. Sad because of what it means for all of collegiate athletics.

On April 5, SIU assistant basketball coach Stafford Stephenson resigned after admitting he knew of payments that were made to 6-foot-11-inch senior center Kenny Perry by a Carbondale chiropractor, Dr. Roy S. White. SIU's investigation into the payment of $900 a month to Perry is still going on. A report is expected to be delivered to the NCAA in several weeks. Until the results of the investigation are made public, this Downstate college community is left to ask, "Whom do you trust?"

Do you trust basketball coach Allen Van Winkle, who resigned Tuesday while insisting he knew nothing about the payments to Perry? Do you trust booster White, who said he gave the money to Perry with Van Winkle's knowledge and consent?

SIU has a struggling, low-visability basketball program that has had trouble recently recruiting players who haven't been to another college first. SIU's booster club is not a powerful organization. It's mostly a social club of 500 that engages in almost no fund-raising.

This is not the sort of place one would expect to find high-finance shenanigans in athletics, and in fact, as Perry's brother Clint told a Carbondale newspaper, The Southern Illinoisan: "They got a blue-chipper for cheap. It was no big money. If you have a wife and kid [as Perry does], you can't live off air and water."

Kenny Perry did not get rich from this scheme, but he certainly broke the rules in a big way. And the Salukis, who in recent years have not been able to compete on the basketball court with big-time programs, are suffering through a big-time scandal. . . .   [Chicago *Tribune*]

By Russ White

There are 42 head coaching jobs in professional football—28 in the National Football League, 14 in the United States Football League.

Some of the men in these jobs are winners, some losers. Some of them have had two or three different head jobs in pro ball. The only thing these guys have totally in common is that each one is white.

It has been that way in pro football for nearly three-quarters of a century. Fritz Pollard, who played and coached in the NFL's embryonic years in the 1920's, is the only black head coach the NFL has had. In modern times there have been no black head coaches and only a handfull of black assistants.

Some facts:

* Although 52 percent of the players in the NFL today are black, only 31 percent of 281 coaches are black. Four NFL teams did not have a black coach in 1984. The San Francisco 49ers, however, had three.

* Although 54 percent of the players in the USFL [1984 season] are black, only 12 of 130 coaches are black. Seven USFL teams did not have a black coach. . . .   [Orlando *Sentinel*]

From rock and country music to the fine arts, there also is plenty of serious in-depth reporting getting done these days on arts beats, as these leads to long stories suggest:

By Steve Morse

Michael Jackson and Boy George one year, then Tina Turner, Cyndi Lauper and Prince the next. And now Madonna, Wham! and Julian Lennon. In the seeming blink of an eye, they've been swept into a chaotic roller coaster of record industry hype and media overkill that can celebrate them one day, savage them the next. A star such as Jackson can gain tens of millions of fans, then be vulnerable to instant decline of the sort that caused his 1984 Victory Tour to ebb drastically as the year wore on.

The rock industry has always seen meteoric successes, dating back to Elvis Presley in the '50s and the Beatles and the Rolling Stones in the '60s. But those were isolated cases, back when pop culture was nowhere near as ubiquitous. Radio stations and celebrity-crazed magazines were fewer, and there was no such video network such as MTV to pump rock stars into living rooms 24 hours a day.

But the machinery to create stars—and to overexpose them and numb the public quickly—has never been greater than it is today and has turned the record industry into a surreal pinball game.

Fear of overexposure is why Madonna and Julian Lennon have recently stopped giving interviews. They're following the lead of Michael Jackson and Prince, who haven't given interviews in three years, even though they're still dogged by media hounds, exemplified by the litany of hotshots who turned Jackson's 1984 Victory Tour into a circus. . . .   [Boston *Globe*]

By Jack Hurst

Nashville record executives are starting to run scared, and the direction they're starting to run is backwards.

Small wonder.

From its fat Urban Cowboy days of 1980—when acceptance of country-crossover records by pop radio pushed the country sales to 16 percent of the whole U.S. record market, making country second only to rock—country in 1983 fell to 13 percent, and some fear the yet-to-be-released 1984 figures may plummet to 11 percent or less.

There, far below rock [35 percent in '83] and "pop & easy listening" [14 percent], country would be battling black music to stay out of fourth place.

So Nashville record bosses appear to be changing gears. They're retreating from their former pop crossover strategies at a pace that's becoming almost disorderly. The sequence of events prompting the turnaround went this way. . . .   [Chicago *Tribune*]

By James Harper

"Our goal is to achieve a new standard of excellence," Lynne Hardin Kearney, the chapeau-adorned president of the Florida Opera beamed during an elegantly catered press conference last fall.

With those optimistic words, Mrs. Kearney declared that the opera's years of struggling against financial uncertainty were over. The 8-year-old company (formerly known as the St. Petersburg Opera and Florida Opera West) was beginning its most ambitious season ever. And indeed, Tampa Bay opera-goers were treated to a short but sweet season of bold artistic risk and satisfying achievement.

But now, the company has announced that seven out of nine performances next season will be devoted not to opera but to revivals of Broadway musical comedy. A much ballyhooed performance of Carlisle Floyd's contemporary opera *Susannah,* with Floyd conducting, has been canceled. The one legitimate opera that remains on the schedule, Verdi's *La Traviata,* has been scaled down. Mrs. Kearney and her general manager Thomas Palmer say ticket sales have never been better. But there are others who see the company's plans as a startling reversal.

The Florida Opera, they say, has lost its nerve. . . .   [St. Petersburg *Times*]

By Barbara Isenberg

Never has Los Angeles seen such a boom in theater construction and renovation.

All over the city, theaters are being planned to improve neighborhoods, humanize shopping centers, massage egos—and even stage plays. From Venice to Northridge, Santa Monica to downtown, enterpreneurs talk optimistically of opening 30 theater spaces in the next several years.

All that's missing are the plays to fill the stages, the money to produce the plays and the audiences to see them.

"There are lots of facilities not being filled on a regular basis now, and we're talking about building new ones," says Edward Weston, western regional director of Actor's Equity. "I'm fearful that we've returned to the edifice complex of spending money on buildings rather than building acting companies."

The theatrical landscape is changing fast. . . .   [Los Angeles *Times*]

The challenges of work on entertainment beats of modern American newspapers rapidly are becoming the same as challenges on other beats. No longer is entertainment the preserve simply of the good writer or the acerbic commentator. Today, a core requirement is the capacity to dig into the politics, ethics, sociology, economics and history of entertainment—to deal with the subject as part of our society, to look for answers to the questions of how and why, and to interpret the significance of popular culture in our lives.

Epilogue

American daily newspapers, whose editors in the 1980s have fretted greatly about tailoring a "marketable product," are among the most profitable industries in the United States. According to one report based on filings with the Securities and Exchange Commission, newspapers closed the first half of the 1980s with profit margins 2.2 per cent higher than at the start of the decade. Their pre-tax operating-income margins reached 17.9 per cent in 1984. Their revenues grew 64 per cent in the first half of the decade. Because they were so profitable, there were many newspaper takeovers, some by newspaper groups and some by outsiders. And many of the largest newspaper groups were buying up broadcast properties as well.

There were plenty of entry-level jobs in newspapers for young would-be reporters willing to "pay their dues" at small to medium-sized dailies. And for those young reporters who did good work, wrote well and kept learning at the outset of their careers, there were good opportunities to move to challenging positions paying from $30,000 a year and up.

From both right and left on the political spectrum, from spokespeople for big businesses to liberal scholars in universities, the work of mainstream journalists often was criticized. And there were more libel suits seeking larger amounts of damages. The criticism reflected a widening perception of the growing power of the news media as influences in American life, especially in deciding not so much what people think as what they think about. Those in other institutions with great power realized they had to deal with the power of the press. Public relations—the quest for good images in the media, for getting one's version of the truth into the public mind—became an increasingly big business, too. Because of the clash of powerful interests within and around the news media, there was growing public skepticism of what they reported, something that worried publishers and their editors. And that worrying became part of the daily working environment of reporters, who report to editors even as they try to report for a larger public.

All of this, coupled with the many vital issues facing American and global society, makes the task of reporting more stimulating, more rewarding, more demanding and more influential than perhaps ever in the history of American newspapers. There is a lot of action, much of it complex and not easy to detect or adequately interpret. And reporters today, from small cities to sprawling metropolitan areas, are where that action is.

It is work that is both fun and interesting if you enjoy trying to understand theories in action, to analyze human nature as it operates in rapidly changing situations, to clearly and imaginatively write for a general audience with much at stake in how well you do that writing.

But while the forms of reporting and its institutional settings are changing, the basics remain the same as they always have. The key is still what questions reporters decide to ask about what and of whom. Even though it is a 'high-tech' age, that is no work for robots, but rather for human beings. So, too, once the questions are framed and asked, is the search for answers a chore that humans must do.

And when the answers are collected as carefully as possible from as many diverse sources as possible, there also is the human work of putting those answers into a larger context, attempting to illustrate their significance and to do so in words that are clear, compelling and crackling with their human dimensions. All reporting is, by its nature, interpretative. It always has been and will remain so. The basic duty of reporters is to provide that interpretation in the most intelligent, thorough, caring, accurate and fair way that they can. Thus, reporters not only need a good education, but they also need to keep educating themselves throughout their careers.

In the clashes of mighty interests playing themselves out within and around the media, reporters have an increasingly difficult, but increasingly important duty. That duty is to remain as independent minded as they possibly can while their bosses push them to slant their interpretations in the interest of greater profits and while various political, economic and social groups prod them to make interpretations that will serve some special interest.

In unthinking or uncaring hands, the inevitable interpretations reporters make can be like a loaded gun pointed at the heart and brain of our society. In intelligent, caring hands those interpretations can become weapons to enlighten the minds and stir the hearts of the citizens of our representative democracy.

Throughout history and throughout the modern world, the rights to inquire, to think and to write freely have been so precious that millions have fought and died for them. Throughout history as today, most people have not enjoyed those rights, which in our society are daily cradled to a great extent in the hands of those doing interpretative reporting. The First Amendment is for all of us, and it should be precious. Preserving it and exercising conscientiously the freedoms it represents constitute the minimum duty and the highest calling of the interpretative reporter.

Index